D0992021

CLASSICAL INFLUENCES ON
EUROPEAN CULTURE
A.D. 1500–1700

CLASSICAL INFLUENCES ON EUROPEAN CULTURE A.D. 1500–1700

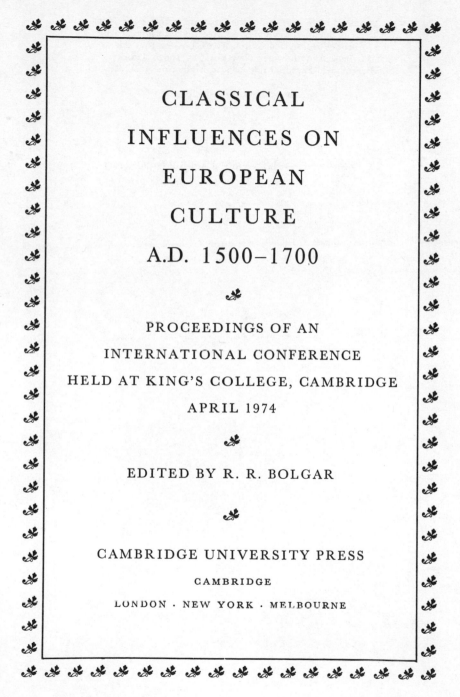

PROCEEDINGS OF AN
INTERNATIONAL CONFERENCE
HELD AT KING'S COLLEGE, CAMBRIDGE
APRIL 1974

EDITED BY R. R. BOLGAR

CAMBRIDGE UNIVERSITY PRESS

CAMBRIDGE

LONDON · NEW YORK · MELBOURNE

Published by the Syndics of the Cambridge University Press
The Pitt Building, Trumpington Street, Cambridge CB2 1RP
Bentley House, 200 Euston Road, London NW1 2DB
32 East 57th Street, New York, NY 10022, USA
296 Beaconsfield Parade, Middle Park, Melbourne 3206, Australia

© Cambridge University Press 1976

ISBN: 0 521 20840 8

First published 1976

Printed in Great Britain at the Alden Press, Oxford

CB
401
.C64

PREFACE
THE KING'S COLLEGE CONFERENCE

The Research Centre of King's College, Cambridge, was conceived
by Lord Annan, then Provost of the College, in 1963. Accommodation
for it was provided in the Keynes Building, completed in 1967. One
of the objects was to enable Fellows of the College to further projects
in which they were interested, whether by long-term group activities
or by short conferences approved by the Managers, who were
empowered by the College to allot financial resources.

In 1969 Dr R. R. Bolgar and I organised a four-day conference
on 'Classical Influences on European Culture, A.D. 500–1500' to take
place on 8–12 April. Twenty-eight guests contributed papers, which
under the above title were edited by Dr Bolgar and published in 1971
by the Cambridge University Press. The function of the Conference,
made clear in the Preface, was 'to bring to light the avenues which,
given the present state of our knowledge, research could most usefully
follow'. Though the book was gratifyingly successful and reviewers
were kind, some of these overlooked this statement, deprecating the
absence of some particular subject or hero. There had never been
any hope or intention of covering the vast field. It had seemed worth
while, however, to give workers in this field a chance to profit from
the experience of a number of authorities, most of them already
well known, others likely to become so.

In 1974 we organised another conference, on exactly the same
lines, from 7 to 11 April. The only significant change was that
fifteen minutes instead of ten were allotted to the shorter papers.
Again we were helped by a committee consisting of Cambridge
scholars, to whom we are very grateful – Dr P. Boyde, Professor
L. W. Forster, Mr (now Professor) E. J. Kenney, Dr Odette de
Mourgues, Mr George Watson and Professor B. A. O. Williams; and
again we had the invaluable advice of Mr J. B. Trapp, Librarian
of the Warburg Institute. The number of speakers was limited, as
before, to a little under thirty by the capacity of the College's private
dining-room as well as by the capacity of an audience to go on
listening. In fact, though the sun shone all the time as in 1969,
attendance was well maintained, and scholars from Cambridge and

LIBRARY
ALMA COLLEGE
ALMA, MICHIGAN

elsewhere, including not a few research students, came in to listen. There was no formal discussion: in the house-party atmosphere informal discussion between interested people was easy. (This arrangement had been warmly approved by those who attended the previous Conference.) Relevant exhibitions were again put on by the University Library and the Fitzwilliam Museum. Our thanks are due for these to Dr J. Hall and Miss Phyllis Giles. We also owe thanks to Mrs H. M. Clark and Mrs E. L. Brown for help with the organisation of the Conference.

This time the title expressed the object of the Conference more explicitly: 'Classical Influences on European Culture, A.D. 1500–1700: What Needs to be Done?' The vast field was narrowed by the exclusion of science, but it remained vast. There proved to be little overlapping, though no suggestion had been made as to topics. It seemed better to choose the authorities, a few representative ones or ones whose subjects called for slides being allotted half an hour. We are naturally aware that even the collective knowledge of our committee must have overlooked some scholars who had a good claim to be invited and must regret that a number who were invited were unfortunately unable to accept. We are also particularly sorry that Professors A. Momigliano, W. J. Ong, R. H. Popkin and F. Schalk and Dr Ida Calabi-Limentani were prevented at the last minute from coming. We are glad however that Professor Popkin's paper could be read (with great spirit, by Professor Bernard Williams) and that we have received Professor Ong's and Professor Schalk's papers for publication. The Proceedings, again edited by Dr Bolgar, are now offered to the interested public.

L. P. WILKINSON

EDITOR'S NOTE

As with the Proceedings of the 1969 Conference, the papers do not follow here the order in which they were delivered. They have been arranged in groups according to subject. But many speakers covered a wide range of topics, as can be seen from the Introduction, so that this arrangement, which has involved placing a paper under one heading rather than another, is often crude and arbitrary. The Index should be consulted by any reader who wants to discover all that was said on a particular subject.

Authors were asked to correct their contributions and have added substantial notes in some cases. But Mrs Carlotta Griffiths, who read a most interesting paper on the sixteenth-century editor, Janus Parrhasius, felt that too much work was needed to make it as perfect as she wanted, and to our great regret refused to allow it to be published. And at a later stage, Professor D. Geanakoplos decided, again much to our regret, to withdraw his paper on early humanist patristic scholarship.

Since the stated purpose of the Conference was to call attention to the gaps in our knowledge about the influence of classical learning, it seems appropriate to mention here the item 'Research Opportunities' in the Index, which lists the pages where some of these gaps are indicated.

Finally, the editor would like to take this opportunity to offer his personal thanks to the Syndics and Staff of the Cambridge University Press; to Dr Lisa Jardine for her indispensable help with the proofs and index; to Dr Elisabeth Bond-Pablé for her help (equally indispensable) in checking some of the German texts; and to Mrs H. M. Clark, Administrative Secretary of the King's College Research Centre without whose ready assistance both with the organisation of the Conference and with the editor's extensive correspondence the papers that make up this volume would never have been assembled.

CONTENTS

Preface L. P. WILKINSON   *page* v

Editor's note   vii

List of plates   xiii

Contributors   xv

Introduction R. R. BOLGAR   I

PART I. CATALOGUES AND EDITIONS OF HUMANIST WORKS

1   1500–1700: the bibliographical problem. A continental
    S.T.C.? DENYS HAY   33

2   Neo-Latin satire: *sermo* and *satyra menippea* J. IJSEWIJN 41

3   An anthology of Renaissance Latin verse: problems
    confronting the editor and compiler J. SPARROW   57

PART II. THE HUMANISTS IN THE RENAISSANCE

4   La première querelle des 'anciens' et des 'modernes'
    aux origines de la Renaissance C. VASOLI   67

A. THE HUMANIST CONTRIBUTION TO THE ARTS OF DISCOURSE

5   Reflections on Ravisius Textor's *Specimen Epithetorum*
    I. D. MCFARLANE   81

6   Commonplace rhapsody: Ravisius Textor, Zwinger and
    Shakespeare WALTER J. ONG   91

7   Commonplaces of law, proverbial wisdom and philosophy:
    their importance in Renaissance scholarship (Rabelais,
    Joachim du Bellay, Montaigne) M. A. SCREECH   127

8   Montaigne's 'Sur des vers de Virgile': taboo subject,
    taboo author D. COLEMAN   135

9   Humanism and dialectic in sixteenth-century
    Cambridge: a preliminary investigation L. JARDINE   141

CONTENTS

10 Poetics, rhetoric, and logic in Renaissance criticism
W. S. HOWELL *page* 155

11 Lucan in der Kritik des 16. und 17. Jahrunderts
H. DÖRRIE 163

12 Petrus Lotichius Secundus and the Roman elegists:
prolegomena to a study of Neo-Latin elegy W. LUDWIG 171

13 From the *Ciceronianus* to Montaigne M. MANN PHILLIPS 191

B. HUMANISM AND RELIGION

14 The humanist idea of Christian antiquity and the impact
of Greek patristic work on sixteenth-century thought
E. F. RICE JR 199

15 John Colet, his manuscripts and the ps.-Dionysius
J. B. TRAPP 205

16 Erasmus, the early Jesuits and the classics
A. H. T. LEVI 223

17 Juan Vivès and the *Somnium Scipionis*
DOMINIC BAKER-SMITH 239

18 Vivès, lecteur et critique de Platon et d'Aristote
J.-C. MARGOLIN 245

19 Zur Rolle der Mythologie in der Literatur des Siglo de
Oro F. SCHALK 259

20 The development of religious scepticism and the influence
of Isaac La Peyrère's pre-Adamism and Bible criticism
R. H. POPKIN 271

C. HUMANISM AND POLITICAL THOUGHT

21 Livy > Tacitus J. H. WHITFIELD 281

22 Vivere sotto i tiranni: un tema tacitiano da Guiccardini
a Diderot A. LA PENNA 295

23 Utilisation et critique de *La Politique* d'Aristote dans
La République de Jean Bodin H. WEBER 305

CONTENTS

D. THE CONTRIBUTION OF THE HUMANISTS TO THE USEFUL AND THE FINE ARTS

24   Die antike Literatur als Vorbild der praktischen Wissenschaften im 16. und 17. Jahrhundert G. OESTREICH   *page* 315

25   Les Loges de Raphaël: répertoire à l'antique, Bible et mythologie N. DACOS   325

26   Criticism of ancient architecture in the sixteenth and seventeenth centuries T. BUDDENSIEG   335

27   Baroque architecture and classical antiquity ANTHONY BLUNT   349

Index   355

PLATES

(*between pp.* 334 *and* 345)

1 *a* Loggias of Raphael. Detail of pilaster IX. (*Photo: Savio, Rome*)

1 *b* Domus Aurea. Detail of the *Volta delle civette.* (*Photo: Gabinetto fotografico nazionale, Rome*)

1 *c* Domus Aurea. Detail of the *Volta nera*, after the Codex Escurialensis, fol.14v

2 *a* Hercules and Admetus. Loggias of Raphael. Detail of archivolt XI. (*Photo: Savio, Rome*)

2 *b* Paintings on a Roman columbarium portraying especially Hercules and Admetus. After the Codex Pighianus, fol.333. (*Photo: Warburg Institute, London*)

3 *a* Dionysus and child. Loggias of Raphael. Detail of archivolt VII. (*Photo: Savio, Rome*)

3 *b* God creates woman. Loggias of Raphael, vault II. (*Photo: Gabinetto fotografico nazionale, Rome*)

3 *c* Noah's Ark. Loggias of Raphael, vault III. (*Photo: Gabinetto fotografico nazionale, Rome*)

3 *d* Visitation of the dramatic poet by Dionysus. Hellenistic relief. London, British Museum. (*Photo: British Museum*)

4 *a* Jacob on the road to Canaan. Loggias of Raphael, vault VI. (*Photo: Gabinetto fotografico nazionale, Rome*)

4 *b* Dionysus in triumph. Roman sarcophagus. London, British Museum. (*Photo: British Museum*)

4 *c* Allegorical representation of Peace. Loggias of Raphael. Detail of archivolt X. (*Photo: Savio, Rome*)

4 *d* Allegorical representation of Peace. Roman coin. (*Photo: Deutsches Arch. Inst., Rome*)

5 *a* Piccolomini Library. General view of the vault. Siena Cathedral

5 *b* Loggias of Raphael. General view of vault X. (*Photo: Savio, Rome*)

6 *a* Joseph and Potiphar's wife. Loggias of Raphael, vault VII. (*Photo: Gabinetto fotografico nazionale, Rome*)

6 *b* Apollo and Daphne. Woodcut from the 1488 edition of Ovid's *Metamorphoses*

7 *a* Gozzoli workshop. Capital. Rotterdam, Museum Boymans–van Beuningen. (*Photo: Alinari*)

7 *b* Boccati. Madonna col Bambino. Detail. Perugia Pinacoteca

7 *c* Bernardo della Volpaia. Codex Coner fol.94. Capital. London, Sir John Soane's Museum

7 *d* Cronaca, Palazzo Strozzi. Cornice. Measured drawing

7 *e* 'Pseudo-Cronaca'. Measured drawing after Florence, Bibl. Naz. MS II.1.429, fol.50

8 *a* Rome. S. Costanza

8 *b* G. da Sangallo. S. Costanza. Bibliotheca Vaticana, Cod. Barb. lat. 4424

8 *c* Bernardo della Volpaia. Codex Coner. S. Costanza. London, Sir John Soane's Museum. (*Photo: Courtauld Institute of Art*)

8 *d* 'Master C' of 1519. S. Costanza. Vienna, Albertina AH. 9v

9 *a* C. Fontana. 'Republican' Pantheon

9 *b* C. Fontana. 'Republican' Pantheon

9 *c* J. Boumann. French Church, Potsdam, 1752

10   G. Romano. Sculptor destroying his statues. Fresco. Vatican, Sala di Costantino

11 *a* Scamozzi. Project for S. Maria delle Celestia, Venice (?). Chatsworth, Duke of Devonshire

11 *b* Raphael. 'Praxiteles'-horse, Quirinal. Chatsworth, Duke of Devonshire

12 *a* Borromini. Rome. S. Ivo della Sapienza

12 *b* G. B. Montano. Reconstruction of an ancient temple. Drawing. London, Sir John Soane's Museum. (*Photo: Courtauld Institute of Art*)

13 *a* Baalbek. Circular temple. (*Photo: Courtauld Institute of Art*)

13 *b* Polidoro da Caravaggio. Designs for a circular building. Drawing. Berlin, Staatliche Museen. (*Photo: Courtauld Institute of Art*)

14 *a* G. B. Montano. Reconstruction of an ancient temple. Engraving. (*Photo: Courtauld Institute of Art*)

14 *b* Borromini. Rome. Palazzo Spada. Plan of colonnade

15 *a* Roman artist, early seventeenth century. Reconstruction of a Roman theatre. Drawing. Royal Library, Windsor Castle. (Copyright reserved)

15 *b* Sabratha. Theatre. (*Photo: Courtauld Institute of Art*)

16 *a* The handwriting of John Colet, from the Register of Doctors' Commons (p.211)

16 *b* The 'red annotating hand' from the Mercers' Hall copy of the Statutes of St Paul's School (p.211). (*Photo: Warburg Institute*)

16 *c* The 'red annotating hand' and the hand of Peter Meghen, from MS Corpus Christi College Cambridge 355 (p.217)

16 *d* The handwriting of the British Library transcript of the Statutes of St Paul's School, MS Add.6274 (p.212). (*Photo: Warburg Institute*)

CONTRIBUTORS

Dr DOMINIC BAKER-SMITH is University Lecturer in English and Fellow of Fitzwilliam College, Cambridge.

Sir ANTHONY BLUNT is Professor Emeritus of the History of Art in the University of London and was Director of the Courtauld Institute. He is the author of various works on French sixteenth- and seventeenth-century art including *Nicolas Poussin* (1966) and has a book on Neapolitan Baroque architecture in the press.

Dr R. R. BOLGAR is Reader in the History of the Classical Tradition and Fellow of King's College in the University of Cambridge. He is the author of *The Classical Heritage and its Beneficiaries* (1954) and editor of *Classical Influences on European Culture A.D. 500–1500* (1971).

Professor T. BUDDENSIEG is Professor of Art History in the Free University of Berlin.

Mrs D. COLEMAN is Lecturer in French and Fellow of New Hall in the University of Cambridge. She is the author of *Rabelais: a critical study in prose fiction* (1971).

Dr NICOLE DACOS holds a research post at the Fonds National de la Recherche Scientifique de Belgique and lectures on the history of art at the Free University of Brussels. She is the author of *Peintres belges à Rome au XVIe siècle* (1964) and *La découverte de la Domus Aurea et la formation des grotesques à la Renaissance* (1969). She is about to publish a monograph on Les Loges de Raphaël.

Dr H. DÖRRIE is professor of Classical Philology in the University of Munster/Westfalen. He is the author of *Der heroische Brief* (1968), *Untersuchungen zur Überlieferungsgeschichte von Ovids Epistulae Heroidum* (1960, 1972), *P. Ovidius Naso: Der Brief der Sappho an Phaon, mit literarischem und kritischem Kommentar* (1974).

Professor DENYS HAY is Professor of Medieval History at the University of Edinburgh. He is the author of *Polydore Vergil* (1952), *The Italian renaissance in its historical background* (1961), *The medieval centuries* (1964), *Europe in the fourteenth and fifteenth centuries* (1966).

Professor WILBUR SAMUEL HOWELL is Professor Emeritus of Rhetoric and Oratory, Department of English, Princeton University. He is author of *The Rhetoric of Alcuin and Charlemagne*

xv

(1941), *Problems and Styles of Communication* (1945), *Fénelon's Dialogues on Eloquence* (1951), *Logic and Rhetoric in England, 1500–1700* (1956), *Eighteenth-Century British Logic and Rhetoric* (1971) and *Poetics, Rhetoric, and Logic: Studies in the Basic Disciplines of Criticism* (in the press).

Professor J. A. M. K. IJSEWIJN is Professor Ordinarius and Director of the Seminarium Philologiae Humanisticae in the University of Louvain. He is the editor of *Humanistica Lovaniensia* and the European editor of *Neo-Latin News*.

Dr L. JARDINE is Fellow of King's College, Cambridge. She is the author of *Francis Bacon: Discovery and the Art of Discourse* (1974).

Professor A. LA PENNA is Professor of Latin Literature at the University of Florence and lectures on Latin philology at the Scuola Normale Superiore di Pisa. He is the author of *Properzio, saggio critico* (1951), *Orazio e l'ideologia del principato* (1963), *Virgilio e la crisi del mondo antico* (1966), *Sallustio e la rivoluzione romana* (1968), *Orazio e la morale mondana europea* (1969) and *Properzio ovvero l'integrazione difficile* (1970).

Professor A. H. T. LEVI is Buchanan Professor of French Language and Literature in the University of St Andrews. He is the author of *French Moralists, Theory of the Passions, 1585–1649* (1964), and the editor of *Humanism in France at the end of the Middle Ages and in the Early Renaissance* (1970). He has also edited the English translation of Erasmus's *Praise of Folly* for Penguin (1971).

Dr WALTHER LUDWIG is Professor of Greek and Latin and Chairman of the Department of Greek and Latin at the Columbia University in the City of New York. He is author of *Sapheneia* (1955), *Struktur und Einheit der Metamorphosen Ovids* (1965), *Antike Komödien* (1966), *Ioannis Harmonii Marsi Comoedia Stephanium* (1971) and of articles in the fields of Hellenistic poetry, Greek and Roman comedy, Augustan poetry and Renaissance Latin Literature.

Professor I. D. MCFARLANE is Professor of French Literature, and Fellow of Wadham College, Oxford. He is the author of *The 'Délie' of Maurice Scève* (1966) and *Renaissance France 1470–1589* (1974).

Mrs MARGARET MANN PHILLIPS is Honorary Lecturer at University College London, and formerly Fellow of Newnham College, Cambridge and Reader in French at King's College,

London. She is the author of *Erasme et les Débuts de la Réforme française* (1934), *Erasmus and the Northern Renaissance* (1949) and *The Adages of Erasmus* (1964).

Professor J.-C. MARGOLIN is professor at the University of Tours where he is in charge of the Department of the Philosophy and History of Humanism in the Centre d'Études Supérieures. He is the author of two volumes of Erasmian bibliography (1963 and 1969), a critical study of Erasmus's *De pueris* (1966), two essays on Erasmus (1965), an essay on Bachelard (1974) and of *L'acte humain de vérité* (1969).

Professor G. OESTREICH is Professor of Early Modern History at the University of Marburg, West Germany. He is the author of *Antiker Geist und moderner Staat bei Justus Lipsius (1546–1606)*. *Der Neustoizismus als politische Bewegung* (typescript 1954), *Geschichte der Menschenrechte und Grundfreiheiten im Umriß* (1968) and *Geist und Gestalt des frühmodernen Staates* (1969).

Professor WALTER J. ONG, S.J. is Professor of English and Professor of Humanities in Psychiatry at Saint Louis University. He is the author of *Ramus, Method, and the decay of dialogue* and *Ramus and Talon inventory* (both 1958), *The presence of the word* (1967) and *Rhetoric, Romance and Technology* (1971). He has also written introductions to facsimile editions of P. Ramus and A. Talon, *Collectaneae praefationes, epistolae, orationes* (1969) and P. Ramus, *Scholae in liberales artes* (1970).

Professor R. H. POPKIN is Professor of Philosophy and Jewish Studies at Washington University in St Louis, editor of the *Journal of the History of Philosophy*, co-director for the International Archives of the History of Ideas, author of the *History of Scepticism from Erasmus to Descartes* and many articles on the history of ideas from the Renaissance to the Enlightenment.

Professor E. F. RICE Jr is Professor of History at Columbia University. He is the author of *The Renaissance idea of wisdom* (1958) and *Foundations of early modern Europe 1460–1559* (1971).

Professor F. SCHALK is Professor of Romance Philology and Director of the Romanisches Seminar and Petrarca-Institut in the University of Cologne. He is the author of *Moralisti italiani del rinascimento* (1940) and *Das Publikum im italienischen Humanismus* (1954) and the editor of *Die Celestina* (1959) and *Alberti: vom Hauswesen* (1962).

Dr M. A. SCREECH is Fielden Professor of French Language and Literature, University College, London. He is the author of several studies on Renaissance authors.

Mr J. SPARROW is Warden of All Souls College, Oxford. He contributed an article, 'Latin Verse of the High Renaissance' to *Italian Renaissance Studies* (ed. E. F. Jacob, 1962).

Mr J. B. TRAPP is the Librarian of the Warburg Institute, University of London.

Professor C. VASOLI is Professor Ordinarius of Moral Philosophy at the University of Florence. He is the author of *Guglielmo d'Occam* (1953), *Due studi per Alano di Lilla* and *La filosofia medioevale* (both 1961), *La dialettica e la retorica dell'Umanesimo* (1968), *Studi sulla cultura del Rinascimento* (1968), *Umanesimo e Rinascimento* (1969), *Profezia e ragione* (1974).

Professor H. WEBER is Professor of French Literature at the Université Paul Valéry, Montpellier. He is the author of *La création poétique au XVe siècle en France* (1955) and *Le langage poétique de Maurice Scève dans la Délie* (1958).

Professor J. H. WHITFIELD was Serena Professor of Italian Language and Literature in the University of Birmingham (1946–74), Chairman of the Society for Italian Studies, Senior Editor of *Italian Studies* and is author of *Petrarch and the Renascence* (1943), *Machiavelli* (1947), *Dante and Virgil* (1949), *Giacomo Leopardi* (1954), *A Short History of Italian Literature* (1960), *Discourses on Machiavelli* (1969), etc.

Mr L. P. WILKINSON is Fellow of King's College, and was until 1974 Brereton Reader in Classics and Orator, in the University of Cambridge. He is the author of *Horace and his Lyric Poetry* (1945), *Letters of Cicero* (1949), *Ovid Recalled* (1955), *Golden Latin Artistry* (1962), *The Georgics of Virgil* (1969) and *The Roman Experience* (1974).

INTRODUCTION

R. R. BOLGAR

By the beginning of the sixteenth century, the special sort of interest in Greek and Roman antiquity that we call humanism had been in existence for close on two hundred years. The aim of the humanists was to reshape the intellectual activities of their day in line with ancient practice. Their success was notable; and as a result of their endeavours, European culture had become so deeply indebted to ideas and techniques derived from the Greco-Roman past that, after 1500, the influence of classical learning cannot be studied any longer as an isolated phenomenon. While in medieval and again in modern times men turned occasionally to their ancient heritage in an effort to redress contemporary short-comings, this intermediate period, comprising roughly the sixteenth and seventeenth centuries, saw the flowering of a culture that was in many respects an actual product of that heritage. What it is fruitful to consider in this exceptional context are developments that often stand at several removes from the immediate impact made by a Greek or Roman author, and that involve the action of numerous other factors. The choice of the sixteenth century as the starting-point of the second King's College Conference meant therefore that the participants had to struggle with topics that could not be understood without reference to the general history of late Renaissance culture.

The historical problems associated with that culture are notoriously thorny. Attempts to discover a single pervasive tendency behind its various manifestations have traditionally and deservedly ended in failure. It is true that at the point when the Middle Ages changed into the Renaissance, one can identify certain trends of a more or less general character. But these were orientations of feeling rather than consciously held purposes or values. Functioning moreover within a complex matrix of institutions, techniques, bodies of knowledge and frameworks of interpretation inherited from the medieval past, they soon lost whatever coherence they had originally possessed and issued in a great variety of specific interests. Such movements as Ciceronianism, Neoplatonism, Anti-Scholasticism, the *devotio moderna*, classicism in art and architecture, the cult of political liberty, and what was hard to reconcile with it, the cult of efficient government, developed independently under their own steam, and by the sixteenth century the connections that had existed between them, deriving from the common matrix from which they originated, had lost all importance. Variety, not uniformity was the characteristic feature of the late Renaissance. A conference whose output was limited to under thirty papers could not hope to cover the diverse manifestations of classical influence in such a perplexingly complex period. All we tried to do therefore was to draw attention to certain obvious gaps in our present-day knowledge of the subject and to indicate certain topics that appeared to offer fruitful possibilities for future research.

A student who wants to master the cultural history of a literate age must begin by finding out what was being written and what was being read. He needs an accurate and comprehensive catalogue of the works that were in circulation during his period, and also accurate copies of these works. The section that opens this book deals therefore with these basic requirements of scholarship. The catalogues at our disposal for the study of humanism do not cover the ground adequately and are often far from correct; so we have Professor Hay's eloquent plea that efforts should be made to compile a Continental S.T.C. He sums up in a pregnant sentence the distressing extent of our ignorance: 'Our knowledge of the unspectacular publications of the sixteenth century (by unspectacular I mean works by unspectacular authors) is certainly much less than our knowledge of medieval MSS.' Once we move outside England, there exists no easily accessible record of what was published, and even such works as have been safely preserved often lie unnoted or wrongly described on obscure library shelves.

Catalogues however are not our only need. To be aware that a book can be found in a remote library does not necessarily represent a great advantage. If you are a beginner, trying to find a subject for research or simply collecting background information, you cannot afford to cross a continent or to purchase a microfilm in order to take a quick look at a text. What would help in such a case would be a widely available critical edition. Professor IJsewijn stresses the

2

importance of this fact in his survey of Neo-Latin satire – a field where, as he tells us, almost everything is still to do. He lists some forty authors of *sermones* as well as twenty who composed Menippean satires and adds that of this large number only seven have been reprinted in modern editions, although such satirical writings with their fund of contemporary references offer material that is of interest to social as well as to literary historians. He reminds us too that early Renaissance texts – and this applies to printed books as well as to MSS – are often physically awkward to read. Moreover, as we have no notes to guide us over difficult passages, references can remain obscure, and the meaning far from plain. Classical scholars, Professor IJsewijn remarks, would not do very well if they had to study their Persius or their Juvenal in the form in which we meet the sixteenth-century satirists.

Some of the other papers also mention these same problems, if more briefly. Professor Rice invites us to deplore the fact that the editions and translations of the Early Fathers that were produced during the Renaissance have not been properly listed; and Professor Oestreich devotes the final paragraph of his paper to pointing out that if we want to understand how much the humanists contributed to the technological advances of the sixteenth and seventeenth centuries, we must explore their many editions and adaptations of the relevant classical texts; and here again our first requirement is a comprehensive catalogue. Finally, in a narrower context, we have Mr Trapp, who tells us about a particular scholar – John Colet – and has reason to mention the defects he finds in the nineteenth-century edition of Colet's works. The case is instructive because it demonstrates that even where an editor has been at work in what must count as relatively modern times, there is room for improvement, though improvement may not be easy to achieve. Mr Trapp's erudite analysis of the Colet MSS makes it plain that editors of Renaissance texts, lacking autographs and faced with undated copies, can have problems that would have taxed a Housman or a Wilamowitz.

Since the Amsterdam Erasmus has now reached its sixth volume, since the Toronto Erasmus in English has begun to appear, and we can take advantage of such useful publications as the Gregg Press reprint of Vivès, it could be argued that the Conference did not do justice to recent progress in the editing of Renaissance Latin. But if it failed in general to draw attention to the brighter side of the picture, one important enterprise did come in for notice. Mr Sparrow gave an enticing account of that long-awaited anthology of Neo-Latin verse which he hopes to publish in the near future. Planned to cover more than eighty poets writing between the beginning of the fourteenth and the latter half of the sixteenth century, this anthology will provide us with a compendious view of the Neo-Latin poetic tradition. We are to be introduced to the Great Unknown, that body of literature which everybody recognises as the source from which the vernacular poetry of the Renaissance drew much of its inspiration, but which few of us have explored. No poem is good unread; and the reputation of Neo-Latin writing has suffered a great deal from its not being easily accessible. Mr Sparrow's anthology promises to remedy this defect.

The papers mentioned so far, which discussed the instruments of scholarship, formed only a fraction of the work of the Conference. The majority of the participants centred their attention on the history of thought and literature, and something must now be said about their choice of topics.

The early humanists cherished clear-cut and relatively simple aims. They wanted to make the whole range of classical literature available to their contemporaries in an easily readable form. They wanted to master the art of writing classical Latin and dreamt of composing works of merit in the better-known ancient genres. By the third decade of the sixteenth century these aims had been largely achieved, or achievement had reached a point beyond which progress was difficult. All but a few of the ancient authors whose works have survived had been resurrected and printed. The knowledge they contained had been made available to the modern world, and there was little that second, third or fourth editions could add. It is true that editorial techniques improved, but it was not often, except perhaps in the case of mathematics, that a new, more correct text added to the first slipshod version something that was of real interest to the imitator, the specialist or even the general reader. And when we turn to the writing of Latin, we see that success there led to sterility in an even more obvious way. Thanks to the lead given by Lorenzo Valla men had learnt to write classical Latin with reasonable accuracy by the end of the fifteenth century, but attempts to progress beyond this measure of general competence then merely

4

gave rise to futile debate. Should one follow Cicero? Or some
other author? Or should one employ all idioms sanctioned by ancient
usage? The third main current of humanist endeavour, that of
producing works of literary value, could not for obvious reasons
find success a bar to further advance, but it came up against a bar
from another quarter. The humanists had learnt to imitate classical
modes of writing successfully in a number of genres. They had produced works of solid merit, and in some cases they had actually
surpassed their Latin models. Alberti had learnt from Lucian a skill
in the composition of dialogues that no Roman author had attained.
Erasmus, drawing on the same Greek source, had produced in the
Praise of Folly an unmatched example of the paradoxical encomium.
But by this time, the spread of education was producing a readership that preferred its mother tongue to Latin, and men with literary
ambitions were not blind to the change. The vernaculars came to
attract the best creative talents of the age; and by the end of the
sixteenth century, hardly anyone still believed the language of the
humanists to be the surest road to fame.

In view of these developments, it is not surprising perhaps that so
little was said at the Conference about textual criticism – in spite
of the triumphs of men like Joseph Scaliger and Casaubon – or
about the notorious Ciceronian controversy. These no longer belonged to the mainstream of cultural advance, though the influence
exercised by the latter on vernacular style did have some importance[1]
and came in for mention in Mrs Phillips's paper. Creative writing
in humanist Latin, the other great interest of the preceding centuries,
could not be – and was not – so readily dismissed. Mr Sparrow
and Professor Ludwig praised its merits warmly. It remained influential as a source of ideas; and although after 1550 Latin no
longer mobilised the same creative energies as the vernaculars, its
use by writers of eminence as an alternative to their mother tongue
is a topic that amply deserves attention.[2] But the main concern of

[1] The Ciceronian debate appears marginal to the live issues of the period, because both
the Ciceronians and their opponents spent the best part of their time discussing problems
that had relevance only for Neo-Latin, and the use of Latin as a literary language was
on its way out. But they did incidentally produce statements about the nature of
language and about prose style that were to prove important for the development of
the vernaculars. See I. Scott, *Controversies over the imitation of Cicero* (New York, 1910);
G. Williamson, *The Senecan amble* (Chicago, 1951); M. W. Croll, *Style, rhetoric and
rhythm*, ed. J. M. Patrick et al. (Princeton, 1966).
[2] Discussing the issues raised at the Conference, Mrs Helena Shire called attention to the
many problems connected with Renaissance bilingualism that have so far received

the Conference lay elsewhere. It centred on the contributions the Humanists made to the new Europe that was developing around them; and we find these conveniently summarised in Professor Vasoli's paper, which touched on so many themes that it could not be included in any particular section. It has therefore been placed at the head of the central portion of the book.

The paper begins by giving us a brief history of humanism. Petrarch's somewhat uncritical admiration for antiquity, his cult of an eloquence based on everyday discourse and his rejection of the logic-dominated culture of his day characterised the first stage of the movement. The second found its principal representatives in Bruni and Lorenzo Valla. Bruni took the view that the scholastic disregard for correct Latin had led men to misunderstand the lessons of the ancient world and had also left them unable to communicate effectively one with another. The arts, learning and religion were all corrupted by this; and their corruption was then aggravated by the loss of political freedom; for it is only in a free republic that culture can truly flower. Valla reaffirmed Bruni's analysis, but introduced a more decided note of hope. He had done much to promote the revival of correct Latin along lines suggested by Manuel Chrysoloras,[1] and he saw this work as the prelude to a new age of creative

---

little attention. Many sixteenth- and seventeenth-century writers used both their mother tongue and Latin. Milton is an obvious example among poets. The Pole, Jan Kochanowski is another. In prose, we have Bembo and Bacon. What determined their choice of language in any particular instance? Was it the readership they envisaged – national on the one hand, international on the other? This was certainly a consideration of some importance, especially in countries where the vernacular readership was small. Learned works in northern and eastern Europe appeared almost invariably in Latin. But even in the south and west almost simultaneous publication in Latin and the vernacular was not unknown, as for example in the case of Calvin's *Institutio*. Bodin translated his *De la république* into Latin after ten years, and Bacon's *De augmentis* appeared after an even longer lapse of time as an enlarged version of the *Advancement of learning*. Hog's Latin version of *Paradise Lost* may have been the work of an over-sanguine crank, but with *The cherrie and the slae*, written in Scots 1597–1610 and published in Latin *ca.* 1620 by the Benedictines of Würzburg, we must look for a more serious purpose. In all these cases, it is reasonable to assume the existence of a wish to appeal to a wider public. But was there also a feeling sometimes that certain themes, certain genres called for Latin? When people were choosing in which language to write verse, was the nature of the poem the deciding factor? And what significance should we attach to the fact that some poems are known to have been composed in Latin before they were composed in English? We forget that educated men in the Renaissance were effectively bilingual, and that this must have had important implications.

1 Manuel Chrysoloras, who was familiar with the techniques used in Byzantium for teaching Attic Greek, seems to have been responsible for introducing his Florentine

imitation which would compensate for the shortcomings of the past. What we are shown in effect is that these two pioneers introduced the themes that were to occupy the attention of their sixteenth- and seventeenth-century successors: the value of clear expression and creative genius, the reform of religion and the cult of political liberty. Valla was also responsible for a practical innovation of great importance. In his *Dialecticae disputationes*, he set out to reorganise the teaching of dialectic. Instead of exploring the complications of the syllogism, it was to help men to understand the forms of argument that are used in everyday life. This was the humanist dialectic that Rudolph Agricola was to develop, and whose later forms Dr Jardine examines in her paper.

But it is in outlining the change that came over humanism in the sixteenth century that Professor Vasoli produces his most interesting insights. By that time, the men of the Renaissance had become self-confident. The standards they had established now seemed to them to possess an independent validity; and they were prepared to submit the classical authorities they claimed to follow to the same rigorously critical examination that they applied to their scholastic foes. They were even prepared to regard Greece and Rome as just two civilisations among many, so that they turned when opportunity offered to other and apparently older sources of knowledge. In the scientific field and in the vernacular literatures, these attitudes were to lead to a rapid advance as soon as the lessons of antiquity were to some extent mastered.

The papers that follow Professor Vasoli's, arranged under the headings: Discourse, Religion, Politics, Technology, the Fine Arts, fill out his picture. These were the directions in which humanism developed during the second half of the Renaissance.

Discourse inevitably takes first place. The Renaissance was above all the age of the written word. The humanists' interest in writing well and the humanists' love of the ancient world were indissolubly linked. Petrarch could not have dissociated his admiration for Cicero's style from his admiration for Cicero as a thinker and a man. For this reason perhaps, imitating ancient authors meant for the

---

pupils (1396–1400) to the idea that an ancient language could be precisely imitated. It is in this sense that Guarino calls him the man responsible for the revival of Latin studies. Guarinus Veronensis, *Epistolario* ed. R. Sabbadini (Venice, 1915–19), vol.2, pp.580–1, 583, 588.

Renaissance not only reproducing the rhythms and idioms of the classical language or experimenting with classical genres, but also – and perhaps more particularly – using ideas and facts taken from ancient sources; and when, as happened by the end of the fifteenth century, scholars had largely mastered the problems set by language and genre, they turned eagerly to the problems of *inventio*, the finding (in this case, the borrowing) of subject-matter. The method recommended by Erasmus for the use of schoolboys has some relevance in this context. They were to collect in a notebook epithets, idiomatic phrases, figures of speech that they came across in their reading (*copia verborum*), and in another notebook they were to collect witty sayings, anecdotes, myths, historical incidents of moral interest (*copia rerum*).[1] These practices were not confined to the classroom. Everybody who composed in Latin was anxious to have at hand lists of useful words and even more surely collections of *sententiae* and *exempla*.

It is interesting to note that even professional scholars who in earlier generations had seen themselves primarily as the pioneers of new ideas, now turned to the amassing of facts and anecdotes. An interesting instance of this was given to the Conference by Mrs Carlotta Griffiths's account of Janus Parrhasius, which to everyone's regret it has not proved possible to print in this volume. Parrhasius was a mediocre practitioner who for that reason affords a good example of the general tendencies of his times. His major work, a commentary on Claudian's *De raptu Proserpinae*, set out to dazzle his readers with a fantastic display of erudition. He had married the homely daughter of Demetrius Chalcondyles to gain unlimited access to the latter's MSS and advice; and the fruits of this *contubernium*, as Mrs Griffiths put it, are evident on every page of the Claudian commentary. It turned into an anthology of Greek learning, drawn for preference from the more obscure authors.

But while men like Parrhasius foraged more or less at random, others, more alive to the general mood, made systematic attempts to satisfy what had emerged as a public need. The sixteenth century was the first great age of anthologies and dictionaries, collections and compendia of all sorts, in which extracts from classical writers were made more easily accessible for quotation and reproduction. Erasmus's *Adagia* and *Apophthegmata*, Raphael Maffeius's *Commentaria*,

---

[1] Erasmus, *De copia verborum et rerum*, chap.7 in *Opera omnia*, vol.1 (1703 edn).

Textor's *Epitheta* and *Officina*[1] came on the market, and they were just the first of an army.

Textor's *Epitheta*, which is discussed both by Professor McFarlane and by Professor Ong, was a monstrously amplified *copia verborum* notebook. The first edition covered some 2,800 words, each with a list of appropriate epithets. *Apollo*, we are told, rated 113, *amor* 163, and some suggested epithets were validated by supporting quotations. The whole constituted a vast rag-bag for the use of intending versifiers; and there seems little reason to doubt that the poets of the day actually used it. We cannot admittedly demonstrate in any particular case that a classical reference comes from a source other than the original; but Professor McFarlane produces some very suggestive instances where conjunctions of words in Buchanan correspond closely to the phrasing of Textor. And if Buchanan reached for the *Epitheta* when he was composing, what must lesser men have done?

Textor's next work, the *Officina*, was a collection of commonplace material intended to provide its readers with *copia rerum*. It was just as popular as its sister volume and just as much of a rag-bag. Professor Ong speaks of its 'studied pursuit of conspicuously useless detail' and its 'zany confusion'. But handbooks of this sort, crude and clumsy as they were, formed the foundations on which greater things were built; and if we want to understand the Renaissance, we cannot push them aside as so much rubbish. They had a part to play in developments that proved ultimately to be of the first importance: in the remarkable flowering of new literatures and in the formulation of new techniques of expression and study.

The contribution the handbooks made in the literary field is a fairly obvious one and should perhaps be considered first. It had some weight both in the writing of Latin and in the vernaculars.

Until Mr Sparrow's anthology inspires scholars to undertake that extensive study which Neo-Latin literature must receive before we can form a settled conviction of its merits, we cannot decide whether the effort to build a new Latin literature with fragments taken from the old was a success or not. But when we turn from Latin to the better understood, because more deeply considered, vernaculars,

[1] Erasmus, *Adagiorum collectanea* (Paris, 1500); *Apophthegmatum opus* (Basle, 1531); Raphael Maffeius, *Commentarii* (Rome, 1506); J. Ravisius Textor, *Epitheta* (Paris, 1518); *Officina* (Paris, 1520).

all doubt vanishes. A Rabelais takes a passage from Textor, a Ben Jonson builds on a colourless entry in Charles Estienne's *Dictionarium poeticum*, and their borrowings are transmuted into gold.[1] It could be argued that this use of the classical heritage to bring about a sudden and brilliant transformation of the vernacular literatures was the outstanding achievement of the sixteenth century.

That we know so little about the inner mechanics of this achievement is therefore a matter for surprise. Some progress has been made with tracing the sources which were used; but *Quellenforschung* never does more than tell the uninteresting part of the story. How these sources were adapted, the precise conditions in which their adaptation proved effective, are what we have to elucidate. Professor Screech and Mrs Coleman pioneer this fruitful field. Writing as literary critics primarily concerned with interpretation, they both stress the point that one cannot understand a sixteenth-century text, if one has not the equipment to recognise the classical allusions. For some texts at any rate this is certainly true. Professor Screech presents the problem in general terms. He analyses a number of classical allusions that occur in authors like du Bellay and Montaigne, and shows that some of these cannot be understood without reference to their original context. Others make sense in their French setting, but can further supplement its meaning if we can remember the Latin passage from which they were taken. They can help us for example to choose between a straightforward and an ironic interpretation. Mrs Coleman in her paper focused on what might be called a creative use of quotation. Taking three passages where Montaigne cites Martial in his essay *Sur des vers de Virgile*, she claims that remembering the context in each case helps us to add further steps to Montaigne's argument by introducing taboo subjects like homosexuality or sexual incompetence. She also notes that Montaigne sometimes changes the order of his Latin originals and will even add or alter words in order to create fresh associations for a reader who knows both Latin and French. What Mrs Coleman's *jeu d'esprit* helps us to realise is that the old was worked into the texture of the new. The relationship between the classical and modern cultures was much more subtle than the simple concept of one borrowing from

---

[1] For Rabelais's borrowings see L. Delaruelle, 'Ce que Rabelais doit à Erasme et à Budé', *Revue d'histoire littéraire de France* (1904); for Jonson's, W. T. Starnes and E. W. Talbert, *Classical myth and legend in Renaissance dictionaries* (Chapel Hill, 1955).

the other immediately conveys. Educated men in the Renaissance – certainly those who were bilingual – lived in two distinct, if over-lapping, intellectual worlds; and the precise effect of this is something we have yet to discover.

But it is time now to return to the handbooks and to consider how they served as the starting-point of another line of development, which was quite as important as the one we have been examining. Textor's works had some serious shortcomings when they first appeared. They were not easy to consult, and they came nowhere near satisfying any wish men may have had to see facts ordered in an intelligible form. The first of these shortcomings was rapidly eliminated. In the later editions of the *Officina* and the *Epitheta*, the alphabetical arrangement is more exact, and it is easier to find the item one happens to want. Simultaneously compendia whose text did not lend itself to such ordering were furnished with alphabetical guides to their contents, which became progressively fuller and more precise. This was an innovation of the first importance. Indexes of a sort had existed in the Middle Ages, but as they had to be made specially for each MS, they had remained highly selective and were of no great value. As Professor Ong points out, it was the invention of printing that made efficient indexing possible. Once you had a large number of copies of a work that corresponded page by page, the labour of constructing a detailed alphabetical guide to their contents became for the first time worth while; and once the usefulness of the technique was recognised, its improvement was rapid. By the latter half of the sixteenth century the problem of ensuring the relatively easy retrieval of information could be regarded as solved.

The further problem of organising this information in a rational way was to prove a harder nut to crack. Professor Vasoli, Dr Jardine and Professor Ong make some pertinent observations on this point. They take us back once again to Lorenzo Valla. His belief that dialectic should serve the needs of everyday discourse had an important corollary. It implied that everyday discourse was, or ideally ought to be, rational; and at the time, this was a novel conception. The educated of the Middle Ages, whose training made them over-estimate the value of the syllogism, had regarded reasoning as an activity confined to philosophical speculation. They certainly did not look for it in literature. Valla therefore must count as an innovator of note. He stands at the beginning of that trend in

Renaissance thought which was to insist on the supreme value of Reason, as Petrarch had insisted on the value of Style and the rhetoricians who eventually found a mouthpiece in Erasmus insisted on the value of *copia*.

A wish to see the life of the intellect ordered in a rational way does not however constitute a very precise programme; and so it is not surprising to find that the trend initiated by Valla's nascent Rationalism led in the event to a number of distinct, if vaguely connected, developments. The most notable of these was that new approach to dialectic that we associate with Rudolphus Agricola. Born a generation after Valla, he elaborated certain features of the latter's teaching in a treatise to which he gave the name *De inventione dialectica*: and the conjunction of terms is significant. The ancient rhetorical technique of *inventio* has some bearing on the organisation of knowledge. What it proposes is essentially a mnemonic aid for finding ideas. An orator was trained to keep in mind certain general propositions appropriate to the type of subject he was tackling. In a political speech, for example, one is necessarily concerned with the question of what is advantageous; and the advantages one must look for fall into two classes: they concern security or honour. (So says the *Ad Herennium*; a modern theorist would have surely added 'wealth'.) Then these headings can be further subdivided. Honour, for instance, accrues from actions in accordance with Wisdom, Justice, Courage or Temperance; and the *Auctor* goes on to furnish us with specific examples for each. It is just to pity the innocent, to repay the deserving with gratitude and so forth.[1] One presumes that an orator would pass these lists in review when composing his speech to see if any heading suggested an idea that fitted the situation he wanted to talk about. But these mnemonic aids that the traditional teaching on *inventio* offered were limited in their scope. They covered only subjects which belonged to judicial, deliberative or epideictic oratory; and Agricola saw that if dialectic was to serve the needs of everyday discourse as Valla had recommended, the scope of *inventio* would have to be widened to cover a much larger variety of topics. So, taking the *Topics* of Aristotle and Cicero as his starting-point, he moved boldly from rhetoric into what had been a minor province of dialectic. Instead of trying to list various kinds of just deeds or courageous deeds as the *Ad Herennium* does, he focused

---

[1] *Rhetorica ad Herennium* Bk3, ch.2–9.

attention on characteristics that could apply to any entity or concept one might wish to discuss: definition, genus, species, efficient and final causes, place, time, similarities, dissimilarities and so forth. Much of this analysis was traditional, but Agricola differed from Aristotle in the positive nature of his approach. Aristotle's topics are primarily pigeon-holes from which you can derive objections to an opponent's statements. Agricola saw them as sources of ideas, from which we can build up a rational understanding of whatever notion we may be considering.

As education came under the control of men with humanist sympathies, which happened generally during the first half of the sixteenth century, Agricola took his place among the authors set for university study;[1] and those who believed in Valla's ideal must have felt this to be a substantial triumph. But it did not give them all they wanted. *Inventio*, the discovery of appropriate subject-matter, is not the only aspect of discourse to which reasoning can be applied. It can be applied also to the types of proof one uses, to the way one analyses situations, to the way one constructs an argument, so that the humanists pressed for – and eventually obtained – a dialectics course that took into account how these activities were carried out in literary composition and even in everyday speech. Among the most vigorous advocates of such a course were Vivès and Ramus; and it is with the Ramist, Gabriel Harvey, the hero of Dr Jardine's instructive paper, that we see the new dialectic (which was based partly on Agricola, but covered a wider field than his) triumphing in Cambridge, a humanist dialectic closely linked with the study of the classical literatures.

By the end of the sixteenth century, Valla's dream of a reformed dialectic had been largely realised. But Reason is a demanding ally who will take an ell if you give her an inch; and as soon as the importance of the rational element in discourse had come to be recognised, there were pioneers eager to rationalise other fields of intellectual activity. Ramus, the *enfant terrible* of the mid-century learned world, won his great reputation as a theoretician of educational method – perhaps the first that ever was. Where Agricola had been interested in dialectic primarily as an aid to expression, Ramus was keenly

[1] L. Jardine, 'The place of dialectic teaching in sixteenth-century Cambridge', *Studies in the Renaissance* (XXI, 1974), and 'Humanism and the sixteenth-century Cambridge Arts Course', *History of Education* (4, 1975).

interested in its potentialities as an aid to learning and to the reasoned discovery of facts. His zealous adoption of the general principle that discovery proceeds from the universal to the particular played a key role in his career, since it provided him with an analytical technique, which unlike Agricola's could be applied to whole departments of knowledge as easily as to single objects. The famous Ramist Method was intended to provide a rational way of teaching the standard academic subjects. But Professor Ong's amusing account of Zwinger's *Theatrum* shows that its applications have no great claim to be considered efficient. Zwinger's 5,000 pages of historical excerpts do not represent a substantial advance on the confusions of Textor's *Officina*. The schematic order is imposed on the subject-matter from outside and does not help us to understand it. The educational programme of Ramism was more important for the problems it brought to man's notice than for the jejune solutions it offered.

Of the developments we have been discussing under the heading of Discourse, the quest for *copia* has been recognised as one of the main avenues of classical influence, since W. F. Smith and L. Delaruelle identified the sources of Rabelais more than fifty years ago.[1] The role of Dialectic has come into prominence more recently thanks largely to the early work of Professors Ong, Howell and Vasoli.[2] But important as they are, the innovations in these fields do not exhaust the humanist contribution to literary development. The age valued precept just as highly as practice. The humanists were also responsible for some interesting new departures in critical theory; and these were touched upon in several of the papers read to the Conference.

Professor Howell provides a general survey which introduces the central problem:

There was in the Renaissance a literature which owed its primary allegiance to what critics of that time called dialectic or logic; there was a literature which owed its primary allegiance to rhetoric, in the full classical sense of that term; and there was a literature, the most remarkable of all, which owed its primary allegiance to

[1] W. F. Smith, 'Rabelais et Erasme', *Revue des études rabelaisiennes* 6 (1908). For Delaruelle see above, p.10, n.1.
[2] W. S. Howell, *Logic and Rhetoric in England 1500–1700* (Princeton, 1956); and 'Ramus and English Rhetoric 1547–1681', *Quarterly Journal of Speech* 37 (1951); W. J. Ong, *Ramus, Method, and the decay of dialogue* (Cambridge Mass., 1958); C. Vasoli, *La dialettica e la retorica dell'Umanesimo. 'Invenzione' e 'Metodo' nella cultura del XV e XVI secolo* (Milan, 1968), but see also his more recent *Profezia e ragione* (Naples, 1974).

poetical theory, or to poetics, or to what was called poesy in the critical writing of that time.

The distinction between these three literatures may not have been as sharp as Professor Howell suggests. The erosion of the frontiers between rhetoric and dialectic was, as Professor Vasoli and Dr Jardine demonstrate, one of the more important consequences of the humanist concern for the efficient use of language; and techniques developed in the rhetorical field certainly exercised a pervasive influence on creative writing. But at another level, Professor Howell's analysis is undoubtedly correct and suggestive. One can trace three approaches to the art of writing that correspond to his three divisions: the emphasis being now on clarity of explanation, now on persuasive force, now on a particular type of subject-matter, the fabulous or fictional, that did not so much serve a definable end as carry its value within itself. In making these distinctions, the Renaissance critics did not, admittedly, explore their subject in depth. They realised that fiction had a didactic dimension, whose importance varied from instance to instance, but which was always present in some degree, so that fiction shared with logical and rhetorical writing the characteristic of providing its readers with instruction, and if it was seen to give pleasure or to act on the emotions, that was a further link binding it to rhetoric. But for all that, at a lower level of generality, fiction could be seen to stand in a class by itself. The pleasure it offered was not subordinated to its didactic purpose as was the case in rhetorical writing; and if its make-believe universes corresponded in their elements to the world of fact (since man cannot imagine anything wholly outside the range of human experience), the relation they bore to observable reality was devious, incomplete and often distorted.

Even the relatively incompetent critics of the time could see that imaginative writing, such as one finds in poetry, was governed by special laws. Aesthetic pleasure, they noted, was not an inevitable accompaniment of the fictional. It was present only when certain conditions were satisfied; and to establish these conditions was recognised to be an important task. Similarly, the relationship between fact and fiction was seen to require clarification; and that is why the problem of verisimilitude came in for so much discussion with the end of the sixteenth century.

The critical theories of these Castelvetros and Scaligers were not considered specifically by anyone at the Conference. Again, it was felt perhaps that they had received more than adequate attention from scholars in the past. But there were some interesting comments on the impact that their normative rules and precepts made in various fields. Professor Dörrie's paper on Lucan, for example, illustrates one of the marginal effects of the adoption of such rules in the case of the epic. He shows how Lucan, surely the most rhetorical of the Roman poets, was admired for his animation and pathos until the middle of the seventeenth century. But when the austerely classical principle that Art should follow Nature (in the sense that it should avoid all excess) came to be generally accepted, he stood condemned and lost his place in the canon of worthwhile authors. Professor Dörrie admits that one can find other reasons for Lucan's disgrace. He was a notorious champion of political liberty, and by the sixteen-sixties Europe was moving into the Age of Absolutism. Was the Sun King to tolerate a voice that Nero had silenced? But literary considerations had certainly counted for something in Lucan's loss of favour.

By contrast, Professor Ludwig and Mrs Phillips presented the influence exercised by critics as largely beneficial, perhaps because they dealt with areas of literature in which critical pronouncements had remained tentative.

In the fifteenth century there had been a fashion for imitating Tibullus, Propertius and Ovid's *Amores*. Many of the humanist writers of elegiacs (Janus Pannonius was a notable exception) produced collections of middle-sized poems addressed to some alluring girl. A hundred years later however, when critical theories had taken a stronger hold, the discrepancy between this fashion and the grammarians' definition of elegy as a poem of mourning began to cause concern. Fortunately, some of the more reputable Roman writers had already in their day rebelled against their pedantic contemporaries' etymologizing; and now even the redoubtable Scaliger was not tempted to go beyond a decent compromise. Elegy, he came to assert, could legitimately express both rejoicing and complaint. His view had some currency even before the publication of his *Poetice* (1561), and Professor Ludwig illustrates its influence on the man who gained the title of *princeps poetarum Germanorum*, the melancholy Petrus Lotichius. Scaliger's conclusion chimed in well enough with classical practice, as the example of Ovid's *Tristia* shows, and adapting it gave Lotichius a breadth of scope his pre-decessors had mostly lacked. Some of his finest verses are descriptive of his travels. Nostalgia lent these the necessary touch of sadness, and he was able to develop Latin elegy along the same lines as his contemporary, du Bellay, developed the French sonnet.

The precepts whose history Mrs Phillips examines related not to a particular literary genre, but to prose style in a general way. She tells us how an account given by Erasmus of the characteristics of good writing was reproduced first by an obscure Neo-Latin poet called Dampierre, and then by Montaigne; and how Montaigne in his essays put Erasmus's recommendations into practice. The inter-est of her paper derives in part from the light it sheds on the chances that governed the diffusion of ideas. But it also shows how statements that seem unexciting when we meet them in Latin could take on a varied, personal colour in a French context; and this is not a fact we can afford to disregard. The rejuvenation of ancient conceptions in the vernaculars is the most fascinating feature of the Renaissance.

The next section of the Conference's proceedings includes the papers that discussed or exemplified the relations of humanism and religion. If the main concern of the humanists was to endow their contemporaries with the knowledge and skill in discourse that had been at the disposal of the ancient world, this was not a concern whose validity they could comfortably take for granted. They lived in a Europe whose roots lay in that first Christian society which had triumphed under Constantine, and which had been inclined to reject pagan culture altogether. It had not been without difficulty that the good sense of men like Basil of Caesarea persuaded their co-religionists to accept even a limited part of their classical heritage. There had been a struggle between those who wanted to learn from pre-Christian Greece and Rome and those who regarded all pagan learning as tainted. The struggle had ended in compromise, but then it was renewed time and again during the Middle Ages. Consequently, when the humanists set themselves up as champions of a more com-plete revival of classical culture than any previously attempted, they faced distrust and hostility, and even their own consciences were not always at ease.

Given their situation in a Christian society and their aim to revive the ancient past, the humanists were bound to take an interest in the writings of the Early Fathers. Here was a body of work come

17

down from antiquity, which they could study without laying themselves open to disapproval. Also some of the Fathers had struggled with the problem of finding room for pagan values in a Christian world. We can see why the humanists should have turned to patristic studies with considerable eagerness. But until recently this interest of theirs has received little notice. Sandys, for example, who devotes eighteen lines to discussion of the *De recta latini graecique sermonis pronuntiatione* dismisses Erasmus's work on the Fathers in a brief sentence: 'He also produced recensions of S. Ambrose, S. Augustine and S. Chrysostom, with three editions of S. Jerome.'[1] The fact that at the present Conference one paper in every four treated of the Christian approach to pagan learning indicates a considerable change in perspective. The humanism of the Renaissance was for good or ill a Christian humanism. Its champions were men determined to reconcile their studies with their faith; and the ways in which they tried to do this certainly merit our attention.

They dreamt of combining holiness with learned eloquence, so as to achieve the ideal to which Petrarch had given the name of *docta pietas*; and they looked to the Fathers to provide them with a model. Modern studies in this field have not proceeded far enough for us to trace in close detail the evolution of the Petrarchan ideal, but reading the paper by Professor Rice, one comes to suspect that the combination of religious belief and studious zeal that Petrarch had in mind was substantially different from the one worked out in the end by Erasmus.

Petrarch was concerned with the rival claims of *otium* and *negotium*, with his wish to be a contemplative and his liking for involvement in public affairs. What he hoped to find in the Fathers was a clue to a way of life that would enable him to satisfy these contrary urges. He wanted to reconcile the irreconcilable. After his time, the patristic studies of the humanists centred for about a century on treatises that justified pagan learning or emphasised the links between pagan and Christian thought: on Basil's *Ad adolescentes* and Eusebius's *Preparatio evangelica*.[2] So long as life in this world was viewed essentially as a preparation for the life beyond, the only justification one could offer for humanist learning was to demonstrate that it could

---

[1] J. E. Sandys, *A history of classical scholarship*, vol.2 (Cambridge, 1908), pp.130–1.
[2] L. Schuhan, *Das Nachleben von Basilius Magnus 'ad Adolescentes'*, Travaux d'Humanisme et Renaissance 133 (Geneva, 1973).

help the propagation of the Christian faith or the understanding of Christian doctrine.

What transformed this situation in the second half of the fifteenth century was the growing importance of northern humanism, deeply rooted in the *devotio moderna*. To exponents of the *devotio*, the ideal Christian life was still a preparation for what awaits us beyond the grave, but you prepared for God's judgement by doing good here and now. The emphasis in the Christian tradition was shifting from contemplation and worship to charity and the imitation of Christ; and as the theologians of the later Middle Ages had not paid much attention to active benevolence, men like Erasmus turned to patristic literature in the hope of finding a picture of the Christian life that would be more to their taste. Their expectations were not disappointed. If the Christianity of the Fathers was not precisely that of the *Imitatio Christi*, it opened horizons beyond the logic-chopping of the medieval tradition; and if men's view of religion altered between 1350 and 1500, so did their concept of humanism. For Petrarch, being a humanist had meant loving the ancient literatures, imitating Virgil and Cicero and hoping to discover the inner secrets of ancient wisdom. For Erasmus too, it meant all that, but in addition it meant the ability to use certain scholarly techniques that enabled him to fix the correct form of ancient texts and to interpret them accurately, techniques that could be applied outside the classical field. Where Petrarch had envisaged humanism as able to offer at best a propagandist eloquence and a knowledge of ancient philosophy in the service of his other-worldly religious beliefs, Erasmus envisaged it as a method that could be applied to the whole heritage – pagan and Christian – of the ancient world and would help men to recover a Christian ideal that the centuries had tarnished.

Erasmus was such a polymath that it is just possible to regard his excursions into patristic scholarship as a great man's hobby; and Sandys seems to have taken that misleading view. But in Colet's case no such illusion is possible. He was a humanist. His contemporaries were unanimous in hailing him as such. He had an enthusiasm for classical studies which led him to found the first of the humanist grammar schools; but his treatises discussed religious subjects and his commentaries elucidated the Pauline epistles and the pseudo-Dionysius. Mr Trapp's survey of his surviving manuscripts leaves us in no doubt. Colet was not a humanist who happened to be also a patristic scholar. He was a humanist because he was a patristic scholar.

It was Erasmus, we are told, who finally formulated the principles of Christian humanism in a truly convincing way; and the view he took of the role of classical studies in a Christian society is generally credited with having been very influential. The range of his influence is something we do not need to question. T. W. Baldwin demonstrated many years ago how great a part his ideas had played in shaping the curriculum of the English grammar schools,[1] and we have Professor Levi suggesting here that what was true in the Protestant sector of education may have been true in the Catholic also, that the educational ideas of Ignatius Loyola may have been directly influenced by the Dutch humanist. But we have always understood the details of Erasmus's educational programme better than the arguments he used to justify his blend of humane studies and pious training, so that the most welcome part of Professor Levi's paper is perhaps his analysis of Erasmus's Christian humanism. This, he pertinently reminds us, evolved over many years and did not reach its definitive form until the last decade of the great scholar's life, which accounts for some of the contradictory statements that have been extracted from the Erasmian corpus. Erasmus began, as Petrarch did, with an aesthetic enthusiasm for classical eloquence and had difficulty in finding room for this in a life whose aim ought to be, he felt, a simple devotion to God. His final position, which he reached after years of pondering, was a good deal more complex. It rested on a series of assumptions, but they were assumptions which reason and learning could defend. Erasmus believed that the best form of Christianity yet known to man had existed during the first few centuries of our era. Knowledge of this primitive Christianity – our finest guide to right conduct – comes to us from books: from the Bible and the writings of the Fathers. But to understand what these books have to say one needs to know Greek and Latin, which further implies knowing the Greek and Roman world as far as that can be known. One has also to be able to decipher and collate manuscripts, to disentangle complexities of expression and to know what solutions scholars had devised for the problems of philosophy, history, law and the like. In short, some men at least in every genera-

[1] T. W. Baldwin, *Shakspere's small Latine and lesse Greeke* (Urbana, 1944).

tion will need to have at their finger-tips the resources of humanist scholarship, which can be gained only through a careful study of the Greek and Roman writers. These assumptions were already sufficient to validate a classical curriculum, but Erasmus added another as a sort of corollary. He was convinced – and Professor Levi maintains that the Jesuit educators shared his conviction – that many of the classical writers can provide us with moral instruction of great value, if we make allowance for the fact that they wrote without the guidance of Revelation. And with this we arrive at the principle that is the key to Erasmus's final position. Our reading of the classics – whether for their own sake or as a preparation for patristic studies – must be carried out in full awareness of their historical role. They were the products of a pagan civilisation with all the shortcomings paganism implies.

Dr Baker-Smith and Professor Margolin add to this picture of Christian humanism by showing us how these principles were applied. They both write about Vivès, who was perhaps the most distinguished of the disciples of Erasmus. In 1520, at a relatively early stage in his career, Vivès wrote a commentary on that famous fragment, the *Somnium Scipionis*, in which Cicero had given a description of his moral ideal: that our life has a transcendental aim, and that the roads leading to perfection in the service of that aim are art (notably eloquence), philosophy and a statesman's care for the public good. If one is prepared to widen the scope of philosophy to embrace Christian Revelation – and Dr Baker-Smith shows Vivès doing just that – the Ciceronian picture corresponds well enough to the views held by Erasmus at that point in his development which preceded the definitive formulation of his humanist credo. We learn from Dr Baker-Smith's paper that Vivès in his preface and commentary laid great stress on the value of eloquence and peaceful good government whose importance Erasmus had come to recognise under the influence of Thomas More. The educational merits of ancient philosophy are praised, but we do not yet hear about the need to allow for the pagan origin of ancient ideas; and if the ceremonial and moral hollowness of the sixteenth-century Church are condemned in favour of a simpler charity, the connection between this purified religion and the work of the early Fathers is not yet emphasised.

Professor Margolin's more broadly based paper gives us a Vivès who has adopted Erasmus's final position and has in some respects

gone significantly beyond his mentor. The subject of the paper is
Vivès's attitudes to Plato and Aristotle, which can be seen to reflect
the principles Professor Levi attributes to the later Erasmus. Vivès
remains profuse in his admiration for the two great philosophers,
but refuses to treat either of them as an infallible authority. He makes
it clear that he is prepared to criticise them, and that in his eyes they
are products of their times: an approach fully in line with Erasmus's
suggestion that the ancient literatures should be read with a critical
awareness of their pagan character. But while Erasmus was a writer
of genius as well as a moralist possessed of vast learning – and in all
this Vivès was his inferior – Vivès had a much firmer grasp of the
technicalities of philosophy. Professor Margolin's citations make it
abundantly plain that the Spaniard was too much of a professional
thinker to be able to limit his criticisms to an application of Christian
criteria; and at the same time he seems to have gone much further
than Erasmus in taking historical influences into account. Erasmus
distinguished between ideas that developed in a pagan and those
that developed in a Christian context. If this involved a chronological
distinction, it was a very rough one. Vivès was more subtle, and one
might say remarkably modern for his times. He seems to have been
very much aware of the master–pupil relationship between Plato
and Aristotle, seeing in the latter a would-be corrector of the former's
ideas; and he even put forward the view that Aristotle's opinions
may have altered in the course of his career.

So far the papers we have discussed under the heading 'Humanism
and Religion' have been concerned with the theoretical reconciliation
of these two ideologies, though Dr Baker-Smith does describe
Vivès using mythological figures in his satire and so incidentally
demonstrates the kind of result this reconciliation produced in the
literary field. But now we come to a paper whose orientation is
wholly literary. Professor Schalk takes as his subject the handling
of mythological concepts by Lope de Vega and Calderón. We have
here two Christian poets coming to grips with the most obtrusively
pagan element in the classical heritage. The Renaissance found the
Greek myths abundantly attractive. They were excellent stories,
very well told; for otherwise, as G. S. Kirk points out, they would not
have survived.[1] Their fictions had a considerable sensuous and indeed

[1] G. S. Kirk, *Myth: its meaning and functions in ancient and other cultures* (Cambridge, 1970), p.254.

sensual appeal; and by the end of the fifteenth century it was widely realised that they embodied profound truths about human experience. At the same time however, the enduring Christian prejudice against the Olympian gods raised difficulties when authors wanted to introduce figures or incidents from ancient mythology into contemporary works.

Professor Schalk exemplifies two popular solutions. He takes first of all three poems by Lope de Vega. These present isolated scenes taken from famous stories, and the emphasis in all three cases is firmly on the human situation. A terrified girl bound to a rock awaits a monster. A boatload of adventurers escape from danger. Another girl on the back of a bull is carried out to sea. Although there are mentions of Nereids, Nymphs and Sea-gods, and although the bull is plainly more than a bull, we are not confronted with pagan beliefs in any systematic sense. We do not move beyond the idea of a world open to the action of mysterious forces; and in any case the patent unreality, the decorative character of what is described, discourages us from relating anything but the central human experience of fear or excitement to life as we know it.

Lope escaped censure by limiting the scope of his pagan references. Calderón, whom Professor Schalk takes as his second example, attempted a different treatment, which allowed him to use mythological detail on a much larger scale. The analysis of *El verdadero Dios Pan* shows Pan as Christ wooing Luna who is the human soul, but simultaneously also Diana and Persephone. The Devil appears as a Great Beast and is vanquished by Christ who then restores to Luna the Lamb whose loss she mourns. Personifications of Paganism, Judaism and Apostasy function as a chorus. They attribute the victory over the Devil to Luna and hail her respectively as Diana, Judith and Man's unconquerable soul. Calderón has taken a central theme of considerable generality, the struggle of Good and Evil for man's soul; he has given it objective expression in terms of Christian, pagan and Judaic myth (not only is Luna identified with Judith, but the Lamb has its parallel in Gideon's fleece); and he has then blended his mythical interpretations, shifting rapidly from one to the other. He could be held to suggest that different religious beliefs are all just alternative statements of the same basic verities. But he does appear to give Christianity pride of place, and the audiences of his day would certainly have taken him to imply that their religion was the true one, of which pagans and Jews had caught only a partial glimpse. Calderón may be regarded as a writer firmly within the traditions of Christian humanism.

Professor Popkin's paper, the last in this section, shows the effects that followed a century later from the hypothesis advanced by Erasmus that the intellectual achievements of Greece and Rome should be considered in their historical setting as the products of a particular stage in man's history. This suggested that other stages of development, other civilisations might not be without interest. We have seen that towards the end of the fifteenth century, a passion for accumulating facts, inspired by the needs of rhetoric, drove men like Parrhasius to hunt after what was odd and rare. Their researches brought into notice societies like the Egyptian, the Babylonian and the Indian, which had existed on the margins of the classical world, and some of which derived added fascination from their connections with the Old Testament. Men became eager to learn about unfamiliar cultures, and their eagerness increased even further when geographical discoveries revealed the existence of peoples whose traditions differed greatly from the European. If all these half-recognised civilisations were to be regarded as deserving of study, each being the product of a particular set of historical conditions, men were bound eventually to challenge the special place allotted to the Hebrew tradition in Western culture. Professor Popkin traces the growth of this challenge and its culmination in pre-Adamism, which he claims played a decisive part in launching the irreligion of modern times. The argument that Erasmus had used to justify Christian humanism had carried within the seeds of a future upheaval.

From Religion we must move to Politics; for that was another field in which humanism proved influential. The belief that men should serve the state, and that education should prepare them for this task had been a vital element in the humanist programme from the time when it was first formulated by Petrarch.[1] But right from the beginning, this ideal of public service had found itself coupled with another that was to prove awkwardly controversial. Because their favourite

---

[1] See for example L. B. Alberti, *I libri della famiglia*, ed. C. Grayson in *Opere volgari*, vol.1 (Bari, 1960); Matteo Palmieri, *Della vita civile*, ed. S. Battaglia (Bologna, 1944); but especially P. P. Vergerio, *De ingenuis moribus*, ed. A. Gnesotto (Padua, 1918). Eng. tr. in W. H. Woodward, *Vittorino de Feltre and other Humanist educators* (Cambridge, 1905).

Athenian and Roman writers recommended democratic forms of government, the Humanists – or many of them – felt it their duty to advocate political liberty.

This general predilection showed itself in an intensified form during the power struggle between Milan and Florence, which produced the polemics Hans Baron has analysed. Professor Whitfield's paper provides some telling quotations mirroring this phase of humanist development. We see Poggio prepared to blame not only mis-government, but also the decline of literature on the loss of liberty. The fifteenth century was still an age of hope when Livy's influence was paramount, and it seemed that republican institutions had some chance of working. With the sixteenth – Professor Whitfield sees 1527 as the turning-point – the balance swung decisively in auto-cracy's favour, and many Italian humanists were faced with the prospect of a painful personal adjustment. The theories of Toffanin, depicting Machiavelli as a disciple of Tacitus, are sharply attacked by Professor Whitfield, who makes out a strong case for assuming that Machiavelli retained confidence in republican institutions. Despair set in only after the disasters of 1527–30 and can be traced in Guicciardini, for whom the tyranny of the Medici came almost as a relief after the tyranny of the people.

Professor La Penna writes about the problems individuals faced under an autocracy. An independent spirit could outrage, obsequi-ousness could disgust an all-powerful ruler. The courtier's problem was to find a middle way, and here Tacitus's descriptions of life under the Caesars proved a useful guide. The situation was ugly enough; but both Professor Whitfield and Professor La Penna point out that an acceptance of autocracy was made easier by the fact that by this time most intellectuals admitted it to be the best available form of government. The alternative was no longer the moderate populism of the Florentine past or the oligarchically controlled democracy of Athens, but anarchy of a frightening kind.

In northern Europe, the situation was easier. Where political liberty had never existed, it was not acutely missed. The passage Dr Baker-Smith quotes from Vivès's commentary on the *Somnium Scipionis* shows Erasmus and his circle mentally prepared for com-promise: 'our Senate and people will assume the leadership of the world by intellectual and cultural endeavour, introducing humane laws to all nations, communicating a civilised mode of life to rude and barbarous peoples, and bringing the scattered race of men into unity through the fellowship and bond of language'. The government envisaged here is efficient, just, peace-loving and motivated by high cultural ideals. But the only reference to popular rule is in the set phrase 'senate and people'; and that cautious mention is immediately cancelled out by talk of the imposition of peace on subject peoples.

One is not surprised therefore to find Bodin in the next generation correcting Aristotle's *Politics*. Professor Weber's careful analysis shows Bodin to have been far to the right of his Italian contemporaries. This French theorist does not strike us as a man who came to terms with an unwelcome reality. He was that reality's convinced apologist. We see him rejecting Aristotle's distinction between constitutions that do and constitutions that do not take the good of the community into account; and one suspects he was unwilling to label 'good' any constitution other than the monarchical. We see him attacking the very foundations of democratic rule when he declares that in any assembly the bad inevitably outnumber the good. He learnt much from Aristotle: what categories to use (even though he rejected some of them), how to assemble evidence, how to analyse it; but his conclusions, dictated by the needs of the monarchical system under which he lived, were altogether different from those of his model.

The kind of pressure that was exercised by the absolutist state is even more evident in another humanist treatise, which Professor Oestreich describes for us. Where Bodin wanted to work out a theory that would justify centralised power, Lipsius in his *Politica* took the existence and desirability of that power for granted and was concerned to use classical knowledge in its service. Rome, as Professor Oestreich reminds us, provided the only known example of a centralised state that was adequately documented, and the humanists of the late sixteenth century set themselves to collect all that classical historians can tell us about the way it had functioned. The *Politica* assembles in its six volumes a huge body of data on the administrative and fiscal procedures of the ancient world. The reader sees that Lipsius has moved beyond the theorising of his predecessors in two important respects. He has come to understand that institutions matter in government, and at the same time he has realised that if institutions are to work, they must have the support of a favourable climate of opinion. He laid great stress on the respect the Romans felt for authority and discipline; and the *Politica* recommends that Renaissance rulers develop this habit of respect in their subjects.

Professor Oestreich mentions Lipsius's political ideas in a wide-ranging paper that discusses how the practical knowledge of the ancients was used in the sixteenth century. Describing developments in law, military science and agriculture, as well as in the art of government, it puts forward a strong case for regarding the humanists of that time as primarily interested in forwarding the acquisition of useful skills. This is an important corrective to the picture we have so often been given of humanism as a backward-looking literary movement whose sole concern was to imitate Cicero's style, the Virgilian epic or Greek tragedy. This practical aspect of the humanist achievement has however remained to the present virtually unexplored, and there are a large number of opportunities for further research. Not only do the relevant classical texts require closer study than they have been given but we have also to establish how the ancient authorities helped with the solution of Renaissance problems in each particular field. This will involve careful enquiry into the detail of translations, commentaries and adaptations; and since many of these are not known to us even by their titles, once again our first need is for an accurate bibliography.

Classical influences in the field of the fine arts have not been neglected to quite this extent. But past research has centred on identifying the Greco-Roman originals used by Renaissance artists or on tracing the impact of classical theories; and consequently there is much that still needs to be done. As in the case of the literature of the period, we have to establish what elements were generally selected for borrowing, and how it was that the borrowed material proved fruitful. Mme Dacos writes about the loggias of the Cortile di S. Damaso in the Vatican, whose stucco-reliefs and paintings constitute one of the richest collections of classically inspired designs that can be found anywhere. Comparison with the invaluable Warburg census of classical works known before 1520, which was drawn up by Mme Phyllis Pray Bober, suggests that practically all the Greco-Roman material available to artists at that time was exploited by Raphael's team. Dispersed over this wide area, their debt to antiquity took two substantially distinct forms: they imitated a great number of specific motifs, and they adopted a style. We see details from classical reliefs that depicted mythological scenes reappearing in new, often biblical contexts. Dionysus turns up as Noah. A satyr astride an ass becomes Jacob astride an ass. And at the same time, we see that the artists made their own the Romano-Hellenistic style of the works they copied, and managed to do this to such an extent that on occasions when they used models of a later and stylistically inferior period, which were themselves imitations of Hellenistic originals, they were able to clear away tasteless accretions and recreate a lost splendour. Mme Dacos then makes a final point of some importance. In Raphael's masterpieces, the classical elements are still clearly recognisable. They play a creative role without being themselves radically transformed. Raphael, like Racine or Ronsard at his best, struck a happy balance between imitation and originality. After his time, we find a much larger gap between artists' sketches from the antique and the works these influence. Classical models still provide inspiration, but at the cost of losing their identity. We have problems here that are of great interest both to the critic and to the historian of culture. The impact made by classical antiquity did not just increase and decrease. It made itself felt in a variety of ways, which are perhaps not directly comparable.

Professor Buddensieg deals with a simpler question. He discusses not the results of imitation, but men's changing attitudes to the classical past. Starting back in the early medieval period, he traces through six stages the development of opinion about the architectural remains of antiquity. An ignorant hostility that regarded the Pantheon as the work of devils persisted through the greater part of the Middle Ages and was succeeded in the fifteenth century by an equally ignorant admiration. Paintings of that time show us classical buildings of great magnificence, but these are little more than glorified versions of contemporary churches and palaces. Then about the turn of the century, the architects took a hand. Men like Giuliano da Sangallo the elder began to make careful analytical drawings of Roman monuments of a type that professional architects could use. They incorporated classical elements in their plans, but still showed a marked tendency to alter what they borrowed in accordance with their own ideas of correct architecture. These pioneers, whose work was described by Dr Howard Burns at the 1969 King's College

Conference,[1] were succeeded by a school of theorists whose criticisms of the antique were based not on their own somewhat Gothic tastes, but on a Vitruvian dogmatism. Accurate reproduction and a true respect for the antique came only with Raphael. He is Professor Buddensieg's hero as he was Mme Dacos's. In his work, the mounting graph of classical influence reaches its peak, and the simplicity favoured by the latter half of the sixteenth century under the impact of Borromeo's aesthetic Puritanism must be taken as a decline.

Finally, Sir Anthony Blunt's paper takes us back to Professor Whitfield's astringent remarks about the supposed unity of the classical tradition. We cannot treat classical literature as if it had been written by a single man; and classical art was not created by a single artist. Sir Anthony points out that what is generally regarded as a Baroque transcendence of classical norms may have been no more than a shift from one sector of a rich tradition to another; that when a Borromini affirmed that his works were based on a study of ancient buildings, his claim was justified. He had merely turned from Vitruvius to the exceptions collected and recorded by that Autolycus, Montano. In so far as this is true (and its truth is affected by the fact that not all Montano's drawings show buildings or monuments that really existed, some being 'reconstructions' where imagination has filled out a ruinous original), the conclusion reached in the last two papers, that Raphael was the supreme classical artist, ought perhaps to be modified. Raphael could be seen as representing not the whole, but one important trend of the classical tradition.

Humanism went through three stages: the extent of the classical heritage was brought to light; it was assimilated by Renaissance culture; and then men used what they had learnt to create something new. These stages manifestly overlapped. Who would argue that Petrarch, the first pioneer of humanism, failed to assimilate classical learning or to use it in a creative way? Or who would argue on the other hand that Casaubon two and a half centuries later added nothing fresh in his *Athenaeus* to our knowledge of the ancient world? Progress moreover occurred at different rates in different sectors of the classical field. Interest in literature came first, preceding by a century or more any close study of language or philosophy. Interest in classical architecture and sculpture came later still, while the

[1] H. Burns 'Quattrocento architecture and the antique' in *Classical Influences on European culture A.D. 500–1500*, ed. R. R. Bolgar (Cambridge, 1971).

revival of ancient science and technology lagged even further behind. By and large however, it can be said that the exploration of the classical heritage was the dominant activity of the fourteenth and fifteenth centuries, and that a forward movement from the positions attained through humanist endeavour was typical of the sixteenth and seventeenth.

The period covered by the papers in this volume is therefore very much the age of new departures. But with the exception perhaps of Professors Ludwig, La Penna and Weber, our contributors do not so much investigate the character of these new departures as point to the need for such investigation. The existing research, which they record, has been largely concerned with analysing how assimilation occurred and the factors which influenced its progress. Among these factors the most notable perhaps was the rise of the vernaculars, which in the sixteenth century replaced international Latin as the main beneficiaries of Humanist learning. Others of almost equal importance were the emergence of powerful centralised states and the change in the Christian ideal from monastic withdrawal to active benevolence. All these receive ample attention. Humanism emerges as a many-sided movement developing in a number of ways within a highly complex civilisation. The simplicities of Burckhardt seem a long way behind us.

PART I

CATALOGUES AND EDITIONS OF HUMANIST WORKS

1

1500–1700: THE BIBLIOGRAPHICAL PROBLEM. A CONTINENTAL S.T.C.?

DENYS HAY

In the summer of 1950 I was still collecting material for my book on Polydore Vergil and I spent a few days looking at copies of printed books in the Bibliothèque Nationale in Paris. It was laborious to find out what the Library held. At that point the published catalogue went only as far as STOSKOPF; for authors later in the alphabet one consulted a series of manuscript catalogues arranged by subject – *Histoire, Belles Lettres* and so on.[1] I saw a fair number of Vergil's printed books but nervously knew that others had probably evaded my search. I am still sure that is the case, but no longer feel particularly nervous. My visit to Paris coincided with the IX International Congress of Historical Sciences, that quinquennial marathon which moves around the world. One of its subdivisions, meeting in a dingy room somewhere in the Sorbonne, provoked me to a passionate plea for a Short Title Catalogue, like our own S.T.C., for continental countries, and ideally for the continent as a whole. I recall scepticism when I described our S.T.C., for I appealed to Mr Lawrence Stone, then a don at Oxford, for confirmation of its existence. And that is all I remember.[2]

The position today is little better, although it is true that a fair number of librarians and bibliographers are concerned, and a few are trying to do something about it. I shall mention some of these initiatives presently. First may I remind you what the situation is at the moment? For books published before 1500 we are handsomely treated, as a result of incunabula having been collector's items for many years. I am not a bibliographer, but I appreciate that much

---

[1] Publication began in 1897. The latest volume (1973) goes as far as WALTARAMUS.

[2] This must, I think, have been in the section 'Méthodes et documents' and during the discussion of a paper by De La Fontaine Verwey (Amsterdam): 'La bibliographie du XVIe siècle. Projet d'une coopération internationale'. I have no recollection of this communication, but I have benefited greatly from reading a paper by Mme Veyrin Forrer dealing with the problem of a union catalogue of sixteenth-century French books.

scientific revision is needed to make the union catalogues of incunables better. But I wish some of the energy still lavished on
incunables could be deflected to books published between 1500 and
(say) 1700. Our knowledge in particular of the unspectacular publications of the sixteenth century (by unspectacular I mean works by
unspectacular authors) is certainly much less than our knowledge of
medieval manuscripts. Some significant discoveries may yet be found
in the neglected folios of the older libraries. I do not mean that the
missing decades of Livy will turn up in a cumbersome Spanish
treatise on theology. Lesser finds there will be, but I am more concerned with the way an overall view will be obtained of cultural
changes in early modern Europe.

Of the libraries with very large holdings of such books – I mean
pre-1700 books – only one has a complete printed catalogue, that of
the British Museum Library, or the British Library, as we must now
learn to call it. I never cease to be proud of Britain when I look along
the shelves of my university library at that remarkable photographic
reprint of the catalogue in the B.M. Reading Room. This enables a
scholar almost anywhere in the world to be almost as well-informed
as if he were actually in Bloomsbury. The British Museum has over
many years in addition put in its debt a range of researchers who
could not find the space, let alone the money, to possess the printed
catalogue. I refer to the series of short title abstracts published for
the main regions of Europe: France, Italy, Germany, Spain, Netherlands.[1] For anyone working in the Renaissance field these volumes
are as indispensable as the S.T.C. of the Bibliographical Society,
extended down to 1700 by Wing. Alas they are no longer as in-
expensive as when they first began to appear. But they are worth
saving up to possess. We can also look forward, shortly it is to be
hoped, to the revised and amplified version of the Bibliographical
Society's S.T.C.

Of course there are hundreds of printed catalogues of old libraries
all over the world. In my own town of Edinburgh such catalogues
exist for the University Library, the National (formerly the Advocates) and the Signet (though some of the older books of this latter
collection have been dispersed). But these catalogues and scores like
them have grave limitations: they are without exception old and

[1] *Spain* (London, 1921); *France* (1924); *Portugal* (1940); *Spanish America* (1944); *Italy* (1958); *German-speaking countries* (1962); *Netherlands etc.* (1965).

they are by no means readily available. The only way to discover what books are in Edinburgh libraries is to go to Edinburgh and look, although since 1970 we have had an admirable S.T.C. of foreign books earlier than 1600 in the National Library.

Remarkable as the holdings of the British Library are, they account for only a modest proportion of the total output of continental presses. In the preface to the *Short Title Catalogue of Books Printed in France to 1600*, the second of the British Museum's series *in usum scholarum* (1924), Alfred W. Pollard wrote: 'considerable as the collection is, it represents probably not much more than a fifth of the editions known to have been printed at Paris, and less than a sixth of the output of the French provinces'. Mr A. F. Johnson, discussing the sixteenth-century Italian books in the British Museum, after bemoaning the absence of printed catalogues of continental libraries, guessed that the Museum's holdings represented perhaps 'a quarter of the known books'.[1] The items in the British Museum S.T.C. for Germany are slightly more numerous but still only a fraction of the total.

The need, then, is pretty obvious and there have been scores of partial attempts to deal with the problem. None of these is fit to be compared for scope and usefulness with the British contribution of Pollard and Redgrave plus Wing. Individually some are remarkable works, such as Mr Adams' survey of Cambridge holdings of sixteenth-century books, which gives collations and other details in more summary lists and which shows, incidentally, that about 44 per cent of books in college libraries are not in the University Library.[2] Mrs Goldsmith's S.T.C. of French books of the seventeenth century in the B.M. has encountered technical criticism but is nonetheless very useful,[3] and for Americans there is the *S.T.C. of Books printed in Italy and of Italian Books printed abroad, 1501–1600*.[4] Finally we must remember the *Répertoire des ouvrages imprimés en langue italienne au XVIᵉ siècle conservés dans les bibliothèques de France*.[5] And there is the

[1] *The Library*, 5th ser., XIII (1958), 161.
[2] H. M. Adams, *Catalogue of books printed on the Continent of Europe, 1501–1600, in Cambridge Libraries* (Cambridge, 1967).
[3] V. F. Goldsmith, *A Short Title Catalogue of French Books 1601–1700 in the Library of the British Museum* (London–Folkestone, 1969–73). See the review by R. A. Sayce, *The Library*, XXVIII (1973), 249–52. Mrs Goldsmith has just (1974) published a similar work covering Spanish and Portuguese books. [4] 3 vols. (Boston, 1970).
[5] Suzanne and P.-H. Michel, *Répertoire des ouvrages imprimés en langue italienne au XVIe siècle, i. A–Ba* (Florence, 1970), is parallel to the above work, which has reached K, restricted to French Library holdings (Paris, 1967–).

very considerable enterprise known as 'Project LOC', which aims to make available a comparison of the holdings of all libraries at Oxford and Cambridge, and of the British Library, of printed books before 1801; all of this, facilitated by a handsome grant from the Old Dominion Foundation, and a use of computers in ways I do not really comprehend, has produced a sample (the letter O). The upshot of this has been to show what one would have, I suppose, guessed: extrapolating the results of the 'O' sample, pre-1801 holdings of the B.M. (nearly 600,000) are nearly three times the Bodleian and four times C.U.L. What was surprising was that college and other libraries at Oxford (about 500,000) and Cambridge (240,000) were really extremely large. All in all there was estimated to be a grand total of 1,650,000 volumes; approximately 750,000 different works were involved.[1]

I have said enough to show that many partial efforts have been made to catalogue in some form of retrievable way (including good old print) scores of libraries in Britain and elsewhere, and those I have mentioned are only a selection. You will all feel I have not even mentioned your own favourite list. Mine, I think, are the collective catalogue of the big Italian libraries which has, alas, only reached AZZ in seven volumes and twelve years; and some specialised library catalogues such as that of the Warburg Institute.[2] I do *not* include, I am afraid, the *Index Aureliensis*, which has begun to be noticeable in antiquarian booksellers' catalogues.[3] My point is simply that a colossal amount of capital has been invested in bits and pieces of cataloguing. I believe that the problem deserves co-ordinated action on a continental scale – at least.[4] Some of you may

[1] I refer to the 'Report' issued in July 1972. Cf. also the University of Lancaster Library Research Unit's 'National Library Coverage' study of August 1971.

[2] *Primo catalogo collettivo delle biblioteche italiane*, 7 vols. (Rome, 1962–); with a DANTE volume published out of turn. *Catalog of the Warburg Institute Library*, 2nd ed., 12 vols and supplement (Boston, 1967–71).

[3] *Index Aureliensis. Catalogus librorum sedecimo saeculo impressorum* (Aureliae Aquensis = Baden-Baden, 1962 ff.). This, published by the Fondation Index Aureliensis, Geneva, is distributed by B. de Graaf, Nieuwkoop, Netherlands. It has reached BUCKE (1973). My reservation relates mainly to the claim that the *Index* lists holdings of representative libraries.

[4] There are a fair number of partially realised or projected bibliographies of which the following may be instanced: *Gesamtkatalog der preussischen Bibliotheken*, 2 vols (Berlin, 1931–9), as far as BEETH; W. Nijhoff and M. E. Kronenberg, *Nederlandsche bibliographie van 1500 tot 1540* (The Hague, 1919–61) continued in E. Cockx-Indestege and G. Glorieux, *Belgica typographica . . . 1541–1600* (Nieuwkoop, 1968 ff.); L. Desgraves (ed.), *Répertoire bibliographique des livres imprimés en France au XIVe siècle* (Baden-Baden, 1968–). But there are a very large number of individual libraries in Britain and

recall that there has recently been agreement on the establishment of a joint fund by the research councils of sixteen European countries.[1] It looks as though this (which unfortunately does not contain new money) will go mainly to the physical sciences. I can think of no fitter use of some of the arts money in the projected scheme than a collaborative bibliography of older books – perhaps in periods of a century at a time – based on the latest techniques (such as those I dimly comprehend in LOC, magnetic tape typewriters, computers, 'finger printing' and so on).

I am sure that I am preaching to the converted, and indeed there are some present who are professionally better informed on all these questions than I am. I must, however, not conceal that were such a wide bibliographical survey to come about it would serve the interests of a far wider group in the world of learning than those who are primarily interested in 'classical influences', the express concern of this Conference. It would illuminate the whole field of changing taste, changing patterns of book acquisition and marketing, changes in education. It would enable us to have a yardstick with which to measure the range and purpose of the older libraries which have been frozen, so to speak, in their pristine state – for instance the Corsiniana in Rome, or indeed any library for which we have an early catalogue.

It would also enable us to refine our generalisations about cultural centres. You will remember that the Pollard and Redgrave S.T.C. has been redigested under years by the energy of Mr William A. Jackson and under printers by Dr Paul Morrison. Such analyses of continental publication would be an invaluable way of watching in Italy the fall of the Venetian printer during the sixteenth century and the rise of the influence of the Roman press. At present all one can give is a 'guesstimation' which suggests that in the period as a whole Venice produced nearly five times as many books as Rome. It would enable us to evaluate the relative importance from time to time of Italian, German and French centres. At the moment it looks as though France, Italy and Germany all produced about the same number of titles – Germany a little more if we add in Basle.[2]

---

abroad, with printed catalogues of their earlier books. More general bibliographies exist (I am informed) for Denmark, Iceland, Norway, Sweden and Russia.

[1] See announcement in *The Times* of 27 September 1973 and subsequent correspondence; cf. *The Times Higher Education Supplement*, 16 November 1973.

[2] *The Library*, XIII (1958), 162.

Another important matter which deserves close scrutiny, and one which can only be tackled by a bibliographical approach which is widely based, is the effect on the circulation of books of censorship of various kinds. The most important effects of censorship were induced by the successive steps taken by ecclesiastical authorities, which culminated in the Roman *Index librorum prohibitorum* of 1559 and its later elaborations and reissues.[1] That this distorted the book trade is notorious, but its effects are very hard to estimate.[2] If the existence of an official list of undesirable works made them difficult to get in Roman Catholic territories, this was not uniformly so. It was easier to obtain works from tainted sources in Protestant Leyden if you lived in France than if you lived in Italy; the Spanish book-collector was even more at the mercy of the Inquisition. There were, of course, all sorts of devices for the ingenious to use. The Italian scholar could look for surreptitious help from a friend in more liberal France; there was the equivalent of the diplomatic bag; and there were some officials of the Holy Office who were more amenable than others. At the other end of the spectrum there were Protestants who looked on the appearance of a continental work in a Roman Catholic Index as a certificate of orthodoxy and importance; Thomas James when he was Bodley's librarian urged Protestants in this direction.[3]

I said a moment ago that the history of education would be illuminated if we knew more about publishing and book buying after 1500. As it is, some things seem evident even from the sporadic forays already made. M. Martin suggests that Geneva in the later sixteenth century is a more important source of learned texts than Roman Catholic Paris.[4] Of Italy Mr A. F. Johnson has written 'the order of popularity of the Latin classics remains in the sixteenth century as reported by Dr Scholderer (for the fifteenth). Cicero was easily the most popular author, especially his Letters, and is followed by Ovid, Vergil, Terence and Horace in that order . . . The chief difference is that after 1500 there is a higher proportion of versions in Italian.'[5] This, incidentally, is borne out more or less by Cambridge libraries.[6]

[1] F. Reusch, *Die* Indices Librorum prohibitorum *des 16 Jahrhunderts* (Tübingen, 1886).
[2] Cf. H. J. Martin, *Livre, pouvoirs et société à Paris au XVIIe siècle* (Geneva, 1969), I. 6–16; and Antonio Rotondò, 'La censura ecclesiastica e la cultura', in the Einaudi *Storia d'Italia*, 5. *I documenti* pt.2 (Turin, 1973), pp.1399–1492.
[3] See *Dict. Nat. Biog.* x (1921–2 ed.), pp.659–60.   [4] *Livre, pouvoirs et société*, I, 29.
[5] *The Library*, XIII (1958), 165.   [6] *The Library*, XIV (1959), 220.

Perhaps you find this unsurprising and I dare say it is the order one would expect as an educator. But the LOC project has thrown up a more unusual piece of information: 'Latin is overtaken by English between 1621 and 1640 . . . a surprisingly early change when it is remembered how closely [university] libraries were tied to academic needs and how pedagogically important Latin remained to the Universities.' A continental-wide survey is needed because long after the Reformation the learned books of Europe tended to be printed not for national consumption but for an international public. We cannot before the eighteenth century deal adequately with publication on the basis of patriotism or parochial loyalties.

I conclude this amateur survey on a lugubrious note. The western world is entering on a period of austerity. The old days when Bodley or the British Museum bought an old book because it was not already on their shelves or a new book because it was important are over. In filling gaps and in adding new stock the great libraries of Europe and North America will have to specialise and collaborate. We cannot begin to do this until we know the strengths and the weaknesses of the holdings of our big libraries. In a way, a depressing way, this is the ultimate pressure behind my plea for a continental S.T.C.[1]

[1] I must thank a number of scholars who have helped me with facts and saved me from blunders. Among them I must name Miss Alison Harvey Wood and some of her colleagues at the National Library of Scotland (Miss King, Mr McGowan, Mr Kelly and Mr Holland); Professor J. IJsewijn; Mr J. B. Trapp; and Mr R. O. MacKenna.

2

NEO-LATIN SATIRE: *SERMO* AND *SATYRA MENIPPEA*

J. IJSEWIJN

The purpose of this contribution is to serve as a first introduction to a scarcely explored field of Neo-Latin literature, which owes its main characteristics to the Roman satirists, yet in most cases is intimately connected with contemporary life in the sixteenth and seventeenth centuries.

Since space is limited it would be impossible to speak of the many different kinds of satirical writing to be found in Renaissance and modern Latin prose and poetry, such as epigrams,[1] letters,[2] dialogues,[3] *declamationes*,[4] or long poems in either elegiac or heroic verse;[5] and for this reason we will limit ourselves to formal satire in hexameter verse after the example of Horace, Persius and Juvenal, and secondarily to *Satyrae Menippeae* and *Satyrica*, the models for which were Seneca's *Apocolocyntosis* and Petronius.

In many respects, the chronological limits chosen for the King's College Conference (1500–1700) do not coincide with those of Neo-Latin satire. To begin with, we lose the whole fifteenth century,

---

[1] Good satirical epigrams were written e.g. by the Germans Ulrich von Hutten and Euricius Cordus, by the Welshman John Owen (Audoenus), the Italians Antonius Beccadelli (Panormita) and Joh. Campanus, etc. See from the recent literature Fr.-R. Hausmann, 'Untersuchungen zum neulateinischen Epigram Italiens im Quattrocento', *Humanistica Lovaniensia*, XXI (1972), 1–36; H. C. Schnur, 'The Humanist Epigram and its Influence on the German Epigram', in *Acta Conventus Neolatini Lovaniensis*, ed. by J. IJsewijn and E. Kessler (Leuven–Munich, 1973), pp.557–76; K.-H. Mehnert, *Sal Romanus und Esprit Français: Studien zur Martial-rezeption im Frankreich des 16. und 17. Jhts* (Bonn, 1970).

[2] First of all the *Epistolae Obscurorum Virorum*. See H. Rogge, *Fingierte Briefe als Mittel politischer Satire* (Munich, 1966), a historical survey and anthology of the genre.

[3] Fine specimens are the dialogues of Johannes Jovianus Pontanus, Ulrich von Hutten and Erasmus's *Colloquia*.

[4] It may suffice to mention Erasmus's *Laus Stultitiae* as the example *par excellence*. Many others are less well known, e.g. the *Laus Ululae ad conscriptos ululantium patres et patronos* of Conradus Goddaeus, Claucopoli, s.a. (Amsterdam, *ca* 1664). See *Admiranda Rerum Admirabilium Encomia* (Nijmegen, 1677).

[5] Among others the *Grobianus* of Fr. Dedekindus and the *Franciscanus* of Buchanan are still famous in literary history.

and that means losing the heyday of Italian humanism, which produced quite a few modern Horaces and Juvenals, not to speak of the
immense amount of work done by philologists such as Gaspar
Veronensis,[1] Domitius Calderini,[2] Johannes Baptista Cantalycius[3]
(and many others) who laboured to procure a better text and to
promote a better understanding of the Roman satirists. Fortunately,
for Italy we possess an excellent book by Vittorio Cian, *La Satira*
(Milan, 1945), which offers a reliable introduction to satirists in
both Latin and the vernacular. Nevertheless, I want to stress here
that there is a most urgent need precisely for the Quattrocento of a
critical and annotated edition of the hundred satires by Franciscus
Filelfus, which were completed before 1448 and were printed several
times from 1476 onwards; and some of which were even introduced
into early sixteenth-century school anthologies.[4]

On the other extreme of our chronological boundaries, we have
Neo-Latin satire continuing its life uninterruptedly down to the
In stultitiam satura and the supplement to Juvenal's last satire, written
in the sixties of this century by the American Harry C. Schnur[5]
or to the satires on the permissive society by the German poet Josef
Eberle, published as late as 1970.[6] Many other examples could be
given of this late flowering of the old Roman genre: in England Neo-
Latin satire was rather assiduously cultivated in the time of Pope,
e.g. by William King;[7] Switzerland can boast of a fine satirist,
Petrus Esseiva, in the late nineteenth century,[8] while the most

---

[1] His autograph comments on Persius and Juvenal are in MS Vat. Lat. 2710. According to
Dorothy Robathan, he is to be identified with Martinus Phileticus. See V. Cian, *La
Satira* (Milan, 1945), p.410 and P. O. Kristeller, *Iter Italicum* (London–Leiden, 1963),
II, p.314.

[2] R. Malaboti, *Domizio Calderini: contributo alla storia dell'umanesimo* (Milan, 1919).

[3] V. Zappacosta, 'Cantalycii in Ibin Ovidianum Labyrinthum interpretatio', *Latinitas*,
XXI (1973), 269–85 and the literature quoted there.

[4] E.g. in Wimpfeling's *Scoparius* and *Adolescentia*.

[5] Schnur's satires are to be found in (1) C. Arrius Nurus, *Pegasus Tolutarius*, edidit et
scholiis doctis ornavit Harry C. Schnur (Oudenaerde, 1962), 53–60 ('In Grammaticum
periurum satira; Eichmann': this poem in distichs); (2) *Carmina Certaminis Poetici
Hoeufftiani* (Amsterdam, 1963), 53–71: 'In stultitiam'; (3) 'Satirae XVI fragmentum
nuperrime repertum', in *Silvae. Festschrift für E. Zinn* ed. by M. von Albrecht and E.
Heck (Tübingen, 1970), 211–15.

[6] Iosephus Apellus P. L., *Echo Perennis: Elegiae/Satirae/Didactica, cum versione Germanica//*
Josef Eberle, *Nie Verstummendes Echo* (Stuttgart, 1970).

[7] See in general Bradner, Leicester, *Musae Anglicanae: A History of Anglo-Latin Poetry
1500–1925* (New York–London, 1940).

[8] His poems are to be found among the *Carmina Certaminis Poetici Hoeufftiani* between
1878 and 1892, and in his *Carminum libri IX* (Freiburg-Sw., 1894), a copy of which is
in the Vatican Library. Esseiva was born in Freiburg on 3 April 1823 and died there

important Latin satirists of the Slavic world, the Pole Antonius
Łoz Poninski[1] and the Croatian Junius Resti[2] belong to the eighteenth and nineteenth centuries.

I am coming now to the sixteenth and seventeenth centuries, for
which almost everything remains to be done. To begin with, so
far as I know there is no list or survey of Neo-Latin satirical works
available for this period. Consequently, I have drawn up for myself
a list of about forty writers of *sermones*, ten authors of small Menippean satires after the manner of Seneca and ten authors of bigger
satyrica. This list is undoubtedly very incomplete, since the only way
to find such texts is by reading hundreds of old books and a great
number of bio-bibliographical dictionaries, catalogues of antiquarian booksellers[3] and the like. But of those I found, only five
poets and two *satyrica* are available in modern editions, as can be
seen from the list appended to this article.

From all this, it will be clear that a definitive study of Neo-Latin
satire is far from being in sight of completion. It would take months
and years to collect copies and to interpret the innumerable allusions even if such an attempt at interpretation was confined to the
most important texts. Therefore I repeat again my call for editorial

---

on 9 May 1899. Notices on his life and work are in *Monat-Rosen, Organ und Eigentum des Schweizerischen Studentenvereins* 28 (1884), 200–17, 281–94, 361–72, 518–20; in *Nouvelles Etrennes fribourgeoises: Almanach des villes et des Campagnes* 34 (1900), 108–11; and in J. Baumgartner, *Die Lateinische und Griechische Literatur der Christlichen Völker* (=Ge-schichte der Weltliteratur, Bd. IV), (Freiburg-Br., 1925[2]). The satires are: 'Satira ad iuvenem'; 'Satira ad procum'; 'Satira de mulieribus emancipatis'.

[1] His *Sarmatides seu Satyrae cuiusdam equitis poloni* appeared in 1741 (in Warsaw?) under the pseudonym of J. M. Królikiewicz. Influence by Pope is possible. Cf. R. Pollak (ed.), *Piśmiennictwo Staropolskie*, Bibliografia Literatury Polskiej 'Nowy Korbut' 3 (Warsaw, 1965), 115–17; Paulina Buchwald-Pelcowa, *La Satire de l'époque des rois Saxons* (Wrocław, 1969). Copies are in the University Library of Łódź and in the Jagellonian Library in Kraków (the last one is missing quire b, i.e. the latter part of the Praefatio).

[2] Resti's *Carmina* were edited by F. M. Appendini (Padua, 1816), two years after the death of their author (Dubrovnik, 1755–1814). Cf. V. Gortan–Vl. Vratović, *Hrvatski Latinisti*, II (Zagreb, 1970), 770–831.

[3] A few examples chosen at random in recent catalogues. In Catalogue 222 (Livres Anciens et Modernes) of the Librairie Paul Jammes in Paris, published autumn 1973, a satire is offered on p.57, nr.594: *Hippolytus redivivus, id est remedium contemnendi sexum muliebrem, autore S.I.E.D.V.M.W.A.S.*, s.l., 1644, 96 pp. in–12. In Catalogue 2 (Rare books and some manuscripts) of Richard von Hünersdorff in London, published spring 1974, one finds a satire of German origin on the sexual behaviour of students, cloaked in the form of a university dissertation: *Theses de cochleatione eiusque venenosa contagione et multiplicibus speciebus, quas sub praeside Hasione Leflero . . . Pro privato et domestico exercitio sui, defendet Volucrinia Lepida Stutzerensis: In Collegii huius facultatibus penetralibus in frequentia utriusque sexus*, 1627, in–4; 6 lvs.

and exegetical work on Neo-Latin literature. Can you imagine today a classicist compelled to read Juvenal in manuscript or only in a rare *editio princeps*? But this is the uneasy situation in which a Neo-Latin scholar frequently finds himself. Moreover I want to stress that those editions that are produced should be in accessible collections or journals[1] and that the notes should be written either in Latin or in a major Western language.

I will now illustrate as far as possible some trends and aspects of Latin satire in the period we are considering.[2] Apart from traditional moralising on human vices and other ancient themes, the modern satirists devoted particular attention to religious, literary and also medical topics. Their stylistic models were most frequently their Roman predecessors, including Lucilius, whose influence becomes noticeable after Franciscus Dousa's first edition of his collected fragments (Leiden, 1597). It goes without saying that Martial is also omnipresent. It even happened that *sermones* were written in a purely heroic style, e.g. a 'Satyra in sicarios ac impiissimos latrones, quorum nuper quidam compraehensi sunt, qui Reverendiss. in Christo principem & Dominum D. Melchiorem Zobel Episcopum Herbipolensem, ac Franciae Orientalis Ducem ex insidiis adorti, Anno Domini 1558, die vero 15 Aprilis, perfide & crudelissime interfecerunt', the author of which is Caspar Stiblinus.[3] Sometimes

---

[1] The *editio princeps* of Simon Rettenpacher's satires by P. Leonhard Klinglmair in the *113. Jahresbericht Schuljahr 1970 öffentliches Gymnasium der Benediktiner zu Kremsmünster* is almost unobtainable outside Austria since it is not for sale. The copy for the library of Louvain was acquired after several vain efforts through the helpful intervention of a colleague in Vienna.

[2] Some useful works are: G. Hess, *Deutsch–lateinische Narrenzunft. Studien zum Verhältnis von Volkssprache und Latinität in der satirischen Literatur des 16. Jahrhunderts* (Munich, 1971); U. Limentani, *La satira nel Seicento* (Milan–Naples, 1961); H. Schaller, 'Parodie und Satire der Renaissance und Reformation', *Forschungen und Fortschritte*, 33 (1958), 183–8, 216–19; D. J. Shaw, 'More about the "Dramatic Satyre"', *Bibliothèque d'Humanisme et Renaissance*, 30 (1968), 301–25.

[3] One may judge by a sample of the text, ll.65–72 on p.Aiij:

> Iam quater exacto Phoebus sua tempora cursu
> Conficit, horrendum facinus cum cerneret amnis
> Qui riguis Francas undis late alluit urbes,
> Insons cum tristi Francorum funere princeps,
> Princeps Nestoreo longe dignissimus aevo:
> Insidiis, Stygioque dolo, furiisque latronum
> Indigne oppressus cecidit, terramque momordit
> Ore premens, multo et fudit cum sanguine vitam.

A copy of the original edition is in the University Library of Freiburg/Breisgau. We thank our friend Dr B. Coppel, who provided us with a photocopy.

we find in one and the same satire a blend of many different poetical styles, as in the first satire of Janus Dousa, where we can see successively reminiscences of Catullus:

> Cui damus hanc? Gulielme, tibi! Tu namque putare
> Esse meas aliquid tricas apinasque solebas . . .

of Horace:

> Exceptos tandem hospitio Gravesanda Britanno . . .

of Persius and Virgil:

> Quadrupedante Ultraiectum quatit ungula, et omnes . . .

etc.

As to the contents of the *sermones*, no one will feel surprised, to be sure, that the century of the Reformation and Counter-Reformation was rich in religious satire; and that often this satire was also political, cultural and social in character. No better example of this mixture of religion and politics exists than two satires by the first curator of Leiden University, Janus Dousa, against making peace with the Duke of Alva, the Spanish governor of the southern Netherlands. The most famous specimens of satire from the Reformation camp are the *Satyrarum libri quinque priores*, written by Thomas Naogeorgus and printed at Basle in 1559. There is no modern edition, although one may be expected in the next few years as a part of the Berlin edition of Naogeorgus's works launched by Professor G. Roloff.[1]

A very interesting sub-division of religious satire is provided by the *sermones* against ecclesiastical censorship and on behalf of poetical liberty. Let me quote an example from my own country: the first satires of the Catholic Antwerp patrician Petrus Scholirius, edited in 1623, are directed against the censors at the university of Louvain, where Scholirius got his degree. Echoing Persius in his wording, Scholirius wrote:[2]

> Nam quid rancidius quam me Tritonidis hastâ
> Carmina vertentem, bis terque quaterque citari
> Parte Facultatis, Rectoris parte citari . . .!

[1] Th. Naogeorgus, *Werke*, ed. by H. G. Roloff. The first volume *Tragoedia nova Pammachius*, with German translation by J. Tyrolff was announced for 1974.

[2] I used the edition of the collected satires: Petri Scholirii equitis et senatoris Antverpiensis *Sermonum Familiarium libri III* cum commentariis Alberti Le Roy (Antwerp, 1683). The verses quoted are from satire 1.11–13 (p.6) and 38–9 (p.9). That his freedom of speech has its limitations appears from the very end of the satire, where Apollo gives his wise advice (116–17): 'Promiscua ludite, Vates, | De reliquis caute, de Principe relligiose.'

and further on he concludes

> ... Libertas aurea vatum
> Tuta sit in terris.

It is interesting to notice that this poet earned fervent praises from Erycius Puteanus, the successor of Lipsius in the chair of Latin at Louvain[1] and himself author of a Menippean satire in the popular form of a dream: *Comus sive Phagesiposia cimmeria: de luxu somnium* (Louvain, 1608).[2]

A second class of considerable importance is the literary satires: they remind us, naturally, of the literary *sermones* of Horace (1.4 and 10; II.1), of the first piece of Persius, of Juvenal's attacks on the *recitationes* and, in modern literature, of the Satires of Boileau. Their interest lies in the fact that the Neo-Latin satirists engage in discussions on contemporary literature. For example, the first Dutch satirist, Petrus Montanus, whose poems went through several editions during the first decade of the sixteenth century,[3] wrote a satire *De discrimine inter divinum poetam et versificatorem*, a subject often mooted in the debate between medieval and humanist literature ever since the Italian Trecento, and whose lasting topicality, at least this side of the Alps, is sufficiently proven by many passages of the *Epistolae obscurorum virorum*.

In the late sixteenth and early seventeenth century the humanists were more than ever divided by questions of what style to use in Latin. The old Ciceronian school was far from dead, as is proved by the educational programme of the Jesuits. At the other extreme we find authors who swear by the style of Plautus and Apuleius, enriched with all kinds of archaisms found in Nonius and the like. Very suitably they called themselves *antiquarii*.[4] One of them, the German J. Lauremberg, wrote a drama *Pompeius* (1610) using almost exclusively Lucilian Latin. He even excused himself for so

---

[1] See his letters to the poet of 17 March 1623 and 25 January 1627, to be found among the *Judicia doctorum virorum* in front of Le Roy's edition.

[2] It is also included in the *Elegantiores Praestantium Virorum Satyrae* (Leiden, 1655). C. Sobry published a French and a Dutch translation: 'Comus ou la Ripaille cimmérienne. Récit en prose et en vers d'E.P.', *Latomus*, I (1937), 113–40, 211–29; E.P., *Comus of de Kimmerische Zwelgpartij* (Antwerp, 1938).

[3] J. Prinsen, 'Petrus Montanus', *Nijhoff's Bijdragen*, 3 (1903), 113–47; *Nieuw Nederlandsch Biografisch Woordenboek*, III (1914), col.878–9. Six satires were printed (s.l.) 1501 and Zwolle, 1506; four of them in Strasbourg, 1529.

[4] See e.g. epigrams XII and L of Adeodatus Marivorda, *Humanistica Lovaniensia*, XVII (1968), 17 and 25.

doing, since Pompeius certainly did not speak that Latin himself.[1] Whereas in earlier days the battles of style were generally fought in prose (think of Erasmus's *Ciceronianus* or Ortensio Lando's dialogues *Cicero relegatus* and *Cicero revocatus*),[2] from the late sixteenth century on we find *sermones* for and against archaism or classicism. A striking example is the first satire of Michael Abel from Frankfurt/Oder, whose slim volume of Latin verse was published in Prague in 1591.[3] He ridicules the archaist poets, whom he calls a *Versificatorum compagnia* – note here the ironical neologism! – and whose language he perfectly imitates:

> Dicite, Lucilli spurium genus Paccuvique
> (Carizare iuvat quoniam cum Care) quis auctor
> Vos citat in graciles tali cacoethe Camoenas? . . .

and he ends his satire with the verse:

> Interea id Musae pignus meminentis habessint.

But from the opposite side, another German, Paul Fleming, an outspoken partisan of Pacuvius, fulminates about 1630 against the Ciceronianism of the schoolmasters, whose device is and remains for ever:

> Noster erat et erit Cicero! Ciceronis enim (Pax!)
> Sola triumphatrix sermonis palma Latini est![4]

In such cases humanist studies come dangerously close to being a kind of pedantic esoterism, as is shown not only by Latin verses of Fleming[5] but also by others as e.g. the French bishop P. D. Huet, not unknown in literary history.[6]

At the end of the period which concerns us in this conference, we find the work of a man, who was perhaps the greatest among the

---

[1] The only known copy of the original edition is in the town library of Schwerin, DDR. A microfilm copy is kept at Louvain.

[2] D. Gagliardi, *Il Ciceronismo nel Primo Cinquecento e Ortensio Lando*, Quaderni di 'Le Parole e le Idee', VI (Naples, 1967).

[3] *Musae undecimae seu ineptae versificatoriae delibatio*. Cf. J. Hejnic–J. Martinek, *Enchiridion Renatae Poesis Latinae in Bohemia et Moravia cultae*, I (Prague, 1966), 24–5.

[4] *Satira*, 77–8. Cf. Paul Fleming's *Lateinische Gedichte*, ed. by J. M. Lappenberg (Stuttgart, 1863), 6–9. Also typical are the verses 56–8: 'Tempus erat, quo Plautus erat bona regula linguae | Et princeps Latiae. Sed quantum distat ab illo | Hoc nostrum, Superi! . . .'

[5] The ninth book of the *Silvae* is characteristic in this respect.

[6] His *Poemata Latina et Graeca* were published in Utrecht in 1694 and in augmented editions Paris 1709 and 1729.

modern Latin satirists, the Italian Monsignore – no priest in spite of his title – Lodovico Sergardi or 'Quintus Sectanus' as he called himself in Latin. Most of his satires owe their origin to an uncompromising enmity towards Gianvincenzo Gravina, one of his fellow members in the then recently founded academy 'Arcadia',[1] who had laughed at one of his verses. We urgently need a critical edition of the Latin text of his eighteen satires,[2] since the last study of this work was based upon an old Italian translation.[3]

Many other aspects of literary satire could be mentioned and studied. I will limit myself to one, since it has some general importance. In his third satire Janus Dousa supports a friend, a physician, against his colleagues who deem poetry unworthy of serious men in that discipline. Now, this throws a remarkable light on the social attitudes of the time. It was not exceptional for doctors to write Latin verse, and some of them were very famous poets; we have only to remember Hieronymus Fracastorius. In general one reads their praises; but here we learn that their colleagues in the faculties of medicine did not always share this favourable opinion.

Speaking of medicine, we arrive at a third group, medical satire, which is not rare at all. Already Petrus Montanus, whom we mentioned above, has a short *satyra de medicis*, in which he depicts an *exemplar vere boni medici*. But as far as we have been able to ascertain, medical satire developed particularly from the seventeenth century onwards. At that time, Latin satire tended to become more and more of an academic distraction and less and less a real and effective comment on contemporary life. This does not mean that medical satire was necessarily merely academic, but the subject lends itself better to such an evolution than religious satire. In 1651 the *Medicinae gloria per satyras duo et viginti asserta* was published in Munich, a collection in which the famous Jesuit poet Jacob Balde anticipated several of the motives, which Molière was to elaborate so brilliantly twenty-two years later in his *Malade imaginaire*, though Balde thinks better of doctors than the French playwright did. Balde did not attack medicine and its practitioners onesidedly. If he stigmatises their vices, he does the same with the sick, and on the

---

[1] I. Carini, *L'Arcadia dal 1690 al 1890* (Rome, 1891).
[2] The satires were written between 1683 and 1718 and published from 1694 on. The best complete edition is Lucca, 1783.
[3] A. Quondam, 'Le satire di Ludovico Sergardi. Contributo ad una storia della cultura romana tra Sei e Settecento', *La Rassegna della letteratura italiana*, 73 (1969), 206–72.

other hand he praises skilful doctors such as Vesalius.[1] This is also the opinion of Simon Rettenpacher, an Austrian Benedictine, who wrote at the end of the same century and who begins his second satire: 'Nobilius nil est medico, nil maius in orbe'.[2]

In the course of the seventeenth century, members of religious orders appear more and more often among the satirists: Jesuits, Benedictines, later also Fathers of the *Scholae Piae*. This naturally increased the part played by moralising satire; but it should be stressed that our satirists never shirked their duty, or what they thought to be their duty of satirising the seamy side of life, though it is true that satire now took a more outspokenly Roman Catholic (Counter-Reformation) or Stoic colour.

I will now add a few words on satire in mixed prose and verse. Menippean satire in its shorter form became popular again thanks to the example, I believe, of Lipsius's *Somnium: Lusus in nostri aevi criticos* (Antwerp, 1581), a perfect specimen of *parodia docta* after Seneca's *Apocolocyntosis*. Lipsius tells us how, in a dream, he and his friend Dousa witnessed a trial in the Roman senate of those audacious philologists who venture to 'correct' ancient texts according to their own fantastic imaginations. Here Lipsius touched upon a sore point in contemporary philology, since we find analogous complaints about foolhardy *correctores* in the preface to Fulvio Orsini's edition of Arnobius and elsewhere. Lipsius's satire proved to be a success. It was widely read and imitated in Europe, and was assigned the first place in the famous collection, *Elegantiores praestantium virorum satyrae* (Leiden, 1655), where it was put before Seneca himself!

Long satirical novels in Menippean form were reintroduced into Latin literature early in the seventeenth century by John Barclay, a Scotsman born and educated in France. One wonders which model he imitated. The title of his work *Euphormionis Lusinini Satyricon*[3] and some of his statements suggest Petronius, but the idea that he imitated this author would explain the Menippean aspect of his work

---

[1] Professor C. J. Classen (Göttingen) read a paper 'Jakob Balde's medizinische Satiren' during the second international congress of Neo-Latin studies, Amsterdam, 1973.

[2] See p.44 n.1 above. On Rettenpacher see now the article of M. Enzinger in *Tausend Jahre Österreich. Ein biographische Chronik*, ed. by W. Pollak, 1 (Vienna–Munich, 1973), 250–4.

[3] John Barclay, *Euphormionis Lusinini Satyricon (Euphormio's Satyricon) 1605–1607*. Translated from the Latin with introduction and notes by D. A. Fleming. Bibliotheca Humanistica & Reformatorica, VI (Nieuwkoop, 1973).

rather than his composing a long work of fiction. One should not forget that the greater part of Petronius, namely the *Cena Trimalchionis*, was discovered only forty years later. Possibly Barclay was influenced by French literature and works such as Rabelais's *Gargantua* or even the *Satire Ménippée du Catholicon d'Espagne* of 1593, although this latter is not a novel but, for the greater part, a series of speeches and poems. The point has still to be settled and even after the studies and edition of David Fleming much research remains to be done on this *satyricon*, which was a best-seller for many generations. Several other *satyrica* followed: for example, a most curious French *Gaeomemphionis Cantaliensis Satyricon* (1628), now available in an excellent critical edition and French translation,[1] and the Dutch *Satyricon in corruptae iuventutis mores corruptos* of Janus Bodecherus Benningius or Hermophilus Tanugriensis (Leiden, 1631), which claims to be a realistic picture of student life at Leiden University. Finally (and although it belongs to the mid-eighteenth century I want to mention it here) we have the last of the great Neo-Latin works in Menippean form:[2] the *Nicolai Klimii Iter Subterraneum* of Ludvig Holberg from Bergen, Norway, which is one of the real masterpieces of Neo-Latin literature and is worthy to stand next to the roughly contemporary work of Jonathan Swift. A few years ago a new edition with Danish translation appeared at Copenhagen.[3]

If much work has already been done on men like Barclay and Holberg, nothing has been done on other *satyrica*. Let me conclude with one example of this. The B.L. owns a copy of a *Satyricon Asini vapulantis, authore Redivivo Menippo*. According to the British Museum Catalogue it was written about 1630 by a certain Alexander Iulius Torquatus a Frangipani. I do not know where the author of the catalogue got this information. In the book we find a letter dated 1662, but this may be a fictitious date. Moreover it is clear that the work belongs to the mass of polemical literature exchanged between

---

[1] *Gaeomemphionis Cantaliensis Satyricon 1628*. Texte latin établi, présenté et annoté par Juliette Desjardins. Roma Aeterna v (Leiden, 1972); François Guyet, *Le Roman satirique de Gaeomemphion du Cantal*. Traduction française présentée et annotée par J. Desjardins. Classiques Néo-Latins 1 (Geneva, 1972).

[2] The very last short Menippean satire seems to be Harry C. Schnur, *Vallum Berolinense. Menippea* (Avignon, 1962; also in the September issue of that year of *Vita Latina*), on the building of the Berlin wall.

[3] Ludvig Holberg, *Niels Klims Underjordiske Rejse 1741–1745*, ed. A. Kragelund (Copenhagen, 1970), 3 vols.

the Jesuits and Protestants in northern Germany. It is, of course, full of allusions which are difficult to interpret. This text alone, I believe, will require long investigation before it can be understood correctly and appreciated in its true historical context and value. *Ab uno disce omnes!*

SERMONUM seu SATYRARUM Scriptores Latini

Saec.XV–XX.

ca 1300   MUSSATUS Albertinus, *Epistolae seu sermones.*

ca 1350   DA STRADA Zanobius, *Satyra in leguleium.*

1429/33   CORRARIUS Gregorius Venetus, *Liber Satyrarum.*
         (Ed. princeps: J. J. Berrigan, Humanistica Lovaniensia, XXII (1973), 10–38.)

14../48   PHILELPHUS Franciscus Tolentinus, *Satyrarum opus = Satyrae centum distinctae decem decadibus.*
         (Ed. princeps: Mediolani, Id. Nov. 1476, prima decas; edd.: Venetiis, 1502; Parisiis, 1508; Tubingae, 1513 ...)

ante 1439   DE LUSCHIS Nicolaus Vicentinus, *Satira in Philelphum.*

ca 1460/70   TRIBRACHUS Gaspar, *Satirae VIII.*
         (Ed.: Tribraco, Gaspare, *Satirarum liber, dedicato al duca Borso d'Este.* A cura di G. Venturini. Deputazione provinciale ferrarese di storia patria: Atti e Memorie, serie III, vol.XIV (Ferrara, 1972).)
         VERINUS Ugolinus, *Satirae* (Florentiae).

ca 1475   LIPPIUS Laurentius Collensis, *Libellus satyrarum ad Laurentium Medicen* (Firenze, Bibl. Riccard. 3022)
         (Ed. partim G. Bottiglioni, *La lirica latina in Firenze nella seconda metà del secolo XV* (Pisa, 1913).)

14..   STROZZI Titus Vespasianus Ferrariensis, *Sermonum libri III.*
         (Ed.: Strozzii poetae pater et filius (Venetiis, 1513).)

14../90   CARARIENSIS Iohannes Mich. Alb. Bergomas, *Sermones Obiurgatorii XV* (Bergamo, Bibl. Civ., Λ 1.18).
         (Ed. partim J. B. Giraldi, *J. M. A. Carariensis Opera* (Novara, 1967), 45–68.)

1489   HASSENSTEINIUS a LOBKOWIC Boheslaus Bohemo-germanus, *Ad Sanctum Venceslaum Satira, in qua mores procerum, nobilium et popularium patriae suae reprehendit.*
         (Ed.: Thomas Mitis, *Farrago Poematum* (Pragae, 1570); K. Hrdina, *Bohemia Latina* (Pragae, 1931), 47–52, etc.)

ca 1494   URCEUS CODRUS Antonius Rubieranus, *Satyrae II.*
         (Ed.: *Opera* (Basileae, 1540), 363 73.)

ca 1500   KEMPO THESSALIENSIS, *Carmina et epigrammata pulcherrima* (Zwolle).
         The first poem is: 'De dolis Gallorum satyra'.

1501   MONTANUS Petrus Batavus, *Satyrae*, s.l.; Suollis, 1506; Argentorati, 1529.

ante 1503   CALENTIUS Elysius Johannes, *Satyrae II.*
         (Ed.: *Opuscula* (Roma, 1503).)

1504	BEBELIUS Henricus Iustingensis, *Satyra contra detractores et perversos hominum mores.*
	(Ed.: *Opera* (Phorce = Pforzheim, 1504); *Opuscula* (Argentorati, 1512).)
ante 1513	HUTTENUS Ulrichus, eques Germanus, *In tempora Julii satyra.*
	(Ed.: *Opera omnia,* ed. E. Böcking, vol.III (Leipzig, 1862), 269–70.)
1507/14	GELDENHAUER Gerardus Noviomagensis, *Satyrae VIII* (Lovanii, 1515).
	(Ed.: J. Prinsen, *Collectanea van G.G.N.* (Amsterdam, 1901).)
15..	POLLIUS Johannes Wesphalus, *Ecclesiastomoria digesta sermonibus IIII* (in: *Opuscula piissima et eruditissima* (Tiguri = Zürich, s.a.)).
1532	ANYSIUS Janus Neapolitanus, *Varia Poemata et Satyrae* (Neapoli; ed. auctior 1536).
1538	VALERIANUS Pierius, *Sermones* [Basileae].
ante 1539	BENESSA = BENESIC Damianus Ragusinus, *Sermonum liber* (MS: Dubrovnik, Bibl. Fratrum Minorum).
	(Vide V. Gortan–Vl. Vratovic, *Croatici auctores qui Latine scripserunt,* 1 (Zagreb, 1969), 517–19.)
ca 1545	ROYZIUS Petrus Maureus in Polonia, *De arte adulandi sermo.*
	(Ed.: B. Kruczkiewicz, *Carmina,* 1 (Cracoviae, 1900).)
ca 1550	CASA Iohannes Italus, *Satyra* (in eos qui, cum nequissimam vitae rationem inierint, ipsum quod deses sit et quod amet accusent).
	(Ed.: *Opere,* IV (Venezia, 1728), 7 sqq.)
1552	HORTENSIUS Lambertus Montfortanus, *Satyrae VIII* (Ultraiecti).
1555	NAOGEORGUS Thomas Straubingensis, *Satyrarum libri quinque priores* (Basileae).
1559	NAOGEORGUS Thomas Straubingensis, *In catalogum haereticorum nuper Romae editum satyra, adjectis etiam aliis eiusdem argumenti* (s.l.).
1562?	STIBLINUS Caspar Amtzellanus, *Satyra in sicarios . . . qui D.D. Melchiorem Zobel episcopum Herbipolensem . . . interfecerunt* (Wirceburgi?)
1569	DOUSA Janus Nordovix, *Epigrammatum libri II, Satyrae II . . .* (Antverpiae).
1576	BILSCIUS Joachim, Polonus, *Satira in quendam Dantiscanum.*
	(Ed.: Th. Bieńkowski, *Carmina Latina* (Warszawa, 1962), 91–4.).
1576	VULPA (= VOLPI), Joannes Antonius, *Satirae II* in J. M. Toscanus, *Carmina illustrium poetarum Italorum* II (Lyon, 1576–7).
1584	CLARIUS Joannes Tunger, *Satyra in Gulielmum Nassoviae.*
1591	ABEL Michael Francofurto-Viadrinus, *Musae undecimae seu ineptae versificatoriae delibatio* (Pragae, 1591) = *Satyrae* II.
15..	PIERIUS Christianus Coloniensis, *Satyra.*
	(Ed.: Ranutius Gherus, *Delitiae poetarum Germanorum,* III (Francofurti, 1612), 805–17.)
1607	FRISCHLINUS Nicodemus Balingensis, *Adversus Jacobum Rabum Novitium catholicum apostatam impiissimum . . . Satyrae VIII* (Gera).
1612	BARTHIUS Caspar Germanus, *Satyrarum liber* (in: *Opuscula varia,* Hanau).
1615	SCIOPPIUS Gaspar Neomarcanus, *Corona regia*: satyra in Iacobum I Angliae regem.
1621–7	HAVRAEUS Joannes Gandavensis, *Arx virtutis sive de vera animi tranquillitate satyra* (Antverpiae, 1621; Gandavi, 1621; Ipris, 1623).
	IDEM, *Satyrae tres* (Antverpiae, 1627).

ca 1622   PIECZKONIDES (Pecka) Michael Bohemus, *Petri Ribaldi Peruani Satyrarum liber prior* ... Impressum Utopiae ...

1623–6   SCHOLIRIUS Petrus Antverpiensis, *Sermonum Familiarium liber* I (Antv. 1623), II (ib. 1624), III (ib. 1626).
(Ed.: *Perpetuis* ... *commentariis illustrati, opera et studio Alberti Le Roy*, (Antv. 1683).)

ante 1629   DE VILLANIS Nicolaus Pistoriensis, *Satyrae II* (MS: Firenze, Bibl. Naz. Centr. II, x, 53).

ca 1630   FLEMING Paulus, *Satyra in grammaticos.*

1636   LAUREMBERGIUS Johannes Rostochius, *Satyra* (Sorø).

1651   BALDE Jacobus Alsatinus S.J., *Medicinae gloria per satyras duo et viginti asserta* (Monachii).

1654   SANGENESIUS Joannes Avenionensis, *Poemata* (Parisiis): i.a. satirae.

1656   BALDE Jacobus S.J., *Satyra contra abusum tabaci* (Noribergae).

1672   LUCCHESINI Joannes Laurentius Luccensis S.J., *Specimen didascalici carminis et satyrae* (Romae).

1694–1700   SECTANUS Quintus (SERGARDI Lodovico) Senensis, *Satyrae XVIII.* (Ed.: 1694; 1696 (XVI); Amstelodami, 1700; Lucae, 1783.)

1692–6   RETTENPACHER Simon Cremifanensis O.S.B., *Satyrae X.*
(Ed.: A. Klinglmaier, 113. Jahresbericht Schuljahr 1970 öff. Gymnasium der Benediktiner zu Kremsmünster (1970), pp. 7–56).

1699   CEVA Thomas (= Callimachus Neridius) Mediolanensis S.J., *Fragmentum satyrae. Ex prolusione habita ad Rhetores initio anni litterarii: De cogitationibus inanibus,* in: *Silvae* (Mediolani, 1704, 1718, 1723; Venetiis, 1732).

ante 1700   NATALIS Antonius S.J. Panormitanus (+1701), *Poemata et Satyrae* MSS.

1702   ANON. *Satyra in poetastros O--c--enses* (Londinii).

1703   NOMI Fridericus Anghiarius, *Liber satyrarum sexdecim* (Lugduni Batavorum).
DE AQUINO Carolus (= Alcon Sirius) Neapolitanus S.J., *Satyrae XII,* in: *Carminum tomus IIIus,* Romae (iterum 1708).

ca 1705   (GRENAN Benignus, Satyras x et xi Nicolai Boileau latine vertit, Parisiis).

1710–51   Nederduitsche en Latijnse Keurdigten, met de vervolgen I–II (Rotterdam).

1722   FRANK DE FRANKENAU Georgius, *Satyrae medicae XX* (Lipsiae).

1729   UMBRITIUS CANTIANUS, *Poemata* (Londinii) = *Satyrae* III.

1733   KELCZ Emericus S.J., *Simulatio per satyras deducta* (Tyrnaviae).

1735   D.G. (Batavus?), *Satyrae quattuor* (Londinii).

1737–42   CORDARA Julius Caesar (Panemus Cisseus) Alexandrinus S.J., *L. Sectani Q. f. de tota Graeculorum huius aetatis litteratura ad Gaium Salmorium Sermones IV* (Genevae); ... Sermo Vus (s.a.); Sermo VIus (Corythi, 1742). Saepius edit.
In Cordaram nonnulli scripserunt: vide 1761 et 1764.

1738/39/40   KING William, *Satyrae III* (Londinii).

ante 1741   GALLENFELS Carolus Carinthius S.J. (+1741), *Satyrae octo de studio litterarum,* MSS.

1741   ŁOZ PONINSKI Antonius Polonus, *Sarmatidae seu Satyrae* (IX) *equitis cuiusdam Poloni* (Varsaviae).

1742–55   GUGLIELMINI Bernardus Italus, Schol. Piar., *Sermonum libri III* (Romae) – cum adiectione duorum librorum (Vratislaviae, 1755).

1758   HEERKENS Gerardus Nicolaus (ps. Marius Cyrillus), *Satyrae* (Groningae).

1761   *Raccolta di Composizioni diverse sopra alcune controversie letterarie insorte nella Toscana nel corrente Secolo* (s.l.).

1764   'Castruccius (= Petrus Josephus) Bonamicus', *Operum pars altera* (Augustae Vindelicorum), 81–118: 'L. Sectani Q. Fil. de causis superiorum quattuor sermonum ad eundem Gaium Salmorium sermo primus'.

1772   NICOLAUS Franciscus Locrensis, *Sermones II*, in: *Carmina* (Neapoli), pp.63–75.

1789   PREMLECHNER Johannes Baptista, S.J., *Satyra in adolescentes formae studiosos*, in: *Lucubrationes poeticae et oratoriae* (Vindobonae), pp.126–30.

1791   BREGOLINI Ubaldus Tarvisinus, *Satyra de coelibatu ecclesiastico* (Patavii). (Ed.: Aem. Piovesan, *Humanistica Lovaniensia*, XVIII (1969), 144–50.)

ante 1815   RESTIUS Junius, *Satirae XXV* (Dubrovnik; ed. F. Appendini, *Carmina*, Patavii 1816).

1872/75/80   ESSEIVA Petrus Helvetus, *Satyrae ad Iuvenem* (1872), *ad Procum* (1875), *in Mulieres Emancipatas* (1880). (Edd.: Amstelodami, in certamine Hoeufftiano; *Carminum libri* IX (Friburgi Helv., 1894).)

1877   FERRUCCIUS Aloisius Chrysostomus, *Epistolae satyricae XX* (Imola).

1882   MOLTEDO Franciscus, *Civi monita* (in: *Carmina*, Florentiae; iterum Amstelodami in cert. Hoeufft., 1916).

1940   DAMSTE Petrus Helbertus Batavus, *Satira* (ed.: *Carmina minora*, fasciculus secundus, Zwolle, 1940).

1962/64/69   SCHNUR Harry = Caius Arrius Nurus, Americanus, *Satyrae IV* (a) Satyrae II in: *Pegasus Tolutarius* (Aldenardae, 1962), pp.43–50 ('In grammaticum periurum; Eichmann'). (b) *In Stultitiam satura* (Amstelodami, Hoeufft, 1964). (c) *Iuvenalis Saturae* XVI *fragmentum nuperrime repertum* (ib. 1969).

1970   EBERLE Josephus = APELLUS J., *Echo Perennis: Elegiae–Satirae–Didactica cum versione Germanica* (Stuttgart), pp.63–74: De Paradiso reperto; Dresstease.

SATYRICA

1605   BARCLAIUS Johannes, *Euphormionis Lusinini Satyricon*, Pars I (Paris).

1607   Id. Pars II (Paris).

1617   CASAUBONUS Isaac (+1614), *Misoponeri Satyricon*. ANON, *Virtus Vindicata sive Polieni Rhodiensis Satyra in depravatos orbis incolas*.

1619   COLLARDEAU Julianus, *Larvina. Satyricon in chorearum lascivias et personata tripudia* (Paris).

1625   MORISOT Claudius Bartholomaeus (?), *Alitophili Veritatis Lacrymae sive Euphormionis continuatio*.

1628   GUYET Franciscus (?), *Gaeomemphionis Cantaliensis Satyricon*.

1631	BODECHERUS BENNINGIUS Ianus, *Hermophili Tanugriensis Satyricon in corruptae iuventutis mores corruptos* (Leiden).
1637	ERYTHRAEUS Ianus Nicius, *Eudemia libri VIII* (Leiden).
1642	Id. *X* (Amsterdam).
1654	BOURICIUS Johannes, *Satyricon in corruptos huius saeculi mores* (Leeuwarden).
16..	'Menippus Redivivus,' *Satyricon Asini Vapulantis.*
1693	NODOTIUS Franciscus, *Petronii Satyricon nunc demum integrum* (Paris).

3

AN ANTHOLOGY OF RENAISSANCE LATIN VERSE: PROBLEMS CONFRONTING THE EDITOR AND COMPILER

J. SPARROW

The last half-century has seen a remarkable growth in the interest taken by students in the Latin poetry of the Renaissance. To satisfy this interest, scholars have edited texts of many individual poets[1] and of the poets of particular nations,[2] and a large body of critical and exegetical work has been published in learned journals. Yet there is no book available to the student that gives an adequate idea of the range and quality of the verse that was written all over Europe during the two centuries that succeeded the Re-birth of Letters.[3] There seems, therefore, to be room for a collection that does for the Latin verse of the Renaissance what Dr Raby's *Oxford Book of Mediaeval Latin Verse* does for the Latin verse of the Middle Ages. This paper gives some account of the problems that confront one who sets out to compile and edit such an anthology.[4]

SCOPE, IN PLACE AND TIME

First, the compiler must determine the limits, geographical and temporal, to be set to the contents of his collection. Plainly, it should cover the whole of Europe, and it seems equally clear that it should

[1] See e.g. the texts mentioned on p.60, n.1.

[2] E.g. *Poeti Latini del Quattrocento*, ed. F. Arnaldi, Lucia Gualdo Rosa, and Liliana Monti Sabia (Ricciardi, 1964); *Lateinische Gedichte deutscher Humanisten*, ed. H. Schnur (Stuttgart, 1967).

[3] Miss F. A. Gragg's *Latin Writings of the Italian Humanists* (New York–Chicago, 1927), contains a small but admirably chosen collection of specimens of prose as well as verse, with brief biographies of the authors; but her book has long been out of print and is now quite unprocurable.

[4] Professor Alessandro Perosa, of the University of Florence, and the present writer have prepared for the press such an anthology, which it is hoped may be published in the near future. This article is, in effect, a record of their joint experience in preparing that anthology.

begin with the beginnings of the Latin poetry that can truly be called 'Renaissance' as distinct from 'medieval'. Since the Renaissance began to bear fruit at different times in different places, the result of applying this rule over the whole of Europe will be to produce different starting-dates for the collection in different countries: Italy, for instance, will begin with Petrarch, who was born in 1304; England with Sir Thomas More, who was born in 1478.

A more difficult question is, when to bring the collection to a close. It should be co-terminous, presumably, with the Renaissance itself. Of course, the Renaissance did not really ever 'end', anywhere; and in so far as it did end, it ended at different times in different places. But anyone who studies the Latin verse written in Europe in the sixteenth century will perceive that a change came over this kind of writing, that a poetical phase or period came to an end, with the Counter-Reformation. This change is difficult to describe and impossible to date, or (so to speak) to locate, precisely: it came later, of course, in some countries than in others. Here the compiler must be arbitrary: for our collection we fixed 1550 as the terminal date for every country.

Whatever your *terminus*, there will of course be border-line cases – poets who began to write before, and continued after, the chosen date. In dealing with this problem, an editor cannot but allow himself some latitude; there seems to be no virtue in a rigid rule, and it would be difficult to frame a satisfactory rule and to apply it uniformly.

ORDER AND ARRANGEMENT OF CONTENTS

On what general plan should the contents of the collection be arranged? Of course this depends on the editor's aims, on what kind of book it is that he wants his book to be. If it is intended not merely to give pleasure to its readers, but also to provide them with a conspectus of a certain kind of poetry, to illuminate the history of Latin verse during the given period, the principle governing the order in which the authors themselves are set out must be a chronological one. But to string them out in a single series extending from Petrarch to Buchanan would be to obscure the answers to many significant questions that may be asked about the development of Renaissance

Latin verse in Europe: Were there centres (so to speak) of production? What were they? How far did they coincide with national boundaries? When did production begin at each of them? Were some more prolific than others? Did each have a character of its own?

With these considerations in mind, we kept together the poets of each country, arranging the poets of each country chronologically, according to their birth-dates. In dealing with each author, however, we felt free to arrange his poems simply in the order that seemed to us the most effective.

To speak of 'countries' in this context is, of course, to be guilty of an anachronism: Italy and Germany, for instance, as we think of them today, did not then exist; and it might have given a truer picture had we grouped our poets, for Italy at any rate, by the towns or courts or districts that they belonged to or frequented. To attempt this would have raised questions and involved complications that we were anxious to avoid, so we arranged the poets in what may seem rough and ready national categories – Italian, German, Hungarian, Dalmatian, Polish, and so on.

Then comes the question: In what order should the countries be placed? On all counts, Italy claims the first place; thereafter, we have placed the countries in an order that seems to us to reflect the spread of Italian influence.

One result of arranging the poets by reference to the countries of their birth, and the countries in the order that we have chosen, is that great prominence is given to Italy, which not only stands first in the book, but also has by far the largest volume of poetry (46 poets out of 84, and about 7,000 out of about 11,600 lines of verse). This is as it should be: the position and the volume of the Italian component reflects the primacy of Italy, as the country where this kind of poetry was first written and where it flourished most prolifically.

SUPPLEMENTARY MATTER

Clearly the book must have an introduction and a bibliography; what other supplementary matter should there be?

First, should one provide an English translation? To do so would mean choosing between doubling the size of the book and cutting down the text by something like one half. It is said that with an English translation a book of this kind would have a larger sale. While this might be true in English-speaking countries, it is by no means certain that elsewhere the inclusion of an English translation would not have the opposite effect: many people would rather have a book with (say) 10,000 lines of Latin verse than one with 5,000 lines of Latin and a translation in a language other than their own. Had it been necessary to include a translation in order to get the Anthology published, we would no doubt have yielded to necessity; but we would not include a 'crib' simply for the sake of procuring additional readers who depend upon it for their appreciation of the text, and we are fortunate in having found in Messrs Duckworth a publisher who is prepared to print our text in full without a translation.

Translation or no translation, clearly the reader will need a short biographical account of each author and notes explaining obscurities of language and topical allusions, which abound in poetry of this kind. Where should the biographies and notes be placed? To put them at the end would split the book into two and make the notes less easy to refer to and therefore less likely to be read; it seemed best, therefore, to print a short biography before the work of each poet and to put the notes at the foot of each page. This arrangement has its disadvantages, especially in the case of poets represented by only one or two short pieces: there is a risk in such cases that the biography and notes may swamp the text; both, therefore, may have, for such authors, to be kept disproportionately short.

TEXTS

What principles ought the editors to follow in constituting their text? Different poets offer, in this respect, different problems. The following paragraphs set out the principles by which we ourselves were guided in the three kinds of case that present themselves.

(1) For some poets there exists a nineteenth- or twentieth-century critical edition which provides a text established on scholarly principles.[1] For them, we made this text the basis of our own, check-

---

[1] E.g. Boecking's edition of the Latin poems of von Hutten in vol.III of von Hutten's *Works* (Leipzig, 1859–70); Pindter's editions of Celtis' *Amores* (Leipzig, 1934) and his *Odae* (Leipzig, 1937); Bolaffi's edition of Ariosto's *Carmina* (Modena, 2nd ed. 1938); Oeschger's edition of Pontano's *Ecloghe Elegie Liriche* (Bari, 1948) and Monti's edition of his *Naeniae* (Naples, 1970); Perosa's edition of Marullo (Zürich, 1951); and Reedijk's *Poems of Desiderius Erasmus* (Leiden, 1956).

ing it with such manuscripts and early editions as we were able to examine, and recording (and explaining) every instance of divergence from it.

(2) There are many poets of whose Latin verse no scholarly edition has been published for the last 200 years. During the eighteenth century, however, there appeared (for the most part in Italy) a crop of editions in which the Latin verse of a Renaissance poet (or, sometimes, more than one poet) was collected, together with a life, testimonia, and a survey of earlier editions and (occasionally) manuscripts.[1] Many of these were very scholarly productions. While we made use of such editions where no modern edition existed, wherever possible we went for the text of our selection from these poets to the original sources, printed or manuscript, not all of which were in every case accessible to the eighteenth-century editor. Where such an edition has remained the standard edition of the author in question, then, even if we did not follow its text, we usually adopted its numeration of the poems when referring to them in our notes.

(3) Some poets have never been edited, though they may have been reprinted, since they first came out in the fifteenth or the sixteenth century. For such poets, we took our text from the original editions, checking it with any manuscripts to which we had access.

Whichever of the three above-described categories an author belongs to, we made it our aim to state (*a*) what authorities exist for the text of the poems we selected from his work, (*b*) which of those authorities we followed, and (*c*) where, and why, we differed from the text they offer. We did not attempt to provide anything like a full *apparatus criticus*, but recorded important variants in our notes.

SPELLING AND PUNCTUATION

Should the editors reproduce in every case the spelling and punctuation of the text they follow? To do so, in a book composed of texts

---

[1] E.g. J. B. Mencken's edition of Campano's *Epistolae et Poemata* (Leipzig, 1707); P. Vlaming's edition of de l'Hôpital (Amsterdam, 1732); Pierantonio Serassi's editions of Zanchi (Bergamo, 1747) and of Molza (Bergamo, 1747, 1750); Zaccaria Betti's edition of Niccolò d'Arco's *Numeri* (Verona, 1762); and the editions of Fracastoro, Navagero, and others, published by Volpi and Comino at Padua in the second and third decades of the century.

drawn from sources so various and belonging to dates so far apart, would be to present the reader with a bewildering and irritating diversity of 'styles'. Moreover, in many cases the original spelling and punctuation have no authority except the printer's. It seemed right, therefore, uniformly to modernise the spelling and punctuation, and unnecessary to record textual divergences that were due simply to the enforcement of this uniformity.

PRESENTATION

One or two minor, but none the less troublesome, questions about the presentation of the text confront the editor of an anthology of Renaissance Latin.

(a) *Titles of poems*. Writers of the period did not usually give distinctive titles to their poems. Should the editor supply titles? We decided to do this, if only as a harmless indulgence to the ordinary reader. A succession of hundreds of poems, with nothing but a number prefixed to each, presents a drab and lifeless appearance; an English title at least gives the reader a hint of what the poem is about and tells him something of what he is to expect of it.

(b) *Names of poets*. There is another problem of nomenclature, which relates to the poets themselves: are they to be given their real vernacular names or the assumed Latin names under which they wrote? In this matter it seems most sensible not to attempt consistency, but to call each poet by the name by which he was best known to his contemporaries or is best known today; du Bellay, not Bellaius; Thomas More, not Morus; Francesco Petrarcha, not Franciscus Petrarca (so, at the head of the page or piece; but 'Petrarch' in the English context of the biography and notes); Poliziano, not Politianus or Ambrogini (but 'Politian' in the biography and notes); on the other hand, Camerarius, not Leibhard; Joannes Secundus, not Jan Everaerts; Janus Pannonius, not Csezmiczei János; and Conrad Celtes, not Conrad Pickel.[1]

---

[1] Excellent guidance in this difficult matter is given by Bywater in his paper 'The Latinizations of the Modern Surname', *Journal of Philology*, xxxiii (1918), 76–94.

J. SPARROW

PRINCIPLES OF SELECTION

When the editor has to make his choice of poems, within the
limits adumbrated above, what criteria is he to apply? He cannot
allow himself to be guided by literary quality alone, to choose simply
the best poems, if he is to produce an anthology that is fairly representative of the Latin poetry of the time. I say 'fairly representative': to give an absolutely faithful sample of the whole mass of
Renaissance Latin poetry would be to produce a book the greater
part of which would be unreadable. For a great part of the Latin
poetry written in Europe in the fifteenth and sixteenth centuries is
worthless as literature and intolerably dull – as no doubt is most of
the vernacular poetry of the period, and as the bulk of classical Latin
poetry would surely have proved to be had it survived: students of
the classics are fortunate in that chance and the taste of succeeding
generations have eliminated all but a small and choice remnant
of the literature of ancient Greece and Rome.

To reprint a due proportion of the endless didactic and epic
Latin poetry of the Renaissance would be to inflict a cruel posthumous punishment on those who wrote it, and a still crueller punishment on the readers who would be confronted with it today. Hardly
more readable, in bulk, are the amatory, bucolic, and 'occasional'
poems then published so profusely. An editor must, if only out of
sheer human concern for the reader, have some regard to the quality
of the verse that he reprints.

We therefore made it our aim to provide a balanced selection of
the good and the interesting Latin verse of the time, allotting plenty
of space not only to true poets, such as Pontano or Marullo, Joannes
Secundus or Michel de l'Hôpital, but also to competent and fluent
versifiers (who sometimes achieve true poetry) like Marcantonio
Flaminio, Fracastoro, Vida, and to poets who are celebrated in
other fields than Latin verse – Bembo, Ariosto, Castiglione, Etienne
Dolet, Joachim du Bellay, Erasmus, Melanchthon.

When it came to choosing poems as distinct from choosing poets,
we found room not only for individual pieces that are specially moving or beautiful – like (to mention only a few) More's lines to his
children and to his youthful love, Niccolò d'Arco's memorial poem
to his mother, Vida's lament for his parents, Sepinus' invocation of
Death, and Telesio's reflections on the firefly – but also for verse

that is interesting for the picture it gives of the world in which it was written – Filelfo's Satires, and the descriptive or topical verses of Franchini, Valeriano, Molza, Nicolas Bourbon, and the Germans, who excel in poetry of this kind.

If an anthology thus selected gives a flattering picture of the Latin verse of the Renaissance generally, it may also be said somewhat to distort that picture as between one country and another. In Italy (and to a lesser extent in Germany and France) a host of respectable, if not remarkable, poets are competing for inclusion: one could remove a dozen of the minor Italians – here represented by two or three poems apiece – and find several dozen others who could take their place without affecting the level of quality of the collection. Not so with the Poles, the Dalmatians, the Hungarians, and the English: no competition there – any poet who reaches the required standard is assured of his place.

The table that follows presents an over-all view of the contents of the collection, with the names of the first and the last poet chosen from each country.

Italy	46 poets	208 pieces	about 7,000 lines	Petrarch (1304–74) G. B. Amalteo (1525–73)
Hungary	1 poet	4 pieces	about 120 lines	Janus Pannonius (1434–72)
Dalmatia	4 poets	7 pieces	about 200 lines	G. Sisgoreus (ca 1440–1509) L. Pascalis (ca 1500–51)
France	11 poets	37 pieces	about 1,200 lines	R. Gaguin (1433–1501) M. A. Muret (1525–85)
Germany	11 poets	43 pieces	about 1,200 lines	S. Brant (145?–1521) S. Scheffer (ca 1530–?)
Netherlands	2 poets	12 pieces	about 550 lines	Erasmus (1467–1536) Joannes Secundus (1511–36)
England	3 poets	11 pieces	about 300 lines	Sir T. More (1478–1535) Walter Haddon (1516–72)
Scotland	1 poet	5 pieces	about 150 lines	G. Buchanan (1506–82)
Spain	1 poet	1 piece	about 70 lines	Garcilaso de la Vega (1503–36)
Portugal	1 poet	2 pieces	about 70 lines	H. Cayado (?–1508)
Poland	3 poets	13 pieces	about 750 lines	N. Hussovianus (ca 1480–ca 1533) J. Kochanowski (1532–84)

82 poets; 343 pieces; about 11,600 lines.

PART II

THE HUMANISTS IN THE RENAISSANCE

4

LA PREMIÈRE QUERELLE DES 'ANCIENS' ET DES 'MODERNES' AUX ORIGINES DE LA RENAISSANCE

Sur le sens que les principaux représentants de la culture humaniste ont donné aux concepts de 'ancien' et 'moderne', entre la moitié du XIVe et la fin du XVIe siècle, nous avons eu, ces derniers trente ans, des études très interessantes[1] qui ont eu le mérite de mettre en relief certains points 'cruciaux' dans l'histoire de ces deux topoi si significatifs. Des travaux très différents comme méthode et comme orientation ont déjà isolé les phases déterminantes d'une évolution

[1] V., à ce propos: W. K. Ferguson, *The Renaissance in Historical Thought. Five Centuries of Interpretation* (Cambridge, Mass., 1948, 1960²) (et aussi: id. 'Humanist Views of the Renaissance', *American Historical Review* (1939-40), 1-28; mais cfr.: D. Philips, 'Ferguson's History of the Periodic Conception of the Renaissance', *Journal of the History of Ideas* (1952), 266-80; H. Weisinger, 'The Self-Awareness of the Renaissance as a Criterion of the Renaissance', *Papers of the Michigan Academy of Science, Art and Letters* (1944), 561-7; id. 'The Renaissance Theory of the Reaction against the Middle Ages as a Cause of the Renaissance', *Speculum* (1945), 461-7; id. 'Renaissance Accounts of the Revival of Learning', *Studies in Philology* (1948), 105-18; H. Baeyens, 'Begrip en Problem van de Renaissance. Dijdrage tot de Geschiedenis van hun onstaan en tot hun Kunsthistorische Omschrijving', *Recueil de travaux d'histoire et de philologie de l'Université de Louvain*, s.iii, f.8 (Louvain, 1952); H. Schulte Nordholt, 'Het Beeld der Renaissance: Een historiographische Studie', *Porta-Reeks, Bibliotheek voor Teoretische en Cultuurgeschiedenis van het Historisch Seminarium der Universiteit van Amsterdam*, 1 (Amsterdam, 1948); *Il Rinascimento. Significato e limiti. Atti del III Congresso internazionale sul Rinascimento* (Firenze, 1953); P. O. Kristeller, *The Classics and Renaissance Thought* (Cambridge, Mass., 1957); *The Renaissance. A reconsideration of the Theories and Interpretation*, T. Helton ed. (Madison, 1964); *The Renaissance Debate*, D. Hay ed. (London–New York, 1965); *Zum Begriff und Problem der Renaissance*, A. Buck ed. (Darmstadt, 1969); E. Garin, 'Medio Evo e tempi bui: concetto e polemiche nella storia del pensiero dal XV al XVIII secolo', dans *Concetto, storia, miti e immagini del Medio Evo*, a cura di V. Branca (Firenze, 1973), 199-224.

Mais v. aussi: D. Cantimori, 'Sulla storia del concetto di Rinascimento', *Annali della R. Scuola Normale Superiore di Pisa*, s.ii, 1 (1932), 229-68 (et, maintenant, *Storici e storia* (Torino, 1971), pp.413-62) et, surtout pour la culture humaniste française: F. Simone, *La coscienza della rinascità negli umanisti francesi* (Roma, 1949); id. *Il Rinascimento francese. Studi e ricerche* (Torino, 1965²); id. *Umanesimo, Rinascimento, Barocco in Francia* (Milano, 1968); id. 'Une entreprise oubliée des humanistes français: de la prise de conscience historique du renouveau culturel à la naissance de la première histoire littéraire', dans *Humanism in France at the end of the Middle Ages and in the early Renaissance*, A. H. T. Levi ed. (Manchester University Press, 1970), pp.106-31.

sémantique très complexe qui, pendant deux siècles, changea complètement la valeur des termes utilisés auparavant pour indiquer d'une façon polémique les protagonistes présumés d'un conflit extrême entre 'civilisation' et 'barbarie'. Mais ce qui compte davantage c'est que l'on a mis désormais en évidence le changement progressif de tout le cadre historique dans lequel on doit reconstruire le sort différent réservé aux *antiqui* et aux *moderni*, c'est-à-dire le passage des premières allusions critiques très précises dans leurs objectifs et très limitées dans le temps, d'abord à un jugement 'global' qui entraînait toutes les formes de la culture de la fin du Moyen Âge et, enfin, à l'affirmation orgueilleuse d'une civilisation 'nouvelle' qui n'hésitait pas à se confronter à ses 'modèles' et à proclamer sa propre supériorité. Cette longue 'querelle' se présente donc aujourd'hui à l'historien dans une perspective très différente de celle que lui proposaient certains travaux plus soucieux de dénoncer le caractère tout 'littéraire' et 'rhétorique' de la réforme humaniste que d'interpréter le sens réel de cette discussion qui s'étend à tous les domaines de la culture. Je crois, en effet, que l'on peut affirmer aujourd'hui que, à l'origine de cette polémique, comme dans ses développements les plus complexes et les plus poussés, on trouve les raisons fondamentales d'une culture 'alternative', opposée non seulement aux méthodes et à les doctrines prédominantes dans les institutions officielles de cette époque, mais aussi à l'idée de l'homme et de son destin qui y était sous-entendue. Pour peu que l'on tente d'approfondir la continuité et, en même temps, la diversité des façons dont on a caractérisé le rapport dialectique entre *antiqui* et *moderni*, il en résulte clairement que l'opposition se fit surtout dans le domaine spécifique des *artes sermocinales*, à la recherche de modes de pensée et d'expression capables de donner vie à une image d'intellectuel très différent et lié aux problèmes et aux tâches d'une société en évolution.[1]

[1] V.: E. Garin, *La cultura filosofica del Rinascimento italiano* (Firenze, 1961); id. *Scienza e vita civile nel Rinascimento* (Bari, 1965); id. *La cultura del Rinascimento* (Bari, 1967); id. *L'età nuova. Ricerche di storia della cultura dal XII al XVI secolo* (Napoli, 1969); id. *Dal Rinascimento all'Illuminismo* (Pisa, 1970). Mais v. aussi: H. Baron, *The Crisis of the Early Italian Renaissance* (Princeton, N.J., 1955, n. éd. 1966); id. *Humanistic and Political Literature in Florence and Venice at the Beginning of the Quattrocento. Studies in Criticism and Chronology* (Cambridge, Mass., 1955); L. Martines, *The Social World of the Florentine Humanists* (Princeton, N.J., 1963); M. P. Gilmore, *Humanists and Jurists. Six Studies in the Renaissance* (Cambridge, Mass., 1963); P. Herde, 'Politik und Rhetoric am Florenz am Vorabend der Renaissance', *Archiv für Kulturgeschichte* (1965), 141–220; H. Baron, *From Petrarch to Leonardo Bruni. Studies in Humanistics and Political Literature* (Chicago, 1968).

Quelles que soient les origines et les causes de la 'révolte' humaniste contre les 'modernes', un fait est donc presque certain: la critique de la logique et du langage scolastique et l'apologie de la poésie et de l'*eloquentia* d'autre part, n'ont été que les premiers pas vers la recherche d'une nouvelle dimension philologique et historique de la culture qui devait, à la fin, remettre en question les critères mêmes sur lesquels s'était basée la proposition humaniste du retour aux *auctores* classiques. On ne s'étonnera donc pas du fait que, de génération en génération, le conflit entre les *antiqui* et les *moderni* ait acquis une portée toujours plus étendue au point d'engendrer le mythe historiographique des 'siècles obscurs', de la période barbare s'étendant pendant mille ans, entre l'*humanitas* des anciens et son retour providentiel; ni du fait que de là soit née la conscience progressive des droits de la culture 'renaissante' par rapport à tout le passé, s'exprimant d'abord dans l'idée d'une imitation 'libre', dégagée de tous les canons absolus, renforcée plus tard par la critique ouverte de certains fondements de la tradition classique et enfin conclue avec la proposition de nouveaux langages, de nouvelles méthodes et de nouvelles sciences. L'image humaniste du 'nouvel Adam', qui a trouvé dans l'exemple des anciens l'inspiration et la force pour vaincre la 'sombre ignorance' des 'modernes', se transforme, en un siècle, dans une 'personnalité' bien différente, celle de l'historien-philologue habitué à juger tous les évènements du passé avec la rigueur de sa science, à en éliminer les traits conventionnels et les 'archétypes' mythiques. Ainsi, au delà des limites que le savoir scolastique avait tracées pour préserver son encyclopédie millénaire, on voit vite se profiler une nouvelle région, un autre âge de l'histoire humaine qui, bien que continuant la bataille humaniste contre la 'barbarie' de l''âge du milieu', n'est pas moins consciente de son éloignement par rapport au monde ancien, reconnu désormais dans ses dimensions historiques plus réelles.

Ces considérations expliquent, ou du moins peuvent aider à comprendre, les difficultés que présente une recherche qui prétend vraiment à un éclaircissement dans une situation aussi complexe, dans laquelle jouèrent un rôle souvent déterminant un grand nombre d'instances culturelles, mais aussi politiques et religieuses, différentes les unes des autres, mais liées par la même aspiration à un renouvellement profond de la civilisation européenne. Justement pour cela est-il probable que l'on a accepté, avec trop de facilité, un 'cliché' historiographique assez commode qui, quand il ne réduit pas la dispute humaniste entre les *antiqui* et les *moderni* à un simple exercice rhétorique, la diminue dans son développement temporel, en la réduisant à la monotone succession de certains 'lieux communs', obligée à une signification trop univoque et de ce fait privée d'une vérification historiographique sérieuse.[1] Il n'y a aucun doute que certaines recherches, basées du reste sur le fondement exclusif d'un choix très limité d'auteurs et de textes, ont souvent transformé la réaction humaniste en faveur des *auctores* et contre la 'réduction' scolastique de la tradition classique en un combat entre les 'vrais' philosophes et hommes de science (considérés volontiers comme les précurseurs de Galilée et de Descartes) et les pétulants *grammatici*, les rhéteurs élégants mais si vains qui étaient à la tête des écoles humanistes ou des académies seigneuriales et princières.[2] On ne peut pas trouver non plus du reste de grande utilité certaines perspectives rapidement tracées à grands traits, où des textes éloignés dans le temps et des moments de développement intellectuel très différents ont tous été choisis comme témoignage d'une soi-disant 'conscience révolutionnaire de la nouvelle culture', toujours pareille pendant les deux siècles plus décisifs pour l'histoire de notre civilisation.[3] En réalité, le problème à affronter est beaucoup plus complexe, et il exige une approche historiographique très prudente, bien définie dans le temps, précise et systématique dans la considération des auteurs et de leur culture, sensible aux multiples raisons qui sont à l'origine de tant de rappels péremptoires à l'enseignement de la civilisation classique comme de polémiques contre l''imitation servile'. Mais surtout il serait bon de définir, tout d'abord, certains points importants pour l'interprétation correcte, afin d'indiquer clairement: (1) la portée et les intentions fondamentales des premières polémiques humanistes contre les 'modernes'; (2) le passage à une critique assez cohérente et organique des fondements de tout le 'système' culturel de la tradition scolastique; (3) ses résultats, au cours du XVIe siècle, en face d'une crise historique décisive, destinée à provoquer des fractures irréversibles et des changements profonds dans toute l'organisation politique, religieuse et culturelle de la société occidentale.

[1] V., à ce propos, les observations de E. Garin, 'Medio Evo e tempi bui', pp.202–10.
[2] V., par example, l'interpretation de H. Haydn, *The Counter-Renaissance* (New York, 1950).
[3] V., encore, ce qui écrit Garin, 'Medio Evo a tempi bui', pp.207–9 (à propos de la méthode de Ferguson).

Ceci veut dire – à mon avis – que cette 'querelle', comme elle se présente déjà à la fin du XIVe siècle, mais aussi dans certains de ses développements plus significatifs, doit être considérée, en premier lieu, comme une fracture linguistique et logique qui concerne toutes les formes et les modes de vie intellectuelle.[1] Ce n'est pas par hasard que les premiers textes de la polémique – bien connus, car ils sont dus à la plume de Pétrarque, de Boccace et de Salutati – se servent justement de la contraposition programmée de deux langues et de deux types de 'discours', de la 'pensée barbare' des Écoles, s'exprimant dans la 'dure' dialectique des 'sophistes britanniques' et de l'*eloquentia* définie dans les formes de la tradition rhétorique, oratoire et poétique.[2] Et il ne s'agit pas non plus seulement d'un 'nostalgique rêve' littéraire, mais du refus d'une méthode qui semble impliquer la *reductio ad logicam* de tous les arts et de toutes les disciplines, surtout de ceux qui ont un rapport très étroit avec l'expérience 'civile' des hommes. Mais si, du moins au début, la rébellion a des objectifs limités et semble dirigée, en premier lieu, contre les hommes et les doctrines contemporaines (ou, tout au plus, contre les tendances dominantes de la culture des Écoles, de la fin du XIIe siècle au milieu du XIVe) elle change ensuite de direction, ses propos se modifient déjà chez les hommes de la seconde génération humaniste, chez Bruni ou chez Valla. Il est vrai que Pétrarque avait lié son appel aux *antiqui* et son âpre invective contre tous les modernes (les logiques 'britanniques' ou les *physici* de Padoue ou de Bologne, élèves d'Aristote et d'Averrhoès) aux mythes eschatologiques et aux rêves historiques de la 'renaissance' de Rome requis par l'aventure emblématique de Cola de Rienzo.[3] Mais même les 'invectivae' de Pétrarque n'ont pas encore cette dimension historique précise et caractéristique que l'humaniste d'Arezzo fixe dans certaines pages des *Dialogi ad Petrum Istrum* ou de la *Historia florentini*

[1] V., à ce propos, les observations souvent originales de N. S. Struever, *The Language of History in the Renaissance* (Cambridge, Mass., 1968); et cfr. D. J. Wilcox, *The Development of Florentine Humanist Historiography in the Fifteenth Century* (Cambridge, Mass., 1969).

[2] V. les textes et les auteurs présentés et analysés par E. Garin, *L'età nuova*, pp.181–90 (mais v. aussi: C. Vasoli, *Studi sulla cultura del Rinascimento* (Manduria, 1968); *The Three Crowns of Florence* ed. and trans. by D. Thompson and A. F. Nagel (New York, 1972).

[3] Cfr.: K. Burdach, *Reformation, Renaissance, Humanismus, zwei Abhandlungen über die Grundlage moderner Bildung und Sprachkunst* (Berlin, 1926), pp.56 ss. (et aussi: id. *Vom Mittelalter zur Reformation. Forschungen zur Geschichte der deutschen Bildung* (Berlin, 1912 ss.); et l'essai vraiment importante de J. Macek, 'Pétrarque et Cola di Rienzo', *Historica* (1965), 5–51).

populi.[1] Ici les 'barbares' ne sont plus seulement les obscurs et insidieux 'sophistes' d'Oxford ou de Paris qui ont détruit la pureté et la vérité de la langue latine, corrompant aussi la 'vraie et sainte philosophie' des anciens et des Pères. Non; pour Bruni, les raisons de la 'barbarie' sont beaucoup plus lointaines et beaucoup plus profondes; et même si elles sont surtout évidentes au niveau révélateur de l'expression linguistique et des techniques logiques, elles ont leurs racines réelles dans de longs siècles de décadence politique et civile. La corruption de la langue et la perte de la 'sagesse' antique coïncident, au contraire, avec l'éclipse de la liberté républicaine de Rome, avec l'écroulement de ses institutions et la disparition des conditions essentielles de toute expérience culturelle valable. La bataille des *antiqui* et des *moderni* s'est donc déjà transformée en une recherche des causes des longues 'ténèbres' qui, pour les humanistes de la seconde génération, ont obscurci la tradition classique, des nombreux *monstra* qui barrent la route au retour d'un idéal culturel, éthique et aussi politique bien défini. Et voici justement, dès le début du XVe siècle, que se profilent des *topoi* déjà différents de ceux qui dominaient dans les pages de Pétrarque et de Salutati; ils servent à recueillir, sous un seul dénominateur commun, tous les vices des 'modernes', qu'il s'agisse du langage scolastique barbare, des insidieuses techniques de la dialectique, de la mauvaise lecture des classiques, ou bien de la décadence de toutes les libertés politiques, de la corruption de la vie ecclésiastique, ou, encore, de la mauvaise théologie contaminée par la science, 'vaine et inutile' des *magistri*, incapables de comprendre l'expérience morale et l'illumination sapientiale cachées dans les oeuvres des *poetae theologi*. Ce n'est pas tout: avec les mêmes mots on peut maintenant condamner aussi la *deformitas* de la *littera moderna* opposée à l'élégance mesurée de l'*antiqua*; et on célèbre la renaissance d'un art qui a redonné à la peinture, à la sculpture et à l'architecture leur 'pureté' originelle, opposée à la *roçeza* des 'modernes', que ce soient les byzantins décadents ou les 'horribles Goths et Lombards', tandis qu'Alberti écrit les louanges des artistes de son siècle capables enfin de rivaliser d'élégance et de beauté avec les *exempla* des anciens. Ce sont certainement des motifs dont il est inutile de rappeler le

---

[1] V. surtout: *Dialogi ad Petrum Istrum*, a cura di E. Garin, *Prosatori latini del Quattrocento* (Milano–Napoli, 1950), pp.39–99; *Historia florentini populi*, a cura di E. Santini, *R.I.S.* n. éd., xix, 3.

long succès, jusqu'aux stéréotypes historiographiques du 'grand siècle' ou des illuministes.[1] Je crois cependant que pour saisir la nouvelle dimension que la 'querelle' a assumée, il faut plutôt se pencher sur l'apport décisif de Lorenzo Valla.[2] Son oeuvre devrait être étudié, de ce point de vue, dans tous ses aspects essentiels: de la critique philologique à l'analyse logique et rhétorique, de la polémique historique et juridique à ses discussions théologiques et religieuses. Pour Valla la corruption 'moderne' de la langue latine n'est plus, en effet, un accident limité dans le temps, aux deux siècles derniers surtout, après les mourants splendeurs de l'époque d'Alain de Lille et de Jean de Salisbury: au contraire il y trouve les symptômes d'une maladie qui remonte au moins au siècle de Boèce, le grand corrupteur de la philosophie et de la morale chrétienne, le principal responsable de la sombre décadence qui, pendant le 'millénaire' barbare a perverti les lettres et le droit, la vérité scripturale, les arts et les disciplines humaines. C'est justement parce que les *magistri* sont désormais incapables de comprendre le grand *sacramentum* de la langue latine (et ils ont, donc, perdu la clef indispensable à la compréhension du sens premier d'une vérité et d'une tradition) que ces 'barbares' modernes sont, tout à la fois, les victimes et les porteurs les plus redoutables d'une corruption radicale qui a conduit aussi à l'égarement de l'Église de Jésus Christ et de ses pasteurs, impliqués dans le naufrage général de la *sapientia* classique et chrétienne. Et l'on comprend pourquoi, dans son appel renouvelé à la pureté de la langue et à la philosophie 'humaine' et 'rhétorique' des anciens, dans ses allusions à Quintilien et à la suprématie des 'arts du discours', le philologue lie, de façon irréductible, toutes les raisons de sa polémique consciente. Si bien qu'il est difficile de dire où la philologie de Valla cesse d'être le tentatif d'une nouvelle reconstruction du passé pour devenir une arme de contestation historique, où l'aspiration sincère à la pureté du message évangélique primitif se tranforme en une proposition théologique résolue, et où l'élaboration d'une 'dialectique' simple et 'usuaire', jointe à l'usage grammatical et rhétorique des langues classiques,

---

[1] Il n'est pas inutile de rappeler les célèbres pages de Voltaire, *Essai sur les moeurs*, éd. R. Pomeau (Paris, 1963), II, pp.87 ss.

[2] Pour une nouvelle et très documentée interpretation de l'oeuvre intellectuelle de Valla, dans tous les domaines de la culture de son temps, v.: S. I. Camporeale, *Lorenzo Valla. Umanesimo e teologia* (Firenze, 1972) (et v. aussi: Ch. Trinkaus, *In our Image and Likeness. Humanity and Divinity in Italian Humanist Thought* (London, 1970)).

cède la place à une critique philosophique qui attaque décisivement la tradition même de la 'science' péripatéticienne. Un fait ressort, avec une clarté indiscutable, de la méditation de Valla : la conscience philologique renouvelée des valeurs du *sermo*, tirée de l'étude des *auctores*, est le fondement d'un type de culture différent et original, d'une 'imitation créatrice' qui a comme but véritable un renouvellement radical s'étendant à toutes les sollicitations de la vie spirituelle.

J'ai insisté sur le tournant pris par Valla parce que je pense que c'est de lui que partent certains thèmes principaux de l'interprétation du rapport *antiqui/moderni*, comme cela se précise avec les changements rapides de nouvelles situations culturelles, religieuses et politiques que l'on ne peut pas ramener à l'horizon de la civilisation humaniste du XVe siècle. Tout d'abord c'est bien de ses *Dialecticae disputationes* que provient la vaste littérature 'dialectique' humaniste du XVe siècle, qui renvoie constamment aux textes capitaux de la rhétorique ancienne, à Cicéron, à Quintilien et à Hermogène, mais qui ne renonce pas à l'enseignement des maîtres byzantins et à l'expérience décisive des écoles italiennes du Quattrocento.[1] Et il s'agit – notons bien – non seulement d'un phénomène culturel d'une grande importance à cause de son extension et de son influence (comme les études de M. Howell, de M. Gilbert et du P. Ong l'ont bien montré), mais de la tentative de construire un nouvel 'instrument' des 'arts', comme une alternative à la logique traditionnelle s'opposant, avec une ferme décision polémique, aux techniques typiques de l'enseignement et de la doctrine scolastiques. De Rodolphe Agricole à Erasme, de Vivès à Mélanchthon cet 'art' (qui se trouve étroitement lié aux techniques rhétoriques et grammaticales) changera évidemment dans ses intentions et dans ses moyens, il accentuera tantôt l'un et tantôt l'autre de ses différents fondements historiques et textuels, et il pourra même assumer une attitude différente en face du *Philosophus* et des doctrines confiées à son *Organon*. Mais ce n'est pas par hasard que l'usage systématique des instruments de la dialectique et de la rhétorique s'associe souvent à l'intention déclarée de vouloir 'guérir', de cette façon, la confusion profonde, l'incertitude et l'"obscurité' des formes linguistiques dont dépendrait aussi le chaos général qui règne dans toutes les disciplines

[1] V. W. J. Ong, *Ramus, Method, and the Decay of Dialogue* (Cambridge, Mass., 1958); N. W. Gilbert, *Renaissance Concepts of Method* (New York, 1960, 1963²); C. Vasoli, *La dialettica e la retorica dell'Umanesimo. 'Invenzione' e 'Metodo' nella cultura del XIV e XV secolo* (Milano, 1968).

et, partant, la crise des *bonae artes* et la 'nuit' de la théologie, des sciences et des doctrines philosophiques. Une analyse – aussi rapide soit-elle – des nombreux textes humanistes de dialectique apparus pendant la première moitié du siècle pourrait facilement confirmer cette affirmation et démontrer le rapport étroit qu'il y a entre la formation de cette nouvelle texture dialectique et la transformation parallèle de la polémique contre les 'modernes' en un projet de réforme générale de toutes les méthodes. Je crois, au contraire, que certaines pointes polémiques plus aiguës, comme celles que présentent les textes de Vivès et de Ramus, témoignent, mieux que tout autre argument, de la nouvelle dimension que la critique humaniste a déjà assumée, bien au delà des limites des premières batailles contre les 'sophistes'. Pour Vivès,[1] en effet, l'égarement des sciences, la décadence de la théologie, la perte de l'*humanitas* coïncident parfaitement avec la *ruditas duarum linguarum* et l'*imperitia pseudodialecticorum*, plus grossiers et corrupteurs à mesure qu'ils se sont éloignés des origines de la 'sagesse' et de l'usage limpide et éloquent des techniques du discours. Pierre de la Ramée, d'autre part, joint sa condamnation non seulement des 'modernes' logiques, mais aussi – surtout dans ses oeuvres de jeunesse – de la tradition même de la logique aristotélicienne, à la louange des 'écoles nouvelles' où tout le savoir est en transformation, grâce au retour des témoignages classiques bien vivants et où refleurit la vérité évangélique obscurcie par la contamination injustifiée de doctrines philosophiques impures et étrangères. Sur un ton encore plus péremptoire et radical, Mario Nizolio[2] (qui reprend un grand nombre des thèmes d'Occam) célèbre la supériorité incontestable des arts et des méthodes rhétoriques et oratoires par rapport aux autres disciplines qui ne peuvent renaître et progresser sans le renouvellement de la langue; et l'aristotélicien Giacomo Aconcio aussi se trouve d'accord pour exiger que la réforme méthodique du savoir procède grâce au recours à la clarté de la langue. Les nouveaux logiciens comme les nouveaux théologues et les nouveaux philosophes prennent, certes, les anciens comme guides linguistiques et stylistiques suprêmes et comme paradigmes méthodologiques, mais ils n'en expriment pas moins clairement, dès à présent, leur droit d'exercer une critique libre par rapport aux 'modèles' mêmes, qu'il s'agisse d'analyser les textes de l'*Organon* ou de la *Poétique* d'Aristote, de discuter de la

---

[1] V.: Vasoli, *La dialettica e la retorica,* ad ind.　　　　　　[2] V.: ibid. Appendice.

prééminence ou seule autorité stylistique de Cicéron, ou bien d'examiner, avec une rigueur de plus en plus grande, les canons méthodologiques de Galène ou les procédés d'Euclide. La compréhension philologique des *antiqüi*, la capacité de reconstruire les expériences linguistiques et doctrinales effectives sont également, en effet, les raisons qui poussent les intellectuels du XVIe siècle à définir aussi les limites et les conditions historiques de la civilisation classique dont on voit clairement les nombreuses possibilités de développements divergents. Et c'est justement pour cela que les nouvelles générations humanistes élargissent leur 'éventail' des *auctores* dans des directions différentes de celles que préconisaient leurs maîtres du XVe siècle.

C'est un fait significatif que, tandis que la polémique antiscolastique s'enrichit de nouveaux contenus théologiques et de sollicitations réformatrices radicales, la recherche de la vérité primordiale aussi tend à se déplacer vers des origines plus mystérieuses et fabuleuses, vers les régions ancestrales de l'Orient méditerranéen et asiatique, dans les terres des Chaldéens, des Egyptiens ou dans le mystérieux trésor du savoir des *secretiores theologi* juifs.[1] L'extraordinaire succès, au XVIe siècle, de la tradition hermétique, des mythes historiographiques attribués au pseudo-Bérose et des *Oracula chaldaica*, joint à l'impressionnante diffusion des techniques cabalistiques que l'on trouve dans beaucoup de milieux religieux et philosophiques sont vraiment autant de témoignages de l'horizon historique plus vaste où se développe la nouvelle conception du rapport entre *antiqui* et *moderni*. D'une part il semble désormais certain que la civilisation gréco-latine n'est pas la seule expression de la *sapientia* dont on recherche aujourd'hui les racines primitives, au delà des *exempla* classiques, dans les oeuvres des philosophes, des poètes,

---

[1] V., à ce propos: A. J. Festugière, *La révèlation d'Hermès Trismégiste*, 1 (Paris, 1949); P. O. Kristeller, *Studies in Renaissance Thought and Letters* (Roma, 1956, 1969²); E. Garin, *Studi sul platonismo medioevale* (Firenze, 1958); *Umanesimo e simbolismo. Atti del IV Convegno internazionale di Studi umanistici, Venezia 1958*, a cura di E. Castelli (Padova, 1958); D. P. Walker, 'Orpheus the Theologian and Renaissance Platonists', *Journal of the Warburg and Courtauld Institutes* (1953), 100–19; id. 'The "prisca theologia" in France', ibid. (1954), 204–59; id. *Spiritual and Demonic Magic from Ficino to Campanella* (London, 1958); *Umanesimo ed esoterismo. Atti del V Convegno internazionale di Studi umanistici, Oberhofen, 1960*, a cura di E. Castelli (Padova, 1960); E. Garin, *La cultura filosofica*, pp.127–228; F. Yates, *Bruno and the Hermetic tradition* (Chicago, 1964); F. Secret, *Les Kabbalistes chrétiens de la Renaissance* (Paris, 1964); E. Garin, *L'età nuova*, pp.261–92; Ch. B. Schmitt, '"Prisca theologia" e "Philosophia perennis": due temi del Rinascimento italiano c la loro fortuna', dans *Il pensiero del Rinascimento e il tempo nostro* (Firenze, 1969), pp.211–36; D. P. Walker, *The Ancient Theology* (London, 1972).

des 'mages' qui les ont précédés. D'autre part, l'enrichissement aussi rapide et tumultueux des connaissances et des expériences contemporaines provoque la conscience, de plus en plus nette, des choix que la nouvelle culture doit opérer en face des suggestions différentes et contrastantes proposées par les 'antiquités infinies', dans une perspective temporelle toujours plus lointaine et indéfinie; de même que c'est une opinion courante que les 'modernes' ont le droit d'utiliser librement et de façon critique tous les modèles stylistiques et les techniques méthodologiques multiples dérivées de l'enseignement des classiques. Les hommes des 'temps nouveaux', qui ont été depuis plus d'un siècle à l'école des *antiqui*, sont, en somme, parfaitement conscients de leur droit de juger le passé humain tout entier, avec l'intention d'étendre leur vérification aux origines des nombreuses traditions et révélations qui ont composé leur hérédité culturelle. Pour cela aussi, les mythes qui ont accompagné (et continuent à favoriser) le retour à la science ancienne et le succés plus récent de la *prisca theologia* sont déjà critiqués et effacés par une analyse subtile, capable de se servir de tous les instruments philologiques mis au point par l'école humaniste. Et il est naturel que la critique, que l'on a utilisée contre tant d'aspects et tant de traditions du Moyen Âge, conteste avec toujours plus d'insistance une image de l'antiquité dont on constate le peu de fondement historique. À ce propos une étude systématique qui analyserait, dans leur ensemble, les différentes phases de la discussion sur les diverses 'antiquités' fantastiques et leurs soi-disant documents, apporterait certainement une contribution décisive pour la connaissance de la nouvelle attitude devant chaque 'témoignage' du passé, typique des courants les plus avancés de la culture du XVIe siècle. On ne devrait pas négliger non plus les résultats et l'incidence historique de tant de disputes qui semblent limitées à des problèmes très circonscrits mais qui, en fait, contribuent à rendre de plus en plus fragile l'hypothèse mystique de la 'vérité primordiale', confiée à la doctrine inspirée des *antiqui*.

En fait, à la fin du XVIe siècle, grâce à la complète diffusion de la culture humaniste dans une grande partie d'Europe, grâce à la crise de la Réforme, grâce aux bouleversantes nouveautés des découvertes géographiques et des conquêtes technologiques, le rapport entre le monde antique et la civilisation 'nouvelle' assume déjà une dimension plus historique, liée – et ce n'est pas par hasard –

à l'idée d'une coupure irreversible. Les auteurs les plus représentatifs sont tous d'accord pour insister surtout sur la 'nouveauté' d'une situation humaine qui, pour eux, n'a rien à voir avec le passé, sur la 'lumière' qui brille désormais grâce à la victorieuse bataille contre toutes les 'ténèbres' et les 'superstitions' des siècles obscurs. Ils sont certains que la conscience historique, l'exercice des arts libéraux et des sciences, le progrès des techniques n'ont jamais été plus avancés et parfaits; et il se sentent à même de célébrer leur temps, *aetas aurea*,[1] même en face de leurs anciens maîtres, sans aucun sentiment d'infériorité ou de dépendance, mais fièrement conscients que le renouvellement de la langue, des méthodes et des doctrines qui s'est effectué dans le courant du siècle a donné toutes les conditions pour aller au delà des traditions et des vérités des anciens. Platon, Aristote, comme Pythagore, Epicure et Plotin (et, dans d'autres domaines, Euripide, Démosthène, Cicéron, Quintilien, ou bien Galène, Hippocrate et Pline) sont, à présent, non pas les porteurs d'un savoir absolu et incontesté, mais surtout les points de repère obligatoires des analyses et des disputes dans lesquelles on voit se préciser des attitudes et des choix qui ont toujours un rapport précis avec les idées et les aspirations du 'nouveau' siècle. C'est pour cela que Nicolas Copernic peut faire appel aux philosophes les plus éloignés dans le temps et aux hommes de science grecs (Philolaos, Nicète, Ecphantus ou Héraclide du Pontus), mais seulement pour renverser l'*imago mundi* que l'antiquité avait transmise à la culture occidentale. C'est dans un esprit pas différent que les *philosophi naturales* du XVIe siècle (par exemple, Bernardino Telesio) redécouvrent dans les doctrines de la philosophie présocratique ou dans les idées atomistiques une alternative à la longue prédominance de la physique peripatéticienne. Et je crois que c'est dans cette perspective qu'il faut toujours considérer un autre événement fondamental de la vie intellectuelle du XVIe siècle: le retour massif des textes mathématiques grecs autour desquels, chaque année, se multiplient les interprétations, les discussions et les études méthodiques.[2] Il s'agit certainement de conceptions, idées et attitudes très variées, parfois même contradictoires, et toujours liées cependant à

[1] V., à ce sujet: H. Levin, *The Myth of the Golden Age in the Renaissance* (London, 1969).
[2] V.: A. Koyré, *Les sciences exactes, dans Histoire générale des sciences*, II (Paris, 1958); M. Boas *The Scientific Renaissance, 1450–1630* (London, 1962); E. Garin, 'Gli umanisti e la scienza', in *L'età nuova*, pp.449–76. Mais v. aussi, en général: R. R. Bolgar, *The Classical Heritage and its Beneficiaries* (Cambridge, 1954).

la naissance d'exigences éducatives originales, aux besoins opératifs d'une societé en rapide expansion et aux problèmes que posent, quotidiennement, les découvertes et les connaissances nouvelles dans tous les domaines du savoir. Il est significatif que le repêchage de la grande science grecque (après celui des 'lettres', de l''éloquence' et de la tradition religieuse et philosophique du monde ancien) signifie presque toujours une occasion précieuse pour reprendre une tradition interrompue et affronter des problèmes et des études dont on reconnaît la nouveauté effective. Les sciences mathématiques, comme toutes les autres formes de connaissance, ont donc eu leur 'saine' origine dans l'antiquité; mais en face du problème et de la recherche de la vérité il n'existe pas, et il ne peut pas exister, aucune autorité exclusive, et n'ont de valeur que les méthodes développées et renouvelées par les 'contemporains'. Comme le dit Giordano Bruno, dans une page mémorable de *La cena delle ceneri*, 'la raggione de l'antico e nuovo' est hors de propos là où l'on veut discuter sur la science et comprendre vraiment la nature des choses. Et s'il est vrai 'qu'il n'existe rien de neuf qui ne puisse devenir vieux, et rien de vieux qui n'ait été neuf', la question des *antiqui* et des *moderni* peut se conclure maintenant, en affirmant que la vérité est plutôt du côté de ceux qui ont pu tirer profit des expériences de nombreux siècles et regarder au delà des 'anciens', grâce à l'accumulation progressive des connaissances et des découvertes.

Il est évident que le nom de 'moderne' perdra donc aujourd'hui les stigmates négatifs dont l'avait marqué la première polémique humaniste. On ne peut s'étonner non plus du fait que – quand le mythe humaniste du 'millénaire des ténèbres' a déjà pris le sens d'une périodisation historique définitive – l'image opposée de l'antiquité, source de tout le savoir, subisse les premières attaques décisives de la part d'une culture désormais consciente de ses propres fins et des tâches qui l'attendent. Du reste, la revendication du 'moderne' par rapport à l''ancien' s'accompagne à l'intention, précisée par les intellectuels les plus représentatifs, de soumettre tous les domaines et les méthodes du savoir à une révision radicale, de réorganiser et de restaurer, suivant d'autres critères, l'immense trésor culturel que toutes les civilisations passées nous ont transmis comme une hérédité précieuse, mais aussi redoutable. Dans un monde qui, en moins d'un siècle, a vu se transformer les paramètres habituels de l'expérience humaine, apparaître de nouveaux continents et des traditions historiques inconnues, s'ébranler les 'systèmes' les plus respectés de l'univers, se briser l'unité millénaire de la *christianitas* et naître des institutions et des formes de vie inédites, la leçon des anciens perd, nécessairement, cette autorité presque sacrée que les premières générations humanistes lui avaient attribuée. A présent, une fois terminé l''âge barbare et obscur' que l'on s'imagine avoir condamné à jamais, les nouveaux 'modernes' se tournent plutôt vers un futur encore informe dans lequel ils projettent les archétypes et les valeurs humaines que leur a légués l'école des 'classiques'.

5

REFLECTIONS ON RAVISIUS TEXTOR'S *SPECIMEN EPITHETORUM*

I. D. McFARLANE

In the field of Neo-Latin poetry Renaissance France has been a Cinderella; and though she failed in her bid to outdo the Italian humanists at their game, she forms an important part of the pattern of humanist verse. There is little recent research of note in the period 1520–60, though there are encouraging signs of renewed interest; much remains to be done in the study of language, metrical practice, stylistic aspects. In this period, younger humanists were aware of a gap between themselves and the generation of Robert Gaguin and his fellow pioneers, and rightly so; there are marked differences of a thematic and linguistic nature. Critical judgements, in the past, tended to be made with an eye on the classical poets they so often imitated, but these humanist writers owed a great deal too to their Neo-Latin predecessors in Italy. A balanced view of their latinity will not be possible until scholars embark on critical editions of the more important figures, examine the conditions in which their latinity took shape, and in this context take a look at the pedagogic background as well as at the poetic antecedents.

It is therefore important to bear in mind the role, perhaps difficult to define but very real, of the *instruments de travail* which were current in the colleges and were used by the teachers as well as by the pupils. In the humanist effervescence of the 1520s, the provision of new or up-dated manuals assumed a high priority; but though France distinguished itself more especially in the field of lexicography, it was probably less successful in producing manuals likely to withstand the ravages of time. Certain foreign works tended to corner important parts of the market: the most obvious is the series of textbooks published by Despauterius who none the less was greatly indebted to medieval sources; and for all the mutterings and grumblings of pedagogues such as Nicolas Bourbon and Hubert Sussannée, he remained firmly in the saddle for a long time to come. Other foreign manuals were welcome: Perotti's little book on Horatian metres, the writings of Ulrich von Hutten or Murmellius, Mantuan's eclogues, Linacre's *Rudimenta* and of course the various works by Erasmus. Native efforts in France were less impressive: Nicole Dupuys (*Bonaspes*), Guy de Fontenay, Martin Dolet, all very ephemeral, but there were exceptions. Mathurin Cordier's textbook *De corrupti sermonis emendatione* was to become standard, and there were the very popular compendia from the pen of Ravisius Textor. Here I wish to speak mainly about one of his manuals, even though it is concerned with a limited aspect of poetic language, the epithet.

Textor's *Specimen* or *Opus* first appeared in 1518, 'quae tibi & lectoribus incredibilem pariet voluptatem'.[1] The author expressed his admiration for the work done by Lefêvre d'Etaples and Erasmus, whose pedagogic ideas no doubt underpin his work. So successful was the manual that it was reprinted under various titles, some-times with additional material – such as Textor's own *Synonyma* or Sabinus's little treatise on prosody – at other times in epitomised form, over the next hundred and fifty years.[2] In the sixteenth century, Paris and Basel appear to share the main load of printing, with the latter becoming gradually more prominent. At the end of the century London begins to figure, with Lyons, Douai and Rouen playing the leading roles in the first quarter of the seventeenth century; later on, the manual seems to appeal mainly to an English audience. I shall confine myself here to its success in France during the sixteenth century.

The first edition had some 2,800 nouns for which epithets were provided: some entries would be minimal (e.g. *zelus*, one), others

---

[1] *Specimen Epithetorum Ioannis Rauisij Textoris Niuernensis, omnibus artis Poeticae studiosis maxime utilium* (Paris, Regnault Chauldiere (for H. Estienne), 1518) (copies in British Museum and Cambridge University Library). The work also appeared in the same year under the title *Epithetorum Opus* from the house of H. Estienne: there is a copy in Besançon which I have not seen.

[2] A casual check of standard repertories and library catalogues yields the following editions, the list of which would certainly be lengthened after systematic inquiry; I do not differentiate between the different presentations of the basic work: 1518 Paris; 1524 Paris; *ca* 1540 Basel; 1541, 1548 Lyons; 1549, 1555, 1558 Basel; ? 1564 London; 1565 Basel, also Avignon; 1573 Basel; 1574 Antwerp; 1579 London; 1580 Paris; 1583 Venice; 1587 Paris, also Geneva; 1588 London; 1592 Basel; 1594 Basel; 1595 London, also Paris; 1599 Basel; 1605 Lyons; 1607, 1608 Rouen; 1608 London; 1611 Lyons; 1612 Douai; 1616, 1620 Lyons; 1621, 1623 Rouen; 1624 Evreux; 1626 London; 1630 Douai; 1634, 1642, 1657, 1664, 1673, 1682 London; 1664 Geneva. I am grateful to Mr Philip Ford for checking some bibliographical points for me in Cambridge University Library.

like *Apollo* had over one hundred. At the beginning of each letter of the alphabet, the entries would be accompanied by quotations, but as time went on the epithets ceased to be substantiated and the order was often far from alphabetical, hence the addition of an index. When the substantive received the full treatment, there might be a *praefatio*, offering suitable historical, cultural and mythological information, occasionally defining a noun and possibly including a substantial piece of verse, often by Textor himself. An entry like *Gallia* might have quite detailed statements on the obscure origin of the country, a reference to Berosus, or to the legend of the Gallic Hercules. This would be followed by the *testimonia*, in which the quotations were numbered to correspond to the list of epithets preceding the *praefatio*; sometimes a periphrasis or *antonomasia* would be provided.

Very soon, a rather different pattern of presentation comes into being and will be generally maintained in successive editions.[1] (1) All nouns are supplied with quotations in support of the epithets recommended and in roughly chronological order, though after-thoughts may be introduced; (2) the *praefationes* are drastically curtailed, but, in compensation, cover a wider range of proper nouns (and sometimes technical terms); (3) greater efforts are made to arrange the nouns alphabetically; (4) a list of authors cited is given, though it tends to be incomplete. The *Epitome*, which still ran to some four hundred pages, compared with the average of eight hundred pages of the later full editions, saves space by reducing quotation and reference to authors.[2] What is of considerable interest is the variety and nature of the sources used.

(1) Occasionally, prose writers are pressed into service, but discreetly since the volume is destined for budding writers of Latin verse. We find examples from Cicero, Columella, Budé; and there are, curiously, a few 'Latin' quotations from Greek poets such as Theocritus and Sophocles.

(2) From the classical world of poetry we have predictably a substantial representation of Virgil and Ovid, as well as of the satirists, in particular Martial who provides a useful domestic vocabulary.

---

[1] I am much obliged to Dr Peter Sharratt for checking some points for me concerning the copy of the 1524 edition (now rather rare) in Edinburgh University Library.

[2] The earliest edition I have so far seen reported of the *Epitome* is Basel *ca* 1540 (Folger); two editions soon follow it in Lyons (1541 and 1548).

(3) Particularly notable is the presence of the Silver Latin poets: Claudian in modest measure, but impressively Statius and Lucan, with Silius Italicus, Sidonius Apollinaris, Valerius Flaccus not all that far behind. A similar pattern will be found in Textor's *Synonyma*, though this is a much smaller manual.[1] Statius and Lucan appeal for their historical interest, but they remain important models of rhetoric. Catullus and Horace, in the *Specimen*, are penumbral, partly because Textor is thinking in terms of elegiac verse and heroic metre, partly because Catullus (who is also castigated in the Sabinus treatise) is suspect, while Horace the lyric does not come fully into his own until the 1530s. Of course, 'technical' writers such as Lucretius and Manilius are well represented.

(4) Medieval authors are not totally absent: Boethius and Martianus Capella appear from time to time.

(5) Then we have the moderns, and quantitatively they are impressive:

(a) A handful of non-Italians: Conrad von Keltis in particular, More.

(b) More substantial, the Italians: Petrarch, especially the Eclogues, Radinus, Pamphilus Saxus, Cleophilus, Politian, Pontano, the Strozzi, Augurellus, Beroaldus, Mantuan, Quintinao Stoa; and Faustus Andrelinus who had settled in France.

(c) Poets closely connected with France: (i) various writers of Flemish origin, though not Gaguin: Michael Anglicus, Remacle d'Ardenne; (ii) French poets, for the most part colleagues of the author: Nicolas Barthélemy de Loches, Gulielmus Castellus, Salmon Macrin, Valeran de Varanne, Textor himself.

At this stage, two points are borne in on the reader. In the first place, the proportional representation of these poets is far from 'classical', as a few random samples will suggest:

Aestus: 10 classical examples, 19 modern; *Chelys*, 4 classical, 33 medieval and modern; *Cithara*, 5 classical, 23 modern; *Phoebus*, 22 classical, 3 medieval, 42 modern; *Tenebrae*, 24 classical, 22 modern, plus 4 from Lactantius and Juvencus. *Barbiton* appears in classical times in the ablative and dative, but Textor gives his examples

---

[1] Bodley holds a copy of the 1528 edition. Among the authors cited, Ovid has a clear lead, followed by Statius with Virgil a rather modest third, though still well ahead of the rest of the field. Sidonius Apollinaris, Silius Italicus, Lucan and Pliny form the only other bunch of well-represented authors; the also-rans are allowed rarely more than three or four references.

(often with other cases) from the moderns: Keltis 3, Augurellus 1, Faustus 1, with one from Quintilian. The entry for *saltus* is supported by quotations from Virgil, Lucan, Varro, Lucretius, Ovid, Silius Italicus, Claudian, Manilius, Pontano, Radinus, Strozzi senior, Livy (4), Crinitus, Mantuan, Juvenal, Catullus. Such samples reveal the massive presence of the 'moderns' and make one wonder what may have been the impact, conscious or otherwise, on the latinity of the college pupil. In the second place, once the pattern of the volume is established, there is very little change, so that on the one hand, the great advances in latinity during the heyday of French scholarship (Turnèbe, Muret, Lambyn, Passerat, Dorat, Scaliger) are not reflected in any serious revision, and on the other hand, Neo-Latin authors after 1520 or so are simply not represented. The average schoolboy is being offered a mixed bag of Latin authors, some of whom are very obscure and jostle with the great names of Golden latinity, but without much indication of critical distinctions.

So far, I have confined myself mainly to description, but the manual does prompt reflections and queries about its possible impact in the classroom, at an early stage in the budding humanist's career.

There is no need to labour the importance of the epithet in poetic composition: Quintilian had had something to say on the score,[1] as had Erasmus in *De duplici copia*;[2] the lesson is thrust home by Textor himself and by Nicole Bérault in a preliminary letter,[3] but a textbook of this sort, perhaps more than the numerous precepts afforded by authorities, was likely to impress on the young humanist mind the need to exploit the epithet in elegant verse. The manual no doubt provided fringe benefits: one may suppose that the rudiments of, say, classical mythology were very easily picked up here; and information, often curious, might be gleaned about foreign countries. The entry on *Aegypti* is weird enough, but not so weird as the remarks on *Scoti*, which of course go back to St Jerome:

Scoti, truces. Scoti populi sunt occidentales. Hi aetate beati Hieronymi vescebantur humanis carnibus. Et quanquam per syluas porcorum greges & armentorum repetirent, tamen pastorum nates & foeminarum papillas sollebant abscind-

---

[1] *Institutio Oratoria* (Camb., Mass. (Loeb), 1953), VIII, vi, 40 ff.
[2] *De duplici Copia verborum ac rerum commentarij duo* (Paris, Simon de Colines, 1526), fol.89v.
[3] See 1518 edition, fol.***vi v (Bérault) and fol.308v–309v (*J. Ravisius Textor ad Candidum Lectorem*).

ere, & has solas ciborum delicias arbitrari. Hi nullam propriam habebant coniugem, sed pro libidine more pecudum lasciuiebant.[1]

So much for the auld alliance in the late sixteenth century. The selection of epithets (and indeed the nouns they accompany) may be determined by a variety of factors. No doubt, there is a built-in temptation to note down all the epithets that come one's way – the collector's mania of the magpie humanist; but conscious and unconscious values may also play their part. A perusal of the entries *amor* and *fortuna* reflect the unfavourable attitudes of certain humanist minds, and a sociological analysis of such an *instrument de travail* (which has, for instance, no entries for *mater* or *pater*) might prove rewarding. From a totally different point of view, quotations would, obliquely and not always overtly, tend to justify certain metrical practices, the ordering of words here or there in the line, and the placing and use of polysyllables, the attitude to hellenisms and so forth; one might go further and ask oneself whether this (and other manuals of Latin rhetoric and poetic practice) did not have some influence on the techniques of poets in the vernacular. Another point that strikes me is the question to what extent the frequency of certain types of adjective (in structure and suffix) may have been determined, in Latin as well as in the vernacular (where transference is feasible), by the recourse to a manual like Textor's. Certain suffixes are very much in evidence: *-ifer*, *-iger*, *-osus*, *-abilis*, *-ibilis*, *-atilis*, but also the present participial form (a device much used by Ronsard), and especially the compound form: *undisonus*, *flammiuomus*, which will also be much exploited by the Pléiade, and the diminutive is already having a good innings in Neo-Latin verse before the appearance of Joannes Secundus's *Basia*. In 1518 *Alpes* was supported by five examples of *-ifer*, *-iger* and eight of *-osus*; if one looks up *oculi* (including *ocelli*) one will find among the epithets *stillantes*, *nictantes*, *rosei*, *orbiculares* (Textor himself), *protuberantes* (no doubt for *innamorate* with thyroid problems), *rutilantes*, *luciduli*, *fulgidi*, *radiantes*, *splendiduli*, *petulci*, *dulciculi*, *procaces*, *flammantes*, *flammiferi*, *crassiculi*, *flammeoli*.

A volume such as Textor's not only offers us a fascinating glance at the poetic reading of a humanist in the early days of Francis I's

---

[1] This quotation occurs in the Paris 1580 edition, which I use as well as the 1518 and 1524 editions, precisely because it brings out the extraordinarily conservative nature of the manual, once the pattern had been established.

reign, it also reflects the range and type of poets that probably appealed to other members of that generation. One fact that emerges, for instance, is the impressive reputation of Pontano,[1] confirmed of course from other sources. The manual, precisely because of its schoolroom prestige, might well guide poetic tyros towards certain authors from a tender age; it might also maintain, in fossilised form, tags from authors, who with the passage of time were sinking into oblivion. At all events, we shall find many of the poets represented in Textor leaving their mark on the coming generation. From our point of view today, it often helps us to accelerate our identification of these sources. When we read Salmon Macrin's play on words:

> Abstrusam latebris tenebricosis
> Sepultam tenebris latebricosis[2]

we shall no doubt get on the track of Pontano without much trouble, partly because the word play is obvious, partly because we know that Macrin was particularly interested in that poet; but Textor conveniently reproduces both quotations; and if that example is a simple one, there are others where Textor can help us to cut more difficult corners.

This leads on to a more important matter, however speculative it must remain: the extent to which the young poet himself used Textor to save himself trouble or to improve on a tentative version of his own – chiefly in the field of the epithet, though the quotations would offer help in other respects. Of course, reservations will immediately spring to mind: the astonishing memory of so many humanists, the knowledge that this or that author was specially well versed in Virgil or Statius, the tendency to reread certain poets if one is working in a particular genre or topic, the difficulty of establishing whether a classical echo is directly remembered, or recalled through some other Neo-Latin intermediary (Pontano, Marullus), or picked up in some dictionary or manual, the realisation that a Neo-Latin poet of some class may well instinctively produce the 'right' solution to his problem. Against this one can bring some counter-arguments: the impression that Textor could have guided humanist rhymesters towards certain authors rather than others,

[1] M. Pierre Nespoulous, of the University of Toulouse, is engaged on a study of the reputation and influence of Pontano in France.
[2] See 1518 edition of the Textor, fol.278r. Significantly, only the early Macrin is represented; the more interesting author of the *Carminum libellus* (1528) and other 'lyric' works does not figure in later editions of the manual.

encouraged them in their choice of vocabulary or in a preference for certain adjectival forms, the fact that many of them were college tutors, the presence of echoes in Textor from poets unlikely to have come otherwise to the notice of the reader, the proof that an author is striving to conceal his source, the law of least resistance, the practice of using Textor and other manuals, as we use Littré, Lewis and Short, the *O.E.D.* and so on. Clearly, common sense and judgement must play their part and one must curb one's enthusiasm which tends to find what one is looking for; but it is remarkable how frequently classical and modern echoes do turn up in Textor, and one experiences a certain cumulative impression that his manual was often on the desk of the humanist poet at work. In order to illustrate these points, I shall conclude by offering some examples from one poet, George Buchanan, who taught for many years in various French colleges, who indeed learned Latin verse composition in Paris shortly after the Textor was published,[1] who composed much of his verse in France between *ca* 1530 and *ca* 1560, and whose poems do seem to have been affected on occasion by a knowledge of the Textor.

Clearly, Buchanan will not bother to consult Textor when he wishes to embellish some thematic material, say, in the *Sphaera*: if Hyginus affords the basis for his passage on the Zodiac,[2] he will reread his Aratus and Pontanus; and his memory of a Virgilian tag in the first invocation was no doubt already present in his mind.[3] A less clear-cut case occurs in *Elegia* IV, ll.53–4:

> Qualia pinguntur miseris simulacra figuris
> Terrificae Mortis, mortiferaeque Famis.
> At neque Tastaeus, nec Tevius assidet, ore
> Suauiloquo longum qui vetet esse diem.[4]

---

[1] 'Ibi [i.e. in Paris] cum studiis literarum, maxime carminibus scribendis, operam dedisset partim naturae impulsu, partim necessitate (quod hoc unum studiorum genus adolescentiae proponebatur) . . .', *Vita ab ipso scripta biennio ante mortem* in *The Trial of George Buchanan before the Lisbon Inquisition*, ed. James M. Aitken (Edinburgh and London, 1939), p.xiv. Buchanan's first sojourn in Paris lasted from 1520 to 1522.

[2] *De Sphaera*, III, ll.120–277. The text may be conveniently found in the Ruddiman–Burmann edition of the *Opera Omnia* (Leyden, 1725), vol.II, pp.468–73.

[3] *De Sphaera*, I, 7, *Rerum sancte parens, audacibus annue coeptis*. The second hemistich is lifted from *Georg*. I, 40: the first hemistich may be an echo of Avienus, 23, *ipse parens rerum*.

[4] *Opera Omnia*, vol.II, p.315. See Textor under *Mors* and *Os*. The second tag occurs in Mantuan's fourth Eclogue, ll.9–10. See *The Eclogues of Baptista Mantuanus*, ed. W. P. Mustard (Baltimore, 1911). One must ask oneself also to what extent Mantuan helped to fashion habits in Latin verse composition (e.g. lavish use of the epithet (as in *Ecl.* IV, ll.124–30), or indulgence in the compound adjective).

88

These lines certainly echo tags from Mantuan (Baptista Spagnuoli):

> Terrificam Mortem facit ignorantia rerum

and, with the same enjambement:

> ... et ore
> Suauiloquo visus cunctos praecellere patres.

Both these tags appear in the Textor; did Buchanan remember Mantuan anyhow, given his schoolroom popularity then, or did he use the manual for one or both of the references? When in *Silva* II, l.87 he writes:

> Siue per aestiferas Libyae sitientis arenas[1]

he may be conflating two memories of Lucan:

> Sicut squallentibus arvis | Aestiferae Libyes

and

> Per calidas Libyae sitientis arenas[2]

There is plenty of evidence that Buchanan was thoroughly familiar with Lucan and used him frequently, but these two quotations, to be found cheek by jowl in Textor (under *Lybia*), might have been exploited after his reaching for the manual. More conclusive, I think, is a case from *Elegia* II, l.76:

> Ingemit extinctum tinnula Mater Ityn[3]

Now, in Textor, there is a quotation from the little-known Cleophilus who does not appear to be anybody's bedside reading:

> Et gemit enectum garrula mater Ityn (under *Progne*)

I am not aware that there is any classical source for this; in any case, the structure of the Buchanan line is so close to Cleophilus: on the one hand, *Ingemit* shows a desire on the poet's part to get away from *Et gemit*; more decisively, a manuscript in the Bibliothèque Nationale in Paris reveals that *tinnula* was later substituted for *garrula*.[4] Elsewhere, especially in the case of Virgilian tags, we have manuscript evidence of Buchanan hiding or blurring his tracks, either by verbal substitution or by syntactical variation, and the technique appears to be repeated in this instance. In other cases,

---

[1] *Opera Omnia*, vol.II, p.329.

[3] *Opera Omnia*, vol.II, p.306.

[2] Lucan, I, ll.205–6 and 368.

[4] See B. N. ms. lat.8140, fol.95ff.

Textor does seem to provide the simplest answer: *populatrix flamma* (*Sphaera*, 1, 173) might be original and so might *ignigenae facis* (*Epigram.* lib. 1, xxix, 3); but both appear in Textor, from Bartholinus and Remacle d'Ardenne respectively.[1] And if in the *Franciscanus*, l.198,[2] the tag *Riphaeae frigora brumae* can be seen as a blend of Claudian and Valerius Flaccus, one may also wonder whether a perusal of the Textor did not come up with a quotation from Columella: *Post ubi Riphaeae torpentia frigora brumae.* One final comment on Buchanan: does Buchanan's very marked preference for adjectives endowed with certain suffixes (*-iger, -ifer,* and so forth) have anything to do with his acquaintance with this manual?

In offering a few examples, which could be easily augmented, I have merely sought to reproduce the rhythms of my own cumulative impressions as I read Buchanan and sometimes consulted the Textor. One may feel that these instances are suggestive rather than conclusive, or alternatively that Buchanan may lend himself to this sort of demonstration more easily than other poets and that one Scots humanist swallow hardly makes a Textorian summer. Nevertheless, it does seem to me that the continued and successful presence of such a textbook raises important questions about the latinity of French poets in the Neo-Latin field, about the ways in which they developed their techniques and reading, and about the fringe benefits of such familiarity with current *instruments de travail*. But until the basic research into these problems is conducted, we shall remain in the dark. The function of this symposium was to suggest areas where further work was required; and to the question 'What needs to be done in this particular field?', the answer is simple and short: everything.

[1] See under *Flamma* and *Fax* respectively.   [2] *Opera Omnia*, vol.II, p.262.

6

COMMONPLACE RHAPSODY: RAVISIUS TEXTOR, ZWINGER AND SHAKESPEARE

WALTER J. ONG

COMMONPLACES AND THEIR SIGNIFICANCE

Writing in *Chapters in Western Civilization*, Professor Paul Oskar Kristeller notes that 'the frequency of quotations and of commonplaces repeated in the moral literature in the Renaissance gives to all but its very best products an air of triviality that is often very boring to the modern critical reader'.[1] The Renaissance exploitation of commonplace material is of course not restricted to moral treatises. Such material shows everywhere through the Renaissance, from speculative theology and medical treatises to lyric and dramatic poetry, where, however, its use is often less cumbersome than among the moralists. And at its best, in the 'pointed' style which derives in part from Seneca, such material becomes brilliant, 'illustrating' the subject with flashes of insight and wit.

A great many studies treat in one way or another what we may here style the commonplace tradition. Looking for the roots of the literary heritage of the West, in his *European Literature and the Latin Middle Ages* Ernst Robert Curtius devotes a great deal of attention to the various 'topics' (*topoi* or *loci*, places, commonplaces) which have provided both themes and ways of managing themes to writers from classical antiquity on. Thus he treats the 'topics of consolatory oratory', 'historical topics', 'topics of the exordium', and other 'topics' explicitly labelled as such.[2] Many of his chapter headings indicate that individual chapters are devoted to the discussion of

[1] Paul Oskar Kristeller, 'The Moral Thought of Renaissance Humanism', in *Chapters in Western Civilization*, ed. by the Contemporary Civilization Staff of Columbia College, Columbia University, 3rd ed. (New York and London: Columbia University Press, 1961), I, 305.

[2] Ernst Robert Curtius, *European Literature and the Latin Middle Ages*, translated from the German by Willard Trask, Bollingen Series, xxxvi (New York: Pantheon Books, 1953), pp.79–105.

further individual topics. Thus, 'The Goddess Natura', 'Heroes and Rulers', 'The Ideal Landscape', 'Poetry and Philosophy', 'The Book as Symbol', and so on. A brief but tightly packed study by August Beck, *Die 'Studia Humanitatis' und ihre Methode*, explains a great deal directly on the use of commonplaces, especially as prescribed in works on education, from Rudolph Agricola and Erasmus on to the time of Montaigne.[1] Studies of sixteenth- and seventeenth-century writers, particularly by American scholars, who constitute the largest group by far of experts on the rhetorical tradition, often treat the commonplaces in various ways. One of the most thorough-going of such treatments is T. W. Baldwin's monumental landmark, *William Shakspere's Small Latine and Lesse Greeke*, which works patiently through large numbers of commonplace collections in use in Shakespeare's milieu by schoolboys as well as by adults.[2] Sister Joan Marie Lechner has provided an invaluable survey of Renaissance views and practice in her *Renaissance Concepts of the Commonplaces*.[3]

Out of these studies there emerges a major question: Why was the commonplace tradition once so important, since it now seems so affected and boring and aesthetically counter-productive? None of the studies just mentioned, nor others like them, really broach this question. The question can be answered only by situating the commonplace tradition in the broader perspectives of noetic history, examining how the tradition relates to the evolution of means of accumulation, storage, and retrieval of knowledge, and thus eventually how it relates to the history of the human psyche and of culture. This is what the present study undertakes to do, working with a certain few significant Renaissance writers. Until the commonplaces are related to the evolving noetic economy, they remain antiquarian curiosities, quaint phenomena, whose obtrusiveness in the past is no more explicable than their eclipse in the present.

'Commonplace' of course has several, more or less related, senses, some of them quite technical.[4] But in all its senses the term has to do

---

1 Bibliothèque d'Humanisme et Renaissance, xxi (1959), 273–90.
2 Two vols. (Urbana, Ill.: University of Illinois Press, 1944).
3 (New York: Pageant Press, 1962); now out of print, but scheduled to be reprinted.
4 See Walter J. Ong, *The Presence of the Word* (New Haven and London: Yale University Press, 1967), pp.56–66, 79–87, etc.; Lechner, *Renaissance Concepts of the Commonplaces*. In *European Literature and the Latin Middle Ages*, Curtius is concerned largely, sometimes explicitly and sometimes implicitly, with the central commonplace tradition of the West.

in one way or another with the exploitation of what is already known, and indeed often of what is exceedingly well known. The 'places' provided access to a culture's noetic store. In classical rhetorical doctrine, places (*topoi* in Greek, in Latin *loci*) refer to the 'seats' or, as we today would commonly conceptualise them, to the 'headings' to which one betook oneself to draw out of the stock of knowledge the things one could say concerning a given subject. These headings implemented analysis of one's subject: for a person, one might, by a kind of analytic process, consider his family, descent, sex, age, education, and the like; or, more generally, for all sorts of things, one could look to definition, opposites, causes, effects, related matters, and so on. This meaning of *topos* or *locus* or 'place' is approximated still in our present term 'topic' (from *topikos*, the Greek adjectival form corresponding to the noun *topos*). In his *Rhetoric* (1.ii.21–1358a) Aristotle notes two classes of 'places': (*a*) 'common' places, headings providing materials for any and all subjects, and (*b*) 'special' places, headings offering matter for certain individual subjects, such as law or physics. But this distinction was too fastidious to survive the hurly-burly of rhetorical doctrine and practice, where 'places' (*loci*) and 'commonplaces' (*loci communes*) were often used interchangeably.[1]

A 'commonplace' might also have another meaning, somewhat deviously related to this first: a 'commonplace' could be a standard brief disquisition or purple patch on any of hundreds or thousands of given subjects – loyalty, treachery, brotherhood, theft, decadence (Cicero's *O tempora! O mores!* passage is a commonplace on this subject), and so on; these prefabricated disquisitions were excerpted from one's reading or listening or worked up by oneself (generally out of material taken or adapted from others). Quintilian explains this meaning of *locus communis* in his *Institutiones oratoriae* x.5.12 – cf. *ibid.* 1.11.12. – after treating other usages of *locus* earlier in the same work (v.10.20).

Even in antiquity, as Quintilian testifies, commonplaces in the sense of standard brief disquisitions or purple patches were often committed to writing, and by the Middle Ages and the Renaissance came to be regularly stored in commonplace books or 'copie' books or copybooks (books assuring *copia*, or the free flow of discourse essential for oratory). The medieval *florilegia* or collections of

---

[1] See Ong, *The Presence of the Word*, p.82.

exempla and other useful bits for use in subsequent discourse belong to this tradition. To it can also be assimilated collections such as Erasmus's *De duplici copia verborum et rerum*, where the entries are often less than disquisitions, being in many instances quite short expressions, mere phrases or turns of diction, such as the Latin equivalents of 'white as snow', 'soft as the ear lobe', for these phrases, too, are presented as stock ways of treating a particular subject, however briefly, got together for subsequent use.[1]

It is helpful sometimes to refer to commonplaces in this latter sense of garnered standard disquisitions or purple patches on a set subject as 'cumulative' commonplaces, and to places or common-places in the earlier sense of headings as 'analytic' places or common-places. By the term 'commonplace tradition' I shall refer here to the practice, more or less reflective, of exploiting both analytic and cumulative places or commonplaces. 'Commonplace collections' here refers to assemblages in writing or print of cumulative common-places, these latter being understood to include both lengthy passages and briefer expressions, down to mere *modus dicendi*, as in Erasmus's *De copia*, stocked in formulaic fashion out of the extant store of knowledge for further exploitation as occasion might demand.

As Eric Havelock has shown, the noetic economy of an oral culture demands that knowledge be processed in more or less formulary style and that it be constantly recycled orally – otherwise it simply vanishes for good unless it be discovered anew.[2] The whole common-place tradition, an organised trafficking in what in one way or another is already known, is obviously part and parcel of the ancient oral world, the primitive human noetic universe, to which the Renaissance rhetorical doctrine of imitation also obviously relates. Elsewhere I have undertaken to show that the persistence of such material in more or less conspicuous form provides one rule-of-

[1] Many of Erasmus's works are collections of what in one way or another is basically commonplace material: thus his *Adagia*, his *Apophthegmata*, his *Colloquia*, the *De duplici copia verborum et rerum*, the *Epigrammata* and the *Parabola sive Similia*. Moreover, his editions of collections of brief lives by Epiphanius, Sophronius, St Jerome, and Plutarch are primary sources of commonplace *exempla*, as are also his editions of Lucian of Samosata's *Dialogi* and other works. As was the case with most humanists, Erasmus regarded reading generally as furnishing commonplace grist for the reader's own rhetorical mill. A great deal of his influence as an educator was due to the fact that he was the most influential collector of commonplace material the Western world has ever seen.

[2] Eric A. Havelock, *Preface to Plato* (Cambridge, Mass.: Belknap Press of Harvard Press, 1963), pp.36–60.

thumb indication of how oral or residually oral a given culture may be – which is also to say how oral or residually oral the culture's typical personality structures and its state of consciousness itself may be.[1]

IOANNES RAVISIUS TEXTOR: EXEMPLARY COLLECTOR

As an instance of some of the workings of the commonplace tradition in the Renaissance and a point of departure for reflection on the tradition, I should like to adduce here two collections of commonplace materials got up by a much neglected sixteenth-century French Neo-Latin writer, Jean Tixier, Seigneur de Ravisi, who latinised his name as Ioannes Ravisius Textor. Although Ravisius Textor was familiar to sixteenth- and early seventeenth-century schoolboys across western Europe – including, it would appear certain, William Shakespeare[2] – he remains a neglected figure today and indeed promises to be neglected even more effectively in the future, for he published in Latin and the knowledge of Latin is becoming less and less common even among scholars – a fact which we should by now frankly admit is severely warping many studies of the Renaissance.

Ioannes Ravisius Textor was born very likely around 1470, but perhaps as late as 1480, probably at Saint-Saulge in the Nivernais. He studied at the University of Paris under his compatriot Jean Beluacus in the Collège de Navarre, with which Textor's entire life was thereafter identified. There it was that he became professor of rhetoric, helping to make this college the best of all the Paris colleges for the study of humanities. In 1520 he was elected Rector of the University and in 1524 he died in Paris. Although a Nivernais by birth and a Parisian by adoption, Ravisius Textor, like many humanists, was international in his reputation and influence: editions of his works appear not only in Paris, Rouen, and Lyons, but also in Basel, Venice, Antwerp, Douai, and London.[3] Few

---

[1] Walter J. Ong, *Rhetoric, Romance, and Technology* (Ithaca and London: Cornell University Press, 1971), pp.23–47.

[2] See T. W. Baldwin, *William Shakspere's Small Latine and Lesse Greeke* (Urbana, Ill.: University of Illinois Press, 1944), II, 391, 414–16; cf. the many other references to Textor locatable through Baldwin's indexes.

[3] Including one London edition not listed in the Pollard and Redgrave *Short-Title Catalogue*, namely *Epistolae Ioannis Ravisii Textoris non vulgaris eruditionis: nunc recens in*

studies of Ioannes Ravisius Textor have ever appeared, and there is no definitive study at all, so far as I can ascertain.[1] Textor's published works – all Latin, as we have just noted – include mostly productions of a routine humanist sort: dialogues (written to be staged, as they indeed often were), epigrams, letters, and editions of Ulrich von Hutten's *Aula* and *Dialogus* and of other authors' works, including a collection of short pieces on distinguished women by various writers. The two works of Textor's to be glanced at here are his *Officina* (a title which can be rendered into English as *Workshop*) and his *Epitheta* (*Epithets*). These continue the copybook

gratiam studiosae iuventutis multo quam antehac unquam emendatiores in lucem editae (London: ex Typographia Societatis Stationariorum, 1628). I have not seen a copy of this edition, but a copy was listed for sale in Maggs Brothers (London), *Catalogue No. 901* (January 1966).

[1] See Maurice Mignon, *Études de littérature nivernaise: Tixier de Ravisy, Augustin Berthier, Adam Billaut, Cotignon de la Charnaye, Jules Renard* (Gap: Editions Ophrys (1946)), esp. pp.9–10. An earlier work by J. Vodoz, *Le Théâtre latin de Ravisius Textor 1470–1524* (Winterthur: Imprimerie Geschwister Ziegler, 1898), treats Textor's *Dialogi*, which were written to be staged as *moralités, soties, et farces*, but, as would be normal or even inevitable at the time this work was done, of course says nothing about the influence of epithet-collecting or commonplaces on Textor's work. Vodoz cites (p.137) the *Roman de la rose* as a frequent source for Textor's ideas, but the complexity of Textor's sources is so little adverted to that one is unsure as to how directly operative this medieval romance as such actually was. A still earlier doctoral dissertation by L. Massebieau, *De Ravisii Textoris comoediis seu De Comoediis collegiorum in Gallia praesertim ineunto sexto decimo saeculo disquisitionem Facultati Litterarum Parisiensi proponebat L. Massebieau* (Paris: J. Bonheure et Compagnie, 1878), goes into the staging of Textor's comedies (that is, his *Dialogi*). Massebieau notes (pp.47–8) some antecedents of Hamlet's gravedigger scene in Villon, Carolus Aurelianensis, Ravisius, and Reuchlin, but without reference to Ravisius's *Officina* or *Epitheta*. He is aware of Textor's reliance on the commonplace tradition, as his remarks about what Textor takes 'ex communi fonte' here shows (p.56): 'Quaecumque autem Ravisius aut excogitavit aut ex communi fonte hauserit aut quidem imitatus sit, at omnia libero impetu, vividisque verbis expressit, raro paganis nominibus respersa nec umquam circuitionum elegantiis oppressa.' The late Professor Don Cameron Allen, in his *Francis Meres's Treatise 'Poetrie': A Critical Edition*, University of Illinois Studies in Language and Literature, vol. XVI, nos. 3–4 (Urbana, Ill.: University of Illinois Press, 1933), pp.32–7 and *passim*, notes that in the 'Poetrie' section of his English-language work *Palladis Tamia* Francis Meres borrows much of his material directly from Ravisius Textor. In reviewing ways by which Meres might have known Textor – and these are vast, for many editions were in circulation – Allen makes no mention of Thomas Johnson's work *Cornucopiae, or Divers Secrets: wherein is contained the rare secrets in man, beasts ... plantes, stones, and such like ... and not before committed to be printed in English, newlie drawen out of divers Latine authors ...* (London: for W. Bailey, 1595). Both the title and the content of this work – it lists places which abound in various things and places which lack various things, just as Textor's *Cornucopia* does (as explained here below) – suggest direct derivation from Textor. But the interweaving of commonplace collections makes such derivation a little less than certain unless someone checks out the matter, as I have not myself done. Hyder Rollins, in his 'Deloney's Sources for Euphuistic Learning', *PMLA*, LI (1936), 398–406, notes that Thomas Deloney's erudite anecdotes come from, among other sources, Johnson's *Cornucopiae*. And so the *loci* yield their hold to generation after generation.

(*copia*-book) tradition of Erasmus, whom Textor much admired, as his prefatory letter to his 1519 edition of Hutten's *Aula* makes clear,[1] and as his brother Jacobus (Jacques Tixier de Ravisi) also indicates in his own prefatory letter to his 1524 edition of Ioannes's *Epitheta*.[2] The *Officina* and the *Epitheta*, like several of Erasmus's works, arrange in collections for subsequent use[3] bits and pieces out of Latin writers.

Essentially the *Officina* is simply a dictionary of classified excerpts or mini-excerpts from extant writing – 'examples', such as Erasmus's copybook programme calls for. The excerpts present students with things to say and Latin words to say them with. No Greek as such appears anywhere in the work. Everything originally in Greek is put into Latin. The sources are mostly the ancients, such as Virgil or Ovid, but also extend to Textor's own contemporaries or near-contemporaries, such as Pontanus or Erasmus, with medieval writers of course scrupulously excluded. The content of the examples in at least ninety per cent of the cases is concerned with antiquity even when the citation is from one of Textor's contemporaries, but on rare occasions citations from the later writers will have to do with a contemporary or near-contemporary matter, such as an event in the life of King Ferdinand of Spain.

The *Officina* first appeared in Paris in 1520 and apparently was not reprinted until 1532.[4] But after this date editions of the work in its entirety and in epitomes multiplied. More will be said of the

---

1 *Ulrich de Hutten Equitis Germani Aula. Dialogus.* Textor emaculavit. (Paris: Antonius Aussurdus, 1519), fol.*2.

2 *Ioannis Ravisii Textoris Nivernensis Epitheta . . . ab authore suo recognita et in novam formam redacta* [ed. Jacobus Ravisius Textor] (Paris: Reginaldus Chauldière, 1524), fol.2.

3 Collections of commonplace materials were used not only by orators, poets, 'philosophers' (including natural scientists), physicians, divines, and others getting up 'original' works under their own names, but even more assiduously by other collectors in their own commonplace collections, published as well as unpublished. As the late Professor Don Cameron Allen points out (see p.96, n.1 above), in his 1933 edition of the 'Poetrie' section of Francis Meres's *Palladis Tamia* or *Wit's Treasury* (1598), a commonplace collection of similes in English which gives us so much of our biographical material on some of the colourful literary hacks of sixteenth-century London, all of Mere's historical examples (for his similes) come from Ravisius Textor's *Officina*, as most of his similes themselves come from Erasmus's *Parabola sive Similia*.

4 *Io. Ravisii Textoris Officina partim historicis partim poeticis refertis disciplina . . .* ([Paris:] Reginaldus Chauldière, 1520) – copies in British Museum and Cambridge University Library. *Ioan. Ravisii Textoris Officina . . . auctior additis ab ipso authore ante quam e vita excederit rebus prope innumeris . . . cui etiam accessit index copiosissimus . . .* ([Paris:] Reginaldus Chauldière, 1532) – copies in the British Museum and the Bibliothèque Nationale, Paris.

editions later. One particular section of the *Officina* appeared frequently as a separate work under its own section title, *Cornucopia*. I have record of some thirty editions of the *Officina* in whole or in part, the last in 1626, with most editions appearing before 1600. Some editions, revised by Conrad Lycosthenes (Wolffhardt), appear under the title *Theatrum poeticum atque historicum: sive Officina*.

Certainly the *Officina* of Ravisius Textor is in many ways one of the most intriguing collections of commonplace material that was ever assembled. If the work were in French or English or German or any other modern vernacular rather than in Latin, it would certainly be a constant point of reference for literary commentators or curio seekers, or for connoisseurs of the unconsciously comic. In its studied pursuit of conspicuously useless detail it rivals even Burton's *Anatomy of Melancholy* or Sterne's *Tristram Shandy*, and in its nose for the bizarre it can compete with Rabelais. Textor is somewhat apologetic about the zany confusion of his work and in a set of elegiacs to the reader at the beginning sets out to disarm criticism by protesting that the *Officina* is not for 'learned poets' but 'for uneducated boys' (*rudibus pueris*) who are for the first time 'sweating in the dust and still imbibing words in the course of elementary instruction'.[1] It is hard, however, to imagine the collection as being put directly into the hands of little boys, for, other reasons aside, the earlier editions of the *Officina* are large folios which would be very expensive even for masters. Probably masters used the work for self-improvement and as a teacher's manual.

As a dictionary of quotations the *Officina* differs from today's dictionaries most spectacularly in the nature of its headings. There are some 350 subject headings in the first edition of the book, with often large numbers of entries under each heading. The reader opening the first edition is plunged into a blood-bath perhaps suggesting that Textor was projecting into his subject matter some of the aggressions against oneself which the gruelling work of a lexicographer can well generate (witness the case of Samuel Johnson, who in his *Dictionary* wryly defines a lexicographer – that is, himself and those like him – as a 'harmless drudge'). Here are the first two dozen or so entries under which Textor ranges his selections of materials from writers in classical antiquity, translated from Textor's Latin and presented in exactly the sequence in which he gives them,

---

[1] *Officina* (1532), fol.[Ai^v].

beginning right after his preface. The reader (in Textor's plan, a little boy! *puer*) encounters first a list of suicides (all the cases from classical antiquity that Textor can find), then parricides, drowned persons, those who have given their names to bodies of water by being drowned in them, persons killed or dismembered by horses, persons killed by the fall of horses, those killed by serpents, those killed by boars, those killed by lions, those killed by dogs, killed by other beasts, individuals struck by lightning, dead from hanging and crucifixion, dead from thirst and hunger, consumed by fire, persons cast off precipices, dead from falling staircases, people swallowed up by the earth, individuals done away with by poison, victims of sudden death (such a heading shows that Textor's standards for close timing were pretty high), dead from joy and laughter, dead from too much food and drink.

Under each of these headings Textor gives a list of the individual cases he has read of. His research was not casual. He exhibits one hundred and eighty-five suicides, eleven killed by dogs, and so on. Each instance is accompanied by an explanation which provides a varying amount of circumstantial detail for the case in question, together with references and quotations in many cases, though not in all.

In the particular sequence of headings just given, like items tend to cluster together, but elsewhere sampling of the classics is more random. One finds, for instance, a fairly sustained section on learned persons, and in rather intelligible succession such items as stone-cutters (*sculptores*), engravers, statuary sculptors, marble cutters, painters, and pigments. But on the other hand one also encounters sequences such as the following (and I am giving these in the order in which they occur); trainers of monsters and wild beasts, the four elements, sycophants, buffoons, parasites, fat and thin men, famous and memorable gardens, public criers, sleepy people (*somnolentes*), fullers, the columns of Hercules. Every so often Textor avails himself of catch-all headings, such as 'those famous for various things'. He has further sections on geometricians, astrologers, various types of measures, lousy distemper (*morbus pedicularis*), men who smelt bad (a *topos* which I have found recurrent in collections of this sort), dwarfs, pigmies, the four harpies, various types of haircuts, brute animals to which statues were erected, arguments drawn from the impossible, various kinds of excrement, descriptions of a long time, descriptions of night, and a long strung-out list of various kinds of worms.

The part of the *Officina* labelled *Cornucopia*[1] is a little curio in its own right, constituting a major section of the book that outranks in size the sections under other headings. The title *Cornucopia*, or horn of plenty, is employed because this section is devoted exclusively to a catalogue of things which can be found in great abundance in specified places. Thus the reader here learns what countries abound in bees or cheese or cinnamon or whales, ants, iron, marble, and so on. The *Cornucopia* concludes with its own contrary, listing various things not found in various places. There is no gold in the Nile, alone of all rivers (a sweeping bit of information, but backed by classical references), there are no deer in Africa, no bears either, no swine in Arabia, 'especially in the country of the Scaenites'. (This transcendentalising of an absolute denial seemingly defies logical clarification; there are none at all, especially in this place!) There are no eagles in Rhodes, no woodpeckers in the fields around Tarentum, there is no thyme in Arcadia, there are no mice in the island of Paris, no mountains in Portugal, no moles in Coronea, and finally, in England there is no oil or wine, only beer.

Ioannes Ravisius Textor's *Epitheta* is a somewhat different but equally fascinating work. It is a collection of standard qualifiers and substitutes for nouns which a writer of Latin poetry imitating the classics might use – and of course which writers of French and Italian and English and German and other poetry also might use and did use, following the Latin. The first edition of the *Epitheta*, called *Specimen epithetorum* (*An Exhibit of Epithets*) was put out in 1518 during the lifetime of its author.[2] The second edition, although its title notes that it represents a revision done by its original author, came out posthumously in 1524, as mentioned earlier, under the supervision of the author's brother, Jacobus Ravisius Textor, who with quaint heartlessness observes in his introduction, 'My brother was brought to an end before his revision was.'[3]

In accord with Erasmus's example, as Jacobus Ravisius Textor tells us in his somewhat defensive introduction to the posthumous

[1] *Officina* (1532), fols.LIX^v–XCIIII^r.
[2] *Specimen epithetorum Ioannis Ravisii Textoris Nivernensis, omnibus artis poeticae studiosis maxime utilium* (Paris: Henricus Stephanus pro Scholis Decretorum, 1518). For the 1524 edition, see p.97, n.2 above.
[3] *Epitheta* (1524), fol.*2^v.

second edition, Ioannes collected his *Epitheta* for boys an academic cut higher than those for whom he says the *Officina* was designed, that is, for those in the highest class in rhetoric engaged in doing exercises in themes for declamations or for dialogues, or other prose or verse.[1] The thinking behind the collection is obviously of a piece with the classical idea of rhetorical ornamentation. The *Officina* proffers more or less bare, hard ideas, 'naked' thoughts, whereas the *Epitheta* provides an assortment of options for giving the presumably bare or 'naked' thought of the rhetorically untrained weaver of words a richer, more attractive – which is to say more commonplace! – texture.

The collection of epithets which Ioannes Ravisius Textor assembled is sizable. It runs to 311 leaves (that is, 622 pages) of folio size in the 1518 edition. Textor's industry appears to have flagged as he worked through the alphabet. *A* to *L* (10 letters, no *J* or *K*) take up fols. 1–206, *M–Z* (11 letters, but only two entries under *X*) take up only fols. 207–303, despite all the *S*s. (In comparison, large Latin dictionaries commonly divide almost evenly between *A–L* and *M–Z*.)

Running through these individual entries is far from a boring occupation today. The coins which Textor proffers have been worn smooth by use, but they still ring true in countless associations. In the *A*s the searcher for epithets can find 113 of them referrable to Apollo, and 163 for *amor* (love). The complementary *bellum* or war merits a 36-page entry, and death (*mors*) has 95 epithets. Achilles warrants 48 epithets, such as – translated into English – tireless, untamed, trusted, furious. Africa is glowing, fertile, full of fords, bristling, teeming with wild beasts. The associations which countless poems and prose writings had established with Arabia are well recorded here. The inhabitants of the land, the Arabs, are rich in odours, palm-bearing, incense-collecting, tender, Oriental, wealthy, ardent, opulent, and so on. One thinks of Othello's dying declamation full of Arabia, wealth, odours, gums, and tender feelings. Coleridge's River Alph is here too, *Alphēus* in Latin. It is not sacred but it is definitely alien, clear, and swift. One could find here the accoutrements and often the substance of thousands of poems of western Europe through the Renaissance and indefinitely later.

---

[1] Iacobus Ravisius Textor, prefatory letter to Ludovicus Lassereus, in *Epitheta* (1524), fol.*2ᵛ: 'supremae classis rhetorices, quos convenit assiduis declamationum dialogorumque thematibus omnique tum solutae tum numerosae orationis genere exerceri'.

RENAISSANCE INTERACTIONS WITH THE
COMMONPLACE TRADITION

The management of commonplace material has a long and complex
history, which can be sketched here and then brought into focus
around Textor's and related works. The source of the tradition, as
we have noted above, is ultimately the primitive oral culture of all
mankind. Memorable sayings from this culture – and in an oral
culture, expression, and thought as well, not mnemonically patterned
for recall to all intents and purposes does not exist – from simple
turns of expression, epithets, and anecdotes to highly sophisticated
aphorisms, gnomes, apophthegms, moralistic fables, and brilliant
paradoxes, are woven from the ancient oral store into early writing,
which in its most artistic forms continues the oral practice of re-
iterating and embellishing the already known. In this morass of
commonly shared mnemonically structured knowledge there is no
footing for anyone seeking an answer to the question, 'Who first
said . . .?' Everybody is quoting everybody else, and has been for
tens of thousands of years before the written records began, on
purpose and with a feeling of achievement.

In classical antiquity, which remained always close to the primitive oral world, the use of commonplace material was not always
conspicuous but eventually, with the help of writing, had become
the object of elaborate reflection, some of it more speculative, as in
Aristotle's *Topika*, and some of it more practical, as in Cicero or
Quintilian or Dionysius of Halicarnassus or Hermogenes. Despite
the currency of writing, however, compilation of commonplace
material, though not unknown in antiquity – conspicuous examples
of compilation would be the Sapiential books in the Old Testament –
was not highly developed before the Middle Ages. Ancient Greek
and Roman authors wrote collections of biographies, such as
those by Plutarch, and vaguely 'encyclopedic' works treating individual words and subject matters (as in Pliny's *Natural History*).
They did relatively little in the way of collecting excerpts.[1] By
contrast, the *Speculum* of Vincent of Beauvais (*ca* 1190–1264), a
famous medieval 'encyclopedia', consists chiefly of excerpts from
other writers. Following beginnings in the patristic period, the Middle

---

[1] A good summary treatment, with references, can be found in the article 'Encyclopaedia',
Encyclopaedia Britannica, VIII (Chicago: Encyclopaedia Britannica, 1973), 364–5.

Ages specialised in *florilegia*, collections of gnomic quotations, *exempla* (illustrative stories, historical or fictional), sermon excerpts, and other kinds of bits and pieces, culled from sources as distant as the Far East (the *Panchatantra*, a collection of beast fables ultimately from India, was taken over deviously by the Middle Ages in Europe as the *Directorium vitae humanae*). The number of *florilegia* is so vast that no even moderately complete study of the genre, of even monograph size, has ever been published, nor has even an inventory of known or extant *florilegia*.[1] Titles would certainly run into the hundreds. Despite their scribal provenience, however, the contents of the inscribed medieval *florilegia* were often presented as 'sayings' or orally conveyed narrative and were intended to be recycled through the oral world, just as the education in the universities, despite the fact that in many ways it was far more text-centred than education in classical antiquity,[2] was calculated nevertheless to provide basically an oral formation for the student.[3]

During the Renaissance, the commonplace heritage of antiquity and the Middle Ages became in many ways more important than ever before. First, by comparison with classical antiquity, the Renaissance needed to become even more self-conscious about commonplace material because Latin, normally the only language one studied and used in school (except for a generally quite small amount of Greek),[4] was a foreign language to all its users, and had been so for roughly a millennium. Unlike schoolboys in ancient Greece or Rome studying their vernacular Greek or Latin, and unlike schoolchildren today who address themselves to their own vernaculars in the classroom, Renaissance schoolboys normally came to the Latin which was the *pièce de résistance* of their academic menu with no store at all of common expressions or sayings from ordinary Latin conversation. These had to be artificially cultivated in academic circles.

[1] Art. 'Florilegia', *New Catholic Encyclopedia* (New York: McGraw-Hill, 1967), v, 979–80.
[2] Ong, *The Presence of the Word*, pp.58–61.
[3] See István Hajnal, *L'Enseignement de l'écriture aux universités médiévales* (Budapest: Academia Scientiarium Hungarica Budapestini, 1954), p.64.
[4] Robert R. Bolgar, *The Classical Heritage and Its Beneficiaries* (Cambridge, England: The University Press, 1958), p.359, reports that, although in later editions of the Jesuit *Ratio Studiorum* Greek was to be begun simultaneously with Latin, in fact it was given only about one-sixth of the time given to Latin at the Jesuit college at Messina. Such proportioning of time appears typical of the better Renaissance schools – in the less good schools Greek got even shorter shrift. See Bolgar, ibid. pp.332–3, etc.

Secondly, although the Middle Ages, for much the same reasons as the Renaissance, had had to exploit artificially a store of common Latin expressions or sayings, the Renaissance felt the need somewhat more keenly because of its keener and more self-conscious ambition to echo the Latin of classical antiquity. One· had to be relatively sure that one's idiom, which included various *modus dicendi*, turns of expressions, Latin proverbs and comparisons and sayings, was more or less of a piece with that of classical antiquity. We need not exaggerate the Renaissance drive to Ciceronianism, which was usually relatively restrained in various ways, but we must acknowledge the existence and the real force of a desire to imitate ancient Latin quite closely. Good Latin writers, such as Erasmus, wrote not purely Ciceronian language but they did not write in medieval style either, though they were influenced by the latter. They wrote their own classically toned Latin.

Thirdly, in settling on the corpus of classical work as its more or less strict norm, the Renaissance fixed its attention on material visually stored and retrievable. Its lexical and linguistic base was not an orally possessed language as such, but a body of texts – a controlled and closed field, at least in principle more or less explicitly bounded. The adoption of this base was crucial in the history of commonplace materials, for it was to mark the beginning of the end of the commonplace tradition. Commonplaces had their deepest roots in the noetic needs of an oral world. The Renaissance preoccupation with texts, inherited from the Middle Ages but intensified by print, tended to shift the focus of verbalisation from the world of sound to the surface of the page, from the aural to the visual. This is not to say there were not competing tendencies in the Renaissance, such as the accentuation of the oral fostered by the cult of the classical orator, but the effect of print was ultimately to prove overwhelming.

Various arrangements for visual retrieval of material in texts had been physically possible since writing was invented. Indeed, this was what writing was all about: words, though irreducibly sounds, could now be recovered by the eye (for reconstitution as sounds). But writing is far less effective than print in fixing verbalised material in space for widespread storage and ready visual access.

Once a fixed order is established in print, it can be multiplied with little effort almost without limit. This makes it more worthwhile to do the arduous work of elaborating serviceable arrangements and – what is all important – of devising complex, visually serviceable indexes. A hundred dictated handwritten copies of a work would normally require a hundred indexes, for the material would appear on different pages in different copies, whereas five thousand or more printed copies of an edition of a given work would all be served by one and the same index. Within a few generations after the invention of print, the index became a conspicuous feature of printed commonplace collections, much advertised on title pages.[1]

Besides facilitating retrieval through indexing, the printed page also facilitated retrieval simply because it normally proved easier to read than most manuscripts. This was, of course, less true at the beginning of print. Earlier printed books kept close to the format and style of the manuscript with which they were competing: the pages were indubitably handsome, but not necessarily adapted to speed reading. However, as it gradually dawned on consciousness that printing was not just imitation handwriting, solid pages of close-set type gave way to pages with well spaced words, the paragraph in the modern sense of this term – a unit of thought visually advertised by an indentation – was invented and became functional, and in countless other ways the feeling gradually developed that words could be arranged on a surface in ways facilitating visual retrieval (albeit for processing in one way or another through the auditory world – for words remain at root always sounds).

Development of the feeling for visual retrieval can be seen everywhere, but most spectacularly in the title pages of Renaissance books. Everyone familiar with Renaissance editions will recall how an early title page will often split even its principal words with hyphens, printing successive parts of the same word on successive lines in different sizes and/or different founts of type. An example – one of hundreds – would be the title page of the first edition (Paris: Andreas Wechel, 1572) of Peter Ramus's final revision of his *Dialectica*.[2] The full title of this edition is: *P. Rami Regii Professoris Dialecticae libri duo* (*The Two Books of the Dialectic of Peter Ramus, Regius Professor*). On the 1572 title page, the words are dismembered. The first line presents, in upper-case type about 24-point in size, the

---

[1] I have given a few instances in *The Presence of the Word*, pp.85–6.
[2] I cite this title page because it can be found reproduced in facsimile in Walter J. Ong, *Ramus and Talon Inventory* (Cambridge, Mass.: Harvard University Press, 1958), opposite p.192.

fragmented 'P. RAMI RE-'; the next line drops to smaller upper-case type, about 18-point in size, in which it presents the last two syllables of one word and the first three of another: 'GII PROFESSO-'; the third line, in 14-point upper-case type, provides the fourth syllable of one word and the whole of another, 'RIS DIALECTICAE', and the following line, in 10-point upper-case type, concludes the title with the two words 'LIBRI DUO'. This last line is the first of the four to present the reader with words not chopped into pieces.

The over-all visual appearance of this title page is far from unpleasant. Quite the contrary, as an inverted pyramid arrangement of black marks on a white surface, the page, which includes the printer's mark and imprint, is aesthetically very pleasing and decorative. It would be attractive framed. It is, however, by present-day standards, not easy to read. As soon as it is read aloud, it is understandable, but it does not come into the visual field in such a way as to facilitate apprehension in lexical units with the ease which later typography would demand. There is no sense of what printers and advertisers today would call 'display'. The reason is that the words are not thought of primarily as being picked off the page as units by the eye, but rather as being made into units within the auditory imagination – or more likely, within the voice box, since many of Ramus's contemporaries were, it seems, still reading aloud or in a mumble when they read to themselves – with only casual relation to the visual. Presentation was improving somewhat. Words came soon to be set with very evident spaces between them, as they were often not in early print, but the verbal visual unit as such was still relatively weak.

In the gradual movement from the state of affairs typified by this 1572 title page toward a more functionally visual economy of verbalised knowledge, collections of 'places' prove to be a recognisable focus of development. Vision is a fractioning sense, as Merleau-Ponty[1] and others have remarked. So in its own way was the commonplace tradition, which, even in its original oral roots, had tended to fragment discourse into the bits assembled by oral narrators and orators – 'rhapsodisers' or 'stitchers', in the original Greek meaning of this term, who sewed together the commonplace bits out of which thought and discourse were made. It was

[1] Maurice Merleau-Ponty, 'L'Oeil et l'esprit', *Temps Modernes*, 18, nos.184–5 (1961), 193–227.

not on the face of it unlikely that the fragmenting possibilities of
the visual field would be exploited somehow when commonplaces
were subject to the visual regimen of print. Some of the more complex ways in which this exploitation was carried out will be discussed
here shortly, but it will be well to note initially here the central
interaction of the old oral commonplace tradition and the newly
improved visual medium. This took place in the development of
the index, just mentioned. Our present term 'index' itself is an
abridged form of the earlier *index locorum* (index of places) or *index
locorum communium* (index of commonplaces) which one meets with
in early printed books.[1] The elements into which an index breaks
down a book are, basically, 'places' in the text and simultaneously
topics or 'places' (*topoi, loci*) in the mind – in the physical world
and in the conscious world both – thought of as pieces out of which
a whole is constituted. The rhetorical and dialectical term 'place'
(*topos, locus*), conceptualised as some kind of vague region in consciousness or in a 'field' of knowledge,[2] here acquires a truly local
habitation, becoming a gross physical reality, the locale on a
surface, now with typography far more operative in noetic management, for the locale was identical now upon thousands of surfaces,
where a 'unit' of verbalisation and thought could be pinned down.

At this point an older primary oral world is dying out in a certain
sense within consciousness and a new visual–verbal world is gaining
credibility. The effects on the accumulation, storage, and retrieval
of knowledge will be vast, as will the effects on the kind of knowledge
to which the mind shapes itself. In the noetic economy, purportedly
inert 'facts' rather than intrinsically evanescent sayings will have the
ascendancy as never before.

EVOLUTION OF VISUAL RETRIEVAL:
TEXTOR, THEODOR ZWINGER AND OTHERS

If we look at Textor's *Officina* and *Epitheta* in terms of knowledge
storage and retrieval – there are of course other ways of looking

[1] See Walter J. Ong, *Ramus, Method, and the Decay of Dialogue* (Cambridge, Mass.: Harvard
University Press, 1958), pp.313–14.
[2] Not without some vague reference to a text at a very early period, it must be said, for
topos and *locus* could in antiquity also mean a place in a written text, though this meaning
was less obtrusive than the rhetorical and dialectical meaning connected with invention
(*inventio*) or 'finding' arguments, as earlier noted here.

at them – their editorial history shows them to be in a way between the two worlds we have just mentioned, that of the old oral economy of all early human cultures (to which composition by formula was indigenous) and the new visual world of the inscribed word, which had come into germinal being with the invention of writing and which in Textor's day was finally maturing through the newly developing alphabetic print of the West.[1]

In the ancient world of letters, which had remained more dominantly oral than its medieval or Renaissance counterparts, the commonplace tradition had kept the noetic store alive and accessible largely through actual oral performance. One mastered commonplaces largely by hearing them. Although it is true, as has been noted earlier, that Quintilian and others report and advocate some use of writing to implement oratory, antiquity did not compile written lists of things that had been said with the fervour later obsessing medieval Europeans, who, as we have just noted, set out to establish massive textual – which is to say visual – bases, such as *florilegia*, within their own attenuated latter-day orality. The Renaissance, for all its programmatic rejection of the Middle Ages, was actually generated and kept alive largely by the medieval addiction to texts as such. What we have seen in Textor is a sweeping design for textual (visual) management of the noetic store: precipitate out of all classical texts all the suicides, haircuts, sleepy people, astrologers, worms, or whatever, so that all of each class can be grouped together in space. The growing appetite for beginning the study of any field of knowledge with 'history' in the sense of patiently recorded 'examples' from the given field providing grounds for 'induction', such as was advocated, for instance, by Francis Bacon,

[1] Modern cultures emerging from orality into print and into electronic culture – at a rate hundreds of times faster than Europe's and with full consciousness, impossible in early Europe, of the evolution being undergone – are manifesting the same passion as that of the European Renaissance for collecting in print the proverbs and other formulaic sayings on which the earlier oral cultures always relied. Thus, for example, at Onitsha, Nigerian printers have been flooding the popular market with printed collections of proverbial materials. See Emmanuel Obiechena, *An African Popular Literature: A Study of Onitsha Market Pamphlets* (Cambridge, England: The University Press, 1973); Bernth Lindfors, 'Perverted Proverbs in Nigerian Chapbooks', *Proverbium* xv (1970), 62 (482)–71 (487). Like their Renaissance counterparts, producers and users of these popular collections in Nigeria appear unaware that print makes cultivation of proverbs outmoded or even counter-productive, though Nigerian scholars are often exquisitely aware of this fact, as their Renaissance counterparts were not. The novels of Chinua Achebe, and of other African writers, counterpoint proverbial materials against growing technological developments, with great literary success.

is certainly here receiving some encouragement which has seldom if ever been attended to. 'Induction' is being encouraged here, subtly but really, by typographically supported developments within the commonplace tradition. The units are not individual observations or experiments, but bits of texts.

These developments show that the age's concern with particularities is not due simply to interest in physical science, that is, to interest in 'induction' from individual experienced instances such as will lead to a universal scientific principle or 'rule'. Speculation about scientific induction there was in plenty in the Renaissance, as, for that matter, there had been in earlier ages. But concern for particulars in the extramental world of the Renaissance was patently intermingled with a concern for textual particulars, which, though outside the mind, on paper or parchment, in fact had to do with the mental world, since texts represented thought and its formulation and expression. In the case of Theodor Zwinger, to be discussed below, we see the two concerns mingled or confused.

The new world of humanism and print in which Textor operated did not, however, immediately maximise all the fuller possibilities which print offered for particularised knowledge storage and retrieval. The new medium was too new, and many of the new procedures which it would ultimately make operative were slow to be realised. Successive editions of Textor's *Officina* and *Epitheta* only gradually implement the possibilities of rapid visual retrieval inherent in print from the beginning. But this makes them all the more interesting, for, despite the inertia in all cultural institutions, they do move eventually and inexorably toward more effective implementation.

We have already noted the often chaotic sequence of materials in the original text itself of the *Officina*. Comparable chaos rules the finding apparatus provided in the volume for pulling items out of the text. In the first edition of the *Officina* (1520), the headings are arranged at the beginning of the book in an index or table of chapters, not alphabetically but simply in their order of occurrence in the work. Visual retrieval is a matter of concern here, but not of urgent concern: the effort to expedite such retrieval is, by later standards, half-hearted. The 1532 Paris edition and subsequent editions, however, take visual access more seriously: they provide an introductory alphabetical index. The later editions of the *Officina* prepared by

Lycosthenes further implement visual access by organising the body of the collection itself into clearly defined sections.[1]

Similarly, in the original edition of the *Epitheta*, entries themselves are presented in alphabetical order, but in a way which again shows that visual retrieval of material was still not attended to with full seriousness by later standards. Alphabetisation is by first letter only: all the 'a's are together, but 'al-' might occur before 'ag-' or 'ab-'. This could indicate, and perhaps does to some degree indicate, haste in getting the material together. But that is not all. It is quite clear that alphabetic ordering as such is quite low in Textor's priorities, for he himself deliberately puts the entry on 'Apollo' first of all and explains that he does so because, although alphabetically 'Apollo' strictly belongs a little further down among the 'a's, it is most fitting that a collection of epithets for writing poetry should start with epithets that apply to the patron of poetry, Apollo.[2] Hierarchy and the realities of the human lifeworld take ready precedence over mechanical alphabetic arrangement, which is to say over arrangement for fully implemented visual access.

Instances of casual visual organisation of materials in this period can be multiplied indefinitely, as can instances of progressively better organisation for visual retrieval. We shall content ourselves with some few more samples here. A work of the scholar and translator Raffaele Maffei (Raphael Maffeius Vollaterranus, 1455–1522), who is credited by Zwinger with being one of Ravisius Textor's chief sources,[3] presents us with a clear case of alphabetisation by sound rather than by letter. In his *Commentariorum urbanorum libri octo et triginta* (Rome: Ioannes Besicken Alemanus, 1506),[4] a great mass of commonplace material, encyclopedic in scope and again, judged by later editorial standards, only partly digested, is introduced by various indices in which the letter *H*, not pronounced in Italian and no doubt considered by many Italians to be pronounceable only by barbarians, is printed but disregarded. Thus, for example, on fol.*3ʳ we find this alphabetisation: 'Alyza, Halyzones, Haliartus, Alifa . . .' The procedure makes sense, of course, but it also shows a

[1] Don Cameron Allen's statement in his edition of Francis Meres's treatise *Poetrie*, p.23, that Textor's *Officina* is divided into seven major sections shows that he was using one of Lycosthenes's editions: the sections do not exist in Textor's original work.
[2] *Specimen epithetorum* (1518), fol.1.
[3] *Theatrum humanae vitae* (Basileae: per Sebastianum Henricpetri, 1604), fol.[]:( ):(4).
[4] The British Museum copy – shelf mark 1487. w.3 – which I have used here, has no title page, but it does have a colophon.

disposition to store the words on the page in terms of what they sound like rather than what they look like. Later Italian reference works, though they traffic minimally in the letter *H*, nevertheless commonly acknowledge its existence if not as a sound at least as a visually apprehensible item on the same footing with other letters, and alphabetise it accordingly. It will be noted also in this series of words, that the letters *I* and *Y*, being pronounced alike, are also treated as the same letter; 'Halicarnassus, Halyz, Alyza, Halyzones, Haliartus, Alifa . . .'.

The casual alphabetisation of Textor and the phonetic alphabetisation of Maffeius would not be without precedent in manuscript tradition, and thus it is not impressive to find either kind in print. The point about their appearance in print is their brief tenure: this sort of thing is doomed by the new medium, which enforces strictly visual regularity as handwriting had not done. Today no editor would tolerate the casual approach to alphabetisation taken in Textor's and other early printed works.

We can turn to a final sample which shows both the intense drive to assemble vast masses of commonplace excerpts and an attempt to organise them in another way for visual retrieval. The Basel physician and polymath Theodor Zwinger the Elder (1533–88) undertook what was in many ways certainly the most comprehensively ambitious compilation of commonplace excerpts up to his time. His *Theatrum humanae vitae* is perhaps the world's largest single collection of commonplace excerpts. It went through five progressively enlarged editions between 1565 and 1604,[1] running to over 5,000 double-column folio pages of small type by the posthumous 1604 edition. In this collection Zwinger marshals tens of thousands of single excerpts from extant writings to try to produce what today would be called groundwork for 'scientific' history – he calls it the

---

[1] *Theatrum vitae humanae* (Basileae: per Ioan. Oporinum, Ambrosium et Aurelium Frobenios fratres, 1565); *Theatrum vitae humanae* (Basileae: ex officina Frobeniana, 1571); *Theatrum humanae vitae* (Basileae, 1576 – I have never seen a copy of this edition, and the only notice of it I have is its listing in *Antiquariats Katalog Nr. 159* (1963) of the bookdealer Joseph van Matt, Stans, Switzerland, who had sold the volume by the time I had contacted him but who assured me by letter dated 3 February 1964, that the 1576 imprint is indeed correct); *Theatrum humanae vitae* (Basileae: per Eusebium Episcopium, 1586–7); *Theatrum humanae vitae* (Basileae: per Sebastianum Henricpetri, 1604). The *Biographie universelle*, under Zwinger, lists a 1596 edition, of which I have found no other trace. This work of Zwinger's was widely distributed: in libraries at Cambridge University alone I have found twenty-four complete copies of one or another edition. King's *Intercollegiate Catalogue* at the Bodleian Library lists fourteen copies in libraries at Oxford.

work of 'historian-rhapsodists' (*rhapsodi historici*),[1] who ferret out and 'stitch together' (*rhapsōidein* in Greek) the units of history, as the epic poets or other narrators 'rhapsodised' or 'stitched together' the themes and formulas out of the commonplace tradition in their oral performances. In Zwinger a new feel for the management of the textual store of knowledge in terms of constituent particulars is simultaneously in contact with the commonplace tradition (itemise and classify for re-use in discourse) and with some kind of more or less Baconian notion of scientific induction (itemise and classify to discover 'rules' or 'laws').

Zwinger's ponderous work is a product of the Basel milieu, not only financially, but also psychologically and genealogically. Zwinger's mother was the sister of the Basel printer Iohannes Oporinus and Zwinger had close personal connections with other printers: he lodged in Lyons for three years with the printer Bering, was financed on a trip to Italy by the Basel printer Peter Perna, and married Boniface Amerbach's sister-in-law.[2] The *Theatrum humanae vitae* (or, in the first two editions, 1565 and 1571, *Theatrum vitae humanae*) builds largely on the compiling work undertaken earlier by Zwinger's father-in-law, Conrad Lycosthenes (Wolff-hardt), a continuator of Erasmus's compilations who has been noted here earlier as editor of some late printings of Ravisius Textor's *Officina*.

In the last edition (1586–7) of the *Theatrum humanae vitae* to appear before his own death, Zwinger lists 510 authors as sources. His son Jakob slightly enlarged the posthumous 1604 edition, which is dedicated to the Triune God – who else? Probably no mere creaturely dedicatee could have survived the now over 5,000 dense pages. Jakob added new *exempla*, especially recent ones, and – an important

---

[1] Theodor Zwinger, *Theatrum vitae humanae* [in later editions, *Theatrum humanae vitae*] (Basileae, 1571), p. 11. Zwinger may have picked up the term from Sabellicus, one of his many sources. See *Enneades Marci Antonii Sabellici ab urbe condita ad inclinationem Romani Imperii* (Venetiis, 1498), where Sabellicus uses the term *rhapsodia historiarum*, 'a rhapsody of histories', in headings (e.g. fol.aaii) as well as in his *Prefatio* and his concluding 'M. Antonius Sabellicus Democrito'. But I find no evidence here of any theory of his about *rhapsodia*. Sabellicus refers to various sources and has a general feeling that history is 'woven' out of *exempla* ('fartum et tectum inde opus', 'a Venetiae civitatis conspectu totam . . . texui historiam' – fol.[GGviiiᵛ]).

[2] For a biographical account of Zwinger, besides the ordinary bio-bibliographical reference works, see Johannes Karcher, *Theodor Zwinger und seine Zeitgenossen: Episode aus dem Ringer der Basler Ärzte um die Grundlehren der Medizin im Zeitalter des Barocks*, Studien zur Geschichte der Wissenschaften in Basel, 3 (Basel: Verlag von Helbling und Lichtenhahn, 1956).

point noted earlier and to be returned to later – improved the indices. These list 601 authors.[1] The *Theatrum*, in all its editions, undertakes to treat universal history in terms of the good and evil of mankind,[2] and consists entirely of short excerpts from published sources. By history in terms of the good and evil of mankind Zwinger appears in fact to mean a large proportion of everything that has ever happened, since there is little in the world which cannot be related directly or deviously to man, for his good or evil. Zwinger's range is quite as indiscriminate as Textor's. The various sections of the work treat good and bad things of the soul, of the body, good and bad chance occurrences, instruments of philosophy (grammar, rhetoric, poetic, logic), practical philosophical habits (including legislation, history, and worth or dignity), temperance and intemperance, money, refinement (as opposed to flattery and fastidiousness), religious and secular justice, mechanical skills (in artists, workmen, craftsmen), the solitary, academic, religious, political, and economic life of man, not to mention other headings.

In all subjects Zwinger casts his net wide. For example, his chapter 'De prudentia inventrice bellica sive de strategematis',[3] a title which we can render 'On Inventive Prudence in Warfare, or Strategems', he includes material under the following classifications: conscription of strong men; elimination of the cowardly; conscription willy-nilly; conscription by wager; segregation of the suspect and perfidious and rebellious; military haircuts and beards; deception of the enemy by simulated victory, retreat, peace, friendliness, or by use of smoke, snow, or statues, of fire, gestures, clubs, and noises of all sorts, or by use of the human voice, either through shouting or through the utterance of enigmas; the amassing and conservation of resources; treachery and desertion, the use and misuse of fortifications; the crossings of seas, lakes, rivers; avoidance of wild animals and snakes; kindness toward one's own forces; avarice and desire for booty; the hope of happiness, glory, victory, freedom; etc. His *exempla* include items such as an account of a betting system to recruit oarsmen for galleys[4] and an anecdote (vol.VII, lib.iii) from Frontinus telling how Hannibal induced his reluctant elephants to

---

[1] The 1604 edition, with some slight variations, is largely a page-for-page resetting of the 1586–7 edition.
[2] *Theatrum vitae humanae* (1571), p.10, 'Proscenia'.
[3] *Theatrum humanae vitae* (1586–7), vol.VII, lib.iii.
[4] Theodorus Zwingerus, *Theatrum humanae vitae* (1586–7), p.1768 (vol.VII, lib.iii).

cross the Rhône by having one of his men slash an elephant under the ear and then run to the river and swim across with the enraged elephant and all his elephant friends in pursuit.[1] A little later (vol. VII, lib.v) Zwinger is off in another direction with a series of anecdotes on the fervour of the Anabaptists.[2] He apologises in his introduction for not doing a more comprehensive job, noting that collectors of 'special places' (in Aristotle's sense, as contrasted with 'common' places), such as those having to do with oratory or grammar or poetry or sepulchres or marriages or banquets, can do more thorough work than those who, like himself, are 'rhapsodists' of universal history and thus attempt to excerpt and string together everything that was ever said on anything.[3]

In breaking down into excerpts and reorganising the extant noetic store, Zwinger's aims and his epistemology are beyond a doubt not only typographically but also topographically conditioned. His title *Theatrum . . .*, matched in scores of other late sixteenth- and seventeenth-century 'theatre' titles,[4] advertises his visualist noetics. He explains that the twenty volumes of the *Theatrum* are in fact twenty scenes.[5] Zwinger thinks of the printed page as a map on which knowledge itself is laid out. Over and over again he compares his work to that of geographers and cartographers. Like geographers, he describes only the larger places (*loci*) into which he wants to 'distribute' his materials, relegating the 'little places' (*locula*) to special supplements.[6] The spatial implications in the classical notion of the *loci* as mental 'places' where arguments can be located are realised with a vengeance here, as is true throughout the Ramist tradition[7] in which, to a significant degree, Zwinger operates. The original 'places' in the mind, a highly metaphorical conception, have here been transmuted into physical places on the printed page. Zwinger's ranging of *exempla* under titles (*tituli*) is likened to the plotting of travels such as those of Alexander the Great and of Ulysses, and to the geometrical work of Archimedes.[8] In

---

[1] Theodorus Zwingerus, *Theatrum humanae vitae* (1586–7), p.1811.   [2] Ibid. p.1946.

[3] Theodorus Zwingerus, *Theatrum humanae vitae* (Basel: Sebastianus Henricpetri, 1604), fol.[]:( ):(5ᵛ].

[4] I have accumulated, incidentally, a collection of several dozen such titles: theatres of botany, of chemistry, of celestial wisdom, of universal nature, of peace, of consumption (diseases), of God's judgements, of hydrotechnic machines, of politics, of poetry, etc.

[5] *Theatrum humanae vitae* (1571), p.32.

[6] 'In suos locos distribuenda' – *Theatrum humanae vitae* (1604), fol.[]:( ):(5ᵛ].

[7] See Ong, *Ramus, Method, and the Decay of Dialogue*, pp.310–13.   [8] Zwinger, ibid.

a like vein Peter Ramus had undertaken to organise knowledge in accordance with 'Solon's Law', a building code for ancient Athens specifying how far apart houses and walls and other structures had to be – the different bodies of knowledge were to be kept separate from one another in a similar way.[1]

Zwinger's concern for a topography of the mind goes hand in hand with an interest in physical topography. His works include a *Methodus apodemica*, in which he undertakes an outline of how to travel and to describe what one encounters. The work is remarkable for, among other things, a Ramist approach to art and art history: in a typically Ramist dichotomised diagram Zwinger analyses Verocchio's equestrian statue of Bartolomeo Colleoni in Venice, plotting the statue in terms of its four causes (material, formal, efficient, and final) so thoroughly as to include a full historical treatment even of the vandalism to which the statue had been subjected.[2] The Basel physician was an omnibus dissectionist in the tradition which gives rise to, among other things, Burton's *Anatomy of Melancholy* and the scores of other 'anatomy' titles of the age.[3]

Zwinger is an outspoken admirer and follower of Ramus, whom he had known when the latter was visiting in Basel in 1569 and who praises Zwinger's *Theatrum* in his *Basilea*[4] – one of the rare Ramist

---

[1] Ong, *Ramus, Method, and the Decay of Dialogue*, pp.280–1.

[2] Theodor Zwinger (Zwingerus), *Methodus apodemica in eorum gratiam qui fructu in quocumque tandem vitae genere peregrinari cupiunt, a Theod. Zwinger Basiliense typis delineata et cum aliis tum quatuor praesertim Athenarum vivis exemplis illustrata, cum indice* (Basileae: Eusebii Episcopii opera atque impensis, 1577), p.398 (lib.IV, cap.ii – the chapter consists entirely of the dichotomised outline, with no other text). The four 'Athens' which Zwinger treats are Basel (the Swiss Athens), Paris (the French Athens), Padua (the Italian Athens), and Athens (the Greek Athens). The book is not unlike a modern travel guide in the miscellaneous information it conveys, although a modern traveller would be put off by Zwinger's procrustean organisation (the causes, accidents, and species of travel) and by finding himself presented not with 'travel suggestions' but with 'rules' (*regulae*) for travellers.

[3] The number of 'anatomy' titles from the mid-1500s through the 1600s has never been calculated, so far as I know. I have accumulated some thirty or so, quite incidentally, mostly of English works – anatomies of the mind, of valour, of abuses, of a lover's flatteries, of fortune, of sin, of the world, etc. There are many more anatomy titles of course in Latin and the other vernaculars. Passing references to the anatomy literature are to be found in L. A. Beaurline, 'Ben Jonson and the Illusion of Completeness', *PMLA*, LXXXIV (1969), 51–9, and in Karl Josef Holtgen, 'Synoptischen Tabellen in der medizinischen Literatur und die Logik Agricolas und Ramus', *Sudhoffs Archiv für Geschichte der Medizin und der Naturwissenschaften* (Wiesbaden: Franz Steiner Verlag), Band 79, Heft 4 (December 1965), 371–90 – this latter study treats Zwinger at some length and explicitly connects the 'anatomy' with Ramist dichotomised tables.

[4] *Petri Rami Basilea ad senatum populumque Basiliensem* ([Lausanae: Ioannes Probus] 1571), pp.18–19.

doctors of medicine, for physicians were commonly the most adamant of Ramus's numerous opponents. Zwinger undertakes the organisation of his (ultimately) more than 5,000 pages of material through Ramist dichotomised outline charts, which introduce each section of the *Theatrum humanae vitae* to show how the heads within the section and the quotations under each head all articulate. Charts on successive pages are linked to one another by asterisks or daggers or other typographical symbols, one of which will be affixed to one of the final brackets of a given page and then will recur at the head of the bracket display on a subsequent page to indicate where the subsequent outline is to be hooked onto the preceding to continue the dichotomised divisions.

Visually neat, the result is so complicated as to be psychologically quite unmanageable. The reader is paralysed by overorganised structural detail. And, in fact, although his *Theatrum humanae vitae* consists entirely of a fabric of citations in the full-blown commonplace tradition, Zwinger has lost all sense of the oral roots of the tradition. His excerpts are hardly conceived of as serving 'invention', as providing matter to be fed back into the stream of discourse, the way Textor's had been. Rather, Zwinger's aim is to tidy up knowledge by collecting in snippets everything everyone has said with a view to arranging all the snippets in proper, visually retrievable, order, so that, in a historical 'rhapsody', as explained here above, one can at long last find out why things are the way they are. Good Ramist that he was, Zwinger felt that somehow the thousands of quotations ranged 'logically' in his text represented in some vague way the 'structure' of the human life-world, the microcosm, and thus in some fashion, no doubt, the macrocosm as well.

The idea of diagrammatic organisation has overwhelmed Zwinger without his quite knowing what has happened to him. The same idea would overwhelm many of his Swiss compatriots, for the typographic collecting drive and also the Ramist dichotomised outline appear to have enjoyed a vogue in Basel and elsewhere in Switzerland which they never quite achieved in other parts of the West. Zwinger's mentality may appear today curiously bemused in its addiction to noetic cartography, but the same drive toward consummate tidiness which produced this cartography would continue to manifest itself through the next two centuries in the Cartesian addiction to clarity and distinctness, and, even more conspicuously in the folding chart of knowledge, the *système figuré*, which at the opening of Diderot's and d'Alembert's *Encyclopédie* (1751–72) epitomises Enlightenment noetics.

In fact, the use of Ramist dichotomised outline diagrams, by Zwinger and so many others, for all its somewhat zany ineffectuality, was not entirely wrong-headed even though it had more limitations than Ramists might allow. For the Ramist outline would eventually have its day. In its binary organisation, as anyone who knows computer programming sees immediately, the Ramist dichotomised outline is in fact nothing other than a computer flow chart. One can, however, hardly have a successful computer operation until one has a computer. This neither Ramus nor Zwinger had, but there can be little doubt that both would have welcomed one.

Ravisius Textor and his congeners, such as Zwinger, I hope it is clear, had no way of viewing what they were doing in the perspectives suggested here – which, it might be noted again, are by no means the only perspectives for viewing the commonplace enterprise of the Renaissance. These perspectives appear useful largely because they help show how, with the emergence of typography, the human imagination, conditioned for thousands of years in the orally grounded commonplace methods of processing the noetic stores of a culture, was evolving new ways of organising this store outside consciousness, in the silent tidiness of exactly duplicable, printed texts. Yet, even after print, storage processes proper to the original oral culture or manuscript culture, with the latter's very heavy oral residue, persisted through many generations: that is to say, the drive to consider what had been said as demanding perpetual reiteration continued strong. Academia still felt the last thrust of the drive in *gradus ad Parnassum* or metrical Latin phrase books which persisted through the nineteenth century, providing schoolboys with set excerpts and expressions for the construction of Latin verse. Today in technological cultures, however, commonplace collections, or their equivalents, are quite peripheral to serious discourse, being restricted largely to dictionaries of jokes and of quotations compiled basically for desperate after-dinner speakers rather than for the serious playwrights, teachers, scholars, and scientists for whom Renaissance collections (and earlier collections) were typically prepared. In the Renaissance, the commonplace material to which Kristeller rightly draws attention was still part of the grist demanded for even the first-rate intellect.

An oral culture can make no lists of commonplaces, for lists demand writing, but, as has been suggested in the first section of this study, following Havelock, such a culture has as its commonplace collections the formal oral performances such as orations or narrative poetry or prose or other poetry, for these performances are mostly beautifully woven ('rhapsodised') textures of formulaic materials. The *Iliad*, it will be remembered, not only weaves together fixedly thematic and formulaic materials ('the rosy-fingered dawn', 'the wine-dark sea', and so on) but actually includes a nearly four-hundred-line roster of the Greek leaders and their followers. This roster is presented in formulaic fashion itself, but it is a kind of oral equivalent of a list, an oral version of Ravisius Textor's and Zwinger's printed compilations. An oral culture's poems are the equivalent of commonplace collections (though they are other things besides).

It is of considerable interest that the Renaissance itself still preserved a strong sense that this is what poems and/or other 'inventions' were, *inter alia* – assemblages of commonplace materials to which other poets could resort for the matter of their own poems. The Elizabethan anthology is typically presented to its reader not simply as an anthology would be presented today, that is, as a collection of works to enjoy. It is also presented as a collection of materials to be used. *Anthologia* is the Greek word for which the Latin *florilegium* is a calque: both mean etymologically 'flower collection', for which the English equivalent is 'posies', a term which figures in not a few Elizabethan collections of poems. The conceptual apparatus of 'flowers' and 'collecting' is tied in with the massive tradition of rhetorical invention (which includes poetic invention) running back into classical antiquity and thence to the oral sources of literature. 'Flowers' imply the busy rhetorical 'bee' who goes through the garden (or, at times, the forest) of invention to visit the 'places' (*loci, topoi*) from which 'arguments' are to be extracted. From the garden he gathers nectar to make honey (orations or poems). These themselves can be constituted as bouquets of flowers, in which 'arguments' are artfully arranged now rather than naturally grown, and which are still interesting to industrious bees. One goes to an anthology thus conceived not merely to enjoy oneself but also to make out of what one can extract from the 'inventions' there other 'inventions' or poems of one's own. This is the ideology in play in the titles of anthologies such as John Bodenham's *Belvedere, or the Garden of the Muses* (1600) or John Proctor's *A Gorgeous Gallery of Gallant Inventions* (1578) or Clement Robinson's *A Handfull of Pleasant Delights* (1584).

In this tradition, with a certain effort, not entirely unwarranted, the commonplace book itself can be viewed as a kind of literary genre. If narratives taking shape within oral cultures, such as the *Iliad* or the *Odyssey* or *Beowulf* (or, in the present, the countless similarly formulaic tales and other verbal performances being transcribed in oral cultures everywhere today, particularly in the Third World), are collections of commonplaces in the sense of formulaic materials stitched together in a narrative frame, or if the classical oration is largely a collection of commonplaces framed for persuasion, the commonplace book is a collection of similar materials ranged in a more abstract frame. To this extent, Textor's two collections examined here and Zwinger's more ponderous assemblage and the hundreds of other collections like these three, are in a way more of a piece with the original oral epic than later epics are, such as Milton's *Paradise Lost* or even Virgil's *Aeneid*.[1] The collections of stock materials and the old epics belong to the same noetic world – the world of commonplace thinking. Milton has his share of stock epithets, but he was literate enough to want to minimise them if not to avoid them totally; for fully literate cultures, by contrast with oral cultures, teach their members that verbalisation should avoid clichés. (In *The Faerie Queene*, however, it might be noted, for reasons which have never thus far been fully explained or even gone into, Spenser uses epithets with many of the techniques and with almost all the abandon of an oral poet, though this is a conspicuously literate poem.)

In these perspectives Textor and even Zwinger appear, if not as poets, which they certainly are not, at least in some sense as typographical equivalents of Homer – weavers, if not of tales, then at least of the elements of tales. For Homer, and oral poets generally, are more than poets are in technological cultures: they are also encyclopedists, the repositories for the culture's noetic store which

---

[1] For the way in which Virgil studiously adapted orally based Homeric similes to the demands of written composition, see Gregory Carlson, *Die Verwandlung der homerischen Gleichnisse in Vergils Äneis* (Heidelberg: Ruprecht-Karl-Universität zu Heidelberg, 1972).

they retrieve and organise by 'weaving'. It is interesting that Textor
in Latin actually means 'weaver', a meaning which its French form
Tixier (Tissier – cf. *tisser*, to weave; *tisserand*, weaver) at least suggests.
An individual's identity is deeply wrapped up in his name, and who
knows the deeper forces of consciousness or of culture which may
have helped steer this sixteenth-century humanist into his sometimes
bizarre achievements?[1]

EFFECTS ON RENAISSANCE LITERATURE:
A SONNET OF SHAKESPEARE'S

Robert R. Bolgar has made the point that much Renaissance teaching of rhetoric, and particularly the doctrine of imitation, implies
that a literary work consists of an assemblage of individually conceived parts.[2] Although too much can be made of implications, this
same piecemeal view of literary composition is obviously also implied
by the doctrine of the commonplaces here discussed, and in a special
way by the studied exploitation of epithets. For epithets – standard
or expected qualifiers or substitutes for given nouns, encoding a
certain amount of lore (the *sturdy* oak, the *clinging* vine, the *vain*
braggart, etc.) – by and large, are the simplest or at least the smallest
bits, the least divisible particles in a rhapsodiser's repertoire. A
commonplace disquisition on, say, loyalty might run to a thousand
words. An epithet is generally one word, a least common denomi-
nator, an atom, in commonplace composition. This is doubtless why
Ravisius Textor's collection and others like it were useful for relative
neophytes in the art of rhetoric. These collections provided the
elemental particles of discourse.

If only because of this paradigmatic status of the epithet in the
commonplace tradition, the effects of epithet collections on literature
is a subject which warrants far more attention than it has received.
Renaissance literature often intoxicates itself on epithets. In book
III, chapter 38, of *Gargantua and Pantagruel*, Pantagruel and Panurge
become dithyrambic over Triboulet's unparalleled qualifications as
a fool, heaping up some 207 different epithets (some of them quite
bizarre, rather than standard, qualifiers, but forced ironically to

---

[1] One thinks immediately also of Ramus, whose name in both this Latin form and in its
original French form, La Ramée, means 'branch' and who specialised in branched
dichotomised outlines or 'ramifications' of knowledge, as has been noted here above.
[2] Bolgar, *The Classical Heritage and Its Beneficiaries*, pp. 271–3.

serve as epithets anyhow) to specify exactly what kind of a fool
Triboulet is. This is only one of many such chains of epithets in
Rabelais's work. It would be interesting to check such epithetic
dithyrambs in detail against individual epithet collections and interesting, too, to check John Lyly's, Thomas Nashe's, or by contrast,
Thomas Deloney's prose against such collections. So, too, with
poetry: a recent study views epithetic poetry as a minor genre
under which some of George Herbert's sonnets can be classified.[1]

In the study of the effects of epithet collections on literature Ravisius Textor's *Epitheta* must be accorded close attention. T. W. Baldwin
has shown at great length that this work was one of the most esteemed
and most used books for the writing of Latin and English in Shakespeare's day, and that Shakespeare himself might well have used
it.[2] Ascham's invective against the book itself attests clearly to
Textor's popularity, at the grammar school level especially.[3]

In a programmatically repetitive milieu such as that of the
commonplace books, one must be careful, of course, in ascribing any
given literary production to a particular commonplace book as a
source. But sometimes startling instances of correspondences leap
to the eye, especially in works or passages which are largely cascades
of epithets. Such an instance is one of Shakespeare's best known
poems, his Sonnet 129, which suggests how deliberately and directly
Textor's *Epitheta* may at times have been used. The sonnet treats of
lust and its consummation – but in reverse: first briefly (one and one-
half lines) of the consummation of lust ('lust in action') and then
retrospectively, in the rest of the poem, of lustful desires ('till action,
lust').

> Th'expense of spirit in a waste of shame
> Is lust in action; and till action, lust
> Is perjur'd, murd'rous, bloody, full of blame,

[1] Virginia R. Mollenkott, 'George Herbert's Epithet-Sonnets', *Genre*, v (June 1972), 131–7.
[2] *William Shakspere's Small Latine and Lesse Greeke*, 1, 714; 11, 366, 414–16, 455, 508.
[3] 'Grammar schools have few *epitomes* to hurt them, except *Epitheta Textoris*, and such beggarly gatherings as Horman, Wittinton, and other like vulgars for making of Latins' – Roger Ascham, *The Schoolmaster* (1570), ed. by Lawrence V. Ryan (Ithaca, N.Y.: Cornell University Press, 1967), pp.106–7. It is clear from the context that Ascham is taking 'epitome' to refer to any edition of Textor's *Epitheta* or *Officina*, not simply to the abridged editions of the *Epitheta* got up by later editors under the title *Epitome epithetorum*. Indeed 'epitome' for Ascham refers pretty much to commonplace collections in the wide generic sense in which I have been using the term 'commonplace collections' here.

> Savage, extreme, rude, cruel, not to trust;
> Enjoy'd no sooner but despised straight;
> Past reason hunted; and no sooner had,
> Past reason hated, as a swallow'd bait
> On purpose laid to make the taker mad:
> Mad in pursuit, and in possession so;
> Had, having, and in quest to have, extreme;
> A bliss in proof, and prov'd a very woe;
> Before a joy propos'd, behind, a dream.
> All this the world well knows; yet none know well
> To shun the heaven that leads men to this hell.

This poem is almost entirely a piling up of epithets.[1] If we turn in Textor's *Epitheta* to the two key terms with which Shakespeare is concerned, *luxuria* or *luxuries* (both these forms occur in Latin) for 'lust in action' and *libido* for lustful desires ('till action, lust'), we find striking equivalents for every epithet in this sonnet, and indeed often two or three Latin terms for one or another English word. Shakespeare's keynote for his sonnet, lust's wastefulness, is sounded loud and clear by the very first epithet supplied by Textor under *luxuria* (*luxuries*), the epithet *prodiga* (spendthrift, extravagant, wasteful), represented in Shakespeare's first line by 'expense' and by 'waste'.

Some of the correspondence between Textor's Latin and Shakespeare's English can be noted here, with Textor's Latin terms beneath the word (italicised) in Shakespeare's text which they suggest.

> Th'*expense* of spirit in a waste of *shame*
>   prodiga   prava, nefanda, infamis,
>   turpis, impudens
> Is *lust* in action, and *till action, lust*
>   (LUXURIES)   (LIBIDO)
> Is *perjur'd, murd'rous, bloody,*   *full of blame*
>   fallax   scelerata flagitiosa probrosa, vitiosa, nefaria
> *Savage,*   *extreme,*   *rude,*   *cruel, not to trust*
> immoderata, intemperata refrenanda saeva fallax
>   indomita
> *Enjoyed no sooner* but *despised straight*
> blanda   odiosa

---

[1] Other connections of the poem have been pointed out which do not invalidate or contravene the connection with the commonplace tradition examined here and which, indeed, often corroborate or further specify this connection. See, for example, Douglas L. Peterson, 'A Probable Source for Shakespeare's Sonnett CXXIX', *Shakespeare Quarterly*, V (1954), 381–4, which notes relationships between the sonnet and rhetorical schemes such as those discussed in Thomas Wilson's *Arte of Rhetorique*. The schemes Peterson treats are admirably suited to the exploitation of epithets, and are themselves from commonplace books.

Past reason hunted, and no sooner had
inconsulta, intemperans, avida
Past reason hated, as a *swallowed bait*
foeda   occulta, personata, astuta
On purpose laid to make the taker *mad*
                    rabida, insana, furens, vecors
Mad in pursuit,   and *in possession so*
praeceps, effrenata,   saeviens, dira
  impetuosa
Had, having, and in quest to have, *extreme*
                infrenata
A bliss in proof, and prov'd a *very woe*
blanda, fervens   aerumnosa, intolerabilis, noxia
Before a joy proposed; *behind, a dream*
illecebrosa   perdita, vana
All this the world well knows, yet none knows well
To shun the *heaven*   that leads men to this *hell*.
      carnis amica   perniciosa, damnosa

This exploitation of epithets, encouraged by Textor and the commonplace tradition generally, can strike an age committed to romantic originality and 'creativity' as devastatingly artificial, unrelated to the human world. But to Shakespeare the use of epithets seemed quite the opposite, eminently human and urbane. 'All this the world well knows.' How? By experience? Yes, certainly. But by direct experience? Hardly. The store of experience with which Shakespeare's sonnet resonates would certainly take a great deal of time to accumulate. Moreover, as Roger Ascham (1515 or 1516–68) had just reminded readers of *The Schoolmaster* (1570 – published posthumously by Ascham's widow), experience is the worst teacher: too many die from it before they learn, or even after they have learned, for the lessons experience teaches can prove fatal.

Learning teacheth more in one year than experience in twenty, and learning teacheth safely, when experience maketh more miserable than wise. He hazardeth sore that waxeth wise by experience. An unhappy master he is that is made cunning by many shipwrecks; a miserable merchant, that is neither rich nor wise but after some bankrupts. It is costly wisdom that is brought by experience.[1]

A mature person must have a lot of experience – indeed, more than anyone can have time for directly – but if a person is truly mature, he or she can, and must, supplement direct experience by vicarious and empathetic experience. Even direct experience is normally the richer for the vicarious experience brought to it. Shakespeare was

[1] Ascham, *The Schoolmaster*, ed. Ryan, p.50.

hardly so callow as to believe that all readers of his sonnet would have experienced directly all the degrees of disillusionment that his sonnet deals with, or that they needed to have experienced them directly, or even that it would have been helpful if they had. Experiences of the sort he is concerned with here would not always leave the sensibility intact enough to appreciate this sonnet or any other. Many would normally be destructive experiences, even though not always irreparable.

'All this the world well knows.' How then, if not simply from direct experience? From Ravisius Textor, of course, or from his equivalents and thus from the total experience of the vast culture which Textor's excerpts sample. That is to say, from all the literature of classical antiquity – a literature based indeed in one way or another on experience, direct and/or indirect, matured over hundreds of years of classical and post-classical, largely Christian, reflection, and by reflection on reflection. The age's restriction of its references – in principle if not in full actuality – to classical antiquity of course strikes us today as quaint and parochial. There was, after all, much more to mankind's experience than what Mediterranean civilisation provided. But at least the civilisation built around and in great part out of Mediterranean classical antiquity was large enough in time and in space to provide a sizeable body of experience, the most sizeable and viable body in fact that anyone in Shakespeare's West had access to. You work with the best you know.

In these perspectives Shakespeare's value becomes once more that of a skilful conservator and reflector of the amassed wisdom of a sizeable portion of the human race. Like his contemporaries generally, Shakespeare was not original in the way in which poets since the romantic age have often programmed themselves to be original. He did not 'create' from nothing. He did not want to, nor did he even consider the possibility. (There is no such possibility.) He wanted to rework the old wisdom in an always fresh and meaningful way. Shakespeare is perhaps our most quotable author in English, or at least the most quoted. It is, or should be, a commonplace that the reason he is quotable is that his text consists so much of quotations – not grossly appropriated, but nuanced, woven into the texture of his work more tightly than is normally possible in any performance, no matter how sophisticated, in the oral tradition, in which the practice of composing out of other compositions is nevertheless grounded, as has been seen. Shakespeare appropriated the oral tradition and exploited it with the condensation and pointedness made possible by writing and even more by print.

And yet the tradition which Shakespeare here exploits in Sonnet 129 and elsewhere in his works – the individual reader can study out for himself where else and how – was moribund at the very time Shakespeare was using it to the maximum. By now it is gone, at least in its Renaissance form. We cannot compose in this way any more. When the heritage of the past is exploited with comparable deliberateness and calculation today, and with comparable effect, it comes out, as in James Joyce's *Ulysses* or *Finnegans Wake*, woven into infinitely more complications than even Shakespeare managed – or wanted to manage – and into different kinds of complications. Shakespeare's world was not what ours is in its relationship to the store of human knowledge – which store itself was different from ours, though not discontinuous with ours. Shakespeare belonged to a world in which typographical culture had not had its full impact, a world in which the accumulation of circumstantial information, vast as it was, could not match that at hand today, and in which information could not be codified so neatly as it can in our superindexed books and supercatalogued libraries and super-programmed electronic computers.

But Shakespeare's world was moving toward ours. With typography and the possibilities it brought of greater codification, the age of intensified information-collecting was beginning to succeed the age more given to utterance-collecting. Soon commonplace collections, which were essentially collections of what persons had said (or, later, written), would be absorbed and superseded by encyclopedias in the modern sense, beginning with the primitive 'methodised' works of John Heinrich Alsted and terminating in such works as today's *Britannica*, which set before the reader stores of 'data' and 'information'. Encyclopedia users today commonly do not advert to the fact that even today encyclopedia articles, and even dictionary definitions, still represent something that someone 'says' (writes) about a subject. There is no way to lay hold of a 'fact' without some kind of intervention of voice. But we live in a world which tends to feel that pure 'facts', without voice, are there, 'contained' in the silent, visible words which are contained in the sentences which are contained in the paragraphs which are contained in the pages which are contained in the volume which is contained in the set which can be located with the help of a trustworthy and convincingly abstract system (Dewey or Library of Congress) upon a specified shelf contained in the library.

Shakespeare lived on the verge of this supercodification or super-localisation of the noetic world. But in Shakespeare's day, the codifying, localising process was in great part still turned primarily not toward purportedly nonvocalised 'data' but quite overtly toward sayings, which had been the proper preoccupation of the original oral culture of mankind and which remained a major preoccupation of the residually oral culture of the Renaissance. Without decrying our vast expansion of the noetic world and our need to deal with 'facts' – perhaps more gingerly and critically than we usually do – we can ask ourselves whether any poetry or literature can forgo delving into the commonplace world of sayings, of communal memory, from which Shakespeare and Ravisius Textor drew, whether it can bypass the wisdom stored in what men and women out of the past have said about actuality and about their experience, matured by subsequent reflection, and sharpened and driven home. It would appear quite feasible to demonstrate that where modern literature is at its peak it retains a living connection of some sort with the commonplace tradition, and when it is poor its poverty is due to its failure to establish this connection – which is to say to its ignorance of itself, of how it comes to be where it is. The older we get, the more mature our literature deserves to be.

7

COMMONPLACES OF LAW, PROVERBIAL WISDOM AND PHILOSOPHY: THEIR IMPORTANCE IN RENAISSANCE SCHOLARSHIP (RABELAIS, JOACHIM DU BELLAY, MONTAIGNE)

M. A. SCREECH

What must we do to enable the next generation of scholars to contribute to our studies?

The most urgent future problem of sixteenth-century scholarship may well be the neglect of meaning or even contempt for it. The reasons for this contempt or neglect may include a decline of the knowledge of the classical languages; a decline of the knowledge of the literatures written continuously in those languages from classical, through Christian to nearly modern times: a growing ignorance of biblical and theological matters. This may well be true also, where literary scholars are concerned, of some of the basic knowledge of sixteenth-century writers in the whole encyclopedia of their studies, including law and medicine.

This means that even the clearest of appeals by a Renaissance author to an authoritative commonplace may not be recognised; or if recognised, its importance may not be grasped.

A further source of error is the tendency to divorce medieval and Renaissance studies, so that universities may be forced to 'train' Renaissance scholars who have no knowledge whatsoever of medieval languages and what they contain. Something may be termed 'typically Renaissance' when it is in fact a medieval commonplace, still valid in Renaissance times.

In his search for meaning a sensitive scholar welcomes studies which stress the extraordinary difficulties of hermeneutics, whilst he will remain sceptical of any study which takes it for granted that (say) Rabelais's meaning is unrecoverable, expressed in an article or book which itself claims conceptual validity for its words.

The 'shareable verbal meaning' (to use Hirsch's expression) is what we are not entitled to ignore or distort. Its recovery is a *sine qua non* of a valid literary judgement. A clear example of this concerns commonplaces. For commonplaces are, by definition, passages of general application, a leading text cited in argument, used precisely because it will be recognised as generally authoritative. Often the wisdom of a commonplace is proverbial; sometimes it is not so much a question of proverbial wisdom as the standard opinion or authority in theology, medicine, law, morals etc., held either to settle the point at issue or at very least to sum up a recognised position.

The greatest risk of error that we run where commonplaces are concerned is when a combination of insensitivity, carelessness or prejudice reinforces our ignorance. If one starts from an over-confident assumption about (say) Rabelais's or Montaigne's meaning this may lead to an undervaluing of whatever does not fit in, stopping one short in one's long labours towards grasping the meaning of the text. An awful warning concerns two juxtaposed notes in the *Edition Critique* of the *Tiers Livre de Pantagruel*. Rabelais wrote:

Appeler (dist Pantagruel) jamais on ne peult des jugemens decidez par Sort et Fortune, comme attestent nos antiques Jurisconsultes, et le dict Balde, *L. ult. C. de leg.* La raison est pource que Fortune ne recongoist poinct de superieur auquel d'elle et de ses sors on puisse appeler. Et ne peult en ce cas le mineur estre en son entier restitué, comme apertement il dict in *L. ait praetor.* § *ult. ff. de minor.* (EC p.103).

The Edition Critique notes assert that the first allusion is to a *titulus, De legibus* and goes on to correct Rabelais (it is in fact a reference to the *Communia de legatis & fidei commissis*), and adds: 'On peut juger oiseux ce déploiement d'érudition de légiste.' Yet this is not 'érudition' but authoritative legal commonplace which dominates the overall intellectual structure of the *Tiers Livre* – hardly surprising in a book whose privilege invokes the 'gens sçavans et doctes du Royaulme'; whose *Prologue* invites comparison with Budé's *Annotationes in Pandectas* by drawing from it the theme of Diogenes and his barrel, and which resolves the intellectual problem of the book in terms of Christian folly with a detailed borrowing from the same *Annotationes in Pandectas*, from the authoritative commentary of Budé on the paragraph 'Si servus inter fanaticos non semper caput jactaret et aliqua profatus esset' (*Opera Omnia*, Gregg, III, 251–2). This itself becomes a commonplace.

The recognition of these authoritative commonplaces as being what they are is not simply a matter of finding a source; it can guide us towards meaning and literary judgement.

Commonplaces may turn up virtually anywhere in a Renaissance author. Let me give some examples. In the *Prologue* to *Gargantua* we can read those famous words commented upon by scholar after scholar:

Puis, par curieuse leczon et meditation frequente, rompre l'os et sugcer la substantificque mouelle – c'est-à-dire ce que j'entends par ces symboles Pythagoricques.

The allusion to Erasmus's adage (1.1.2) *Pythagorae symbolae* is duly noted. But there are no less than two more commonplaces in these few words. They are readily accessible in Charles de Bouelles's *Proverbia* of 1531 (Book II, no.li):

> *mandere ad usque ossa*
>   manger jusques aulx os.
> *ossa infringere,*
>   Rompre les os.
> *Eruere medullam*
>   Tirer la mouelle des os.

Bouelles comments as follows:

Quadrant haec ad plurima. Cum primis ad discumbentium inhonestatem nihil in mensa residui facientium pręter ossa, & escam canum; deinde ad principum tyrannidem erodentium plębem. Postremo ad subtiliorem pastum refectionemve esurientis animi. Animus enim rebus in arduis haud literali contentus sensu, nec satis sibi esse ducens solidam duntaxat palpare, et erodere ossium substantiam subtili ingenii acumine, ipsa etiam ossium adyta & interiores cryptas adit. Quinimmo ossa refringens latentioris intelligentiae medullam inde eruit, qua esuriem temperet suam, Et inclyte siti medeatur occulta, & arcana quaeque noscendi.

(fol.1 xx iij v°)

The relevance of this to what Rabelais is saying is, I suggest, clear and important.

The same can apply to large-scale questions of interpretation. The *Tiers Livre* can be shown to be concerned with φιλαυτία as a major theme. Should one need supporting evidence I would suggest a study of a work entirely composed of connected commonplaces: the *Bellum discors Sophiae ac Philautiae, Veritatis ac Falsitatis* (Antwerp, 1530) (B.M., 527, b2(1)). Readers of the *Tiers Livre* will feel particularly at home I think on leaves D 6 v° and D 7 Ro.

An awareness of these interconnected proverbial commonplaces and their meaning will lead also I suggest to the conclusion that the mock encomium of debts, when Panurge sets out to 'manger son bled en herbe' is a means of condemning him against the proverbial wisdom of the Adage *Messe tenus propria vive*, and so on.

Commonplaces such as these were so current that Rabelais can innocently refer (in the *Tiers Livre* at any rate) to the 'mot vulgaire ἐχθρῶν ἄδωρα δῶρα'. It was, of course, a *mot vulgaire* for the readers of the *Tiers Livre* (if not for us) appearing for example in Alciati's *Emblemata*.

The rôle of this kind of proverbial commonplace in poetry is sometimes very significant. I take my example from Joachim du Bellay's *Regrets*. As these poems are sonnets, they partake (for many Renaissance authors) of the nature of the *épigramme*: hence the frequency of proverbial wisdom in their salty tails. It makes a great deal of difference, conceptually and aesthetically, whether or not one recognises the last line of sonnet 90

– C'est vrayment de les voir le salut d'un jeune homme –

as an allusion to Terence (not the least comic of authors) in the *Eunuch* (934–40)

Nosse omnia haec, salus est adulescentulis.

It will also alert one to the sustained indebtedness of du Bellay to the *Eunuch* at this point in the *Regrets* and enable us to have a different 'feel' for the poem.

Many of these commonplaces were pointed out in the TLF *Regrets*. But not all. One (which fell out, inexplicably, during printing) concerns sonnet 140:

Ayme donques (Ronsard) comme pouvant haïr.
Haïs donques (Ronsard) comme pouvant aymer.

The allusion is to a mime of Publilius's mentioned by Aulus Gellius in the *Attic Nights* (XVII.14):

Ita amicum habeas posse ut facile fieri hunc inimicum putes.

Nicolas Bonaspes renders it thus in his *Proverbia communia* (B.M., 1305, aa.18: sig.D.iii v°):

> Ayme tellement ton amy
> Pensant qu'il peut estre ennemy.

And of course Montaigne refers to it too.

There are other proverbs passed over unexplained in the TLF *Regrets*, simply because I did not recognise them or could not trace them. Sonnet 142 ends thus:

> La souris bien souvent perit par son indice,
> Et souvent par son art se trompe l'artisan.

The word *indice* is not attested in French in any relevant sense. It is, in fact, another allusion to Terence's *Eunuch* (v.6.23):

> Egomet meo indicio, quasi sorex, hodie perii.

Erasmus duly explains it (*Adages* 1.3.65): *Suo ipsius indicio periit sorex*. Donatus (as Erasmus points out) treats it as a proverbial condemnation of a man betrayed by his own words, perhaps because the shrew-mouse (*sorex*) makes shriller cries than the ordinary mouse. This is a real help towards grasping the meaning both of the word *indice* (which is possibly a hapaxlegomenon in this sense) and of the poem as a whole. It has, after all, been taken to refer to a mouse's droppings, which alters – and wrongly alters – the whole feel of the sonnet.

There are many other examples that I could give. But I want to pass rapidly to Montaigne, where the question is I think of even more fundamental importance.

A special feature of Montaigne's style and meaning is his refusal (normally) to state his sources and authorities. This is quite deliberate: he likes the ideas to be weighed *in vacuo*; he likes to tempt the reader to condemn him, only to have it revealed to his embarrassed ignorance that that particular gem of wisdom was not Montaigne's own creation but a borrowing from an authoritative Ancient. Because of this, pages of Montaigne which contain authoritative commonplaces crying out for recognition are often passed over in silence.

I will give only two examples, both of which are important, but for different reasons.

Chapter ix of Book 1 of the *Essays* is entitled 'Des menteurs'.

Yet it deals mainly with lack of memory, not lying as such. About half-way through the chapter one can see why, when Montaigne writes:

Ce n'est pas sans raison qu'on dit que qui ne se sent pas ferme de memoire, ne se doit pas mesler d'estre menteur.

Students take it to be an allusion to a 'popular saying' if they think of it at all. Yet here we have an authoritative commonplace going uninterruptedly back to the great Quintilian (IV.3.91):

Verum est quod vulgo dicitur: mendacem memorem esse oportet.

The 'Seraphino Calbasy' of the Almanach for 1544 (which I do *not* think was by Rabelais) remembers it in his first paragraph:

En ce peu de papier quil [*sic*] restoit blanc, je respondroys vouluntiers a la calumnie daucuns ocieux. Car lon dict communement *Quod opportet mendacem esse memorem.* Et puis vous savez que tout homme est menteur –

where, in addition to Quintilian, we have David (Psalm 116.11):

Ego dixi in excessu meo, *Omnis homo mendax.*

The chapter *Des menteurs* is primarily about failures of memory because the currency of Quintilian's remark as a proverbial commonplace made the association almost inevitable.

But to end with may I point out an example of a commonplace which we need to recognise to understand the greatest of all chapters of the *Essays* (III, xiii, 'De l'experience'), where the thought of this serene post-Tridentine catholic Christian gentleman breaks like a great wave at the end of his quest.

'De l'experience' starts thus:

Il n'est desir plus naturel que le desir de connoissance. Nous essayons tous les moyens qui nous y peuvent mener. Quand la raison nous faut, nous y employons l'experience.

The opening words of this great resolving chapter are the best known of all metaphysical commonplaces, being an allusion to the first sentence of the first paragraph of the first book of Aristotle's *Metaphysics*: πάντες ἄνθρωποι τοῦ εἰδέναι ὀρέγονται φύσει. Treatises without number began with these words in medieval times. One, pointed out to me by my friend and colleague Miss Tootill, is *Li Bestiaires d'Amours* of Richard of Furnival:

Toutes gens desirent par nature à scavoir.

It was not spurned by the learned. It was commented on by Thomas
Aquinas, explained by Albertus Magnus, vulgarised by Isidore of
Seville, and so on. Dante – just like Montaigne – uses it as the
starting-point of his *Convito*:

Si come dice lo Filosofo nel principio de la Prima Filosofia, tutti li uomini desi-
derano di sapere.

Rabelais uses it in the *Almanach* for 1535 in such a way as to show that
it had long since become a text establishing by natural reason the
immortality of the soul. So too Montaigne:

> Nostre fin est en l'autre monde.

That Montaigne should start his last chapter, and his most
profound, with a *sententia* (following in this the advice of the treatises)
is not unimportant. That the commonplace is from *Metaphysics* 1.1.1
is more so. That this commonplace was associated with reflections on
immortality is vital to know. But most important of all, Montaigne
often (despite his coyness about sources) goes back to his originals
(at least in Latin translation). This chapter is entitled *De l'experience*.
And what is the first chapter of the first Book of the *Metaphysics*
about, if not that! Other animals live by the ability to register
impressions (φαντασία) and by memory (μνήμη) alone. Unlike man,
they have virtually no share in experience (ἐμπειρία). It is through
this experience (διὰ τῆς ἐμπειρίας) that man acquires his science and
his art. These are just the concerns of Montaigne in the opening
pages of this chapter. The student is discouraged from going into
this by Hugo Friedrich's assertion in his justly celebrated book:
'Schwach sind die Spuren einer Aristoteles-Lektüre in den *Essais*' –
especially when he adds that that is what one expects from a
sixteenth-century author! (*Montaigne* (Berne, 1949), p. 75).

It makes a difference to know that this chapter starts with a
public bow towards Aristotle's *Metaphysics*, as a prelude to going
beyond it; it makes a difference to the meaning of the memorable
statement later in the same chapter:

Je m'estudie plus qu'autre object. C'est ma metaphysique, c'est ma physique

– as well as to other specific allusions to Aristotle and his works in
this chapter.

And it makes an equally important difference, almost, if one
realises that when Montaigne asserts at the climax of the chapter

that 'Nature est un doux guide, mais non pas plus doux que prudent et juste . . . je queste partout sa piste', that he has Cicero's *De officiis* in mind and, indeed, that the very expression *vestigia naturae* was Ciceronian. Other – medieval – philosophical commonplaces, such as *naturalia non sunt turpia* also help to guide us towards Montaigne's meaning in this chapter.

I would suggest that, as Renaissance scholars, we should be concerned – above all else – to provide the next generation with the means of learning 'Both the Languages', to enable Hebrew and Arabic to be learned when needed or desired; to expand our knowledge of the medieval and Renaissance encyclopedia. A wider knowledge of medicine, theology (especially Eastern and Western Patristics) and – the most neglected of all – the law would be fruitful, not least for students of literature.

One of the ways (not the most nor the least important) is from the study of commonplaces. But it is only one. The Renaissance in Europe fed upon Antiquity. The writings of Greece and Rome and their medieval heirs; the legendary wisdom of Egypt; the scholarship of Christendom and Islam, were the very stuff from which they created that new and vigorous culture which it is still our privilege to enjoy and to pass on to others, who, perhaps, will understand it better than we can.

8

MONTAIGNE'S 'SUR DES VERS DE VIRGILE': TABOO SUBJECT, TABOO AUTHOR

D. COLEMAN

The taboo subject that Montaigne tackles here is sex.[1] We remember him saying in the 'Avis au Lecteur' (which he hardly touched up since its appearance in the first edition of 1580),

> Mes defauts s'y liront au vif, et ma forme naïfve, autant que la reverence publique me l'a permis. Que si j'eusse esté entre ces nations qu'on dict vivre encore sous la douce liberté des premieres loix de nature, je t'asseure que je m'y fusse très-volontiers peint tout entier, et tout nud. (I, p.2)

In this essay – III.5 – dating from 1588 in the first instance, he is breaking the public taboo on the discussion of sex. If sex matters at all to Montaigne its meaning must be seen in the context of his whole life and his experience *vis-à-vis* the way of thinking about and feeling the sexual act. Towards the end of this essay Montaigne firmly asserts that sex is central to his self-portrait,

> Chacune de mes pieces me faict esgalement moy que toute autre. Et nulle autre ne me faict plus proprement homme que cette-cy. Je dois au publiq universellement mon pourtrait. (V, p.149)

And there is a statement in the Bordeaux edition which harks back to the 'Avis au Lecteur' in a vital way so that the interconnection between his portrait and the subject matter is made quite clear. There are two versions of the personal statement,

---

[1] The subject of sex has been largely avoided in Montaignian criticism. But recently Richard Sayce in *The Essays of Montaigne. A critical exploration* (London, 1972), pp. 127–33, analyses this essay sympathetically. Other writers who have dealt with sex are, for example, Donald M. Frame, *Montaigne's Essais: a study* (New Jersey, 1969) and Philip P. Hallie, *The scar of Montaigne: an essay in personal philosophy* (Middletown, Conn., 1966). The page references are to the Plattard edition, *Les Textes Français*, VI vols. (Paris, 1931). The Bordeaux edition has been consulted particularly for the Martial quotations and references given under the letters EM (Edition municipale: Montaigne, *Essais*, ed. F. Strowski, F. Gebaix, P. Villey, Bordeaux, 1906–33).

1° Ma preface liminere [*liminere* was added later] montre que ie n'esperois pas tant. Les plus sages et sains escris des auteurs m'ont enhardi. Et le recueil qu'on a faict a mon premier proiect [followed by two words which are unintelligible] ie me suis pique a rompre la glace et montrer a nos [the end of this variant is unintelligible and later Montaigne modified the statement to . . . auteurs et le recueil qu'on a faict a ma proposition m'ont enhardi si que ie me suis piqué . . .] 2° Et les praeceptes de nos maistres et leurs exemples portent que tout esprit ~~dont~~ qui par fois ne se sente agite de quelque allegresse foliante . . . (EM III, p.132)

Thus Montaigne, wanting to make his position less ambiguous, added, crossed out and tried to find words that would express his personal statement: his beloved ancient authors provided the authority, and a reading public – the selling of his first editions – furnished the audience.

Sex is and always has been important in a human being's life. The 'unserious' treatment of it is an attempt at denying its significance by converting it into entertainment. It is utterly wrong to say, as the American scholar Barbara Bowen has said, that 'The Latin quotations are erotic but not explicit, and in French Montaigne "dares to say" a great deal less than Rabelais, Des Périers, Nicholas de Troyes, or Brantôme.'[1] Montaigne is the only author in sixteenth-century France to realise that the kinds of language that are most important for discussing copulation are unquotable, that language is at its poorest in this area and that though all words are ambiguous, those concerning sex are especially so. Hence his use of bilingual – French and Latin – modes of communication.

In 'Sur des Vers de Virgile' he dovetails sex to the context of his life as a whole. The way he 'proves' that it is a 'serious' subject is partly through the circular structure of the essay, the quotations from Virgil and Lucretius forming the hub of the wheel, and the leitmotivs are interconnected spokes leading out of the centre which is sex (e.g. the contrasting thematic pairs, youth and age, health and disease, knowledge of oneself and knowledge of the human condition, Latin language and French language, sincerity and dishonesty, essence and appearance, words versus things and so on); partly through his use of concrete language to create layers of language around sex; and partly through the comic and ironical attitude which is so characteristic of Montaigne. All this 'proves' that sex is vital to him and, incidentally, that Christian values are rejected here. For Christianity would like sex to be a mere appendix

[1] *The Age of Bluff* (Chicago, London, 1972), p.153.

to the life of an individual human being: it can be removed by an operation and the patient will continue to live.

The Latin quotations are essential for Montaigne to communicate what he wants to say about copulation and sex. To quote Sayce, 'A point of particular importance . . . is the use of quotations to slip in subversive thoughts.'[1] The whole texture of this essay is woven around Latin and French words: it is a poetic composition rather than a discourse on sex.

In the light of this perspective we can now ask how and why Montaigne uses nine quotations from Martial's *Epigrammata*.[2] Martial is still a taboo author: until the new edition of the Loeb one could not read certain epigrams in English.[3] Many are crude and obscene. But let us not forget that Montaigne was aware of the defects and advantages of using Martial. For instance, in II.25 he says that 'Il y a un epigramme en Martial qui est des bons (car il y en a chez luy de toutes sortes) . . .' And as Latin was his mother tongue and not French he can say with some confidence in II.35 that Martial is 'bien vif en son naturel et d'un sens plus riche'. But in II.10 he can contrast him with Catullus (and other writers of the Augustan era),

Si n'y a il bon juge qui les trouve à dire en ces anciens, et qui n'admire plus sans comparaison l'egale polissure et cette perpetuelle douceur et beauté fleurissante des epigrammes de Catulle que tous les esguillons dequoy Martial esguise la queue des siens.

The advantage in using Martial was seen by Villey who said that in addition to Horace 'Il faut nommer . . . Martial, qui a pu lui aussi . . . aider Montaigne à baisser le ton et à parler de lui-même.'[4]

As usual, Montaigne manipulates ancient authors at will and often changes the value of a Latin statement by introducing an *Et* or a different tense or indeed a different person of a verb. Thus we can watch him re-texturing the context of a quotation and using it for a purpose which is his own. He is concerned with sexual fulfilment throughout this essay, and I shall take three examples

[1] *The Essays of Montaigne*, p.37.
[2] In this essay Virgil is quoted 14 times, Horace 13 times, Catullus 12 times, Ovid 11 times and Martial 9 times. Lucretius is quoted 3 times. The relative importance of Martial is thus seen.
[3] French translation in the sixteenth and seventeenth centuries avoided certain words altogether and themes such as homosexuality, buggery, prostitution and sexual fulfilment were absent.
[4] *Les Sources et l'Evolution des Essais de Montaigne* (Paris, 1908), t.II, p.142.

to demonstrate *how* and *why* the Martial quotations are part of the texture of the essay.

The context of my first example is an attack on philosophers who divide the soul and body of man and make themselves repulsive. Montaigne approves of a *sagesse gaye et civile* and hates austerity: then comes a quotation from Buchanan,

> Tristemque vultus tetrici arrogantiam.
> (Et la tristesse arrogante d'un visage renfrogné)

followed immediately by a line from Martial, VII.58:

> Et habet tristis quoque turba cynaedos.

Montaigne has made one alteration – changing Martial's *Sed* to an *Et*. *Cinaedos* – 'catamites' – is the operative word. The context in Martial is satire on a woman who is always marrying homosexuals. 'Look out for some fellow who is always prating of the Curii and Fabii, shaggy, and with a savage look of stubborn rusticity: you will discover him; *but even the grim tribe has its catamites*: it is difficult, Galla, to marry a genuine man.' In the 1588 edition the Martial quotation was immediately followed by 'La vertu est qualité plaisante|voluptueuse . . .' (*voluptueuse* was later scratched out). By comparing the two contexts in Martial and Montaigne we can see that Montaigne is indicating that both wisdom and virtue are *voluptueuses* and that the grim tribe of philosophers are useless in the participating action of sex as distinct from talking about it. Furthermore Martial's philosophers are humbugs: that is, they preach austerity and practise (not natural but unnatural) pleasure. Montaigne makes no comment but leaves homosexuality and philosophers 'in the air' around the reader.

The context of my second example is Montaigne's assertion that in marriage, which is intended to stop females burning with lust, the males play with sex outside the marriage door, thus making their wives worse off than virgins or widows. The Martial quotation, from XII.97, is interesting: there are three lines, but with their order changed – 10, 7, 11. Changing the order is typical of Montaigne throughout the essays. For instance, in 'De l'Amitié' (1.28) he uses two poems of Catullus and almost 'creates' a different poem out of the parts he uses. Montaigne does not translate the Martial lines but simply puts them there,

Sit tandem pudor, aut eamus in jus:
Multis mentula millibus redempta,
Non est haec tua, Basse; vendidisti.

The epigram recounts how Bassus exhausts himself making love to long-haired youths instead of to his wife; and in this, he is guilty of fraud, because through her dowry, which he now spends on these youths, she has bought his penis. The homosexuality of Bassus's fraud is prominent in Martial. Montaigne has widened the scope and made the irony question the male/female position more generally in marriage. The Martial quotation is followed by the story of Polemon, also with a homosexual theme. But Montaigne makes no comment; instead he has brought into the texture the three Latin lines and relies on the reader knowing both contexts. He questions the values that man has about sex; he asserts that society itself is created by man for the enjoyment of sex by man and it is precisely because of this that women have to be chaste. There is an ironical view on males here: we males say that marriage is a good thing and yet we know that females are more lustful than we are and so when we marry we are automatically joining the cuckoldry queue. Again homosexuality plus the opening up of whole new dimensions around male and female rôles in sexual matters is left in the reader's mind.

The third example is from epigram VII.95, lines 10, 11 and 14. Again we notice the leaving out of lines 12 and 13 and 'creating' a quotation for his own use,

Cuius liuida naribus caninis
Dependet glacies rigetque barba:
Centum occurrere malo culilingis.

But Martial has *cunnilingis* whereas Montaigne has *culilingis*. Villey (EM IV, p.390) remarks, 'On trouve partout la forme cunnilingis et non culilingis' but does not go into the problem at all. As far as I know the form *culilingis* does not occur in Latin.[1] The context in Martial is again homosexual: 'put off your wintry osculations, Linus, till the month of April'. There is nothing rich in the context;

[1] According to etymology, A. Ernout and A. Meillet, *Dictionnaire étymologique de la langue latine*, 3rd edition (Paris, 1951), under *culus*: 'un mot populaire (satiriques, graffiti, priapées), mais non plautinien. Cf. cunnus' and under *cunnus*: 'sinus muliebris quem vulgo cunnum appellant. On l'évite en parlant, au dire de Cicéron.' There is the possibility that *cunnus* and *culus* are of the same family of words. Cf. *cul* and *con* in modern French.

there is no problem to be solved and Martial, as is his usual attitude, is lasciviously witty and writes an epigram as easily as if it were falling into bed. Montaigne could not have simply dropped *cul* out of a hat. Is he therefore consciously refraining from extreme lewdness in altering the word from licking female pudenda to arse-lickers? It does seem from the context that Montaigne was talking in French, before the quotation, about the ceremonious kissing embedded in French custom, a custom which he cannot stand. The context is richly ambivalent. In French he is dealing with one kind of kissing. In Latin he is dealing with another. Now it may be that Montaigne was stating that kissing – from the cere- monious gesture, through family kissing showing affection to the intensely physical kissing with the tongue – is basically the same. There is no such thing as a 'platonic' kiss; in pressing your lips to someone you are applying the same movements as copulation. In quoting three lines from Martial Montaigne seems to be not going as far as him and is deliberately toning down the quotation by avoiding the extreme gesture.

Montaigne has 'dared to say' a lot through the use of quotations from Martial. By altering the actual Latin words he is in fact creating his own Latin quotations. The contexts are important, the order of lines, the words used and the complete lack of logical con- nectives at first reading. It is only with a certain knowledge of the writing of bilingual people that one begins to 'hear' Montaigne's tone aright. The implicit suggestions are more pregnant than the explicit statements – which is what one would expect from Mon- taigne. For after all did he not say 'Je ne dis les autres, sinon pour d'autant plus me dire.'

HUMANISM AND DIALECTIC IN SIXTEENTH-CENTURY CAMBRIDGE: A PRELIMINARY INVESTIGATION

L. JARDINE

If there is a single work which stands as a landmark in the development and clarification of the pedagogic aims of the humanists, that work is Lorenzo Valla's *Dialecticae Disputationes*.[1] This elegant little treatise deserves more attention than it has hitherto received.[2] Its particular importance lies in Valla's choice of *dialectic*, traditionally the focal discipline within the *trivium*,[3] as the appropriate

[1] Here, and throughout this paper, I use the term 'humanism' in a sense consistent with Aulus Gellius's definition in the *Noctes Atticae*: 'Qui verba Latina fecerunt quique his probe usi sunt "humanitatem" non id esse voluerunt quod vulgus existimat quodque a Graecis φιλανθρωπία dicitur et significat dexteritatem quandam benivolentiamque erga omnis homines promiscam; sed "humanitatem" appellaverunt id propemodum quod Graeci παιδείαν vocant, nos "eruditionem institutionemque in bonas artes" dicimus. Quas qui sinceriter percupiunt adpetuntque, hi sunt vel maxime humanissimi. Huius enim scientiae cura et disciplina ex universis animantibus uni homini data est idcircoque "humanitas" appellata est' (XIII, xvi; Loeb edn, II, 456).

[2] P. O. Kristeller, *Eight Philosophers of the Italian Renaissance* (Stanford, 1964), pp.33–5, in a brief passing discussion of this work, notes its importance in intellectual history: 'His work is historically important as a first attempt to apply the standards of humanist thought and learning to a philosophical discipline other than ethics' (p.35). And later in the same paragraph he remarks: 'Keeping these later developments [the impact of the dialectical innovations of Agricola and Ramus] in mind, we might say that among all philosophical disciplines outside ethics, logic was the most strongly affected by the impact of Renaissance humanism.' In an earlier paper in this conference Professor C. Vasoli picked out the *Dialecticae Disputationes* as providing 'the starting point for a new approach to dialectic in the sixteenth century' (see p.74). See also Vasoli, 'La retorica e la dialettica umanistiche e le origini delle concezioni moderne del "metodo"', *Il Verri*, 35/36 (1970), 256.

[3] On the central position of dialectic and of the *trivium* as a whole in late medieval curricula see J. A. Weisheipl, 'Curriculum of the faculty of arts at Oxford in the early fourteenth century', *Mediaeval Studies*, 26 (1964), 143–85; 'The place of the liberal arts in the university curriculum during the XIVth and XVth centuries', *Actes du Quatrième Congrès International de Philosophie Médiévale* (Montreal, 1969), pp.209–13. A widely used medieval dialectic manual which gives a clear idea of the material covered in the course, and the emphasis on disputing techniques for university debating exercises is Petrus Hispanus's *Summulae Logicales* (1246). On the *Summulae* see J. P. Mullally, *The Summulae Logicales of Peter of Spain* (Notre Dame, 1945); T. Heath, 'Logical grammar, grammatical logic, and humanism in three German universities', *Studies in the Renais-*

curriculum study to carry an outspoken account of the goals and objectives of an intellectual programme in the liberal arts remodelled in accordance with humanist principles. In the *Dialecticae Disputationes* Valla urges that the study of dialectic (the analysis of existing utterance and the principles of argumentation) should concern itself exclusively with language as it is used in ordinary (literate) discourse: 'For philosophy and dialectic are not accustomed nor ought they indeed to depart from the most regularly used conventions of speech, and, as it were, from a path frequented by the public and well-paved.'[1] It is neither the business of the dialectician to explore in detail general philosophical concepts (like 'identity' and 'number'), nor is he required to provide analysis of contrived philosophical discourse that a grammarian would dismiss out of hand as ill-formed. According to Valla, investigations of the former sort belong to the specialist academic discipline of metaphysics; dialectic should support grammar as a practical guide to composition and criticism. The model that Valla proposes for such a dialectic (dialectic as a true *ars* amongst the *artes sermocinales*) is Quintilian's *Institutio Oratoria*.[2]

In his reappraisal of dialectic Valla reacts against the traditional teaching texts of Boethius, and the treatment of the subject in manuals like Peter of Spain's widely used *Summulae Logicales*,[3] rather than directly against the logical works of Aristotle.[4] In the three books of his treatise he considers in turn the primitive concepts on which dialectic is founded (*primordia*), the interpretation of terms

sance, 18 (1971), 9–64; L. Jardine, 'The place of dialectic teaching in sixteenth-century Cambridge', *Studies in the Renaissance* (XXI (1974), 31–62). On late scholastic debating exercises and their relation to dialectic see H. Schüling, *Die Geschichte der axiomatischen Methode im 16. und beginnenden 17. Jahrhundert* (Hildesheim, 1969), chap.6.

[1] *Dialecticae Disputationes* (Coloniae, 1541), p.24: 'At philosophia ac dialectica non solent, ac ne debent quidem recedere ab usitatissima loquendi consuetudine, et quasi a via vulgo trita et silicibus strata.' This emphasis on 'usitatissima consuetudo loquendi' as the proper subject of dialectic is echoed by Vivès in *In Pseudodialecticos* (*Opera*, (Basileae, 1555), I, 272–86, especially pp.273, 279): 'quapropter praecepta dialectices non minus, quam grammatices atque rhetorices ad usum loquendi communem aptanda sunt' (p.274).

[2] On Quintilian's influence on Valla's *Dialecticae Disputationes* see S. Camporeale, *Lorenzo Valla: Umanesimo e Teologia* (Florence, 1972), pp.33–67.

[3] On the content of Petrus Hispanus' manual see Jardine, 'The place of dialectic teaching'.

[4] For a clear account of the sort of logical issues to which Valla takes exception see A. J. Ashworth, *Language and Logic in the post-medieval period* (Dordrecht, 1974). On topics like 'modality' Valla makes direct use of conventional teaching as a foil for his own approach. Vivès uses the same technique in his attack on advanced *suppositio* theory in his *In Pseudodialecticos*.

in propositions (*interpretatio verborum*), and argumentation (*ratio argumentandi*).[1] At every stage in his treatment of these topics critical issues are decided on grounds of language *usage* ('quanto satius erit sequi communem loquendi consuetudinem'[2]). On the issue of 'priority', for instance, Valla maintains that the complex scholastic discussions of the various orders of priority depend on careless use of words: 'priority' is a temporal concept; any other type of 'priority' should, to avoid confusion, be designated by some alternative term, as suggested by the conventions of elegant written Latin:

They say that the whole is 'prior' to the part; genus is 'prior' to species; species is 'prior' to the individual; the state is 'prior' to the household or 'prior' to the individual men; good is 'prior' to evil. Why do they not say more appropriately: 'more advantageous', 'more worthy', 'greater in magnitude', 'greater in extent', 'superior to', 'more excellent', 'more to be honoured', 'more distinguished'. Whereas as I see it, each part was 'prior' to the whole in writing, building and doing [prior in time]. And a single man was 'prior' [temporally] to a single family, and that family to a single state, and Adam to the species 'man'. For to such an extent these philosophers seem indiscriminately to contrive niggling questions about things by sophisms of words.[3]

Similarly, Valla holds that negative propositions should be formed 'not so much in accordance with the precepts of the art of grammar as in accordance with the usage of the erudite and elegant':[4]

There are those, however, who place the negative where it cannot legitimately be upheld, as 'not a certain man reads', which is grammatically absurd. But

[1] Ed. cit. p.7: 'Quare illis contemptis ac spretis si qua sunt quae quam in Aristotele melius dici possent, ea tentabo ipse melius pro mea virili dicere, non hominis (quod absit) insimulandi gratia, sed honorandae veritatis, idque potissimum in Dialectica, repetitis necessario altius huius rei primordiis quae liber primus: nam secundus verborum interpretationem, tertius argumentandi rationem continebit.'

[2] Ibid. p.96: 'Quis etiam isto inquam modo loquutus est? quod ne dici quidem ratio permittit, aliud est enim lignum fieri posse arcam, aliud est esse arcam potentia cum dicimus, fieri arcam posse, iam negamus esse arcam: quia quod est, fieri rursus non potest cum iam factum sit, quanto satius erit sequi communem loquendi consuetudinem, hoc lignum potest effici arca, scilicet quod forma figuraque huius ligni mutabilis est in formam figuramque arcae.'

[3] Ibid. p.114: 'Si enim de alia re quam de tempore agunt, cur non aliis vocabulis utuntur? Totum est inquiunt prius parte, genus prius specie, species prior individuo, civitas prior domo aut prior singulis hominibus, bonum prius malo. Cur non potius dixerunt, satius, dignius, maius, amplius, superius, excellentius, honoratius, praestantius. Quanquam prius fuit pars (ut sentio) quam totum, ut in scribendo, aedificando, fingendo. Et prius unus homo, quam una familia, et una familia, quam una civitas, et Adam, quam species homo. Usque adeo enim videntur isti philosophi verborum captionibus passim struere rerum quaestiunculas.'

[4] Ibid. p.176: 'nobis quidem ad normam grammatices loquendum est, nec tam grammatice quam latine loquendum, hoc est, non tam ad praecepta artis quam ad consuetudinem eruditorum atque elegantium, quae optima ars est.'

I would certainly not dare to say thus, 'not someone', 'not anyone', 'not a certain one reads', unless in verse, where transfer of words is allowed.[1]

And in his treatment of syllogistic he discards the last five modes of the first figure of the syllogism and all the third figure syllogisms as grammatically grotesque:

[the seventh mode of the first figure] which they call Dabitis is similar to this . . . 'every animal is a substance, some man is an animal, therefore some substance is a man'. The correct conclusion should be 'therefore some man is a substance', which they put forward inverted and perversely, like boys who walk backwards for fun, and like certain entertainers who, using their hands as feet, walk on their hands to amuse.[2]

It is, according to Valla, language used in contravention of custom and eloquence which creates most of the problems traditional logic was developed to handle. Such problems are simply irrelevant to a revised dialectic of 'natural' language, and the technical tools of such a logic correspondingly more simple. On the other hand, Valla gives considerable attention to induction, enthymeme and example, the weaker forms of argument commonly used in oratory (elegant discourse), but virtually ignored by Peter of Spain as lacking in inferential rigour. The implications of Valla's approach are far reaching. It is not his intention, as historians of logic have suggested, to subordinate dialectic to rhetoric.[3] They see Valla as riding rough-shod over subtle medieval logical issues, with apparent disregard for their finer points, and are suitably appalled. But we can understand why a man of Valla's intellectual calibre, himself apparently trained in scholastic logic,[4] adopted this strategy if we consider what

---

[1] Ibid. pp.174–5:' Sunt tamen qui applicent ibi negationem ubi haerere non potest ut non quidam legit, quod dictu absurdum est. At ego ne sic quidem loqui ausim non aliquis, non ullus, non quispiam legit, nisi in carmine, ubi traiectio est permissa verborum.'

[2] Ibid. p.260: 'Tertium huic simile est particulariter assumens concludensque quod vocant Dabitis, omne animal est substantia, quidam homo est animal, ergo quaedam substantia est homo. Vera conclusio erat, ergo quidam homo est substantia, quam isti inverse ac praepostere proferunt similes pueris qui per lusum retrorsum incedunt, similes scaenicis quibusdam, qui manibus tanquam pedibus utentes, ludicri gratia ipsis manibus ambulant.'

[3] For the standard judgement that humanists like Valla 'rhetoricised' dialectic see e.g. W. and M. Kneale, *The Development of Logic* (Oxford, 1962), p.300; W. Risse, *Die Logik der Neuzeit*, Band 1 (Stuttgart, 1964).

[4] Apart from the ability to handle (or strategically mishandle) key logical issues which he displays in the *Dialecticae Disputationes* (for instance, in his discussion of, and rejection of the scholastic treatment of modals he shows himself conversant with subtle scholastic distinctions; *Dialecticae Disputationes* in *Opera* (Basileae, 1540), 1, 717), Valla

his model, Quintilian, offers in the way of dialectical instruction which is not to be found in, say, Peter of Spain's textbook.

First and foremost, such treatment of selection and organisation of material as there is in the *Institutio Oratoria* is focused squarely on the practical exigencies of 'arguing on one's feet', and in particular on the needs of the lawyer and politician. The *Institutio Oratoria* is, after all, a self-contained scheme of education for the public servant as opposed to the professional academic. When, therefore, Valla elects to model his treatment of dialectic on those books in which Quintilian outlines the minimal formal apparatus which will provide a rigorous foundation for such a training, he is making a polemical and essentially pedagogic point about the purpose of dialectical instruction within the curriculum.

Valla takes it for granted that any complete educational programme needs as its basis a formal intellectual training (such as medieval dialectic was designed to provide). If oratorical instruction (that area of studies within the curriculum for which humanists were responsible[1]) is to be autonomous, and is to provide a real alternative scheme of education to that of the philosophy schools and traditional metaphysically oriented curricula, then it must provide its own replacement for traditional dialectic. The course which Valla devises in the *Dialecticae Disputationes* provides the formal foundation for a programme of study which ignores or skirts philosophical issues of the sort central to scholastic training, and concentrates instead on the practical problems of cut-and-thrust argument in politics and law. It is hardly surprising, therefore, that wherever he compares Boethius's exposition of a topic with Quintilian's, Quintilian's inevitably emerges as the more sensitive and appropriate approach.[2]

Gabriel Harvey was public lecturer in rhetoric at the University of

also shows familiarity with Albertus Magnus's logical works elsewhere in his writings (see Camporeale, *Lorenzo Valla*, pp.122–3).

[1] At university level 'humanists' were teachers of rhetoric and oratory whose position in the academic community was inferior to that of teachers of logic and philosophy. I would argue that some of the impetus for a new *dialectic* stemmed from the humanists' desire to move into the centre of the teaching area.

[2] See, for example, Valla's treatment of induction, in which he contrasts extremely cleverly the narrow, impractical treatment given by Boethius (criticising it for failing to account for areas of discourse which Boethius regarded as outside the scope of his discussion) with the broad, essentially applied treatment of the topic in Quintilian. *Opera* (Basileae, 1541), I, 757.

Cambridge from 1574 to 1576.[1] In his published introductory orations (the *Ciceronianus* and *Rhetor* (Londini, 1577))[2] Harvey insists on two points in particular concerning the balance and nature of the *artes sermocinales*. He is adamant that dialectic provides the formal structure for all discourse, and hence that the instruction he offers in rhetoric presupposes a firm grounding in dialectic (in the *Rhetor* Harvey indicates that his rhetoric lectures followed those by a colleague in dialectic[3]). According to Harvey the priority of dialectic over rhetoric does not hold merely in the context of the formal academic debates in which every student participated to obtain his degree (and for which scholastic dialectic had traditionally prepared him). Dialectic is also crucial as the basis for all critical analysis and composition in what we would call 'literature'. Rhetoric, according to Harvey, provides instruction in embellishment, style and delivery to enhance and complete discourse which must always have been composed in accordance with the formal rules of dialectic.[4] However good the model, neither slavish imitation of its style, nor a wealth of knowledge of the tropes and schemes which decorate it can provide a substitute for a clear grasp of the principles of argumentation on which it is constructed.[5] The second point which Harvey makes in the *Rhetor* is that it was the Roman orators (Cicero and Quintilian) who fully appreciated the relation of Greek logic

[1] Gabriel Harvey (1550–1630). For a justification of the dating of Harvey's tenure of the professorship of rhetoric see H. S. Wilson's introduction to C. A. Forbes's translation of the *Ciceronianus*, *University of Nebraska Studies* (Nebraska, 1945), pp.1–34, especially pp.2, 8; Wilson, 'Gabriel Harvey's orations on rhetoric', *Journal of English Literary History*, 12 (1945), 167–82; G. C. Moore Smith, *Gabriel Harvey's Marginalia* (Stratford-upon-Avon, 1913), pp.1–76.

[2] On the precise dates of delivery of these orations see Wilson's introduction to *Ciceronianus*, pp.5–10.

[3] *Rhetor*, fo.Bii r–v: 'Ut igitur ad comparandum Dialecticam (id quod est heri commodissime a meo collega explicatum) ut ad res, artesque omnes, vel usu, fructuque necessarias, vel amplitudine ac dignitate illustres adipiscendas: sic ad accuratam et splendidam dicendi rationem, id est eloquentiam siquis pervenire velit, huic triplici est opus instrumento, Naturae, Artis, Exercitationis . . .'. The Cambridge Statutess of 1570 make dialectic the central study of the arts course as follows: 'Primus annu, rhetoricam docebit: secundus et tertius dialecticam. Quartus adjungat philosophiam', *Documents Relating to the University and Colleges of Cambridge* (London, 1852), I, 459.

[4] It should perhaps be said here that Harvey was a Ramist, and that this careful distinction between the provinces of dialectic and rhetoric was a basic tenet of Ramus's reformed curriculum. But as I have argued elsewhere, Ramus's dialectic presents the ultimate simplification and schematisation of 'humanist' dialectic as envisaged by Valla, and hence makes particularly clearly points which are sometimes not fully articulated in earlier dialectics like Agricola's (whom Ramus claims as his inspiration). See Jardine, 'The place of dialectic teaching'.

[5] See particularly *Ciceronianus* (Londini, 1577), pp.48–55.

to the practical business of public speaking and communication in all fields. For Harvey, Cicero's *De Inventione* and Quintilian's *Institutio Oratoria* bear out his own views on the relative weight to be attached to dialectic and rhetoric studies in the training of a politician and lawyer. Both, according to Harvey, can be read as advocating dialectic as the key study, and both provide models for the sort of adaptation and simplification of Greek dialectic appropriate for a liberal arts training.

In the *Rhetor* Harvey singles out one humanist in particular, Rudolph Agricola, as having recognised and reconstructed the Roman view of dialectic.[1] Agricola's *De Inventione Dialectica*[2] was prescribed in the 1535 Cambridge University Statutes and in the 1560 Trinity College Statutes as the text from which dialectic was to be taught to students.[3] Like Valla's work in the same field, Agricola's manual is something of a manifesto. It combines actual instruction in the analysis and composition of reasoned discourse with an extremely lucid account of the structure and goals of a liberal arts course, and the revised rôle of dialectic within such a programme. Agricola's commentator Phrissemius makes it clear that Agricola's work owes a great deal to Valla's, not just for its general inspiration (which Agricola acknowledges), but also in the details of the alternative Roman-style dialectic programme proposed.[4]

[1] *Rhetor* (Londini, 1577), fo.Hi r–Hiv r.
[2] On Agricola's *De Inventione Dialectica libri tres* (first published in 1513) see C. Vasoli, *La dialettica e la retorica dell'Umanesimo* (Milan, 1968).
[3] For the Trinity Statutes see J. B. Mullinger, *The University of Cambridge* (Cambridge, 1884), appendix to vol.II; for the University Statutes see *Statuta Academiae Cantabrigiensis* (Cambridge, 1785), pp.137–8.
[4] On Valla's direct influence on Agricola see Vasoli, *La dialettica e la retorica*, pp.166–82. A clear indication of the way in which Agricola's dialectic was used as a stick to beat Petrus Hispanus with (on grounds of the incompatibility of the latter's treatment with humanist ideals) is given in Phrissemius's commented edition of the *De Inventione Dialectica*. See, for instance, *Rodolphi Agricolae Phrisii de inventione dialectica libri tres, cum scholiis Ioannis Matthaei Phrissemii* ([Colonie], 1528), fo.a3 r: 'At dialectico, hoc est ei, qui probabili accurataque de re quavis uti velit oratione, et in umbra ac schola discere ea, quae postea de civilibus causis disserenti aliquem allatura sint fructum: ei ego (quemadmodum dicere coeperam) tam esse haec necessaria duco ut nihil magis: quippe sine quorum accesione, parum admodum profutura ei sint omnia ea, quaecunque vel de argumentis inveniendis, vel de usu argumentorum traduntur. Et quod de his rebus verbum facit Petrus Hispanus? Ubi horum illi in mentem venit? Quid de his affert? quid docet? quid monet? Quid de motione affectuum praecipit? Quid de oblectatione? Quid, quomodo collocanda disponendaque oratio? Quae omnia cum non erudite minus quam copiose ac eleganter explanet Rodolphus, qua tu fronte illud mihi dices homo impudentissime, nihil esse in libris viri huius, quod in summulis non doceat Petrus Hispanus?'

The key charge levelled by Agricola against the *doctissimi viri* who teach dialectic in the schools is that their techniques have no application to discourse other than contrived debating exercises:

So they teach like boys telling riddles, which not even when they have told them, either those who tell them, or those who hear them are able to understand. I have very often heard these complaints of the most serious and learned of men, who in a greater age, or with greater ability would know better; who have caused the order of the most beautiful arts to be severely distorted, and their parts confused.[1]

If you ask such men what conceivable use their instruction is in the arts of which they call themselves *doctores*, they will answer that it trains and taxes the mind of the student in preparation for his other studies.[2] But this view is totally unacceptable to Agricola. Dialectic must itself provide specific rules and precepts which will guide the student in all those fields (law, politics, theology) which may broadly be considered to be concerned with *moral* questions, and which for Agricola must be the central preoccupation of an educated man.[3] In his commentary on this chapter of the *De Inventione Dialectica* Phrissemius makes the burden of this requirement for instruction in dialectic vivid by means of an analogy:

[1] *Rodolphi Agricolae Phrisii de inventione dialectica libri tres, cum scholiis Ioannis Matthaei Phrissemii* ([Colonie], 1528), p.143: 'Docent itaque, quemadmodum pueri solent in aenigmate proponere, quae ne tum quidem quum docuerint, vel ipsimet qui docent vel illi qui didicerint, sciant. Has ergo persaepe querelas audivi gravissimorum doctissimorumque hominum, quos vel grandior aetas, vel acrior ingenii vis, meliorum admonebat: qui ferebant graviter pulcherrimarum artium ordinem turbari, membra confundi.'

[2] Ibid. pp.143–4: 'Si quem ergo eorum quos doctores artium vocant, arripias, rogesque, dic quaeso vir doctissime de dialectice (quando illam vel solam vel maxime omnium artium, quas vos numeratis liberales, videris prae te ferre) cui usui discendam putas? ... Hoc ergo pacto si quem interroges, dicat [dicet] fortasse, ut pleraque quae in ipsa dialectice praecipiuntur, vel non prosint ad percipiendas reliquas artes, vel ita praecipiuntur ut non prosint: hoc tamen iuvant, quod agitatione quadam et versatione mentem exacuant, et flexibilem praebeant, quo facilius reliquis se possit accommodare.'

[3] See in particular '[epistola] Eiusdem Rodolphi Agricolae Phrisii | De formando studio. Epistola elegantissima', in *Rodolphi Agricole Phrysii . . . nonnulla opuscula . . .* (Antuerpiae, 1511): 'Censeo ut ad philosophiam te conferas hoc est euitaris [enitaris] ut recte de rebus omnibus sentias et que sentis commode et possis eloqui. Sentire autem recte duplex est proinde et duplex conditio rerum quas inquirimus. alie namque res ad actiones moresque nostros pertinent. quibus omnis ratio vite recte riteque degende continetur quam philosophie pars ea que moralis vocatur tradit. huius prima nobis et praecipua habenda est ratio: hec autem est petenda tibi non modo a philosophis: qui literis eam tradere [tradidere]. ut sunt Aristoteles. Cicero. Seneca: et si qui sunt alii vel latini vel latine ita redditi. ut digni sint qui legantur. sed ab historicis etiam et poetis et oratoribus quoniam hi et benefacta laudando: et que contra facta sint vituperanda [vituperando]. non docent quidem: sed quod efficacissimum est. exemplis propositis que recte secusve fiant. velut in speculo ostendunt per hec gradus ad sacras litteras faciendus est. et ad illarum praescriptum dirigendus vitae nobis ordo saluberrimisque illis ducibus de nostra salute credendum' (fo.cviii v–di r).

Those who teach armed combat do not content themselves simply with outlining verbally the general way to strike an adversary, or to avoid the blows he aims. Seizing a weapon, they start with a mock combat, so that now the student becomes not just a listener, but a spectator of that art. Nor indeed is that all. Next they hand over arms to him, and teach him the correct grip, the correct stance. They teach the conventions of retreating from and advancing towards an adversary.[1]

In just the same way, an effective dialectic must present precepts which can be 'fitted to civil use and public life' and which are such as 'either encourage virtue, or deter from vice, or otherwise may be seen to be pertinent to the formation of moral conduct and the regulation of life.'[2] And once again, it is Quintilian whom Agricola singles out as having attempted in the restricted context of civil lawsuits (civiles quaestiones) to provide just such a programme for dialectic.[3]

Harvey's own copy of Quintilian, now in the British Museum, is copiously annotated.[4] These annotations make it clear that when Harvey read and reread the Institutio Oratoria he did so in the light of two particular works which he regarded as authentic 'modern' expositions of Quintilian's key themes. These works are Valla's Dialecticae Disputationes and Agricola's De Inventione Dialectica. It is extremely telling that both these works should be explicitly concerned with dialectic, and that the annotations which refer to them are not confined to the sections of the Institutio Oratoria on argumentation. For Harvey, the Institutio Oratoria as a whole is sufficiently dialectical in focus to be directly comparable with the two specialist texts.

---

[1] Agricola, De Inventione, ed. cit. p.150: 'Qui docent . . . artem gladiatoriam, ii non sat habent verbis modo praescribere, qua ratione vel adversarium ferias, vel ictus ab illo intentatos cludas. primum ipsi arrepto telo in ludicrum certamen illud descendunt: ut iam non solum auditor, sed spectator etiam artis suae fiat is, qui se illis in disciplinam tradiderit. At ne id quidem satis. Tradunt deinde arma discipulo, docent aptare manus, docent gradus componere: docent quo pacto, nunc fugere antagonistam, nunc insequi debeat: quando fidendum viribus, quando arte utendum . . . Quam docendi rationem putant observandam esse etiam in dialecticis: quorum si quis alius sit usus praeter istos gymnasiorum conflictus, hunc aiunt indicari oportere eis qui doceantur: neque tam referre illorum, ut adversus praeceptum quodque plaustra aliquot convehas obiectionum: quam ut commodis in singulorum explicatione utare exemplis, demon-stresque, quo pacto alii hac aut illa praeceptione sint usi, quo modo ipsis utendum.'
[2] Ibid. p.151: 'ita et dialecticis illud curae esse debere, ut quaecunque explicandis praeceptis suis, vel effingant ipsi, vel aliunde sumpta adducant, ea semper eiusmodi sint, ut ad civilem usum communemque hominum vitam accommodari queant.'
[3] Ed. cit. p.145.
[4] The edition is M. Fabii Quintiliani oratoris eloquentissimi, Institutionum oratorium libri XII (Parisiis, 1542). Moore Smith, Gabriel Harvey's Marginalia, transcribed some, though by no means all, of the marginalia in this volume.

On the opening pages of his copy Harvey cites two celebrations of Quintilian from the *Dialecticae Disputationes* (quoting one at length and giving the reference for the other).[1] At the end of the proemium he compares the *Institutio Oratoria* directly with the *Dialecticae Disputationes* as follows:

First [the *Institutio Oratoria*] and after the three books of Valla's *Dialecticae Disputationes*: as clearly put together and freely pervaded with the same acute and critical spirit. Nor does either the former or the latter displease to be read thoroughly many times with much fruit and pleasure. They are such indeed, that they will please if repeated ten times. As you already know to be the case for the former.[2]

And against the index, at the end of the work, he writes: 'No author, not even Valla, shares more in material, form or end with Quintilian than my Rodolphus Agricola, *De Inventione Dialectica*. Therefore look at Rodolphus together with Quintilian.'[3] In a further annotation Harvey acknowledges Valla and Quintilian together as the direct inspiration for Agricola's *De Inventione Dialectica*.[4] And in a marginal synopsis of the content of the *Institutio Oratoria* he makes clear the way in which he sees the work as centred round a humanist-style treatment of dialectic supported by rhetoric:

The first two bookes, preparative.
The five next, Logique for Invention, and disposition.
The fower following, Rhetorique for Elocution, and pronunciation: Logique for memory: an accessary, and shaddow of disposition.
The last, A supplement, and discourse of such appurtenaunces, as may otherwyse concerne an Orator to knowe, and practise. As necessary furniture, and of no less vse, or importaunce in oratory Pleas, then the Praemisses.[5]

---

1 Marginalia on p.2 of Harvey's Quintilian, at the end of the dedication (not transcribed by Moore Smith): '*Laurentius Valla* in extremo libri primi Dialecticarum Disputationum. Nonne ubicunque *Quinctilianum nuncupo*, videor velut *Achillem inter Heroas* nuncupare? . . . ut coeteris Graecis, ad ultima redactis, animum, ardoremque restituam [*Dialecticae Disputationes* (Coloniae, 1541), pp.133–4]. Consimile etiam Quinctiliani Elogium, 1°.2.c.20. earundem disputationum.'
2 Moore Smith, p.110: 'Ante, et post Vallae dialecticarum disputationum libros tres: eodem fere acri, criticoque spiritu tam disserte concinnatos; quam liberrime effusos. Nec vel huius, vel illius piget, tanto cum fructu, ac iucunditate toties perlecti. Talia vero, decies repetita placebunt: ut scite ille.'
3 Moore Smith, p.123: 'Nullus scriptor, ne Valla quidem, Quinctiliano affinior vel materia, vel forma, vel fine, quam meus Rodolphus de inventione dialectica. Ergo ad Rodolphum cum Quinctiliano.'
4 On p.315 of Harvey's Quintilian (not in Moore Smith): 'Ecce etiam insigne caput de delectatione, Libro 3. Rodolphi de inventione dialectica. Ut sunt pleraque illius artificiosa et praeclara capita; suisque digna singularibus magistris, Quintiliano, et Valla.'
5 Moore Smith, p.110 (this note is in English).

Harvey was an assiduous annotator. A wide range of printed texts densely packed with marginalia in his clear and unmistakable hand survive, as well as some commonplace book jottings, evaluations of ancient and contemporary authors, recommended courses of study for students, and odd lecture notes.[1] From these one can piece together Harvey's general intellectual attitudes and something of his picture of the purposes and goals of higher education. The Greek and Latin classics and the best of contemporary European literature provide the broad foundation both for his own habits of thought and for his projected schemes of study for students. The practical fields towards which his interests are directed are politics and law (which Harvey studied for his higher degree[2]). There can be little doubt that Harvey derives his intellectual outlook from Cicero and Quintilian. And it is also clear from his textual annotations (in particular, of his Quintilian) that he sees the dialectical works of Valla and Agricola as key texts in the articulation of the educational ideals of the Roman authors for the sixteenth century.[3]

In his commendation of Valla and Agricola as exponents of dialectic Harvey assigns them the title *Critici*, astute and sensitive in their response to language and the way it should be used. He

[1] There are also two printed Greek lectures which Harvey gave to students at Pembroke Hall; *Lexicon graecolatinum Ioannis Crispini* . . . (Londini, 1581), fo.Nnnnvi r-Ooooii r. These were first identified by T. W. Baldwin, *William Shakspere's Small Latine & Lesse Greeke* (Urbana, 1944), I, 436–7 (the lectures are published anonymously, initialled G.H.). Baldwin cites the second of these lectures as providing a list of 'most recommended' books for students; this is incidentally true, but slightly misleading, since what Harvey in fact gives is a list of frequently encountered books with *Greek titles* (e.g. Mantuan's *Eclogae*, Erasmus's *Apophthegmata*) of which the student with no Greek will be unable to appreciate the significance (fo.Nnnnviii r).
   An excellent survey of the work done to date on Harvey's marginalia, together with a detailed discussion (and transcription) of the marginalia in Harvey's copy of Erasmus's *Parabolae sive Similia*, is to be found in J.-C. Margolin, 'Gabriel Harvey, lecteur d'Erasme', *Arquivos do Centro Cultural Português*, IV (1972), 37–92. W. G. J. Colman, of the Department of English Literature, University of Ghent, Belgium is in the process of transcribing all the marginalia in works known to have been owned by Harvey, in English libraries. He intends to produce a much needed new edition of the so-called 'letter book' in the Sloane collection.
[2] See V. F. Stern, 'The *Bibliotheca* of Gabriel Harvey', *Renaissance Quarterly* (1972), 13.
[3] Some of the most interesting marginalia are in Harvey's Quintilian; Joannes de Sacro Bosco, *Textus de Sphaera* (Parisiis, 1527); *Gnomologiae; sive sententiae collectaneae, et similia, ex Demosthenis orationibus et epistolis* . . . (Basiliae, no date). For a characterisation of Harvey's literary interests see Moore Smith, pp. 52–6; Margolin, 'Gabriel Harvey', pp.40–5.

extends this title to one other 'modern' pedagogue, Angelus Decembrius, author of the *Politia Literaria*:[1]

Angelus Decembrius (at one time orator at Milan) calls [Quintilian's] Institutes 'mirificus' in his *Politia Literaria*. That Angelus comes next after Valla as Critic, nor would anyone today claim otherwise. After him came Rodolphus Agricola, also a most acute Critic in his time: also a distinguished eulogist, imitator, emulator, and occasionally censurer of Quintilian. But as fair as he was frank.[2]

Decembrius's work is a collection of widely ranging comments and observations on the comparative merits of various Greek and Latin literary classics, the best works to read in pursuit of literary elegance (*politia literaria*), the case for the authenticity or inauthenticity of dubious classical texts, and points of Latin and Greek philology and etymology. It is written in the form of a series of pseudo-Socratic dialogues, which are supposed to be conducted between the members of the circle of humanists led by Guarino Veronese under the patronage of Leonello d'Este in fifteenth-century Ferrara.[3] In the sixteenth-century editions of the *Politia Literaria* much is made of the light shed by the work on the activities and attitudes of classic Italian humanism.[4] The models which Decembrius chooses for the task are Aulus Gellius's *Noctes Atticae* and Quintilian's *Institutio Oratoria*.[5]

[1] Angelus Decembrius (*ca* 1415–*ca* 1466). The *Politia Literaria* was published in 1462. See M. E. Cosenza, *Biographical and bibliographical dictionary of the Italian humanists . . . 1300–1500*, 6 vols. (Boston, Mass., 1962–7), II, 1195. I have used the edition of 1562, published in Basle. Harvey praises Decembrius's work repeatedly, and ranks him with Valla and Agricola as the great followers of Quintilian. See e.g.: 'Interest doctiorum, esse exemplaria indoctorum. Turpe eruditis ab indoctis superari. Vel solus Quinctilianus praeclare docebit eruditos egregie vincere ineruditos. Ut quidem eximie docuit Vallam, Decembrium, Rodolph*um*, nonnullos alios, suis maioribus conspicue praecellentes' (Moore Smith, p.113).

[2] Harvey's Quintilian, p.2 (not in Moore Smith): 'Mirificus illius institutiones appellat Angelus Decembrius, orator olim Mediolanensis, in sua ad eruditissimum pon¹'ficem politia literaria. Proximus Vallae Criticus accedebat ille suorum Angelus, nec hac aetate contemnendus. Postea emersit Rodolphus Agricola, acerrimus etiam suo aeuo Criticus: idemque praeclarus Quintiliani et praedicator, et imitator, et aemulus, et interdum Censor. Sed tam candidus, quam liber.'

[3] The only secondary source on the *Politia Literaria* is A. della Guardia's rather anecdotal little work, *La Politia Literaria di Angelo Decembrio e l'umanesimo a Ferrara nella prima metà del sec. XV* (Modena, 1910). On Decembrius's debt to critical attitudes of Guarino see R. Sabbadini, *La scuola e gli studi di Guarino Guarini Veronese* (Catania, 1896), pp.52, 153–4.

[4] See, for example, *Angeli Decembrii . . . de Politia literaria libri septem . . .* (Basiliae, 1562), fo.α3 r. The frontispiece to the edition of Augustae Vindelicorum, 1540, shows Guarino, Vegius, Decembrius, Aretinus, Poggius and Gualengus in earnest debate round an open book. For Gualengus see Cosenza: 'Gualengo, Giovanni: in the literary "circle" of Guarinus at Ferrara: Sabbadini; "Scuola", p.153'.

[5] Angelus Decembrius, ed. cit. p.4: 'Quae quidem ingentes virtutes tuae a nobis eo maiore preconio dignae viderentur, quo minor esse soleat in ecclesiae nostrae pontificibus anti-

As a group, therefore, the three works of Valla, Agricola and Decembrius singled out by Harvey are presented as offering genuine insight into a humanist tradition in education,[1] with dialectic as the crucial field for clarifying the issues at stake.

It is striking that for Harvey *dialectic* continues to occupy a crucial position in a literary and humanistic programme of study, and that he regarded this as not merely consistent with, but directly modelled on the example of Quintilian. Nor do I think that Harvey is exceptional in holding this view (although as a pronounced radical he may lie on the extreme wing of contemporary pedagogic thinking). From the inventories of books owned by students in the four-year arts course in Cambridge at this time (preserved amongst the probate records in the University Archives) one learns that most owned Aristotle's *Ethics* and *Politics*, Terence, Cicero's *Orations*, Virgil, Horace, and Ovid's *Metamorphoses*, and that the majority owned at least one humanist dialectic manual, usually Agricola's. Many owned little else apart from an assortment of dictionaries, Bibles, elementary Greek grammars, catechisms, arithmetic primers and collections of commonplaces.[2] Far from suggesting a scholastic

quae Romanaeque scribendi familiaritas; inde optimo consilio effectum est, ut quam librum eius principis perpetuo nomini dicandum arbitrarer, non minus gloriae tuae immortalitati conficerem. Cuius futuram seriem ut brevibus intelligas, seu ad opus A. Gellii Noctium Atticarum, seu potius ad Quintiliani institutionem oratoriam formatus est, partium et librorum opportunitate eadem fere servata.'

[1] In the passage in the *Politia Literaria* in which Quintilian's *Instituto Oratoria* is called 'mirificus', book ten of that work is singled out for attention: 'Et quoniam ulterius de Ciceronis etiam operibus mentio fiet, ad huius oratoris de eloquentia praecepta, Quintiliani mirificas institutiones non indigne censeo associandas: quanquam ex eis fuere qui librum duntaxat decimum, vel certe aliis praestantiorem, eligerent. Eius vero declamationibus in tali genere nihil aeque comparabile legitur, quasi id opus pro rhetorica et arte oratoria summa, ad Ciceronis aemulationem composuerit. Sane multo elegantius quam Seneca suas edidit' (ed. cit. pp.33–4). To judge from the marginal annotations in Harvey's Quintilian, he gave particular attention to the study of book ten, and appears to have lectured from it in his capacity as professor of rhetoric. It is at the end of book ten, which is particularly heavily annotated, that Harvey has inscribed in a careful hand: 'Gabriel Harvejus, Rhetoricus Professor Cantabrig. 1573. 1574. 1575.' Against the second page of this book in his edition (wrongly paginated 497) Harvey notes: 'Liber, istorum omnium maxime singularis' (not in Moore Smith). For further influence of Decembrius on Harvey, compare the etymological argument in Harvey's published Greek lectures with Decembrius's discussion of the usefulness of Greek studies for understanding Roman culture (etymology of borrowed words, etc.), and his praise of Homer as inspirer of Virgil with Decembrius's comments on the same subject.

[2] See Jardine, 'Humanism and the sixteenth-century Cambridge arts course', *History of Education* 4 (1975), 16–31. Some members of the university, of course (particularly older members), had much more extensive, specialist libraries. But the smaller, non-specialist collections are remarkably alike in their content.

conservatism, the fact that dialectic, the reformed dialectic of Valla and Agricola modelled on Cicero and Quintilian, retained its central position in the four-year arts course in Cambridge goes a considerable way towards justifying the claim that this was essentially a humanist programme of study.

10

POETICS, RHETORIC, AND LOGIC IN RENAISSANCE CRITICISM

W. S. HOWELL

I

The interrelations of poetics, rhetoric, and logic in Renaissance criticism are so imperfectly understood by present-day British and American literary scholars as to suggest that we need either to cease expressing opinions altogether about this aspect of literary history or to re-examine it with a view to discovering what its true contours really were. I propose to follow the latter course and try to describe those contours. In line with the stated objectives of the Conference, I shall limit myself to the consideration of what needs most urgently to be done in connection with my own particular topic.

II

As I see it, Renaissance criticism recognised three distinct literatures and took the differences and similarities among them so much for granted that the modern literary student might at first glance be unaware of them as three distinct entities. These literatures relate to my present topic. That is to say, there was in the Renaissance a literature which owed its primary allegiance to what critics of that time called dialectic or logic; there was a literature which owed its primary allegiance to rhetoric, in the full classical sense of that term; and there was a literature, the most remarkable of all, which owed its primary allegiance to poetical theory, or to poetics, or to what was called poesy in the critical writing of that time. These three literatures define the boundaries within which my present topic falls.

III

Logical writings and rhetorical writings of the Renaissance may respectively be called the literature of the fist and the literature of the open hand. I derive these names from what Zeno the Stoic had originally said and Renaissance writers had often repeated, in describing the differences between logic and rhetoric. Logic is to rhetoric, declared Zeno, as the fist to the palm. This neat metaphor became a kind of refrain in the critical writings of the British Renaissance. Thomas Wilson echoed it, as did Francis Bacon, John Donne, and many others.

Since these two literatures are the subject of a book I published in 1956,[1] and since we are asked to speak in the present conference, not of what has been, but of what needs to be, done, I am not going to discuss them at any length here. All I should like to do for them now is to remind you that each of these literatures sought to convert the sum of things, that is, the meanings which men gave things, into statements that would exactly match those meanings; and that the matching process, the fitting of language to idea, produced in the case of logic a plain and naked style, and a literary form called argumentation, whereas in the case of rhetoric it produced a style full of fresh colours and goodly ornaments, and a literary form called oratory or persuasions.[2] It was Francis Bacon who distinguished memorably between these two literatures by making logical writings the typical mode of address for the learned audience, and rhetorical compositions, the typical mode for the popular audience. Logic differs from rhetoric, said Bacon, 'not only as the fist from the palm, the one close the other at large; but much more in this, that Logic handleth reason exact and in truth, and Rhetoric handleth it as it is planted in popular opinions and manners'.[3] And he amplified this precept by adding that 'the proofs and demonstrations of Logic are toward all men indifferent and the same; but the proofs and persuasions of Rhetoric ought to differ according to the auditors'. The target of both rhetoric and logic, Bacon said, was the human reason, capable in itself of perceiving the difference between truth and falsehood, disposed by its nature to follow truth, able on many occasions to prevail upon the human will to accept the truth, once

[1] *Logic and Rhetoric in England, 1500–1700* (Princeton, New Jersey: Princeton University Press, 1956); (New York: Russell & Russell, Inc., 1961). Cited below as Howell. For references to Zeno's metaphor, see pp.15, 33, 51, 141, 208–9, 293, 315, 320, 341, 365, 374, 377.

[2] Howell, pp.14–15, 98–108.

[3] *The Works of Francis Bacon*, ed. James Spedding, Robert Leslie Ellis, Douglas Denon Heath (Boston, 1860–5), VI, 300. Cited below as *Works of Bacon*.

it has been perceived, but constantly threatened in the latter endeavour by the rival influence upon the will of the human imagination and human passions. These latter faculties, Bacon held, are also disposed to follow goodness and truth, but they cannot by themselves distinguish between the transient and the permanent values in those conceptual states, only the reason being able to do that.[1] Thus logic, in Bacon's total view, is the literature that addresses itself to the reason alone, when such an address is sufficient to prevail upon the will; and rhetoric, the literature ˙which seeks '*to apply Reason to Imagination* for the better moving of the will', on those occasions when the imagination and passions are driving mankind towards the goals of transient rather than permanent goodness.[2] As to the rôle of rhetoric in these transactions, Bacon made clear that it does not play the part of evil minister. It does not play self-servingly upon the passions or the imagination. It is not hostile to truth and reason. It simply does what needs on many occasions to be done if human conduct is to realise the highest potentialities of the human soul – it brings the imagination, in Bacon's words, 'to second reason, and not to oppress it'.[3]

In connection with Renaissance logic and rhetoric, and with Renaissance poetics, too, for that matter, it should always be remembered by present-day scholars that Aristotle was the great authority behind what Renaissance criticism took as its basic doctrines. The six books of Aristotle's *Organon*, and in particular the *Topica*, were the ultimate source of Renaissance treatises on logic. It was Aristotle's *Rhetoric* which taught Bacon that rhetorical compositions had as their characteristic target 'an audience of untrained thinkers',[4] and that the units of thought in the literature of the open hand must be identified as statements and proofs.[5] And it was Aristotle's *Poetics* which taught Renaissance criticism that oratory, history, and scientific exposition were set apart from genuinely poetic literature by a certain unique element in the latter.[6] Modern scholars have forgotten that unique element, with the result that they speak of Renaissance poetics as if it were a branch of rhetoric.

---

[1] *Works of Bacon*, VI, 297–9.   [2] Ibid. VI, 297.   [3] Ibid. VI, 298.
[4] *Rhetorica*, 1357a10–12. Trans. W. Rhys Roberts, in *The Works of Aristotle*, ed. W. D. Ross (Oxford, 1924), XI.
[5] Ibid. 1414a30.
[6] *De Poetica*, 1447b10–20; 1451a–b. My discussion of Aristotle's *Poetics* is based upon the translation by Ingram Bywater in *The Works of Aristotle*, ed. W. D. Ross (Oxford, 1924), XI.

Let us now examine that unique element and its consequences for Renaissance criticism.

IV

Although Zeno's metaphor indicates to perfection the spirit of the relations between logical composition and rhetorical composition as Renaissance critics saw these two literatures, the contrast between fist and palm cannot be made to shed light upon what those critics believed poetical composition to be. They never said, for example, that poetry stated the tightfisted truths of logic in the openhanded style of rhetoric. For them, such a statement could not have finally differentiated poetry from oratory. What they did instead was to envisage poetry as a particularly gifted way of revealing truth through the linguistic forms of stories or fictions, whereas oratory and learned argument revealed truth through statements and demonstrations.

The key idea of Renaissance critics is that poetry is fable, and fable, poetry. To them fable was equivalent to the Latin word *fabula*, and it meant primarily a narrative of imagined characters taking part in imagined events. The characters could be gods, or heroes, or kings, or nobles, or knights, or commoners; they could also be monsters, or animals, or even inanimate things, speaking and acting like human beings. The events could be mythical, or legendary, or fictitious, or quasi-historical, or historical. The imaginings could be presented in realistic terms, or in terms of romance, or allegory. The end sought could be amusement with or without barbs of meaning capable of pricking the ordinary conscience or the conscience of a hearer-king. But regardless of its particular guise on a given occasion, the fable was understood to be the principle which made poetry what it was, and which distinguished it from all other literary kinds, that is to say, from all compositions falling within the two literatures just discussed.

Renaissance witnesses to the existence of this theory of poetry are numerous and influential. I do not have space here to quote their opinions on the nature of the poem, nor to discuss them. But I shall at least name some of thcsc witnesses, even if with this audience such a procedure is hardly necessary. For one, there is Thomas Wilson, who in his *Arte of Rhetorique* found occasion to define poetry as fable, and to rest his judgement upon Plutarch, Basilius Magnus,

158

and Erasmus.[1] For another, there is Sir Philip Sidney, whose *Defense of Poesy* has been said to be a rhetorical approach to its subject, but who confounds that judgement completely not only by repeatedly insisting upon the generic difference between the poem and the oration, but also by stressing time and again that poems proceed by fictions, not by the less-complicated rhetorical method of direct statements.[2] In addition to Sidney, there is Sir John Harington, who read Sidney's *Defense* in manuscript, and who subscribed fully to Sidney's view that fiction and poetry are one and the same thing.[3] Then, too, there is Sir Francis Bacon, whose theory of poetry is so often underemphasised or disparaged by literary scholars of the twentieth century. Bacon defined the substance of the poem by calling poesy feigned history, that is, imagined narrative as distinguished from historical narrative.[4] And above all there is Ben Jonson, who in his *Timber* remarked that 'the Fable and Fiction is (as it were) the forme and Soule of any Poeticall worke, or *Poeme*'.[5]

The source of this theory of poetry, as Renaissance critics repeatedly acknowledged, is Aristotle's *Poetics*. In that work, Aristotle taught that poetry involved mimesis and mythos, that is, imitation and plot; and the Renaissance view that poetry is fable or fiction is a brilliant synthesis of those two Aristotelian concepts. Nowhere is the connection between Renaissance poetical theory, on the one hand, and Aristotle's *Poetics*, on the other, more perceptively recognised than in Mr Leonard James Potts's evaluation of the definition which I just now quoted from Ben Jonson. Says Mr Potts: 'Jonson himself was a conscientious scholar, inclined more than any of our other great writers to be guided by critical principles in his own poetry and drama, and he came as near to a correct interpretation of Aristotle's general theory of poetry as any of them has. He saw clearly that by poetry Aristotle meant *fiction* . . .'[6] These words are, I believe, a dependable guide for the modern scholar in search of the Renaissance conception, and the Aristotelian conception, of poetry. These words occur in the introduction to

1 *Wilson's Arte of Rhetorique 1560*, ed. G. H. Mair (Oxford: Clarendon Press, 1909), pp.47, 195.
2 Sir Philip Sidney, *The Defense of Poesy*, ed. Albert S. Cook (Boston, 1890), pp.3, 8, 11, 23, 25, 36.
3 G. Gregory Smith, *Elizabethan Critical Essays* (Oxford, 1904), I, xcii; II, 201, 204, 422.
4 *Works of Bacon*, VI, 202–6; VIII, 439–69.
5 *Ben Jonson*, ed. C. H. Herford, Percy and Evelyn Simpson (Oxford, 1925–52), VIII, 635.
6 L. J. Potts, *Aristotle on the Art of Fiction* (Cambridge: University Press, 1968), pp.6–7.

Mr Potts's English translation of Aristotle's *Poetics*, first published at Cambridge in 1953. Mr Potts deserves great credit, not only for speaking as he did of Ben Jonson, but also for having the creative genius to bring his translation out under the title *Aristotle on the Art of Fiction.*

v

The functions assigned to poetry by Renaissance critics, that is to say, by Sidney, by Harington, by William Webbe, by Thomas Nashe, and by Ben Jonson, were centred in the idea that poetry should teach and delight. Indeed, this aspect of my present subject is so well known as barely to require mention. Also well known is the fact that Renaissance poetics acknowledged its having borrowed these two terms from Horace's *Ars Poetica*. But what is not often remembered is that Aristotle's *Poetics* also recognises that poetry has these same two functions. Aristotle mentions the pleasure that narrative poetry gives its readers, and he mentions the delight which all of us find in works of imitation; but, by explaining this latter reaction as the product of our feeling that the imitation is teaching us something at the moment when we take delight in it, Aristotle plainly indicates that the aesthetic and the didactic functions of art operate simultaneously upon us.[1] Furthermore, there can be no doubt whatever that the pity and fear aroused by a tragic drama were considered by Aristotle to be not only a deeply emotional response on the part of spectators in the theatre but also an experience which taught them values and insights previously half guessed and half understood. Thus, when Horace recognised the didactic as well as the aesthetic dimensions of poetry, he could claim to be following the authority of Aristotle's *Poetics*. Modern scholars have often said that Horace borrowed from Ciceronian rhetoric the idea of a didactic function for poetry, and that, in so doing, he gave his *Ars Poetica* a dominantly rhetorical cast, which Renaissance criticism is to be condemned for having thoughtlessly adopted.[2] This argument

[1] *De Poetica*, chs.4, 23.
[2] See, for example, M. H. Abrams, *The Mirror and the Lamp* (New York: Oxford University Press, 1953), pp.15–16; also Brian Vickers, *Classical Rhetoric in English Poetry* (London: Macmillan and Co., Ltd, 1970), pp.25–6; also M. T. Herrick, 'Rhetoric and Poetics', in *Encyclopedia of Poetry and Poetics* (Princeton, New Jersey: Princeton University Press, 1965), p.702.

seems, however, to reflect more of a tendency to disparage than to understand what Aristotle intended rhetoric to be. A poetical theory would be rhetorical, in Aristotle's view, only if it asserted that poetry should proceed to its pleasurable and didactic ends by statement and proof rather than by mimesis or fiction. And by that standard Horace's *Ars Poetica* and the most influential of Renaissance poetical theories are not rhetorical to the slightest degree.

VI

What then needs to be done by modern scholarship in its approach to Renaissance literary theory? The answer is clear. Modern scholars must recognise rhetoric for what it was in classical times and in the Renaissance, not for what our present-day prejudices towards it would make it out to have been. Modern scholars must also recognise logic for what classical and Renaissance authors held it to be when they wrote about it and used it to guide one important part of their literary activity. But above all modern scholars must recognise poetics in classical and Renaissance terms if they want to speak instructively of Renaissance poetical theory. And if they really adopt those terms, they will not be inclined to find rhetoric lurking alone behind every figure of thought and speech in the plays of Shakespeare or Marlowe. Figures of thought and speech are the common property of oratory and poetry, and a common property of these two separate arts cannot fairly be claimed to have the capacity to change either one of them into the other. Figures of thought and speech are necessary for the statements and proofs of rhetoric, if an oration is to influence a popular audience. Figures of thought and speech are necessary for the fictions of poetry, too. But the function of figurative language in a rhetorical statement is less complicated than in a mimesis; for in the mimesis the figure must have a rhetorical function within an imagined plot, and a poetic function in contributing to the poet's desire to make that plot take hold of his own proper audience in theatre or study. In short, a figure in a poem has two different functions with two distinct audiences; but a figure in an oration reaches only one audience and thus has only one function, that of making a reasonable statement appealing to the imagination of the hearers addressed. These nuances of the classical period and of the

Renaissance, and the other nuances which I have been discussing, must be recovered by modern scholarship if we are to see the proper relations of rhetoric and logic to poetics in the literary theorising of British authors of the sixteenth and seventeenth centuries.

11

LUCAN IN DER KRITIK DES 16.
UND 17. JAHRHUNDERTS

H. DÖRRIE

Lucan ist in den nach-humanistischen Jahrhunderten zum ersten Beispiel dafür geworden, daß man eine bis zur Ablehnung kritische Haltung einem lateinischen Autor gegenüber gewann. Zuvor hatte alles, was aus der Antike überkommen war, unbestritten Wert und Geltung; wohl hat man stets verglichen, oft auch differenziert; immer ist Lucan neben Vergil gestellt, aber eben in Relation zu Vergil auch anerkannt worden. Jetzt wird – aus Gründen, die hier dargestellt werden sollen – dem Lucan abgesprochen, daß er unter die Dichter gerechnet werden dürfe. Das 18. Jahrhundert hat das zuvor umstrittene Verdict Lucans nahezu einmütig übernommen.

Nun hat es im 16. und im 17. Jahrh. an positiver, oft an Begeisterung grenzender Stellungnahme für Lucan nicht gefehlt. Selbstverständlich ist es in erster Linie die Bewunderung für Lucan, die auf die Dichtung jener Jahrhunderte gewirkt und vielerlei Responsion hervorgerufen hat. Aber es wurden Stimmen laut – und diese Stimmen sollten hernach durchdringen – die eben vor derart von Emphase getragener Bewunderung warnten.

Die knappe Skizze dieser Entwicklung, die ich hier vorlegen möchte, wird die Kontroversen um Lucan in drei Schritten darstellen. Die Bewunderung für Lucan wurde aus zwei Quellen gespeist; neben eine rein literarische Würdigung Lucans (von der zuerst die Rede sein soll), trat ein politisch motiviertes Bekenntnis zu Lucan; denn in ihm sah man den Dichter, der für die republikanische Freiheit und gegen Tyrannen aufrief. Hiervon soll an zweiter Stelle die Rede sein. Drittens endlich habe ich darzustellen, wieso Lucan durch die Wertungen einer rational begründeten Poetik vom Parnass verwiesen wurde.

I

Die vielfältige Diskussion, die im 14. und 15. Jahrh. über Lucan geführt wurde, kann hier nicht nachgezeichnet werden; schon Petrarca war sich des ungemeinen Abstandes bewußt, der Lucan von Vergil trennt. Hernach sind die Humanisten zu differenzierendem und dabei ausgewogenem Urteil über beide gelangt. Denn noch wurde die gesamte antike Dichtung als eine Schatzkammer angesehen, von deren Kostbarkeiten die neuen Dichter angemessenen Gebrauch machen sollten. Es war also legitim – und Petrarca ist in seiner Africa darin vorausgegangen – Lucan auszuwerten, wenn die Stilhöhe, die man einzuhalten beabsichtigte, das als angemessen erscheinen ließ. Im Ganzen genommen kam es nicht so sehr darauf an, über einzelne Dichter objektive Urteile zu fällen, als vielmehr zum richtigen Gebrauch der durch ihr hohes Alter empfohlenen Dichter anzuleiten.

So ist Lucan bis weit in das 17. Jahrh. hinein der Lehrmeister des pathetischen Stiles gewesen. Was Ed. Fraenkel vor allem für Petrarca und seine Zeitgenossen aufgezeigt hat, das gilt für alle Dichter – vor allem für Italiener und Deutsche – die in seiner Nachfolge stehen.

Kaum einer von diesen ist bei textgerechter Wiedergabe einzelner Figuren Lucans stehen geblieben. Sondern hier herrscht das Gesetz, daß man Lucanisches nicht einfach nachahmt, sondern daß man es, von Lucan inspiriert, überhöht und überbietet.[1] Hugo Grotius gab mit einem gewissen Stolz zu,[2] daß er dichtend vom Geiste Lucans erfüllt sei. Bald wurde es zum Ehrentitel, *Lucano ipso lucanior*[3] zu schreiben. Es wäre ungenügend, das, was da stattfand, eine Rezeption zu nennen. Wer immer sich dem Lucan öffnete, wurde eben dadurch genötigt, ihn zu überbieten. Dieser Satz gilt ganz besonders für die Übersetzungen, die im Zeitalter des Barock erschienen.[4]

---

[1] Das hat Cl. Schlayer gut und klar für die spanische Literatur nachgewiesen. Mit Recht hat sie sich nicht auf den Nachweis textlicher Gleichungen beschränkt, sondern sie hat gerade das oft Hypertrophe der lukanisierenden Umsetzungen hervorgehoben. Eben dieser Vorzug ihrer Arbeit ist von mehreren Kritikern verkannt worden.

[2] So in der Vorrede zu seinen opera omnia: 'agnosco me ipse . . . Lucani spiritus plenum . . .'

[3] Das war ein Wort der Kritik, das zunächst gegen die Lucan-Übersetzung von G. de Bréboeuf (1655) gerichtet worden war – ein Wort, das ein wohl hörbares und zugleich wohl gehörtes Lob einschloß.

[4] Zu den Übersetzungen von Jauregui (spanisch: 1640 abgeschlossen, 1684 veröffentlicht), G. de Bréboeuf (1655) und Veit Ludwig von Seckendorff (gest. 1692, veröffentlicht 1695) sind Monographien erschienen, deren Verfasser unabhängig von einander und mit kaum verhohlenem Erstaunen eben dies feststellen: Nicht Übersetzungen, sondern Nach- und Neu-Dichtungen – also Versionen im eigentlichen Sinne liegen dort vor.

Schon jetzt ist die Zahl der Belege, da Reminiszenzen aus Lucan auf andere Stoffe übertragen wurden, kaum mehr zu überblicken; jede Analyse, vor allem von Zeugen manieristischer Dichtung, fördert Weiteres zu Tage. Zugleich aber eröffnete sich ein Wirkungsbereich, der zuvor nicht zur Verfügung stand – das war die Tragödie. Längst war Lucan als ein *poeta tragicus* anerkannt[1] – was Wunder, wenn man aus dem vielfach geeigneten Stoff der *Pharsalia* ganze Gruppen von tragischen Stoffen gewann – den Tod des Pompeius,[2] das Leid der Cornelia,[3] die Verherrlichung Catos,[4] das skandalöse Zusammentreffen von Caesar und Kleopatra.[5]

Durch solche Zeugnisse, die in großer Zahl vorliegen, scheint dem Nachwirken Lucans eine Breite und eine Intensität attestiert zu sein wie kaum je zuvor; es kann garnicht geleugnet werden, daß das Pathos in der Dichtung, vor allem in der Tragödie, nur zum Teil von Seneca, in hohem Maße aber von Lucan beeinflußt ist.

II

Zugleich gewann Lucan eine unbestreitbare politische Aktualität; man hätte also meinen sollen, daß eine derartige, zuvor nicht geübte Nutzanwendung antiker Dichtung auf Aktuelles das Ansehen Lucans erheblich hätte stärken müssen.

Denn als im 17. Jahrh. über Machiavelli hinaus und oft schon in Opposition zu Machiavelli[6] die Frage neu erörtert wurde, wo denn die rechtliche Grundlage zu suchen sei, ist sogleich die

---

Der englische Übersetzer, Thomas May (1626), als solcher weit wörtlicher als die zuvor Genannten, nahm in anderer Richtung die Autonomie des Nachvollzuges in Anspruch: Er dichtete die *Pharsalia* bis zum (von Lucan vielleicht gewollten) Ende weiter: Bis zum Tode Caesars.

[1] D. Heinsius: *De tragoediae constitutione* (1610, im Anhang zur Ausg. von Aristoteles' *Poetik*): '*Pharsaliam* inter tragoedias numerare audeo sive actionem sive elocutionem video.'

[2] Hier ist P. Corneille: *La mort de Pompée* (1643) von zentraler Bedeutung geworden, obwohl er mit solcher Wahl des Stoffes keineswegs am Anfang steht.

[3] So Robert Garnier: *Cornélie* (1574).

[4] Hier muß auf den großen Widerhall hingewiesen werden, den die Cato-Tragödie von Addison besonders in Italien fand.

[5] Es würde lohnen, im Einzelnen darzustellen, wie bewußt und wie vollständig G. B. Shaw sein Stück *Caesar and Cleopatra* in Gegensatz zu Lucan gerückt hat; ihm ist eine gänzliche Delucanisation gelungen.

[6] Im 7. der *Gesichte Philanders von Sittewald* führt Moscherosch staatsrechtliche Argumentationen ein, die er aus Lucan herübernimmt. Denn Lucan läßt im 8. Buche seines Epos den Pothinus das Dogma von der Staatsräson vortragen, die das Verbrechen an Pompeius rechtfertigt. Moscherosch macht sein Zitat aus Lucan ganz deutlich: Sein Photinus tritt in der Rolle eines Mephisto auf; was er mit ständiger Beziehung auf Lucan ausführt, kennzeichnet *e contrario* die Überzeugungen Moscherosch's.

Gegensätzlichkeit der großen Dichter erkannt und beleuchtet worden: Aus Vergil war in der Tat eine Begründung dafür zu gewinnen, wieso göttlicher Ratschluß den Friedenskaiser Augustus in sein Amt berief. Lucan dagegen führt – für das 17. Jahrh. vollauf verständlich – den Gedanken des Gottesgnadentums *ad absurdum*: Die Götter haben sich geirrt, ja sie waren zu schwächlich, als sie Caesar den Sieg gewährten. Nicht das Urteil der Götter, sondern das Urteil Catos hat objektive Gültigkeit:

victrix causa deis placuit, sed victa Catoni.[1]

Zudem sollte man nicht übersehen, daß die Zeichnung von Caesar und seinen Erfolgen, so wie Lucan sie darstellt, die Leser des 16. und 17. Jahrh. auf das frappanteste an die Condottieri der jüngsten Vergangenheit erinnern mußte. Dann aber kam der Staatsgründung durch Caesar und seinen Nachfolger nicht mehr an Legitimität zu als den Gründungen der damals gegenwärtigen Glücksritter.

Vor allem ist Lucans gewaltiges Pathos, das sich für die Freiheit und gegen die Unterdrückung einsetzt, als etwas ganz Wichtiges zu veranschlagen. Wenn Montaigne an Lucan nicht so sehr die Vortrefflichkeit des Stiles, sondern vor allem 'la vérité de ses opinions et jugemens' rühmt, dann ist der Hintergrund solchen Lobes unverkennbar. Alle Urteile – 'jugemens' – die Lucan äußert, zielen ja auf die Frage nach dem, was Recht und was Unrecht ist.[2] Weit deutlicher hat sich Hugo Grotius ausgesprochen,[3] der Lucan als Freiheitsdichter – *poeta phileleutheros* – rühmt und der sich einen Beitrag zur politischen Erziehung davon verspricht, wenn seine Landsleute Lucan lesen.[4] G. de Bréboeuf endlich empfiehlt Lucan seinen Lesern darum, weil Lucan offen habe tun dürfen, was die jetzt Lebenden nicht wagen dürfen – nämlich einen Tyrannen anzugreifen und an den Pranger zu stellen.[5] In der Form viel maßvoller, und ohne den Versuch zu machen, Lucan für Einzelnes

---

[1] Lucan, *De bello civili*, 1.128.
[2] Dieses General-Thema gliedert sich in mehrere Unter-Themen auf, von denen die wichtigsten diese sind: Cato und die Republik, deren Gegner, die Halbherzigkeit derer, die zur Verteidigung der Freiheit aufgerufen waren, und endlich der Unrechtsstaat in Ägypten.
[3] Die hierzu einschlägigen Äußerungen hat Oudendorp in der *praefatio* zu seiner Ausgabe (1728) zusammengestellt.
[4] Hierzu spricht H. Grotius dieses aus: 'in summa dignus quem mei Batavi legant ut quo magis amant vatem Hispanum, eo Hispanum regem implacabilius oderint'.
[5] So in der Vorrede zum 4. Teil der Übersetzung (1655). Das wurde geschrieben zwei Jahre nachdem der gegen Mazarin frondierende Adel in Frankreich unterlegen war.

zu aktualisieren, sprechen Thomas Farnaby[1] und Thomas May.[2] Durch sie kommt ein Humanismus zu Wort, der aus und durch Lucan Grundlagen einer politischen Erziehung gewinnen möchte.

III

Hiergegen ist kaum Widerspruch geäußert worden.[3] Und auch der literarische Rang Lucans ist nicht, wie damals üblich, durch ein Streitgespräch, eine *querelle*,[4] zur Person und zur Sache geklärt worden. Sondern es ist, fast unversehens, eine Entscheidung auf Lucan angewendet worden, die im Bereiche des Grundsätzlichen gefallen war.

Mitten in der Barock-Zeit ist die Frage nach der Regelhaftigkeit von Kunstwerken gestellt worden. Und diese Frage ist keineswegs 'im barocken Sinne' beantwortet worden. Sondern man ließ sich von Kriterien leiten, die man antiken Autoren, vor allem Aristoteles und Horaz, entnahm.

Hier las man, daß alle Dichtung einfach, wahr und der Natur (also auch der Vernunft) gemäß sein solle. Damit sind die Werte bezeichnet, auf die man – vom älteren Scaliger bis auf Boileau – die Forderungen der Poetik gründete. Folgerichtig war Julius Caesar Scaliger[5] der erste, der Lucan schlechthin verwarf. Und rund 200 Jahre nach ihm gab Marmontel[6] Rechenschaft darüber, warum sehr viele Lucan ablehnen: 'Ceux qui n'ont lu que Boileau, méprisent Lucain': eindeutig ist damit – jedenfalls für Frankreich – Boileau als der Urheber des Lucan verdammenden Urteils bezeichnet.[7]

Zuvor bezogen sich literarische Urteile vorwiegend darauf,

---

[1] Thomas Farnabius, in der Vorrede zum Kommentar zu Lucans *Pharsalia*, 1618.

[2] Thomas May, Vorrede zur Übersetzung Lucans, 1626.

[3] Erst später (1740) rügte P. Burman, daß Lucan Caesars Bild in unerlaubter Weise verzeichnet habe. Durchaus bemerkt wurde die entschiedene Ablehnung durch Ludwig XIV in Person: Dieser untersagte es, Lucans Gedicht unter die Bücher *ad usum Delphini* einzureihen; von dem Gift, das dieses Buch enthält, sollte der Dauphin nicht infiziert werden.

[4] Soviel ich sehe, hat einzig Palmerius = Jacques Le Paulmier die Formen der *querelle* gewahrt; er schrieb 1629 eine *apologia Lucani* gegen das Urteil des Joseph Justus Scaliger über Lucan.

[5] So in der *Poetik* (= *poetices libri septem*), 1. Aufl. 1561.

[6] So in den *éléments de littérature*, den Beiträgen zur Enzyklopädie, die Marmontel 1765–7 verfaßte, und die 1787 gesammelt veröffentlicht wurden.

[7] Hinter der unbestreitbaren Festellung ist einige Ironie verborgen: Die Verächter Lucans haben ein zu schmales Fundament; ihr Urteil ist einseitig auf Boileau gegründet. Denn etwas Anderes haben sie nicht zur Kenntnis genommen.

wie ein antiker Dichter von modernen Dichtern genutzt werden könne oder solle. Jetzt aber sind Urteile gefällt worden, denen man absolute Gültigkeit zuerkannte. Was Lucan anlangt, so war dessen Kontrast zum Kanon des Wahren, Einfachen und Vernunftgemäßen so krass, daß daraus eine schwerwiegende Folgerung gezogen wurde: Lucan war kein für die Jugend geeigneter Dichter.[1] Die Kritik am Dichter Lucan fällt notwendiger Weise mit der am Menschen Lucan zusammen. Denn das *ingenium* eines Dichters, der vom Kanon des Einfachen, Wahren und Schönen abweicht, muß deformiert sein. Maßlosigkeit und Unnatürlichkeit können aber nicht Vorbild für die heranwachsende Jugend sein – weder im Stilistischen, noch im Moralischen. Das ist eine Beweisführung, die seit J. C. Scaliger auf Lucan angewendet wurde, und die im 19. Jahrh. noch viel nachhaltiger auf Ovid angewendet werden sollte.

Durch diese neue Wertung entfernte man sich vom Humanismus bisheriger Prägung um einen Schritt, der sich als folgenreich erweisen sollte: Das antike Erbe wurde einer Wertung unterworfen, mit dem Ergebnis, daß es in der antiken Dichtung auch Schädliches[2] gibt. Wer eine auf absoluten Werten gegründete Poetik forderte, schloß damit aus, was diesen Werten und Bewertungen nicht entsprach.

Diese Entscheidung ist damals widerspruchslos hingenommen worden. Sie war auf der einen Seite durch beste antike Zeugnisse, vor allem durch die *ars poetica* des Horaz, gestützt. Sie war auf der anderen Seite in sich schlüssig – sie anzugreifen hätte bedeutet, sich zum Anwalt des Entgegengesetzten – also des nicht-Einfachen oder des Unnatürlichen zu machen. Hier liegt der Grund, warum ab und an Stimmen laut werden, die Lucan verteidigen, warum es aber zu einer auf das Grundsätzliche gerichteten *querelle* nicht kommen konnte.

Die Preisgabe Lucans erfolgte allmählich – wahrscheinlich ist man dabei im Jesuiten-Orden vorangegangen, wo Ovid eine geringere Gefahr zu sein schien als Lucan. Noch immer übt Lucan Impulse aus auf die zeitgenössische Dichtung – aber es gibt zu denken,

---

[1] So rückte man im Jesuiten-Orden seit etwa 1600 von Lucan ab. Wohl waren Bidermann wie Balde noch mit Nachdruck auf die Vorzüge Lucans hingewiesen worden. Beide machen aber nur mehr im Formalen Gebrauch von Lucan; zu einer Kontroverse über den Wert Lucans vgl. Joh. Müller: *das Jesuitendrama* etc. (Augsburg, 1930, 1, 27 f.)

[2] Pierre Bayle erklärte im *Dictionnaire* die Silberne Latinität als eine *dépravation du goût*, die er in enge Verbindung zur gleichzeitigen 'Dépravation' der Sitten rückte.

daß unter Ludwig XIV. keine Stimme mehr zu Gunsten Lucans hörbar wird – und wie emphatisch hatten zuvor Corneille und Bréboeuf gesprochen! Das 18. Jahrhundert jedenfalls ist in der Ablehnung Lucans nahezu[1] einig gewesen, bis man – von den 70er Jahren an – Lucan als einen Dichter des Genialischen entdeckte.

So ist Lucan zu einem lehrreichen Beispiel dafür geworden, wohin es führte, als man begann, poetische Forderungen auf absolute Werte zu gründen; die anfangs blühende, vielerlei poetische Kräfte freisetzende Wirkung Lucans hat davon eine tief reichende Beeinträchtigung erfahren. Der barockeste aller lateinischen Dichter ist just zu der Zeit, als das Barock in Europa seinen Gipfel erreichte, vom Parnass verbannt worden. Rationale Grundsätzlichkeit hat sich dabei als schlechthin überlegen erwiesen. So lässt sich am Beispiel Lucans ablesen, wie die barocke Freude am Pathetischen abgelöst wurde durch das Dogma der beginnenden Aufklärung – jenes Dogma, das Rationalität und Geradlinigkeit forderte.

BIBLIOGRAPHIE

Friedrich Gundolf: *Caesar. Geschichte seines Ruhms* (Berlin, 1924).

Eduard Fraenkel: 'Lucan als Mittler des antiken Pathos', *Vorträge der Bibl. Warburg* 4 (1924), 229–57 = *Kleine Beiträge zur klass. Philologie* 2 (Rom, 1964), 233–66.

Clotilde Schlayer: *Spuren Lukans in der spanischen Dichtung*, diss. phil. Heidelberg, 1928.

Walter Fischli: *Studien zum Fortleben der* Pharsalia *des M. Annaeus Lucanus*; Beilage zum Jahresbericht der kantonalen höheren Lehranstalten (Luzern, pro 1943/44).

---

[1] Hier ist vor allem auf die völlig negativen Urteile von Gottsched und von P. Burman zu verweisen. Erst Marmontel ist in der *Poétique françoise* (1763) gegen diese einhellige Ablehnung aufgetreten.

12

PETRUS LOTICHIUS SECUNDUS AND THE ROMAN ELEGISTS: PROLEGOMENA TO A STUDY OF NEO-LATIN ELEGY

W. LUDWIG

Elegy is one of the oldest poetical genres. The earliest extant examples date back to the middle of the seventh century B.C., and it is a term which is still used for poetical productions in our own times.[1] One might like to know how this ancient literary genre which went through surprising changes even in its Greek and Roman history, survived through the ages and how it preserved or changed its characteristics in the various European literatures; but if one expects to find a monograph or a competent article which outlines the development of that genre in its decisive steps from a comparative point of view, one will be seriously disappointed. No attempt has been made to describe the history of elegy by taking into account all the relevant European literatures, and the scholars who have dealt with the history of elegy within the borders of a national literature have been amazingly unaware of or unconcerned with the elegies produced in the neighbouring countries and read perhaps not only there.[2] Often these studies are also preoccupied with an unhistoric notion of what they consider the elegiac principle or

---

[1] The *New York Times Magazine* published a poem by J. Berryman titled 'Formal Elegy' on 4 November 1973. On modern forms of elegy see A. F. Potts, *The Elegiac Mode. Poetic Forms in Wordsworth and Other Elegists* (Cornell U.P., Ithaca, 1967), and K. Weissenberger, *Formen der Elegie von Goethe bis Celan* (Bern, 1969).

[2] To give two examples, the article 'Elegy' in the 1971 *Encyclopaedia Britannica* edition, whose part on modern elegy was written by J. W. Tibble and designed to give a panoramic view, contains, after a 24 line description of English elegies from the sixteenth to the nineteenth century, the laconic statement 'In German literature, elegy as poetry of lamentation does not exist.' A quick look into F. Beissner's *Geschichte der deutschen Elegie* (1st edn Berlin, 1940, 3rd edn 1965), which is still the best description of the history of the genre within the limits of a national literature, would have taught differently. But Beissner too did not pay enough attention to the elegiac production of Italy, France and England and its impact on literary development in Germany.

das Elegische, instead of investigating which concepts of elegy existed in different times and countries, how they developed, and in what way they influenced the reception and production of the poems which were called elegies.[1] Further, no study has adequately explored the Neo-Latin elegy of the fifteenth and sixteenth centuries, although modern elegy started in the Neo-Latin form.[2] The few attempts in the history of Neo-Latin poetry do not compensate for that deficiency.[3] The neglect of the Neo-Latin origins of modern elegy has obscured its very beginnings. I should like to make first a few points in this respect.

Friedrich Beissner emphasised in his monograph titled *Geschichte der deutschen Elegie* that it was a continuation of the medieval *aetas Ovidiana* and its predilection for elegiac distichs, when the humanists used them as their favourite metre.[4] But one should also see that the elegiac distich was certainly used in medieval times for many purposes, but never for a group of middle-sized poems collected within one artistically arranged book and, at least to a large extent, dealing with the passionate and devoted love of the poet for a specific girl. Such books of elegy, which were often titled with the girl's real or poetical name and which tended to consist of a cycle of elegies describing the love affair from its beginning to its end, were written in Italy from the first half of the fifteenth century onwards. Sometimes they also contained a few poems in other metres. The oldest examples which I know are the *Angelinetum* of Giovanni Marrasio, a book of nine elegies, written in Siena before 1429, when the poet was in love with an Angelina Piccolomini,[5] and the *Cinthia*

---

1 The general methods and concepts of research in the history of literary genres have recently been discussed by Klaus W. Hempfer, *Gattungstheorie – Information und Synthese* (Munich, 1973). See his remarks on 'elegy' on pp.130 f.

2 F. Beissner's chapter 'Die Elegie im Zeitalter des Humanismus', pp.46–53, is the weakest in his monograph. J. Wiegand, in *Reallexicon der deutschen Literaturgeschichte* (2nd edn Berlin, 1958), vol.1, pp.332–4 (*s.v.* 'Elegie'), has two short sentences on the elegy of the humanists, and these are wrong. Chr. M. Scollen, *The Birth of the Elegy in France 1500–1550* (Geneva, 1967), offers a short appendix 'Marot's creation of the Elegy and the Neo-Latin elegy', pp.153–6. G. Luck, *The Latin Love Elegy* (2nd edn London, 1969), deals, contrary to expectations which the title could raise, exclusively with the Latin elegy of classical times to which it provides an excellent introduction.

3 The survey of P. van Tieghem, *La littérature Latine de la Renaissance* (Paris, 1944), is too general in its purpose, and the monumental work of G. Ellinger, *Geschichte der neulateinischen Literatur Deutschlands im sechszehnten Jahrhundert*, 3 vols. (Berlin, 1929–33), shows little interest in the concept of poetic genres and their development.

4 See F. Beissner, *Geschichte der deutschen Elegie*, p.47.

5 A. Altamura, *I carmi Latini di Giovanni Marrasio* (Palermo, 1954) (Biblioteca del Centro di Studi Filologici e Linguistici Siciliani 3).

of Enea Silvio Piccolomini.[1] Some time later, around the middle of the fifteenth century, Christophoro Landino wrote his *Xandra*, Tito Vespasiano Strozzi the *Eroticon* which represents his love for a certain Anthia, and Basinio Basini the cycle of love elegies titled *Cyris*. Other humanists followed, including Pontano with his *Amores*.

The basis for this new fashion was a new awareness of and a new interest in the Roman elegists, not just as composers of exemplary elegiac distichs, but as writers of personal love poetry. It would be worthwhile to explore how much the Roman elegists helped these humanist poets to express and articulate their experiences and sentiments and how much the humanists' concept of love and the artistic structure of their elegies owed to Catullus, Tibullus, Propertius and Ovid. But another poetic ancestor should not be overlooked: Petrarch's *Canzoniere*. It contributed motifs and concepts to the humanistic love elegies in varying degrees, and these elegies may even be considered as the humanistic answer to Petrarch's vernacular love poetry. Italian humanists of the fifteenth century who in their love for Latin were looking out for a mode of expression which could be taken as a classical equivalent to the *Rime* had to come upon the Roman elegies and the collection of Catullus, because only there in Latin literature did they find books of poems which described and glorified the prepossessing love of a poet for his *domina*. Thus, elegy was discovered as the Latin equivalent to the Italian sonnet. Matteo Maria Boiardo, the nephew of Tito Vespasiano Strozzi, confirmed this equation from the opposite side, when he chose to write Petrarchan sonnets about his love for Antonia Caprara, by giving his collection the Ovidian title *Amorum libri tres*.

The beginnings of modern elegy should be seen and investigated within these horizons.[2] In addition, it seems important to me to

[1] J. Cugnoni, 'Aeneae Silvii Piccolomini Senensis qui postea fuit Pius II Pont. Max. Opera inedita', in *Atti della R. Accademia dei Lincei anno CCLXXX* (1882–3), ser.III, memorie vol.8 (Rome, 1883), edited the *Cinthia* on pp.658–64 (see also pp.325–8).

[2] J. Sparrow, 'Latin Verse of the High Renaissance' (in *Italian Renaissance Studies, A tribute to the late Cecilia M. Ady*, ed. by E. F. Jacob (London, 1960), pp.354–409), in an article which is a masterly introduction to Italian Latin poetry in general, points in passing to the Petrarchist sentiments in the Latin poetry of the late fifteenth and early sixteenth century, without further exploring the problem (see p.381). L. Forster, 'On Petrarchism in Latin and the Role of Anthologies' (in *Acta Conventus Neo-Latini Lovaniensis*, ed. by J. IJsewijn and E. Kessler (Leuven and Munich, 1973), pp.235–44), discussed it in more detail, again focusing on late fifteenth- and sixteenth-century poetry. The point which I should like to stress is that Neo-Latin elegy was from its beginnings related to Petrarch's love lyrics.

realise that ancient literary theory was no less influential than the productions of the Roman elegists for the further development of modern elegy in its Neo-Latin as well as in its later vernacular forms.

The theory that elegy was originally a poem of mourning had found its way through the *Artes versificatoriae* of the Middle Ages and reappeared in the many poetics of the sixteenth century.[1] They all quote Horace's famous lines 'versibus impariter iunctis querimonia primum,|post etiam inclusa est voti sententia compos' (*A.P.* 75 ff.) and usually also, from the beginning of Ovid's elegy on the death of Tibullus, 'flebilis indignos, Elegia, solve capillos;|a, nimis ex vero nunc tibi nomen erit' (*Am.* III.9.3 f.). The literary critics could not fail to notice that there was an inconsistency between ancient theory and practice.

Within the range of the transmitted classical elegies, Ovid's elegy on the death of Tibullus is almost the only one which represents elegy according to the alleged true meaning of the word as a poem of mourning (in Cat. *c.* 68 mourning has been blended with other elegiac themes). The usual practice of the Roman elegists could be described much better by another quotation from Ovid: 'blanda pharetratos Elegia cantet Amores' (*Rem. am.* 379). As a matter of fact, it seems that Ovid himself was quite aware that he deviated from his reader's expectations in regard to the subject-matter of the Roman genre, as it had been established by his immediate predecessors and by himself, when he used elegy to mourn Tibullus. He fittingly did so, not only because there had been a few earlier elegies on the death of some beloved one (like the lost poem of Catullus's friend Calvus on the death of his wife), but also because Tibullus was best bemoaned in the poetic form characteristic for him, and Ovid could, in addition, wittily justify his choice by an allusion to the grammarians' theory of the etymology and origin of Greek elegy. Horace too probably alluded to it, when he wrote the strophe 'Albi, ne doleas plus nimio memor|inmitis Glycerae, neu miserabilis|decantes elegos cur tibi iunior|laesa praeniteat fide', (*c.* 1.33.1 ff.). The *elegi* are here called *miserabiles*, because Albius Tibullus piteously deplored the infidelity of his beloved in them. These *elegi* were amatory elegics, but the situation provided

[1] There is no exhaustive collection of the theoretical statements on elegy. For a selection see I. Behrens, *Die Lehre von der Einteilung der Dichtkunst vornehmlich vom sechzehnten bis neunzehnten Jahrhundert. Studien zur Geschichte der poetischen Gattungen* (Halle/Saale, 1940) (Beihefte zur Zeitschrift für Romanische Philologie 92).

Horace with a pun in respect to the alleged threnetic origin of the old Greek elegy. *Miserabilis* could be taken as a reference to one of the proposed etymologies of the word *elegeia* which connected it with ἔλεος, that is in Latin *miseratio*. Diomedes understood it so,[1] and Isidore of Seville said afterwards that the *versus elegiacus* is the appropriate metre for the laments of the *miseri*.[2]

It is important for the understanding of the modern theories on elegy to see upon which ancient testimonies they were built. The *querimonia*, which Horace gave as its primary function, had nothing to do with amatory elegy. The statement was based on grammatical theory, not on contemporary practice. In speaking of the *miserabiles elegi* of Tibullus, Horace jokingly connected amatory and mourning elegy. And in the elegy on the death of Tibullus, Ovid included, under exceptional circumstances, a mourning elegy among his amatory poems. Thus, later theoreticians faced a puzzling situation. They read that elegy was a plaintive poem of mourning, but did not find very many examples of them, whereas its theoretically unexplained use as an amatory poem was prevalent. In the Middle Ages this was not too bothersome. Authors of *Artes* usually chose either the *querelae* or the *amores* for their definition of elegy. Only Joannes de Garlandia, who wrote a *Poetria* in the first half of the thirteenth century, may have seen the problem. His definition 'elegiacum id est miserabile carmen, quod continet et recitat dolores amantium' is the first definition of elegy in the sense of *querimonia amantium*.[3] His wording suggests that Horace's ode to Tibullus helped him to this compromise.

For the theoreticians and the poets of the sixteenth century the problem was more acute. They tried to bridge the chasm between *querimonia* and *amores* by interpreting the theoretical statements in the light of ancient practice and vice versa. In this way they established a connection between the two types of content which became very influential for the modern concept of elegy. Scaliger, for instance, gave two solutions.[4] In the first book of his *Poetice* he

---

[1] *Ars Grammatica*, p.484 K.   [2] *Etym.* 1.39.14 f.
[3] See I. Behrens, *Die Lehre*, pp.55 f.
[4] See J. C. Scaliger, *Poetices libri septem*, Faksimile-Neudruck der Ausgabe von Lyon 1561 mit einer Einleitung von A. Buck (Stuttgart–Bad Cannstatt, 1964), pp.52 and 169. Scaliger's theory on elegy does not seem to have been discussed in recent scholarly literature. For a bibliography see R. M. Ferraro, *Giudizi critici e criteri estetici nei Poetices libri septem (1561) di Giulio Cesare Scaligero rispetto alla teoria letteraria del Rinascimento* (Chapel Hill, University of North Carolina Press, 1971).

states that elegy was probably first used at funerals. Later its use was transferred to something quite different: *ad amores*. This, as he says, was done not without reason: 'nam et frequens conquestio in amoribus et verissima mors'. In love affairs the lovers often complain, and love can truly be considered as equal to death, since the lover loses all his senses, pining away with desire. From unhappy love, the subject-matter of elegy was then further extended to include the happy lover as well, whose wishes have been fulfilled. Scaliger here is giving the Horatian statement in the *Ars Poetica* a new interpretation. Horace had mentioned as a secondary use of the elegiac distich *voti sententia compos*, a term with which he probably referred to the dedicatory epigram. But Scaliger, like other critics and poets of his time, understood *vota* as the wishes of the lover and *voti sententia compos* as expression of their fulfilment. He quotes Ovid's *Amores* II.12 'Ite triumphales circum mea tempora lauri etc.', where the poet boasts in line 13 'me duce ad hanc voti finem me milite veni'. The transition from mourning for the dead to the expression of happy love is achieved by the thought of certain common characteristics of the mourner and the unhappy lover. Thus, elegy as poetry of love is justified within the framework of the Horatian theory.[1] Scaliger had second thoughts and modified his reconstruction in his third book. There he rejects the idea that elegy started with

[1] Scaliger does not mention the elegies of Joannes Secundus in this context nor in his sixth book *Hypercriticus*, but Secundus's first book of elegies, titled *Iulia* and printed for the first time in 1541 (*Opera nunc primum in lucem edita*, Utrecht; facsimile reprint Nieuwkoop, 1969), shows strong similarities in its concept of elegy. The book opens with two programmatic elegies, the first modelled on Ovid's *Am.* 1.1, the other explicitly claiming Ovid as Secundus's poetical predecessor. It closes with elegy 11, a dedication of the book to Venus and Cupid (the terminologically important words *moesta querela* and *vota* occur in ll.33 and 38 f.). As in Ovid's *Amores* the beloved girl appears first in the third elegy, then elegies 3–10 develop the love story in three steps. (1) In 3–6 Secundus expresses his love for Julia and his desire to win her – *vota* in the sense of Scaliger's *Horace*. The metaphorical identity of *amor* and *mors* is thematic in elegy 5. (2) In 7–9 a rival has entered the picture who successfully takes her away from the poet: 'querulo mihi carmine flenda es' (7.27), 'in venis flebile vulnus alo' (9.26), and 'semper in absenteis suspiro moestus amores' (9.27) show that Secundus could have labelled these elegies as *querimonia*. (3) Elegy 10 opens with 'Ite procul moestum lachrymae genus, ite querelae... cinge triumphanteis victrici fronde capillos... misit in amplexus illam Venus aurea nostros.' It is Secundus's *voti sententia compos*. Ov. *Am.* II.12 is the model, the same poem which Scaliger later used as an example for this Horatian term. Secundus's special twist is that the reader learns towards the end of the poem that the fulfilment happened only in a dream. In summary, the *Iulia* not only presents an actual love affair of Secundus in the language and style of Ovid and other Roman elegists, but it also conforms to a special interpretation of Horace's statement which we later find in Scaliger's *Poetice*. The parallel may not be accidental.

mourning altogether. He now prefers to assume that the original use was for *amantium commiserationes*, as they may have been expressed in front of the closed doors of the beloved girls. Afterwards elegy was extended to the praise of the fulfilment of the lover's desires, as if to thank the poem for having attained its original purpose. In this interpretation, Horace's whole statement refers to love elegy, whereas *Epicedia*, *Epitaphia* and *Epistolae* are mentioned by Scaliger only at the end of the chapter as belonging to the elegiac genre in a wider sense.

These explanations as well as those of other literary critics were influenced by and had their impact on the contemporary production of elegies. The general effect was that *querimonia* and *voti sententia compos* were not considered as necessarily belonging to two different kinds of elegy. Practice and theory showed that love elegy in itself contained the expression of sadness and joy, of desire and fulfilment. Thus, contrary sentiments became a characteristic of elegy. Critics of the eighteenth century took a further step by declaring that a mixture of these sentiments is essential. Elegy should not only contain them in a chronological sequence in different poems, but as a mixture within the same poem, where sadness is mitigated by the revival of joy, where grief and hope are mingled, and where desire longs for a lost or unreachable ideal, whose visualisation causes not only nostalgia, but also a certain consolation. The development of the concept of elegy may thus be seen as a continuous line of interpretations and re-interpretations of the basic statement of Horace, the elements of which were transformed so much that they were barely recognisable at the end and that even the theorists sometimes did not realise in which tradition they stood. Especially for the vernacular literatures which did not always try to reproduce the elegiac distich, these poetological theories were essential for the definition of elegy.

It is obvious that the poetics and the Neo-Latin elegies of the Renaissance played a crucial rôle in this process, which is not yet sufficiently explored. But let us now turn our attention to a specific elegist of the sixteenth century in order to see more precisely what we may gain by a closer study of the Neo-Latin elegists for the knowledge and appreciation of European literature.

The work of Petrus Lotichius Secundus is worthy of serving as an example.[1] He was born in 1528 in a little village about 50 miles north-east of Frankfurt/Main as the son of a peasant and died in 1560 as Professor of Medicine at the university of Heidelberg.[2] Besides other *carmina*, he published his first book of elegies in Paris in 1551, the second in Lyons in 1553, and a third in Bologna in 1556. His hitherto published works were re-edited immediately after his death in 1561. Before his death he had worked on a revised version of his three books of elegies. This version, along with his other poetical works, was published from his manuscript by his brother Christianus and his friend Joachimus Camerarius in 1563, whereupon ten other editions followed up to 1622, six new ones between 1700 and 1773, and one in 1840.[3] The printing history reflects his fame and the eclipse of it. Immediately after his death and by the next two or three generations he was considered to be *princeps poetarum Germanorum*. He was ranked with Joannes Secundus in the Netherlands and with Pierre Ronsard in France,[4] and Martin Opitz not only called him once 'unser *Lotichius*, der Fürst aller Deutschen Poeten', but even translated one of his poems and named him in his *Buch von der Deutschen Poeterey* as one of the masters of elegy along with Ovid, Propertius, Tibullus, Sannazaro and Secundus.[5]

If Lotichius had such a reputation one may suppose that his

[1] When he went to school, he abandoned his German name Peter Lotz (etymologically a dialectical short form of Ludwig) in favour of Petrus Loticius or Lotitius and added Secundus in order to distinguish himself from his uncle and teacher who had first adopted this name. In his student years, upon the advice of Melanchthon, he changed this to Lotichius for euphonic reasons and connected it etymologically with the lotus plant (cf. *El.* 11.5.85; 6.53).

[2] For detailed accounts of his life see *Allgemeine Deutsche Biographie s.v.*, the literature listed by H. Rupprich, *Die deutsche Literatur vom späten Mittelalter bis zum Barock. Zweiter Teil, Das Zeitalter der Reformation 1520–1570* (Munich, 1973), p.498, and K. A. O'Rourke Fraiman, *Petrus Lotichius Secundus, Elegiarum liber primus*, edited with an Introduction, Translation and Commentary (Diss. Columbia University/New York, 1973), pp.1–8.

[3] A list of the editions in A. Heimpel, 'Quellen und Verzeichnisse zum Leben und zu den Werken von Petrus Lotichius Secundus', *Unsere Heimat* 21 (Schlüchtern, 1929), 34–6, 55–6, and Fraiman, *Petrus Lotichius Secundus*, pp.18–34. In this paper, quotations of Lotichius refer to the annotated edition of P. Burmannus Secundus, *Petri Lotichii Secundi Solitariensis poemata omnia . . .* (Amsterdam, 1754), 2 vols.

[4] J. Camerarius wrote in the *epistula nuncupatoria* of the 1561 edition (Burmannus, vol.2, p.52): 'fuit autem Petrus Lotichius talis poeta qualem sua aetas et nostra natio alterum non tulit.' The term *princeps* or *primus poetarum Germanorum* became a commonplace (cf. Burmannus, vol.2, pp.231 f., 255 ff.). Janus Dousa Pater praised Lotichius and Joannes Secundus as *principes utriusque Germaniae poetarum* (Burmannus, vol.2, p.259) and Nathan Chytraeus compared him with Ronsard (Burmannus, vol.2, p.268).

[5] See M. Opitz, *Lob des Feldtlebens* (1625), in *Deutscher Poematum Erster Theil* (Breslau, 1628), p.122; he published a translation of Lotichius's *El.* 11.4 in 1631 (Burmannus, vol.2, pp.284–9).

works had an influence on the poetic production of Opitz and other German lyricists of the Baroque age, especially because several of them wrote both German and Latin poems. But this problem has so far not been touched by Germanists except for a few isolated observations.[1] What is more, Lotichius himself remained in the no-man's-land between Classicists and Germanists. One may find in a handbook of German literature that he is considered to be the greatest lyric poet in Germany before Klopstock,[2] but no one has tried to substantiate this verdict by a detailed literary interpretation of his poems. Ellinger and others praised the sincerity with which he expressed his sentiments.[3] The sequence of his elegies was seen as a unique poetical diary, which was exploited for its autobiographical content. Then Karl Otto Conrady approached the poems from another angle and emphasised that the contemporaries of Lotichius applauded above all his mastery in imitating the ancients.[4] Conrady's book *Lateinische Dichtungstradition und deutsche Lyrik des 17. Jahrhunderts* is one of the very few attempts to integrate the study of Neo-Latin and German lyrics, but a literary appreciation of the individual character of Lotichius's poetical production was not within its more general aims. Thus, Conrady did not try to explain why Lotichius's art of *imitatio* was superior to the similar tendencies of other Neo-Latin poets.[5]

A first step towards understanding why Lotichius was unanimously considered to be the best German poet of his age is obviously to study the criteria on which such an appraisal was based. Camerarius, for instance, stated that Lotichius exceeded all his German contemporaries 'elegantia et suavitate et exprimendi vetustatis simili-

---

[1] See, for instance, R. Haller, *Geschichte der deutschen Lyrik vom Ausgang des Mittelalters bis zu Goethes Tod* (Bern, 1967), p.89, concerning Paul Fleming. Haller unfortunately decided to exclude the treatment of Neo-Latin lyrics from his monograph (cf. p.110: 'Die Lateindichtung läßt sich nicht in die Entwicklung und das Gefüge der deutschen Literatur einordnen.').

[2] Rupprich, *Die deutsche Literatur*, p.308. Within the short space of one and a half pages, Rupprich gives an excellent report on Lotichius's poetical works.

[3] See Ellinger, *Geschichte der neulateinischen Literatur Deutschlands*, vol.2, pp.340–95, and A. Schroeter, *Beiträge zur Geschichte der neulateinischen Poesie Deutschlands und Hollands* (Berlin, 1909) (Palaestra 77), pp.36–128.

[4] K. O. Conrady, *Lateinische Dichtungstradition und deutsche Lyrik des 17. Jahrhunderts* (Bonn, 1962) (Bonner Arbeiten zur deutschen Literatur 4), pp.185 f.

[5] B. Coppel, 'Marginalien zu dichterischen Berührungspunkten zwischen Petrus Lotichius Secundus und C. Valerius Catullus', in *Acta Conventus Neo-Latini Lovaniensis*, edited by J. IJsewijn and E. Kessler (Munich, 1973) (Humanistische Bibliothek 1.20), pp.159–70, gave a critical response to certain exaggerations of Conrady's point of view.

tudinem contentione', terms which reappear in later evaluations.[1] *Elegantia* and *suavitas* are the special virtues of Tibullus's elegies according to Renaissance poetics.[2] The terms have a distinct meaning. We find their definition in the *Praecepta de carminibus ad veterum imitationem componendis*, written by Georgius Sabinus, a friend of Lotichius and Camerarius, and published ten times between 1551 and 1632.[3] There we read that the most desired qualities of a poem in regard to *aurium voluptas* are *elegantia sermonis* and *suavitas compositionis* and that the first consists in the special way that words and phrases are selected, whereas the latter is achieved by the *structura* in which the words are smoothly joined together, by the appropriate use and arrangement of epithets and by the *concinnitas pedum, numerorum, membrorum et figurarum*, a term which covers a variety of requirements, among others that sense and rhythm should be correlated so that the verses are fittingly adjusted to the *res* and *affectus* which they ought to express. These categories are clearly deduced from the rhetorical theory and poetical practice of the ancients. We should use them for our interpretation of Lotichius and other Neo-Latin poets in order to gain a better appreciation of their qualities.

As for the *contentio exprimendi similitudinem vetustatis*, it is good to remember that Lotichius even in his early years had been admonished by his teacher Joannes Pedioneus to imitate Cicero and achieve *exprimendo similitudinem aliquam non quidem ut simius hominis, sed ut filius patris*.[4] From the biography of Lotichius by his friend

[1] Cf. the statements of G. Fabricius, J. P. Lotichius and Burmannus Secundus (vol.1, p.3; 2, pp.47, 172). Camerarius alluded in his evaluation to a statement of Lotichius himself who had written in the dedicatory letter to the edition of 1551: 'sum enim in hoc scribendi genere . . . non ignarus quam in eo ipso difficile atque arduum . . . cogitationes suas sic illustrare ac eloqui posse, ut ad veterum in eo genere suavitatem atque elegantiam simile quiddam expressum esse videatur.'

[2] Cf. J. Vadianus, *De poetica et carminis ratione* (Vienna, 1518) (re-edited by P. Schaeffer, Diss. Princeton University, 1970), *tit.* 29: . . . 'ego (sc. Propertium) ut Tibullo elegantia et suavitate inferiorem esse puto, ita doctrina multifaria . . . et verborum nonnullorum gratiosa quadam novitate Tibullo priorem statuo.'

[3] See the list of editions in M. Töppen, *Die Gründung der Universität zu Königsberg und das Leben ihres ersten Rektors Georg Sabinus* (Königsberg, 1844).

[4] For Joannes Pedioneus see K. H. Burmeister, 'Johannes Pedioneus Rhetus (*ca* 1520–50). Biographie–Werkverzeichnis–Briefe', *Humanistica Lovaniensia* 20 (1971), 121 ff. The quotation is from a letter of Pedioneus (Burmannus, vol.2, pp.81–2, and Burmeister, pp.143–4). The image of son and father goes back to Seneca (*ep. ad Luc.* 84.8) via Petrarch (*ep. ad Fam.* 23.19); see A. Buck, *Italienische Dichtungslehren vom Mittelalter bis zum Ausgang der Renaissance* (Tübingen, 1952) (Beihefte zur Zeitschrift für Romanische Philologie 94), p.55. The image of the ape was used by Petrarch in the same letter; for

Joannes Hagius we know that Ovid and Tibullus were his favourite poets, whose works he always carried with him when, during his student years, he went to the countryside for relaxation.[1] All his critics agreed that he, born to be a poet, achieved a most felicitous *imitatio* of Tibullus and Ovid in his elegies.[2] We still have to become more sensitive to this art. The wording of the verses, the mood, the motifs, and the structure of the poems, and even their arrangement within the books are influenced by the Roman elegists, and we should distinguish between the general use of the poetical Latin vocabulary, specific allusion to certain classical passages, and the re-use of certain themes and structures which could be done without any verbal parallel. But the poems are, at the same time, new literary creations, coherent in form and with a sense of their own. Lotichius did not ape Tibullus and Ovid, nor did he just mix the ingredients of their elegies kaleidoscopically. He used some of their literary forms, because he felt that some of his thoughts and experiences could be best expressed with the help of these forms. That is, he had something to say and he said it in the elegiac code which he admired and which had become his own by his relentless study of it. Classical elegy acted as a mould for his own experiences and their artistic expression. It restricted, but it also offered possibilities which he otherwise would not have had. His elegies became a unique amalgam. As a consequence, our interpretation is confronted with the methodo-logical difficulty that we should always see the features of the father, but only within the new individuality of the son.

These considerations lead us to the main task of future research on Lotichius, the literary interpretation of his poems. A critical edition of his works would be enormously useful for that purpose, especially because of the different versions in which his poems are transmitted. He changed the first printed version of his elegies considerably by substitutions, eliminations and expansions within

its medieval and ancient antecedents see E. R. Curtius, *Europäische Literatur und lateinisches Mittelalter* (Bern, 1948), pp. 437–8 (yet Curtius missed Hor. *Sat.* 1.10. 18 and Sen. *Contr.* 9.3.12, the oldest ancient examples for *simia/simius* in the sense of the unintelligent imitator).

[1] The passage deserves to be read in its context, because it shows in what way Ovid and Tibullus were part of Lotichius's very existence; see Burmannus, vol.2, p.84 (cf. Joannes Secundus, *El.* III.6). The account of Hagius (Hagen) was condensed and interpreted in the light of the poetical imagery of the ancients by J. P. Lotichius (Burmannus, vol.2, pp.168–9).

[2] Burmannus, vol.2, collected the judgements on Lotichius's poetry made by contemporary and later critics.

existing elegies, by the composition of new ones, and by rearranging their order in the three books. A study of these changes provides the opportunity to observe what artistic principles guided a Neo-Latin poet at his work.[1]

The three books have eleven, twelve, and ten elegies, and are clearly intended to form a literary unity together.[2] The locality of the first book is north-eastern Germany, where he served as a soldier during the Schmalkaldian war (1546–7), the locality of the second is central and southern France, where he was a student and tutor from 1550 to 1554, the locality of the third is mainly Italy, where he studied at Padua and Bologna from 1554 to 1556. During all these years and in all the books he expressed the desire to return to his homeland near the Main valley, a wish which is finally going to be fulfilled in the last elegy of the third book after, as he says, *duo lustra* of wandering and hardship.[3] He not only sees himself as a returning Ulysses, but also wants to be compared with Conradus Celtes, whose *Quattuor libri Amorum secundum quattuor latera Germaniae* were written during a *decennalis peregrinatio* too.[4] Moving from the

---

[1] Fraiman, *Petrus Lotichius Secundus*, took the first step with her dissertation on the first book of his elegies. She compares the two printed versions on pp.60–82.

[2] Lotichius was preparing these books for a definitive edition when he died. The conventional fourth book contains seven elegies put together by Camerarius for the edition of 1563. Most, but not all of them were composed in Lotichius's last years. The fifth book appears for the first time in Burman's edition of 1754. It consists of twenty-one poems in elegiac distichs which originally had been published in Lotichius's *carminum libellus* (1551) and in various other places. Burman also added three elegies to the second book (II.13–15). A modern literary critic has to be aware that Lotichius did not place all his elegiac writings into his three *Elegiarum libri*, but selected specific pieces for them according to his thematic and structural concept.

[3] See *El*. III.10.13 f. 'nunc requies erroris adest finisque laborum,| post duo fas tandem lustra redire domum'. He had used the term *duo lustra* before in *El*. III.1.43 ff., where the origin of the phrase is clearly Ov. *ep. ex Ponto* IV.10.10 'exemplum est animi nimium patientis Ulixes,| iactatus dubio per duo lustra mari'.

[4] Cf. the editions Nürnberg 1502 and F. Pindter, Leipzig 1934. Various parallels indicate that Lotichius consciously competed with Celtes's *Amores*. (1) The books follow the distinct geographical pattern of the adventures. The period of ten years is emphasised by both elegists (for Celtes see *praefatio* and *Am*. 1.3.69 f.). Both features have no parallel in Classical or, as far as I know, other Neo-Latin elegy. (2) Celtes's *Am*. 1.1 and Lotichius's *El*. II.8 have an identical thematic structure: the poems give a description of the poet's horoscope, starting with an announcement thereof and continuing with an indication of the time of birth which leads to a full presentation of the positions of the planets and the zodiacal signs within the individual horoscopes. Both horoscopes are explained in regard to their astrological meaning, and in both poems gods are used to predict the poet's destination. Both times Apollo reveals that the baby will become a poet, and the other figure shows his future fate in regard to love. The dependence of Lotichius is obvious, but an interpretation could demonstrate his artistic superiority. He placed the poem deliberately in the centre portion of his collection (cf. too *El*. III.1

north-east to the west and from there to the south of Europe, Lotichius succeeded in giving an impressionistic picture of the various regions, their landscape, climate, and cities, and the way they affected his life. In this he outdid the analogous attempt of Celtes by far. But unlike that poet, he was not primarily interested in writing amatory elegy – only five of the thirty-three elegies may be classified as such.[1] His poetry encompasses a much broader spectrum of life.

The main themes of the first book are the toil of his *militia*, his disillusionment with the war, his longing for peace, and the realisation of his proper vocation, a life dedicated to the Muses. The concluding elegy, jubilating since peace has finally come, is a *voti sententia compos*.[2] Lotichius found in Tibullus, in whose footsteps he was now walking, the same contrast of inclination versus reality, the combination of being a soldier against his will and a poet by destiny. He also felt his own circumstances were a kind of exile and saw his sentiments reflected in the *Tristia* of Ovid.[3]

The *querimonia* of the first book is followed by *amores* in the second.[4] The first of its elegies takes the scenery from Ovid's *Amores*,[5] and in the last Lotichius wishes to be crowned with the myrtle of Venus.[6]

of Georgius Sabinus). (3) *Am.* 1.3 and *El.* iii.1 begin with an astronomical indication of springtime and a description of the spring, whereupon Celtes starts his trip to Cracow, Lotichius his travel homewards. (4) In *Am.* iii.14 and *El.* iii.3 the poets mourn the death of their beloved girl, whom no physician could save and whose ghost appears to them in a dream. Other parallels could be listed which are too specific to be explained by the common elegiac tradition.

[1] These are *El.* ii.1, 3, 9; iii.3, 5.
[2] For a detailed analysis of the thematic structure of *El.* i see Fraiman, *Petrus Lotichius Secundus*, pp. 46–59.
[3] Fraiman, pp.83–105, discusses the classical sources of *El.* i.
[4] The first elegy of *El.* i in the edition of 1551 (Burmannus, *El.* v.17) announces *querimonia* as the theme of the following elegies (cf. esp. ll.2, 18, 20, 23, 33, 59, 62). This elegy was eliminated in the revised edition, probably because of its too theoretical style, and replaced by an elegy which calls Lotichius's military service in north-east Germany *tristia . . . exilia* (l.63). For the description of this area Lotichius used colours taken from the description of Ovid's place of exile in *Trist.* iii.10. The *Tristia* were obviously considered to be Ovid's *querimonia*. Lotichius believed he was following Horatian theory in his progression from *El.* i to ii.
[5] *El.* ii.1.1 borrows from Ovid's epilogue *Am.* iii.15.1 and from *Am.* 1.6.12, but the main picture, the poet's speech to Cupid and the answer of Venus, originate from *Am.* 1.1 (cf. also *Am.* 1.1.29 'cingere litorea flaventia tempora myrto' and *El.* ii.1.13 'viridi cinxit mea tempora myrto'). Lotichius introduces himself as a new poet, a poet of love (cf. also *El.* ii.1.17 'voti compos nova carmina feci'). He was probably aware that *El.* i.1 of Joannes Secundus was also modelled on Ov. *Am.* 1.1.
[6] *El.* ii.12 takes again motifs from *Am.* 1.1 and iii.15. Lotichius rejects a crown of laurel (he connects the laurel with the higher form of lyrical poetry, the ode) and asks Carolus Clusius (Charles de l'Ecluse, 1525–1609): 'tu mihi vel myrti nectas e fronde coronam,| vel caput hoc circa moesta cupressus eat' (ll.3 f.), hinting with this at the

Two elegies deal with past and new love,[1] but others with the desire to return to his homeland,[2] with his birthday and destiny,[3] and with the separation from friends.[4] Lotichius admires the ancient monuments in and near Nîmes,[5] expresses, in imitation of a Greek epigram, sympathy for a dead dolphin found ashore,[6] and enjoys the beauty of landscape and vegetation around Montpellier, where he hopes to

two principal kinds of elegy (cf. Ov. *Am.* 1.1.29 quoted above; Dominicus Marius Niger explains this line in his commentary, published in Venice in 1518, with the remark 'myrtea corona, ut amatoria canens' and quotes for a contrast Statius's *Silv.* v.1.135 f. 'tempus nunc ponere frondes, Phoebe, tuas maestaque comam damnare cupresso'. In Joannes Secundus's *El.* iii.7, *Elegia* appears to the poet as *dea bina*, two sisters, one crowned with cypress, the other with myrtle.)

[1] *El.* ii.3 should be compared with Propertius's iii.21. The common theme is the attempt to liberate oneself from love by travelling to a distant place, where one intends to study. The passion of Catullus was foreign to Lotichius's more moderate emotions, but in *El.* ii.9.85 he tries to take advantage of a famous Catullan line: 'nec precor, ut contra solum me diligat illa' (cf. Cat. 76.23), inadvertently showing with the continuation how far he is from Catullus's feelings: 'dum modo sit penitus non aliena, sat est'. Nearer to Catullus are the hendecasyllabic poems among his *carmina*; see B. Coppel, 'Marginalien zu dichterischen Berührungspunkten'.

[2] See *El.* ii.2 and 11. The theme is *animi vota*, as *El.* ii.11.62 states. A major source of inspiration for this elegy was Tib. 1.1. Tibullus lent the idyllic colours for the longed-for homeland.

[3] *El.* ii.8. For the birthday as an elegiac theme compare Ov. *Trist.* iii.13, written on the occasion of the poet's birthday, to which the opening of *El.* ii.8 alludes.

[4] *El.* ii.5. This elegy is modelled on Tib. 1.3. A comparison shows not only that Lotichius used the opening lines, where the verbal parallels are most frequent, starting with the almost identical, but in its meaning reversed, first line, but that the structure of Tibullus's elegy is generally imitated. It is interesting to observe how Lotichius fitted the poetical structure of his classical model to the exigencies of his own situation.

[5] *El.* ii.10, 'De monumentis in agro Nemausensi', contains the description of the Pont du Gard and the temple of Diana with the fountain nearby, two passages which were enthusiastically praised by later critics. Lotichius justified this as a proper theme of elegy by referring to the aetiological elegies of the fourth book of Propertius. His statement that he would like to describe 'varias gentes et nomina prisca locorum' (l.15) alludes to Prop. iv.1.69 'sacra diesque canam et cognomina prisca locorum'. The themes mentioned in the first half of the Propertian line were deliberately rejected (ll.11 f.) and reserved for the addressee of the elegy, Joannes Stigel (1515–62).

[6] *El.* ii.7, the *epicedium* for a dolphin, is a special experiment. The primary model was *Anth. Pal.*, vii.216, transmitted in the *Planudea* and known to Lotichius probably by the annotated edition of Joannes Brodaeus (Jean Brodeau), Basel, 1549 (A. Alciati had earlier given a partial Latin translation in his *Emblematum liber*, Augsburg, 1531). Lotichius may have heard stories about dolphins from his teacher and friend Gulielmus Rondeletus (Guillaume Rondelet, addressee of *El.* iii.3) who published his famous work *De piscibus marinis* in 1554 (see pp.459–73 *De delphino*, esp. p.469, where he mentions that he has himself seen a dead dolphin ashore). That the topic was suitable for an elegy was proved by Ov. *Am.* ii.6, the *epicedium* on a parrot, which Lotichius therefore took as secondary model. The verbal artistry was enhanced by the allusion of the opening line to Prop. iii.7.57, where the shipwrecked Paetus cries to the *di maris*. The poem is neither listed by G. Herrlinger, *Totenklage um Tiere in der antiken Dichtung mit einem Anhang byzantinischer, mittellateinischer und neuhochdeutscher Tierepikedien* (Stuttgart, 1930), nor by J. Hutton, *The Greek Anthology in France and the Latin Writers of the Netherlands to the Year 1800* (Cornell U.P., Ithaca, 1946).

find rest.[1] The war in Germany reappears in the recollection, in a dream and in messages from afar,[2] and the death of a friend is to be mourned,[3] but on the whole, the second book shows not only a greater variety of elegiac topics and sentiments, but also a somewhat brighter mood than the first.

This is again succeeded by a generally darker atmosphere in the third. The forced stay in Italy delays his home-coming. Unhappy love (the death of his girl and his frustrated new love), the plague at Padua, the death of his patron and dearest friend, and his own illness give the dominant gloomy accents,[4] against which the two poems with lighter colours, the description of his studies and of his idyllic retreat, provide only a frail counterpoint.[5]

The third book is framed by two travel poems, *El.* III.1 and 10. The first, one of his very best poems, narrates the travel of the poet from France to Germany, where war brutally prevented him at the last moment from reaching his home-town. It is a unique *hodoeporicon*,[6] in so far as it describes a trip which did not reach its aim and because Lotichius is neither sightseeing nor entertaining with

[1] Cf. *El.* II.6 (*Ad Montem Pessulanum*), 89 f. 'te propter tantos libuit perferre labores, | tu requies Musis, tu decus omne, meis'. The salutation of Montpellier and its paradisiacal surroundings is a bright and cheerful moment in the centre of the collection – *voti sententia compos*, one could say.

[2] The most famous poem of Lotichius became later *El.* II.4, the dream of the siege and occupation of Magdeburg, because the 'prophecy' seemed to be fulfilled in 1631. References to the war also in *El.* II.2.

[3] The death of J. Altus is mentioned only in parenthesis in *El.* II. 3.41 ff. and 5.65 ff.

[4] See *El.* III. 3, 5, 6, 7, 9. The elegy *In obitum Danielis Stibari* is noteworthy for an artistically perfect example of an *epicedium*. The classical motif of grieving from morning to night (cf., e.g., Virg. *Georg.* IV. 465 f.) provided the structural skeleton for the whole elegy which shows Lotichius deploring the death of his patron during the course of a day. The poet is represented as sitting at the mouth of the Po. The river occasions a dominant mythological image, the mourning *Heliades*. The times of the day and the corresponding changes of nature cause a division into three major units in which expressions of praise and grief alternate. The progress from dawn to sunset is paralleled by allusions and references to Stibar's life, beginning with a *praeteritio* of the deeds of his ancestors and ending with the reception of his *spiritus* into heaven. The numerous Neo-Latin *epicedia* have generally been neglected by historians and literary critics alike, but they not only offer valuable biographical material, they also deserve attention as works of literary art.

[5] *El.* III.4 and 8. The latter was not included in the 1556 and 1561 editions. Its addition may have been caused by Lotichius's wish to lighten the gloomy second half of the book.

[6] The Neo-Latin genre of the elegiac or hexametric *hodoeporicon* deserves a monographic study; cf. J. IJsewijn, *s.v.*, in: *Moderne Encyclopedie der Wereldliteratuur*, vol.3 (Gent, 1965), p.639. Two early and influential examples from Germany, not mentioned by IJsewijn, are Helius Eobanus Hessus, *A profectione ad Des. Erasmum Roterodamum Hodoeporicon* (Erfurt, 1519), and J. Micyllus, *Hodoeporicon* (Wittenberg, 1527) (reprinted in J. Classen, *Jacob Micyllus, Rector zu Frankfurt und Professor zu Heidelberg von 1524–1558* (Frankfurt/Main, 1859), pp.276–313).

his adventures. His poem is more concerned with his inner emotions which condition the selection of the points on his route and the way he sees them. There is a movement from wintry coldness to the warmth of spring, symbolic for his way homewards and his increasing joy of anticipation, which culminates in an implicit comparison with the homecoming Ulysses. But the message about the war in progress abruptly kills all his hopes and precipitates him into utter despair, in which he wishes he had died before[1] and even considers, for a moment, emigration to America.[2] Turning backwards, he remembers the distant past, when he left the Main valley with a vow for his safe return (his situation seems now similar to that of Achilles in *Il.* 23.144 ff.), and concludes with a pathetic wish that he will, at least, be buried in his home-town at the end of his days. He reaches his homeland only in his memory and in his expectation. The structure of the poem as a whole, with its reversal of mood and its various changes in the time level, is very much Tibullan.

It may be instructive to quote briefly from this elegy of eighty-four lines in all, in order to give an immediate impression of Lotichius's poetical art. The quotation starts towards the end of the narration of the journey, when the poet, travelling through the Rhine valley from the Swiss border, reaches the Palatinate and its capital Heidelberg (ll.37 ff.; a few interpretative hints are given in the notes):

> Iam procul aerios montes, procul alta videbam
> templa Palatinis conspicienda iugis;[3]
> ergo salutabam loca nota deosque locorum
> et Nicri colles Pieriamque domum.[4]   40
> Mille pererrabant tacitam mihi gaudia mentem,
> ante oculos patriae cum foret ora meae,[5]

[1] See ll.59 ff. and cf. *Od.* 5.298 ff, and Verg. *Aen.* 1.93 ff.

[2] See ll.65 f. and cf. *El.* II.2.17 f. and A. Flaminius, *carm.* V.1.27 ff.; 45.22 ff.

[3] The anaphorical *procul* indicates the heightened joy of anticipation. Note the additional emphatic alliteration *aerios . . . alta. templa* seems to refer to the churches on top of the Heiligenberg near Heidelberg. Cf. Ov. *Fast.* V.552 'templaque in Augusto conspicienda foro'.

[4] *Pieriamque domum* refers to the University of Heidelberg. Cf. Ov. *Trist.* I.1.70 f. 'scandere te iubeam Caesareamque domum?|ignoscant augusta mihi loca dique locorum'. Lotichius strengthens the emotional overtones by transferring phrases with which the homesick Ovid characterised his beloved Rome to Heidelberg and its surroundings.

[5] Propertius had used the phrase 'patriae . . . ora tuae' in reference to his Umbria (IV. 1.122). In the description of the journey (ll.21–40), the poet's emotions were only implicitly shown. Note the tension in 'Mille . . . tacitam . . . gaudia mentem' – the exuberance of joy has not yet found its verbal outlet. It is the moment of unrestrained happiness.

et velut, Ioniis cum navita fessus ab undis
post duo natalem lustra revisit humum,
laetitia exsultat caraeque dat oscula terrae   45
exilii recolens taedia longa sui,[1]
sic ego fortunae tot tempestatibus actus
mollia concipiens otia laetus eram,[2]
cum mihi Fama volans inopinos retulit hostes
castra super ripas, Moene, locasse tuas   50
deletasque acies et totas funditus urbes
ignibus eversas procubuisse solo.[3]
Quid loquar ereptos profugis cultoribus agros
praediaque ad dominos non reditura suos?[4]
I nunc, finge animo reditus finemque malorum   55
teque puta casus exsuperasse tuos!
Exul inops erro, nec honore carentia mortis
matris adhuc licuit busta videre meae.[5]

---

[1] The climax is underlined by a classical simile *velut . . . sic . . .* Ulysses is indicated by periphrasis (see p.182, n.3 above); l.45 translates *Od.* XIII.353 f. with Ovidian vocabulary (cf. *oscula terrae Met.* III.24, VII.631, XIII.420, and *Met.* XIV.158 *taedia longa laborum*). Lotichius identifies himself with Ulysses coming home to Ithaca. The classical prototype expresses the depth of his happiness.

[2] Cf. Virg. *Aen.* III.709 'pelagi tot tempestatibus actus', referring to Aeneas, the second classical prototype. The imagery of the sea – in its proper sense in l.43 – has been transformed into a symbol in l.47. Note the contrast between the storms of the past and the conceived *mollia otia* of the future, paralleled by the harsh *f-, t-* and *st-*sounds in l.47 and the dominant *m-* and *l-*sounds in l.48. The four distichs, ll.41–8, which contain the simile of Ulysses embedded within a personal frame constitute the emotional summit of the elegy, reached by a slow but steady upward motion, and now, in a moment, suddenly lost by a plunge into utter desolation.

[3] *Fama volans* is taken from Virg. *Aen.* XI.139 ff. 'et iam Fama volans, tanti praenuntia luctus,|Euandrum Euandrique domos et moenia replet,|quae modo victorem Latio Pallanta ferebat.' Lotichius implies that the news was as much of a shock to him as the news of Pallas's death to Euander. He refers to the military actions of Albert Alcibiades, Margrave of Kulmbach-Bayreuth, in 1552–4. The message itself is phrased in epic language (cf. Virg. *Aen.* XI.898 'deletas Volscorum acies', II.746 'quid in eversa vidi crudelius urbe?', Ov. *Met.* XIII.169 'ingentem evertere Troiam', 175 f. 'mea concussa putate|procubuisse solo Lyrnesia moenia dextra); l.52, consisting of only four words, sounds heavy and definitive.

[4] The rest of the message is given in the form of a *praeteritio*. After mentioning the camp of the enemy, his bloody victories on the battlefield, and the destruction and devastation of whole cities, Lotichius causes the reader to envisage the terror on the countryside at large. The four items provide together a climactic sequence of horrifying news on the war and its effects.

[5] In reaction to the news, Lotichius pushes aside his former optimistic comparison with the home-coming Ulysses. The sarcastic imperative *i nunc* is common to Virgil, Propertius and Ovid, cf. especially Prop. III.18.17 'i nunc tolle animos et tecum finge triumphos'. Not *laetitia*, but *exilium* is his fate, pointedly expressed in *exul inops erro*. The phrase is taken from the list of deprecations in Ov. *Ibis* 107 ff. (113 *exul inops erres*). Lotichius sees himself as being under a curse. He is even unable to pay a visit to the grave of his mother who died in his absence (Virg. *Aen.* VI.333 'mortis honore carentes' refers to two Trojans who have not been buried; Lotichius transferred the expression to the prevented visit of the tomb).

The quoted passage is central to the elegy not only because it contains the turn from optimism to pessimism, but also because here the narration of the journey changes into the expression of Lotichius's emotional reaction to the news which prevents him from coming home, a topic which fills the rest of the elegy.

The pendant poem, *El.* III.10, then shows the poet saying goodbye to Venice before he sets out on his new and final journey homewards. He predicts the way he will take and ends with the hope he will finally return to his native rivers and fields where he wants to live *contentus cultu paupere.* The Tibullan tag in the last line serves as a final reverence to the elegiac poet whom Lotichius liked most and whose ideals in poetry and life he believed he shared.[1]

This survey may have given an idea of the variety and comprehensiveness, the structural composition and the overall unity of this collection of elegies. All its topics may, in some way, be considered as legitimate elegiac themes on the grounds of classical practice and contemporary theory. But Lotichius expanded the thematic scope of Roman elegy too, insofar as he often chose topics for his main themes which had only been subordinate motifs in Roman elegy. The elegies as a whole do not seem to reflect a limited section of the poet's life, rather they present the poet in his elegiac existence. They give an elaborate and full picture of the poet's personal life, of his experiences and adventures during the crucial period from 1546 to 1556, unfolding in three well arranged and interconnected cycles. Lotichius mentions with high esteem the outstanding contemporary Neo-Latin poets of Italy,[2] and his poetry was influenced by some of them, most clearly by Antonius Flaminius and Franciscus Molza,[3] but compared with the influence of the classical poets

---

[1] *El.* III.10 was added in the second version (ed. 1563) in order to serve not only as a happy conclusion, but also as a counterpart to *El.* I.1. Many parallels and deliberate contrasts between the two poems may be noticed.

[2] See *El.* III.4.19 ff.; 8.39 ff., and *Carm.* 1.22.6 ff.

[3] The sickness of the poet had been an elegiac theme since Tib. 1.3, and Lotichius wrote accordingly *El.* 1.6 *De se aegrotante,* and III.9 *Ad Joannem Sambucum, cum gravissimo morbo laboraret Bononiae.* F. Molza's elegy *Ad sodales, cum morbo gravi et mortifero premeretur* belonged to the same tradition. It left its imprint on *El.* III.9 in various phrases and motifs. Lotichius used the same elegy of Molza, when he later wrote *El.* III.8 (cf. ll.21 f. and Molza's ll.49 ff., going itself back to Virg. *Ecl.* 7). Further, he followed at least two elegies of Flaminius: (1) *Ad Alexandrum Farnesium Cardinalem* (*carm.* II.4), a poem which is indebted to Tib. I.1. When Lotichius imitated this poem of Tibullus in his *El.* II.11, he also alluded to the elegy of Flaminius. (2) *De se proficiscente Neapolim* (*carm.* II.7). As a travel poem, it should be compared with *El.* III.1 (esp. ll.1 ff. of Flaminius with ll.71 ff.), but it was influential for other elegies of Lotichius too (e.g. *El.* III.7.36 and 92; cf. Flaminius's ll.50 and 39 f.).

their imprint is of a very minor sort, and it may be said that none of them nor any of the German Neo-Latin poets of his time produced an elegiac work of such scope.

The collection contains more actual and specific autobiographical information than any of the classical collections of elegies, and therein lies one of its essential differences from them. But the works of the Roman elegists, above all the books of Tibullus and the *Tristia* and *Amores* of Ovid, stimulated him to create this work.[1] They influenced him in his reactions to the circumstances of his life, guided him in the selection of the material for his elegies, helped him in their composition and gave him models for their artistic arrangement in a sequence of books. His imitation of the Roman elegists was so successful because he used their classical art for the expression of his own personal experiences.

It is here not possible to observe in more detailed interpretations of single elegies how the different components worked together and how Lotichius created new works of original beauty partially with, so to speak, prefabricated parts. Characteristic of him is a simple and straightforward style which avoids far-fetched images, display of striking conceits, and a rare or grandiose vocabulary.[2] The implied allusions to classical texts add another dimension, but the poems are also understandable for readers who do not always recognise them. Lotichius used mythological pictures rarely and an extended allegory[3] only once; in most cases he wrote about his actual experiences.

---

[1] The preference of Tibullus above Ovid is explicitly stated in *Carm.* iii.36.27 ff. Propertius was not among Lotichius's principal models. His style, in the Renaissance famous for its *doctrina* in regard to rare Greek myths, for its daring neologisms and its passionate abruptness, was contrary to the stylistic tendencies of Lotichius. But he imitated some of his elegies and adapted various phrases. E.g. in *El.* 1.8, Prop. 1.18 provided a structural frame and background for his *querelae* on the cruelty of war; compare also p.183, n.5, p.184, n.n.3 and 4 above, and in general for the verbal borrowings, Burman's commentary.

[2] In this, he was in agreement with the doctrine of Eobanus Hessus who wrote in his *Explicatio in J. Murmellii tabulas de ratione faciendorum versuum*, explaining the term *exiguos elegos* in Hor. *A. P.* 77 (ed. Nürnberg, 1552, fol. g6 v): 'decet enim Elegiam versu et leni et quotidiano et minime assurgenti esse conflatam, ut sua sponte et naturali vena ex nostro ore prodire videatur; quare exiguos, id est humiles vocat'.

[3] In *El.* ii.4, the besieged Magdeburg appears as a speaking personification, whereupon a fight between an eagle and a rooster allegorises the war between the emperor and the king of France (cf. H. C. Schnur, *Lateinische Gedichte deutscher Humanisten* (Stuttgart, 1966), p.454; Burmannus *ad loc.* wrongly takes the rooster as an allegory for the elector of Saxony). Lotichius made only one experiment in this unclassical style. He probably was under the influence of two older Neo-Latin poets from Germany. Georgius Sabinus had introduced a speaking *Roma* in his elegy on the sack of Rome (*El.* v.1), and Ulrich von Hutten had played with the same animal allegory in numerous poems of his *Ad Caesarem Maximilianum epigrammatum liber.*

He had a talent for vivid description and narration, but did not use it for facts or events which were not related to him personally. Nature reflects his own feelings, and outward events parallel or foreshadow his emotions. His favourite image, appearing in many elegies, is the running water of a river. His voice is sincere and unpretentious, his perception sensitive and tender. Neither involved in the religious controversies of his time nor politically engaged, except for a general German patriotism, he lived and wrote according to his motto *simpliciter, sine strepitu.*

He once expressed his artistic ideal in the following lines:

> Odi ego qui vastis torrens exaestuat undis;
> qui fluit exiguo murmure rivus amo.[1]

The contrasting image of the foaming torrent and the lovely creek was used in Lotichius's time to differentiate Propertius from Tibullus.[2] It has its Roman origin in the ode of Horace, where he compares Pindar with a swollen river rushing down from the mountains. But Lotichius may also have known its ultimate provenience from the Assyrian stream of Callimachus.[3] His hymns had just been translated and edited by Franciscus Robortellus who was a teacher and friend of Lotichius at Padua,[4] and Lotichius may have been interested in becoming acquainted with the poet whom he knew to have been the Greek *princeps elegiacorum.*[5]

---

[1] *El.* III.8.43 f. The framing *Odi ego* . . . | . . . *amo* alludes, of course, deliberately to Cat. 85.

[2] Cf. J. Vadianus, *De poetica et carminis ratione*: 'adsimilis Tibullus est amni placido, plano alveo per floridos agros defluenti, limpidae undae et suavis haustus; at Propertius torrenti similior, ad iniqua saepe illisus littora, atque ipso asperior vado, celeriorque decursu, cuius tamen undas ex montanis plane fontibus derivari dixeris.'

[3] Cf. Hor. *carm.* IV.2.5 ff. and Call. *h.* II.105 ff.

[4] F. Robortellus (Professor at Padua 1552–7) was the addressee of *El.* III.10. Together with his commentary on Aristotle's *Poetics*, he had published the *Explicatio eorum quae ad elegiae antiquitatem et artificium spectant* (Florence, 1548). His edition of Callimachus's hymns, with the Greek *scholia* and his own Latin translation, appeared in Venice in 1555.

[5] Cf. J. Vadianus, *De poetica et carminis ratione, tit.* 8: '. . . ab hoc elegiaci nominati principes apud Graecos Callymachus et Philetas' (according to Prop. III.1.1 and Quint *Inst. or* X.1.58).

13

FROM THE *CICERONIANUS* TO MONTAIGNE

M. MANN PHILLIPS

The point I want to make is that more investigation is needed on the relationship between discussions on Latin style in the sixteenth century and discussions on French style. Without wishing to suggest that Erasmus is always at the bottom of everything, I think it is undeniable that he had a great hand in the change of taste which came about in the second half of the century, and this was not only in one direction. Erasmus's own attitude to the classics was not a simple one, and his influence can be discerned as operating on several fronts. Dr Bolgar[1] was the first to point out the effect that *De copia verborum et rerum* must have had on several generations of French scholars and writers, who were all likely to have read it at school, since we know that in a forward-looking school it was on the curriculum for the fourth grade, and it is easy to imagine its effect on Ronsard ('tu doibs travailler estre copieux en vocables')[2] and on du Bellay ('Ceste elegance et copie qui est en la grecque et latine').[3] Relevant to their training, too, was the warning in the *De copia* that the object of *copia* was not so much richness as power of selection, the right word in the right place.

But Erasmus went to the heart of the literary problem of his century when he discussed from several angles the effect of the reading of the classics. His characteristic *via media* supplied, or at least symbolised, two opposite trends of imitation. Professor Higman has lately given us telling examples of the change from a flowery allegorical vocabulary to a severely intellectual one, from Gerson to Calvin; and a comparison between the Latinised vocabulary of the early writers of the century (e.g. Jean Lemaire de Belges) and Calvin or Amyot shows that the influence of Latin, from being

---

[1] R. R. Bolgar, *The Classical Heritage and its Beneficiaries* (Cambridge, 1954), pp.272–5, 297–8, 320 ff.

[2] *Abbregé de l'Art Poetique.*   [3] *Deffence et Illustration*, I.IX.

purely external and decorative, had become internal and structural – a way of thinking rather than a process of ornamentation.

This transformation is much in keeping with the lifelong labours of Erasmus to procure a purified Latin usage resulting from the reading of the best authors, and the trumpet call for it is in the *Antibarbari*. But there was another side to the question, and later in life Erasmus came to insist as much on freedom from the classics as on agreement with them. This is the aspect I want to illustrate here, because the results of the Ciceronian controversy seem to have been far-reaching and to have had their effect on French. The servile attitude to classical style and vocabulary affected by the Ciceronians, whether Italian or French, provoked the scorn of Erasmus expressed in the *Ciceronianus* of 1528 and in many of his letters. To him imitation was not true imitation unless it aimed at reproducing the very soul of the model, and we are in fact given the same advice in the *Ciceronianus* as in the *Enchiridion militis christiani*, where we are urged to imitate the virtues of the Apostles rather than kiss their relics. When Joachim du Bellay said 'Mais entende celuy qui voudra imiter, que ce n'est chose facile que de bien suivre les vertus d'un bon auteur, et quasi se transformer en luy',[1] he was echoing, consciously or not, the end of the *Ciceronianus*:

> I welcome imitation, the sort of imitation which aids nature and does not violate it, which corrects natural gifts and does not ruin them. I approve of imitation when it is in agreement with your own mind, or at least not alien to it. Then I like imitation when it does not tie itself down to one model, not daring to stray from it by a line, but rather selects from all authors, or at least the most distinguished, what is best in them, and nearest to your own mind ... So your speech will not seem like an anthology or a mosaic, but the living and breathing image of your inmost feelings, a stream flowing straight from your heart.[2]

The slavish copying of the verifiable words of Cicero was for Erasmus the antithesis of true imitation, and in his proposals for a modern use of Latin, which would be a living, developing international language, supple and adequate for the needs of the modern world, he was pleading for a new vernacular. His attempt failed as far as Latin was concerned, but its results can be traced in the work of later French authors and particularly in that of Montaigne.

I have had occasion before to refer to the engaging example of this pointed out by Hugo Friedrich in his *Montaigne*, published in

[1] *Deffence et Illustration* I.VIII.   [2] *Erasmi Opera* (Leiden), I, 1022C.

1949.[1] In a note on the famous definition of style in the essay *De l'Institution des Enfans*, he shows how Montaigne's list of desirable qualities follows point by point an Erasmian definition in a letter of 1527. There can be little doubt of the connection between the two passages; but Dr Friedrich prudently avoids drawing conclusions. He asks whether Montaigne had read this letter, first published in 1529 and many times subsequently, or whether both Erasmus and Montaigne were harking back to a common source, perhaps Quintilian.

Some light on this may be found in the work of a Neo-Latin poet, famous in his day but soon almost forgotten: Jean Dampierre. I think this may not be the only instance in which a Neo-Latin poet of the mid-sixteenth century may be seen to stand in some way as an intermediary between earlier humanism and later developments.

Jean Dampierre was a native of Blois, a friend of Nicolas Bourbon, an older contemporary of Dolet, and familiar with the circle of poets at Orléans including Viart and Truchon. Scévole de Ste. Marthe writes a touching elogium of him,[2] and tells us that he was a brilliant lawyer and achieved success in this line at Blois and in Paris, but suddenly threw over the law and became a Franciscan. He was a good preacher and finally became Prior of La Madeleine near Orléans. Here he died in 1550, and his friends, particularly Germain Audebert, tried to prevent his works from sinking into obscurity, but in vain. They circulated in manuscript but were never printed, until some of them found their way into Gruterus, *Delitiae Poetarum Gallorum*, in 1609.[3]

Dampierre's convent was a house of the order of Fontevrault. It is hard to imagine that he never met Rabelais. He was much admired, and his friends called him Magister Hendecasyllabôn, because he usually wrote in this metre in imitation of Catullus. He was in fact a Catholic humanist, who had grown up in liberal circles before the upheaval of 1534 imposed a choice on Frenchmen, and he had remained (like Bourbon) an ardent Erasmian.

The poem I am interested in was reprinted by Gruterus. In this I think Dampierre was lucky. It is hard to see now what his friends so much admired in him. Scaliger[4] perhaps strikes a true note in

[1] Hugo Friedrich, *Montaigne* (Bern, 1949), p.493.
[2] *Elogia doctorum Galliae virorum* (Jena, 1596), p.24.
[3] *Delitiae C. poetarum gallorum . . .* collectore Ranutio Ghero (Gruterus) (1609), pp.833–61.
[4] J. C. Scaliger, *Poetices libri septem* (1580), p.789.

saying that Dampierre's verse was so facile that it seems hardly to be in verse at all, and had so many verses that it cannot be called easy. But he adds in extenuation that there is no smell of cloister or of cowl, and that the ideas are persuasive.

This poem of over seven hundred lines[1] begins with an epitaph on Erasmus written by Nicolas Bourbon, to the effect that France and Germany vied with each other in claiming Erasmus for their own, but Death intervened and said: He is mine. This epitaph was written on a false rumour of Erasmus's death in 1533, and it was not included in the *Nugae* of that year, though it figured in a correspondence between Bourbon and Erasmus.[2] It came out in the 1538 edition, which helps us to date Dampierre's poem, unless he too had seen the epitaph in manuscript.

Dampierre begins with a refutation: Erasmus has not died, the Fates can claim nothing of his. The works remain. Some people, Dampierre admits, would dispute this on the grounds of his not being a Ciceronian, and the true subject of the poem emerges: it is a defence of Erasmus in the Ciceronian quarrel. The relations between Erasmus and Cicero are debated for ten pages, in a style of which one extract will suffice:

> Esto:
> Nempe nec Cicero est Erasmianus.
> Erasmum sinant esse Erasmianum,
> Sinant Tullium ut esse Tullianum.

If Cicero had lived in our times, he would have written like Erasmus, and conversely, if Erasmus had lived in Cicero's time he would have written like Cicero. Dampierre is conscious of labouring the point of this quarrel of the Ancients and Moderns, and he apologises constantly for his many repetitions ('ut ante dixi'). One wonders if this poem was a happy choice if it were to be one of the few to survive.

But we may be glad it did. There are many longueurs, but it improves, and there are two passages when the whole thing springs to life. The second of these is my real subject, but the first is an unexpected bonus, a contemporary vignette: the account of a visit of one of Dampierre's friends to the home of Erasmus at Basle, and his rapturous, astonished pleasure at being so well received.

More important for us is the passage towards the end where

---

[1] Gruterus, pp.834–62. [2] *Erasmi Epistolae*, ed. P. S. Allen, 2789.

Dampierre attempts to be judicious about the Erasmian style of writing. He agrees that it is not to be followed in preference to any other, even if it has many good qualities, of which he proceeds to make a list. This list is the identical one given by Erasmus in the letter to Vergara written in 1527,[1] just at the time when he was preparing to defend himself against the Ciceronians. 'What does this boastful noise in the name of Cicero mean?' asks Erasmus. 'I'll tell you in your ear. They are using it as a cover for their paganism, which is dearer to them than the glory of Christ.' He goes on to say that he would not have wished to copy Cicero, even if he had been able to do so, because he preferred a more direct form of speech. It is natural and to be expected that Dampierre should use this strongly anti-Ciceronian letter in his poem, and merely proves that he knew his Erasmus. But it is interesting to see the reappearance of the Erasmian definition of the preferred style both in Dampierre and Montaigne.

To put the three passages together: Erasmus says

malim aliquod dicendi genus solidius, astrictius, nervosius, minus comptum magisque masculum.[2]

Montaigne says:

Le parler que j'ayme, c'est un parler simple et naif, tel sur le papier qu'à la bouche; un parler succulent et nerveux, court et serré, non tant delicat et peigné comme vehement et brusque ... plutot difficile qu'ennuyeux, esloigné d'affectation, desreglé, descousu et hardy ... plutot soldatesque.[3]

Let us now look at Dampierre's version:

> Illorum haud ita damno furorem
> Ut sequi libeat, genusque solum
> Dicendi illud Erasmicum probare,
> Quantumvis lepidum facetum acutum,
> Fucatum minus at nec invenustum,
> Astrictum solidumque masculumque,
> Sic cutim haud adeo comamque curans,
> Firmis ossibus ut sit atque nervis.[4]

In other words: I do not condemn the frenzy of these people (the Ciceronians) so far as to say that solely the Erasmian style of writing is to be followed and admired; even though it may be engaging, merry and shrewd, not highly coloured (painted up), yet beautiful,

---

[1] Ibid. 1885.
[3] *Essais*, ed. Thibaudet et Rat (Paris, 1962), p.171.
[2] Ibid. ll.142–3.
[4] Gruterus, p.855.

short and sharp, solid and masculine, not over-careful about preening and combing, firm in bone and sinew.

He has copied the passage of Erasmus exactly, but also added what Erasmus did not need to add, the attraction of humour and irony. The expression *fucatus* or *picta fucis* is a favourite with Erasmus (cf. *Adages* III.1.1). The presence in each case of the metaphor of uncombed hair, *minus comptum, non peigné, haud adeo comamque curans*, is sufficiently striking.

A few very obvious conclusions arise from this. First, I think, it disposes of Friedrich's doubts; Montaigne must be quoting the letter, either because he had read it in one of the many editions, or because it was a well-known source from which others like Dampierre had quoted. It is unlikely in the circumstances that Montaigne knew the poem of Dampierre, unless Buchanan or some other enthusiast had put it in his way in his schooldays. This definition of style had for some reason lingered in his mind. But there is a further and wider implication: it links Montaigne with the theme of anti-Ciceronianism. Both Dampierre and Montaigne go on from this passage to develop the theme of negligence. Dampierre does not seek to excuse Erasmus from the imputation of negligence, but he remarks that in some ways negligence has its own charm, especially in Christian matters (and here the argument of the *Ciceronianus* is plain to be seen). He then writes an interesting passage on the place of studied negligence in a work of art. Like women, he says, who bind up their hair and let stray locks flutter here and there, so negligence has its own carefulness, its own attention. We are reminded of Ben Jonson:

> Give me a look, give me a face
> That makes simplicity a grace,
> Robes loosely flowing, hair as free,
> Such sweet neglect more taketh me
> Than all th'adulteries of art . . .

This is what Dampierre calls *negligentia diligens*, and it has its equivalent celebration in the passage of Montaigne immediately following our quotation, where he tells us that he was happy to copy the careless dress of the youth of his time, the coat flung on askew, the cape over one shoulder, the wrinkled stocking, symbols of a proud disdain for externals. Even more, he says, freedom and negligence in speech are the marks of the gentleman.

So we follow the meanderings of the anti-Ciceronian argument.

From being in Erasmus the defence of the right of a Christian society to use language in its own way, it becomes in Montaigne the defence of the non-professional, the writer who is free, against the narrowness of the specialist. Both are vindicating the human spirit. The classics must be friends, not masters; they enrich Christian thought for Erasmus, for Montaigne they help to create the ideal of the *honnête homme*. Dampierre, leading us back to the same fountainhead, links two aspects of a fight for freedom.

I think other pointers of this kind might well be found in the Neo-Latin poets.

14

THE HUMANIST IDEA OF CHRISTIAN ANTIQUITY AND THE IMPACT OF GREEK PATRISTIC WORK ON SIXTEENTH-CENTURY THOUGHT

E. F. RICE JR

The reappropriation in the Renaissance of the works of the Greek Fathers has been less carefully studied than the fortunes of Greek literary, philosophical and mathematical texts. An abundance of important and entertaining problems await investigation and solution.

What we need to have first is more of the kind of bibliographical data gradually being made available to us in the *Catalogus translationum et commentariorum*, the vast enterprise initiated by Paul Oskar Kristeller and directed now by Professor Edward Cranz. The *Catalogus* will comprise annotated lists of the manuscripts and editions of all translations and commentaries of Greek texts produced in the Latin West before 1600. It will give us for the first time a precise, quasi-statistical knowledge of what Greek patristic works were known in the West, who translated them and when, who wrote commentaries on them, and how wide or limited was their diffusion in manuscript and print.

Certain conclusions seem fairly clear already: enthusiasm for pagan literature was from the beginning of the so-called 'revival of antiquity' inseparable from an enthusiasm for ancient Christian literature; most Greek patristic works became a living part of western culture only in the fifteenth century, in Italy, through Latin translations by Italian humanists and Greek émigrés; editions of the Greek texts and direct familiarity with them became relatively common among the learned only in the sixteenth and later centuries.

Bibliographical data are fascinating and indispensable, but they will not explain adequately that intensity of interest in patristic literature so charactcristic of fifteenth- and sixteenth-century humanist thought. Why did Cardinal Cesarini tell Ambrogio Traversari that 'if he lived to be as old as Methusalah he could do nothing so useful as spend night and day translating Basil's *Adversus Eunomium*'? How shall we explain the revived interest in Origen; the immense popularity of Leonardo Bruni's translation of Basil's *Ad adolescentes*; or the at least forty-five surviving manuscripts and numerous printed editions of George Trebizond's translation of Eusebius's *De praeparatione evangelica*? Why did Erasmus, from his earliest study of St Jerome to the posthumous edition of the *Opera* of Origen, devote the bulk of his time and energy to patristic studies?

To answer these questions we will need further research on individual translators and editors like Cono of Nuremberg or Zanobio Acciaiuoli, Dominican of San Marco in Florence and Prefect of the Vatican Library, who between 1501 and 1519 translated a number of texts previously unknown in the West: Eusebius, *In Hieroclem*, Olympiodorus's *Commentary on Ecclesiastes*, and Theodoret of Cyrus's *De curatione Graecarum affectionum* and *De providentia Dei*. We will need to know more about celebrated scholars like Erasmus as well. It is astonishing how little attention has been given to the patristic scholarship that was the core of his intellectual life. We will need imaginative studies of the reception and influence in the early modern centuries of individual fathers and of single important texts, the *De homine* of Nemesius of Emesa, for example, or the *De vita perfecta* of Gregory of Nyssa. Naturally, too, the works of a great many authors not themselves patristic scholars in the strict sense are useful sources for investigating sixteenth-century conceptions of Christian antiquity, the primitive church and the periodisation of ecclesiastical history. An attractive subject would be the study of these and related ideas in the works of German humanists like Reuchlin, Konrad Peutinger, Beatus Rhenanus and Mutianus Rufus.

The results of these special studies will be interesting and various. Cardinal Cesarini wanted Basil's *Adversus Eunomium* translated because he believed it to support the Latin position on the procession of the Holy Spirit. One reason Zanobio Acciaiuoli translated Theodoret of Cyrus's *On the Maladies of the Ancient Philosophers* was that it repeated from Clement of Alexandria and Origen the idea of a 'Christian Socrates', divinely inspired, foreknowing Christ, ignorant but supremely wise, an idea recaptured in Italy in the fifteenth century and a cliché by the end of the sixteenth century. 'Socrates', as Theodoret put it, 'was practically illiterate and made himself conspicuous by stammering like a child when called on to read or write. Yet this uneducated, unlearned man was more worthy of respect than all the rest.' Basil's *Ad adolescentes* justified the study of the pagan classics and the humanist educational programme. The *Hexapla* of Origen became an inspiration and model for the critical study and correction of the Bible in its original tongues. The idea of the dignity of man in its later fifteenth- and sixteenth-century formulation had as its immediate nourishing sources pages of Gregory of Nyssa and Nemesius of Emesa. Many Greek patristic works, finally, were admired and pillaged because they were treasure houses of new facts about ancient history, philosophy and religion, both pagan and Christian, and of quotations from classical works now lost. This was clearly part of the appeal of Eusebius's *Praeparatio evangelica*, as a book like Polydore Vergil's *De inventoribus rerum* makes clear.

More generally, I should like to suggest that sixteenth-century humanist intellectuals admired the fathers because they found in their works (or thought they had) a particular style of piety and religious sensibility, one already distilled in the Petrarchan phrase *docta pietas* and in the formula used by many humanists to describe their religious programme: the union of wisdom and piety with eloquence. Peutinger, to cite a single example, explicitly connected the humanist ideal to patristic practice: 'Prisca illa christiana eruditio quae semper eloquentiam ipsam cum divina illa sapientia coniunctam habere voluit.'

The fathers were eloquent because they wrote, as Francis I's confessor put it early in the reign, 'before ancient eloquence began to totter with the tottering Roman empire'. Many of them had been themselves poets, orators and friends of philosophers. To imitate the pagan classics was to follow the example of the Fathers; to imitate the Fathers was to imitate stylists of the great periods of classical letters.

Inevitably humanists used the Fathers as polemical rods with which to beat the scholastics. For not only was the style of the theologians of the recent past said to be barbarous and therefore incapable of persuading men to love God and their neighbours, the *summae* were thought to be unnecessarily complex. When scholastic theologians raised knotty difficulties, opposed authorities *sic et non*, probed *quaestiones* in disputations and reconciled them by a subtle logic, they were rather pandering to their own dialectical pride than serving the faith; indeed, they were contaminating theology with profane philosophy. Humanists pictured themselves as Hercules vanquishing the Hydra or Alexander cutting the Gordian knot. To the discredited theology of the schoolmen they opposed the piety of the Fathers (which they conveniently claimed to have prefigured their own) and which they understood to be simpler, more pure, more personal and emotional, more humbly and accurately dependent on the divine text, directed less to the presumptuous and inevitably disputatious goal of trying to know God in his fullness than toward the more human and possible aim of ardently loving him, more persuasively concerned with moral teaching, closer to the source of truth. The scholastics sought to make theology a science, that is, to establish a systematically ordered body of true and certain knowledge derived from the certain but undemonstrable principles of revelation. This effort too humanists typically attacked as misguided, arrogant and dangerous because it produced only sophistry, arid intellectualism, emotional poverty and lack of charity. The learned and eloquent piety of the fathers, on the other hand, was not a science but a positive wisdom, a holy rhetoric derived from the holy page of scripture. The simple biblical piety Renaissance thinkers attributed to the Fathers justified their own aversion to scholastic method, their insistence on a return to the sources in the original languages, the normally exegetical form of their own theological work, and the end they sought – an eloquent and warm personal piety joined to moral probity.

The Protestant reformers echoed the humanist attack on the sophists; they did not share the humanists' respect for the Fathers' piety and exegetical authority. *Sola scriptura. Omnis homo mendax.* 'The Word of God teaches its own truth', wrote Luther. Zwingli included the Fathers (when he disagreed with them) among the 'rabble of carnal divines' (*der fleischlich Geistlichen*). Calvin distinguished the ancient Fathers from the 'sounder schoolmen' (among whom he included St Bernard and Peter Lombard) and from 'the more recent sophists', less sound as 'they are farther removed from antiquity'; but he was even more cutting about the free-willish Greeks: 'The Greeks above the rest – and Chrysostom especially among them – extol the freedom and ability of the human will. Indeed all the ancients, save Augustine, so differ, waver, or speak confusedly on this subject that almost nothing certain can be derived from their writings.'

Catholics understandably quoted the Fathers against the Protestants, as Erasmus had quoted Origen against Luther. Protestants replied that Catholics 'worshipped only the faults and errors of the Fathers. The good things that these Fathers have written they either do not notice or misrepresent or pervert.' The debate continued into the seventeenth century. Scholars from both camps studied the Fathers. But it was post-Tridentine Catholics who had the weightier motives to do so systematically and in detail. My conclusion is speculative. Patristic scholarship in the decades between 1560 and 1640 is an almost unexplored intellectual landscape.

15

JOHN COLET, HIS MANUSCRIPTS AND THE PS.-DIONYSIUS

J. B. TRAPP

'As for John Colet, he hath never a word to show, for he wrote no works.'[1] Thomas Harding's retort upon John Jewel, Bishop of Salisbury, in 1566, if less than just to the great Dean of St Paul's, was true enough as far as he could have known. It was not until three hundred years later that the labours of one man made it clear that Colet wrote far more than he published, in any conventional sense of the word publication. Until J. H. Lupton, Surmaster of St Paul's School a century ago, made them available (and translated them into English) the Latin texts had lain in manuscript, unprinted, for three hundred and fifty years.[2]

Lupton's achievement, to which he added an excellent biography of Colet[3] besides a still indispensable edition of Sir Thomas More's *Utopia*,[4] is remarkable. He brought Colet out of oblivion, and besides providing good current texts of all his works, identified – in many important instances – the sources of what he borrowed from else-

---

[1] *Rejoinder to M. Jewel's Replie* (1566), fol.44.
[2] The most up-to-date bibliography of Colet is that in the *Cambridge Bibliography of English Literature*, rev. edn, vol.1 (Cambridge, 1974), pp.1790–1; but the fullest and most useful, though it unaccountably fails to mention the *Treatises* (or, as I shall call them, the Commentary) *on the ps.-Dionysius* and the treatise *De sacramentis ecclesiae*, is in Sears Jayne, *John Colet and Marsilio Ficino* (London, 1963), pp.149–59. In their order as edited by Lupton the works are: *Opus de sacramentis ecclesiae: A Treatise of the Sacraments of the Church* (1867); *Super opera Dionysii: Two Treatises on the Hierarchies of Dionysius* (1869); *Enarratio in Epistolam B. Pauli ad Romanos: An Exposition of St. Paul's Epistle to the Romans* (1873); *Enarratio in Primam Epistolam S. Pauli ad Corinthios: An Exposition of St Paul's First Epistle to the Corinthians* (1874); *Opuscula quaedam theologica: Epistolae ad Radulphum: Letters to Radulphus on the Mosaic Account of the Creation, together with other Treatises (De compositione corporis Christi mystici: On the Composition of Christ's mystical Body. Epistolae B. Pauli ad Romanos Expositio: Exposition of St Paul's Epistle to the Romans. Enarratio in Primam B. Petri Epistolam: Commentary on the First Epistle of Peter)* (1876) with a Bibliography of Colet, pp.307–14, especially valuable for its account of previous publication. See also A. B. Emden, *A bibliographical Register of the University of Oxford to A.D.1500* (Oxford, 1957), vol.1, pp.462–4.
[3] First published in 1887; 2nd edn 1909.
[4] First published in 1895.

where. Lupton's books are the foundation for all later work on the subject, though it is hardly to be expected that they are not now in need of revision. This paper is an attempt to clear the ground through a re-examination of the manuscripts written by or for Colet, both those known to Lupton and those unknown. It operates in rather close detail, but only to suggest that the manuscripts can be made to yield more (and different) information than they have so far been made to do. Much of the evidence – it must be admitted at the outset – leads to no sure or startling conclusion. A bald, bibliographical account is nevertheless worth while for what it can contribute to our knowledge of Colet's grave, restless, quest for the amendment of life and his position in the evangelical humanist movement.

I

Only one work of John Colet's seems to have been printed in the lifetime of its author: the Latin 'reform' sermon to the Convocation of Canterbury in 1511/12. Even here there is room for uncertainty. Richard Pynson's undated printing is usually assigned to 1513, on no grounds (I suspect) except the inference that it would have been published soon after it had been preached.[1] Possibly, it was not printed until well after Colet's death – perhaps not until some time nearer 1530, the presumed date of publication by Thomas Berthelet of its English translation.[2] It would fit better into the context of anti-clerical publishing at that moment, though the greater part of that activity was in English, and though its original Latin would have limited its circulation.[3] It is also possible that Colet's *Aeditio*, a little Latin accidence in English for his newly founded St Paul's School, had been printed more than once – like his first High Master William Lily's companion grammar books – while its author

---

[1] *Oratio habita ad Clerum in Convocatione*, A. W. Pollard and G. R. Redgrave, *A Short-title Catalogue of Books printed in England . . . 1475–1640*, no. 5545; repr. in Samuel Knight, *Life of Dr. John Colet* (1724, edn 1823), pp.239–50; cf. Jayne, *Colet and Ficino*, p.149 for printings after the first.

[2] *The Sermone of Doctor Colete, made to the Conuocacion at Paulis*, STC 5550; repr. in Knight, *Life* (edn 1823), pp.251–64; and in Lupton, *Life*, pp.293–304. Jayne, p.150, gives a useful list of later printings and translations. He records a manuscript in Lambeth Palace Library, but no manuscript exists. The Lambeth sermon is a copy of Berthelet's printing.

[3] Cf. *The Apologye of Syr Thomas More Knyght*, ed. A. I. Taft (Early English Text Society, O.S. 180), (Oxford 1930), p.66.

lived. The first extant edition dates from 1527, but schoolbooks are notoriously bad survivors.[1]

That is the best one can do for the Dean to clear him from Harding's charge. Add the editions of his *Right fruitful Monition* to make up the list of what had been published before Harding's day,[2] and it is still short enough – nothing at all if set against the half-million or so words that More saw in print before his execution.

Much of what Lupton published so long after Colet's death at the age of about fifty-two in 1519 must have survived in the memories of those who had heard it as Oxford lectures – particularly on First Corinthians and on Romans.[3] These were delivered in the late 1490s and the first years of the sixteenth century, between Colet's return to Oxford in 1496 from his studies in Italy and France and his departure for London in 1504 to take up his duties as Dean of St Paul's. His prowess as a preacher, too, gained him a large reputation. Were all Colet's works indeed lost, the testimony of Erasmus to his eloquence and holiness, to his effectiveness as a biblical commentator of a new and acceptable kind, one who went straight from his texts to an exposition of their moral value, would command respect for him. The association of the two, documented in Erasmus's published accounts of their friendship, their agreements and their controversies, of the spiritual and material help he received from the Englishman from the time of their first meeting in Oxford in 1499, is responsible for much.[4] It is remarkable how much of our view of Colet comes through Erasmus's eyes, how much we owe, for example, to his obituary letter to Justus Jonas of 1521.[5]

[1] See V. J. Flynn, 'The grammatical Writings of William Lily', in *Papers of the Bibliographical Society of America*, xxxvii (1943), 85–113; C. G. Allen, 'The Sources of "Lily's Latin Grammar": a Review of the Facts and some further Suggestions', in *The Library*, 5th ser., ix (1954), 85–100; id. '*Certayne briefe rules* and "Lily's Latin Grammar"', in *The Library*, 5th ser., xiv (1959), 49–53.

[2] *STC* 5547 [1534]; 5548 [1563]; repr. Lupton, *Life*, pp.305–10. The work is not cited in Jayne's bibliography, pp.149–53.

[3] Sears Jayne, *Colet and Ficino*, pp.23 ff.; P. A. Duhamel, 'The Oxford Lectures of John Colet', in *Journal of the History of Ideas*, xiv (1953), 493–510.

[4] E.g. the fragment quoted in his *Disputatiuncula de taedio et pavore Christi*, first printed in the *Lucubratiunculae* (Antwerp, 1503); the letters conveniently listed by Jayne, *Colet and Ficino*, pp.157–9; and the Colloquy *Peregrinatio religionis ergo*, for which see the trans. by Craig R. Thompson, *The Colloquies of Erasmus* (Chicago, 1965), pp.285–312.

[5] Erasmus, *Opus epistolarum*, ed. P. S. Allen (Oxford, 1906–58), (hereafter Erasmus, *Epp.*), no.1211; trans. by J. H. Lupton in *The Lives of Jehan Vitrier and John Colet by Desiderius Erasmus* (London, 1883), pp.19 ff.

II

One area where it would be valuable to see further and where the manuscripts tell us very little more than Erasmus specifically allows us to know, is Colet's encouragement of the preparation of a new Latin translation of the Greek Testament. If it was the discovery of Lorenzo Valla's *Annotationes in Novum Testamentum* in 1504 that set Erasmus to work,[1] it was Colet who, when Erasmus came again to England in 1505, helped him to make a beginning, significantly enough with the Pauline and Catholic Epistles.[2] But only one extant biblical manuscript can be directly connected with him. This is in three great volumes, with miniatures and illuminations, written for him in a bulky, upright humanist script by Peter Meghen (or, as he sometimes signed himself, Magius) Monoculus, the one-eyed Brabantine from Bois-le-Duc,[3] employed as scribe and messenger by other English prelates as well as by Erasmus.[4] Of these volumes, two are in the British Library and one in Cambridge.[5] All have elaborate colophons. The British Library volumes are dated 1 November 1506 (the Epistles) and 7 September 1509 (Luke and John); the Cambridge volume 8 May 1509 (Matthew and Mark). The dates immediately pose a problem. The main text of these volumes is the Vulgate, with Erasmus's new Latin version written in the margins with equal clarity and elegance, if in a slightly smaller size. J. P. Gilson and Sir George Warner thought that Erasmus's translation had been written into the margins later, in space deliberately left.[6] P. S. Allen's inclination to the view that Erasmus's translation

---

[1] The most convenient short account is P. S. Allen's in Erasmus, *Epp.*, II, pp.182–4.

[2] Ibid., no. 181.

[3] For Meghen, see G. Dogaer in *National biographisch Woordenboek*, I (Brussels, 1964), cols.707–8, with bibliography. To the list of fifteen manuscripts established by O. Pächt in his 'Holbein and Kratzer as Collaborators', in *Burlington Magazine*, LXXXIV (1944), 137, n.6, several more may be added. See my 'Notes on MSS. written by P. Meghen', in *The Book Collector*, XXIV (1975), 80–96.

[4] For example, Christopher Urswick and Cardinal Wolsey (see below, p.210, n.1, p.217, nn.6 and 7). For manuscripts written for Urswick see F. K. Gale, 'Christopher Urswick, 1448–1522' (London University M.Phil. dissertation (Warburg Institute), 1974), pp.38 ff.

[5] MSS Royal I.E.V. in the British Library (J. P. Gilson and G. F. (Sir George) Warner, *Catalogue of the Western MSS. in the old Royal and King's Collections* (London, 1921), vol.I, pp.19–20; cf. the exhibition catalogue *Erasmus en zijn Tijd* (Rotterdam, 1969), no. 106); and Dd. VII.3 at Cambridge (*Catalogue of MSS. in the University Library, Cambridge* (1856), vol.I, p.321; cf. *Erasmus en zijn Tijd*, no. 104).

[6] Loc. cit.

was complete when he left England in 1506 and that the delay in completing the other two volumes was due to the scribe would make this hypothesis unnecessary.[1] According to Allen, this and another English manuscript version of Erasmus's translation are bolder in their retranslations than the text of the first printed edition of the *Novum Instrumentum* (1516).[2] Not until his second edition of 1519 did Erasmus venture so far in print. The inference is – if Allen is correct – that Erasmus was prepared to be more radical in helping the Greekless Colet to an exact understanding of the sense of the Epistles and the Gospels, than he felt able to be to the world at large until he had gauged the strength of his public's opinion. We might be in a better position to judge the matter if we knew when and for whom Meghen wrote three other Bible manuscripts: the smaller, more elegant two volumes of the New Testament, the Vulgate in black and Erasmus in red on alternate lines, now belonging to Corpus Christi College Oxford;[3] the two (originally five) large volumes of the Vulgate Pauline Epistles with alternative readings in red at appropriate places;[4] and the Gallican Psalter and Canticles, glossed as far as Psalm 51,[5] all now in the British Library. The illuminations of the Corpus Christi manuscript must be after 1514 and may stylistically be dated as late as 1520.[6] Assuming that decoration and transcription are contemporary, it is possible that the Erasmus version in this manuscript was copied by Meghen from the printed New Testament of 1519. Scribal copying of printed books was common enough at this time, and especially so in the circle served by Meghen.[7] The evidence of the British Library – Cambridge University manuscript cannot be set aside in the same way.

Further study will let us know more about Erasmus and Colet

---

[1] In Erasmus, *Epp.*, vol.II, pp.182–4.   [2] Ibid.

[3] MSS E.4, 9–10 (13–14); Erasmus, *Epp.* vol.II, p.182; H. O. Coxe, *Catalogus codicum mss. qui in Collegiis Aulisque Oxoniensibus hodie adservantur, pars ii* (1852), Sect.xiii, p.4; cf. *Erasmus en zijn Tijd*, no.105.

[4] MS Royal I.D.XI–XV; *Catalogue of the Royal MSS.*, i, p.18.

[5] MS Royal I.E.III; *Catalogue*, i, p.19.

[6] Pächt, in *Burlington Magazine*, LXXXIV (1944), 137 n.6, gives the date 1514 as *terminus a quo*. In a letter inserted into the MS itself, which he kindly allows me to cite, Professor Pächt gives the *terminus ad quem* as *ca* 1520.

[7] Cf. MS Princeton University Library 89 (C. U. Faye and W. H. Bond, *Supplement to the Census* [by Seymour de Ricci] *of medieval and Renaissance MSS. in the U.S.A. and Canada* (New York, 1962), p.309; and W. K. Ferguson in *American Historical Review*, XXXIX (1933–4), 696–9). For the practice of scribal copying of printed books, see Curt F. Bühler, *The fifteenth-century Book: the Scribes, the Printers, the Decorators* (Philadelphia, 1960), pp.15 ff.

from these manuscripts. Meantime, the British Library–Cambridge University manuscript is a witness of Colet's reverence for the sacred page, of the pride of place he gave to St Paul and of his determination to get at the true message of the whole New Testament by means of the most accurate rendering of the literal sense he could command. It is an index, too, of his taste. The colophons suggest that it was also written as a memorial to Sir Henry Colet, twice Lord Mayor of London, whose death in 1505 had made his son and heir a very wealthy man.[1]

With some of this wealth John Colet was shortly to rebuild and endow St Paul's School,[2] in the churchyard of the cathedral, for the instruction of one hundred and fifty-three boys 'of all nations indifferently' in Greek and Latin, and inculcation of the 'pure chaste eloquence' with 'good Christian life and manners'.[3] At his death the endowment was to increase. Meantime he conveyed certain property to the Mercers' Company (his father's associates) as trustees for the school[4] and drafted statutes setting out the qualifications and duties of the masters, the curriculum that was to be taught and the behaviour expected of the pupils. These statutes

[1] They must have been written in memory of Sir Henry, not for him as stated by W. Schwarz, *Principles and Problems of Biblical Translation: some Reformation Controversies and their Background* (Cambridge, 1955), p.139, and J. K. McConica, *English Humanists and Reformation Politics* (Oxford, 1965), p.69 (among others). He had been dead more than a year when the colophon to the first volume was written. Nor were they the only manuscripts written by Meghen as memorials to a named person: two large, handsome codices in Wells Chapter Library were commissioned in memory of Sir John Huddleston by his executor Christopher Urswick, for Hayles Abbey, as the colophons state. Meghen finished the first – a glossed Psalter with the Canticles and Creed – in 1514; and the second – St John Chrysostom's *Sermones in Evangelium secundum Matthaeum* – in 1517. Cf. C. M. Church, 'Notes on the Buildings, Books and Benefactors of the Library of the Dean and Chapter of the Cathedral Church of Wells', in *Archaeologia*, LVII, pt.2 (1901), 215–16.
[2] The actual foundation date is a vexed question. M. F. J. (Sir Michael) McDonnell, *The Annals of St. Paul's School* (London, 1959), p.32 notes that the preface to the volume of *Evidences of Dean Colet's Lands*, belonging to the Mercers' Company and written out – as far as this time is concerned – by William Newbold, Clerk to the Company and formerly Colet's servant, gives 1508 as the year building was begun. The document giving this date is written in Colet's own person. The first legal instrument to mention the school is dated 1 July [1509]; and the first mention in the Acts of Court of the Company is 9 April 1510 (McDonnell, ibid.) A. F. Leach, 'St. Paul's School before Colet', in *Archaeologia*, LXII (1910), 230 ff. prints extracts from the Book of Evidences and elsewhere. See also L. Lyell and F. D. Watney, *Acts of Court of the Mercers' Company, 1453–1527* (Cambridge, 1936), pp.360 ff. The Statutes and the *Book of Evidences* agree on the date 1512 for the completion of building.
[3] Statutes, as printed in Knight, *Life* (edn 1823), pp.307, 310; Lupton, *Life*, pp.277, 279, 280.
[4] Leach, loc. cit. and *Report of the Charity Commissioners*, Appendix Q, pp.585–6.

are well known and figure in all accounts of English Renaissance education. A dozen manuscript copies survive,[1] but no one has yet succeeded in printing a completely accurate text. None is autograph, and there are textual differences between the two most interesting of them. Both these have inscriptions stating that they have been deposited at the school to be preserved and observed there, and repeatedly professing themselves to be in the Founder's own hand, but neither (I believe) bears any trace of Colet's own rapid, small, firm script (Pl. 16a,b). One set of inscriptions is perhaps more nearly contemporary than the other, and is in the hand, rather like the Dean's but larger, which annotated other manuscripts of Colet's after his death. The copy of the St Paul's School statutes which bears this hand is dated internally 1514, the year in which Colet made a second will in the school's favour.[2] Probably a slightly later transcript, it is preserved at Mercer's Hall in an Elizabethan binding with a portrait of the Founder attributed to William Segar. The other manuscript with inscriptions is now in the British Library:[3] dated internally 1512, the year of the rebuilding, it was transcribed some time after the mid-sixteenth century, on the evidence of its

[1] Probably in 1512, Colet petitioned Pope Julius II for a bull to annul the statutes of St Paul's relating to the Chancellor's power over schools and scholars and to confirm the statutes of the new school (*Book of Evidences*, fol.29; printed in Leach, pp.237–8). I have not found any trace of Colet's supplication or of any other document concerning the school in the Vatican Archives, in spite of every assistance, especially from the Reverend Charles Burns. On 17 July 1512, according to the Acts of Court of the Mercers' Company, Colet 'shewed furth and read' the statutes to the Court of Assistants of the Company (McDonnell, *Annals of St. Paul's School*, p.47, citing earlier publications). I hope to deal at length with the statutes and other documents concerning the foundation, in collaboration with Miss Jean Imray, Archivist of the Mercers' Company, to whom I am grateful for much help.

[2] Three wills of Colet's are known, but the first, dated 4 November 1511, is not to my knowledge extant in a contemporary manuscript. It is printed in Samuel Knight's *Life* (edn 1823), pp.282–5; cf. *Letters and Papers domestic and foreign of the Reign of Henry VIII*, ed. J. S. Brewer and others, vol.1 (1862), no. 1933; 2nd edn (1920), no. 931. Colet probably intended it for the Court of Husting of the City of London, though McDonnell, *Annals of St. Paul's School*, p.45 regards it as a draft. In the form given by Knight it is certainly truncated. A longer and fuller will was proved in the Court of Husting on 10 June 1514 (Guildhall Record Office, Hustings Roll 241(32)). There is a translation in the Report of the Charity Commissioners, Appendix Q, pp.586–7; cf. McDonnell, p.45. Like its predecessor, this will disposed of lands and tenements in favour of the school. Colet's moveable goods and some other lands are elsewhere bequeathed in another will, made five years later, just before his death (see below, p.214, n.1). As a freeman of the City of London, Colet was entitled to make his will for probate in the Court of Husting, and it was not unusual to make two wills. For the procedure, see R. R. Sharpe, *Calendar of Wills proved and enrolled in the Court of Husting, London, 1258–1668* (London, 1889–90), I, pp.iii ff.

[3] MS Add. 6274. The subscriptions are reproduced in Jayne, *Colet and Ficino*, pl.5.

handwriting (Pl. 16*d*). It seems to represent the first stage of Colet's intentions for St Paul's School.

Of other documents connected with Colet, two deserve mention. Both are evidence of that reforming zeal which made him sometimes 'out with the chapter'[1] at St Paul's and both apparently date from the first year or two of his deanship.[2] The first is extant. Now MS Tanner 221 in the Bodleian Library, it is a collection of letters patent, ordinances, charters, deeds and accounts of the Guild of Jesus in the Crowds [crypt] of St Paul's,[3] founded in 1459. This Tanner MS begins with the new vellum book provided by Colet in 1507 for the guild to record its statutes and other documents.[4] The second has disappeared from view. It was seen in private hands in 1890 by W. Sparrow Simpson, who published its contents.[5] From his description, this manuscript was most likely written out by Peter Meghen.[6] It consisted of excerpts put together by Colet from the cathedral statutes relating to the government of the chantry priests and other clergy and it was intended to be placed in the choir so that no one henceforth could plead ignorance of his obligations.

It is time to turn to those manuscripts which do bear the hand of Colet himself. The first must be the incunable, discovered in the library of All Souls' College by Mr N. R. Ker in 1952, of Marsilio Ficino's *Epistolae* (Venice, 1495), which is copiously annotated by Colet. This volume makes certain what Lupton had long ago postulated: that Ficino was the most substantial contributor – far more than Pico della Mirandola – to Colet's knowledge of the Florentine Platonists. Letters drafted and transcribed by Colet on to its flyleaves

---

[1] Lupton, *Life*, p.133.

[2] For documents concerning St Paul's Cathedral during Colet's deanship, see W. Sparrow Simpson, *Registrum statutorum et consuetudinum ecclesiae cathedralis Sancti Pauli Londinensis* (London, 1873), esp. pp.xlv–xlix; Book II, items xi (epitome of the Statutes), pp.217–36; item xii (*Exhibita* to Wolsey), pp.237–48; Book V (Guild of Jesus), pp.433–62 (see below).

[3] See A. Hackman, *Catalogus codicum . . . Thomae Tanneri* (Oxford, 1860) (*Catalogi codd. mss. Bibliothecae Bodleianae*, iv). Colet's purchase seems to have comprised the first sixteen vellum leaves; the accounts, which run from 1514 to 1534, are on paper.

[4] If the apparently contemporary note 'a° 1507' at the head of the inscription on fol.1 v recording Colet's purchase is to be credited.

[5] See his 'On a newly discovered Manuscript containing Statutes compiled by Dean Colet for the Government of the Chantry Priests and other Clergy in St Paul's Cathedral', in *Archaeologia*, LII, pt.1 (1890), 145–74.

[6] Loc. cit. p.161: 'The manuscript . . . is composed of twenty-three leaves of vellum . . . The height of a page is 12¼ inches, and the width 8 inches . . . The handwriting is very clear and distinct, the character not unlike Roman letters. There are fourteen lines to a full page; some capital letters being ornamented with red and blue . . .'

seem also to confirm the suspicion that the two men never met and that – contrary to nineteenth-century opinion – Colet never visited Florence. (There is still just room, I think, to believe that older opinion was right.) These annotations have been edited, with a long introduction, by Professor Sears Jayne,[1] but more remains to be done about their significance, especially their relation to the Commentaries on St Paul and the ps.-Dionysius.

The letter drafts in the All Souls' Ficino are the only extant autograph letters of Colet's. There are transcripts of letters in a manuscript in Cambridge;[2] in another manuscript at Princeton;[3] and in the Public Record Office.[4] The rest of his correspondence – with Erasmus,[5] and with Thomas More[6] for example – we know only from printed editions.

To complete the tally of minor specimens of Colet's hand, there are his subscriptions in registers – one in Rome and one in London – and his annotations of deeds and charters. On 14 March 1493 Colet subscribed the *Liber fraternitatis* of the Hospital of S. Spirito in Sassia at Rome.[7] On 3 May 1493 his name was entered, probably by another hand, in the register of the English Hospice at Rome.[8] At an unknown date but probably about 1511 in London, Colet subscribed the admission book of Doctors' Commons.[9] The charters and deeds I leave aside.[10]

The All Souls' Ficino is the only extant printed book which once formed part of Colet's library. He mentions a Jerome 'and other

[1] *Colet and Ficino.* A page annotated by Colet and a page annotated by another hand (I believe) are reproduced there (pls.2, 4).
[2] To Richard Kidderminster, Abbot of Winchcombe, MS University Library Gg. iv.26, fols.61–2; there is a transcript in Knight, *Life* (edn 1823), pp.265–8.
[3] To Christopher Urswick, Princeton University Library MS 89, fol.1; W. K. Ferguson, 'An unpublished Letter of John Colet, Dean of St. Paul's' in *American Historical Review*, XXXIX (1933–4), 699.
[4] To Cardinal Wolsey; Public Record Office SP 1/16; see *Letters and Papers . . . Henry VIII*, ed. J. S. Brewer and others (London vol. II, 2, 1864), no.3834.
[5] See the table in Jayne, *Colet and Ficino*, pp.157–9.
[6] *The Correspondence of Sir Thomas More*, ed. Elizabeth Frances Rogers (Princeton, 1947), nos.3, 8.
[7] Ed. P. Egidi, in *Necrologi e libri affini della provincia romana*, II, *Necrologi per la città di Roma* (Fonti per la Storia d'Italia, xlv), (Rome, 1914), p.276.
[8] Archives of the Venerable English College at Rome, Lib. 17. For a convenient assemblage of the literature on these entries, see Jayne, *Colet and Ficino*, p.17.
[9] Lambeth Palace, Archives, MS S.R. 136, fol.8r; Jayne, pp.135–6, pl.3.
[10] E.g. British Library, Add. Charters 826 and 828 (see J. B. Trapp, 'Dame Christian Colet and Thomas More', in *Moreana: Bulletin Thomas More*, XV–XVI (1967) (*Hommage à Miss E. F. Rogers*) pp.102–13); and St Paul's Cathedral Archives.

printed books' in his will[1] – and that is all. On his reading and his sources, much remains to be done: the admiring testimony of Erasmus needs to be sifted and examined. Besides his deep study of the Bible, Erasmus tells us, Colet had read Plato, Plotinus and all Cicero, as well as taking most pleasure in the early Fathers – the ps.-Dionysius, Origen, Cyprian, Ambrose and Jerome. To Augustine he was *iniquior* than to any others. Scotus and Aquinas he read with distaste for their defining habit, which had led men away from the true message of the scriptures.[2] Is it pure coincidence that most of Colet's favourites, according to Erasmus, were also favourites of Erasmus? Other Fathers, of course, Colet read – St John Chrysostom for example[3] – a favourite of the time because of his habit of commenting on the biblical text by going straight from that to the moral enlightenment to be derived therefrom. Gulielmus Durandus, Bishop of Mende,[4] Pico della Mirandola,[5] Marsilio Ficino,[6] the Renaissance Cabbala[7] he knew and quotes from. Perhaps he had read some Savonarola.[8] Such scattered and incomplete remarks only indicate the need for investigation of Colet's reading and his intellectual and spiritual formation.

To come at last to Colet's own commentaries and other works, some survive as autograph versions, some as transcripts, some as part one and part the other. Almost all are corrected or enlarged by Colet and/or another hand: Colet was obviously as diligent a rewriter and second-thinker as the next man. The manuscripts are:

[1] That is the third will (above p.211, n.2), now in the Public Record Office, P.C.C. Ayloffe 19; printed in Knight, *Life of John Colet* (edn 1823), pp.400–9; a copy is in the Archives of St Paul's Cathedral: see *Ninth Report of the Royal Commission on Historical MSS.*, Appendix 1 (London, 1883), p.48, item 72. But Thomas Lupset was left 'suche bookes prynted as may be most necessary for his lernyng' (Knight, p.401).

[2] Letter to Justus Jonas, p.207, n.5 above.

[3] Lupton, *Life*, p.249n.

[4] Cf. Colet on the *Ecclesiastical Hierarchy*, 1, 1, ed. Lupton (1869), pp.57, 203.

[5] Most of all the *Heptaplus*; cf. Jayne, *Colet and Ficino*, pp.27, 28, 44, 49, 105; and the *Apologia*, cf. *Ecclesiastical Hierarchy*, v, 1, ed. Lupton (1869), pp.xviii, 109, 236.

[6] See especially Jayne, *Colet and Ficino*, passim; and Colet, *Celestial Hierarchy*, ed. Lupton (1869), pp.xviii, 36–47, 187–96.

[7] Via Pico della Mirandola, cf. n.5 above.

[8] On the circulation of Savonarola (the Meditations on the Psalms 'In te Domine speravi' and 'Misereri mei Deus') among Colet's associates, see J. K. McConica, *English Humanists and Reformation Politics* (Oxford, 1965), pp.71, 195–6; and now F. K. Gale, 'Christopher Urswick' (unpublished M.Phil. dissertation, University of London (Warburg Institute), 1974), pp.39 ff. It is just possible that MS Corpus Christi College 547 (Savonarola's Meditation on Psalm 50), was written for Colet: it is certainly in Meghen's hand.

1. Cambridge University Library MS Gg.iv.26, containing the *Commentary* on I Corinthians, the *Enarratio* on the whole of Romans, the treatise *De corpore Christi mystico*, the Commentary on the *Celestial Hierarchy* of the ps.-Dionysius the Areopagite, with its 'Postscript', and a letter.[1] It is a paper manuscript, partly in Colet's own hand and partly in that of a scribe (perhaps Meghen) corrected, augmented and annotated by Colet. It reached the University Library in 1649, via the collection of Richard Holdsworth, Master of Emmanuel College.

2. Emmanuel College Cambridge, MS iii.111.12, a transcript on vellum by Meghen, without annotation, of the *Commentary* on I Corinthians, made from the University Library manuscript.[2] It was presented to the college by Anthony Tuckney, Master from 1645 to 1659.

3. Corpus Christi College Cambridge, MS 355, a transcript on vellum by Meghen with annotations by Colet and by the 'red annotating hand' of the Statutes, of the *Expositio* of Romans i–v and the *Letters to Radulphus on the Mosaic Account of the Creation*.[3] It formed part of the collection of Matthew Parker (1504–75), Archbishop of Canterbury.

4. The manuscript belonging to the Duke of Leeds, at present British Library MS Loan 55/2, a transcript on vellum by Meghen with annotations by Colet and headings and annotations by the 'red annotating hand', of the *De sacramentis Ecclesiae*, and of the *Commentary* on both the *Celestial* and the *Ecclesiastical Hierarchies*, with the 'Postscript' to the former.[4] The *Commentary* on the *Celestial Hierarchy* and the 'Postscript' are transcribed from the Cambridge University Library manuscript. It once belonged to Lord Burghley, who probably acquired it after 1574, since its binding bears his arms within the Garter.[5]

---

[1] *Catalogue of the MSS. in the Library of the University of Cambridge*, vol.iii (Cambridge, 1858), pp.171–2.

[2] M. R. James, *A descriptive Catalogue of the Manuscripts in the Library of Emmanuel College, Cambridge* (Cambridge, 1904), no.245.

[3] M. R. James, *A descriptive Catalogue of the Manuscripts in the Library of Corpus Christi College, Cambridge* (Cambridge, 1912), no.355; see the Correction by C. A. L. Jarrott, in *Proceedings of the Cambridge Bibliographical Society*, vol.v, pt.ii (1970), pp.149–50.

[4] 27 × 18 cm (10⅝″ × 7″); 142 fols. (a–r⁸ˢ, s⁶), 22 lines per page; d⁵⁻⁶, o³ blank. Spaces for initials, but none inserted.

[5] I am grateful to Mr Howard Nixon of the British Library for this identification of the arms and for dating the binding, independently of them, as '1590s or thereabouts'. It was lot 59 among the 'MSS latini in folio' at the sale of Burghley manuscripts in

5. The St Paul's School manuscript, a later transcript on paper of 4, including the headings but not the annotations.[1] It was presented to the school in 1759 by a pupil, Robert Emmot, and bears the signature of Peter Fanwood, probably from the end of the sixteenth century.[2]

6. Trinity College Cambridge MS O. 4.44, suspected by Lupton of being a work of Colet's, and including the Commentary on I Peter.[3] A later transcript on vellum, not annotated, by an unnamed scribe, which I leave aside here because of its doubtful status. Thomas Gale (1635–1702, High Master of St Paul's School from 1672 to 1697) believed it to be Colet's.

Of these, 1–4 can be said with certainty to belong to Colet's lifetime; 5 is probably a little later and 6 later still. The Cambridge University Library manuscript is neatly written and is a sort of fair copy, a pre-final version as it were. 2, 3 and 4 form part of what may be called the 'collected edition' of the Dean's works. It seems at least likely that copies on vellum, written out with clarity and some elegance by Peter Meghen, once also existed of the *Enarratio* on the whole of Romans and the *De corpore Christi mystico* of the Cambridge University Library manuscript.

Like Christopher Urswick, Henry VII's Great Almoner and Dean of York and Windsor, to whom he once sent a book,[4] Colet seems to have had a rich man's preference for manuscripts over printed books, joined with a reluctance to publish. When he finally decided to give his works a more permanent dress, he went no further than to commission Meghen to make this sort of uniform, authorised edition in a single copy. Whether those works which we know only from Bale's[5] and John Pits's[6] reports ever existed in this (or in any) form, I do not know. Lupton, it seems, did not grasp the significance of the 'collected edition'. Colet valued this enough to mention it

---

1687 (*Bibliotheca illustris sive Catalogus ... bibliothecae viri cuiusdam praenobilis ...*, p.83).

[1] 25 × 19 cm (9⅞″ × 7⅜″); 114 fols. (a–i¹²ˢ, k⁶, lacking a⁴⁻⁵, c⁴); 26 lines per page. Secretary hand.

[2] Colet, *Opuscula quaedam theologica* (1876), p.311.

[3] M. R. James, *A descriptive Catalogue of the Manuscripts in the Library of Trinity College, Cambridge* (Cambridge, vol.III, 1902), no.1274; Lupton, *Life*, p.62n.

[4] See above, p.209, n.7, p.213, n.3.

[5] John Bale, *Scriptorum illustrium Maioris Brytannie ... Catalogus* (Basel, 1557), p.609; cf. id. *Index Britanniae Scriptorum ...* ed. R. L. Poole and M. Bateson (Oxford, 1902), p.195.

[6] *Relationum historicarum de rebus Anglicis tomus I* (Paris, 1619), p.692.

specifically in his will, in which he leaves his 'Newe Testament, and oder of myne owne makyng wryten in parchement, as Comentis on Paulis Epesteles and Abbreviacions with many such other' at the disposition of his executors.[1] Bale records the discovery of the manuscripts after Colet's death, 'divaricatis pagellis, in secretissimo suae bibliothecae loco'.[2] What happened to them next we do not know; but a sad note in the Corpus Christi College Cambridge manuscript[3] records that many others of the works had perished *incuria puerorum* (Pl. 16c). This note and others in the same manuscript are in the same hand, using the same red ink as that which copied Colet's subscriptions on to the Mercers' Hall copy of the St Paul's School statutes and added headings and annotations to the Duke of Leeds's 'collected edition' manuscript. This hand can therefore not be Colet's, as it is frequently said to be; and I doubt whether it is Cuthbert Tunstal's, as a perhaps sixteenth-century note in the Corpus Christi manuscript asserts.[4] I suspect that it may belong to the mid-century, when some attempt was made to put together some of Colet's manuscripts[5] – but I have no evidence.

It is not clear when Colet ordered Meghen to make these fair copies, since none of them is dated. Not before 1504, it seems, when Meghen's presence in this country is first documented[6] and Colet was translated to the Deanery of St Paul's. Perhaps not before the 1510s. The mention of vellum manuscripts of his own works in Colet's will and the occasional presence of additions and annotations in his own hand in the 'collected edition' makes it impossible that they were written by order of his executors, though Meghen was active as a scribe in England until the end of the 1520s.[7] Occasional gaps

[1] Knight, *Life* (1823), p.401.   [2] Bale, *Catalogus*, p.608.   [3] P.194.
[4] P.58; James, *Catalogue*, loc. cit., accepts the identification.
[5] W. Sparrow Simpson, *Registrum Statutorum . . . Cathedralis S. Pauli* (1873), pp.xlvi–xlvii.
[6] In the colophon to MS V.a.84 (olim Smedley 7), in the Folger Shakespeare Library, Washington D.C., written for Christopher Urswick (De Ricci, *Census*, vol.i, p.443. I thank R. J. Schoeck for supplying particulars of the manuscript). See also MS Douce 110, in the Bodleian Library, also written for Urswick – the earliest dated manuscript executed by Meghen, according to Pächt's list, *Burlington Magazine*, LXXXIV (1944). This has a colophon dated 28 November 1505, but also, for good measure, giving the regnal year as 20 Henry VII, which would be 1504, Henry's reign dating from 22 August 1485.
[7] When he wrote the two opulent lectionaries for Wolsey, now MS Christ Church 101; and Magdalen College Oxford 223 (not 233 as in Pächt) as well as the little manuscript, a New Year's gift for Henry VIII, of Nicolas Kratzer's *Canones horoptrici*, now Bodleian Library MS Bodley 504. The Magdalen lectionary can be dated – at least as far as its illustration is concerned – 1529 by Wolsey's arms, several times repeated, impaling

in them where Meghen presumably could not read the Dean's handwriting were sometimes filled, sometimes not.

III

So much for Colet's manuscripts in general. What of the manuscripts of his *De sacramentis ecclesiae* and his commentary on or Abstracts of the *Hierarchies* of the ps.-Dionysius? In the first place, Lupton's edition of these works is by far his least satisfactory. He took as the basis of his text the St Paul's School manuscript, which besides being a later transcript of the Duke of Leeds's 'collected edition' manuscript, lacks three leaves. He collated the readings of the school manuscript with those of the Cambridge University Library codex as far as possible, that is for the *Celestial Hierarchy*, and made up two of its three missing leaves from the same source. About the gap in the *Ecclesiastical Hierarchy* he could do nothing. His edition was published in 1867–9, so that he could have known of the Duke of Leeds's manuscript only by chance. Mention of it is made in the Report of the Historical Manuscripts Commission for 1888,[1] but as far as I know Lupton never later acknowledged its existence[2] and it has never been collated by any student since his day. As the fullest and most authoritative text, it must form the basis for any edition.

Even so, much that we should like to know about Colet's dealings with the ps.-Dionysius remains obscure. Is his Commentary the Abbreviations named in his will? What Latin translation from the Greek was he using? No answer seems at present possible to the first question. To the second the reply is that, characteristically, he based himself on the new translation, that of Ambrogio Traversari. As for the edition – if he did indeed use a printed text – opinion is divided between the two possibilities. Professor Jayne seems to

York and Winchester; and the Kratzer must be New Year 1528/9 (Pächt, in *Burlington Magazine*, LXXXIV (1944), 134). J. K. McConica's statement (*English Humanists . . .*, p.70) that 'by far the largest number of commissions surviving and identified . . . are associated with the name of Christopher Urswycke' needs modification: according to my count of manuscripts in which Meghen certainly had a hand the score is Urswick six, Colet five.

1 *Eleventh Report of the Royal Commission on Historical MSS.*, Appendix VII (London, 1888), p.40 (the arms on the binding not identified).

2 It is not in the bibliography in *Opuscula quaedam theologica . . .* (London, 1876), p.311, nor in the *Life*, 1909; nor in E. W. Hunt, *Dean Colet and his Theology* (London, 1956), with bibliography pp.131–3; nor in Jayne, *Colet and Ficino*.

indicate that it was the *princeps* (Bruges, 1480), Professor Eugene Rice thinks it was Lefèvre d'Etaples' recension, first published at Paris in 1498/9 – and to my mind Professor Rice has the better arguments.[1]

When Colet wrote the work, which he says he did in a few days, is unclear. It seems to belong to the context of his Pauline lectures at Oxford, which in turn seem to belong to the time when he was reading Ficino's *Epistolae* with such close attention.[2] Lupton long ago pointed out the direct borrowing from the *Epistolae* in what looks like a postscript to the *Celestial Hierarchy*.[3] Clearly, for Colet, the ps.-Dionysius had a Platonic authority equal to Ficino's, and he read both with fervour – but this does not necessarily help to reach certainty about when the *Commentary* was written. It seems to me likely that it belongs to the very last years of the fifteenth century or the very first years of the sixteenth, at about the time when, as far as we know, William Grocyn began to deliver his famous lectures on the ps.-Dionysius.[4] (Grocyn began his course in the belief that he was lecturing on the convert of St Paul, but changed his mind as he proceeded, and ended on the side of Valla and Erasmus, who had denied the identity.) One of our difficulties is that we know neither when the earliest of Colet's ps.-Dionysian manuscripts was written down nor what stage of his work it represents. Another is that we do not know exactly when Grocyn's lectures were given. Sir Thomas More calls them 'recent' in a letter that can hardly be later than very early in 1502 (since he calls the London entry of Catherine of Aragon recent also, and that took place in November 1501);[5] and Erasmus (never strong on dates and figures) says in 1532 that they had been given thirty years earlier.[6] Nor can we say whether John Jewel was right in counting Colet with those who doubted the identity of the ps.-Dionysius with the Pauline Dionysius of Acts xvii[7] – for Colet nowhere gives any indication of his views. That he included his Commentaries on the *Hierarchies* in the works he

[1] Jayne, p.29; E. F. Rice, review of Jayne, in *Renaissance News*, XVII (1964), 108–9.
[2] Jayne, pp.29 ff.
[3] *Two Treatises on the Hierarchies* (1869), pp.36–47, 187–96.   [4] Jayne, pp.29 ff.
[5] Jayne, p.29; *Correspondence of Sir Thomas More*, ed. E. F. Rogers (Princeton, 1947), no.2.
[6] *Declarationes Des. Erasmi Roterodami ad censuras Lutetiae vulgatas sub nomine Facultatis Theologiae Parisiensis* (Basel, 1532), p.264; cf. *Opera* (edn Leiden, 1703–6), vol.IX, cols. 916–17.
[7] *Reply unto M. Harding's Answer* (1611), p.8; ed. J. Ayre (Parker Society, London, 1845), pp.113–14.

commissioned Meghen to write suggests either that he continued to accept the quasi-apostolic authority of these writings or – as seems more likely – that he found that the ps.-Dionysius's value for a Neo-Platonic justification of the order of created being, the hierarchy of the church and its sacraments, was sufficient in its own right to outweigh the loss of that authority.

This, I believe, is the most important instance where the examination of the manuscripts adds something to what we can say of Colet. It is, perhaps, not a great deal and Meghen's fair copy does not substantially alter what might already be said about the ps.-Dionysius and Colet's Neo-Platonic search for reform and perfection. On the other hand, that is only because what has so far been done is so inadequate.[1] The importance of the ps.-Areopagite for one of the most important shifts in Colet's thinking, his reversal of the two first members of the Pauline triad so that it reads, in ascending order, hope, faith and charity has not been fully recognised.[2]

The fact that this work of Colet's was the only one of the 'collected edition' to be retranscribed perhaps indicates the value placed on the author of its original. It is worth noting that the annotations in the 'red' hand in the Duke of Leeds's manuscript all concern the *Ecclesiastical Hierarchy* – an indication of the relative importance of the *Hierarchies* to sixteenth-century readers which needs further investigation. Bellarmine's wrath with Valla, Erasmus and the other know-alls who doubted the apostolicity of the ps.-Dionysius must have derived some of its warmth from the implied danger to church government.[3]

We need a much fuller and more detailed account of the presence of the ps.-Dionysius in the Renaissance, of the use of the various translations and commentaries, for example, and of his wider

[1] Lupton apart, E. W. Hunt's, in *Dean Colet and his Theology* (London, 1956), esp. pp.112 ff., is the fullest treatment. The matter is touched on by Jayne, *Colet and Ficino*, pp.29 ff.; and Leland Miles, *John Colet and the Platonic Tradition* (London, 1962), passim.

[2] Colet, it seems, was still wavering when he wrote out that particular section of Cambridge University Library MS Gg.iv.26; in one place, he began to list them in their conventional order, but recollected himself and, crossing out *fides* as the first element in the triad, wrote in *spes* instead.

[3] St Robert Bellarmine, *Opera omnia* (Naples, 1872), VIII, p.21 (after a list of ps.-Dionysius's works): 'Soli haeretici Lutherani et quidem scioli Erasmus, Valla, et pauci alii, opera supra nominata negant esse sancti Dionysii Areopagitae.' I take the quotation from D. P. Walker, 'The *Prisca Theologia* in France', in *Journal of the Warburg and Courtauld Institutes*, XVII (1954), 217n. The essay has been reprinted in Walker's *The Ancient Theology: Studies in Christian Platonism from the fifteenth to the eighteenth Century* (London, 1972).

influence, than any now in existence. We need a new edition of Colet's Commentary on the *Hierarchies* to act as the corner-stone of the English section of this account. We need a new edition of Colet's other works, such as we expect to receive from Professor Bernard O'Kelly for the Commentary on First Corinthians.[1] When we have all this, we need a new intellectual biography of John Colet.[2] It should not take longer to do than a lifetime.

I am obliged to the following for allowing me to see manuscripts in their charge: The Keeper of Manuscripts, the British Library; the Keeper of Western Manuscripts, the Bodleian Library (where I am especially grateful for the help of Dr A. C. de la Mare); and to the Librarians of the following: at Cambridge, the University Library, Corpus Christi College, Emmanuel College and Trinity College; at Oxford, Christ Church, Corpus Christi College, Magdalen College, University College; in London, St Paul's School; at Wells, the Chapter Library; in Washington D.C., the Folger Shakespeare Library.

[1] P. B. O'Kelly, 'A Commentary on First Corinthians by John Colet' (unpub. Harvard University dissertation, 1960).
[2] What his early university training contributed to his intellectual formation may need re-examination in the light of W. Robert Godfrey's contention that Colet's undergraduate years were passed at Cambridge: see his 'John Colet of Cambridge' in *Archiv für Reformationsgeschichte*, LXV (1974), 6–18.

16

ERASMUS, THE EARLY JESUITS AND THE CLASSICS

A. H. T. LEVI

Erasmus has long been esteemed for the breadth of his classical learning and for his enthusiasm for the culture and style of classical antiquity. He acquired Greek painfully, added during the whole of his adult life to his *Adagia*, making that work one of the great sixteenth-century compilations of philological learning, and became the best-known classical scholar of the northern European Renaissance. The early Jesuits made the classics the basis of the curriculum in their schools and used them to provide perhaps the best education widely available in Europe towards the end of the sixteenth century. The historical image of both Erasmus and the early Jesuits has been changing in recent years. But we still need to explain how the conciliatory Erasmus and the counter-reforming Jesuits came to have so much in common.

It has long been known that Ignatius of Loyola disliked and distrusted the subtle, doubtless devout but also ambiguous humanist. Ignatius's early biographers, Maffei, Polanco and Ribadeneira, all tell us how Ignatius felt his ardour grow cool on attempting to read the *Enchiridion*, how he put the book aside and forbade the reading of Erasmus to the early Jesuits. But recent historians have tended to suspect the early biographers of more than a little mythologising. It is the similarities between Erasmus and Ignatius that are now emphasised rather than the differences. There is however one text, apparently unnoticed, which seems to me capital not only for explaining the apparent similarity of attitude towards the classics of Erasmus and the early Jesuits, but also to demonstrate the nature of Erasmus's influence on the central formulation of Jesuit spirituality. It is to this text that I wish first to draw attention.

Modern historians of Jesuit spirituality have come to trace Ignatius's central inspiration to a mystical experience which he underwent beside the Cardoner river in the autumn of 1522, called by Jerome Nadal, his most trusted lieutenant, the *eximia illustratio*. This experience determined both Ignatius's own spirituality and the principles of the Jesuit order to be embodied in its *Constitutions*. Its essence was an understanding of how life could be conducted under the certainty of divine guidance through a series of choices or 'elections' based on the discernment of spirits. The celebrated *Spiritual Exercises* are essentially a practical guide to the making of such elections, and at their heart are the famous 'Rules for the discernment of Spirits' which lay down the basic principle of discernment which constituted the intellectual insight of the Cardoner experience.[1]

The discernment of spirits was not a subject unknown to earlier spiritual writers, and the tradition goes back to St Paul who, in warning the Corinthians against false prophets, said that even Satan could change himself into an angel of light.[2] The question was how to recognise Satan in disguise. Gerson touched on the subject, and in 1519 Menot's sermon at Tours on Septuagesima Sunday gives a graphic illustration of Satan appearing as an angel to Saint Simon Stylites.[3] But no one before Ignatius formulates systematic rules of discernment.

However, in 1546 the *Tiers Livre* of Rabelais puts into the mouth of Pantagruel at the end of the discourse on dreams in the fourteenth chapter the following statement, 'souvent l'ange de Sathan se transfigure en ange de lumière . . . l'ange maling et séducteur au commencement resjouist l'homme, enfin le laisse perturbé, fasché et perplex'. Pantagruel's view is disconcertingly similar to that of Ignatius, for whom also the bad angel transforms himself into the angel of light, at first counterfeiting the effects caused in the soul by God, which are 'vera laetitia et gaudium spirituale', in order finally to reach his end, 'trahendo animam in suas fraudes occultas ac perversas intentiones' and so to destroy 'eiusmodi laetitiam, et consolationem spiritualem, adducendo rationes apparentes, subtilitates, et assiduas fallacias'.[4] Ignatius had certainly not read the

---

[1] On the complex evidence for this interpretation of Ignatius's spirituality, see José Calveras, 'La Illustración del Cardoner y el Instituto de la Compania de Jesús según el P. Nadal', *Archivum Historicum Societatis Jesu* (1956) ('Commentarii Ignatiani', 1556–1956), 27–54, and Leonardo R. Silos, 'Cardoner in the Life of Saint Ignatius of Loyola', *Archivum Historicum Societatis Jesu* (1965), 3–43.
[2] II Corinthians xi, 13–14.   [3] *Sermons choisis*, ed. Josephe Nève (Paris, 1924), p.14.
[4] The quotation is an amalgamation of the first and fourth rules for the second 'week', which assume that the soul is detached from serious sin (*Spiritual Exercises*, §§329 and 332).

Tiers Livre, and Rabelais could not have known the as yet unpublished *Spiritual Exercises*. It seems likely that there was a common source. It may well have been Erasmus.

At the beginning of 1522 Erasmus was at Basle. The *Paraphrasis in Evangelium Matthaei* was ready for, or already at, Froben's press and, to fill the opening sheet, which Allen thinks was 'evidently printed after the rest of the book', Erasmus composed an 'appendix', addressed to the reader and dated 14 January, to follow the formal dedicatory letter to Charles V, dated the previous day, 13 January.[1] The *Paraphrasis* appeared dated 15 March in a folio edition, and there was an octavo of the same month. The prefatory appendix is one of Erasmus's more outspoken pleas for the reading of scripture, in translation if necessary, as a foundation for Christian piety. It does however formally pose the question of the *discretio spirituum*, refer to Satan's ability to change himself into an angel of light, and propose as a solution that the spirit of Christ brings peace and harmony, whereas 'ubicumque dissidium est, ibi Diabolus est'. More important perhaps is the long passage starting 'Dicet mihi quispiam: Difficilis est discretio spirituum.' Erasmus talks not only of Satan transformed into an angel of light, but also of the primacy of interior sentiment, the opposition between the followers of the world and the followers of Christ, the way in which the good spirit disturbs the wicked, blinded by their attachments, the importance of interior guidance, the need to approach the scriptures with a spirit of piety. Erasmus also here proposes the meditative reconstitution of the scenes of Christ's life and the use of the interior senses in prayer, 'Tanquam pius Jesu discipulus, assectetur illum per omnia vestigia: observet quid agat, quid loquatur; suboderetur, vestiget, scrutetur singula.' Above all Erasmus encourages the simple Christian to taste and feel the *tranquillitas* of the Gospel message against the storms of those attached to worldly values.[2]

There is here such a confluence of ideas and even words to be found in the *Spiritual Exercises* that it is impossible to deny some form of influence of this prefatory appendix on the text of the *Exercises*. Ignatius centred his doctrine on what Erasmus, early in the year of the Cardoner experience, called the problem of the *discretio*

[1] *Opus Epistolarum Desiderii Erasmii*, ed. P. S. Allen and H. M. Allen (Oxford, 1924), vol.5, p.4.
[2] The prefatory appendix to the *Paraphrasis in Evangelium Matthaei* is printed in the *Omnia Opera*, vol. VII (Leiden, 1706), in the prefatory material without page numbers.

spirituum. The rules for discernment adopted by Ignatius are those explicit in this prefatory appendix and, in fact, used subsequently by Erasmus when, for instance, in the 1523 preface to the edition of Cicero's *Tusculanae Quaestiones*, he talks of the marked spiritual elevation he gains from reading Cicero.[1] The primacy of interior sentiment, the way in which good and bad spirits act respectively on those attached to worldly values and on sincere Christians, the need to approach the reading of scripture with prayer and, above all, the imaginative reconstruction of scenes from Christ's life to stimulate the affections and the interior senses are all quite fundamental to Ignatius's *Spiritual Exercises*. It is unlikely that the written text of the *Exercises*, at least, did not depend on Erasmus and specifically on this text.[2]

---

[1] The *discretio spirituum* as developed by Ignatius was by no means limited to the discernment of extraordinary movements of the soul caused through the external agency of 'good' or 'bad' spirits, but was extended to all the 'variae motiones quae in anima excitantur' (*Exercitia Spiritualia*, §13, versio litteralis). All the early biographers show how Ignatius extended the principle of discernment to every sort of choice with which he was confronted. Polanco describes the effect of the 'subita quadam et insolita lux' of the Cardoner experience as extending 'ad discretionem etiam spirituum bonorum a malis in particulari . . . adeo ut omnia divina et humana novis mentis oculis sibi cernere videretur' (see Silos, 'Cardoner in the Life of Saint Ignatius', pp.19–20). Ignatius intended the members of his order to live by the same sort of moral discernment, derived from an intense life of prayer, and was himself doggedly persistent, for instance, in getting ecclesiastical authorities to change their minds in consequence of his personal discernment of the divine will, stopping only at actual disobedience. Erasmus of course does not anchor his own power of moral discernment in mystical experience. But he does heavily rely on it in his dogged prosecution of what he calls the *res evangelica*, and in the second paragraph of the preface to the *Tusculanae Quaestiones* he refers explicitly to it, justifying his pleasure at the prospect of spending some months again with his *veteres amici* among the classical authors, 'Tantum fructus me sensi percepisse ex his libris relectis, non tantum ob stili rubiginem abstergendam . . . verum multo magis ob animi cupiditates moderandas refrenandasque' (*Opus Epistolarum*, vol. 5, p.338).

[2] The case for supposing the direct literary influence of this text of Erasmus on the *Spiritual Exercises* is cumulative. It rests not only on the central importance which Ignatius attaches to Erasmus's problem of the *discretio spirituum* and interior guidance, but also on the similarity between Erasmus's views and Ignatius's rules for the first week (when the good spirit disturbs the wicked) and the second week (with its criterion of *tranquillitas*). It is confirmed by Ignatius's insistence after Erasmus that the reading of Scripture should be approached prayerfully in the interest of stimulating devotion, by the opposition between the followers of Christ and the followers of the world (itself a *topos*, but notably elaborated by Ignatius in the meditation on the Two Standards), and above all by Ignatius's insistence on the use of the senses to stimulate the affections in the meditative reconstruction of scenes from Christ's life in which the exercitant is urged in Erasmus's terms to watch, to follow and even to smell. Some of these characteristic features of Ignatius's spirituality could have derived individually from elsewhere. Their confluence in the *Spiritual Exercises* does however suggest the literary influence of Erasmus's text, which is anyway not inherently improbable. For an important part of Erasmus's text, see the appendix.

It is here however that the difficulties begin. Even if one of the Froben editions of March 1522 had reached Spain by the date of Ignatius's Cardoner experience in the autumn of that year, it is extremely unlikely that he would have come across it, or indeed have read it if he had. We are forced into the somewhat awkward but nevertheless not unlikely hypothesis that sometime between the *eximia illustratio* and the definitive formulation of the *Spiritual Exercises*, Ignatius read the prefatory appendix to the *Paraphrasis in Evangelium Matthaei* and used Erasmian terminology and insight to express his own intellectual illumination in the series of rules and exercises designed to make an election under divine guidance. The *Spiritual Exercises* themselves insist on the distinction between the content of a spiritual experience under immediate divine influence, and the form of words used to articulate the insight after the moment of rapture has passed. We know that the *Paraphrasis* was published in Spain in 1525 and that the *Spiritual Exercises* existed as a document of some sort by 1527. The probability is that their first formal redaction as exercises was partly inspired by the text of Erasmus and occurred after Ignatius had started his humanities at Barcelona. They were most probably committed to paper in the form of rules and exercises at Alcala in 1526, at a place and time, that is, at which Erasmus was widely read, discussed and controverted.

The influence of Erasmus on Ignatius's formulation of his central spiritual attitudes in the *Spiritual Exercises* seems to be historically possible and textually probable. The argument is not of course conclusive, but it does reach out towards a second ambiguity in connection with the possibly Erasmian inspiration of Ignatius, who began to study theology in Paris in 1528 at the reactionary Collège de Montaigu, only to move to the rival and humanist Collège de Sainte-Barbe in 1529. Why did Ignatius move from the stronghold of scholastic reaction to the centre of evangelical humanism across the lane?

Ignatius had started to direct consciences in accordance with his principles of discernment. At Alcala and subsequently at Salamanca he was interrogated by the Inquisition. If he wished to continue to direct consciences he should obtain proper qualifications, study theology and become a priest. In the spring of 1529, Ignatius, now studying grammar at Montaigu, gave a series of spiritual exercises to three Spanish students, all noble, one of whom was already a master of arts, and all of whom gave away books and possessions and took to begging for a living. Ignatius then departed on a quixotically charitable errand to Rouen and returned to a furore on account of what had happened to the three Spaniards. One of them came from Sainte-Barbe and its Principal, Diego de Gouvea, briefly resident in Paris, forbade Ignatius to enter his premises. Yet it was as a *pensionnaire* at Sainte-Barbe, with its humanist style and strong connections with the Iberian peninsula, that Ignatius in 1529 started his philosophy. Here, in spite of an incident that nearly led to a public beating, Ignatius swiftly won over the volatile but pious Diego de Gouvea, later to become a firm friend of the new Jesuit order.

It is probable that Ignatius, who had had to live far from Montaigu, moved to Sainte-Barbe because there he could be a *pensionnaire* and because of the Iberian connection. The Principal, Diego de Gouvea, was an ardent counter-reformer who had studied at Montaigu under Standonck and Beda, who detested Erasmus and regarded his condemnation as a matter of urgency. He was faithful to the scholastic tradition, deeply suspicious of any inclination to Lutheranism and he shared Beda's hatred of the whole evangelical humanist movement. The facts that he recommended Ignatius and his early companions to John III of Portugal for the evangelisation of India in February 1538, that he later helped the Jesuit students in Paris, even going so far as to offer them his college, that in 1553 he defended the Jesuits in their legal battle against the Sorbonne and that so many of the *Regulae Communes* which regulated the domestic order of Jesuit houses were derived from the statutes of Sainte-Barbe, fit in well with the received view that Ignatius and the early Jesuits were counter-reformatory in spirit.[1]

Ignatius's move to Sainte-Barbe is however more ambiguous than it seems. The college was already humanist in 1529. Gelida, Fernel, Buchanan and Postel had already taught there.[2] Diego de Gouvea spent most of his time running diplomatic errands for the King of Portugal, and was in fact away from 1528 to 1531 with the exception of a short period from August to November 1529. During his absence, the college was governed by his nephew Andrea, later to leave Paris

[1] On Diego de Gouvea, see Marcel Bataillon, *Études sur le Portugal au temps de l'humanisme* (Coimbra, 1952).
[2] On the history of Sainte-Barbe, see J. Quicherat, *Histoire de Sainte-Barbe*, 3 vols (Paris, 1860–4).

with Cop and Calvin and to end up as Principal of the famous humanist college of Guyenne at Bordeaux. While Diego urges the condemnation of Erasmus at Valladolid in 1527 or is to be found at Rouen in 1532 in his rôle of peripatetic judge on ecclesiastical tribunals set up to examine accusations of Lutheranism, Sainte-Barbe is in fact in the charge of his evangelical nephew Andrea.

In 1533, when Ignatius was still at Sainte-Barbe, the series of confrontations took place between humanists and scholastics which started with Roussel's Lenten sermons, and passed through the skit on the King's sister at the Collège de Navarre, the condemnation of the second edition of her *Miroir de l'âme pécheresse*, the exile of Beda, Cop's sermon on 1 November 1533 at the beginning of the academic year and the subsequent disappearance of Cop, Calvin and Andrea de Gouvea. It is unlikely that Ignatius remained uninfluenced by the intensely evangelical humanist atmosphere of his college, which had managed to break the ordinary rotation of rectors and to provide in Cop a second in succession. The evangelical humanism of Sainte-Barbe in 1533 was however still firmly Erasmian.

Erasmus's attitude towards the classics came in the end to be dominated by the same concerns which determined the rest of his literary activity. We can, I think, trace its development from an early purely aesthetic delight based on a somewhat self-conscious fastidiousness, through the discovery that the classical heritage was not only compatible with evangelical Christianity but that this compatibility could be used to extend contemporary Christian orthodoxy in a desirable direction. The authority of Jerome helped, of course, but what is most striking in Erasmus's attitude to the classics is the slow movement by which it became integrated into his definitive religious mission. Erasmus's mind moved very slowly and the final powerful view is scarcely discernible before he was nearly fifty. He was excited by the classics in his youth and at Steyn, although even at that date he was inspired by the example of Jerome to integrate his dedication to *bonae literae* with serious piety and a devotion to scripture. At Paris, where he began to learn some Greek, his attitude to the classics was still fastidiously aesthetic, and it was as a poet that Colet received him in Oxford. Colet's influence certainly confirmed the religious mission already clear in Erasmus's own mind but it also introduced him to Florentine Neo-Platonism.

The first decade of the sixteenth century sees Erasmus putting out tentative feelers. His introduction to Origen by Vitrier sowed the really important seed of a possible integration of the classical and the Christian view of man which confirmed what he had by now discovered in Pico. But Erasmus was still groping. His attempts to relate Scotist views to scholastic style and to see the restoration of *bonae literae* as a theological solution to the problems of Christendom were the product of an early enthusiasm and doomed to fail, although the view was popular among a small group of dedicated humanists. The *Enchiridion* seems to be merely of historical interest in the charting of Erasmus's intellectual and spiritual development, interesting chiefly in the light of what was to follow and less important than the prefatory letter to Paul Volz which preceded the re-edition in 1518. The *Praise of Folly* in 1511 is still a very tentative work and, despite Erasmus's provocative disingenuousness, it does not in fact go much further than the *Enchiridion* and the 1508 *Adages* in integrating classical and Christian visions. Even the famous long essays introduced into the Froben 1515 edition of the *Adages*, almost certainly reflecting the influence of Thomas More, still simply juxtapose Erasmus's Christian vision with his philological expertise, although now the social criticism, since it draws at the same time on classical and Christian values, goes much of the way towards integrating them.[1] The full integration is the product of the *Colloquia*, the religious works and classical editions of the 1520s, the polemic with Luther and the *Ciceronianus* of 1528.

Erasmus, I think, only gradually became conscious of the way in which his classical enthusiasm and his Christian vision coalesced into a unified programme. The integration of the two sources of inspiration and enthusiasm progresses from the early years of the century, before the 1508 *Adages*, until after the *Ciceronianus* of 1528. After 1520 he no longer regards classical style as the simple remedy for scholastic logic-chopping. He increasingly emphasises the moral grandeur of the classical figures he admires. Through the various editions of the *Adages* he pursues the popular dissemination of classical wisdom, while through the *Paraphrases* he attempts to broadcast the moral message of the New Testament. He wishes to break down the growing feeling that humanism leads to heresy, and in particular the view that a knowledge of Greek smelt of the

---

[1] For the probable influence of More on the 1515 edition of the *Adages*, see Margaret Mann Phillips, *The Adages of Erasmus* (Cambridge, 1964), pp.96–121.

faggot, a prejudice which became stronger after his death, and which Budé's 1535 *De Transitu Hellenismi ad Christianismum* did little to dispel. It was still felt strongly by Ignatius's early companions.[1]

It is in the context of Erasmus's effort to integrate on the conceptual level his instinctive admiration for certain values upheld by and exemplified in classical authors with the equally instinctive devotion which derived from his monastic experience that we must see the important prefaces to the classical editions of the 1520s, the *de pueris . . . instituendis,* and the reaction against sterile, dilettante and irreligious classicism in the *Ciceronianus.* Certainly the affirmation of Cicero's salvation in the preface to the *Tuscalanae Quaestiones* of 1523 or the suggestion of Socrates's sanctity in the 1522 *Convivium religiosum* indicate Erasmus's views about the 'instauratio bene conditae naturae' and have a bearing on the position he was to take in the 1524 *De libero arbitrio.* But the real importance of such affirmations or suggestions for Erasmus personally was that, irrespective of theological implications he did not much care to discuss, they marked the resolution of the personal dilemma he had been caught up in. By 1516 Erasmus was willing to affirm the spiritual stimulus he gained from reading Seneca, but only later did he come openly to understand how much the classical authors could reinforce the New Testament message against the debased Christianity of the late fifteenth century, and contribute, like the New Testament, to the restoration of a properly Christian moral piety.[2] From 1522 on, Erasmus was prepared to affirm intellectually the necessity of integrating the classical heritage into the Christian one to produce the Christian moral renewal to which his activity became ever more uniquely directed.

The exact nature of the contribution to be made by the classics to the definitive Erasmian programme becomes clear, for instance, in the preface to the second edition of Seneca, a letter to Peter Tomiczki dated January 1529. Erasmus had edited Seneca's *Lucubrationes* in 1515, and the preface on that occasion, a letter to Thomas Ruthall,[3] sheltered clearly behind the authority of Jerome,

[1] See Georg Schurhammer, *Franz Xaver. Sein Leben und seine Zeit* (Freiburg, 1955), vol.1, pp.159–60.
[2] See Erasmus's letter to Peter Gilles of 6th October 1516 (*Opus Epistolarum,* ed. P. S. Allen (Oxford, 1910), vol.2, pp.356–8).
[3] *Opus Epistolarum,* vol.2, pp.51–4.

'quod hunc unum dignum iudicavit qui non Christianus a Christianis legeretur', before it went on to extol Seneca's moral values. In 1529, the tone is different.[1] Instead of the 'nihil huius praeceptis sanctius' of the earlier preface, we have a more formal affirmation of the 'sanctitas praeceptorum'. It is now stated not only that Jerome recommended the reading of Seneca, but that he placed Seneca 'in catalogo sanctorum'. Erasmus insists that Seneca was a pagan, not even a Nicodemite, and that he must be read with this in mind, 'si legas illum ut paganum, scripsit Christiane, si ut Christianum, scripsit paganice'. But Seneca the pagan is none the less useful in the context of the Erasmian programme, and belongs to the *Christi philosophia*, although precisely because he is a pagan he should be read for his moral elevation and not his conceptual vision, with its reiterated *deos deasque*. Erasmus has become perfectly clear on what he wants from Seneca and what in him he rejects. The pagan classics can be integrated into the Erasmian programme only if they are understood as pagan, and their moral message is accordingly distilled from their conceptual universe.

The actual classical authors edited by Erasmus were not necessarily his chosen favourites. Much depended on the demand for proper texts and what his publishers thought they could sell. Similarly the incidence of quotations in the *Adages* reflected more those authors who wrote in *genres* favourable to the coining of aphorisms than Erasmus's own preferences. Even the classical *genres* utilised by Erasmus reflected his literary requirements more than his enthusiasms. He clearly learned much from Lucian's literary techniques, but he became acquainted with them chiefly because he needed texts to practise his Greek on. Erasmus's attitude to the classics should not be invested with an importance it did not have. The early enthusiasm for *bonae literae* became later much more purposeful as he slowly integrated it with his other enthusiasms and consciously formulated his insight, that classical values as well as classical style had more in common with the New Testament message than had the nominalist-based scholastic religion of works. The classics became a tool in the task of procuring the moral renovation of Christendom.

Much the same can be said of the attitude of the early Jesuits towards the classics. No doubt their understanding of the theological

[1] *Opus Epistolarum*, ed. P. S. Allen and H. M. Allen (Oxford, 1934), vol.8, pp.25–39.

issues, while it did not oppose the Erasmian programme of returning to the texts of the New Testament or the Fathers, none the less stopped short of canonising Socrates. But the programmes were very similar, and the similarity was not fortuitous. There is already the probability that the central tenet of Ignatius's spirituality was derived from an Erasmian formula and Erasmian practice. Like Erasmus, Ignatius was clearly influenced by the Florentine tradition of Neo-Platonism in the *Spiritual Exercises*, both in his references to angels and in the final 'Contemplation for obtaining divine love', which progresses from love of earthly things to the love of God. It seems not unlikely that Ignatius transferred from Montaigu to Sainte-Barbe in 1529 partly on account of the evangelical humanism of that college. And without wishing to extend the direct influence of Erasmus on Ignatius beyond the crucial text on the discernment of spirits, there are at least important similarities of attitude and even of syntax between the *Enchiridion* and parts of the *Spiritual Exercises*, notably the 'Principle and Foundation'.[1]

It is at any rate certain that Ignatius rejected the means chosen by Standonck, the Principal of Montaigu, to implement religious reform. Even if his 'Rules for thinking with the Church' borrow from Clichtove via the Council of Sens in 1523, Ignatius's positive attitude to Erasmian reform goes far beyond the increasingly reactionary views of Clichtove. Nadal tells us that Ignatius specially advocated the reading of Cicero for Jesuit preachers, in addition to their formation in the humanities, and it was to become a characteristic of the Jesuit colleges, perhaps in the wake of some Protestant ones, that they put Greek on a par with Latin.[2] A particular feature of the Jesuit *Regulae Concionatorum* was to be the insistence on scriptural formation. Ignatius followed Erasmus in his preference for a forma-tion based on the theological sources, although a generation later he remained more concerned than Erasmus to integrate the scholastic teaching, which Erasmus so disliked, with the sources of revelation. Towards the classics, however, Ignatius's attitude is unequivocal and, no doubt led on by Polanco and relying on Augustine, Ignatius wrote into the Jesuit Constitutions his reliance on the need to treat of the arts and natural sciences to achieve the end of the Society, the

---

[1] On these similarities, see R. Garcia-Villoslada, *Loyola y Erasmo* (Madrid, 1965), pp.31–50, and pp.229–32.
[2] The text of Nadal is quoted by F. de Dainville, *La naissance de l'humanisme moderne* (Paris, 1940), vol.1, p.15.

salvation and perfection of its members and of the world, '[Quoniam] artes vel scientiae naturales ingenia disponunt ad Theologiam, et ad perfectam cognitionem et usum illius inserviunt, et per se ipsas ad eundem finem iuvant.'[1] This was to be a sentiment echoed in scores of Jesuit texts before 1600.

No doubt, much more than Erasmus, Ignatius regarded a classical formation as a stepping-stone to another intellectual level which would ideally be reached *senza tanto Cicerone et Demostene*.[2] Ignatius's dream, realised in the colleges he was at first reluctant to found, was clearly the integration of a classically based culture with a Christian formation which, while based on scripture and the Fathers, none the less encompassed the scholastics. But this extension of the Erasmian ideal is not surprising in the generation of Ignatius, who had scarcely finished his studies when Erasmus died in 1536. However, the reaction typified by the Council of Trent hardened, and the early Jesuits had to grope all the harder for a real synthesis. But even when Erasmus's works were being proscribed, the Jesuits were merely cautious about which of his texts they used, and who was allowed access to the others.[3] Erasmus's texts were never treated in the same way as the heretical writings of the reformers in Jesuit houses. What the early Jesuits never surrendered, whatever prudence and public demand dictated in the way of suppressions, omissions, adaptations and expurgations, was the moral grandeur of the great figures of classical antiquity and the consequent utility of their texts and their example in the pursuit of the great enterprise of religious renewal, even when popular ecclesiastical sentiment had become much more hardened in reaction than ever it was in Erasmus's lifetime.[4]

What I hope emerges from this brief survey of the respective attitudes of Erasmus and the early Jesuits to the classics amounts almost to a total congruence of view modified not by a difference of final aim but by a difference of theological circumstances. Erasmus came to view the classical authors, the restoration of their texts and the popularisation of their views, as a weapon in his concentrated

[1] *Constitutiones Societatis Jesu*, pars IV, caput XII, 3.
[2] Letter from Ignatius to a scholastic of 30 May 1555.
[3] See R. Garcia-Villoslada, *Loyóla y Erasmo*, pp.233–270, on the norms in various Jesuit colleges governing the reading of Erasmus and the availability of his texts.
[4] On the attitude of the early Jesuits to pagan authors, see F. de Dainville, *La naissance de l'humanisme moderne*, pp.217–46.

effort to obtain a renewal of Christianity based on a moral reformation which, as he pointed out, was dictated by scripture and the Fathers, but also taught and exemplified by classical antiquity. His view presupposes the 'instauratio bene conditae' naturae' which made even ancient pagans capable of the *Philosophia Christi*. He was led by his own discernment of moral values wherever he found them. They were almost certainly first suggested to him both by the spirit of the *Devotio moderna* and by the writers of the Florentine Neo-Platonist tradition, and were elaborated through the Neo-Platonist *Enchiridion*, the *Praise of Folly*, More's *Utopia* and the prefatory material of the 1516 *Novum Instrumentum* until the final coherent plan emerged, the integration of the values mediated by the *renaissance des lettres* with those mediated by the sources of the Christian revelation, which of course included the Fathers.

Ignatius of Loyola, like Erasmus, relied in all things primarily on his own discernment of moral values. He was influenced by Erasmus at least in the formulation of the principle of discernment and, even when in the two decades following Erasmus's death the theological conflict hardened into revolution and reaction, he refused to abandon his educational belief in the utility of the texts and examples of the classical authors in the pursuit of salvation and sanctity. In the circumstances of a raging counter-reformation, Ignatius's *Constitutions* remained remarkably faithful to the overall principle of personal discernment under the guidance of divine illumination. The *Constitutions* open with a ringing declaration that it would be preferable to have no formal rules at all, since the conservation, government and propagation of the Order would better be helped by the 'interna caritatis et amoris . . . lex quam Sanctus Spiritus scribere et in cordibus imprimere solet', than by any external constitutions.

After Ignatius's death, the success of his Order brought in its wake an institutionalisation which necessarily detracted from the early reliance of Ignatius and his companions on the direct discernment of God's will. Concessions were made to the more aggressive constraints of the Counter-Reformation, obedience became formalised into the acceptance of instructions from hierarchical superiors and the spiritual freedom of the early days became diluted with the foundation of colleges which could accept revenues rather than of the houses for the professed foreseen by Ignatius, which could not.

The Order became corporately rich, powerful, and to some extent the early ideals became corrupted by power. But Ignatius had been reluctant to include obedience in his arrangements for the new Order and, even when he did, he used it merely to ensure that, in the last resort, the superior's discernment of the subject's spiritual experience should take precedence over the subject's own and possibly mistaken or even paranoiac views about his own mission. This is not how things worked out, but even in changed circumstances the Jesuit colleges did not abandon faith in the utility of the classical authors, even when they were under pressure to expurgate them of everything that appeared to a counter-reformatory sensibility to smack of dangerous moral teaching.

Ignatius above all took Erasmian teaching further by insisting on the integration of scholastic theology with the theology based on the sources of revelation, notably insisting that the scholastics he sent to Paris should study theology with the Dominicans who had early in the sixteenth century undergone the humanist reform of basing the curriculum on the *Summa Theologica*, rather than on the Lombard's *Sententiae*, which were still the basis for lecture-comment-aries at the other three centres in Paris at which the graduate discipline of theology was taught. In the end Erasmus's views, even of classical authors, seem more determined by his desire to effect the moral reformation of Christianity than is sometimes supposed, as Ignatius's views seem more reliant on the capacity of human nature to attain moral heights and to be divinely led than is generally conceded. The sad Dutch humanist was as dedicated in his way as the intense Spanish mystic. Their styles were totally different. But their guiding principles and their views of human nature, as illustrated in their attitudes to the major classical authors, were not so very different, as both were nourished in the same evangelical and partly illuminist tradition, and the one influenced the other more than has ever been admitted.

We still require a formal and full-scale reassessment of the way in which both the reform and the counter-reform in the sixteenth century were related to the evangelical humanist movement, and a new examination of the constraints which led to polarisation across the abyss of schism. Erasmus found some classical authors spiritually stimulating. The Jesuits retained their confidence in the classics as a fitting basis for Christian education. Yet the pressure from extreme wings on both sides of the schism to abandon the classics because they were the product of paganism was strong. What was it in the classical inheritance which ensured its survival as a common cultural basis, ultimately perhaps to become the strongest unitive force in a dangerously divided cultural world?

APPENDIX

The prefatory letter *Pio Lectori* which precedes the *Paraphrasis in Matthaeum* covers four and a third folio pages in volume 7 of the Leiden edition (no page numbers). In the context of the possible influence on the text of the *Spiritual Exercises*, the whole letter is important. The most significant passage however occurs in its fourth paragraph, from which the following extracts are taken.

'Dicet mihi quispiam: Difficilis est discretio spirituum, et Angelus Satanae nonnunquam transfigurat se in Angelum lucis. Fateor: et eam ob causam, nolim esse praeceps judicium. Sed tamen certissimum cuique suffragium est testimonium suae conscientiae. Proximum est consensus Scripturae et vitae Christi. Denique quaedam dilucidiora sunt, quam ut oporteat ambigere, aut requirere interpretem. Et tamen his offenduntur, qui se totos dedicarunt mundo, non ob aliud, nisi quod officiunt institutis votisque suis ... Certe Scripturarum suarum penum nulli pio claudit Christus, etiamsi subulcus esset, qui quondam pastoribus impartiit Spiritum Propheticum. In hujus igitur libris versentur omnes qui venantur Christianam Philosophiam. Si succedit, age gratias Deo. Sin minus, ne protinus abjice animum; quaere, pete, pulsa. Quaerenti continget ut inveniat, petenti dabitur, pulsanti aperiet is, qui habet clavem, qua sic aperit, ut nemo claudat: sic claudit, ut nemo aperiat. Consule proximum, si quid non assequeris: fortasse per illum tibi loquetur Spiritus arcanus, qui non uno modo sese solet inserere mentibus hominum. Adsit quidem pia curiositas, et curiosa pietas, sed absit temeritas, absit praeceps et pervicax scientiae persuasio. Quod legis et intelligis, summa fide complectere. Frivolas quaestiunculas, aut impie curiosas dispelle, si fors oboriantur animo. Dic: *Quae supra nos, nihil ad nos.* Quomodo Christi corpus exierit clauso sepulchro, noli disceptare: tibi satis est quod exiit. Quomodo in sacra mensa sit corpus Christi, ubi ponebatur panis, noli disquirere: tibi sufficit credere quod illic est corpus Domini. Quomodo Filius sit alius à Patre, quum sit una natura, noli scrutari: tibi satis est credere Patrem, Filium et Spiritum Sanctum tres Personas, sed unum Deum. Sed illud in primis cavendum, ne Scripturam tentes ad tuas cupiditates, tuaque decreta detorquere: sed ad hujus regulam potius tuas opiniones ac vitae rationem attempera. Alioqui ex hujusmodi fontibus nascitur asseverandi pervicacia, nascuntur contentiones, nascuntur dissidia et odia, nascuntur haereses, fidei simul et Christianae concordiae venena. Neque tamen protinus arcendi sunt à sacris Libris idiotae, si quis exortus fuerit, qui per hanc occasionem prolapsus sit in errores. Neque enim istud lectionis vitium est, sed hominis. Nec olim ideo vetitum est Evangelium in Templis recitari, quod hinc haeretici prisci hauserint errorum suorum semina. Nec ideo prohibentur apes à floribus, quod ex iis aliquando venenum sugat aranea. Legant igitur omnes, sed qui volet cum fructu legere, legat sobrie, legat non oscitanter, velut historiam aliquam humanam, ad se nihil attinentem, sed avide, sed attente, sed assidue. Tanquam pius Jesu discipulus, assectetur illum per omnia vestigia: observet quid agat, quid loquatur: suboderetur, vestiget, scrutetur singula, et reperiet in simplicissima illa rudique Scriptura consilium ineffabile sapientiae coelestis: videbit in illa stultitia Dei, si fas est ita loqui, prima fronte humili et contemnenda, quod longe superet omnem prudentiam humanam, quamvis sublimem et admirabilem. Nihil autem illic narratur, quod ad unumquemque nostrum non pertinet: nihil illic geritur, quod quotidie non geritur in vita nostra, tectius quidem, sed verius. Nascitur in nobis Christus, nec desunt *Herodes*, qui tenerum adhuc et lactentem conantur occidere. Grandescit et proficit gradibus aetatum. Sanat omne morborum genus, si quis modo cum fiducia imploret illius opem. Non repellit ille leprosis, non Daemoniacos, non sanguinis profluvio impuros, non caecos, non claudos . . .'

17

JUAN VIVES AND THE *SOMNIUM SCIPIONIS*

DOMINIC BAKER-SMITH

Two dominant characteristics of humanism during the Renaissance were a concern for Latin style and a taste for the practical issues of moral philosophy. Such a combination was both a cause and a consequence of studying Cicero, and his description of rhetorical culture emerged as the alternative to the abstractions of late-scholasticism. A significant association between the arts of language and moral philosophy can be seen in Cicero's writings, with particular vividness in that fragment of his *De republica* known as the *Somnium Scipionis*, and it is in any case emphasised by Macrobius in the *Commentarius* by which he preserved Cicero's fragment for later centuries. In his effort to produce a myth of Rome Macrobius transforms Cicero and Virgil – the exponents of golden latinity – into moral guides and the *Somnium* into a compendium of all knowledge. At the very heart of Scipio's vision is the claim that 'Learned men, imitating this heavenly music with stringed instruments and songs, have won for themselves a return to this celestial place, as also those who have devoted their outstanding talents in this life to divine studies' (v.18). Together with the sage and the artist (for we must take the musician here as a representative) Cicero places the man of affairs, the governor, so that the three stand together as tuners of society, recreating in men the harmony of the heavens. Art and ethics are aspects of the same reality.

Thus, quite apart from its interest as a dream allegory, the *Somnium* with its metaphorical resources stands as a model for rhetorical culture. Now an ability to respond to these resources, to recognise them as contributing to a unified scheme of values, is one of the features we might expect to find in humanism; and it is certainly significant that while Schedler's study of the influence of Macrobius in the Middle Ages[1] reveals for the most part interest in isolated facts or

[1] P. M. Schedler, *Die Philosophie des Macrobius und ihr Einfluss auf die Wissenschaft des christlichen Mittelalters* (Munster I. W., 1916).

doctrines, it is in the work of Petrarch, and above all in his *Africa*, that we become aware again of this comprehensive vision, of the poet Ennius and the general Africanus as interpreters of cosmic harmony. In the two centuries that divide the *Africa* from Gerard Vossius's *In Somnium Scipionis Commentarius* (Rome, 1575) there is a vigorous tradition of commentary on the *Somnium* which has so far received slight attention.[1] But from preliminary reconnaissance it is clear that investigation of the *Somnium* and its career during the Renaissance can help to illuminate many intellectual issues of the period.

Among the various commentaries on the *Somnium* composed during the Renaissance the one by Vivès stands out for originality and scope. It was written in 1520 at a time when Vivès was resident in Louvain, heavily engaged in anti-scholastic polemic. A letter from Thomas More to Erasmus, written in May 1520, expresses pleasure at three works by Vivès: the *Somnium*, the *In Pseudo-Dialecticos* and the *Aedes Legum*.[2] *In Pseudo-Dialecticos* is basically an attack on the desiccated theory of language which imprisons the *moderni* in a world of irrelevant abstractions, regardless of those arts – moral philosophy, oratory, politics and economics – which instruct the mind and contribute to life. The *Aedes Legum* contains reminiscences of the *Somnium* and is an elaboration of the Ciceronian theme that 'nothing of all that is done on earth is more pleasing to that supreme God who rules the universe than the assemblies and gatherings of men associated in justice'.[3] Vivès's actual commentary on the *Somnium* brings together both these themes; the *Praefatio* is a brilliantly amusing and ferocious satire on the scholastics, a fictional elaboration of points made in the *In Pseudo-Dialecticos*, while the actual discussion of the *Somnium* stresses its moral force. In the dedication to Erard de la Marck, bishop-elect of Valencia, Vivès concludes 'by this little book the most perfect and absolute prince may be instructed in affairs of state and moulded in character; there is no work in the whole of philosophy more outstanding or more divine'.[4]

The germ of Vivès's satirical fiction can be sensed in a letter he

[1] A notable exception is C. R. Ligota's article 'L'Influence de Macrobe pendant la Renaissance', in *Le Soleil à la Renaissance: Colloque de Bruxelles, 1963* (Brussels, 1965), 465–82.
[2] Allen, *Epistolae Erasmi*, IV (Oxford, 1922), 1106; see also 1108.
[3] *Somnium Scipionis*, III.1. References are to the edition by A. Ronconi (Florence, 1961).
[4] *Opera Omnia* (Valencia, 1782–90), V.63, '... quo libello perfectus et absolutus in republica princeps instituitur, atque formatur, nullumque est in tota philosophia praestabilius opus, atque divinius.'

wrote to Cranevelt, describing his request to the Senate at Louvain for permission to lecture on the *Somnium*. As soon as the Rector and his deputies heard the word '*somnium*' they laughed. This reaction, Vivès suggests, was stirred by their pleasure at the thought of sleep.[1] In his *Praefatio* Vivès is wafted off in sleep to the ebony palace of Somnus. There the silence is shattered by the arrival of Parisian sophists whose incomprehensible language baffles the door-keepers. While efforts are made to eject them they break into a chamber of dreams. It is love at first sight, so the dreams depart with the sophists. But they are shocked to learn that the sophists do not know their way in the world; although familiar with every bush and pond in heaven they cannot navigate from the Petit Pont to Nôtre Dame. Finally when they return to Somnus's house in autumn the doorkeepers cannot distinguish philosophers from dreams. Meanwhile Vivès wanders restively through the palace and stumbles across a chamber filled with Somnus's *compotores*. The party reads as a roll-call of the *moderni*, dominated by the figure of Scotus.[2]

The climax comes in the house of the Fates with a furious debate in the presence of Lachesis between adherents of Clotho, who hold to the thread of scholastic ways, and adherents of Atropos who wish to cut it and return, after a millennium of boredom, to the great authors of the past.[3] Cicero delivers an oration which amounts to a manifesto for the new learning. Compared to the *sapientia* of antiquity, learning now appears to be *stultitia et fatuitas*; Christ's yoke is too heavy for men who are more loaded with ceremony than the Jews ever were. Not even Demosthenes and Crassus could make the moderns live the Gospel. Despite the obstinacy of the Clothici who block their ears, shout and in any case can't understand the oration, the followers of Atropos are confident of success. Virgil seizes his lyre and breaks into song while Cicero is sent to the heavens with Vivès to announce the outcome. This provides an opportunity for Cicero to outline his

[1] H. de Vocht, *Literae ad Franciscum Craneveldium* (Louvain, 1928), Epist. II, p.5. One issue which has a distinctly modern ring was which faculty should be considered responsible for lecturing on *somnia*. Permission was eventually granted and Vivès appears to have repeated his lectures at Paris in May 1520. The printed version appeared at Antwerp in April.

[2] *Opera*, v.80, '. . . Ochamum, Suisethum, Gregorium quendam Ariminensem, Paulum Venetum, Houtisberum, conterraneum meum Petrum Hispanum, Accursium, Bartholum, Baldum, tum vero ad singulares, summasque delicias, Joannem Scotum acceperat, quo homine ferebant Somnium usque ad insaniam delectari . . .'

[3] Significantly the supporters of Atropos include not only Cicero, Virgil, Seneca and Quintilian, but also St Paul and the Fathers (*Opera*, v.84).

intention and to emphasise the platonic inspiration of his brief work, conceived as 'something of value to our youth'.

It is clear that the ethical concern which lies at the heart of the *Somnium Scipionis* constitutes its chief appeal so far as Vivès is concerned. The literary impact and discursive range of this, Cicero's most erudite and elegant work, are justified by this overriding interest. Cicero's moral teaching is wholesome, pure and spiritual to a degree astonishing in a Christian, let alone a pagan; Vivès personally prefers this *cornucopia* to the fat works of other philosophers, and considers it harder to master than the *Physics* of Aristotle, a philosopher second to none though ill-served by the *Pseudo-aristotelici*.[1] The *Vigilia* which contains the main body of Vivès's commentary is composed as a dialogue and the attention given to historical context makes it clear that it is offered as an alternative to the didactic methods of the scholastics. Perhaps the most striking feature of the treatise is its fidelity to Cicero's spirit, so that the Plotinian deprecation of active life which is central to Macrobius's interpretation is quite rejected. Those who preserve the state and enrich its life will attain their reward in the divine city where Africanus dwells. Indeed public duty is the final end of education: by the study of geography and natural science the sage frees himself from the thrall of the mutable. Meditation on the true order of things prepares him for good action and this is necessarily social action – to neglect public duty is to war on nature. The justice of a good man's life expresses the inner harmony he has created, a beauty beyond the conception of evil men. Thus body and soul work in harmony, a microcosm that reflects the harmony of the spheres.

Clearly then for Vivès the *Somnium* offered an intellectual programme which contained the seeds of a better world. 1520 was still a hopeful year for Erasmus's friends and a personal theme that Vivès has injected into the traditional material stands out: the desire for

---

[1] The verdict is stated positively: 'Nulla unquam hominum memoria scriptum est librum (sacros nostrae religionis semper excipio) in quo plus rerum, plus artis, plus eloquentiae, sit comprehensum atque infarctum; nulla portio cujusquam partis aut speciei philosophiae in tantillo deest libello' (p.106). The moral value of the text is especially stressed '. . . quae ad privatos affectus conducit, quam dicunt ethicen, et quae ad regendam rempublicam quam politicen, tam pure, tam integre, caste, religiose, sancte tractat, ut incredibile paene videatur ab Ethnico illa potuisse proficisci, quae etiam a christiano viro dicta non possemus non admirari et adorare.' While Vivès shows great respect for Aristotle he still sees Plato as the master of ethics, 'moralia non poterant sanctius tradere quam a Platone et Cicerone' (p.108). Eloquence is presumably the crucial factor.

peace. Scipio's slaughter of the Carthaginians is depicted as a reluctant course forced on him by his country's desperate situation. When he is shown the tiny size of the world beside the entire cosmos he realises the futility of war.[1] No commentary on the *Somnium* combines erudition with greater faith in its practical relevance; none gives greater support to the alliance between eloquence and virtue. The spirit of Petrarch is present in a passage which recalls the theme of the *Africa* and foretells how, after Rome's ascendancy has been established by Scipio, 'our Senate and people will assume the leadership of the world by intellectual and cultural endeavour, introducing humane laws to all nations, communicating a civilised mode of life to rude and barbarous peoples, and bringing the scattered race of men into unity through the fellowship and bond of language'.[2]

This faith in the regenerative power of classical studies is a primary feature of humanism in its creative phase. At bottom it presupposes the intimate association of art and speculative truth, joint manifestations of platonic reality. The followers of Atropos in Vivès's fantasy desired a return to antique simplicity and this was the simplicity of unity. The specialised disciplines of the schools had become isolated, ends in themselves, and as a result they appeared remote from life. The *Somnium Scipionis* suggested to the sympathetic mind a unified vision of the world in which the entire scope of human potentiality could be realised and contemplation reconciled to action. If philosophy was to be readmitted to the world of the living it had to re-acquire its hold over the emotions; eloquence was the means by which wisdom could be injected into the pulsing arteries of men. The strength of Cicero's *Somnium* lay in its appeal to the affections, the way in which it utilised subjectivity in the service of wisdom. To Petrarch, to Palmieri,[3] to Vivès and its other devotees it offered the humanist programme in embryonic form.

I have described the development of Vivès's satire at length because it shows clearly those values which he considers to be the foundation of humane studies. The commentary provides specific informa-

---

[1] Ibid. p.129, '. . . videbamque omnia non fuisse vel minimo bello, ex iis quae gessimus, digna.'

[2] Ibid. p.113, 'Senatus populusque noster, orbis terrarum imperium mente et cogitatione invaserit, quomodo leges vere humanas cunctis gentibus et nationibus ferat, quomodo victus et humanitatis rationem barbaris et efferatis populis communicet, quomodo linguae commercio et tamquam vinculo dispersum genus humanum congreget et devinciat.'

[3] In his *Della Vita Civile* where the fourth book is based on the *Somnium*.

tion about Roman history, about classical literature and thought, even about geography and psychology, but all contained and ordered by this moral context. Indeed it could be termed a religious context since Vivès tactfully adjusts Cicero's views to Christian principles, an adjustment made in full awareness of his responsibility so that Cicero's teachings may bear yet finer fruit. This attitude to the *Somnium* is by no means isolated: later commentators like Florens Wilson (Volusenus) and Pompeo della Barba describe it as the ideal introduction to that monument of Christian syncretism, Ficino's *Theologia Platonica*. However, della Barba writes in the vernacular on *questo divinissimo sogno*, and in the British Library there is an English translation of 'the dreame of Scipion' by Henry Parker, Lord Morley, which he presented, probably in the late 1520s, to Vivès's pupil the Princess Mary. In contrast to these efforts in the vernacular, Ramus's lectures on the *Somnium* printed at Paris in 1550 and dedicated to the Cardinal Charles of Lorraine, give an extremely dense body of learned information but markedly fail to convey a sense of vision or metaphorical force.[1] All this serves to remind us that the reception of influences is invariably an active process.

The *Somnium Scipionis* is a work of considerable scope and its effects are evident throughout medieval and Renaissance literature. By examining the various commentaries on it (and allusions to it) within a span of time it is possible to learn a great deal about responses to classical literature. Work of this kind can help us to attain greater precision in the discussion of cultural life. There are many texts of fundamental importance in the classical tradition which are amenable to this sort of exploration, and the same can be said of certain major themes: *dignitas hominis* or *tranquillitas animi* would serve as examples. Supported by something like Professor Hay's continental *S.T.C.* – since the greatest difficulty lies in finding the relevant commentaries – such attempts to trace the *fortuna*[2] of seminal works can be a very real aid to our understanding of the classical heritage, particularly at that period when it begins to discharge its resources into the vernacular literatures.

[1] Florentius Volusenus, *Scholia seu Commentariorum Epitome in Scipionis Somnium* (London, Robert Redman, 1534?). Pompeo della Barba, *I Discorsi Filosofici sopra il platonico divin sogno di Scipio* (Venice, G. Bonelli, 1553). Henry Parker, Baron Morley, *The dreame of Scipion* (British Library, Royal MS 18 A. LX). P. Ramus, *Scipionis Somnium . . . praelectionibus explicatum* (Paris, M. David, 2da editio, 1550).
[2] I have borrowed this term from Charles Schmitt's model investigation *Cicero Scepticus: a study of the influence of the 'Academica' in the Renaissance* (The Hague, 1972).

18

VIVÈS, LECTEUR ET CRITIQUE DE
PLATON ET D'ARISTOTE

J.-C. MARGOLIN

A lire, ou même à parcourir les huit tomes de l'édition valencienne des *Opera omnia*[1] de Vivès, nous rencontrons de multiples références à Platon et à Aristote; mieux que des références, d'importants passages, des jugements, quand ce ne sont pas des oeuvres entières ou des fragments d'oeuvre consacrés par l'humaniste espagnol au philosophe de l'Académie ou à celui du Lycée. Tantôt l'admiration paraît sans borne pour l'un, pour l'autre, ou pour les deux; tantôt d'assez vives critiques s'élèvent à leur sujet, ou à l'égard d'un seul d'entre eux. Ces jugements sont-ils conciliables? De quel Platon, de quel Aristote s'agit-il? Questions toujours légitimes quand on s'interroge sur l'influence de la pensée antique sur l'humanisme de la Renaissance, et que l'on évoque les débats de la fin du XVe siècle et de presque tout le XVIe sur la 'concordance' ou la 'discordance' de Platon et d'Aristote.[2] Et lorsqu'on a affaire à un humaniste chrétien, comme c'est ici le cas, le problème n'en est que plus excitant pour l'esprit.

Commençons par évoquer quelques textes d'un Vivès, lecteur admiratif de Platon. Voici, par exemple, au livre XXII.28 de son commentaire de la *Cité de Dieu* de saint Augustin un chant de gloire en l'honneur du philosophe grec: 'Aucuns des nostres aimans Platon, à raison de quelque fort belle manière de parler, et pource qu'en aucune chose il a suivy la vérité, disent qu'il a eu des opinions semblables aux nostres, mesmes de la resurrection des morts . . .'[3]

---

[1] G. Mayans y Siscar, *Vivis Opera omnia* (Valence, 1782). La plus récente réédition (anastatique) est celle de Londres (The Gregg Press, 1964).
[2] On a pu s'en rendre compte au récent colloque international du C.E.S.R. de Tours, au cours des débats sur 'Platon et Aristote à la Renaissance' de juillet 1973. Cette étude sur Vivès vise à compléter le dossier qui a été ouvert à Tours.
[3] *De Aurelii Augustini opus absolutissimum de Civitate Dei, emendatum per J. L. Vivem et dignis commentariis illustratum* (Bâle, 1522). Il en existe une traduction française par Gentian Hervet (Paris, 1570). C'est ce commentaire géant, conçu et élaboré au cours de son séjour à Oxford qui le rangea parmi les plus grands humanistes de son temps. Nous

245

Platon est vraiment le divin Platon, comme son maître Socrate est 'un maître vraiment divin'. Dans une lettre de 1523[1] à Erasme, Vivès recommande aux théologiens la lecture et la méditation de Platon: 'Je m'occupais de matières que nos théologiens ne semblent pas bien connaître, comme l'histoire, la littérature et la philosophie, en particulier la philosophie platonicienne.' Et il justifie la longueur de ses propres commentaires pour des raisons d'ordre pédagogique: il veut faire connaître Platon aux théologiens. Platon est donc bien, en ces années d'enthousiasme érasmien (1520–3), le philosophe sacré, le 'Moïse athénien', qui parle au coeur et à l'esprit. Ce ne sont pas des dialogues de Platon que commente Vivès, mais, en marge de saint Augustin, le *Songe de Scipion*,[2] synthèse éclectique de stoïcisme et de néoplatonisme; c'est ce livre qu'il avait essayé d'introduire à l'Université de Louvain pour ses explications et commentaires d'auteurs. A la vérité l'essai célèbre de Cicéron ne fut pas une découverte de la Renaissance, et Vivès s'inscrit dans une tradition qui était déjà solidement installée parmi les penseurs du Moyen Age, comme les humanistes de l'École de Chartres.[3] Son enthousiasme pour cette harmonieuse synthèse de l'unité cosmique et de la suprématie de l'ordre spirituel sur l'ordre matériel était tel qu'il écrivait dans la préface de son commentaire du *Songe de Scipion* de 1519: 'Jamais, de mémoire d'homme, un livre ne fut écrit (je fais toujours exception pour les ouvrages sacrés de notre religion) qui comprenne et qui distille plus de matière, plus d'art, plus d'éloquence.'[4]

On pourrait multiplier les textes dans lesquels Platon et son 'divin maître' sont admirés et présentés comme ayant ouvert la voie au christianisme. Si l'un des personnages du *Banquet religieux* d'Erasme

citons la traduction de G. Hervet, d'après l'édition parisienne (Michel Sonnius) de 1585 (BN. C 562), p. 718. Texte latin dans l'édition Plantin (Anvers, 1576), p.308 (BN C 829).

[1] *Opus Epistolarum Erasmi*, ed. Allen, t. v (Oxford, 1924), ep.1271, 10–17: 'Ego enim in hoc opere brevitati, quantum potui, studui placere. Incurrerunt quidem loci in quibus id praestari non potuit, ut quum erant res non admodum theologis nostris cognitae, sicut philosophicae, praecipue Platonica. Ideo in octavo et decimo libris longior fui forsan quam oportebat; tum ut recondita illis aperirem et proferrem, tum ut Platonica prorsus non ignorarent, viderentque haec nihil Aristotelicis cedere, et inciperent alios quoque magnos auctores velle cognoscere.'

[2] *In Somnium Scipionis*, commentaire du *Somnium Scipionis* de Cicéron (Bâle, 1519), préface de Vivès, *Opera omnia*, v, pp.64–109.

[3] Cf. Carlos G. Noreña, *Juan Luis Vives* (Martinus Nijhoff, The Hague, 1970), p.165.

[4] *Opera omnia*, v, p.106: 'Nulla unquam hominum memoria scriptum est librum (sacros nostrae religionis semper excipio) in quo plus rerum, plus artis, plus eloquentiae, sit comprehensum atque infarctum.'

s'écriait 'Saint Socrate, priez pour nous', Socrate, 'source sacrée et sublime' de la pensée grecque, aurait bien pu, pour Vivès, remplir l'office de guide spirituel pour des âmes éprises de vérité. C'est ce que nous voyons bien exprimé dans son opuscule *De initiis, sectis et laudibus philosophiae*,[1] où il tente une esquisse d'histoire de la philosophie:

> Socrate est le premier qui ait ramené la philosophie qui se complaisait et divaguait dans les cieux et leurs éléments, vers la cité des hommes et à leur service individuel ... Et tout en étant, à l'affirmation et au sentiment déclarés de tous les mortels le plus savant en de telles matières, il se déclarait néanmoins parfaitement ignorant des choses de la nature, encourageant les hommes à abandonner l'étude immense et désespérante de ces mystères pour se convertir tout entiers à la réforme de leurs moeurs.[2]

C'est là l'image classique de Socrate, moraliste et réformateur, maître de pensée et d'action.

En fait, ces témoignages admiratifs de Vivès se sont plus d'une fois tempérés de critiques, sans que l'on puisse parler, avec Carlos G. Noreña,[3] d'une évolution de sa pensée. Peut-être le pédagogue, l'auteur du *De disciplinis*,[4] est-il moins sensible au style poétique, voire au mysticisme de Platon, dont l'usage répété du mythe donne à ses développements philosophiques un caractère ambigu, auquel les élèves ont souvent du mal à accommoder leur esprit. Toujours est-il que Vivès écrivait, deux ans avant sa mort, dans un texte intitulé *Censure des oeuvres d'Aristote*:[5] 'Platon fut le premier philosophe de l'antiquité à s'exprimer d'abondance en un style élégant et savant, mais difficilement adapté à l'enseignement et à l'instruction.'[6] Que devons-nous penser de cette critique? Vivès perd-il de son enthousiasme pour les spéculations éthico-métaphysiques du philosophe athénien? Il est difficile de le prétendre, d'autant plus qu'il reste fondamentalement socratique ou platonicien dans le problème des rapports entre l'intelligence et le bien: le vice ou le mal n'est pas l'effet d'une nature vicieuse ou mauvaise, mais la conséquence d'un

---

[1] Louvain, 1518. (*Opera omnia*, III, pp.3–24.)

[2] 'Socrates primus philosophiam, in coelis elementisque versantem et divagantem, ad civitatem atque hominum singulorum usus, vitamque devocavit ... et quum esset unus omnium consensu et approbatione rerum eiusmodi scientissimus, affirmavit tamen, se illorum omnium ignarum esse, ut ceteri desperata ... tanta arcanorum scientia, illis relictis, ad morum compositionem totos se converterent' (*Opera omnia*, III, p.15).

[3] Op. cit. p.165.   [4] Anvers, 1531.

[5] *Censura de Aristotelis operibus* (Strasbourg, 1538).

[6] 'Primus omnium Plato eleganter sane multa, et docte, sed ad docendum discendumque parum accommodate.'

jugement faux sur le prix à accorder aux choses; les passions in-
férieures doivent se soumettre entièrement à la direction de la raison.

Qu'en est-il maintenant d'Aristote? Nous devons à la vérité de dire
qu'à la différence de Platon, qui n'a jamais bénéficié d'un tel honneur, Aristote a eu droit à tout un développement élogieux dans une
préface de Vivès à une édition de ses oeuvres. C'est en 1538 dans le
De operibus Aristotelis censura que nous lisons ceci: 'Il ne semble pas
qu'il y ait eu un esprit plus puissant que celui d'Aristote' ('nullum
videtur fuisse ingenium Aristotelico praestantius').[1] Et il poursuit en
affirmant que pour le lecteur attentif et diligent de son oeuvre, une
admiration s'élève à l'égard d'un penseur aussi profond, capable dans
ses déductions de pénétrer jusqu'au noyau intime des choses, et par
son esprit critique, de réfuter les arguments les plus subtils.[2] C'est la
force et la solidité de son raisonnement qui l'impressionne au premier
chef. Mais le pédagogue n'est jamais absent dans ses considérations,
et Vivès mesure l'utilité d'Aristote pour les élèves et les étudiants à
sa concision verbale: 'chez lui, rien de superflu ou d'inutile: tout est
solide, tout est plein; aucune hésitation n'est permise au lecteur,
aucune démarche aberrante. A cet égard on peut vraiment lui appliquer ce que l'on disait à propos de l'Athénien Lysias et d'une cause
mineure: l'édifice tout entier s'écroulera si on lui retire un seul petit
mot, comme on le ferait d'une pierre . . .'[3] De même les argumentations et les matériaux choisis par Aristote défient le temps, on ne peut
rien leur substituer. Dès 1518, dans son histoire critique de la philosophie que nous avons déjà citée, le *De initiis, sectis et laudibus philosophiae*, Vivès avouait une admiration sans borne pour les Péripaté-
ciens: 'Mes philosophes sont les péripatéticiens, dont le chef de file,
Aristote, est incontestablement le plus avisé de tous les philosophes.'[4]
Le terme latin *sapientissimus* désigne à la fois le savoir et la sagesse
théorique et pratique. Un an plus tard, dans ce même commentaire

---

[1] *Censura* (*Opera omnia*, III, p.25).
[2] 'Legenti opera ejus attente ac diligenter, exoritur ingens admiratio, quam ab ultimis
principiis deducit abditissima, et profondissima rerum omnium, quam acute refellit
aliena, quam fortiter communit et corroborat sua, quo ordine digerit singula, et,
quod est in tradendis artibus perutile, quanta frugalitate verborum' (ibid. p.25).
[3] 'Nihil est in eo vacans, aut inane, omnia solida et plena: nusquam sinit lectorem oscitari,
aut aliud agere. De hoc vere dici potest, quod Lysiae Atheniensi minori de causa attri-
buitur, ruituram structuram universam, si vel verbulum unum tamquam lapidem
detraxeris' (ibid. p.25).
[4] 'At vero nostrates philosophi, quorum princeps idem, philosophorum omnium facile
sapientissimus, Aristoteles Stagyrites fuit' (*De initiis, O.o.* III, p.18).

du *Songe de Scipion* où il faisait l'éloge de Platon, il rend hommage à son disciple, et il écrit: 'Nul ne pourrait imaginer que je fasse peu de cas d'Aristote, ce philosophe que je place, sans exception aucune, avant tous les autres.'[1] Et, pour en revenir à la préface à l'édition des oeuvres d'Aristote, dès les premières lignes il reproche à Pline l'Ancien d'avoir dressé à Homère une stèle qui l'élève au-dessus de tous les génies de l'histoire.[2] Entre le poète de l'*Iliade* et de l'*Odyssée* et le philosophe du Lycée, Vivès n'hésite pas à préférer le second.

Les raisons de son admiration sont nombreuses. Peut-être devons-nous y voir d'abord la marque de son éclectisme philosophique et de sa curiosité universelle. Dans cette oeuvre de jeunesse que constitue le *De initiis philosophiae*, Vivès s'enthousiasme pour la curiosité encyclopédique du Stagyrite et de ses disciples, auxquels nul sujet, nul domaine, nul champ de recherches n'était étranger. Aristote a tout étudié, tout résolu à fond, il a soumis à des normes inébranlables et définitives la pensée humaine qui se dissipait et se dispersait à l'aventure. C'est là un thème que l'on retrouve dans de nombreux passages du traité des *Disciplines*, et notamment dans les livres qui traitent de la corruption des arts (*De causis corruptarum artium*). Pour un peu, Vivès appliquerait à l'action d'Aristote la fonction que le philosophe Anaxagore attribuait à l'Esprit, qui 'vint et remit tout en ordre'. Philosophie constructive, philosophie éclectique, philosophie rigoureuse.

Mais Aristote est aussi le philosophe qui s'adapte merveilleusement à un enseignement magistral. On a déjà noté son économie de mots. Écoutons maintenant dans la *Censura*[3] le développement de quelques-unes de ses qualités pédagogiques:

Tous les livres d'Aristote ont un ordre et une structure qui conviennent à l'enseignement et à la discipline pédagogique. Nul ne fut plus habile à transmettre le savoir, car tout ce qu'il a enseigné a été consigné en des formules et en des préceptes certains, et avec une telle concision et une telle densité d'écriture et de pensée qu'on puisse les recevoir et les retenir aisément, et, quand les circonstances l'exigent, les appliquer opportunément. Aucun autre écrivain grec ne possède une telle maîtrise du langage: ses expressions semblent naître du sujet traité; il ne cherche pas à enjoliver les choses ni à parsemer son discours de fleurettes dont le

---

[1] 'Nemo me suggillare Aristotelem credat, quem ego universis philosophis, nemine excepto, antepono . . .' (*O.o.* v, p.107).

[2] 'Plinius Secundus libro septimo naturalis Historiae inquirit, quodnam existimetur maximum fuisse ingenium, ex iis quidem, quorum extet memoria, vel suis ipsorum, vel alienis monumentis. Et eam tantae ambitionis palmam videtur ad Homerum vatem deferre . . .' (*O.o.* III, p.25).

[3] *O.o.* III, pp.25–6.

charme superflu tient le lecteur enchaîné, mais qui le laissent peu après les mains vides . . .[1]

Nous sommes au coeur du grand débat de la vraie et de la fausse rhétorique, que les humanistes de la Renaissance ont repris aux sources helléniques et romaines, et notamment à la controverse indéfiniment recommencée de Socrate avec les sophistes. L'auteur de l'*Organon* a fondé l'art de la parole humaine, il a étudié le langage humain sous son triple aspect grammatical, rhétorique et dialectique, mais il a aussi enseigné l'art de relier les paroles aux choses, le signifiant au signifié. C'est ce dont le loue l'humaniste espagnol, qui s'en est pris, comme on sait, aux faux dialecticiens,[2] à la phraséologie creuse. Et il éprouve le besoin d'établir un parallèle entre Platon et Aristote pour mieux faire apparaître les mérites de ce dernier, véritable inventeur et ordonnateur de la rhétorique :

Bien que les livres de Platon contiennent çà et là des germes multiples de tous les arts et de toutes les disciplines, et que dans ses dialogues apparaissent avec éclat toute la méthode et tous les exercices de la dialectique, il n'existe pratiquement pas, dans sa prose abondante, à l'exception de quelques passages litigieux de l'*Euthydème*, une seule formulation des préceptes dialectiques ; c'est encore plus vrai de Zénon d'Elie, et de Parménide auxquels on attribue l'invention de cet art ; mais c'est indubitablement Aristote qui lui a donné une forme systématique, comme il l'a fait pour la rhétorique.[3]

Ainsi la lecture d'Aristote fournit à Vivès le modèle d'une pensée dialectique, qu'il oppose souvent à la dialectique stérile de toute une catégorie de penseurs médiévaux, dont l'Aristote était passablement différent du sien. Comme un certain nombre de philosophes de la Renaissance, hellénistes et historiens – plus ou moins éprouvés – de l'antiquité, Vivès croyait à un retour à l'originalité, à l'authenticité d'une pensée, enfin débarrassée de ses gloses ou de ses bandelettes

[1] 'Aristotelis omnia ordinem et formam habent institutionis ac disciplinae, nec fuit dexteritas in aliquo ad artes tradendas par, omnia vero sunt illi certis praeceptis et formulis conscripta, ea brevitate ac gravitate verborum et sententiarum ut facile accipi et retineri possint, et ad usum, quum res postulat, accommodari ; verba autem nullus Graecorum habet aeque apposita, ita ut ex rebus videantur nasci, quas tractat ; non persequitur rerum flosculos et orationis deliciolas, quibus inani oblectamento delinitum lectorem teneat, postea remittat vacuum . . .'

[2] Voir notamment son traité *In pseudodialecticos* (Sélestat, 1519) (*O.o.* III, pp.37–68). C'est une longue lettre à son ami Juan Fort, qui réside à Paris, dont l'Université comprend un certain nombre de ces pseudo-dialecticiens.

[3] 'Nam Platonis, etsi magna sunt in illius operibus artium omnium ac disciplinarum sparsa semina, et dialecticae tota ratio ac exercitatio in ejus dialogis eluceat, praeceptum tamen nullum fere disertis extat verbis, praeter litigiosa quaedam in *Eutydemo*, multo minus Zenonis Eleatis et Parmenidis, ad quos refertur artis inventio ; sed indubie Aristoteles eam in artis faciem reduxit, ut et rhetoricam' (*O.o.* VI, p.114).

aseptisées. L'Aristote latin du Moyen Age, l'Aristote des commentateurs scolastiques, est rejeté, ou tout au moins passé au crible au profit de l'Aristote grec. Mais la question qui se pose – et qui se pose aussi bien pour Platon – est celle de savoir si Vivès n'est pas malgré lui tributaire d'une tradition, ou de telle tradition à laquelle la pensée médiévale n'est pas étrangère. On ne fait pas impunément bon marché de près d'un double millénaire d'histoire de la pensée. 'C'est notre paresse ou notre négligence', écrit-il,[1] 'qui nous fait croire à l'obscurité de certains passages d'Aristote. Quand on le compare à ceux qui nous ont précédés, il est plus lumineux que le jour à midi.' Une certaine ambiguïté persiste quant à la signification de l'expression de Vivès 'superioribus collatus'. On pourrait croire tout d'abord qu'il s'agit des philosophes antérieurs à Aristote lui-même, plus obscurs, et par conséquent plus difficiles que le Stagyrite: sens confirmé par d'autres passages, comme on l'a vu et comme on pourrait encore le voir. Mais il paraît plus conforme au contexte où il est question des commentateurs d'Aristote, d'interpréter *superioribus* comme les traducteurs et les glosateurs médiévaux du philosophe grec, ceux qui ont précédé la génération des humanistes, et même des commentateurs beaucoup plus anciens. C'est ainsi qu'Aristote est lumineux, et que ceux dont la mission était d'éclairer sa pensée, sont plus obscurs que lui. Mais écoutons Vivès lui-même: 'Les commentateurs grecs d'Aristote, tels qu'Alexandre, Themistius, Simplicius, Psellus, Philopon, et d'autres encore, utilisent beaucoup de mots qui sont par différents de ceux d'Aristote, lui-même; mais nos anciens commentateurs latins, Apulée, Capella, Augustin, Boèce, ont corrompu sa dialectique et ont fait violence à la langue latine . . . '[2] (langue considérée comme impropre à l'expression de la philosophie). Et encore ce passage dans lequel il condamne les commentaires arabes d'Aristote, notamment celui d'Averroès, qui devait jouer un rôle historique si important en fournissant à l'École de Padoue la base de sa philosophie naturaliste ou matérialiste:[3]

[1] *De initiis* (*O.o.* III, p.19): 'Torpor vero et negligentia nostra efficit ut nonnullae tenebrae in Aristotele esse videantur, qui superioribus collatus, ipse quoque meridie clarior est.'

[2] 'Aristotelis enarratores Graeci Alexander, Themistius, Simplicius, Psellus, Philoponus, et alii, multum habent verborum, sententiarum non aliud quam ipse Aristoteles; Latini nostri prisci illi Apulejus, Capella, Augustinus, Boethius, dialecticam suam depravarunt, et vim attulerunt Romano sermoni . . .' (*De Disciplinis*, 1.3.4; *O.o.* VI, pp.124–5).

[3] Nous renvoyons à ce propos à notre communication du colloque de Tours de juillet 1973: *Cardan, lecteur et interprète d'Aristote*.

Le nom qui lui [à Averroès] fut donné est celui de 'Commentateur', alors qu'en commentant Aristote il ne fait rien d'autre que d'expliciter ses propres idées, qu'il se mit à exposer . . . Qu'apportait-il enfin dans ses commentaires d'Aristote qui pût l'habiliter à cette tâche d'instructeur? Il n'avait pas de connaissance de l'histoire ancienne, il n'avait pas d'idée des opinions exprimées en cette discipline vénérable, il n'était pas au courant des sectes philosophiques dont Aristote fait mention presque à chaque page. C'est ainsi qu'on peut le voir citer abominable-, ment tous les philosophes de l'antiquité, car il n'avait jamais lu un seul d'entre eux, ignorant qu'il était du grec et du latin: au lieu de Proclus il écrit Ptolomaeus, au lieu de Protagoras Pythagoras, au lieu de Cratyle Démocrite; il affuble les livres de Platon de titres ridicules, et il s'exprime à leur sujet de façon telle que même un aveugle peut voir clairement qu'il n'en jamais lu le moindre mot.[1]

Certes, nous avons affaire ici davantage à une polémique contre le philosophe arabe qu'à un éloge d'Aristote, mais on peut quand même ranger ce texte parmi les écrits destinés à défendre la mémoire des grands philosophes de l'antiquité contre l'interprétation abusive qui a été faite de leur pensée.

Au point où nous sommes arrivés de notre recherche, la question se pose de savoir auquel des deux philosophes grecs il accorderait plutôt la palme, et pourquoi. Nous avons déjà noté, à propos de ses préoccupations pédagogiques, qu'il fait peut-être plus entièrement confiance à Aristote qu'à Platon. Mais qu'en est-il au juste? L'examen d'autres textes devrait permettre de préciser notre jugement.

Une chose est certaine: Vivès s'oppose avec fermeté et continuité à la méthode d'autorité, sous toutes les formes où elle peut apparaître. Alain Guy l'a bien noté dans le petit livre[2] qu'il a consacré récemment à l'humaniste valencien. Voici ce que Vivès écrit dans la préface de son immense ouvrage *De disciplinis*, adressée de Bruges à Jean III de Portugal, et où il analyse avec une maîtrise et une sérénité absolues les conditions de la crise de la culture que traverse alors l'Europe intellectuelle: 'Il n'y a pas de doute qu'il est beaucoup plus utile au progrès de la culture d'appliquer la critique aux écrits des grands auteurs que de se reposer paresseusement sur la seule autorité

---

[1] 'Nomen est Commentatoris nactus, homo qui in Aristotele enarrando nihil minus explicat, quam eum ipsum, quem suscepti declarandum . . . Quid tandem afferebat, quo in Aristotele enarrando posset esse probe instructus? Non cognitionem veteris memoriae, non scientiam placitorum priscae disciplinae, et intelligentiam sectarum, quibus Aristoteles passim scatet. Itaque videas eum pessime philosophos omnes antiquos citare, ut qui nullum unquam legerit ignarus graecitatis ac latinitatis, pro Proclo Ptolomaeum ponit, pro Prothagora Pythagoram, pro Cratylo Democritum, libros Platonis titulis ridiculis inscribit, et ita de iis loquitur, ut vel caeco perspicuum sit litteram eum in illis legisse nullam' (*De Disciplinis*, 1.5.3; *O.o.* VI, p.192).

[2] *Vivès*, ed. Seghers, 'Philosophes de tous les temps' (1972), p.21.

et d'accepter systématiquement tout ce que nous offre la foi en autrui.'[1] Ce principe ne saurait souffrir d'exception. Et après avoir, une fois de plus, déclaré son admiration à l'égard d'Aristote dont le génie est immense, il revendique à son propre usage la liberté intellectuelle dont le Stagyrite avait jadis usé à l'égard de son maître Platon: 'Amicus . . . Aristoteles, sed magis amica veritas!' Car la vérité, pour Vivès, n'est ni celle de Platon, ni celle d'Aristote, ni celle d'Augustin. 'Sectateurs de la vérité', s'écrie-t-il, 'partout où vous pensez qu'elle se trouve, mettez-vous de son côté!'[2] Et c'est encore lui qui exprime cette idée, que tout homme de science, tout philosophe, ou même tout esprit foncièrement honnête devrait considérer comme le principe directeur de sa vie: 'La vérité est accessible à tous; elle n'est pas encore conquise. Une grande part en est encore laissée au futur.'[3] Dirons-nous pour autant avec Bernardo Monsegu:[4] 'Vivès est un aristotélicien convaincu, mais il ressentit comme peu d'intellectuels le poids de son temps, qui le menait à voir dans le Stagyrite une idole scolastique qu'il fallait abattre, si l'on voulait en finir avec la barbarie de l'École'? Non, nous ne le dirons pas, car cette transformation d'Aristote en idole, ce culte abusif de la personnalité, est l'affaire de ces héritiers douteux: ni Aristote ni Vivès ne sont concernés. 'Il fut mal interprété par des incapables, qui, en le traduisant en latin, ne firent pas du latin et ne conservèrent pas non plus le grec . . .'[5] Et de citer le proverbe: 'Aristote passe pour avoir un nez en cire, que chacun infléchit à son gré et dans le sens qui lui plaît.'[6]

L'affaire est entendue, mais si Aristote n'est pas responsable de son culte posthume et des délires intellectuels auxquels son nom a fourni le prétexte, il n'en est sans doute pas de même en ce qui concerne la dégénérescence de l'idée de dialectique, ce cheval de bataille de tous les humanistes. C'est là une difficulté certaine, car nous trouvons dans le texte de 1531 des critiques qui paraissent contredire les éloges de cette même dialectique que nous avions trouvés dans les écrits de 1518 ou 1519, mais aussi dans la préface de la *Censura* de 1538. L'*Organon*, lisons-nous au livre III du *De causis corruptarum artium*, comporte des

---

[1] Trad. A. Guy, op. cit. p.21. On notera la dernière formule: 'auctoritate sola acquiescere et fide semper aliena accipere omnia' (VI, p.6).

[2] Ibid. p.7.

[3] 'Patet omnibus veritas; nondum est occupata. Multum ex illa, etiam futuris relictum est' (Préface au *De Disciplinis*).

[4] *Filosofia del humanismo de J. L. Vives* (Madrid, 1961), p.33.

[5] '. . . nec latinum fecerunt, nec reliquerunt graecum' (p.69).

[6] 'Aristotelem habere nasum cereum, quem quilibet, quo velit, flectat pro libito' (p.70).

défauts très graves, car il n'aide pas le lecteur à 'trouver des arguments' ou à 'juger des argumentations'.[1] La justesse et la rigueur des traités de logique ne sont pas mises en cause, mais bien leur puissance d'invention. A la logique d'Aristote il manquerait ce que nous appelons aujourd'hui une métalogique, prenant en quelque sorte ses distances par rapport à l'argumentation ou au tableau des catégories, pour juger celles-ci ou celle-là. D'autre part, Aristote aurait commis l'erreur de confondre dialectique et métaphysique et d'avoir obscurci l'argumentation du vrai. Les catégories elles-mêmes sont arbitraires dans leur choix comme dans leur nombre de dix; elles sont également plus métaphysiques que logiques. La manière dont Aristote les expose n'est pas ordonnée, ni selon l'ordre des essences des choses, ni selon celui de notre pensée. Le *Peri Hermeneias* ou *Traité de l'interprétation*, dont l'inspiration est également résumée dans la *Censura*,[2] mais ici sans volonté de critique, relève davantage de la grammaire que de la dialectique. Quant aux *Premiers analytiques*, le *De causis* leur reproche d'être encombrés de beaucoup de 'superfluités' (*supervacaneis*),[3] comme il reproche aux syllogismes leur complication inutile; c'est au nom de cette même inutilité qu'il critique dans la *Censura*[4] la modalité des jugements, tout en rendant hommage à la pénétration d'Aristote. Beaucoup plus grande est la sévérité que le traité de 1531 réserve aux *Seconds Analytiques* et aux *Topiques*. Le premier traité recèle non seulement des longueurs oiseuses, des difficultés qui excèdent la portée des pauvres humains,[5] mais aussi de graves insuffisances en ce qui concerne les universels, les notions de cause ou de nécessité. Le second traité est taxé de dépotoir, où règne une foule bigarrée d'éléments hétéroclites; beaucoup de renseignements peuvent y être trouvés, mais sans ordre et sans souci d'efficacité pédagogique ou d'application pratique. Nous sommes loin de l'Aristote considéré comme le solide et irremplaçable instituteur de la jeunesse.

Ces critiques sont loin d'être homogènes. Tantôt Vivès se place du point de vue du logicien, qu'il n'est pas vraiment – beaucoup moins qu'Aristote, en tout cas – tantôt du point de vue du pédagogue soucieux d'application pratique.

M. Alain Guy[6] pense que la *Censura de operibus Aristotelis* étant une

[1] *Filosofia del humanismo de J. L. Vives* (Madrid, 1961), p.114.   [2] *O.o.* III, pp.27–8.
[3] *O.o.* VI, p.118.
[4] *O.o.* III, p.28: '. . . magno quidem illa acumine, quis neget? scd inutiliter'.
[5] 'Tiens-tu compte de nous, Aristote, et de notre portée intellectuelle, ou de la nature des choses?' (p.118).   [6] *Vivès*, p.32.

oeuvre de circonstance, dans laquelle Vivès réagit davantage avec son affectivité qu'avec le plein emploi de sa raison critique, il vaut mieux interroger l'oeuvre longuement mûrie qu'est le *De tradendis disciplinis* pour connaître son véritable sentiment ou son sentiment définitif sur le philosophe grec. La question peut se discuter. Tout d'abord la *Censura* donne bien plutôt l'impression que nous avons affaire à un résumé et à une mise au point rapide et objective des oeuvres d'Aristote ou de celles qui lui sont communément attribuées; on a l'impression qu'en dehors du préambule, Vivès met son point d'honneur à ne pas entrer dans une *disputatio* pour ou contre Aristote. Nous ne conclurons donc finalement pas grand'chose de l'examen de cet opuscule dont le ton reste neutre. Il importe donc de poursuivre l'examen des critiques répandues dans le *De causis* et dans le *De tradendis disciplinis*. Elles sont assez nombreuses et variées pour que nous soyons détournés de l'envie de conclure trop uniment.

Dans le chapitre 2 du livre v du *De causis*[1] (qui indique, dans son titre même, que l'auteur loue Aristote, mais s'écarte de ceux qui estiment impie de contredire le maître), nous lisons: 'En vérité, je ne vois pas, dans l'étude de la nature, quelqu'un que je puisse lui comparer',[2] mais il ajoute aussitôt: 'Toutefois nos gens pensent que ses thèses sont telles que l'esprit humain ne peut atteindre rien de plus exact ni de plus certain[3] . . . Sur la faiblesse d'une telle opinion, sur son impudence et même parfois sur son impiété, on ne peut parler autant qu'il le conviendrait.' Ici encore, ce n'est pas Aristote lui-même qui est visé, mais bien le culte inconditionné de sa personnalité. La nature a permis à l'homme de prétendre à la découverte du vrai: pourquoi donc nous asservir à la pensée du vieux maître? Au nom de cette lumière naturelle qui permet à chaque homme d'être le détenteur provisoire d'une parcelle de vérité, il combat le monopole d'Aristote: 'Possède-t-il des vérités telles qu'aucune autre ne puisse être plus vraie? Il en possède indubitablement un grand nombre: qui n'en possède-t-il pas? Et pas seulement chez les philosophes, mais dans le commun des mortels!'[4] N'a-t-il pas d'ailleurs été l'objet

---

[1] *O.o.* VI, p.185.

[2] 'Equidem in inspectione naturae haud video quem possem illi comparare' (ibid. p.185).

[3] 'Opiniones de natura rerum, nostri homines ejusmodi rentur esse, nihil ut humanum ingenium exactius vel certius possit exculpere' (ibid. p.185).

[4] 'An ea quae ad assensum veritatis pertinent, ut veritates habeat quibus nihil possit esse verius? Habet indubie permultas, quis enim non habet? Non modo ex philosophis, sed ex vulgo?' (ibid. p.186).

de maintes critiques? 'Dans ce qu'il a affirmé, tout n'est pas vrai: les philosophes des autres sectes, et parfois même des Péripatéticiens, Galien et de nombreux médecins, des historiens de la nature, des auteurs anciens appartenant à notre religion, ruinent beaucoup de ses thèses avec de grands arguments et des expériences incontestables.'[1] Le temps et la variété des lieux ont révélé la fausseté de certaines de ses vues. Vivès dénonce sans ambages la sotte vanité de ceux qui prétendent qu'Aristote représente 'l'extrême pointe de la nature' ('extremum esse aiunt naturae'), et que sa 'route est la plus droite et la plus sûre de toutes' ('eam rectissimam esse omnium et certissimam in natura viam').[2] Il s'en prend en particulier à la superstition des syllogismes aristotéliciens qui ont (ou qui auraient) la prétention de contenir la nature entière. Ce culte d'Aristote paraît aux yeux du chrétien Vivès attentatoire au culte du Dieu unique, qui 'seul connaît les limites de la nature et de notre esprit, puisqu'il en est dans les deux cas l'auteur'.[3] Aristote lui-même n'a-t-il pas progressé dans sa propre existence? N'en savait-il pas davantage dans sa vieillesse que dans sa jeunesse?[4] C'est toujours l'idée d'une vérité immobile ou immobilisée à un moment donné de l'histoire ou chez un homme, que combat l'humaniste valencien. Et voici l'argument le plus fort, lancé contre les épigones indignes, les commentateurs ou glosateurs anémiques: 'Assurément Aristote lui-même, s'il vivait aujourd'hui ... se moquerait de la stupidité de ces gens et les corrigerait.'[5] Les opinions erronées d'Aristote, lisons-nous dans la suite du chapitre, ne sont pas imputables à la lumière naturelle – car celle-ci, comme on l'a vu, est infaillible, puisqu'elle a été créée par Dieu – mais bien 'aux ténèbres et à une certaine image provenant d'une lumière captieuse'.[6] Ainsi quand Aristote 'se trompe dans l'un de ses arguments, ce n'est pas la splendeur naturelle qui le trompe, mais bien la faiblesse de son esprit ...'. Il lui faudra, pour se rapprocher de la lumière naturelle 'un plus grand effort, plus d'attention, un autre jour, un conseil étranger, des informations'.[7]

[1] 'Sed non sunt tamen vera omnia quae confirmavit: philosophi aliarum sectarum, nonnunquam etiam Peripateticae, Galenus et medicorum complures, historici naturae, prisci religionis nostrae scriptores, multa in eo magnis argumentis et inevitabili experimento convellunt' (ibid. p.186).
[2] Ibid. p.186.
[3] '... solus Deus, qui et naturae terminos et ingenii nostri novit, auctor utriusque, (ibid. p.187).
[4] 'Ipse Aristoteles an non plura assecutus est senex quam juvenis?' (ibid. p.187).
[5] 'Aristoteles ipse, si nunc viveret ... istorum tamen stultitiam irrideret ac castigaret' (ibid. p.188).   [6] Ibid. p.189.   [7] Ibid. p.189.

Voici un défaut plus grave, car il est plus personnel, défaut qui n'est, à la vérité que l'envers d'une qualité: l'ambiguïté, revers de la subtilité. Les adjectifs utilisés par Vivès sont d'une part, *vafer*, qui désigne l'habileté, l'ingéniosité, et *occultus*, qui s'applique à tout ce qui est secret, mystérieux, donc ambigu. Cette subtilité ambiguë, ou cette ambiguïté subtile apparaît principalement dans les définitions.[1] Ne voyons-nous pas poindre ici une nouvelle contradiction chez Vivès? Si seulement les commentateurs d'Aristote avaient choisi des ouvrages plus positifs, dont le sens est patent et l'intérêt évident, comme le traité des *Animaux* ou les *Problèmes*! Mais non! Ils s'embarrassent dans les *Physiques*, le *Ciel*, la *Génération*, les *Météores*![2] Ici encore, la critique d'Aristote débouche sur une critique de la pensée scolastique. Le chapitre suivant[3] traitera du commentaire d'Averroès, dans lequel, cette fois, l'affectivité et l'esprit critique de Vivès seront étroitement associés.

Il est difficile de dire, en définitive, ce que Vivès admire chez Aristote, et ce qu'il lui reproche. Encore plus difficile d'établir un classement *ne varietur* entre Platon et Aristote. Si l'on se réfère au *De disciplinis*, on peut accumuler des jugements aussi dissemblables que ceux-ci: Il a commis de lourdes erreurs en logique (p. 114); il s'est toujours complu dans l'obscurité verbale (p.219); ses meilleurs livres concernent la philosophie naturelle (p.190); on peut faire dire à Aristote ce que l'on veut (p.70) parce qu'il est obscur (p.31); il a écrit de bonnes choses en morale (p.211), mais il est ridicule de s'étonner de ce que tous les philosophes du passé n'aient pas été d'accord en tout point;[4] il est supérieur dans le domaine de l'art et dans ses considérations esthétiques (p.64); on ne peut pas considérer que sa philosophie ou sa religion soient hérétiques (p.90); il a passé au crible tous les auteurs (p.34); il a osé renverser les opinions admises depuis toujours (p.7); Aristote est isolé par les tenants de l'École (p.185), remarque qui concerne davantage les scolastiques qu'Aristote lui-même; saint Thomas a adapté la Dialectique d'Aristote afin qu'elle ne fût pas nuisible à la religion (p.149), remarque qui vise également davantage saint Thomas et son rôle historique que le philosophe grec; il trouble

---

[1] 'Est autem in definiendo vafer et occultus' (ibid. p.190).
[2] Ibid. p.190.
[3] Caput III. *Irruit in Abenroem, et quem non modo Aristoteli, sed et D. Thomae aequiparandum sua aetate homines arbitrabantur, foedissime prosternit . . .*
[4] Ce n'est pas un jugement spécifique sur Aristote.

plutôt qu'il n'aiguise ou stimule les esprits (p.191) : nouveau reproche à l'adresse de ses 'subtilités'; son zèle pour l'étude était admirable (p.57); il a commis des erreurs (p.36).

Ses jugements sur Platon sont moins nombreux et surtout moins contradictoires. Il l'admire pour sa *summa eloquentia*, son style, même s'il fait quelques réserves sur son efficacité pédagogique. On a l'impression que, dans son combat permanent contre la scolastique, il n'a pas eu à rencontrer comme pour Aristote, des commentateurs qui l'auraient contraint de prendre une position nette. Il peut admirer Platon sans gêne. Il n'en est pas de même pour Aristote, car, qu'il le veuille ou non, il traîne avec lui des siècles d'aristotélisme dont il n'est pas si facile de se débarrasser. Le néoplatonisme l'a moins gêné que le néo-aristotélisme, car il n'avait pas à se définir par rapport à lui.

Nous n'établirons donc pas pour conclure de palmarès, nous ne parlerons pas davantage d'une évolution de Vivès dans ses jugements concernant l'un ou l'autre de ces philosophes, car, soucieux tout au long de sa carrière, de s'attacher à une vérité dont l'essence même lui paraissait devoir rejeter tout caractère de fixité, il ne s'est jamais imposé une admiration ou un dénigrement sans faille de ces deux penseurs : il les a rencontrés dans de multiples circonstances de sa vie, de son travail, de son métier de pédagogue, et chaque fois il a réagi à leur appel ou à leur sollicitation avec la lucidité critique que les circonstances exigeaient de lui.

19

ZUR ROLLE DER MYTHOLOGIE IN DER LITERATUR DES SIGLO DE ORO

F. SCHALK

Die Dichter und Maler des goldenen Zeitalters in Spanien waren aufgeschlossen für die Mannigfaltigkeit der Mythologie. Ihre Motive sind bald im Gedicht scharf ausgeprägt dargestellt, bald fanden sie ihre Gestalt im Fronleichnamsspiel und im Drama. Infolge der engen Verbindung aller Gattungen, die stets vertauschbar waren, fliessen die Motive hin und her und offenbaren stets aufs Neue die Neigung der Zeit, die Dichtung mit bekannten mythischen Persönlichkeiten zu verknüpfen. Die immer wieder bearbeiteten grossen Inhalte – Odysseus, Phaeton, Orpheus, Prometheus, Narziss, Perseus und Andromeda[1] und viele andere – wurden Träger einer Entwicklung von grösster Wirkungskraft, durch die die Gegenwart in das Licht einer ruhmvollen Vergangenheit gestellt wird. Einige Beispiele mögen zeugen für die Macht einer ununterbrochenen mythologischen Tradition.

In der Lyrik sind mythologische Themen stets zum Gefäss für wechselnde Inhalte geworden. Lope de Vega hat zwar in seinen Gedichten den Pfad des volkstümlichen Wortes nicht verloren, die gesprochene Sprache lag im Rahmen seiner Kunst und oft und oft fügt sie sich dem Rhythmus des Volkslieds. Aber im Gesichtsfeld zweier Stile – der *poesía popular* und der *poesía culta* – hat Lope nicht entschieden seinen Platz auf dem Boden des Naiven, noch nur in dem Bereich des Prunkvollen und Ornamentalen. Sein Werk bietet Beispiele für beide Stile, beide herrschen bis tief in unsere Zeit und feiern – wie die hermetische Dichtung Góngoras – immer wieder eine neue Auferstehung.

---

[1] Zur Thematik cf. L. Schrader, 'Odysseus im Auto sacramental,' in *Spanische Literatur im goldenen Zeitalter*, Festschrift F. Schalk (Frankfurt, 1973), *El verdadero Dios Pan*, Texto y estudio por José M. de Osma (Lawrence, Kansas, 1949) (dort Skizze der Pansage), *La estatua de Prometeo*, ed. Ch. Aubrun (1965), *Eco y Narciso*, ed. Aubrun (Paris, 1961) (dort weitere Literatur).

Es gibt eine Reihe mythologischer Sonette, in denen der Einfluss griechischer Motive, deren Kenntnis damals eine erstaunliche Höhe erreicht hatte, durchschimmert. So in dem folgenden:

De Andrómeda

Atada al mar Andrómeda lloraba,
los nácares abriéndose al rocío,
que en sus conchas cuajado el cristal frío
en cándidos aljófares trocaba.
    Besaba el pie, las peñas ablandaba
humilde el mar, como pequeño rio,
volviendo el sol la primavera estío
parado en su cenit la contemplaba.
    Los cabellos al viento bullicioso
que la cubra con ellos le rogaban
ya que testigo fué de iguales dichas,
    y celosas de ver su cuerpo hermoso,
las nereidas su fin solicitaban,
que aun hay quien tenga envidia en las desdichas.[1]

Die Gestalt der Andromeda erscheint in mehrfachen Brechungen. Ihre Tränen werden Perlen – Tauperlen. Schon in der ersten Strophe erscheint die weinende Andromeda nicht isoliert in einer feindlichen Welt, sondern als ein Wesen inmitten der Natur, allem zugänglich, was mit ihr geschieht. Das Meer küsst ihre Füsse, die Sonne verwandelt den Frühling in Sommer, um im Zenith sie betrachten zu können, der Wind spielt wollüstig mit ihren Haaren und die Nereiden verzehren sich in Eifersucht in der Betrachtung ihres schönen Körpers. Andromedas Schönheit setzt die Kraft der Natur und der Götter in Bewegung, ihr Wesen ist gekennzeichnet durch den Reichtum einer Vielfalt, die nichts was zur Natur gehört, ausschliesst – Tau, Meer, Sonne und Wind. Es herrscht in dem Sonett ein anderer Ton als in den Wiegen- und Schnitterliedern, in vielen volkstümlichen Weisen, aus denen uns die Luft der Romanzen, die Luft von Lopes Theater anweht, das ihm zur Ausübung seiner differenzierten Kunst so reiche Gelegenheit geboten hat. Das Gedicht atmet vielmehr die Stimmung, für die man bei den Parnassiens Parallelen findet. Aus wenigen Elementen ist es mit Klarheit aufgebaut. Das menschliche Wesen strahlt in die Umwelt hinaus als hielte die Natur den Atem an, um Andromeda zu bewundern.

[1] Lope de Vega, Sonetos no.70: in *Obras Escogides*, ed. F. C. Sainz de Robles (Aguilar, Cuarta Edición, 1964). II, p.56. Für eine Variante dieses Gedichts s. Lope, *Los Palacios de Galiana*, Ak. Ausg. XIII, 184b, in der die Heldin sich ein mythisches Gegenbild erzeugt, durch dessen Medium sie von Andromeda vorbeilenkt auf sich selbst.

Ein zweites Beispiel mag uns weiterführen. Es handelt sich um die Argonautensage, bei deren Schilderung seit der Antike viele Dichter ihre Hand im Spiel gehabt haben:

De Jasón

Encaneció las ondas con espuma
Argos, primera nave, y sin temellas
osó tocar la gavia las estrellas
y hasta el cerco del sol volar sin pluma.

Y aunque Anfitrite airada se consuma,
dividen el cristal sus ninfas bellas
y hasta Colcos Jasón pasa por ellas,
por más que el viento resistir presuma.

Más era el agua que el dragón y el toro,
mas no le estorba que su campo arrase
la fuerta proa entre una y otra sierra.

Rompióse al fin por dos manzanas de oro
para que el mar cruel no se alabase
que por lo mismo se perdió la tierra.[1]

Wieder tritt der Dichter zurück als wäre das Gebot der Allgemeinheit allein massgebend. Trotz Sparsamkeit im illustrativen Detail offenbart sich der Zusammenhang mit der Sage – die Argo, das 'erste Schiff' –, der Kampf mit Stieren und Drachen lenkt auf Höhepunkte der Argonautenfahrt. In den letzten Strophen sind die Fahrt des Schiffes zwischen den Felsen, die Hesperidensage, die in verschiedenen Formen überliefert ist, zur Einheit zusammengerafft. Die Entwicklung der Argonautensage ist auf zwei aufeinanderfolgende Begebenheiten verteilt und in eine bildliche Darstellung zusammengefasst.

Beide Gedichte, Schöpfungen Lopes, sind doch zugleich Produkt einer Epoche, deren Dichter auf ein Publikum rechnen konnte, das in den Stand gesetzt war, antik bestimmte Texte so wie die stete Bezugnahme auf Ereignisse der Vergangenheit zu verstehen. Ein drittes Beispiel, das auf derselben Linie liegt:

De Europa y Jupiter

Pasando el mar el engañoso toro
volviendo la cerviz, el pie besaba
de la llorosa ninfa que miraba
perdido de las ropas el decoro.
Entre las aguas y las hebras de oro

[1] Lope de Vega, Sonetos no.68, op. cit. p.56.

ondas el fresco viento levantaba,
a quien con los suspiros ayudaba
del mal guardado virginal tesoro.
    Cayéronsele a Europa de las faldas
las rosas al decirle el toro amores,
y ella con el dolor de sus guirnaldas,
    dicen que, lleno el rostro de colores,
en perlas convirtió sus esmeraldas,
    y dijo: – ¡Ay triste, yo perdí las flores![1]

Wie die beiden früheren Gedichte, hebt auch dieses erzählend an, begibt sich mitten in die Begebenheit: Jupiter erschien Europa als Stier – engañoso toro. Von Anfang an ist das Gedicht auf die preziöse Pointe gerichtet. Die weinende Europa steht so sehr im Mittelpunkt – ihre Tränen sind Perlen der Wehmut – dass alles sich in gleichem Licht und auf ein und derselben Fläche abzuspielen scheint. Es ist wieder ein Gedicht, das literarischer Vorwurf einer bildlichen Darstellung hätte sein können. Allen drei Gedichten ist gemeinsam die epische Färbung – die Kühnheit der Argonauten, das Schicksal Europas und Andromedas werden durch die knappe Form des Sonetts geläutert und erklärt.

Der Gedanken- und Gefühlswert der Gedichte ist dem des Theaters in Vielem verwandt. Aber es liegt in der Natur der Sache, dass die Bewegung, die durch Fronleichnamsspiel, Drama und Komödie geht, durch die Spannung diametraler Gegensätze hervorgerufen wird. Wieder gestattet die Mythologie einen Einblick in das Innerste der Dichtung. Die mythologischen Motive sind überall zugegen und werden in den verschiedensten Phasen des goldenen Zeitalters in sich wandelnden Dimensionen erfahren und festgehalten. Die entfachte Kraft des vorstellenden Denkens geht in die Antike zurück, ruft die Bilder des Gewesenen herauf und überlässt sich gern der Erinnerung an die Vergangenheit.

Im Theater des goldenen Zeitalters haben die dramatischen Dichter Lope, Calderón, Tirso überall ihre Hauptgedanken durchschlagen lassen. Sie machten von antiken Fabeln und Mythen einen freien Gebrauch, wenn es die Durchführung ihrer Anschauung zu verlangen schien. Nun hatte die antike Mythologie durch das Mittelalter hindurch schon einen günstigen Boden für moralisch-allegorische Entwürfe gefunden; von Fulgentius bis zu Alciat und den moralisierten Metamorphosen geht ein gerader Weg. Die Götter waren Symbole moralischer Ideen und man kennt die Fülle mittelalterlicher

---

[1] Lope de Vega, Sonetos no.71, op. cit. p.56.

Figuren mit antiken Namen. Daran ändert sich im Prinzip nichts durch die Menge mythologischer Handbücher, die seit Boccaccios *De genealogia Deorum* in ganz Europa verbreitet waren: Gyraldis' *De Diis Gentium* (1548), Natalis Comes' *Mythologiae* (1551), Cartaris, *Immagine degli Dei* (1556). Die Fakten waren stets in ein Gefüge eingeordnet, innerhalb dessen jedem Element ein fester Platz und eine bestimmte erbauliche Funktion zugewiesen worden war. Die beiden spanischen Mythologietraktate – Juan Pérez de Moya, *La Philosophia secreta* (1585) und Fray Baltasar de Vitoria, *El teatro de los Dioses de la gentilidad* (1619) – sind in Spanien stets ausführlich zu Rate gezogen worden; das Hinundherblicken zwischen Ovids *Metamorphosen* und mythologischen Handbüchern regte an zu Umbildungen und Erfindungen, Ovid und die mythologischen Handbücher bilden oft wechselseitig den Hintergrund zu den mythologischen Stücken. Pérez de Moya erläutert schon im Titel seine Absicht '. . . donde debajo historias fabulosas se contiene mucha doctrina provechosa . . . es materia muy necesaria para entender poetas y historiadores'. Die Mythologie ist eine geheime Philosophie, die eine reformatorische Aufgabe übernimmt. Deswegen verbindet sich die Erzählung des Lebens der Götter stets mit einer *declaración*, die eine historische, physische und vor allem moralische Interpretation einsetzt, damit der Mensch durch das Studium antiker Mythen sein Ziel zu Gesicht bekommt und lernt, richtig zu leben. Wenn im 6. und 7. Buch die Rede ist von 'fabulas que exhorten al hombre a huir los vicios y seguir la virtud' oder wenn die Analyse dem Zweck unterworfen wird, 'para persuadir al hombre al temor de Dios', so müssen Mythen – wie schon die *Metamorphosen* – moralischen Postulaten genügen.

Es ist kein Zweifel, dass die geheime Philosophie des Pérez de Moya den Dichtern bekannt war. Während Ovid seit dem Mittelalter nie ohne geschichtliche Wirkung blieb, vereinigen die mythologischen Traktate jetzt das ganze mythologische Geschehen in dogmatischer Absicht. Aber die Benützer waren gleichwohl nie der historischen Kontinuität entzogen. Seznec hat in seinem Buch *La survivance des dieux antiques : essai sur le rôle de la tradition mythologique dans l'humanisme et dans l'art de la Renaissance* drei einander ergänzende Traditionen unterschieden: eine historische, durch die Götter als historische Personen erkannt werden, eine physische, d.i. die Gegenwärtigkeit der Götter in der Astrologie, und eine moralische, d.i. die allegorische Deutung der Mythen.

So allgegenwärtig nun auch alles was mythologische Gelehrsamkeit geboten hat, sein kann – im mythologischen Theater kann uns doch auch ein Ton entgegenklingen, der eine Welt der Vielheit und des Wechsels widerspiegelt und sich der doktrinären Behandlung entzieht. Schon L. Schmidt hat in einem noch heute aktuellen Aufsatz bemerkt, dass Calderón die Göttin Diana auf sehr verschiedene Art darstellt. In dem Stück *Celos aun del aire matan* entspricht sie 'obwohl im Einzelnen durch den Synkretismus römischer Vorstellung gafärbt, doch in ihrem Grundcharakter der Stimmung des griechischen Autors in lebendigster Weise'. Hier hat er das Gewebe seiner Kunst nicht aus Allegorien geknüpft. Anderseits hat er trotz der Verstrickung in antike Mythen die antike Naturanschauung zur Seite geschoben, um für die christliche Raum zu haben. Die Verwandlung der Menschen in Tiere, Bäume erschien in seiner Deutung wie der Übergang in eine andere Seinsart, die Ovid'schen Metamorphosen, in denen der Mensch als eine Gestalt der Natur erscheint, verändern im Licht der christlichen Umdeutung ihren Sinn. Die neue Deutung wird, wieviel aus der Überlieferung sie sich auch aneignet, doch nie auf die Grenzsetzung verzichten, die wichtig ist durch das, was sie ausschliesst und die in Entwicklung und Konstellation der Figuren die antike Haltung verlässt, um den Weg zum christlichen Drama und Fronleichnamsspiel anzutreten. Daher die gestufte Gliederung bei Calderón, die den Aufstieg zu Höherem voraussetzt, und einen neuen Aufschwung, durch den der Mensch sich zum Transzendenten erheben kann.

Jenes Transzendente, zu dem die Dichtung den Blick lenken will, zeigt sich mit aller Deutlichkeit in den zahlreichen 'autos sacramentales', die Calderón verfasst hat: *La estatua de Prometeo, El hijo del Sol Faetón, Eco y Narciso, El divino Orfeo, Fortuna de Andrómeda y Perseo*, und andere. Es liegt in der Natur des Fronleichnamsspiels, dass es zur allegorischen Darstellung führt. Innerhalb der begrenzten Zeit der Aufführung soll der Gesamtverlauf des christlichen Weltgeschehens – Sturz der Engel, Schöpfung und Sündenfall, Erlösung durch Christi Opfer und Jüngster Tag – vor Augen gebracht werden. Der Mensch überhaupt tritt an die Stelle des Menschen, denn sonst wäre das Spiel an die menschliche Lebensdauer gebunden. Neben ihm treten Gott und Teufel auf als die Exponenten des kosmischen Dualismus. Calderón hat die Technik der *Autos sacramentales* oft beschrieben. Ein dem Zuschauer geläufiger Vorgang wird in solcher Auslegung vorgeführt, dass er das christliche Universalgeschehen unmittelbar vertreten kann. Ein *concepto imaginado* wird von einem *concepto practico* verkörpert. In dem Auto *No hay más fortuna que Dios*, erhebt sich jene für das goldene Zeitalter in Spanien charakteristische Stimmung der Enttäuschung, Ernüchterung, Desillusionierung (*desengaño*) zur Entwertung des Lebens als etwas Flüchtigem, Nichtigem. Das Stück sieht den Menschen in der Spannung zwischen Wahrheit und Lüge, es bewegt sich zwischen Betrug und Entlarvung. Entlarvt wird der Teufel, der den Menschen von Gott fernhalten will und ihn verleitet, sein Los als eine blinde Zufälligkeit zu erklären – der *desengaño* eröffnet die Aussicht auf eine Anschauung, in der natürliche und göttliche Ordnung untrennbar vereint und korrelativ aufeinander bezogen sind.

Auch die mythologischen *Autos* bieten den christlichen Inhalt, verhüllen ihn im mythologischen Gewand, deuten jedoch durch den Titel schon an, dass die Scheidelinie zwischen dem wahren Gott und den Göttern der Heiden nicht scharf genug gezogen werden kann – daher: *El* divino *Orfeo* – *El* sacro *Parnaso* – *El* divino *Jasón* – *El* verdadero Dios *Pan*. Überall setzt die profane Fabel das christliche Gegensystem in Kraft. Die Religion wird in alles hineingezogen und Bezüge werden hin- und hergesponnen zwischen den verschiedenen Epochen.

In wechselnden Bildern und in wechselnden sprachlichen Ausdrücken hat Calderón Einblick in die Motive seiner Vorliebe für mythologische Themen gegeben. Im *Verdadero Dios Pan* heisst es: die Heiden besassen nur dämmerhafte Kunde von unsern religiösen Wahrheiten und da sie sie blind vernahmen, ohne Erleuchtung durch den Glauben, schrieben sie sie falschen Göttern zu:

> que tuvieron los Gentiles
> noticias, visos y lejos,
> de nuestras puras verdades,
> y como los oigan ciegos,
> sin lumbre de fe, a sus falsos
> dioses las atribuyeron.[1]

Eben wegen jener nur dämmerhaften Kenntnis der Heiden vermag die allegorische Auslegung die in profanen Texten verborgene christliche Wahrheit zu entdecken. Im *Auto sacramental* sind die in der Spätantike und im Mittelalter gültigen Allegorien besonders wirksam. Man verwendet sie entsprechend den Lehren, die die mytholo-

---

[1] Calderón de la Barca, *El verdadero Dios Pan*, p.66.

gischen Handbücher gegeben haben. Steht die Fabel im Dienst der christlichen Wahrheit, so leuchtet, so sagt Calderón in der *Loa* zum *Verdadero Dios Pan*, das Licht heller, wenn man auch die es umgebenden Schatten ins Auge fasst. An einem prägnanten Beispiel, an dem Auto *El verdadero Dios Pan* versuchen wir die Umbildung zu beschreiben, die sich in der Behandlung der antiken Mythologie vollzieht.

Drei stoffliche Anregungen hat Calderón für das 1670 aufgeführte Stück aufgenommen, um sich die Atmosphäre zu schaffen, die er brauchte. Erstens eine Geschichte aus Plutarchs *De defectu oraculorum*, die er vielleicht im fünften Kapitel von Eusebius' *Praeparatio Evangelica* gefunden hat. Zweitens Verse aus Vergils *Georgica* III mit den Erklärungen der Kommentatoren, Servius und Philargyrius. Drittens wirkte die Betrachtungsweise von Lopes Auto sacramental *Maja* auf ihn, insofern sie·ihm das Gesetz des Auto sacramental an einem Beispiel wieder zum Verständnis brachte. Der von Plutarch erzählten Geschichte, dass der grosse Pan gestorben sei, hat Eusebius eine andere Wendung gegeben, indem er vom Sterben der heidnischen Götter unter Christi Einwirkung sprach. Daraus ergab sich die Möglichkeit Pan mit Christus zu assoziieren, ja zu identifizieren. Calderón hat Momente aus der Überlieferung auf verschiedene Szenen und Personen verteilt. Von Plutarch sind nur einige Verse bestimmt, in denen sich jedoch der Kern der Geschichte zusammenfasst: die Götterbilder liegen stumm, und man vernimmt nur das schaurige Echo von Stimmen, die sagen: 'Der Grosse Pan ist tot':

> todos los idolos mios,
> al consultarles su estruendo,
> mudos yacen, y en lejanas
> voces de horrorosos ecos,
> decir se ha oído en varias partes –
> El Demonio (dentro) – El Dios Pan es el que ha muerto[1]

Die Fabel aber knüpft an Vergil an. Calderóns dialektische Virtuosität fand hier einen würdigen Stoff, dem er jedoch einen neuen Gehalt abgewinnt. Vergil (*Georgica* III. 391 f.) sagt: 'Durch das Geschenk eines schneeweissen Vliesses (wenn man dem Glauben schenken darf) hat Pan, der arkadische Gott, dich, Luna, listig verführt, indem er dich in die Tiefe des Waldes lockte; und du verschmähtest ihn nicht.'

---

[1] Calderón de la Barca, *El verdadero Dios Pan*, p.134.

Munere sic niveo lanae, si credere dignum est
Pan deus Arcadiae captam te, Luna, fefellit,
in nemora alta vocans; nec tu aspernata vocantem.

Aber Calderón unterlag nicht nur der Wirkung Vergils. Das Liebens-
abenteuer Pans mit der Mondgöttin als Werben Christi um die
menschliche Seele weist zurück auf Lopes Prolog zu dem Auto *Maja*
und hat hier seine Vorbedingungen. Bei Lope handelt es sich um die
Geschichte von Pan und der Nymphe Syrinx: 'No huya el alma de
vos (Pan–Christus) como aquella ninfa huia.' Und Lope rückt auch
bereits die verschiedenen Bedeutungen der Namen in eine neue
Beleuchtung: der Name des Gottes kann im Spanischen auch Brot
bedeuten, schliesst sich die christliche Bedeutung von der profanen
Gott Pan an – in Dios Pan kann sich das Wort zum christlichen Sinn
erheben und den durch die Transubstantiation in Brot verwandelten
Leib Christi bedeuten. Umspannt ein Wort so Verschiedenes und
Gegensätzliches, so erlaubt es dem Dichter auch, die Kräfte des
Ingeniösen, des Wortspiels einzusetzen. Calderón dachte an die
Bedeutung, die durch das 9. Buch der Etymologien des Isidor von
Sevilla nahegelegt ist: Pan τὸ πᾶν, was den Stoikern erlaubte, in Pan
ihren pantheistischen Abgott zu sehen.

Im einleitenden Gespräch zwischen Pan und der Nacht erläutert
Calderón jene universelle Ordnung des Seins, die sich im Bilde des
Spiegels fortschreitend gestaltet und herstellt. Calderón verwendet
das Bild des Spiegels in vielen Stücken. In *No hay más fortuna que Dios*
sind Hermosura und Discreción Träger verschiedener Insignien: die
Hermosura ist mit einem Spiegel, die Discreción mit einem Buch, d.h.
einem Seelenspiegel (*espejo del alma*) ausgestattet; Spiegel und Buch
werden auf den gemeinsamen Nenner der Eigenliebe – im Gegensatz
zur Gottesliebe – gebracht. Sie spiegeln die eigene Nichtigkeit, die
vanitas des Irdischen wieder. Wechselbegriffe sprechen von verschiedenen Seiten her dasselbe beherrschende Phänomen aus und
lassen die Entlarvung der Wirklichkeit in dem Wesentlichen ihrer
Bedeutung heraustreten: die Allegorie ist ein Spiegel, der das Seiende
in ein Nichtseiendes verwandelt:

La Alegoría non es más
que un espejo que traslada
lo que es con lo que no es;
y está toda su elegancia
en que salga parecida
tanto la copia en la tabla,

que el que está mirando a una
piense que está viendo a entrambas.[1]

Pan bittet nun die Nacht Luna auf den Mondberg zu locken und ihm bei seiner Werbung behilflich zu sein, aber die Nacht, in den Schranken ihrer Schuld gefangen, der Gnade nicht teilhaftig, verschleiert das Motiv ihrer Weigerung. Luna ist die zweite Hauptfigur und vereinigte schon immer in der Dichtung entgegengesetzte Qualitäten: sie ist Luna im Himmel, Diana auf der Erde, Proserpina in der Unterwelt. Und der mögliche ewige Umschlag ihres Wesens entspricht dem Wechsel der Mondphasen. Nun treten in allegorischen Gestalten die Religionen auf, die den Schutz vor einem Dämon erbitten, vor einem Untier, das schon die Hirten in Angst versetzte – nämlich das Heidentum, der Götzendienst, das Judentum, die Synagoge, die Apostasie, wobei die Parallelität von Gentilidad und Judaismo, Idolatria und Synagoge systematischen Charakter hat. Calderón will der Erscheinung der Religionen und dem ihnen zugrundeliegenden Prinzip gerecht werden.

Unter dem Namen Luna erscheint die menschliche Natur als Braut Christi; auf Bitten der Gentilidad lässt sie sich auf die Erde nieder. '¡Esto me parece' kommentiert der Text, 'significa entra el alma a ser huéspedes en la tierra!' Wenn der Teufel als Wolf oder Löwe auftritt, um den Herden der 'Welt' nachzustellen, tritt Pan als Retter auf, um die Seele der Luna zu gewinnen. Im Zweikampf besiegt er den Dämon. Die wieder auftretenden Religionen – die vom Eingreifen Pans nichts wussten – schreiben jedoch den Sieg der Luna zu. Allen scheint die Rettung unter verschiedener göttlicher Leitung zu stehen, die auf die Ereignisse einwirkt: der Gentilidad öffnet sich die Sicht auf Diana, die, mit dem Schild der Pallas und dem Helm der Bellona gewappnet, als Göttin gesiegt hat, der Judaismo spürt im Sieg nur die Stimme der Judith, seiner nationalen Heldin, und der Apostasie scheint die Tat ein Sieg der Seele zu sein. Ungebrochen treten die Anschauungen der Religionen hervor und durchziehen die Reden der Personen. Die Klagen der Luna, die ihr Lieblingslamm, ein weisses mit schwarzgesprenkeltem Fell, verloren hat, unterbrechen die Freude über die Rettung aus Gefahr. Da erscheint plötzlich Pan, ihr das Lamm wiederzubringen. Wieder handelt es sich um eine Szene, die verschieden gedeutet werden kann. Luna – ihre dritte Begegnung mit Pan hat Simplicidad vermittelt – sieht in dem Lamm

---

[1] Calderón de la Barca, *El verdadero Dios Pan*, pp.74–5.

das Wissen um Gut und Böse – Pan jedoch versetzt das Ereignis auf einen andern Boden: es ist die Parabel vom verlorenen Schaf, das wiederzufinden der gute Hirte die 99 andern verlässt, und es ist zugleich verknüpft mit der Geschichte von Jesus und der Samariterin. Analogisch wird die Begegnung Christi mit der Samariterin zur Begegnung Pans mit der Mondgöttin, der Seele, gesehen. Und wieder finden sich in der allegorischen Doppeldeutigkeit zwei Bewegungen zusammen: 'oveja perdida' bedeutet 'verloren' in den Augen Lunas, für Pan aber meint 'verloren' der Sphäre der Sünde verfallen.

Pan, der dreimal sich Luna genaht hat – als Retter, als Wiederbringer der Erkenntnis von Gut und Böse und als Liebender –, beschliesst nun – und die Religionen mit ihm – das Geschenk des Vliesses zu überbringen, durch das die Allegorie der Fabel sich erfüllen soll. Wieder sieht man, wie jeder Punkt des Geschehens nur Durchgangspunkt für die Herstellung einer allgemeinen über ihm stehenden Ordnung ist, das Einzelne ordnet sich als ein Mittel dem Allgemeinen ein. Mit den Religionen erscheinen Idolatrie und Apostasie, Hülle und Einkleidung der Idee der Religion. Die Apostasie überreicht das schwarzgefleckte Fell, Pan das lebendige Lamm. Die Gentilidad überreicht das Vliess des goldenen Widders, das Hermes den Königskindern Helles und Phryxos geschenkt hat und das den Mittelpunkt der Argonautensage bilden sollte. Der Judaismus das weisse Schaffell, das der israelitische Held, Gideon, ausgebreitet hatte unter dem Himmel, um Gottes Zustimmung zu seinem Feldzug zu erlangen. Doch das gefleckte, das goldene und das weisse Vliess werden alle von dem mit Blumen bekränzten, von Pans Geschenk übertroffen. Die Blume, die das Feld ziert, ist eine kostbare Margerite, aber es treten auch Rose und Lilie hinzu. Margerite, Rose und Lilie sind Attribute der Mutter Gottes und symbolisieren ihre reine unbefleckte Jungfräulichkeit. Schon wählt Luna Pan zum 'esposo', als ein letztes Mal der Dämon auftritt, um sich an Simpleza, die auf der Bühne zurückgeblieben war, zu rächen. Der Kampf endet aber mit dem Sieg Pans, der in die Niederlage des Dämons auch das Judentum mit hineinrcisst, nicht nur wird Pan getroffen, sondern auch die hinter ihm stehende Synagoge, und damit die Idee der Auserwähltheit des Judaismus.

In dem Stück nimmt nicht nur die Religion, sondern auch die Theologie einen so breiten Raum ein, dass Darstellung und Beweis eine besondere Aufgabe zu bilden scheinen. Calderón war an den verschiedenen Religionen wie an einem wandlungsfähigen Stoff, an seiner Gestaltung und Umgestaltung interessiert, in der Doppelnatur von Pan sah er eine Vorstufe des Christentums; im Vergleich verschiedener Religionen mit der christlichen stellt sich ihm in prägnanter Weise der Sinn des Weltprozesses dar. In der beständigen Wechselwirkung von Problemen und Problemkreisen greifen Erkenntnis und Bekenntis ineinander über, ebenso wie in der patristischen Beurteilung der nicht christlichen Religionen. Der geistige Kosmos stellt sich im Bilde einer hierarchischen Gliederung geistiger Substanzen dar, die sich gemäss einer Rangordnung des Seins einander über- und unterordnen.

Wie erklärt sich die Wirkung dieses Stücks, in dem Antike mit christlichen Momenten sich zu einem Mosaik zusammenfügt und dem ein komplexes theologisches Ganzes als Voraussetzung zugrunde liegt? Das Publikum konnte folgen, weil der Gedankenfülle die Bilderfülle entsprach. Luna, die den Anruf der Gentilidad erhört, lässt sich in einer Wolke herab, und die Szene, in der das Lammfell überreicht wird, hebt mit Festesklängen an. Der Hintergrund öffnet sich auf zwei Gärten; und dem Chor und den Musikern folgen die Hirtin, die das Lammfell trägt, dann die Apostasie, die Synagoge, die Gentilidad schliesslich die Simplicidad. Es ist eine schwelgerische Darstellung der Kunst im Kunstwerk, als ob die Gedanken in einen kostbaren Faltenwurf gehüllt wären. Die fliessende Bewegung und Entwicklung vieler Figuren verknüpft sich mit dem Gehalt, mit einem komplizierten Gehalt, der sich jedoch in einer reichen und farbigen Umwelt entfaltet.

Verbindungslinien führen von dem *Auto sacramental* zu andern Stücken Lopes und Calderóns, die das Thema des goldenen Vliesses behandeln. In einer sich verändernden geistigen Landschaft findet man den Mythos als beherrschenden Faktor wieder: in Calderóns *El divino Jasón* und *Los tres majores prodigios del mundo*, in Lopes *El vellocino de oro*, in Corneilles *La conquête de la toison d'or* und in Grillparzers *Das Goldene Vliess*.

20

THE DEVELOPMENT OF RELIGIOUS
SCEPTICISM AND THE INFLUENCE OF
ISAAC LA PEYRÈRE'S PRE-ADAMISM
AND BIBLE CRITICISM

R. H. POPKIN

One of the most important new views that led to modern irreligious scepticism was the pre-Adamite theory, especially as stated in Isaac La Peyrère's *Prae-Adamitae* (1655) (English translation *Men before Adam* (1656)). This then revolutionary view that there were men (and women) before Adam, and its attendant consequence that the Bible did not present the history of the origin and development of *all* mankind, grew out of many lines of theological, philosophical, historical and anthropological thought. La Peyrère, 1596–1676, as I have shown elsewhere,[1] worked out his thesis as part of a strange Marrano theology, coupled with a French nationalist Messianism. Here, I should just like to treat those aspects of the theory which grew out of relating new information gained from the voyages of discovery to aspects of classical learning that were being revived during the Renaissance and early seventeenth century. Classical pagan views about the origins and nature of man played a quite significant rôle in making the pre-Adamite theory a most forceful explanation of the dispersed and varied state of mankind revealed through the explorations, and in giving plausibility to a picture of the history and development of mankind apart from the Providential view of Judeo-Christianity.

In my study, 'The Pre-Adamite Theory in the Renaissance',[2] I traced briefly the history of the theory from ancient times. The theory was probably first stated when an ancient Jew or early Christian tried

---

[1] Richard H. Popkin, 'The Marrano Theology of Isaac La Peyrère', *Studi Internazionali di Filosofia*, v (1973), 97–126.
[2] This essay is in the *Festschrift* for Paul Oskar Kristeller, which will appear shortly, to be published by Brill.

to explain the biblical account of man's origins to a Greek or Egyptian or Babylonian. Pagans probably advanced their own historical – mythological accounts, tracing human history far before events recorded in *Genesis*. The earliest case I know of is that Theophilus of Antioch debated the claim of Apollonius the Egyptian in A.D. 170 that the world was 153,075 years old.[1] The problem of Adamism versus pre-Adamism was so severe by St Augustine's time that he had to write two chapters in the *City of God* on 'Of the falsenesses of the History that the world hath continued many thousand yeares' and on 'The Aegyptians abbominable lyings, to claime their wisdom the age of 100,000 yeares'. St Augustine's position, which was subsequently adhered to by practically all Jewish and Christian theologians up to the seventeenth century was that the pagan views of history were fables and myths, and that the biblical view was correct because it was revealed truth.[2]

Occasionally during the Middle Ages the question of whether there were pre-Adamite civilisations or whether Adam had parents or teachers was raised. Some of this speculation came from discussions in Judah Halevi and Maimonides of material in the strange work, *Nabatean Agriculture*, and some from discussions about Greek views about the eternality of the world.[3] A couple of cases are mentioned

---

[1] 'Theophilus to Autolycus', in the *Ante-Nicene Christian Library*, vol.III, bk.III, chap.XVI, p.120. On this and other ancient pagan views about human history, see Paul H. Kocher, *Christopher Marlowe, A Study of his Thought, Learning and Character* (New York, 1962), p.44; and Arthur O. Lovejoy and George Boas, *Primitivism and Related Ideas of Antiquity* (New York, 1965).

[2] St Augustine, *Of the Citie of God*: with the *Learned Comments of Io. Lod. Vivès*, transl. by J. H. (n.p. 1610), bk.XII, chap.10 and bk.XVIII, chap.40; *De Civitate Dei, Corpus Christianum*, Series Latina, XLVIII (Turnholti, 1955), Pars XIV, 2, pp.364–5 and 635.

St Augustine claimed, in the Renaissance English translation, 'For seeing it is not yet six thousand yeares from the first man *Adam*, how ridiculous are they that over-runne the truth such a multitude of yeares? Whom shall wee believe in this, so soone as him that fore-told what now we see accordingly effected? The dissonance of histories, giveth us leave to leane to such as doe accorde with our divinite. The citizens of Babilon indeed, being diffused all the earth over, when they read two authors of like (and allowable) authority, differing in relations of the eldest memory, they know not which to believe. But we have a divine historie to under-shore us, and wee know that what so ever secular author he bee, famous or obscure, if hee contradict that, he goeth farre astray from truth. But bee his words true or false, they are of no valew to the attainment of true felicitie.'

[3] *The Nabatean Agriculture*, written by Ibn Waḥshiyya in A.D. 904, tried to show that Nabatean–Babylonian civilisation was superior to that of Islam. In so doing the author contended that Adam had parents, that he came from India, that there were wise men before him, and that Adam was the founder of agricultural civilisation, but not the founder of mankind.

Both Judah Halevi and Maimonides discussed this theory, as well as Greek views

of fourteenth- and fifteenth-century heretics who were condemned for holding that Adam was not the first man.[1]

It was, I believe, in the beginning of the sixteenth century that pre-Adamism became a serious issue and a serious possibility with radical implications for the Judeo-Christian view of the world. The voyages of discovery and the humanistic rediscovery of the pagan past posed basic problems of explaining in a coherent and consistent manner where people came from and what sort of a historical process or drama they were living through.

Some of those concerned with the revival of classical learning, like Juan Luis Vivès, collected information about ancient pagan historical claims that conflicted with biblical history. Vivès, in his notes to his edition of St Augustine's *City of God* listed Chaldean personages back 470,000 years and Egyptians over 100,000 years ago. Vivès suggested that the pagans concocted these figures to make their civilisations look as if they had created all human achievements. We do not know whether he believed this, or whether he had doubts about the accuracy of biblical history. But, in any case, he and others made available and publicised the ancient data that conflicted with the claims of Judeo-Christianity as the unique history of the world.[2]

The discovery of America raised the problem in a most forceful way. And this followed by the contacts of Europe with Asia, Africa, Polynesia, etc., posed the question of whether all of these widely dispersed and enormously different peoples could have come from the biblical world (which would involve them all as being descendants of the survivors of the Flood). For over two centuries

about the eternality of the world. See Judah Halevi, *The Kuzari*, intro. by Henry Slonimsky (New York, 1964), pt.I, sec.60–7; and Moses Maimonides. *The Guide of the Perplexed*, translated with an Introduction and Notes by Shlomo Pines, with an introductory essay by Leo Strauss (Chicago, 1964), bk.III, chap.29.

[1] One Father Tomás Scoto was accused in the fourteenth century of maintaining that there were men before Adam, and Zaninus de Solcia was condemned in 1459 for saying that Adam was not the first man. Cf. Marcelino Menendez Pelayo, *Historia de los Heterodoxes Españoles* (Madrid, 1956), vol.I, I.iii, c.4, p.593; and *Historia de los Heterodoxes Españoles* (Santander, 1948), vol.VII, Apéndice I, pp.324–5; O. Zöckler, 'Peyrère's (gest. 1676) Präadamiten-Hypothese nach ihren Beziehungen zu den anthropologischen Fragen der Gegenwart', *Zeitschrift für des ges. lutherische Theologie and Kirche* (1878) 38, n.2.

[2] Cf. Juan Luis Vivès's commentary in St Augustine, *Of the Citie of God* (n.p. 1610), bk.XII, chap.10, pp.450–1.

On the possibility that Vivès held heretical views growing out of his Jewish background and his naturalism, see Carlos G. Noreña, *Juan Luis Vivès* (The Hague, 1970).

theories were offered tracing the American Indians either directly to the biblical world, as Lost Tribes of Israel, or derivative from it, from Solomon's Ophir, from the Phoenicians, from the Chinese, the Norwegians, and so on. Some found possibilities in pagan literature, such as that America was Atlantis. Conflicting data, like the Aztec calendar stone, indicating an antiquity of Mexican civilisation far beyond that of biblical or Mediterranean pagan history, was literally buried.[1]

In the debate over the origins of the Indians a few hardy souls proposed a most dangerous theological possibility. Paracelsus, and later Bruno, and probably Christopher Marlowe, Thomas Hariot and Sir Walter Ralegh, advanced the view that the Indians had not come to the New World from anywhere. They were created separately in the New World, and were not Adamites. Paracelsus and Bruno connected this with accounting for the existence of other non-Adamites, nymphs, griffins, salamanders, pygmies, giants, Ethiopians, etc. For Paracelsus the non-Adamites had no souls, while for Bruno they had a different progenitor. Both of these views already suggested that the non-Adamites were not part of the Divine Drama.[2]

The Elizabethans who were accused of holding the pre-Adamite theory, Marlowe, Hariot and Ralegh, may have drawn some of their ideas from Bruno, but probably derived more of them from information about the American Indians, whom Hariot and Ralegh had both met personally. Since no writing of theirs exists stating their pre-Adamite views, and only accusations and comments by their opponents survive, it is hard to tell what opinions they held. One attack on Marlowe, the Baines report, claimed that the playwright had given a lecture to Ralegh and others that stressed the conflict between

[1] See Lee Eldridge Huddleston, *Origins of the American Indians, European Concepts, 1492–1729* (Austin and London, 1970).

The Aztec calender stone was found in 1551, and was buried by the Spanish ecclesiastical authorities in 1558. It was only rediscovered in 1790, Cf. Giordano Bruno, *The Expulsion of the Triumphant Beast*, trans. and edited by Arthur D. Imerli (New Brunswick, 1964), p.307, n.52.

[2] Theophrast von Hohenheim gen. Paracelsus, *Astronomia magna*, in *Sämtliche Werke*, Abt. I, Band 12, edited by Karl Sudhoff (Munich and Berlin, 1929), p.35. See also the texts from Paracelsus on this cited by James Sydney Slotkin, *Readings in Early Anthropology* (Chicago, 1965), p.42; and T. Bendysche, 'The History of Anthropology', *Memoirs read before the Anthropological Society of London, 1863–64*, I, p.354.

Giordano Bruno, *Opera Latine Conscripta*, ed. F. Fiorentino et al. (Naples, 1879–91), vol.I, par.II, p.282, and *Spaccio della Bestia trionfante*, in *Dialoghi Italiani, Dialoghi Morali*, newly printed with notes by Giovanni Gentile, 3rd edn by Giovanni Aquilecchia (Florence, 1958), pp.797–8.

biblical history as 6,000 years old, and Indian and ancient pagan accounts which indicated the world was 16,000 years old.[1]

The sixteenth-century discussions of pre-Adamism and possibly polygenetic origins of mankind contained the basic ingredients that were to be woven together by La Peyrère into a monumentally heretical doctrine which was to play a very great rôle in launching the irreligious modern world view. The pagan accounts and the findings of the explorers were being cast in opposition to the biblical teaching. Along with this, Renaissance scholarship raised the question of whether the text of the Bible then in existence was the accurate text. The academic and theological establishment was able to prevent any serious crisis from arising by offering kosher explanations of some of the data, denying other data, and in extreme cases executing such heretical interpreters of the data as Bruno, and Vanini.[2]

The problem came to a head, and led to immense consequences when Isaac La Peyrère produced his new theological system based on the supposition that there were men before Adam. La Peyrère was not just posing a conflict of biblical, pagan and exploration data. He was offering a theory, a theology, that would encompass all of the data.[3] His theory, however, contained the seeds for the destruction of the Judeo-Christian world.

La Peyrère, in one of his explanations of the genesis of his theory, said he started from internal questioning of the story in Genesis. La Peyrère came from a New Christian family (converts from Judaism from Iberia) in Bordeaux. He was raised as a Calvinist.[4] In his youth he had questioned the origin of Cain's wife. If Adam, Eve, Cain and

[1] The material on Marlowe, Hariot and Ralegh's pre-Adamite views appears in F.-C. Danchin, 'Etudes critiques sur Christopher Marlowe', *Revue Germanique*, IX (1913), 576; Jean Jacquot, 'Thomas Hariot's Reputation for Impiety', *Notes and Records of the Royal Society of London*, IX (1952), 164–87; Paul H. Kocher, *Christopher Marlowe*, pp.34–6; and Pierre Lefranc, *Sir Walter Ralegh Écrivain, l'oeuvre et les idées* (Quebec, 1968), chap.xii, and pp.344–52.

[2] Ralegh and Archbishop Ussher showed how all of human history fitted with the creation of man in 4004 B.C. Menasseh ben Israel, in his *Conciliador* (1632–3) tried to show how the apparently conflicting passages in the Old Testament could be consistently reconciled.

[3] The chief part of La Peyrère's masterpiece *Prae-Adamitae, Men before Adam*, is entitled *A Theological Systeme upon that Presupposition that Men were before Adam*.

[4] On La Peyrère's life and career see Popkin, prefaces to forthcoming photoreproduction editions of La Peyrère's *Du Rappel des Juifs*, and *Men Before Adam* (Olms), and Popkin, 'The Marrano Theology of Isaac La Peyrère', and 'Bible Criticism and Social Science', *Boston Studies in the Philosophy of Science*, XIV (Dordrecht and Boston, 1974), 340–4. The notes in these articles give references to most of the source material regarding La Peyrère.

Abel were the sole inhabitants of the world, then, after Cain killed Abel, how could he go off to another city and take a wife? La Peyrère apparently took this as a starting point for seeking within the Bible evidence that there must have been a source of people other than Adam and Eve and their descendants. La Peyrère was neither a Renaissance scholar, nor a Bible scholar.[2] He became the secretary of the Prince of Condé in 1640, and soon became the intimate of many of the scientists, and scholars in the circle around Mersenne and Gassendi. He produced the first draft of his masterpiece in 1641.[3] By then he had a monumental theory, to wit that there were innumerable men before Adam; that the Bible only deals with Jewish history; that Adam is the first man in Jewish history, not world history; that Moses did not write the Pentateuch; that the biblical text we possess is not the accurate text; that the Bible properly reconstructed and understood is the beginning of the central Divine Drama, the Election of the Jews, which was followed after Jesus by the Rejection of the Jews and which is about to be followed in the mid-seventeenth century by the Recall of the Jews which will usher in the Messianic Age to be presided over by the Jewish Messiah, His secular aide, the King of France, and His court of Jewish Christians. (How this all fits together I have dealt with elsewhere. Suffice to say, I think it all makes sense as a theology for Marranos, Jewish Christians, who play the central rôle in world history in this scenario.)[4]

La Peyrère's evidence for his pre-Adamite theory (which was crucial for him in justifying his separation of Jewish history from world history) was a combination of biblical criticism (of which he was one of the pioneers),[5] ancient pagan information about the origin of the world and the history of mankind, and exploration data. By the time *Prae-Adamitae* was published in 1655, the author had had the benefit of much criticism and consultations with leading scholars in various fields. (La Peyrère had travelled widely in the period 1641–55,

---

[1] Cf. La Peyrère, 'Proeme' to *A Theological System upon the Presupposition that Men were before Adam* (London, 1656), p.F v.

[2] His friend, the great Bible scholar, Father Richard Simon, said that he 'ne savoit ni grec ni Hebreu'. Simon, letter to M.Z.S. in 1688, *Lettres choisies* (Rotterdam, 1702), II, p.27.

[3] A letter of Gabriel Naudé to Cardinal Barberini in 1641, fol.22v, indicates La Peyrère's work was already completed, and that because Cardinal Richelieu had banned the publication of it, people were trying to obtain copies of the manuscript.

[4] Cf. Popkin, 'Marrano Theology of Isaac La Peyrère'.

[5] Cf. Popkin, 'Bible Criticism and Social Science', pp.339–60.

going to Belgium, Holland, Scandinavia, Spain and England, as well as parts of France.) His final case begins with his biblical evidence, and then in book III, chapters V–XI there is a truly amazing compilation of ancient pagan material indicating the independent and pre-Adamitic development of Egyptian, Greek, Babylonian and Chinese histories, along with parallel data from Mexico, and information about the Eskimos (on whom La Peyrère was the leading authority of the day).[1] La Peyrère used materials from Homer, Hermes Trismegistus, Porphyry, Cicero, Ausonius, Pomponius Mela, Claudian, Virgil, Lucan, Iamblicus, Plato, Horace, Varro, Josephus, Diodorus Siculus, Herodotus, among others. It is hard to tell what he actually read since even when he quoted passages, he gave no citations. He often referred to his friend, Claude Saumaise, and to Scaliger, who may have been his sources.[2]

This ancient material is used to show that pagan chronologies go further back than biblical chronology, and that human events prior to Adam are described in ancient pagan literature by reliable authors like Plato, Herodotus and Cicero.[3]

What La Peyrère regarded as the most convincing evidence of an antiquity of the pagan world long before Adam came on the scene was the discoveries by the Egyptians and Babylonians about astronomy and astrology. (If he had known about the Mayans, he probably would have been overjoyed.) The sophistication of their calculations, their theories and interpretations required ages of observation and intellectual development, far beyond the time span available within biblical history. Much of what La Peyrère offered in his chapters on these matters derived from the study of ancient astronomy and astrology of his friend Saumaise, published in 1648, entitled *De Annis Climactericis*.[4] When the book came out, La Peyrère thanked the author on behalf of '*mes pré-Adamties*'.[5] The wealth of learning that Saumaise showed was known to the Egyptians and the Chaldeans, La Peyrère

---

[1] La Peyrère published two works, *Relation du Groenland* (Paris, 1647) and *Relation d'Islande* (Paris, 1663), which are landmarks in anthropology regarding the Eskimos.

[2] Saumaise, for instance, is cited in bk.III, chap.VI, p.168, as the person who is the most learned about Greek, Roman and Egyptian affairs. Scaliger is cited about Chinese chronology in bk.III, chap.vii, p.177.

[3] See, for example, La Peyrère's defence of Critias's history in Plato's *Timaeus*, bk.III, chap.vii, p.172, and of Herodotus as the father of history, chap.vii, p.171.

[4] La Peyrère, *Men before Adam*, bk. III, chap.VIII–XI. Saumaise's work was published in London in 1648.

[5] La Peyrère mentioned this in his letter to P. de la Mare, June 1660, Bibliothèque Nationale Coll. Moreau 846, fol.286 v.

argued, could not have been acquired in the time span between Adam and Abraham or Adam and Moses. (La Peyrère scoffed at the idea that Adam could have arrived on the historical scene with all the requisite scientific knowledge.)

The revived classical learning provided an arsenal of data for La Peyrère's heretical position, which coupled with the internal evidence he found in the Bible, and the explorer data reported from Mexico, China, Greenland and Iceland, led him to put forth his pre-Adamite theory. One of the chief virtues of his position 'which asserts Men to have been before Adam', he proclaimed, is that

the History of *Genesis* appears much clearer, and agrees with itself. And it is wonderfully reconciled with all profane Records whether ancient or new, to wit, those of the *Chaldeans*, *Egyptians*, *Scythians*, and *Chinensians*; that most ancient Creation which is set down in the first of *Genesis* is reconciled to those of *Mexico*, not long ago discovered by *Columbus*; It is likewise reconciled to those Northern and Southern Nations which are not known, All whom, as likewise those of the first and most ancient creation, were, its probable, created with the Earth itself in all parts thereof, and not propagated from Adam.

Again, by this Position, Faith and right Reason are reconciled, which suffers us not to believe that the world had so late an infancy.[1]

A bit later on La Peyrère claimed his view threw great light on the Gospel, St Paul's writings and Genesis, and

That *Genesis*, and the Gospel, and the Astronomy of the Antients is reconcil'd and the History and Philosophy of the most ancient Nations: So that if the Chaldeans themselves should come, those most antient Astronomers, who had calculated the course of the stars, as they say, many hundred thousand years ago; or the most ancient Egyptian Chronologers, with those most antient Dynasties of their Kings: if Aristotle himself come: if with Aristotle those of China come, who are perchance excellent Chronologers and Philosophers; or any Wise men that we may perchance henceforth find amongst those Southern and Northern people, as yet unknown, who have their ages receiv'd and known downward many Myriads of years. They will willingly receive this History of Genesis, and more willingly become Christians.[2]

So the virtues of the theory, according to La Peyrère, were wondrous. The Bible would be understood (with its imminent Messianic message), Jewish history would be separated from world history, the ancient data and the explorer data would be reconciled with the

[1] La Peyrère, 'A Discourse upon the twelfth, thirteenth, and fourteenth Verses of the Fifth Chapter of the Epistle of the Apostle Paul to the Romans', in *Men before Adam*, p.22.
[2] Ibid. pp.60–1.

Bible, and *then* the Gentiles could become Christians, and the Jews would be recalled.[1]

If La Peyrère saw it all so neatly, practically everyone else saw that the price to be paid for all of these benefits was catastrophically high. The biblical text was no longer to be accepted as accurate, and biblical history was no longer world history. La Peyrère's book was burned and banned in many places. The author was jailed until he personally recanted to the Pope and turned Catholic. He then retired as a lay brother in the Oratory collecting more and more evidence for his views. He calmly said that his theory was like Copernicus's. It did not change anything in the world. It merely described or interpreted facts differently.[2]

His different interpretation quickly led later scholars from Spinoza to Bayle, Voltaire and Hume to develop a picture of the human scene in which what happened to the ancient Hebrews had little or no importance, and in which man could be seen a secular man, both in ancient pagan times and modern European ones.[3]

The revival of classical learning about ancient history coupled with the unfolding world outside of the European orbit led to polygenetic speculations.[4] La Peyrère put it all together in a Marrano French nationalist theology,[5] buttressed by his pre-Adamite theory (which

[1] La Peyrère summarised his overall theory in the dedication 'To all the Synagogues of the Jews dispersed over the face of the Earth', in *Men before Adam*. His Messianism is developed at length in *Du Rappel des Juifs* (Paris, 1643).

[2] For details about the reaction to La Peyrère's views, see Popkin, 'Marrano Theology of Isaac La Peyrère', pp.107–10 and the references given there.
   The comparison with Copernicus appears in La Peyrère's *Lettre à Philotime* (Paris, 1658), pp.105–7, and *Apologie de la Peyrère* (Paris, 1663), pp.21–3.

[3] Cf. Popkin, 'Bible Criticism and Social Science', pp.345–53, and 'Menasseh ben Israel and Isaac La Peyrère', *Studia Rosenthaliana*, VIII (1974), 63.

[4] The development of polygenetic theorising and its relation to the rise of racist views are discussed in my forthcoming study, 'The Philosophical Bases of Modern Racism' in *Essays in honor of Herbert W. Schneider*.

[5] La Peyrère's French nationalist Messianism was revived at the time of the meeting of the Napoleonic Sanhedrin in 1806. While the Jewish leaders were meeting, the *Journal de Paris* reported on 29 August 1806 that 'On a découvert un livre aussi rare que singulier, imprimé en 1643, sans nom d'auteur & d'imprimeur, mais que l'on croit avoir été composé par Isaac lapeyrère de Bordeaux. Il est intitulé *du Rappel des Juifs*. L'auteur dit, dans un avis préliminaire qu'il se propose de faire voir, que tous des Juifs seront un jour appelés à la connoissance de l'evangile, & que ce rappel sera l'ouvrage d'un roi de France, auquel tous les autres rois rendront hommage & se soumettront volontairement', p.1775.
   La Peyrère's influence on Messianic views during the French Revolution and the Napoleonic period is discussed in my forthcoming study, 'La Peyrère, l'abbé Grégoire and the Emancipation of the Jews', in the *Proceedings of the American Society for 18th-Century Studies*.

in turn was buttressed in large part by what was then known from ancient accounts of man's origins and development and of ancient science). His successors who no longer shared his theology soon transformed his pre-Adamism into a non-Providential account of man. The secularisation of La Peyrère's reconciliation of biblical criticism, ancient history, explorer finds, and early anthropology was a basic factor in launching the Enlightenment conception of man, seen outside of Judeo-Christianity.

21

LIVY > TACITUS

J. H. WHITFIELD

*Restando verificato che dagli occhi si
levano le sole festuche, non mai le travi.*
Paolo Sarpi

When classicists take time off from detailed articles they write general essays, which get widespread praise because they do not say very much. One of these is Douglas Bush on *Classical Influences in Renaissance Literature*, where he remarks on the convenience of a unified tradition: 'During the Renaissance and well through the nineteenth century, all students all over Europe were brought up on the same body of literature, and study of that literature meant a unified literary, historical, political, ethical, and metaphysical knowledge and understanding.'[1] This comforting dogma is not true. The classics were not all written by one man, nor did fashion miss out on them. The prevalence of one author often means the supersession of another, where *hoc est continuo mors illius quod fuit ante*. This is the case of Livy and Tacitus. I shall not pretend that it is one, according to our rubric, which no one has seen: but it is one which has not been treated as an entity, and which, in its second half, has been productive of the grossest misconceptions; though you will not need my epigraph to tell you that it is the grossest misconceptions which are the hardest to dislodge. I must apologise for trespassing over our datelines, but I shall do this briefly. The fact is that neither life nor literature grows neatly to ordered dates.

The magnitude of Petrarch's contribution for Livy has become apparent through the work of Billanovich.[2] The *Decades* had been separated, he brought them together; they had been reduced, and,

---

[1] Douglas Bush, *Classical Influences in Renaissance Literature* (Cambridge, Mass., 1952), 21.

[2] Cf. Giuseppe Billanovich, *Suggestioni di cultura e d'arte tra il Petrarca e il Boccaccio* (Napoli, 1946); 'Petrarch and the Textual Tradition of Livy', *Journal of the Warburg and Courtauld Institutes* XIV (1951), 137–208; *I primi umanisti e le tradizioni dei classici latini*, Prolusione (1951) (Friburg, 1953); 'Il Boccaccio, il Petrarca e le più antiche traduzioni in italiano delle Decadi di Livio', *Giornale storico della letteratura Italiana* CXXX (1953).

heir to Landolfo Colonna, he made up their total. He began as a young man the purification of their text which Valla was to continue in his *Emendationes* on Petrarch's manuscript.[1] In this way he built a massive platform on which first his own gentle rivalry – the *Africa* and the *De viris illustribus* – and then the tradition of Livy was to rest. Boccaccio took over from him, and added a translation of *Decades* III and IV to the pre-existent version of I (the *Decade* which perhaps was all that Dante knew): the basis of Boccaccio's own style in the *Decameron*. So Livy was passed on to the Quattrocento as the main source of Roman history. Witness that page of Valla in which he defends history against philosophy. 'Nimirum tanto robustiorem esse historiam, quanto est verior. At non versatur circa universalia, immo vero versatur. Nulla enim alia causa huius operis est, quam ut per exempla nos doceat.'[2] The historians whom Valla instances are Sallust and Livy, but when he comes to the examples they are all, naturally, from Livy: 'An fortitudinem, fidem, iustitiam, continentiam, contemptum doloris ac mortis, melius alii docebunt, quam Fabritii, Curii, Reguli, Decii, Mutii, aliique innumerabiles? Quantum enim Graeci praeceptis valent, tantum Romani, quod magis est, exemplis.'[3]

This is the face of the Quattrocento. We may remember Cosimo de' Medici sending a Livy to Alfonso of Aragon, and the fears of his entourage lest it was poisoned, which did not deter him from handling it. Instead, 'Amava assai i literati . . . e sempre, mentre che istava a Napoli, ogni dí si faceva leggere a messer Antonio Panormita le Deche di Livio, alle quali lezioni andavano molti signori.'[4] And similarly for Cosimo Vespasiano lists the historians in his library: 'Delle istorie tutte le Deche di Livio; i Comentarj di Cesare; Svetonio Tranquillo . . .Plutarco; Quinto Curzio . . . Sallustio . . . Valerio Massimo . . . Emilio Probo . . . Eusebio . . . Vincent de Beauvais.'[5] It is an interesting list, both in its order, and, for our purpose, in its omissions.

Rather than proceed to enrich this theme of the predominance of Livy I had better turn to what is the main omission. I hope I may begin with a curious, if distant, fact. Dante, the great proponent of

---

[1] See the catalogue of the B.M. Exhibition, *Petrarch Poet and Humanist* (1974), and cat. no.10 for Petrarch, and Valla's, Livy (with ill.).
[2] Lorenzo Valla, *Historiae Ferdinandi Regis Aragoniae Libri* (1528), Prooemium 6.
[3] Ibid.
[4] Vespasiano da Bisticci, *Vite di uomini illustri del secolo XV* (Florence, 1938), p.102.
[5] Id. p.276.

the Roman Empire, based his belief in its God-given perpetuity upon
Virgil and Livy; and in his ignorance of Tacitus was able, by a curious infelicity, not quite to include, but at least to praise Tiberius in
his *Paradiso*.[1] But it was not just ignorance of Tacitus which made him
disregarded through the Quattrocento. Though the merit of finding
him again has now been given to Zanobi da Strada, it was still
Boccaccio who put him into play. Yet we may note the doubtful
company which Tacitus keeps when Boccaccio displayed his new
acquaintance by revising the *Amorosa visione*:

Ivi con lor mi parve ch'io vedesse	Ivi con lor mi parve ch'io vedesse
Paolo Orosio stare ed altri assai	Tacito ed Orosio stare ed altri assai.[2]

We may contrast this timid intrusion with the unchanged two tercets
for Livy, which correspond to the conception of him as prince of prose
and history.[3] Against the abundance of Boccaccio's tributes and debt
to Livy, there is a meagre gathering of a few scattered cases cited out
of Tacitus. Even more strongly symptomatic is the fact that, though
Boccaccio rediscovers Tacitus, he never, for all his reverence for
Petrarch, or because of it, passed his knowledge on. The latter, in a
redolent phrase, full of his admiration for those examples to be found
in Livy, once remarked, 'Quid est omnis historia nisi romana laus?'
Like that odd matter of Dante having Tiberius on the doorstep to
Paradise, this is something Petrarch might have reconsidered had he
known Tacitus.

Here is the recoil of the early Quattrocento. Leonardo Bruni ration-
alised his view of imperial history, when he interpreted that opening
phrase of the *Histories* ('Postquam bellatum apud Actium atque
omnem potentiam ad unum conferri pacis interfuit, magna illa
ingenia cessere') as the death-knell for all individual greatness.[4]

---

[1]
   Ma ciò che 'l segno che parlar mi face
  fatto avea prima e poi era fatturo
  per lo regno mortal ch'a lui soggiace,
   diventa in apparenza poco e scuro,
  se in mano al terzo Cesare si mira
  con occhio chiaro e con affetto puro;
   che la viva giustizia che mi spira,
  li concedette, in mano a quel ch'i'dico,
  gloria di far vendetta alla sua ira. (*Par.* VI. 82–90)

[2] Boccaccio, *Amorosa visione*, ed. V. Branca (Florence, 1944), Canto V, 64–6. Cf. Attilio
Hortis, *Studj sulle opere latine del Boccaccio* (Trieste, 1879), pp.417–21.

[3] Boccaccio, *Amorosa visione*, Canto V, 55–60, for the unchanged six lines on Livy.

[4] For Leonardo Bruni, v. Hans Baron, *From Petrarch to Leonardo Bruni* (Chicago, 1968),
where the text of the *Laudatio Florentinae Urbis* is printed, pp.232 ff., 247, after the crimes

His contemporary Coluccio Salutati spelt it out more savagely:

Rem enim publicam Romanorum, quam pauper fundavit Romulus et pauperrimi principes ad tantam magnitudinem evexerunt ut imperium oceano, astris vero gloriam terminaret, et eis ad occasum ab ortu solis omnia domita armis parerent, divites L. Silla crudelis, Cinna ferox, ambitiosusque Marius labefactaverunt, et ditiores, M. Crassus, Gn. Pompeius Magnus, ac Gaius Caesar, Lucii Caesaris filius funditus destruxerunt.[1]

In Guarino Veronese, even where he defends Caesar, there is the same general gravamen, while his adversary Poggio echoes Tacitus and Bruni on the end of noble minds.[2] For the transcendency of Livy, I will refer you to that first account of Latin literature by Sicco Polentone.[3] But I shall ask you to hold in mind the last two passages: the one from Tacitus because it will not be until we have the same admission ('omnem potentiam ad unum conferri pacis interfuit') that the climate will be ready for the changeover; and the one from Salutati because, as long as this predominates, even if we are, in time, well into the Cinquecento, we are still within the atmosphere of fifteenth-century humanism. And since you may well fear by now that I have no intention, and you no hope, of progressing over our

---

of Caesar and Augustus, the *monstra, quibus imperium tradidistis*, and the bill of health for Florence, founded while Rome still flourished. 'Nam posteaquam res publica in unius potestatem deducta est, preclara illa ingenia (ut inquit Cornelius) abiere.' Cf. the supporting passage in Bruni's *Historiae Florentini Populi*, ed. E. Santini, *R.I.S.* xix.1, 14: 'Declinationem autem romani imperii ab eo fere tempore ponendam reor, quo amissa libertate, imperatoribus servire Roma incepit . . . si postea Tiberii saevitiam, Caligulae furorem, Claudii dementiam, Neronis scelera et rabiem ferro igneque bacchantem; si postea Vitellios, Caracallas, Heliogabalos, Maximinos et alia huiusmodi monstra et orbis terrarum portenta reputare voluerit, negare non poterit tunc romanum imperium ruere caepisse, cum primo caesareum nomen, tanquam clades aliqua, civitati incubuit.'

[1] Coluccio Salutati, *De seculo et religione*, ed. B. L. Ullman (Florence, 1957), pp.127–8. Cf. Charles Trinkaus, *In Our Image and Likeness* (London, 1970), II, 667.

[2] For the controversy between Guarino and Poggio, v. Hans Baron, *The Crisis of the Early Italian Renaissance* (Princeton, 1955), II, appendices, 465–8, and esp. Poggio Bracciolini, *Defensiuncula*: 'Cum ergo et Senecae verbis, quibus illa praeclara ingenia Ciceronis aetate nata esse, deinde in deterius decrevisse affirmat, et Taciti testimonio asserentis magna illa ingenia post imperium ad unum delatum defecisse apertissime constet quanta iactura sit secuta in literis latinis libertate amissa.' Cf. *Crisis*, 2nd ed. (1966), pp.478 ff.

[3] Sicco Polentone, *Scriptorum illustrium latinae linguae libri xviii*, ed. B. L. Ullman (Papers and monographs of the American Academy in Rome, Rome, 1938), vi,175: 'Omnium qui Romanas res apud Latinos litteris tradiderunt et in scribenda historia sunt laudem maxime assecuti sine dubio fuit iste cum rerum magnitudine et copia tum lactea quadam eloquentia princeps.' 179: 'Ingens quippe id opus . . . Illud autem existimant periti omnes, quod apud Latinos, uti Cicero oratoriam ad rem, uti Virgilius ad poetica, ita noster hic T. Livius exornandam ad historiam et divino quodam munere, gratia, consilio nobis datus.' Contrast the short and modest account of Tacitus, vii.208–9.

starting-line of 1500, I will say now that the date which I shall propose as the first one when Tacitus can begin to shed his long inferiority is post-1530.

As a valedictory, let us sum up the fifteenth-century enthusiasm for Livy with the preface of the 1470 Venice edition: 'Quid multis immoror? non materiae magis Livii Decades felicitate censendae sunt, quam ipse Romanorum inde felicissimus potentatus, quod Livium illi contigit habere praeconem.'[1] As a corollary to which, we may recall the thirty to forty editions of Livy, with translations into the major languages, in the period down to 1530, to be counted against the six or seven for Tacitus, with the first translation to come, of the *Histories* in 1544, of the *Annals* in 1563.[2] And if we count in the place where Tacitus found some employment, in the *Italia illustrata* of Flavius Blondus, it is a neutral use, signifying no greater acceptance of the backcloth of Tacitean history than was implied by Boccaccio's lifting of the death of Seneca, or the fate of Epicharis.[3]

It is time we went back to the discreet essayist with whom we began. I said that he said nothing; but at one point, since it was a fashionable platitude, he had one specific thing to say: 'Although in his chief work Machiavelli drew political lessons for his own time from the pages of Livy, he had much less affinity with that mellow *laudator temporis acti* than with the shrewdly analytical and cynical Tacitus.'[4] What Douglas Bush said suavely, others have said stridently; and since it is hard to keep a bad book down, the place where it was proclaimed most loudly, and most ridiculously, *Machiavelli e il Tacitismo*, written by Toffanin in 1921, is reappearing now in a new edition. By Toffanin it was taken for granted that the restoration of the Medici to Florence in 1512 confirmed a 'trionfante principio monarchico', already established ideally in the mind and heart of Machiavelli, and relieved him of the paradox of having had to work under the popular republic of Florence from 1498 to 1512.[5] So sure

---

[1] Printed in *Bibliotheca Smithiana* (Pasquali, Venezia, 1755), lxxxv. For the rest, Polybius and Appian are quoted as not to be compared, and Tacitus is not mentioned at all.

[2] *Le historie auguste di Cornelio Tacito*, novellamente fatte Italiane (Vinegia, 1544); *Gli annali di Cornelio Tacito*, nuovamente tradotti di latino in Lingua toscana da Giorgio Dati (Venetia, 1563).

[3] Attilio Hortis, *Studj sulle opere latine del Boccaccio*, p.425. The death of Seneca, in the *Commento a Dante* XVI; and Epicharis (with a few other women out of Tacitus) in *De claris mulieribus*; but with, of course, no judgements on Tacitus.

[4] Douglas Bush, *Classical Influences*, p.21.

[5] Toffanin, *Machiavelli e il Tacitismo*, pp.8–9.

was Toffanin of this assumption, that it never occurred to him to look for the evidence of Machiavelli's comfort or discomfort in a republican environment. But though we do not require the evidence here it is easily available for those whose prejudices do not prevent them looking. And as for the triumph of the monarchical principle, we may note that in the *Discursus florentinarum rerum* of 1520 Machiavelli pressed on Leo X the need, and the opportunity, of establishing a republic in Florence; and confirmed this two years later by still pressing it, after the death of Leo, on the future Clement VII.[1] The *Prince*, if you look steadily, is a fleeting moment in the hopes, and thought, of Machiavelli, and if you do not connect it with the horoscope of Italy in the year of its birth (1513) you will land in the topsy-turvy world of Toffanin's arguments. Thus he could explain away the awkward fact that Machiavelli's chief work was a commentary on Livy, by positing a hidden sarcasm, a playing to the surface of the Orti Oricellari;[2] and he could magnify the few quotations from Tacitus which he identified in the *Discorsi su Tito Livio*, as showing as easy an acquaintance with Tacitus as with Livy (the proportions are something like 1 to 99 per cent, so you will see the assumption was preposterous).[3] Meanwhile, since Toffanin was not prepared to attach much importance to the *Discorsi*, the essential fact was that Machiavelli 'leggeva Tacito e scriveva il *Principe*'.[4] And here Toffanin proposed his greatest absurdity, saw the lack of any base to it, and explained it into being by a piece of bluff. The prince is of course Tiberius: but then how do you explain the fact that the first edition of *Annals* I–VI is 1515, two years after the *Prince*? No problem at all: you just assert that the flavour of Tiberius pervades the whole of Tacitus. If you are an *aficionado* you will absorb the appetite for Tiberius from any part of Tacitus.[5]

You will remember that this was not the experience of the Quattrocento: they were repelled by the monsters whom they saw (even without Tiberius).[6] Now as for Machiavelli, the last article on him

[1] One of the rarest of Machiavellian texts. Printed twice in the nineteenth century, 1872 and 1875, it had to wait almost a hundred years for its first printing in this century. V. G. Guidi, 'Niccolò Machiavelli e i progetti di riforme costituzionali a Firenze nel 1522' in *Il Pensiero Politico*, II.3 (1969), 580.

[2] Toffanin, *Machiavelli e il Tacitismo*, p.18.

[3] Id. p.27.   [4] Id. p.35.   [5] Id. pp.35–8.

[6] In the absence of a reading-list for Machiavelli some interest attaches to this one for his close friend Francesco Vettori, especially in view of the date (23 November 1513) and of the comments which he adds in writing to Machiavelli: 'A nocte torno in casa;

and Tacitus rightly recoils from stressing much the links between them; but has some curious reasoning on the two admitted cases (in the twenty-six chapters of the *Prince*) where Machiavelli – once certainly, and once probably – quotes Tacitus.[1] Let us take the open case, where Machiavelli quotes from memory, 'quod nihil sit tam infirmum aut instabile quam fama potentiae non sua vi nixa'. The interesting thing is the neat abstraction of this jewel from its rich setting in the *Annals*. There it comes in the sequence by which Nero strips all her support from his mother Agrippina, and it is followed immediately by words which no *aficionado* could bear to throw away ('statim relictum Agrippinae limen. Nemo solari, nemo adire, praeter paucas feminas, amore an odio, incertum'). Was it not a master-stroke, that last addition, of the cats who came to gloat on Agrippina's nakedness?[2] But Machiavelli is not amused, or engaged; and if you want the proof of this, let us look at two other passages. In *Prince* xvii, in a famous passage, Machiavelli noted the dangers for a new prince: 'Et infra tutti e'principi, al principe nuovo è impossibile fuggire el nome di crudele, per essere li stati nuovi pieni di pericoli.' Who would not think the words of Tacitus ('Novum, et nutantem adhuc Principem') were trembling on his lips? Yet it is Virgil whom he quotes:

Res dura, et regni novitas me talia cogunt
moliri, et late fines custode tueri.[3]

And then, the strangest thing if indeed Machiavelli was prepossessed by Tacitus, in the long chapter where he conducts that most Aristotelian debate (*De contemptu et odio fugiendo*), he plunges into a long excursus on Roman emperors, and does it wholly on the basis of Herodian.[4]

I once made the mistake of asking a colleague in the French department if he read Amelot de la Houssaye very much. He took one look at me, and fled. But all the boiling of Machiavellian scholars have absorbed unconsciously the lesson of Amelot, who first, in 1683,

et ho ordinato d'havere historie assai, massime de'Romani, chome dire Livio chon lo epitoma di Lucio Floro, Salustio, Plutarcho, Appiano Alexandrino, Cornelio Tacito, Svetonio, Lampridio et Spartano, et quelli altri che scrivono delli imperatori, Herodiano, Ammiano Marcellino et Procopio: et con essi mi passo tempo; et considero che imperatori ha sopportati questa misera Roma che già fece tremare il mondo, et che non è suta maraviglia habbi ancora tollerati dua pontefici della qualità son suti e'passati.' (Machiavelli, *Lettere*, ed. F. Gaeta (Milan, 1961), p.299.)

[1] R. C. Schellhase, 'Tacitus in the political thought of Machiavelli', in *Il Pensiero Politico*, IV.3 (1971), 381.

[2] *Principe* xiii; *Annals* XIII.xix.   [3] *Annals* 1; *Aeneid* 1.563–4.   [4] *Prince* xix.

brought out an edition of the *Prince* adorned with citations out of Tacitus.[1] The fact is, that there is no Tacitean element in the *Prince*, which you must explain from other sources, and in other ways. That moves us on to our own private paradox, which is, that while the pack of critics have been barking round the non-existent Tacitism of the *Prince*, they have failed to see the obvious place where the text of Tacitus comes bubbling up unashamedly onto the pages of Machiavelli's *Discorsi*. It is in a chapter from which many have chosen to avert their eyes. But if we hanker for the formula of Toffanin, of the flavour of Tacitus pervasive, so that Machiavelli could breathe it in, why here it is, complete with more palpable echoes of Tacitus's own words than would condemn any criminal to hang. It is *Discorsi* I.x, where Machiavelli contrasts Rome under those emperors 'che vissero sotto le leggi e come principi buoni' (Titus, Nerva, Trajan, Hadrian, Antoninus, Marcus Aurelius) with the bad ones. Now if you write in categories of good and bad, you cannot help committing yourself to the good. So do not be surprised when Machiavelli writes the names of Caligula, Nero, Vitellius, and adds immediately (like Vettori on his reading-list) 'ed a tanti altri scelerati imperadori'. To throw sand in our eyes? But not only does the whole chapter sing with a lyrical enthusiasm the contrast of *gloria* against *biasimo*, and *sicurtà* against *timore*, but it captures and distils the crucial Tacitean texts. On the one side, the golden age, 'dove ciascuno può tenere e difendere quella opinione che vuole' ('Rara temporum felicitate, ubi sentire quae velis, et quae sentias dicere licet'). On the other, all the ills which Tacitus forenounced at the opening of his *Histories*.

Vedrà Roma arsa, il Campidoglio da'suoi cittadini disfatto, desolati gli antichi templi, corrotte le cerimonie, ripiene le città di adulterii: vedrà il mare pieno di esilii, gli scogli pieni di sangue. Vedrà in Roma seguire innumerabili crudeltadi: e la nobilità, le ricchezze, i passati onori e sopra tutto la virtú essere imputate a peccato capitale. Vedrà premiare gli calunniatori, essere corrotti i servi contro al signore, i liberti contro al padrone; e quelli a chi fussero mancati inimici, essere oppressi dagli amici.

... et urbs incendiis vastata, consumptis antiquissimis delubris, ipso Capitolio civium manibus incenso. Pollutae caerimoniae, magna adulteria; plenum exiliis mare, infecti caedibus scopuli. Atrocius in urbe saevitum: nobilitas, opes, omissi gestique honores pro crimine et ob virtutes certissimum exitium. Nec minus praemia delatorum invisa quam scelera ... Corrupti in dominos servi, in patronos liberti; et quibus deerat inimicus per amicos oppressi.[2]

[1] *Le Prince de Nicolas Machiavel*, Traduit & Commenté par A. N. Amelot, Sieur de la Houssaie (Paris, 1683). [2] *Hist.* I.ii; *Discorsi* I.x.156–9 (Feltrinelli).

Since Machiavelli here openly and unashamedly flaunts the words of Tacitus, we may take him at their face value. Especially as he goes on to draw the lesson from them. 'E conoscerà allora benissimo quanti obblighi Roma, l'Italia e il mondo abbia con Cesare . . .' And then a moment later: 'E veramente cercando un principe la gloria del mondo, doverebbe desiderare di possedere una città corrotta, non per guastarla in tutto come Cesare, ma per riordinarla come Romolo.' And then he closes the chapter, and sums up on the two paths, with a last contemptuous epitaph for those who take the wrong turning: 'E in somma considerino quelli a chi i cieli danno tale occasione, come e'sono loro preposte due vie: l'una che li fa vivere sicuri, e dopo la morte li rende gloriosi: l'altra li fa vivere in continove angustie, e dopo la morte lasciare di sé una sempiterna infamia.'[1] Look back from those sharp words to where we started, after the unmeaning knowledge of Boccaccio, with Leonardo Bruni, Poggio and Coluccio Salutati ('guastarla in tutto come Cesare. . . . funditus destruxerunt'). You will see that Machiavelli echoes, in his own and Tacitus's words, their verdict. We need not pursue Tacitus further in the *Discorsi su Tito Livio*, because it is made obvious, in the main place where Tacitus surfaces triumphantly, that Machiavelli, as a looker for examples, will find them, like Valla, in Livy, and not in Tacitus.

Now some Italian critics have stumbled belatedly on the use of Tacitus in *Discorsi* I.x, and have thought this warranted conclusions on the first part of the *Discorsi* not being a commentary to Livy.[2] But obviously Machiavelli threw Tacitus in here because he was throwing him away: or rather, since it is not the same thing, throwing away the history Tacitus related. We can find confirmation in *Discorsi* I.xvii, as in the *Arte della guerra*, in that distinction between the Romans when they were incorrupt, and later, repudiated by Machiavelli, when they were corrupt.[3] Now luckily for Machiavelli, he died in 1527, and so never saw, or suffered, the death-throes of the world which he inherited, and of the values to which he aspired. Something of his idealism lived on, in those who were, to borrow Faguet's phrase, *attardés et égarés*: in Donato Giannotti, or in Jacopo Nardi, who

---

[1] *Discorsi* cit. 159.

[2] See Sergio Bertelli, 'Intervento sulla comunicazione di J. H. Whitfield', in *Studies on Machiavelli*, ed. Myron P. Gilmore (Florence, 1972), p.397.

[3] E.g. *Arte della guerra*, ed. Piero Pieri (Rome, 1937), I, 8: 'pigliare i modi della antichità vera e perfetta, non quelli della falsa e corrotta'. Or II, 69: 'perché, sendo tutta la virtú ridotta in Roma, come quella fu corrotta, venne a essere corrotto quasi tutto il mondo'.

re-translates Livy between 1537 and 1540 for a world no longer at-tuned to him.[1] But if we look to the two most closely associated with Machiavelli, and who have the misfortune to survive him, we shall find a significant shift in attitudes. One of the most puzzling things in Francesco Guicciardini's life has been his acquiescence in the Medici principality, of Alessandro, and then of Cosimo Duke of Florence. It springs from the experience of 1527–30, when Florence (think of that other shift, from the idealism of 1789 to the Terror of 1793) had been taken over by the *arrabbiati*. There had always been a gap between Machiavelli and Guicciardini in their estimate of the people: for Guicciardini, with his ideal of an aristocratic republic, a capricious monster to be distrusted and restrained; for Machiavelli, looking with the spectacles of Livy, a stable element, more constant than a prince. But after the catastrophes of 1527–30, listen to the tone of Guicciardini:

> Perché la libertà non consiste che la plebe conculchi la nobiltà; non che i poveri per invidia cerchino di annichilare le facoltà de'ricchi; non che nelle amministrazioni della Repubblica abbino piú luogo gli ignoranti e imperiti dei governi, che gli uomini prudenti e esperti; né che sotto falso nome di libertà le cose si governino con una dissoluta licenza e temerità come tutto dí accadeva allo stato del popolo.[2]

Or as another Guicciardini, Luigi, put it: 'la nostra ciptà sobto el nome di libertà condocta sí presto in un'altra piú velenosa et piú pernitiosa tyrannide'.[3] From which it is left for Machiavelli's friend and correspondent, Francesco Vettori, to draw the conclusion. What is the question of 1527–30? 'La terza, perché non è la maggiore tirannide né piú crudele che quella del popolo quando diventa tiranno.'[4] Then what the answer? The last quotation was from a letter of Vettori of 1527, the next comes from one of 1532:

> Noi habbiamo a fare con li piú tristi et piú obstinati et piú ignoranti huomini del mondo, e quali non si curorno di ridursi senza pane et senza vino et senza tutte le cose necessarie al vivere et di lasciarsi guastare et di guastare da loro medesimi le ville et le possessione per una loro gara et loro obstinatione. Et se pensiamo

---

[1] For Nardi, see now Sergio Bertelli, *Ribelli, Libertini e Ortodossi nella storiografia barocca* (Florence, 1973), ch. i, 7.

[2] See the important book of Rudolf von Albertini, *Das florentinische Staatsbewusstsein im Übergang von der Republik zum Prinzipat* (Bern, 1955). I quote from the Italian edition, *Firenze dalla repubblica al principato* (Turin, 1970). This text of Guicciardini (from the *Risposta per parte del duca alla querela de'fuorusciti*), It. ed. p.239.

[3] Luigi Guicciardini, *Dialogo* (1530), in the Appendix to R. von Albertini, p.434.

[4] *Lettere di Francesco Vettori a Bartolomeo Lanfredini 1527–1533*, in the Appendix to Albertini, p.437.

che hora non facessino il medesimo, certo c'inganneremo assai se lo pensassimo. A noi bisogna tenere questo stato in virga ferrea, et gastigare e fatti et le parole, et poi fare buona iustitia nel civile . . . Et io non so con quale piú amore lo possa amare et con che gli possa fare piú beneficio che col provedere che questa città non venga piú in mano di huomini libertini, rabbiosi, maligni et ignoranti.[1]

It is the trauma of 1527–30 which drives the patricians of Florence to seek their survival through the despotism of the Medici; and it corresponds to that trauma of Italy in general, which had begun in 1494, and been consummated in the sack of Rome. I shall not attempt historical accountancy, but from now on the weight of monarchy, in the shape of Charles V, is going to press on Italy. For those who survived those shattering experiences the examples of Livy had no further meaning, but they could open the *Annals* of Tacitus, and find something obvious, 'Domi res tranquillae, eadem magistratuum vocabula, etiam senes plerique inter bella civium nati, quotusquisque reliquus qui rempublicam vidisset? Igitur verso civitatis statu nihil usquam prisci et integri moris: omnis exuta aequalitas iussa principis aspectare.'[2] The difference between the moment 1513 and that of 1532 is that the first involves a fleeting opportunity to meet the external threat to Italy, the second a permanent need to contain an internal threat. It is an accident of literary history that Machiavelli's *Prince*, which belongs to the first moment, was published in the second one. But it is only now, after 1530, that we can look for the fulfilment of Alciato's prophetic remark in his edition of Tacitus of 1517, 'sed et nobis prae Tacito sordescet Livius', with those derogatory words which follow on the content of Livy;[3] which we may sample again, more legitimately, in the words of Justus Lipsius, when we have passed resolutely into the world of monarchies: 'Non adfert ille [Tacitus] vobis speciosa bella aut triumphos, quorum finis sola voluptas legentis sit; non seditiones aut conciones Tribunicias, agrarias frumentariasve leges; quae nihil ad saeculi huius usum: reges ecce vobis et monarchas, et velut theatrum hodiernae vitae.'[4]

---

[1] *Lettere di Francesco Vettori* etc. p.463.   [2] *Ann.* i.iii.

[3] For this, see Arnaldo Momigliano, *J.R.S.* xxxviii (1947), 91. And of Arnaldo Momigliano, see also *J.R.S.* xxxvi (1946), 225 and his *Contributo alla storia degli studi classici* (Roma, Ed. Storia e Letteratura, 1955). Andrea Alciato, pref. to edn 1517: 'sed et nobis prae Tacito sordescet Livius, cum ille clarorum virorum exemplo plurimis nos praeceptis instructos dimittit . . . nisi magis mortalibus prodesse longas prodigiorum narrationes aliquis credat, procurataque a pontificibus portenta, tum fusius explicatos annuos magistratus, quorum nomenclatura vel diem dicendo eximere quis posset.'

[4] Justus Lipsius, *Ad Annales Cor. Taciti Liber Commentarius* (1585).

Here, as I told you, Livy is thrown on the rubbish-heap, and Tacitus enthroned in the council-chamber. But take heart, for no fashion remains constant, and for the sake of symmetry (and compensation) I will end by anticipating the next twist of the road, with Kaspar Schoppe's reversion to the view of Bruni and Salutati, so that Tacitus *nil prodest Principi*: 'Si enim in principes illos intuemur, quorum vitas resque gestas describit, quis eos ullius virtutis exemplo nostris Principibus futuros credat? Tiberius scilicet, Caligula, Claudius, Nero, Galba, Otho, Vitellius, generis humani portenta in exemplum Christianis Principibus proponentur, ut cum prudentia et virtute, imperio praeesse discant.'[1] After which it is left for Bouhours, when the *grand siècle* was re-establishing the canon of Virgil, Cicero and Livy, gently to debunk the special claims of Tacitus.

C'est à la vérité un grand Politique, & un bel Esprit que Tacite, mais ce n'est pas à mon avis, un excellent Historien. Il n'a ni la simplicité, ni la clarté que l'Histoire demande: il raisonne trop sur les faits; il devine les intentions des Princes plutôt qu'il ne les découvre; il ne raconte point les choses comme elles ont été, mais comme il s'imagine qu'elles auroient pu être; enfin ses réflexions sont souvent trop fines & peu vraisemblables. Par exemple, y a-t-il de l'apparence qu'Auguste n'ait préféré Tibére à Agrippa & à Germanicus que pour s'aquérir de la gloire, par la comparaison qu'on feroit d'un Prince arrogant & cruel, comme étoit Tibére avec son prédécesseur?[2]

In this climate, we may observe maliciously, the high priest and the idol both go out through the same window.

Il ressemble donc à Lipse, dit Philanthe, qui s'étant mêlé d'éclaircir Tacite, ne fait rien moins que cela, ou fait voir qu'il ne l'entend pas trop lui-même en plusieurs endroits. La comparaison est juste, reprit Eudoxe, en ce point-là, & en d'autres; car le Traducteur de Gracian & le Commentateur de Tacite font tous deux non seulement l'apologie, mais l'éloge de l'obscurité de leurs Auteurs; en disant qu'ils n'ont pas écrit pour tout le monde, qu'ils ne l'ont fait que pour les Princes, pour les hommes d'Etat, pour les gens d'esprit; & que ce n'est pas tant leur faute que celle de leurs lecteurs, si on ne les entend pas. Par malheur, repartit Philanthe, les Princes, les hommes d'Etat, & les gens d'esprit n'entendent pas plus que les autres les passages difficiles.[3]

[1] Sergio Bertelli, *Ribelli*, p.28, for Kaspar Schoppe, *De styli historici virtutibus* (Sorae, 1658), p.18.
[2] Bouhours, *Manière de bien penser dans les ouvrages d'esprit* (Paris, 1715) (but first published 1687), p.408.
[3] Id. pp.473–4. And to show how this caught the contemporary mood, cf. Fénelon, *Dialogues sur l'Eloquence* (Paris 1718 (written 1681–6)), p.372: 'Tacite montre beaucoup de génie, avec une profonde connoissance des coeurs les plus corrompus; mais il affecte trop une brieveté mysterieuse. Il est trop plein de tours poëtiques dans ses descriptions. Il a trop d'esprit: il rafine trop: il àttribuë aux plus subtiles ressorts de la politique, ce qui ne vient souvent que d'un mécompte, que d'une humeur bizarre, que d'un caprice.

You as classicists may make the commentary on this change of fashion out of Horace.

Les plus grands évenemens sont souvent causez par les causes les plus méprisables. C'est la foiblesse, c'est l'habitude, c'est la mauvaise honte, c'est le dépit, c'est le conseil d'un affranchi, qui décide, pendant que Tacite creuse pour découvrir les plus grands raffinemens dans les conseils de l'Empereur. Presque tous les hommes sont médiocres & superficiels pour le mal comme pour le bien. Tibere, l'un des plus méchans hommes que le monde ait vûs, étoit plus entraîné par ses craintes, que déterminé par un plan suivi.'

22

VIVERE SOTTO I TIRANNI: UN TEMA TACITIANO DA GUICCIARDINI A DIDEROT

A. LA PENNA

Le tre menzioni di Tacito che ricorrono nei *Ricordi* del Guicciardini sono di notevole importanza, perché preannunziano di un mezzo secolo circa temi fondamentali del tacitismo e perché, se interpretati nel complesso dell'opera, ci fanno capire bene il terreno su cui il tacitismo è nato.[1]

Guicciardini dovette conoscere Tacito solo dopo l'edizione di Filippo Beroaldo il Giovane, del 1515, la famosa edizione che offrì al pubblico, per la prima volta, anche i primi sei libri degli *Annali*. Ne *Le cose fiorentine*,[2] stese nel 1528, egli dice di Tacito che 'venne alla luce non molti anni or sono': penso che egli abbia riferito a tutto il volume pubblicato dal Beroaldo ciò che andava riferito solo ai primi sei libri degli *Annali*.[3] Dato il posto che i tre *ricordi* hanno nella redazione B (78, 79, 101), si può concludere che essi, fatta eccezione per l'ultima proposizione del secondo,[4] sono anteriori al 1525 o addirittura al febbraio 1523.[5] La posteriorità al 1515 è poi assicurata dal fatto che essi si riferiscono a primi libri degli *Annali*.

L'importanza che gli accenni del Guicciardini possono avere per la storia del tacitismo, è stata intravista negli ultimi tempi;[6] ma innanzi tutto essi vanno interpretati e riempiti di un contenuto: il compito può essere assolto, io credo, richiamando altri *ricordi* del Guicciardini relativi alla tirannia. 'Chi vuole vedere quali sieno e pensieri dei tiranni, legga Cornelio Tacito, quando referisce gli ultimi

---

[1] Cito dall'edizione di R. Spongano, la migliore edizione critica (Firenze, 1951). Se non aggiungo precisazioni ulteriori, la citazione si riferisce all'ultima redazione, la C, del 1530. I tre *ricordi* sono 13 (p.17 Sp.); 18 (p.22 Sp.); B 101 (p.243 Sp.).
[2] P.6 ed. R. Ridolfi (Firenze, 1945).
[3] Nello stesso passo c'è un errore simile anche per Frontino.
[4] Vedi p.297 nota 1 e p.299 nota 1.   [5] Cfr. Spongano, ed. cit. pp.XVI ss.
[6] Cfr. Jürgen von Stackelberg, *Tacitus in Romania. Studien zur literarischen Rezeption des Tacitus in Italien und Frankreich* (Tübingen, 1960), pp.92 s.

ragionamenti che Augusto morendo ebbe con Tiberio' (13, p.17 Sp.).
Quali sono i pensieri dei tiranni? 'Gli ultimi ragionamenti' sono i
supremi sermones di Augusto, che Tacito riferisce molto brevemente in
*Ann.*I.13.2 s.,[1] *sermones* noti a Tiberio, anche se Tacito non afferma che
egli li ascoltasse direttamente, presso il letto di morte:[2] l'imperatore
morente si preoccupava di indicare i personaggi in vista che aspira-
vano al principato, avessero o no le qualità per far l'imperatore, o
che avevano le qualità, pur non avendo l'ambizione. Probabilmente
Guicciardini pensa alla sospettosità inquieta del tiranno verso gli
ottimati, che tiene questi in continuo pericolo. In un altro *ricordo*
(103, p.113 Sp.) egli sottolinea, con una prosa particolarmente raffi-
nata, la diligenza e l'arte con cui il tiranno spia e fa spiare l'animo dei
personaggi importanti.[3] L'insegnamento che dal passo di Tacito
ricava Amelot de la Houssaie non s'accorda male con l'interpretazione politica racchiusa nella riflessione del Guicciardini:

> Un Prince ne peut jamais donner une meilleure instruction à son successeur,
> que de lui marquer ceux d'entre les Grans, dont il se doit défier. Cete connoissance
> est la chose la plus nécessaire a un Prince, qui commence à régner, d'autant que
> c'est dans les commencements qu'il est plus facile à tromper, et les Grans plus
> hardis à entreprendre sur une autorité qui n'est pas encore bien établie.[4]

E il commentatore francese cita Commines per ricordare la sospettosità di Luigi XI verso i personaggi autorevoli del suo regno.[5]

Amelot, secondo il suo metodo solito, confronta i *supremi sermones*
di Augusto con gli ultimi avvertimenti di Davide a Salomone, di
Francesco I a Enrico II, di Carlo V, prima del suo ritiro, a Filippo
II.[6] Avrà avuto in mente anche Guicciardini casi analoghi? avrà
messo nei *supremi sermones* di Augusto, in un ricordo impreciso, più di
quanto essi non contenessero, facendone un piccolo trattato politico
del grande imperatore al suo successore? Non è assurdo supporlo se
si riflette che in un altro *ricordo*, abbastanza legato col precedente

---

[1] Per la numerazione dei paragrafi seguo l'ed. Goelzer (Les Belles Lettres).

[2] In *Ann.* I. 5.5 Tacito non dà per certo che Tiberio, venendo in gran fretta dall'Illirico,
trovasse Augusto ancora vivo; ma neppure in I. 13.2 dà i *sermones* come tenuti direttamente a Tiberio: quindi fra i due passi non v'è quella contraddizione che ancora vi
trovano commentatori moderni, più pedanti che accurati (cfr., per es., E. Koestermann
nel comm. al passo degli *Annali* (Heidelberg, I, 1963), p.81).

[3] 'Fa el tiranno ogni possibile diligenza per scoprire el segreto del core tuo, con farti
carezze, con ragionare teco lungamente, col farti osservare da altri che per ordine suo
si intrinsicano teco . . .'

[4] *Oeuvres de Tacite*, traduites en français avec des notes politiques et historiques, par
M. Amelot de la Houssaie (Amsterdam, Wettstein, 1748[4]), I, p.63. La prima pubblica-
zione cade negli anni 1690 ss.

[5] *Oeuvres*, p.62.   [6] *Oeuvres*, pp.63 s.

(18, p.22 Sp.),[1] Guicciardini indica in Tacito il maestro che 'insegna a' tiranni e modi di fondare la tirannide'. È più prudente, comunque, pensare che qui Guicciardini voglia indicare la lezione di prudenza politica nell'unione di violenza e manipolazione, l'insegnamento machiavellico in senso lato che si può trarre dalla fondazione del principato da parte di Augusto e dal passaggio, non privo di pericoli, del principato a Tiberio. È su gli inizi del principato, su Tiberio, sui primi libri degli *Annali* che l'attenzione si concentra: come accadrà, appunto, nel tacitismo fin dai suoi inizi. Come si spiega ciò nel Guicciardini? È naturale pensare all'importanza di primo piano che hanno nel Machiavelli, specialmente nel *Principe*, i problemi della fondazione di nuovi regimi monarchici e all'esperienza politica contemporanea che è alle radici delle formulazioni teoriche del Machiavelli. Il segretario fiorentino non aveva mancato di trarre anche da Tacito spunti per un'analisi lucida e demistificante della realtà politica, ma nel *Principe* e nei *Discorsi* non conosceva ancora i primi libri degli *Annali*, ed è probabile che direttamente non li conoscesse neppure in seguito;[2] ora Guicciardini indicava ad una meditazione di tipo machiavellico un nuovo campo che doveva rivelarsi fertilissimo e attualissimo: Tacito e Machiavelli cominciavano un lungo viaggio l'uno a fianco dell'altro, rafforzandosi a vicenda. Ma va tenuto molto conto anche dell'esperienza politica diretta del Guicciardini. Quando leggeva Tacito per la prima volta, egli aveva sperimentato il ritorno della repubblica fiorentina sotto i Medici, che non usarono molto tatto: il servilismo era generale, lo spettacolo era deprimente, proprio come quello offerto dai Romani da Augusto in poi: 'Non si meraviglierà dell'animo servile de' nostri cittadini chi leggerà in Cornelio Tacito che i Romani, soliti a dominare el mondo e vivere in tanta gloria, servivano sì vilmente sotto li imperadori che Tiberio, uomo tirannico e superbo, aveva nausea di tanta dappocaggine' (B 101, p.243 Sp.). Spiriti repubblicani non ancora spenti, amarezza per la decadenza morale e politica, consapevolezza dell'inevitabilità del principato, rassegnazione si uniscono senza limiti netti in queste riflessioni su Tacito come in tante altre pagine del Guicciardini: filoni di future contrastanti interpretazioni di Tacito sono ancora

---

[1] Da notare che nella redazione B questo ricordo (C 18 = B 79) segue immediatamente all'altro (C 13 = B 78); ma per l'ultima proposizione di C 18 cfr. p.299 nota 1.

[2] Sull'utilizzazione di Tacito da parte di Machiavelli una trattazione rigorosa e molto convincente in von Stackelberg, *Tacitus*, pp.63 ss.; sulla non conoscenza dei primi libri degli *Annali* pp.66 s.

confusi, ma l'insieme forse riflette lo spirito dello storico antico molto più di quanto non faranno i tacitisti teorici della ragion di stato o gli interpreti antitirannici.

Circa due secoli dopo Guicciardini, Giambattista Vico, che considera Tacito il suo testo fondamentale per conoscere 'l'uomo qual è',[1] ferma particolarmente la sua attenzione sui *suprema Augusti* e gli *initia Tiberii*, visti attraverso la splendida e dissacrante sintesi che lo storico antico ne dà all'inizio degli *Annali*: accanto alla *Germania*, questo è il pezzo tacitiano che egli studia di più.[2] Sembra di vedere sviluppato il *ricordo* 18 di Guicciardini quando si legge questo passo ne *Il diritto universale*: 'Cornelius Tacitus, rerum romanarum sub principatu scriptor incomparabilis, non aliam ob causam "suprema Augusti" et "initia Tiberii" statuit *Annalium* principia, nisi ut lectores moneat quibus artibus respublicae ex liberis transformentur in regias.'[3] Vico osserva questi capitoli di Tacito con gl'interessi di Polibio e ne parte per collocare il passaggio dalla repubblica popolare sfrenata alla monarchia nella sua 'storia ideale eterna'; ma resta pur sempre molto del Tacito osservato con gl'interessi di Machiavelli, cioé del Tacito demistificante, che coglie le forze reali e le necessità politiche al di là delle parvenze legalitarie (ritorna più volte la polemica contro la *lex regia* che avrebbe conferito i poteri monarchici ad Augusto e Tiberio).[4]

Non c'è nessun bisogno di pensare a un contatto diretto di Vico col Guicciardini, da lui pochissimo frequentato. Guicciardini preannunzia il tacitismo, Vico ne è in complesso al di fuori, ma lo presuppone: circa un secolo e mezzo di riflessioni politiche su Tacito uniscono in qualche modo, non casualmente, i due grandi intellettuali italiani, l'uno rassegnato alla monarchia, l'altro, grazie alla 'storia ideale eterna', sostenitore abbastanza convinto.

Nello stesso tempo che come maestro della 'ragion di stato', Tacito

---

[1] Cfr. *Autobiografia* a cura di M. Fubini (Torino, 1965), p.30.
[2] Una buona sintesi dell'interpretazione vichiana di Tacito si trova ultimamente in von Stackelberg, *Tacitus*, pp.149 ss.
[3] *Il diritto universale*, parte I cap.160, 1 (ed. F. Nicolini (Bari, 1936), I, p.169). Il passo è 'tradotto' in *Scienza nuova seconda*, App. IV (*Ragionamenti d'intorno alla legge regia di Triboniano*) cap. I (ed. F. Nicolini di Vico per la collana 'Storia e Testi', vol.43 (Milano–Napoli, 1953), p.899).
[4] Altri passi di Vico interessanti per l'interpretazione dei primi capitoli degli *Annali* sono: *Il diritto universale*, parte I cap. 157, 4 (I, p.163 Nic.); cap. 158, 4 (I, p.166 Nic.); cap. 205 (I, p.238 Nic.); *La scienza nuova seconda*, ed. F. Nicolini (Bari, 1967⁵), I par. 292 (p.105); IV par. 1007 (p.474); 1008 (pp.480 s.); 1084 (p.517); *Conclus.* par. 1104 (p.529).

si presenta a Guicciardini come maestro di prudenza per chi vive sotto i tiranni: il *ricordo* 18, già citato, dice nella prima parte: 'Insegna molto bene Cornelio Tacito a chi vive sotto a' tiranni el modo di vivere e governarsi prudentemente'.[1] Che significa vivere prudentemente sotto i tiranni? Anche qui ci aiutano altre riflessioni del Guicciardini. Abbiamo già citato 103, che descrive il tiranno sospettoso e la sua diligenza nello spiare e far spiare: la constatazione serve a introdurre l'ammonimento: 'guardati con somma industria da tutte le cose che ti possono scoprire, usando tanta diligenza a non ti lasciare intendere quanta usa lui a intenderti'. I *ricordi* da 98 a 101 sviluppano delle riflessioni sull'atteggiamento da tenere verso il tiranno: non collocarti fra i *timidi*, perché il tiranno non si curerà di te e non ne ricaverai alcun vantaggio; non collocarti fra gli 'animosi e inquieti', perché il tiranno penserà di non poter contentarti mai e ti prenderà in odio: la posizione migliore è tra gli 'animosi di cervello quieto', che ti rende rispettabile e dà al tiranno la speranza di contentarti. La questione più attuale e più scottante è se l'uomo appartenente all'*élite* politica e intellettuale debba o no collaborare col tiranno. Guicciardini cerca di giustificare la collaborazione: 'Credo sia ufficio di buoni cittadini, quando la patria viene in mano di tiranni, cercare d'avere luogo con loro per potere persuadere el bene e detestare el male; e certo è interesse della città che in qualunque tempo gli uomini da bene abbiano autorità' (220, p.232 Sp.). Quanto sia attuale il problema per Guicciardini è chiaro dalle righe che seguono: 'E ancora che gli ignoranti e passionati di Firenze l'abbino sempre intesa altrimenti, si accorgerebbono quanto pestifero sarebbe el governo de' Medici se non avessi intorno altro che pazzi e cattivi'.[2] È press'a poco la via tenuta, finché fu possibile, da Agricola sotto Domiziano, Agricola la cui scelta darà a Tacito i valori fondamentali con cui giudicare il comportamento dell'*élite* politica e intellettuale verso i principi; è la via tenuta da Marco Lepido sotto Tiberio, che

---

[1] La seconda parte del *ricordo* 18 ('così come insegna a' tiranni e modi di fondare la tirannide') pare aggiunta in un secondo momento nell'autografo del 1530 (redazione C) (cfr. nota di Spongano). In un primo momento la contrapposizione fra 13 e 18 (collocati di seguito nella redazione B: cfr. p.297 nota 1) dev'essere bastata al Guicciardini; ma poi l'autore è giunto a stringere i due aspetti dell'insegnamento di Tacito in una sola massima, con un'antitesi efficace e una magnifica elaborazione stilistica, e, soprattutto, ha dato alla massima l'amarezza e il sapore di Machiavelli.
[2] Sarebbe qui utile confrontare la redazione B (108), dove si parla anche dell'opportunità di evitare sospetti e pericoli. In B i Fiorentini e i Medici non sono nominati esplicitamente, ma l'allusione è chiarissima.

dimostra come anche sotto i tiranni sia lecito 'inter abruptam contu-
maciam et deforme obsequium pergere iter ambitione ac periculis
vacuum' (*Ann.* iv.20.7). Anche l'attenzione a questo secondo aspetto
dell'insegnamento di Tacito poteva essere sollecitato da qualche
autore precedente: non tanto dal Beroaldo, che troppo generica-
mente nella sua prefazione esaltava Tacito come utile 'cum privatis
hominibus et optimatibus, tum vero etiam principibus ipsis atque
imperatoribus',[1] quanto, ancora una volta, da Machiavelli, che, in-
troducendo la trattazione delle congiure, si appellava a Tacito (*Hist.*
iv.8.4) per esortare a desiderare i buoni principi, ma anche a tolle-
rarli, per evitare rovina a sé e alla patria, 'comunque ei sieno fatti'
(*Discorsi* iii.6). È tuttavia evidente che questa tematica è immersa
più profondamente dell'altra nella riflessione morale e politica propria del Guicciardini. A volere interpretarla e valutarla saremmo
trascinati in quella polemica sull' 'uomo del Guicciardini' (o, come
pensano alcuni, l'italiano immutabile di tutti i tempi), polemica viva
e importante nella cultura del nostro Risorgimento e, grazie all'influenza del De Sanctis, non sopitasi neppure in seguito.

La via indicata da Tacito per servire bene la patria sotto i tiranni
ed evitare nello stesso tempo l'*abrupta contumacia* e il *deforme obsequium*
doveva apparire l'unica giusta a molti intellettuali di rilievo, convinti
ormai della necessità della monarchia, anche quando conservavano
qualche traccia del repubblicanesimo umanista. Citerò due casi
illustri, che si collocano l'uno agli inizi, l'altro verso la fine del tacitismo. Nella sua prima prolusione a corsi su Tacito, tenuta a Roma
il 3 novembre 1580, Marco Antonio Mureto trae una regola di vita,
soprattutto un consiglio alla prudente dissimulazione, dal famoso
passo degli *Annali* su Lepido, or ora citato, e da uno altrettanto
famoso dell'*Agricola* (42.4), che esprime con più pathos gli stessi con-
cetti:

Quamquam autem Dei beneficio aetas nostra Tiberios, Caligulas, Nerones non
habet, prodest tamen scire, quomodo et quatenus etiam sub illis viri boni ac
prudentes vixerint, quomodo et quatenus illorum vitia tulerint et dissimulaverint;
quomodo neque intempestiva libertate utentes vitam suam sine ulla publica
utilitate in periculum obiecerint, neque tamen foeda ac probrosa laudantes sibi
ullam turpitudinem ostenderint.[2]

[1] Ed. del 1525, f.2 v.
[2] Cito da un'edizione lipsiense del 1672 di *Orationes, epistolae et poemata*, pp.345 s. L'ora-
zione è stampata anche in alcune edizioni del commento del Mureto a Tacito (per es.,
in quella di Ingolstadt 1604). Il passo significativo è citato anche da von Stackelberg,
Tacitus, p.111.

Come grandi esempi di vita operosa e gloriosa sotto la tirannia sono richiamati Germanico e Seneca; il richiamo di Seneca va notato, perché il filosofo si ritroverà poi altre volte accanto a Tacito come ispiratore della medesima scelta morale e politica. L'animo di Amelot de la Houssaie non è certo quello del Mureto: egli è un fautore convinto della monarchia assoluta; ma l'insegnamento che egli ricava da Tacito sul comportamento dell'uomo di corte è press'a poco lo stesso: ritroviamo qui la terza via fra il servilismo e la rivolta. Anche per Amelot de la Houssaie il caso di Lepido fornisce un insegnamento molto opportuno: 'Un homme prudent sait aler par un chemin qui ne mène ni au précipice de la liberté, ni à l'abîme de la servitude.'[1] Egli si fa forte di un'osservazione analoga, sullo stesso passo di Tacito, del tacitista italiano Pagliari del Bosco.[2] Un altro personaggio che per Tacito, ma molto di più per il suo fanatico commentatore, costituisce un buon esempio per la stessa morale è Lucio Pisone, che sotto Tiberio, pur essendo illustre, riuscì a morire di morte naturale, 'nullius servilis sententiae sponte auctor et, quoties necessitas ingrueret, sapienter moderans' (*Ann.* VI.10.3). A questo eroe il commentatore scioglie un inno: 'Voilà ... le portrait achevé d'un sage Conseiller d'Etat, d'un bon juge, d'un bon Ministre. Heureux l'Etat, qui en a de tels!'[3] Gli sembra opportuno riprendere qui le riflessioni di Tacito su Lepido: 'Les gens de bien savent garder un tempérament entre une lâche complaisance et une opiniâtre résistance aux volontés du Prince. Les Magistrats peuvent toujours ménager ses bonnes-graces et leur propre dignité, pour qu'ils aient d'envie de faire leur devoir.' E richiama, oltre l'esempio di Lepido, quelli analoghi di Memmio Regolo (*Ann.* XIV.47) e di Cluvio Rufo (*Hist.* IV.43.2).[4]

Poco meno di un secolo dopo, Diderot in vecchiaia (1778) cercherà di giustificare la collaborazione del *philosophe* coi sovrani per mezzo di una lunga apologia di Seneca, spesso avvocatesca e noiosa, qualche volta commovente (*Essai sur les règnes de Claude et de Néron*). Diderot è fuori del tacitismo, ma riprende, tuttavia, un problema della tradizione tacitista. Malgrado tutte le differenze della situazione politica e del clima culturale, il problema è in fondo lo stesso del Guicciardini e del Mureto e la soluzione non è molto diversa. Diderot ci tiene a

[1] *Oeuvres de Tacite*, II, pp.246 ss.
[2] *Oeuvres de Tacite*, II, pp.247 s.
[3] Cito da *Tibère. Discours politique sur Tacite* (pubblicato con uno pseudonimo) (Amsterdam, Elzevier, 1683 (è la prima ediz.)), p.369.
[4] *Tibère*, p.370.

distinguere il *philosophe* dal cortigiano, anche quando, in certe circo-
stanze, la condotta dell'uno e dell'altro è la stessa (*Essai* 1.48):[1]

Malheureuse condition des gens de bien qui vivent à côté d'un prince vicieux!
Combien de fois ils sont obligés de faire violence à leur caractère! Cependant il y a
cette différence entre le courtisan et le philosophe, que l'un épie l'occasion de
flatter, et que l'autre la fuit; que l'un souffre de sa dissimulation, en rougit, se la
reproche; et que l'autre s'en applaudit (*Essai* 1.83).[2]

Come rifiuta il servilismo del cortigiano, così il *philosophe* rifiuta,
finché è possibile, la rivolta sterile di Trasea Peto o il ritiro nella
solitudine e nella meditazione. 'Thraséa reste inutile dans un sénat
déshonoré, et personne ne l'en blâme! Sénèque garde une place
dangereuse et pénible, où il peut encore servir le prince et la patrie,
et on ne lui pardonne pas! Quels censeurs de nos actions! Quels
juges!' (*Essai* 1.86).[3]

Evidentemente, la vitalità di questa tematica tacitiana non è dovuta
all'influenza del Guicciardini. Storicamente la cosa non sarebbe impossibile, poiché i *Ricordi* già nel Cinquecento cominciarono a
diffondersi in Italia e fuori nella 'redazione' A;[4] ma mancano le prove
filologiche, almeno per i temi che ho qui illustrati. Recentemente è
stata formulata l'ipotesi che Guicciardini sia l'intermediario più importante fra Machiavelli e il tacitismo;[5] qualche caso, per es. quello
interessante di Jacopo Corbinelli, il fuoruscito fiorentino che nella
seconda metà del Cinquecento pubblicò in Francia i *Ricordi* del
Guicciardini (1576) e vi diffuse la conoscenza di Machiavelli,[6]
potrebbe farlo pensare; ma in complesso credo che l'ipotesi sia molto
difficile a dimostrarsi e, forse, frettolosa. La vitalità del tema si deve
piuttosto alla situazione dell' *élite* politica e intellettuale nei secoli
delle monarchie assolute: fra il servilismo deprimente del cortigiano,
cioè il *deforme obsequium*, e la sterilità della rivolta o della solitudine,
l'*abrupta contumacia*, lo spazio per altre scelte era molto ristretto: restava
solo una collaborazione prudente e dignitosa. Del resto in generale

---

[1] *Oeuvres complètes* a cura di J. Assézat, *Philosophie*, III (Paris, Garnier, 1875), p.73.
[2] Ed. Assézat, p.125.   [3] Ed. Assézat, p.130.
[4] Metto redazione fra virgolette, perché è difficile parlare di una redazione A confrontabile
come figura complessiva a B e C: ho l'impressione che A sia piuttosto un simbolo per
indicare un insieme di elaborazioni, in gran parte dovute al Guicciardini stesso e anteriori agli autografi del 1528 (B) e del 1530 (C), in parte dovute alla trasmissione del testo.
Ciò non vuol dire, però, che A sia un fantasma. Mi limito ad un'impressione, ben
consapevole delle grosse difficoltà che la questione presenta.
[5] Cfr. von Stackelberg, *Tacitus*, p.93.
[6] Su di lui cfr. G. Procacci, *Studi sulla fortuna di Machiavelli* (Roma, 1965), pp.174 ss.
E' un peccato che il Procacci non conoscesse l'utile opera di von Stackelberg.

chi disprezzava i cortigiani disprezzava anche il volgo e aveva orrore delle sedizioni. Si può dire solo che Guicciardini fu il primo grande intellettuale che soffrì della nuova situazione e trovò in Tacito un conforto alla sua scelta.

Il tacitismo dei teorici della ragion di stato è finito col Settecento e col tramonto delle monarchie assolute: in un'età come la nostra, in cui anche i regimi reazionari sono regimi di massa, ricorrere a Tacito come a maestro della ragion di stato sarebbe ridicolo. Ma la ricerca di una terza via tra il conformismo e la rivolta insieme tragica e sterile può conservare qualche interesse. Se uno si trova a vivere in un sistema ingiusto che non può sperare di cambiare nel corso di una vita umana, se non crede nei valori della vita solitaria e contemplativa, sarà indotto a chiedersi se e fino a qual punto deve adattarsi, se ha un senso ribellarsi per essere schiacciati; e allora potrà trovare in Tacito ragioni per la rassegnazione, ma anche per una vita operosa, non inutile agli altri. Ben inteso, il tentativo di sfuggire al conformismo potrà essere illusorio; ma anche chi sceglie la rivolta, dovrà riconoscere almeno che l'altra scelta non comporta la stupidità, l'abdicazione dell'intelligenza storica.

23

UTILISATION ET CRITIQUE DE LA *POLITIQUE* D'ARISTOTE DANS LA *RÉPUBLIQUE* DE JEAN BODIN

H. WEBER

Depuis la traduction latine de Guillaume de Moerbeke en 1260, *La Politique* ou *Les Politiques* d'Aristote, suivant la transposition latine du titre au seizième siècle, n'a pas cessé d'être au centre des réflexions de tous ceux qui se sont préoccupés d'une étude des gouvernements. Dès sa parution, à la fin du treizième siècle, Albert Le Grand et Saint Thomas d'Aquin l'ont abondamment commentée. Partisans et adversaires de la suprématie du pouvoir ecclésial sur le pouvoir laïque y ont puisé des arguments; dès 1370, Nicolas Oresme la traduite en français pour le roi Charles V et l'oeuvre sera imprimée en 1489.

L'humanisme apporte avec Leonardo Bruni une nouvelle traduction latine faite sur le texte grec; celui-ci connaît, de 1498 à 1556, cinq éditions différentes, en Italie, à Bâle, et en France, tandis que traductions et commentaires latins s'accumulent. Citons, pour la France, celui que Lefévre d'Etaples ajoute à la traduction de Leonardo Bruni entre 1506 et 1511, les traductions latines de Sepulveda (1548), de Denys Lambin (1567) enfin et surtout, en 1568, la traduction française de Louis Le Roy qui s'accompagne elle aussi d'un abondant commentaire encore enrichi en 1576.

L'éclairage philologique apporté par l'humanisme permet une meilleure compréhension de l'oeuvre reliée désormais à l'ensemble de l'histoire et des institutions, située ainsi dans une chaîne de pensées et de réflexions qui s'étend de Platon à Polybe, à Cicéron et Saint Augustin. De la comparaison naît l'attitude critique qui se manifeste, sous sa forme la plus élémentaire, par l'opposition d'Aristote à Platon. C'est encore celle qui domine le traité de Louis Le Roy intitulé: 'De l'origine, antiquité et excellence de l'art politique' qu'il place en tête de sa traduction des *Politiques* en 1568. Il y reconnaît à Platon le mérite de fonder la politique sur la justice et la réflexion morale, à

Aristote celui d'avoir commencé par recueillir les constitutions et les lois existantes pour établir un art de la conduite humaine. Il reproche par contre à Platon ses théories chimériques sur la communauté des biens et la communauté des femmes, à Aristote de se soucier uniquement des choses humaines et de négliger la religion inséparable pour lui de la bonne administration de l'état.

La plupart des commentateurs de *La Politique* à cette époque unissent au souci de l'éclairage historique, le désir d'ajouter des exemples modernes aux types de gouvernement classés par Aristote. Déjà Lefévre d'Etaples, à propos de la royauté, s'appuie sur l'excellence de la monarchie française pour critiquer les réserves d'Aristote, Louis Le Roy ajoute les exemples de la Moscovie et de la Turquie aux exemples de monarchie barbare fournis par Aristote.

L'accumulation de matériaux nouveaux depuis l'époque grecque, ne serait-ce que tout le développement de l'empire romain, la constitution et la systèmatisation du droit romain, la naissance du droit féodal et enfin le développement de monarchies centralisées en Europe oblige les théoriciens à reconsidérer ces classifications et ces distinctions.

Jean Bodin qui publie sa *Méthode de l'Histoire* en 1566, quand Louis Le Roy rédige sa traduction et son commentaire, représente une nouvelle étape de la réflexion critique. C'est le moment où apparaît, après l'époque des commentaires, l'exigence de classifications systèmatiques. L'oeuvre philosophique de Ramus ne tend-elle pas à la recherche de méthodes de classifications scientifiques qui se substituent à la logique purement déductive de la scolastique? Les études juridiques de Conan et Baudouin se caractérisent par la recherche d'une réorganisation systèmatique de l'ensemble du corpus du droit romain.

Aussi Jean Bodin, dès le chapitre six de sa *Méthode de l'Histoire* qui s'intitule *De la Constitution des Républiques*, s'attaque d'emblée à Aristote: 'mais comme il convient de ne pas donner dans la discussion plus de poids à l'autorité qu'aux raisons, il faut d'abord réfuter par des arguments nécessaires les définitions d'Aristote'.[1] Cette critique ne s'appuie pas sur Platon, Bodin s'oriente résolument vers l'analyse des gouvernements existants plutôt que vers la recherche du gouvernement idéal, mais il fait remonter cette ambition à Platon lui-même dont Aristote

---

[1] Jean Bodin, *La Méthode de l'Histoire*, traduction Pierre Mesnard, dans *Corpus Général des philosophes français* v, iii (Paris, P.U.F. 1951), p.350.

n'aurait fait que suivre les conseils, sans réussir pleinement son entreprise.

Ce qui crée finalement la plus grande opposition entre Aristote et Bodin, c'est le monde politique où ils vivent: la cité grecque pour Aristote, les monarchies centralisées pour Bodin. Tout l'effort d'Aristote s'oriente vers la recherche d'un équilibre ou d'un compromis entre aristocratie et démocratie, qu'il appellera du nom de 'politie'; tout chez Bodin vise à assurer l'autorité d'un monarque absolu, mais respectant certains droits fondamentaux de ses sujets et ceci, contre les nouvelles tendances issues des guerres de religions, celle d'Hotman en particulier qui cherche à soumettre l'autorité monarchique à un contrôle d'assemblées, en s'appuyant sur l'histoire des origines de la monarchie française. Chez tous deux pourtant, on trouve l'ébauche d'une théorie relativiste qui fait dépendre la nature du gouvernement des conditions géographiques du climat, de la nature du sol, de l'exposition ou de la situation des villes. Un très long chapitre du livre v de *La République* de Bodin[1] développe ainsi de façon systématique et plus nuancée la théorie un peu sommaire exposée par Aristote au chapitre VII du livre VII de sa *Politique*. Il appartiendra à Montesquieu d'en jouer plus subtilement encore dans l'*Esprit des Lois*.

Dans l'ensemble, *La République* de Bodin va reprendre tous les problèmes posés par Aristote, sauf ceux qui concernent l'éducation et la formation du citoyen. Si le plan de *La Politique* n'est pas respecté, c'est qu'il n'est pas en lui-même satisfaisant. En effet, la plupart des exégètes considèrent cette oeuvre comme un recueil hétérogène de traités ou de cours composés à différentes époques de la vie d'Aristote et rassemblées tardivement.

Il nous faut maintenant, en nous limitant à quelques thèmes choisis dans un ensemble plus vaste, montrer comment Bodin se sert d'Aristote comme point de départ pour en corriger ou en contester les formules.

La définition première d'Aristote est celle de la cité à laquelle il parvient par un processus génétique, s'élevant de la famille au village qui est 'la première communauté formée de plusieurs familles pour les besoins qui débordent la vie quotidienne', à 'la communauté de plusieurs villages: la cité'.[2]

[1] Cf. également dans la *Méthode de l'Histoire* le chapitre v qui réunit déjà tous les éléments repris sur ce sujet dans la *République*.
[2] Aristote, *Politique* (traduction J. Aubonnet, Les Belles Lettres, Paris, 1968), I, chap.II, 5–8.

Bodin nous fournit, dès les premières lignes de *La République*, la définition qui convient aussi bien à un grand état qu'à une cité: 'La République est un droit gouvernement de plusieurs ménages et de ce qui leur est commun avec puissance souveraine.' Dès lors apparaît la différence capitale entre les deux conceptions: à l'idée un peu vague de communauté Bodin substitue l'idée de souveraineté, c'est à dire celle de *potestas* ou d'*imperium* issue de l'évolution du droit romain.[1]

Tandis que, pour Aristote, comme en témoigne l'*Ethique*, l'amitié, le lien social demeure le fondement de la vie politique, pour Bodin, c'est le pouvoir de commander, qui a son origine naturelle dans le pouvoir du père de famille sur ses enfants.[2] Aristote tout en faisant précéder sa définition d'une longue analyse de la famille et des rapports du maître et de l'esclave distingue l'autorité familiale de l'autorité politique, comme La Boétie qui les opposera plus radicalement.

En ajoutant à la définition d'Aristote la formule 'droit gouvernement' Bodin oppose l'état aux sociétés de voleurs ou de brigands; ce qui implique que la notion d'état est liée à celle d'une législation nationale ou internationale. Tout en critiquant certaines formules d'Aristote sur le but de la cité,[3] il se rallie finalement à son point de vue qui ne voit dans la vie politique qu'un moyen d'assurer l'excellence de la vie individuelle, le but suprême ne pouvant être que la contemplation intellectuelle.[4]

Quand il s'agit du citoyen et du magistrat, les critiques de Bodin procèdent du même désir d'adapter les définitions d'Aristote aux réalités de la monarchie du seizième siècle. En effet, la définition du citoyen par 'le pouvoir de rendre la justice, d'exercer la magistrature et de participer aux délibérations' ne convient selon Bodin qu'aux États démocratiques et tend à confondre citoyens et magistrat; pour lui les citoyens sont 'les francs sujets' par opposition aux esclaves ou aux étrangers.[5] Le mot 'sujet' comme le mot 'souveraineté' caractérisent d'ailleurs la pensée essentiellement monarchique de Bodin.

[1] Cf. à ce sujet Jean Bodin, *Méthode de l'Histoire*, p.359; il signale que la notion de souveraineté apparaît incidemment chez Aristote.
[2] Ibid. p.351 'Je commence donc par établir que la famille et le collège sont la véritable image de la république.' Cf. dans la *République* les chapitres II et IV du Ier livre.
[3] Aristote, *Politique* I, chap.II, 11–12.
[4] Bodin, *République* I, chap.I, p.5. (La plupart des éditions de la *République* de Bodin au 16ème siècle, à partir de 1579 nous semblent avoir la même pagination, nos références sont celles de l'édition Lyonnaise de 1593.)
[5] Bodin, *République* I, chap.I, p.5 et Aristote *Politique*, VII, chap.III et chap.XIII.

De la même façon, Bodin juge équivoques et contradictoires les différents essais de définition du magistrat par Aristote.[1] Ce qu'il lui reproche, c'est d'inclure dans la fonction du magistrat les activités délibératives ou législatives comme celles des 'probouleutes' à Athènes. Pour lui, le magistrat est celui qui a le pouvoir de commander. Il faut pourtant remarquer que Bodin se contente de considérer comme unique ce qui était déjà, pour Aristote, l'attribut le plus important du magistrat.[2] Dans toutes ces définitions il y a donc un effort de clarification des plus utiles pour l'établissement d'une science politique, mais aussi une orientation trés précise qui consiste à privilégier la décision unique sur la délibération.

Ces mêmes principes vont conduire Bodin dans la classification des différentes formes de constitutions à refuser de considérer qu'il peut y avoir des gouvernements mixtes. Il renonce d'abord à la distinction traditionnelle entre trois bons gouvernements et trois mauvais gouvernements[3]. Le critère moral semble aboli,[4] il n'y a plus que le nombre des possesseurs du pouvoirs qui distinguent trois formes de gouvernement. Bien que cette évolution se dessine chez Aristote tout au long des livres III et IV de *La Politique*, Bodin rompt nettement avec l'idéalisme traditionnel; en cela, il est bien du siècle de Machiavel, qu'il combat tout en subissant quelque peu son influence. Pour lui, l'aristocratie se définit par le gouvernement d'une minorité plus ou moins restreinte, la démocratie étant le gouvernement d'une majorité qui ne comprend pas nécessairement la totalité des citoyens. Ceci lui permet de définir Venise comme une aristocratie puisque seuls les nobles participent au grand conseil. Une question décisive rend la classification plus claire: qui dispose de la souveraineté? Dans la souveraineté, Bodin unit les trois pouvoirs que Montesquieu s'efforcera de distinguer.[5] La souveraineté a aussi comme caractéristique d'être indivisible et perpétuelle: ceux qui délèguent, même pour un temps déterminé, leurs pouvoirs à un homme restent en fait

[1] Cf. Bodin, *République* I, chap.VI, p.70, *Méthode de l'Histoire*, p.350, Aristote, *Politique* III, chap.I.

[2] Cf. Bodin, *République* III, chap.II, p.373 et chap.III, p.394. Enfin Aristote, *Politique*, IV, chap.XV, 4, 'il faut appeler avant tout magistrature toutes les fonctions auxquelles est attribué dans un domaine déterminé le pouvoir de délibérer, de décider, d'ordonner et tout spécialement ce dernier pouvoir, car donner des ordres c'est plus particulièrement la marque d'un chef'.

[3] Aristote, *Politique* III, chap.VII, 3–5. Cf. aussi *Ethique* VIII, chap.X.

[4] Cf. *Méthode de l'Histoire* p.362, 'La vertu ou le vice n'apportent pas non plus de variétés nouvelles dans les formes du gouvernement.'

[5] Cf. Bodin, *République* I, chap.VIII.

les véritables souverains; ainsi l'empire d'Allemagne n'est pas une monarchie, pour Bodin, mais une aristocratie, la souveraineté reposant dans les grands électeurs qui désignent l'empereur et dans la diète qui doit être consultée pour un certain nombre de mesures essentielles.

Ce nouveau critère permet à Bodin de ruiner la théorie du gouvernement mixte, de celui qui pour Aristote réunit oligarchie et démocratie dans la *politeia* et pour Polybe les trois principes monarchique, aristocratique et démocratique dans la constitution romaine. Contarini au début du seizieme siècle voyait aussi l'idéal du gouvernement mixte dans la constitution de Venise. Bodin est catégorique 'il n'y a point et ne se trouva oncques République composée d'aristocratie et de l'estat populaire et beaucoup moins de trois sortes de République'.[1] Ce souci de clarté théorique dans l'analyse s'accompagne d'ailleurs du désir de réfuter Hotman et tous ceux qui essayent de découvrir à l'origine de la monarchie française une forme de gouvernement mixte où le parlement de Paris représenterait l'aristocratie et, les états généraux, la démocratie. L'indignation de Bodin va jusqu'à considérer comme 'un crime de léze majesté de faire les subjects compagnons du Prince souverain'.[2] Chez un homme comme Louis Le Roy qui admirait tout à la fois la constitution de Venise et la monarchie française, il y avait tendance à les rapprocher comme des modèles de gouvernements mixtes. Bodin se refuse absolument à ce jeu, il énumère toutes les marques de respect, toutes les formules employées dans les arrêts du parlement ou dans les assemblées des états généraux pour soutenir qu'en France la souveraineté ne réside que dans le roi.

La critique du classement opéré par Aristote entre les différentes formes de monarchie procède du même esprit. Aristote en effet se contentait d'étudier les formes successives que lui offrait l'histoire: il distinguait ainsi cinq sortes de monarchie dont celle des temps héroïques, où les rois étaient choisis pour être des juges et des sacrificateurs, puis celle des rois barbares d'Asie caractérisée par le pouvoir despotique et la transmission héréditaire.[3] Dans l'ensemble, la royauté paraît à Aristote une institution du passé, elle est née dans les petites cités où les hommes de mérite dignes d'être rois étaient rares, le développement et l'enrichissement progressif ont entraîné le

[1] *République*, II, chap.I, p.266. [2] *Ibid.* pp.262–3.
[3] Aristote, *Politique* III, chap.XIV, 14.

passage de la monarchie à l'oligarchie puis de l'oligarchie à la démocratie.[1] Pour Bodin, les monarchies assyriennes et babyloniennes
prouvent que la monarchie héréditaire est la plus ancienne. S'appuyant sur l'exemple de Nemrod qui en hébreux signifie à la fois chasseur
et brigand, il fait de la violence l'origine de la monarchie[2] ce qui
annonce la théorie Hobbes.

La tyrannie n'est pas, à proprement parler, une forme de monarchie; pour Bodin, elle se définit par la conduite personnelle du roi qui
refuse d'obéir aux lois de Dieu et de la Nature. Ainsi réapparaît le
principe de distinction morale entre les gouvernements qu'il s'était
refusé à admettre en ce qui concernait l'oligarchie et l'aristocratie.

A toute occasion Bodin reprend les critiques qu'Aristote et plus
encore Platon ont adressées à la démocratie athénienne, après l'époque
de Périclès, mais c'est à la racine même du gouvernement populaire
qu'il s'attaque en déclarant que, dans toute assemblée, il y a plus de
méchants que de bons, que le principe de la majorité pour justifier
la démocratie ou l'aristocratie aboutit à la domination des méchants.
Aristote soutenait que la réunion de plusieurs avis constitue une
somme de connaissances supérieures à celui d'un seul homme si excellent qu'il soit.[3] Bodin, implicitement, paraît admettre le point de
vue d'Aristote: 'le conseil de plusieurs bons cerveaux peut estre
meilleur qu'un, comme on dit que plusieurs voyent mieux qu'un
seul', mais, c'est pour en détruire les conséquences par la distinction
entre le conseil et le commandement 'pour résoudre, conclure et
commander, un le fera toujours mieux que plusieurs: et lors celui qui
aura meurement digéré les advis d'un chacun prendra la résolution
sans débat'.[4] Ainsi en est-il des conseils royaux où chacun opine et le
roi seul décide, il en est de même pour les états généraux.[5]

La clef de l'opposition entre Bodin et Aristote se situe peut-être
dans le rapport du souverain et de la loi. Aristote après avoir exposé
les caractères de la monarchie absolue la juge contraire à l'égalité que
la nature a mise entre les hommes; il est préférable que la loi règne
plutôt que l'un quelconque des citoyens . . . 'exiger le règne de la loi
c'est exiger que Dieu et la raison règnent seuls'.[6] Pour Bodin au contraire, le souverain est au-dessus de la loi puisqu'il en est la source,
qu'il soit roi, peuple, ou aristocratie. A l'exception des lois de la

[1] Ibid. chap.xv, 11 à 13.
[2] Bodin, *République* II, chap.II, p.273.
[3] Aristote, *Politique* III, chap.xv, 7–9.
[4] Bodin, *République* VI, chap.VI, p.966.
[5] Ibid. I, chap.VIII, p.198.
[6] Aristote, *Politique* III, chap.XVI, 5.

nature et de Dieu, que tout souverain doit toujours respecter, le roi
'n'est pas sujet à ses lois, ni aux lois de ses prédécesseurs puisqu'il peut
les changer par d'autres'.[1] Une restriction importante cependant, le
roi doit respecter les conventions, les contrats qu'il conclut avec ses
propres sujets ce qui exige qu'il obtienne leur consentement lors de
la levée de nouveaux impôts par l'intermédiare des états généraux.[2]
Pour Aristote, le problème central de la cité est celui de la lutte des
riches et des pauvres; c'est ce qui lui fait définir l'oligarchie comme
la domination des riches qui sont toujours la minorité et la démocratie comme la domination des pauvres qui sont la majorité.[3] Son
besoin d'équilibre lui fait considérer la domination de la classe
moyenne comme la seule garantie de stabilité, c'est elle qui permet
de constituer la véritable 'politie'. Bodin se refuse à lier aussi caté-
goriquement la définition des gouvernements à la lutte des classes, il
s'efforce de découvrir des minorités gouvernants dans l'intérêt du
peuple et qui devraient être appelés 'démocratie', si l'on suivait
Aristote.[4] Il justifie également ces attaques par une distinction entre
'la forme de gouverner' et 'l'estat d'une république'. Une monarchie
peut ainsi être gouvernée populairement si les offices et les charges
sont donnés aux pauvres aussi bien qu'aux riches.[5] Mais Bodin ne fait
ici qu'adapter au monde moderne une remarque faite par Aristote
lui-même: 'en beaucoup d'endroits il se trouve qu'un régime qui, dans
sa législation, n'est pas démocratique, cependant par l'effet des habi-
tudes et du mode d'éducation, se comporte comme une démocratie'.[6]
En dépit de ces subtilités, il semble surtout que Bodin cherche à
masquer une réalité gênante.

Il est cependant obligé de reconnaître que 'de toutes les causes de
séditions et changement de république, il n'y en a point de plus
grande que les richesses excessives de peu de subjects et la pauvreté
extrême de la plupart',[7] mais il écarte immédiatement les solutions
extrêmes. Pour justifier la société hiérarchisée de son temps, il déclare
qu'il n'y a jamais plus de haine qu'entre hommes qui sont égaux
tandis que le 'pauvre, le petit, le faible ploye et obéyt volontiers aux

---

[1] Bodin, *République* I, chap.VIII, p.155.   [2] Bodin, *République* VI, chap.II, p.880.
[3] Aristote, *Politique* IV, chap.IV, p.19 'ce que l'on considère comme les parties par excellence de la cité, ce sont les riches et les pauvres, de plus, comme d'habitude les riches
sont moins nombreux et les pauvres les plus nombreux, ce sont là parmi les fractions
de la cité les parties manifestements opposées'.
[4] Bodin, *République* II, chap.VII, p.337.   [5] Ibid. p.338.
[6] Aristote, *Politique* IV, chap.XI.   [7] Bodin, *République* V, chap.II, p.702.

grands, aux puissans pour l'aide et proffit qu'il en espère'.[1] Il y a sans doute là encore une critique qui estime que la communauté implique l'amitié et que 'la cité se veut composer le plus possible d'égaux et de semblables' ce qui se rencontre surtout dans la classe moyenne.[2] Cependant, dans le désir d'un équilibre social qui maintienne la différence entre les ordres, sans trop creuser de fossés, Bodin utilise, pour conclure son ouvrage, les deux notions de proportion arithmétique et de proportion géométrique auxquelles Platon et Aristote ont successivement fait appel pour opposer l'égalité démocratique et la répartition des fonctions suivant la richesse ou la noblesse qui caractèrise l'oligarchie. C'est dans l'*Ethique* qu'Aristote définit la justice distributive par la proportion géométrique.[3] Dans la *Politique*, Aristote semble préconiser une combinaison entre l'égalité arithmétique et la proportion géométrique.[4] Bodin invente pour la préciser de recourir à une autre formule mathématique, la proportion harmonique qui combine la proportion arithmétique et la proportion géométrique de telle façon que les extrémités soient toujours unies par un moyen terme, comme dans la série des nombres 4, 6, 8, 12.[5] Ainsi le gouvernement harmonique, au lieu d'isoler les classes sociales, permettra, par des alliances, un passage progressif du menu peuple à la bourgeoisie et de la bourgeoisie à la noblesse en autorisant, par exemple, le mariage d'un gentilhomme pauvre avec une riche roturière.[6] De même le roi distribuera les charges et les bénéfices, tantôt en tenant compte de la naissance, tantôt du seul mérite.

Tel est le compromis entre les aspirations de la bourgeoisie et la puissance de la noblesse dont Bodin se fait le théoricien. Il n'est pas tout à fait sans analogie avec le compromis aristotélicien entre aristocratie et démocratie, mais, répondant à l'inquiétude provoquée par la crise des guerres de religion, il se fixe autour de la notion de souveraineté liée pour lui à la conception d'une monarchie absolue.

Cette orientation fondamentalement neuve, se manifeste à travers l'étude et la critique des définitions et des classifications fournies par Aristote et ses successeurs; il serait utile d'en étudier les cheminements à travers tous les commentaires de *la Politique* d'Aristote qui se sont succédés en Europe du treizième au seizième siècles. Cette invitation est peut-être ce qui justifie la présente communication.

[1] Bodin, *République* v, p.704.
[2] Aristote, *Politique* IV, chap.XI, 8.
[3] Aristote, *Ethique* v, chap.III et IV.
[4] Aristote, *Politique* III, chap.IX.
[5] Bodin, *République* VI, chap.VI, p.1016.
[6] Ibid. p.1017.

24

DIE ANTIKE LITERATUR ALS VORBILD DER PRAKTISCHEN WISSENSCHAFTEN IM 16. UND 17. JAHRHUNDERT

G. OESTREICH

Am Beginn meiner Betrachtungen über das Verhältnis von antiker Literatur und praktischer Wissenschaft des 16. und 17. Jahrhunderts mögen zwei Beispiele aus einem Bereich stehen, der uns Geisteswissenschaftlern wohl zu allerletzt in den Sinn kommt. Ausgang des 16. Jahrhunderts setzte die Verwissenschaftlichung des Krieges und der Kriegführung ein; es war eine grundlegende Militärreform im Gange. In der damaligen Kriegstechnik spielte das Schanzen und Graben eine hervorragende Rolle, und es galt zu entscheiden, ob die Erdbefestigungen von den Soldaten oder von besonderen Schanzgräbern ausgeführt werden sollten. Der Generalstab wandte sich an den klassischen Philologen mit der Frage, wer diese Arbeiten in der Antike verrichtet hat. Auf das Beispiel der römischen Legionäre geht eine Entscheidung von sehr großer Tragweite zurück, daß nämlich den Soldaten der modernen Heere keine Zuarbeiter an die Seite gestellt wurden.[1] Und zweitens: Für das neu einzuführende Exerzieren fehlte es an entsprechenden Kommandos. Hier half die oft wörtliche Übersetzung der in der byzantinischen Literatur überlieferten Befehlssprache. So entstanden die ersten Exerzierreglements der Neuzeit unmittelbar auf der antiken Grundlage.[2]

[1] J. Lipsius an den Greffier der Generalstaaten C. Aerssen, 28 Mai 1590. G. H. M. Delprat, *Lettres inédites de Juste Lipse concernant ses relations avec les hommes d'état des provinces-unies des Pays-Bas* (Amsterdam, 1858), pp.41 f. Die Stelle lautet: 'Alterum quod quaeris; de Fossoribus et operis est, quod in castris et militia adhibemus. Habuerintne eos prisci? Nego habuisse.' Und nun folgt eine ausfuhrliche Darlegung und der Beweis mit Stellen aus Vegetius, Caesar, Plutarch. Die hier angekündigten Notae zum Buch v der *Politicorum libri sex* sind allerdings nie geschrieben worden. Dafür hat Lipsius in *De Militia Romana liber quintus qui est de disciplina* (1595), pp.248 ff. die Schanz- und Feldbefestigungsarbeit der Soldaten als notwendigen Teil der Kriegsdisziplin behandelt.

[2] W. Hahlweg, *Die Heeresreform der Oranier und die Antike* (Berlin, 1941), SS.279 ff., bzw. ders., ed., *Die Heeresreform der Oranier. Das Kriegsbuch des Grafen Johann von Nassau-Siegen* (Wiesbaden, 1973), SS.120–5.

Was uns die beiden Beispiele besonders eindrucksvoll vor Augen stellen, ereignete sich mehr oder weniger bei den meisten technisch-praktischen Wissenschaften des 16. und 17. Jahrhunderts. Ich zähle hierzu Medizin, Astronomie, Kosmographie, Geographie, Bergbau, Technik, Jurisprudenz, Architektur, Agrikultur, Militärwissenschaft und schließlich im weitesten Sinn die politische Wissenschaft, die Lehre vom Staat und politischen Handeln. Die Humanisten edierten die griechischen, byzantinischen und römischen Schriften jener technisch-praktischen Wissenschaften nicht aus literarisch-ästhetischem Interesse, sondern aus ganz realen Gründen des aktuellen Bedarfs und der unmittelbaren Anwendung.[1] Damit wurden die genannten Gebiete verwissenschaftlicht und systematisiert, als Fächer lehr- und lernbar, aber sie wurden nicht theoretisiert. Durch den unmittelbaren Bedarf der Erfahrungen des Altertums entstand eine Wissenschaft mit großer Praxiswirksamkeit. Ernst Cassirer hat auf die methodische Übereinstimmung zwischen Aristoteles und den im Kampf gegen die aristotelische Scholastik stehenden Wissenschaftlern der Renaissance hingewiesen.

Doch geben wir einige allgemeine Belege über Bedeutung und Umfang der Wiederbelebung der klassischen Literatur anhand von Daten über die Editionen, die über den Appell an die antiken Bücher einen überraschenden Aufschluß geben.[2] Von Galen besitzen wir in dem einen Jahrhundert von 1490 bis 1597/8 insgesamt 660 Editionen, davon 18 *Opera omnia*, hauptsächlich erschienen in Paris, Lyon,

---

[1] Die großen Geschichten der Naturwissenschaften nehmen oft wenig Notiz von den Zusammenhängen zwischen antiker und moderner Wissenschaft, wie z.B. S. F. Mason, *A History of the Sciences* (London, 1953), SS.99 ff. Part Three: 'The scientific revolution of the sixteenth and seventeenth centuries'. Im Sachregister fehlen Stichworte wie Humanismus oder Renaissance ganz. Vom philosophischen Standpunkt erörtert das Thema E. Cassirer, 'Die Antike und die Entstehung der exakten Wissenschaft', in: *Die Antike* 8 (1932), 276–300. Vgl. auch knapp G. Harig, 'Die Aneignung des antiken Wissens auf dem Gebiet der Naturwissenschaft in der Renaissance', in: *Renaissance und Humanismus in Mittel- und Osteuropa. Eine Sammlung von Materialien*, besorgt von J. Irmscher (Berlin, 1962), Bd.1, SS.3–15. Wichtig bleibt L. Olschki, *Geschichte der neusprachlichen wissenschaftlichen Literatur*, 3 Bde. (Heidelberg, 1919–27). M. Boas (*Die Renaissance der Naturwissenschaften 1450–1630* (Gütersloh, 1965)) und A. C. Crombie (*Von Augustinus bis Galilei* (Köln 2. Aufl. 1965)) diskutieren die Frage der Nützlichkeit des Humanismus für die Entwicklung der Naturwissenschaften kurz. Zuletzt A. Buck, 'Der humanistische Beitrag zur Ausbildung des naturwissenschaftlichen Denkens', in: *Die humanistische Tradition in der Romania* (Berlin, 1968), SS.165–81. – Zusammenfassend: G. Sarton, *The Appreciation of ancient and medieval Science during the Renaissance (1450–1600)* (Philadelphia, 1955).

[2] Vgl. allgemein F. Russo, *Eléments de bibliographie de l'histoire des sciences et des techniques* (Paris, 2. Aufl. 1969).

Venedig, Basel. Die größte Aktivität findet sich zwischen 1525 und 1560.[1] Bis 1550 erlebte die naturwissenschaftliche Enzyklopädie von Plinius Secundus, *Historiae naturalis libri XXXVII*, mindestens 46 Auflagen. Euclids *Elementa geometricae* wurden bis dahin in 40 Gesamt- oder Teildrucken verbreitet, und 32 Ausgaben von Dioscorides' *De materia medica* liegen im gleichen Zeitraum vor. Das ist schon ein überzeugendes Bild.[2]

Die Beziehungen zwischen der klassischen Literatur und den frühneuzeitlichen Realwissenschaften müssen im Rahmen einer großen allgemeinen Entwicklung gesehen werden: in der Verwissenschaftlichung lange Zeit nur praktisch geübter und tradierter Tätigkeiten. Die Rezeption des römischen Rechts im 16. Jahrhundert ist als ein solcher Vorgang bisher am stärksten erforscht. Im hohen Mittelalter begann die Beschäftigung mit dem *Corpus iuris* in Italien, dann im *Sacrum Imperium Romanum* und griff schließlich über auf andere Staaten des Kontinents.[3] Es ist umstritten, was dieser Vorgang für die Rechtskultur der jeweiligen Staaten und Völker Europas, für ihre gesellschaftlichen und politischen Zustände im einzelnen bedeutet. Der heutige Rechtshistoriker sieht jedoch die allgemeine Bedeutung des Vorgangs nicht mehr vornehmlich in der Rezeption einzelner materieller Regelungen, sondern in dem fundamentalen Prozeß der Verwissenschaftlichung des Rechtsdenkens.[4] Als Symbol dieser Umwälzung trat auf dem Kontinent der römisch-rechtlich gebildete Jurist an die Stelle des unstudierten Schöffen und des Laienrichters.

Die Verwissenschaftlichung anderer weiter Bereiche des praktischen Lebens im 16. und 17. Jahrhundert scheint mir in gleicher Weise mit dem Einwirken der klassischen Literatur zusammenzuhängen. Ich kann in der kurzen Zeit nicht alle Wissenschaften behandeln, weise nur auf die Mathematik und den Bergbau hin und greife dann drei Gebiete besonders heraus: Kriegs- und Heerwesen, Landwirtschaft, Staat und Politik. Zunächst also Mathematik und Bergbau:

Niccolò Tartaglia (1499–1557), einer der bedeutendsten Mathe-

---

[1] R. J. A. Durling, 'A chronological recensus of Renaissance editions and translations of Galen', in: *Journal of the Warburg and Courtauld Institutes* 24 (1961), 230–305.

[2] Vgl. ferner A. Koyré, 'Les sciences exactes', in: R. Taton, *La Science Moderne (de 1450 à 1800)* (Paris, 1958), S.27, Anm. 1 Angaben für Apollonius, Archimedes, Pappus usw.; SS.53 f. Ptolomaios' *Almagest*.

[3] P. Koschaker, *Europa und das römische Recht* (München–Berlin, 3. Aufl. 1958), SS.38 ff.

[4] F. Wieacker, *Privatrechtsgeschichte der Neuzeit* (Göttingen, 2. Aufl. 1967), SS.131 ff.

matiker des 16. Jahrhunderts, der sich den technisch-praktischen Problemen seiner Zeit stellte, rezipierte Archimedes und Euclid als Voraussetzung seiner *Scientia nova* in gleicher Weise wie Rafael Bombelli, der das algebraische Wissen der Zeit zusammenfaßte. Dieser stützte sich auf die Neuentdeckung Diophants von Alexandria, den er aus dem vatikanischen Codex übertrug.[1]

Die Begründung der modernen montanistischen Wissenschaft ist Georg Agricola (1494–1555) zu danken, der die Grundlagen von vier Spezialwissenschaften legte: Bergbau, Hüttenkunde, Mineralogie und Geologie. Sein Hauptwerk *De re metallica* (1556) wurde bis ins 18. Jahrhundert immer wieder neu aufgelegt. 'Für etwa 450 Textseiten Agricolas ergeben sich beiläufig etwa 1575 Berufungen auf die Antike.' Zwei Tendenzen werden offenbar: 'möglichst wenig die antiken Historiker und Dichter, aber möglichst umfassend die antiken Ärzte, Naturforscher und Philosophen heranzuziehen'.[2] Mit dem in der klassischen naturwissenschaftlichen und medizinischen Literatur enthaltenen Material wurde ein ganzer Wissenschaftskomplex errichtet, der den 'aktuellen Interessen' und der 'Lösung praktischer Aufgaben' diente. Der Deutsche Agricola wollte nach eigenen Worten dasselbe für die Montanistik leisten, was der Römer Columella für die Agrikultur vollbracht hatte. Wer erinnert sich nicht an die Bedeutung von Vitruvs Werk für Baukunst und Technik oder an die Begründung der modernen Zoologie durch Konrad Gesner (1516–65) in den sechs Foliobänden *Historia animalium*, die wesentlich das Wissen der Antike zusammenstellten! Doch genug der Daten. Wenden wir uns etwas ausführlicher drei Bereichen meines eigenen Fachgebietes zu.

Ich begann meinen Vortrag mit zwei Beispielen aus der Oranischen Heeresreform, dem Ausgangspunkt der modernen Militär-

---

[1] L. Olschki, *Geschichte der neusprachlichen wissenschaftlichen Literatur*, Bd.III, SS.77 ff. und 105 ff. 'Bei der Wiederentdeckung Diophants und Archimedes' durch Bombelli und Tartaglia ersieht man, wie in der Entstehungsgeschichte moderner Wissenschaften die Antike ihre Hervorbringungen erst dann behauptet, wenn die neuen Kulturen imstande waren, sie zu begreifen und aufzunehmen. Die Kunst, die Philosophie und die Literatur waren den exakten Wissenschaften in dieser Assimilierung antiken Vermächtnisses vorangegangen' (ebda S.107).

[2] H. Wilsdorf, 'Die Auseinandersetzung der Humanisten mit der Antike beim Aufbau der Bergbaukunde', in: *Renaissance und Humanismus in Mittel- und Osteuropa*, a.a.O. I, SS.201–217. Zitate SS.211 und 217. In der Gedenkausgabe von H. Prescher, *Georgius Agricola. Ausgewählte Werke*, 9 Bde. (Berlin, 1955 ff.), sind jeweils die Zitate der Klassiker zusammengestellt. Agricola war wissenschaftlicher Mitarbeiter bei der Herausgabe der Werke Galens im griechischen Original.

wissenschaft. Die niederländischen Reformer studierten für die neue systematische Truppenausbildung, die es in den nur auf kurze Zeit geworbenen Söldnerheeren der frühen Zeiten nicht gegeben hatte, das antike Exerzieren.[1] Sie studierten die römische Militärorganisation, um die Truppenkörper besser gliedern zu können; sie studierten die moralischen Voraussetzungen eines schlagkräftigen Heeres und schufen die neuen Kriegsartikel nach dem Vorbild der *disciplina militaris* der Römer.[2] Der Erfolg war das bewunderte Heer der Oranier, das zum Vorbild für ganz Europa wurde. Die Philologen leisteten dabei wichtige Dienste – an erster Stelle Justus Lipsius, dessen Ausführungen über das Kriegswesen im v. Buch seiner *Politicorum libri sex* (1589) erste Anregungen gegeben hatten. Lipsius legte dann in zwei Spezialwerken, *De militia Romana* (einem Polybius-Kommentar 1595/6)[3] und *Polyorceticon* (einer Beschreibung antiker Kriegstechnik 1596),[4] weitere Grundlagen für das moderne Kriegswesen.

Niederländische Universitätsprofessoren wie Sixtus Arcerius und Johannes Meursius edierten die Schriften des Aelian und Kaiser Leos VI. neu, aus denen u.a. die Sprache für das Exerzieren entwickelt wurde. Aus 'ad hastum declina' wurde 'rechts um!', aus 'ad scutum declina' wurde 'links um!'[5] Man befragte die griechischen und römi-

---

[1] Graf Wilhelm Ludwig von Nassau berichtete an Prinz Moritz von Nassau-Oranien über die Ausbildung der niederländischen Truppen nach den Vorschriften des Ailianos und Kaiser Leos VI. von Byzanz, Groningen 8. Dez. 1594. Der eindrucksvolle Brief ist mehrfach gedruckt: Groen van Prinsterer (1857), L. Mulder (1862), M. Jähns (1890), zuletzt W. Hahlweg, *Die Heeresreform der Oranier und die Antike* (Berlin, 1941), SS.255–64. Hahlweg hat die militärtechnische Seite der Reform sorgfältig untersucht und dargestellt, a.a.O. SS.41 ff.

[2] Vgl. 'Disciplina militaris', in: Pauly's *Realencyclopädie der classischen Altertumswissenschaft* v, 1 Sp. 1175–83. Zur Literatur ist an erster Stelle genannt: Lipsius, *De militia Romana* v.

[3] 5. Aufl. 1630. Wir haben genaue Zahlen über die Auflagenhöhe: die ersten drei Auflagen zu je 1.500 Exemplaren, insgesamt 6.325 Stück. *Bibliographie Lipsienne. Oeuvres de Juste Lipse* (Gand, 1886) – ii, SS.113–25. Die Generalstaaten schickten sofort ein Exemplar der *Militia Romana* des klassischen Philologen an ihren Generalkapitän, den Prinzen Moritz von Oranien. Darüber berichtet Raphelengius aus Leiden an Lipsius nach Löwen: 'Hic omnibus approbatur: Principi praecipue, qui dum in castris contra Dragonium est, unicae deliciae eius lectio; et saepius militum ad eam formam exercitatio.' P. Burmannus, *Sylloges epistolarum a viris illustribus scriptarum*, Tomus i (Leiden, 1724), S.206. F. Raphelengius an Lipsius 24.8.1595. Im gleichen Jahr wird berichtet: 'Comes noster Mauricius interim, dum Hagae in ocio est, milites suos pugnare Romano more docuit.' Burmannus a.a.O. S.744.

[4] 4. Aufl. 1625. Die ersten drei Auflagen gleichfalls je 1.500 Stück, insgesamt 5275 Exemplare. *Bibliographie Lipsienne, Oeuvres de Juste Lipse*, ii, SS.319–32.

[5] Vgl. S.315 Anm. 2. Dazu G. J. D. Aalders, 'De antieke oorsprong van de moderne exercitie', in: *Tijdschrift voor geschiedenis* 58 (1943), 224 ff. Zur ethischen Seite der Reform vgl. G. Oestreich, 'Der römische Stoizismus und die oranische Heeresreform', in: Ders., *Geist und Gestalt des frühmodernen Staates* (Berlin, 1969), SS.11–34.

schen Historiker auf ihre militärwissenschaftlichen Aussagen hin und faßte ihre Angaben zur Nutzung in großen mehrbändigen Sammlungen zusammen.[1] Vegetius erlebte schon während des ganzen 16. Jahrhunderts viele Auflagen.[2] Die niederländischen Reformer selbst forderten neue, bessere Übersetzungen aus dem Griechischen ins Lateinische, beispielsweise zum Sachverständnis des Polybius. Zahlreiche Übersetzungen oder Darstellungen des antiken Kriegswesens erschienen in den europäischen Nationalsprachen. Die Cannae-Studien des Grafen Wilhelm Ludwig von Nassau stellten Vorbilder für eine neue Strategie auf.[3] Nachahmung der Antike bedeutete aber nicht nur blinde Übernahme, sondern auch Umformung und kritische Anpassung. Die Verwissenschaftlichung von Militärwesen und Kriegführung, von Taktik und Strategie begann unter der Patenschaft der Antike.

Die Landwirtschaft als weiteres Beispiel wurde in ähnlicher Weise durch die klassische Agrarliteratur in ihrer Entwicklung und Verwissenschaftlichung im 16. und 17. Jahrhundert bestimmt.[4] Gewiß war die umfangreiche griechische und römische Agrarliteratur schon im Mittelalter bekannt, aber erst im 16. Jahrhundert wurde sie wirklich aktuell und systematisch genutzt.[5] 1539 erschien die Standardausgabe der *Geoponica*, des abschließenden Werkes der griechischen Agrarwissenschaft. Zwei Jahre später gab der Florentiner Humanist Vettori die römischen *Scriptores rei rusticae* in der maßgebenden kritischen Edition heraus. Übersetzungen beider Werke in verschiedene Nationalsprachen folgten. Cato, Varro und Columella, die drei großen römischen Agrarwissenschaftler, aber auch Plinius und Xenophon erlangten damals stärkste Beachtung und praktische Nachahmung. Ihre Werke fanden sich im Original oder in Übersetzungen in den Bibliotheken des europäischen Adels, jener Grundbesitzerschicht, die sich dem Studium ihrer wichtigsten Erwerbsquelle widmete.

[1] Ein Beispiel: Der bekannte Humanist Janus Gruterus veröffentlichte 1624 in zwei Bänden mit über 2.000 Folioseiten antike Kriegsschriftsteller.
[2] Eine Sammlung *Scriptores veteres de re militaria* erschien seit 1487. Sie vereinigte Vegetius, Aelianus, Frontinus, Modestus und später Onosander. Weiteres bei Oestreich, *Geist und Gestalt des frühmodernen Staates*, SS.68 f.
[3] G. L. de Nassau, *Annibal et Scipion ou les grands capitains* (Hague, 1675), herausgegeben von A. C. de Mestre.
[4] Seit 1472 gibt es eine Sammlung *Scriptores rei rusticae*, zusammengestellt aus Cato, Columella, Palladius und Varro. Als Inkunabel bereits fünfmal erschienen.
[5] Für diesen ganzen Abschnitt vgl. ausführlich O. Brunner, *Adeliges Landleben und europäischer Geist* (Salzburg, 1949), SS.260–80. Brunner stellt die Agrarlehre in den Kreis der 'technischen' Wissenschaften, die auf der Antike aufbauen.

Mit der Agrarkonjunktur des 16. Jahrhunderts einher ging eine starke Intensivierung und Rationalisierung der Landwirtschaft. Wein- und Obstanbau wurden nach den Angaben Columellas systematisch betrieben und bildeten wiederum das Muster für andere Kulturen. In Italien und Spanien, in Frankreich, in England und in Deutschland finden wir auf der antiken Literatur aufbauende, aber regionale Eigenständigkeiten berücksichtigende wissenschaftliche Werke. Für Anlage und Bewirtschaftung der *villa* machte Alessandro Piccolomini in seinem Werk über die Erziehung des Adligen 1542 'Columella, Plinius und vor allem Xenophon zu Lehrmeistern der Gegenwart'.[1] So setzte die Verwissenschaftlichung auch der Agrartätigkeit ein. Bekannte Beispiele sind in Frankreich Carolus Stephanus mit seinem lateinischen *Praedium Rusticum*, das als *Maison rustique* ins Französische und dann in andere lebende Sprachen übersetzt wurde, oder Olivier de Serras *Théâtre d'Agriculture*, das zum klassischen Werk der älteren französischen Agrikultur wurde und zwischen 1600 und 1804 einundzwanzig Auflagen erlebte. In Deutschland erschienen entsprechende Werke: *De re rustica* 1570 von dem juristischen Humanisten und Gutsbesitzer Conrad Heresbach und das *Opus Oeconomicum* 1593–1603 von dem Theologie-Professor Jacob Coler mit vierzehn Auflagen.

Hier zeigen sich aber auch gleichzeitig die Grenzen der Übernahme antiker Erfahrungen: Die römische Literatur über die Arbeit auf der *villa* eignete sich nur als Vorbild einer agrartechnischen Rationalisierung für den Großgrundbesitzer mit seinem auf den Marktabsatz eingestellten Gutsbetrieb, nicht aber für die große Schicht der Kleinbauern, die damit noch mehr ins Hintertreffen gerieten.

Als letztes, besonders einprägsames und im Blickpunkt der gegenwärtigen Forschung stehendes Beispiel möchte ich noch die Staats- und politische Wissenschaft erwähnen. Schon länger wird der Späthumanismus als eine den Realien zugewandte Wissenschaftsbewegung betrachtet, deren konkretes Ziel eine konstruktive Hilfestellung zur Überwindung der tiefen staatlichen und religiösen Krise im Zeitalter der Konfessionskämpfe gewesen ist. Im Mittelalter wurde die Politik neben der Oeconomik und der Ethik als dritter Teil der praktischen Philosophie anhand von Aristoteles gelehrt und blieb damit weitgehend im abstrakten Rahmen. Der Aufbau des frühmo-

---

[1] A. Buck, *Die humanistische Tradition in der Romania*, S.296.

dernen Staates aber erforderte eine andere politische Wissenschaft. Im Laufe des 16. Jahrhunderts trat Athen in den Hintergrund; das Interesse richtete sich auf die Institutionen Roms. Die römischen Schriftsteller, die Staatsdenker und Historiker, unter ihnen vor allem Tacitus, bildeten die Grundlage zur Verwissenschaftlichung der praktischen Politik.[1] Nicht umsonst ist das 17. Jahrhundert ein römisches Jahrhundert genannt worden.

Mit Machiavelli und Guicciardini begann die Flut der Betrachtungen über eine moderne Regierungskunst. Wie an der Militärreform um 1600, so hat die niederländische Philologie auch an der Entwicklung des modernen Staates einen kräftigen Anteil. Lipsius schrieb das genannte wichtige Handbuch der praktischen Regierungslehre, die *Politicorum libri sex*, die bis in die Mitte des 18. Jahrhunderts einschließlich ihrer Übersetzungen *ca* 80 Auflagen erreichten.[2] Dieses Werk und die ihm folgende Literatur diente der Unterrichtung von Königen, Fürsten und Regenten, von Staatsmännern und Diplomaten, nicht zuletzt aber der neuen Bürokratie, der Stütze des frühmodernen Staates.

Es handelte sich zumeist um Aphorismensammlungen aus den antiken Historikern und Philosophen – Schatzkammern für den praktischen Staatsmann. Die Realien: die römische Verwaltung, der Aufbau ihres Finanz- und Steuerapparates, aber auch die geistig-ethischen Voraussetzungen des römischen Staatswesens wurden intensiv studiert und bildeten einen besonderen Ausgangspunkt für die Gestaltung des frühmodernen Staates. Die politisch-moralischen Werte Roms, an der Spitze *auctoritas* und *disciplina*, entwickelten sich zu historisch-politischen Grundbegriffen der Zeit. *Auctoritas* und *disciplina* waren es dann auch vor allem, die die öffentlichen Institutionen im Zeitalter des Absolutismus beherrschten.

[1] Die Literatur zum Tacitismus in Europa ist seit dem Buch von G. Toffanin, *Machiavelli e il »Tacitismo«. La »Politica storica« al tempo della controriforma* (Padova, 1921), sehr angewachsen. Ich erwähne nur A. Momigliano, 'The first political Commentary on Tacitus', in: *Contributo alla storia degli studi classici e del mondo antico* 1 (Roma, 1955) 34–54; J. v. Stackelberg, *Tacitus in der Romania* (Tübingen, 1960); E.-L. Etter, *Tacitus in der Geistesgeschichte des 16. und 17. Jahrhunderts* (Basel, 1966); E. T. Galvan, 'El Tacitismo en las doctrinas politicas del Siglo de Oro Español', in: *Escritos* (Madrid, 1971), SS.11–93.

[2] Hierfür das Kapitel 'Der Geist des Machtstaates und die Antike' in: Oestreich, *Geist und Gestalt*, SS.11 156, besonders die Abschnitte 'Justus Lipsius als Theoretiker des neuzeitlichen Machtstaates' und 'Politischer Neustoizismus und Niederländische Bewegung in Europa'. Ich verweise auf die dortigen reichhaltigen Literaturangaben und erspare mir eine Wiederholung. Ergänzend G. Oestreich, 'Justus Lipsius als Universalgelehrter zwischen Renaissance und Barock', in: *Leiden University in the Seventeenth Century* (Leiden, 1975), SS.177–201.

Der Aufbau von Staat und Heer und die Lebensführung der oberen Gesellschaftsschichten richteten sich nach dem Vorbild der Antike. Die stark auf die Praxis ausgerichtete pädagogisch-philosophische Bewegung der Seneca-Rezeption und des Neustoizismus ergänzte nun den rein politischen Tacitismus. Hier wurde die *Constantia* – übersetzt mit Standhaftigkeit oder Beständigkeit – ein Symbol im neuen Wertesystem, bestehend aus römischer Moralistik, stoischer Psychologie und neustoischer Aktivität.[1] Auch im persönlichen Bereich ging es um praktische Lebensmeisterung, nicht um abstrakt-theoretische Reflexionen. Das Idealbild des 17. Jahrhunderts in allen Staaten Europas war der 'politische Mensch' im Sinne von Lebensklugheit und Tüchtigkeit. Realgeschichte, politische und Wirtschaftsgeschichte, Verfassungs-, Rechts-, und Geistesgeschichte stoßen hier zusammen.

Max Weber hat als Kennzeichen der gesamten europäischen Entwicklung den Prozeß der Rationalisierung herausgestellt. Dieser Prozeß ist im 16. und 17. Jahrhundert in besonderer Weise vorangetrieben worden. Das systematische Angehen der Probleme der Zeit führte zur Verwissenschaftlichung von Staatskunst und Kriegskunst, Verwaltungsorganisation und Pädagogik, Landbau und Technik, zu einer Verwissenschaftlichung, die nicht aus eigenschöpferischem Nachdenken, sondern aus dem bewußten Rückgriff auf die Antike erwuchs. Die klassische Philologie sprengte die soziale Einengung des literarisch-ästhetischen Humanismus auf die schmale Schicht der humanistisch Gebildeten, sie erweiterte sich in jener Zeit selbst zur praktischen Wissenschaft und damit zu einer Wissenschaft breiterer Schichten.

What needs to be done? Ich meine, daß die Einflüsse dieser realwissenschaftlichen klassischen Philologie stärker studiert werden müssen. Es ist zu erforschen, in welcher Stärke und in welcher Breite die Antike zur Lösung von Fragen und Problemen der frühneuzeitlichen Gegenwart herangezogen wurde und welche Folgen das nicht nur für die Entwicklung der einzelnen Disziplinen, sondern auch für die Praxis von Ständestaat, Absolutismus und Aufklärung mit ihrer Wirtschaft, Gesellschaft und Kultur hatte. Eine Bibliographie der damaligen Klassiker-Ausgaben und -Auflagen mit der Fülle ihrer Übersetzungen in die modernen Sprachen ist die allererste Voraus-

---

[1] G. Oestreich, 'Das politische Anliegen von Justus Lipsius' De constantia . . . in publicis malis (1584)', in: *Festschrift Hermann Heimpel* (Göttingen, 1971), Bd.i, SS.618–38.

setzung – ein Teil der Aufgabe, die das Referat von Professor Hay schildert.

Die Forschung könnte meines Erachtens darangehen, die bisherigen Einzelarbeiten auf den von mir anfangs genannten technisch-praktischen Wissenschaftsgebieten zusammen mit denen aus dem literarisch-ästhetischen Bereich zu einer umfassenden Kultursynthese zu vereinigen. Künftige Spezialuntersuchungen sollten unter dem Gesichtspunkt der Zusammengehörigkeit von antiker Theorie und moderner Praxis betrieben werden. Ich glaube, daß es möglich sein müßte, die Kontinuität des realen wie moralischen Erfahrungsschatzes menschheitlicher Entwicklung über Umbrüche und Krisen hinweg zu beweisen. Zudem fügt der Blick auf die Realien und die technisch-praktischen Wissenschaften unserer Beschäftigung mit der Antike gerade in der Gegenwart eine weitere Rechtfertigung hinzu. Es gilt, die ganze Breite der kulturellen Überlieferung erneut ins Bewußtsein zu bringen.

25

LES LOGES DE RAPHAËL:
RÉPERTOIRE À L'ANTIQUE,
BIBLE ET MYTHOLOGIE

N. DACOS

Les problèmes dont je désire vous entretenir ont trait aux recherches que j'ai menées depuis plusieurs années sur la décoration des Loges de Raphaël.[1] L'étude de ce monument me paraît en effet particulièrement adaptée au sujet qui nous réunit ici. Déjà lorsque, sous Jules II, Bramante a conçu l'architecture des trois étages de loggias, dont l'ensemble grandiose devait dissimuler le vieux palais médiéval du Vatican, son but devait être de réaliser une succession de portiques à l'antique d'où il fût possible de dominer le panorama de la Rome moderne, et la façade monumentale du Tabularium, d'où l'on embrassait la vue de tout le forum romain, lui était sans doute présente à l'esprit.[2]

Quelques années plus tard, sous Léon X, lorsqu'après la mort de Bramante Raphaël en a pris la succession et a projeté le décor de la galerie du deuxième étage, destinée *al piacere solum del Papa*[3] et à

---

[1] Le livre est maintenant terminé et sera bientôt sous presse. Certains aspects de la décoration des Loges ont été déjà traités dans mes deux articles 'Il trastullo di Raffaello', in *Paragone*, 219 (1968), 3–29 (centré sur le rôle de Jean d'Udine dans l'exécution des grotesques et des stucs), et 'La Bible de Raphaël (Quelques observations sur le programme et sur les auteurs des fresques)', ibid., 253 (1971), 11–36, où il a été déjà question de sources antiques et que je serai amenée à citer plusieurs fois. Mais l'optique y était différente. Comme il n'existe encore aucune publication scientifique des Loges, je ne donnerai pas de référence bibliographique aux détails de la décoration que je traiterai.

[2] Sur l'architecture des Loges de Raphaël, qui n'a fait l'objet d'aucune étude approfondie, voir, en dernier lieu, D. Redig de Campos, 'Bramante e il Palazzo Apostolico vaticano', in *Rendiconti della Pontificia Accademia di Archeologia*, 43 (1970–1), 283–99. Sur le Tabularium, dont on n'a pas souligné suffisamment l'importance, voir F. Fasolo–G. Gullini, *Il santuario della Fortuna Primigenia a Palestrina* (Rome, 1953), p.335, et R. Delbrück, *Hellenistische Bauten in Latium* (Strasbourg, 1907), pp.23–46, qui fait allusion à la connaissance du monument à la Renaissance. Cf. aussi V. Wanscher, *Raffaello Santi da Urbino* (Londres, 1926).

[3] Journal de Marcantonio Michiel, fol.315. Cf. V. Golzio, *Raffaello nei documenti, nelle testimonianze dei contemporanei e nella letteratura del suo secolo* (Vatican, 1936), p.104.

laquelle le nom du maître est resté attaché, il a renforcé encore le ton à l'antique des Loges. Celles-ci sont couvertes d'un réseau de grotesques conçus comme l'équivalent de celui des grandes demeures romaines, la Maison Dorée de Néron et la Villa d'Hadrien, dont les artistes étudiaient alors les vestiges avec enthousiasme. Sur les voûtes, sur les archivoltes, sur les écoinçons, dans les lunettes, sur les pilastres, sur les soubassements et jusque sur le pavement, presque toute l'ornementation est d'origine archéologique. Le fait est bien connu depuis Vasari, mais personne n'en avait jamais entrepris l'étude détaillée.[1] Or l'élaboration d'un catalogue raisonné de tous les motifs avec, pour chacun d'entre eux, l'identification des sources, était indispensable pour comprendre l'attitude de Raphaël et de ses élèves vis-à-vis de l'antique. J'ai entrepris cette enquête de caractère warburghien, pour laquelle j'ai pu me baser largement sur le *census* des oeuvres antiques connues avant 1520, mis sur pied depuis de nombreuses années par Madame Phyllis Pray Bober et dont le matériel peut être consulté à Londres, au Warburg Institute.

Ce problème de l'identification des sources en entraînait deux autres. Tout d'abord, les oeuvres antiques utilisées l'ont-elles été au hasard des connaissances archéologiques de l'époque ou, au contraire, répondent-elles à un choix de la part de Raphaël et de ses élèves, qui illustrerait un goût bien précis? Ensuite, dans quelle optique les modèles ont-ils été transformés et interprétés par les artistes?

Envisageons d'abord la première question. En dressant le catalogue des modèles antiques mis en oeuvre par Raphaël et ses élèves, on est frappé par leur quantité et aussi par leur grande variété. Le maître et l'atelier ont exploité à la fois peintures, stucs, reliefs – dont la plupart sont tirés de sarcophages – monnaies, médailles, gemmes et terres cuites.

Ce sont surtout les peintures romaines, et en particulier celles de la Domus Aurea, qui ont servi de sources pour les principes généraux de l'ornementation. Ainsi, la suite de médaillons stuqués que l'on retrouve sur plusieurs voûtes du monument antique est à

---

[1] Il faut signaler cependant les travaux de W. Amelung, 'Die Stuckreliefs in den Loggien Raffaels und ihre Vorbilder', in Th. Hofmann, *Raffael als Architekt*, IV (Zittau–Leipzig, 1911), col.57–137, et de Fr. Weege, 'Der malerische Schmuck von Raffaels Loggien in seinem Verhältnis zur Antike mit Berücksichtigung der Gesamtdekoration', ibid., col.141–203. Ceux-ci ont eu certes le mérite de montrer la voie à suivre mais leurs tentatives sont limitées, ne dépassent jamais le point de vue strictement archéologique et ne posent pas le problème de l'interprétation des sources.

l'origine de la composition des pilastres des Loges, scandés chaque fois de quatre médaillons de stucs dans la partie supérieure (Pl. 1*a*). Plus exactement, le premier, en forme de bouclier d'amazone, provient de la *Volta delle civette* (Pl. 1*b*),[1] tandis que les trois autres sont tirés de la *Volta nera* (Pl. 1*c*).[2] De même, la disposition générale des archivoltes, en stuc blanc, sur lesquelles alternent les scènes figurées, la plupart du temps rectangulaires, et de petits compartiments ornementaux, décorés de motifs secondaires ou de rosettes, est reprise à celle des grands passages stuqués du Colisée.[3]

Pour les détails des grotesques qui ornent les pilastres et aussi une partie des voûtes, je pourrais multiplier les exemples d'emprunts au répertoire des peintures antiques. Qu'il suffise de préciser que celles-ci ont exercé leur action non seulement du point de vue iconographique, mais aussi technique. Les peintures sont rendues souvent à la manière *compendiaria* des Romains, qui procède par larges touches et que l'on pourrait traduire à peu près par 'impressionniste'.

Parfois aussi les décorations romaines, peintes et stuquées, ont inspiré des scénettes de stuc dans les archivoltes. L'un des cas les plus flagrants est celui des figures d'Hercule et d'Admète, qui vient lui annoncer la mort d'Alceste (Pl. 2*a*). Elles sont reprises à celles d'un columbarium aujourd'hui détruit, qui se trouvait sur la Via Salaria. Dans le Codex Pighianus, qui date des environs de 1550, on en a conservé plusieurs dessins qui permettent de juger de la fidélité de l'emprunt dans les attitudes (Pl. 2*b*).[4] Mais Admète semble transformé en une jeune femme, probablement parce que l'artiste qui a exécuté le stuc – Jean d'Udine – ne se préoccupait pas de comprendre les détails de la légende.

Cependant, le répertoire des stucs des Loges est tiré essentiellement de reliefs. Ainsi, une fameuse plaque illustrant la Visite de Dionysos au poète dramatique (Pl. 3*d*), qui se trouvait au seizième siècle à la Casa Maffei, à Rome, a été exploitée plus de dix fois dans les archivoltes des Loges, où l'on retrouve presque toutes les figures,

---

[1] N. Dacos, *La découverte de la Domus Aurea et la formation des grotesques à la Renaissance* (Londres–Leyde, 1969), p.36 et fig. 41 et 45.

[2] Ibid. p.41 et fig. 59 et 60.

[3] Ibid. p.45 et fig. 68 et 69.

[4] Codex Pighianus, fol.332–7. Cf. O. Jahn, 'Über die Zeichnungen antiker Monumente im Codex Pighianus', in *Berichte der Kgl. Sächsischen Gesellschaft der Wissenschaften*, 20 (1868), 229–31, n°228, et id. 'Über ein römisches Deckengemälde des Codex Pighianus', ibid., 21 (1869), 1–38.

interprétées chaque fois avec de légères variantes (Pl. 3*a*).[1] Un autre modèle particulièrement prisé est un sarcophage représentant le Triomphe de Dionysos (Pl. 4*b*), qui se trouvait depuis le quinzième siècle devant l'église de Sainte-Marie Majeure, à Rome, où presque tous les artistes ont été le voir et l'étudier et qui a inspiré bien douze scénettes des Loges.[2] Les reliefs et les sarcophages qui ont servi de base au répertoire des Loges sont extrêmement nombreux. On note cependant une prédilection pour les thèmes dionysiaques, évoquant le monde des satyres et des faunes, qui reparaît dans les grotesques, et aussi pour les scènes de cavalcade, tirées des amazonomachies et des centauromachies. Mais on retrouve aussi les grands mythes grecs, celui d'Oreste, celui de Médée ou la légende de Pâris. En fait, bon nombre des sujets n'ont pas d'importance; ils ne constituent qu'un répertoire de figures qui sont utilisées souvent indépendamment de leur contexte iconographique.

Il faut tenir compte également d'un autre groupe de sources antiques qui comporte tous les objets de petit format, qui, en dépit des différences de matière et de technique, demandent à être considérés dans leur ensemble et ont exercé une action importante sur l'art de la Renaissance. Dans les stucs des Loges, entre les pilastres en particulier, les emprunts aux médailles, aux monnaies, aux plaques Campana et aux pierres gravées sont légion.[3] A côté des dieux romains, de la personnification de Rome et d'Annone, les représentations de la Fortune, de la Liberté, de la Concorde et surtout de la Paix (Pl. 4*c*, *d*) sont certainement destinées à rappeler les qualités du pontife. Le graveur de la *zecca*, Pier Maria Serbaldi della Pescia, avait gravé une intaille en porphyre à l'effigie du pape avec au revers la même allégorie brûlant des armes et l'inscription, tirée des Psaumes, SCUTA COMBURET IGNI. Le thème de la Paix était aussi

---

[1] Sur le relief antique, voir C. Picard, 'Observations sur la date et l'origine des reliefs dits de la "Visite chez Ikarios"', in *American Journal of Archaeology*, 38 (1934), 137–52. La version du British Museum a été reproduite souvent à la Renaissance. Voir notamment les trois dessins conservés dans le Museum Chartaceum: C. C. Vermeule III, *The Dal Pozzo–Albani Drawings of Classical Antiquities in the Royal Library at Windsor Castle* (Philadelphia, 1966), p.32, n°8488, p.63, n°8023, et p.65, n°8060.

[2] Le sarcophage est conservé au British Museum. Cf. F. Matz, *Die dionysischen Sarkophage* (Berlin, 1968–9), II, pp.204–7, n°88, qui cite une partie des nombreux dessins qui le reproduisent. Deux stucs inspirés par le sarcophage sont reproduits dans N. Dacos, 'Il trastullo di Raffaello', fig. 6a–6b.

[3] Pour les emprunts aux pierres gravées et aux plaques Campana, voir pour le moment N. Dacos, 'Il trastullo di Raffaello', p.11. Sur l'importance des terres sigillées, dont quelques-unes sont exploitées également dans les Loges, cf. l'étude en préparation de T. Yuen.

l'un de ceux que les poètes de la cour développaient le plus fré-quemment.[1] Mais ces allusions sont éparses dans le grand ensemble de la décoration, destiné avant tout à évoquer un monde idéal, où revivent les motifs antiques les plus variés et auxquels se joignent occasionnellement des allusions aux passe-temps que le pape préférait, la chasse, la pêche et la musique, développés en d'éton-nants morceaux naturalistes.[2]

Une fois établi le répertoire d'oeuvres antiques que les artistes ont exploité, il est possible de reconstituer le processus d'après lequel ils l'ont constitué. Pour beaucoup des pièces en question, on a conservé de nombreuses copies qui en ont été prises parfois au quinzième siècle, mais surtout dans le courant du seizième siècle. Curieusement, aucun de ces dessins ne peut être mis en rapport avec la décoration des Loges. Le travail de relevé 'archéologique' avait certainement été confié aux aides et l'on n'a peut-être pas prêté autant d'attention à ces dessins que s'ils avaient été de la main du maître, à moins que très tôt ils n'aient péri en bloc. Mais c'est surtout peu après que se généralise la méthode qui consiste à dessiner ces mêmes antiques et à les consigner dans des répertoires. Dans les Loges, bien que cette documentation n'ait pas été con-servée, on peut affirmer, je crois, que le vocabulaire à l'antique y est alors mis en oeuvre pour la première fois de manière systé-matique. Il restera valable pendant tout le seizième siècle et même jusqu'à l'époque néo-classique.

Comprend-il l'ensemble des monuments antiques connus à l'époque? Malgré l'abondance du répertoire, il n'en est rien. Le matériel extrêmement riche que les artistes ont sélectionné com-portait occasionnellement des oeuvres grecques, hellénistiques, et surtout des dérivations lointaines de celles-ci, d'époque romaine. C'est le cas notamment des sarcophages, exécutés pour la plupart à l'époque impériale par des artisans peu cultivés, sur la base de

---

[1] La Paix apparaît deux fois dans l'archivolte X et à droite du pilastre II. On peut com-parer à titre d'exemple un bronze de Vespasien sur lequel on retrouve l'attitude de la jeune femme, qui porte aussi un rameau d'olivier, son attribut habituel, et met le feu aux armes amassées près d'un autel. Voir H. Mattingly, *Coins of the Roman Empire in the British Museum* (Londres, 1923–67), II, pl. 21, 4. L'intaille en porphyre est reproduite notamment par E. Kris, *Meister und Meisterwerke der Steinschneidekunst in der italienischen Renaissance* (Vienne, 1929), pl.25, n°96. Sur Léon X chanté comme champion de la paix, voir maintenant J. Shearman, *Raphael's Cartoons in the Collection of Her Majesty the Queen and the Tapestries for the Sistine Chapel* (Londres, 1972), p.15.

[2] Sur ces aspects des Loges, voir N. Dacos, 'Il trastullo di Raffaello', notamment pp.4–8.

modèles hellénistiques. Episodiquement l'on retrouve parmi les sources des Loges des oeuvres romaines plus originales ou plus tardives, datant parfois des deuxième et troisième siècles après Jésus-Christ et répondant à une esthétique différente, qui a rompu avec le classicisme. Mais celles-ci sont généralement écartées et, quand elles sont utilisées, elles sont comme filtrées de leur éléments 'impurs' et transformées selon les critères de l'art classicisant, qui restent l'idéal de Raphaël et de son milieu. L'option du maître est bien précise et n'a rien de commun avec les intentions scientifiques d'un Cassiano Dal Pozzo, par exemple, dans son Museum Chartaceum.[1] On assiste à l'élaboration d'un style idéal, qui dépasse de manière décisive la reconstitution archéologique.

Cette grande souplesse de Raphaël, qui interprète les modèles et n'hésite pas à y introduire des oeuvres de son époque ou des scénettes anecdotiques, nous porte à envisager maintenant le cycle biblique qu'il a situé sur les voûtes et sur le mur interne du soubassement et qui, à première vue, semble opérer une rupture totale avec le décor païen qui l'entoure. Pour en expliquer la présence, on pourrait recourir de prime abord à l'union idéale du monde antique et du monde chrétien que Raphaël s'est efforcé de réaliser surtout dans les *Stanze*. Mais si ses intentions s'étaient bornées à l'exigence abstraite de la fusion des deux cultures, le programme des Loges se serait soldé dans une certaine mesure par un échec. Dieu, Adam, Noé, Abraham, Isaac, Joseph, Moïse, Josué, David, Salomon et le Christ auraient cohabité de manière artificielle avec les créatures du monde dionysiaque, satyres, nymphes, ménades, silènes, faunes . . . les dieux et les héros de la mythologie, qui envahissent les écoinçons, les archivoltes, les pilastres, sans qu'aucun lien ne les rapprochât réellement.

Il existe, je crois, une cohérence bien plus profonde entre les deux pôles du décor. Pour la saisir, il faut se rappeler d'abord comment étaient conçus précédemment les décors à grotesques au début du seizième siècle. Deux des dernières oeuvres de Pinturicchio, la voûte de la Libreria Piccolomini et celle du palais Petrucci, en offrent des exemples-types (Pl. 5*a*). Parmi les grotesques sont introduites de petites scènes mythologiques, situées dans un monde de rêve qui prolonge la tradition des *cassoni* ou au contraire rectifiées du point de vue archéologique d'après l'iconographie des sarco-

---

[1] Sur ce processus, voir notamment N. Dacos, 'La Bible de Raphaël', p.18.

phages. Les ensembles à grotesques, qui dans les deux cas ne comprennent que les voûtes et qu'il faut par conséquent dissocier des cycles qui se déroulent sur les parois, sont donc conçus à l'antique tant dans la forme que dans le contenu.[1]

L'orientation est à peu près semblable dans les premiers décors à l'antique conçus par Raphaël. Je ne parle pas de la loggia de Psyché à la Farnésine, où le mythe illustré est emprunté entièrement à la littérature païenne, mais où le décor se compose essentiellement de figures monumentales et ne laisse aucune place aux grotesques. On peut établir une comparaison plus suggestive avec les pièces qui subsistent de l'appartement du cardinal Bibbiena au Vatican, dont Raphaël a dirigé les travaux en 1516 et qui constituent la première tentative de créer un décor qui fût l'équivalent de ceux que le maître avait étudiés dans les ruines romaines. A la *Stufetta* de l'appartement, les grotesques sont singulièrement proches de leurs modèles. Ils couvrent voûte et parois, où le cycle figuré qu'ils entourent illustre l'histoire de Vénus et d'Amour.[2] A la *Loggetta*, les motifs tirés de la Domus Aurea envahissent également toutes les surfaces et, sur le mur interne, le seul cycle figuré se réduit à trois histoires ayant trait à Apollon, copiées de peintures du columbarium antique qui a été également exploité dans les Loges.[3] Dans l'appartement du cardinal, Raphaël donne la version la plus archéologique qu'on lui connaisse du décor à grotesques et ne laisse aucune place à la culture chrétienne.

Mais cette phase n'est qu'un moment expérimental. Aussitôt après, probablement en 1517, dans les Loges du pape auxquelles le nom de Raphaël est resté attaché, le maître change d'optique, mêle le chrétien au païen et projette une Bible. Dans chacune des treize travées de la galerie, il introduit quatre histoires – tirées toutes sauf le dernier groupe de l'Ancien Testament – au milieu d'un décor qui varie: caissons qui rappellent ceux du Panthéon mais sont ouverts sur le ciel, architectures en trompe-l'oeil qui semblent prolonger à l'étage supérieur les éléments réels de la loggia,

---

[1] N. Dacos, *La découverte de la Domus Aurea*, fig. 97 et 99. Dans les ensembles à grotesques du début du seizième siècle, il existe cependant plusieurs cas où les ornements païens voisinent avec les scènes religieuses, notamment chez Gaudenzio Ferrari, à la chapelle Sainte-Marguerite, à l'église Santa Maria delle Grazie à Varallo (N. Dacos, *La découverte de la Domus Aurea*, fig. 136) ou chez Sodoma, au réfectoire de Sant'Anna in Camprena (ibid. fig. 140). Mais les deux types d'iconographie voisinent toujours de manière artificielle et ne constituent nullement des précédents pour Raphaël.
[2] Ibid. pp.101–2.   [3] Ibid. p.105 et fig.170.

tapisseries de grotesques peuplées de putti, de centaures marins, de satyres et de nymphes (Pl. 5b) ou stucs blancs agrémentés de nymphes dansantes. Les histoires bibliques sont liées intimement au décor, dans lequel elles apparaissent comme des fenêtres imaginaires.

Constituées généralement de quelques figures, les histoires sont à peine plus grandes que celles des grotesques ou des stucs des écoinçons et des archivoltes, de sorte qu'elles semblent se mouvoir dans le même cadre idyllique et mythique. En outre, les scènes sont claires et ne posent aucun problème de lecture. Par leurs petites dimensions et par le ton narratif du récit, les scènes de la Bible ne diffèrent donc nullement des récits légendaires grecs et romains qui étaient introduits dans les premiers ensembles à grotesques. Mais il y a davantage. Si par leurs attitudes et par le décor qui les entoure, nombre de figures semblent faire écho à celles qui égaient les stucs et les grotesques, c'est aussi parce qu'elles procèdent de la même culture et sont inspirées souvent de prototypes archéologiques. L'Adam de la Création d'Eve dérive d'une figure de faune qui joue de la double flûte, sur un relief conservé aujourd'hui à la Galerie Borghèse.[1] Jacob en route vers le pays de Canaan, à califourchon sur sa mule (Pl. 4a), n'est autre que le silène du Triomphe de Dionysos sur le sarcophage largement utilisé pour les stucs (Pl. 4b).[2] L'exemple le plus frappant et qui aurait certainement paru blasphème pendant la Contre-Réforme, est celui du Dieu de la Création d'Eve (Pl. 3b), dans lequel on reconnaît Dionysos en personne sur le relief de la Visite du dieu au poète dramatique (Pl. 3d), qui fait partie également du répertoire de base des stucs et qui a inspiré aussi le Noé de la Construction de l'arche (Pl. 3c).[3] Les souvenirs archéologiques sont donc déterminants pour certains héros de l'Ancien Testament et l'on n'a pas encore insisté sur le fait que cette culture contribue encore davantage à la représentation alors tout à fait nouvelle d'une Bible qui soit l'équivalent de la mythologie classique. Dans le Passage du Jourdain, le fleuve est personnifié par un vieillard barbu, comme d'ailleurs le Tigre du Sacre de Salomon, selon le goût de l'allusion érudite, d'origine archéologique, qui ne s'accorde en rien avec l'iconographie religieuse. Raphaël pousse à ce point l'équation Bible–mythologie que, lorsqu'il doit représenter Joseph et la femme de Putiphar (Pl. 6a), il représente la poursuite amoureuse

---

[1] N. Dacos, 'La Bible de Raphaël', p.17 et fig. 9a–9b.
[2] Voir p.328, note 2.   [3] Voir pp.327–8, note 1.

comme celle d'Apollon et Daphné, qu'il connaissait peut-être par une xylographie d'une édition des Métamorphoses (Pl. 6*b*).[1] L'expression angoissée de Joseph n'est autre que celle de la nymphe et le mouvement des bras levés, dont la ligne ascendante accentue le désarroi d'une manière inattendue pour un homme, s'explique par le souvenir des membres déjà feuillus de la nymphe.

Ailleurs les héros bibliques se comportent comme sur les grands reliefs commémoratifs romains. Les modèles n'appartiennent donc plus uniquement au monde des légendes, mais aussi à celui de l'histoire, comme si, par ce truchement, Raphaël avait tenu à renforcer la vraisemblance de son récit. Le Sacrifice de Noé se déroule comme les cérémonies d'époque impériale; c'est près d'un autel de même provenance qu'a lieu l'Onction de David. Les soldats qui assiègent Jéricho ont les boucliers disposés en tortue, comme sur la colonne Trajane. David triomphe sur un bige comme Titus sur le relief de l'arc érigé en son honneur. L'Adam du Péché originel et le soldat qui s'affaisse sous les coups d'un Amorite dérivent des Gaulois blessés du Louvre et de Venise.[2] Même les variantes les plus inattendues du costume, comme les braies de Noé qui rend grâce à Dieu, des figures qui assistent à la Répartition des terres, à l'Onction de David ou à son triomphe, rappellent encore les barbares de la colonne Trajane. Et la liste pourrait être allongée aisément.

En transposant les textes sacrés sur ce ton de légende et d'histoire, Raphaël a saisi que pour actualiser le portique idéal, à l'antique, qu'il devait décorer, il fallait renoncer aux récits mythologiques, qui auraient rendu la galerie trop érudite, et leur substituer des histoires plus appropriées à la dignité pontificale. En interprétant la Bible de la sorte, comme une mythologie des Temps Modernes, il tendait certainement à la vider de ses implications sacrées. Mais simultanément il trouvait ainsi le moyen voilé de l'enrichir d'une dimension actuelle, que je qualifierais presque de politique. Et la réussite a été totale puisque le cycle qu'il a créé a servi de référence constante jusqu'à la fin du dix-neuvième siècle, même pour les artistes les plus éloignés de la culture antique et les plus engagés dans l'iconographie religieuse, tels que les Nazaréens. Sous leur vêtement à

---

[1] Probablement l'*editio princeps*, parue à Venise en 1497 et souvent rééditée par la suite. Les xylographies sont dues à Zoan Rosso. Cf. Y. F. A. Giraud, *La fable de Psyché. Essai sur un type de métamorphose végétale dans la littérature et dans les arts jusqu'à la fin du XVIIIe siècle* (Genève, 1968), pp.251–2 et fig. 3, p.171.

[2] N. Dacos, 'La Bible de Raphaël', fig. 11–13.

l'antique, en harmonie avec la frénésie païenne du décor, par la manière dont elles sont sélectionnées et conçues, les scènes de l'Ancien Testament répondent au renouveau des études chrétiennes que Léon X favorisait à la fin de son pontificat, lorsque l'exigence de réformes se faisait sentir partout en Europe. Mais ceci sort de notre propos.

Si l'on revient maintenant à la question qui est au centre de nos préoccupations dans ce colloque qui nous réunit, *what needs to be done*, j'ajouterai que je ne crois pas que les mêmes problèmes puissent être posés pour la suite du seizième siècle. La fin du règne de Léon X et les Loges de Raphaël sont une époque et un monument charnières dans l'histoire de la survivance de la culture antique dans notre civilisation occidentale. Il s'agit du moment, bien éphémère, où, du point de vue stylistique, l'antique est assimilé à tel point qu'il est confondu avec la culture contemporaine, selon une conception qui témoigne d'un optimisme fondamental et qui, du point de vue du contenu, permet une union spontanée avec les problèmes déjà brûlants de l'iconographie religieuse. Pendant toute la suite du seizième siècle, lorsque les copies d'antiques abonderont dans les cahiers de croquis, la distance augmentera toujours davantage entre les dessins purement archéologiques et les oeuvres que ceux-ci inspireront. Et dans ce cas, c'est cette distance surtout qu'il faudra étudier.

1*a*   Loggias of Raphael. Detail of pilaster IX.

1*b*   Domus Aurea. Detail of the *Volta delle civette*.

1*c*   Domus Aurea. Detail of the *Volta nera*, after the Codex Escurialensis, fol. 14v.

2*a* Hercules and Admetus. Loggias of Raphael. Detail of archivolt XI.

2*b* Paintings on a Roman columbarium portraying especially Hercules and
Admetus. After the Codex Pighianus, fol.333.

3a Dionysus and child. Loggias of Raphael. Detail of archivolt VII.

3b God creates woman. Loggias of Raphael, vault II.

3c Noah's Ark. Loggias of Raphael, vault III.

3d Visitation of the dramatic poet by Dionysus. Hellenistic relief. London, British Museum.

4*a* Jacob on the road to Canaan. Loggias of Raphael,
vault VI.

4*b* Dionysus in triumph. Roman sarcophagus. London, British Museum.

4*c* Allegorical representation of Peace.
Loggias of Raphael. Detail of archivolt
X.

4*d* Allegorical representation of
Peace. Roman coin.

5a Piccolomini Library. General view of the vault. Siena Cathedral.

5b Loggias of Raphael. General view of vault x.

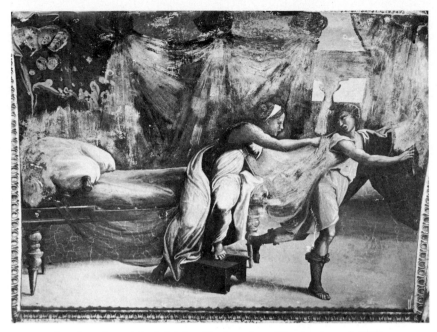

6a   Joseph and Potiphar's wife. Loggias of Raphael, vault VII.

6b   Apollo and Daphne. Woodcut from the 1488 edition of Ovid's *Metamorphoses*.

7a Gozzoli workshop. Capital. Rotterdam, Museum Boymans–van Beuningen.

7b Boccati. Madonna col Bambino. Detail. Perugia Pinacoteca.

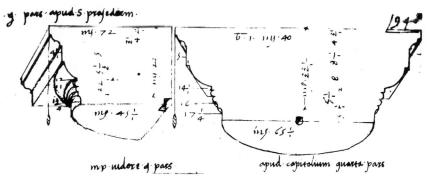

7c Bernardo della Volpaia. Codex Coner fol.94. Capital. London, Sir John Soane's Museum.

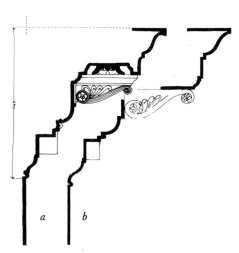

7d Cronaca, Palazzo Strozzi. Cornice. Measured drawing.

7e 'Pseudo-Cronaca'. Measured drawing after Florence, Bibl. Naz. MS II.1.429, fol.50.

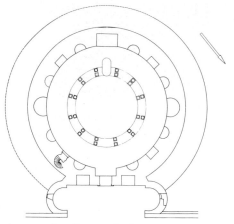

8a Rome. S. Costanza.

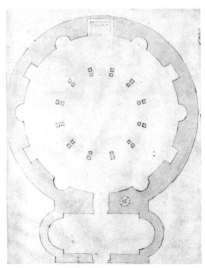

8b G. da Sangallo. S. Constanza. Bibliotheca Vaticana, Cod. Barb. lat. 4424.

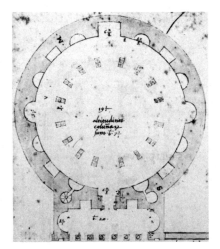

8c Bernado della Volpaia. Codex Coner. S. Costanza. London, Sir John Soane's Museum.

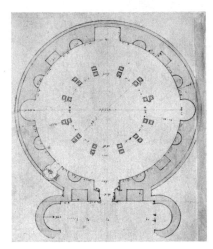

8d 'Master C' of 1519. S. Costanza. Vienna, Albertina AH. 9v.

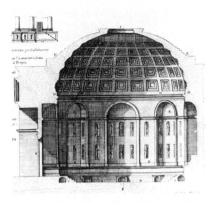

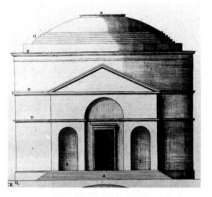

9a   C. Fontana. 'Republican' Pantheon.

9b   C. Fontana. 'Republican' Pantheon.

9c   J. Boumann. French Church. Potsdam, 1752.

10   G. Romano. Sculptor destroying his statues. Fresco. Vatican, Sala di Costantino.

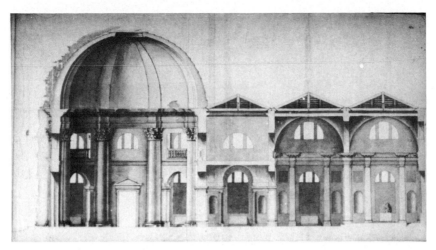

11a Scamozzi. Project for S. Maria delle Celestia, Venice (?). Chatsworth, Duke of Devonshire.

11b Raphael. 'Praxiteles'-horse, Quirinal. Chatsworth, Duke of Devonshire.

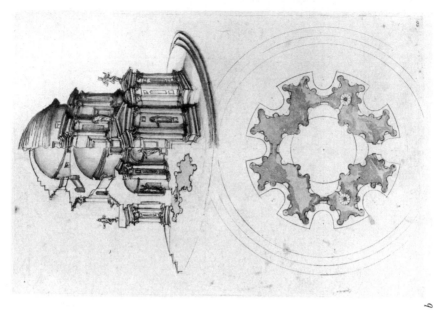

12a Borromini. Rome. S. Ivo della Sapienza.

12b G. B. Montano. Reconstruction of an ancient temple. Drawing. London,

13a   Baalbek. Circular temple.

13b   Polidoro da Caravaggio. Designs
for a circular building. Drawing. Berlin,
Staatliche Museen.

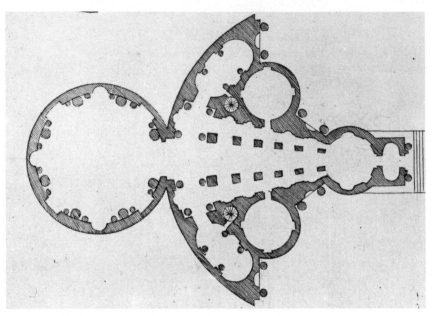

14*a* G. B. Montano. Reconstruction of an ancient temple. Engraving.

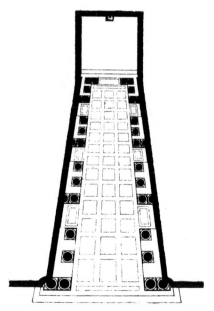

14*b* Borromini. Rome. Palazzo Spada.
Plan of colonnade.

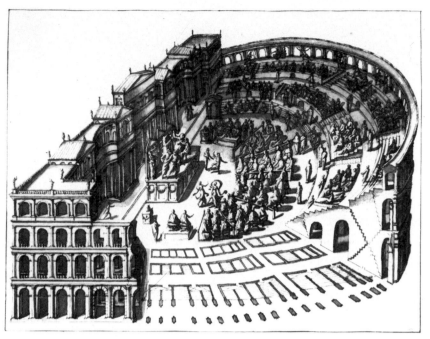

15a   Roman artist, early seventeenth century. Reconstruction of a Roman theatre.
Drawing. Royal Library, Windsor Castle. (Copyright reserved.)

15b   Sabratha. Theatre.

a

b

c

d

16a The handwriting of John Collet, from the Register of Doctors' Commons (p.211).
16b The 'red annotating hand' from the Mercers' Hall copy of the Statutes of St Paul's
School (p. 211). 16c The 'red annotating hand' and the hand of Peter Meghen, from MS
Corpus Christi College Cambridge 355 (p.217). 16d The handwriting of the British
Library transcript of the Statutes of St Paul's School, MS Add.6274 (p.212).

26

CRITICISM OF ANCIENT ARCHITECTURE IN THE SIXTEENTH AND SEVENTEENTH CENTURIES[1]

T. BUDDENSIEG

It is the intention of this paper to point to the rather surprising fact that there are very few instances in fifteenth- and sixteenth-century architecture, where we can speak of a productive identification with the system of values underlying ancient architectural practice or even of an acceptance of that system. During my lecture, I shall have reason to mention only one outstanding architect in this context – and he will not be Palladio.

I shall not tire you with a long list of all the criticisms which were levelled by writers and architects at every stage of the Renaissance against a multitude of ancient buildings in a multitude of European towns. Such an exhaustive account would require a book to do it justice, and perhaps the book is one that ought to be written. But for the purposes of this present survey, I shall make no mention of those disparaging remarks that rested on personal preferences or dislikes, of the type, say, that the Pantheon is too big, too small, too high, too narrow, better seen at full moon than in daylight and so on. I shall try instead to distinguish about seven different types of what appear to be more consistent criticisms levelled against ancient architecture, and I hope you will not object to my going outside the boundaries set by this conference, and referring in part to the paper I gave at the conference in 1969.[2]

---

[1] This paper was written during my unforgettable stay in Cambridge as Slade Professor and Fellow of King's College. My gratitude goes to these institutions and to Michael Jaffé for his hospitality. R. R. Bolgar has kindly looked through my English text.

[2] T. Buddensieg, 'Criticism and praise of the Pantheon in the Middle Ages and the Renaissance', in *Classical Influences on European Culture, A.D. 500–1500*, ed. R. R. Bolgar (Cambridge, 1971), pp.259 ff.

I

There are a few instances of explicit criticism of ancient sculpture and architecture in the general and radical medieval dismissal of ancient architecture and sculpture in the form of pagan temples and idols, as instanced by St Catherine's dislike for ancient statues illustrated in a painting in the Kress Collection of about 1440,[1] or the hostility of St Nicolas depicted in a fresco of the thirteenth century in Bojana, Jugoslavia.[2]

Since the Pantheon is the key monument in the post-antique *Wirkungsgeschichte* of ancient architecture, I may be allowed perhaps to mention briefly a few aspects of its long history. Before its conversion into a church, the Pantheon was called a dirty temple, a house of darkness, inhabited by the Devil. One of its main architectural features, the *opaion* in the cupola, was explained as a hole broken through the roof by the Devil in his desperate attempt to flee from the building at Pope Boniface IV's consecration of the Temple of all Gods to the Mother of God the Virgin Mary, and, as Herman von Fritzlar says, nobody dared thereafter to close the hole. Other chronicles describe the *impluvium*, the large stone in the floor of the Pantheon, as a lid placed by the Devil to cover his escape.

The actual process of building the Pantheon is related in the *Legenda Aurea*: the architect had started that temple on so huge a scale that nobody was able to erect the dome. It was therefore decided to fill the whole building with earth mixed with money. After the dome had been easily completed, the Roman people shovelled the earth out of the temple to get hold of the money, and in a few hours the temple was empty. This story is still told by Vasari in his life of Brunelleschi and by Baglione in his appraisal in 1640 of Giacomo della Porta's cupola of St Peter's: the latter, he claims, has surpassed the Pantheon because Giacomo was able to build his vault without a heap of earth.[3] Vasari's story is more interesting. In their search for the right man to build the cupola of their cathedral, the Florentine *Operai* and *Consoli* had to listen among others to a German architect, who proposed to fill the building with earth, to mix this with pennies, *mescolare quattrini fra essa*, and to

---

[1] G. Fiocco, *L'Arte di Andrea Mantegna* (Venice, 1959), pl. 43.
[2] K. Mijatev, *Die Wandmalereien in Bojana* (Dresden, Sofia, 1961), pl. 58.
[3] See p.260, n.2 of my paper quoted above, p.335, n.2.

build the cupola on that basis. Then the *popolo* were to be 'allowed' to take the earth away, thus saving the cost of emptying the church.

Against this background of fairy tales, Brunelleschi explained his method of vaulting *senza tanti legni e senza pilastri o terra . . . e facilissimamente senza armatura* (scaffolding).[1] His claim to build the cupola without earth is an implicit rejection of the story in the *Legenda Aurea*, and his further promise to need little wood and no scaffolding apparently refers to another tale concerning the Pantheon that aroused the amazement of the medieval chroniclers. In his widely read life of St Dionysius, Hugo of Flavigny writing about 1100 mentions the wickedness and cruelty of the Roman emperor Domitian. To demonstrate his sacrilegious *cultura deorum falsorum* he had built in the fifth year of his reign a *templum sine lignorum ammixtione*, which he called the Pantheon.[2] This building, then, is the creation of a criminal with the help of witchcraft; and to the Monk of Malmesbury in the fourteenth century all the pagan buildings in Rome appeared to be such frightening *miranda vestigia de mirabilibus arte magica constructa.*[3]

Lurking behind these legends of the Pantheon, we are able, it seems to me, to discern a criticism of ancient architecture which is different in the level of its rationality and couched in the guise of fairy tales, but which in the final analysis is as general and total as the Renaissance criticism of the Gothic style. Just as for Raphaël and Vasari, Gothic architecture was the result of a lack of taste and the lack of a sense of beauty due to the general stupidity of the Germans, so for the northern chroniclers pagan architecture was the work of the Devil, and the Pantheon in particular was the house of the Devil before he was expelled from it, and the Virgin Mary moved into a cleaned building.

II

Petrarch and Boccaccio and their disciples brought about a radically different attitude towards the visual remains of antiquity. Once the temples of Rome were no longer *vestigia . . . arte magica constructa*

---

[1] G. Vasari, *Le vite*, ed. Milanesi, II, 345.

[2] *Chronicon*, ed. Pertz in *MGH*, SS.VIII (1848), 291.

[3] A Monk of Malmesbury, *Eulogium historiarum chronicon . . . usque ad a.d. MCCCLXVI*, ed. F. Scott Haydon, in *Rer. Brit. med. aev. script.* I (London 1858), p.410.

as they had been for the Monk of Malmesbury but *testimonio della grandezza, dell'anima di collui chi edificò*,[1] the medieval criticism of ancient architecture was no longer possible. If the Roman statues, those idols and demons of the Devil, could be regarded, as Pope Sixtus IV expressed it in a commemorative inscription of 1471, as the *insignes statuas, priscae excellentiae virtutisque monumentum*,[2] then ancient statuary too had to be accepted once again as virtuous, beautiful, and exemplary and as the visual expression of a glorious past. This early Renaissance acceptance of the remains of classical antiquity led to what one might call a romantic or naïve equation of ancient and contemporary architecture with the result that ancient Roman and contemporary Florentine buildings were supposed to look virtually the same, to be visually without a difference.

Two splendid examples of this equation, which was promoted particularly by Florentine painters, are Gozzoli's *Babilonia* in Pisa[3] and Niccolo Fiorentino's *Massacre of the Innocents* on the High Altar at Salamanca, a composition which dates from 1445;[4] and to this same romantic vision of Roman architecture there belongs the highly interesting, still insufficiently appreciated, group of fantastic reconstructions of Roman buildings, probably Sienese in origin and generally associated with Cronaca, which had a curious and even European fame.[5] There, a faint but recognisable substratum of archaeological information is buried under an architectural vocabulary which is simply a fantastic exaggeration of the Tuscan architec-

---

[1] Boccaccio, Letter to Francesco Nelli, 28 June 1363, in *Opere latine minori*, ed. A. F. Massèra (Bari, 1928), nr.xII, 165.

[2] Forcella, *Iscrizioni* I, nr. 16. E. Müntz, *Les Arts à la cour des Papes*, III (1882), 169, n.1. R. Lanciani, *Storia degli scavi*, I, 76. W. S. Heckscher, *Sixtus IIII aeneas insignes statuas romano populo restituendas censuit* ('s Gravenhage, 1955).

[3] See p.262 and n.2 of my study quoted above, p.335 n.2.

[4] M. Gómez-Moreno, in *Archivo español de Arte y Arqueologia*, IV (1928), I ff., pls. 19, 20; A. de Bosque, *Artistes italiens en Espagne* (Paris, 1965), pp.111 ff., 479 f. in *Catalogo monumental de España*, vol.9; M. Gómez-Moreno, *Provincia de Salamanca* (Madrid, 1967), pl. 83.

[5] See A. Bartoli, *I monumenti antichi di Roma nei disegni degli Uffizi di Firenze*, I (Rome, 1914), figs. 33–42. G. Scaglia, 'Fantasy Architecture of Roma antica', in *Arte Lombarda* XV, II, (1970), 9 ff. The surprising identity between these drawings and the architectural background in paintings by Liberale da Verona (in Berlin and Cambridge) and those by Matteo di Giovanni (in Chicago) point rather, as I have tried to show in papers given at the Bibliotheca Hertziana and the Warburg Institute 1968 and 1969, to a Sienese, not north Italian (Scaglia) origin of the whole series of drawings. The models for the 'romantic' reconstructions of the Sienese Pseudo-Cronaca may go back to the young Francesco di Giorgio. See also the following note. For additional drawings of this group in Bayonne and Oxford, Christ Church, see T. Buddensieg and G. Schweikhart, 'Falconetto als Zeichner' in *Zeitschrift für Kunstgeschichte* (1970), p.39, n.38.

ture of the fifteenth century.[1] The mingling of the echoes of ancient descriptions, medieval *mirabilia* legends and the awesome presence of the ruins of Rome led not to an archaeological examination of ancient buildings but to the naïve belief that they had looked more or less like fifteenth-century architecture, only enormous in size and expensively decorated.

III

This decorative rendering of ancient art and architecture was suddenly superseded by a third phase in the handling of the classical inheritance, which might be called the architects' practical approach. Architects like Giuliano and Antonio da Sangallo the Elder, Simone del Pollaiuolo called il Cronaca, Francesco di Giorgio Martini and Bernardo della Volpaia transformed what Alberti dubbed 'the painters' approach' to architecture[2] into an analytical investigation of its ancient monuments. Purely decorative renderings of ornamental details intended primarily for the use of painters were replaced by measured sections in perspective of architectural elements, useless now for painters but meant to be employed and reproduced by the architect in his own work. The drawing of a capital in Gozzoli's Rotterdam sketchbook (Pl. 7*a*) reappearing exactly in Boccati's *Madonna col Bambino* in Perugia (Pl. 7*b*) may be compared with a drawing of a capital in the Codex Coner (Pl. 7*c*) to demonstrate the fundamental change from a painter's to an architect's rendering of ancient art.[3]

These exact reproductions, which appeared first in the latter

[1] G. Scaglia's attempt to locate the prototype for the 'Pseudo-Cronaca' series in northern Italy, possibly in the circle of Mantegna, does not seem convincing to me. The series of copies mentioned by G. Scaglia, loc. cit., can be considerably enlarged, all being Sienese or Tuscan: so-called Fra Giocondo, Uffizi A 1686 ff. (almost certainly Sienese); Florence, Laur., Cod. Ashb. 1828 App., fols.99, 113, 114 (very close to Francesco di Giorgio); Signorelli, Crucifixion, Washington; P. Cattaneo, Uffizi A 3299; Berlin, Kunstbibl. Hdz 3918 r and v; so-called J. Sansovino, Uffizi A 4331, 4332; Sallustio Peruzzi, Uffizi A 106 r (= Bartoli, op. cit., fig. 693) and v; Neroni (il Riccio), fresco in Monte Oliveto; Taccuino O. Vanocci Biringucci in Siena, Bibl. Comunale, S.IV.I.

[2] L. B. Alberti, *De re aedificatoria* ed. G. Orlandi (Milan, 1966) I, 98.

[3] For the Rotterdam sketchbook see B. Degenhart and A. Schmitt, *Corpus der italienischen Zeichnungen 1300–1450*, pt.I (Berlin, 1968), nr.434, fol.I v, pl. 327b, 479 f. For the Codex Coner see below, p.341, n.I. For the development of Renaissance architectural drawing, see the classic study by W. Lotz, 'Das Raumbild in der italienischen Architektur der Renaissance', in *Mitteilungen des Kunsthistorischen Instituts in Florenz* VII (1956), 218 ff.

half of the fifteenth century, led to actual copies being made of details of ancient architecture, a famous example being Cronaca's copy of an entablature of the Forum of Trajan in Rome for his own cornice of the Palazzo Strozzi in Florence. If one compares the measured profiles of both compositions (Pl. 7d, e), one is struck by the unprecedented closeness and at the same time the subtle deviations of Cronaca from his model, due to the enormous height of the Strozzi Palace and its generally greater dimensions. Unfortunately the beautiful studies of the Forum of Trajan in the Biblioteca Nazionale in Florence used for this composition cannot be attributed to Cronaca as Alfonso Bartoli proposed, because of the handwriting.[1]

This new empirical and analytical method destroyed the naïve belief in the general congruence of ancient and modern architecture. By excavating, measuring and drawing ancient buildings, Francesco di Giorgio and others realised the fundamental differences between their own rules of what was to be considered good, perfect and faultless and the rules apparently underlying a very different aesthetic system in Roman architecture.

Let me demonstrate this with a few drawings after the Roman church, S. Costanza, generally believed in the Renaissance to have been formerly a *tempio di Baccho*.

There exist two drawings of the ground plan by Giuliano da Sangallo the Elder.[2] When we compare the first of these with a modern ground plan (Pl. 8a, b) of the ancient building,[3] we notice that Giuliano changes the niches of the outer wall in such a way that they correspond exactly with the *intercolumnia*. At the same time he systematises the sequence of the niches: the square ones are placed to form a cross and there are two round ones between each pair.

[1] Florence, Bibl. Nazionale, Cod. II, 1, 429 fol.50 r and v; A. Bartoli, 'La recinzione meridionale del Foro Romano' in *Atti della Pontificia Accademia Romana di Archeologia* Ser. III *Memorie* (Misc. G. B. de Rossi) vol.I, p.II (Rome, 1924), 177 ff., pl. 34. For the cornice of the Palazzo Strozzi see C. v. Stegmann and H. v. Geymüller, *Die Architektur der Renaissance in Toscana*, IV (Munich, 1890–1906), fig. 12. J. Durm, *Die Baukunst der Renaissance in Italien* (Leipzig, 1914²), p.290. The drawings pl. 7d and e I owe to Dipl.Ing. G. Kaster.
[2] Chr. Hülsen, *Il libro di Giuliano da Sangallo. Codice Vaticano Barberiniano latino 4424* (Leipzig, 1910), fols.16 and 39.
[3] F. W. Deichmann, *Frühchristliche Kirchen in Rom* (Basel, 1948), pp.25 ff. plan 4 (drawn by M. Stettler). Th. Kraus, *Das römische Weltreich: Propyläen-Kunstgeschichte*, vol.2 (Berlin, 1967), pp.197 f. fig. 40 (F. Rakob). H. Stern, 'Les mosaiques de l'Eglise de Saint-Constance à Rome', in *Dumbarton Oaks Papers* 12 (1958), 157 ff.

This deviation from what Giuliano must have seen in the building cannot be properly explained by carelessness or lack of interest. It seems to me a deliberate criticism of what Giuliano apparently considered a serious lack of correspondence between the inner circle of columns and the system of the outer wall. His rendering of the building is one possible way of correcting that 'mistake'. Then, in the second drawing, he attempts to improve the temple by an alternation of round and square niches and a complete and harmonious relationship between the inner circle of double columns and the rhythm of the outer wall.

Bernardo della Volpaia, the great draughtsman of the Codex Coner in Sir John Soane's Museum in London,[1] tries another solution (Pl. 8c) to the criticised lack of *concordantia* and *conformità* in the composition of the *Tempio di Baccho*. He takes over the number, form and sequence of the niches in the outer wall, but he increases the number of the double columns from 12 to 16 and achieves therewith the correspondence he wants. In addition, he corrects one 'mistake' of the ancient architect after another: the distance of the outer columns to the wall is equal to the width of the *intercolumnium*. The distance of the circle of columns from the outer wall is one third of the radius of the building.

This analysis shows, I hope, the fundamental difference between a Renaissance conception of architectural composition and that of an ancient architect. The latter was interested primarily in the visual relationship of plastic units. He constructed his building to please the eye of a constantly moving beholder, creating changing vistas. He composed it of rhythmically organised horizontal units with little concern for their vertical linear coherence.[2] The ancient architect

[1] Th. Ashby, 'Sixteenth-century drawings of Roman buildings attributed to Andreas Coner', in *Papers of the British School at Rome* II (1904), pl. 20, fol.13. T. Buddensieg, 'Bernardo della Volpaia und Francesco da Sangallo. Der Autor des Codex Coner und seine Stellung im Sangallo-Kreis', in *Jahrbuch der Bibliotheca Hertziana (Festschrift Graf Wolff Metternich)* XV (1974) pp.89 ff.

[2] See above, p.335, n.2 for exactly the same difference in ancient and Renaissance architectural composition, in the Pantheon; also M. Gosebruch, 'Vom Pantheon', in *Römische Quartalschrift* (1966), 161 ff. It should be noted that Paulus Silentiarius in his *Ekphrasis* praises the 'audacity' of the architects of the Hagia Sophia in Istanbul because in the half-round 'conchae' they 'place six columns above two columns' giving the impression that 'they are standing in the air': 391–4:

ἓξ δ' [ὑπὸ Θ]εσσαλικοῖσι καὶ οὐ δύο κίοσι λάμπει.
ἔστι δὲ θαμβῆσαι νόον ἀνέρος, ὅς ποτε δοιαῖς
πῆξατο θαρσαλέως ἐπὶ κίοσι τρισσάκι δοιάς,
οὐδὲ βάσιν κενεοῖο κατ' ἠέρος ἔτρεσε πῆξαι.

341

would have argued against his Renaissance critics that axial relationships, linear connections, equal distances were of limited interest to
him because one could *see* them only on that abstraction, the drawing
of a ground plan. And he might have accused Giuliano and Bernardo
of a basically Gothic architectural practice and aesthetic, in that
they achieved the unity of the building by addition of equal parts.
We have precisely the same Renaissance criticism of ancient
architecture, when Antonio da Sangallo the Younger says of S.
Vitale in Ravenna, taking it for a Temple of Neptune, that it is
fatto di mala compositione, even if he admits that *la fantasia è bella*.[1] In
another context, he acknowledges his esteem for its architectural
detail as being *perfetto in sè*; but says that often a detail is *imperfetto*
with relation to the whole, 'perché resta li, e non seguita, e chon-
pagnia l'opera; quale è cosa pessima'.[2]

In the presence of this widespread controversy about what many
Renaissance architects took to be basic mistakes in the principles of
ancient architectural composition, it cannot come as a surprise that
a carefully measured and correct drawing of a classical building like
the beautiful ground plan of Santa Costanza in the Albertina in
Vienna (Pl. 8*d*) is a great rarity among the thousands of fifteenth-
and sixteenth-century drawings of ancient architecture.[3] But this
will be discussed in the last section of this paper.

IV

With Antonio da Sangallo the Younger we reach the fourth type of
criticism of ancient architecture: Vitruvian dogmatism. Whereas
Giuliano da Sangallo, Francesco di Giorgio and Bernardo della

See P. Friedländer, *Johannes von Gaza und Paulus Silentiarius. Kunstbeschreibungen justini-
anischer Zeit* (Leipzig and Berlin, 1912), 128, 238. I owe advice and confirmation to
my colleague Professor Rudolf Kassel. The text quoted by H. Jantzen, *Die Hagia
Sophia* (Cologne, 1967), p.68. English translation by C. Mango, *The Art of the Byzantine
Empire 312–1453* (Englewood Cliffs, 1972), p.81. It is fascinating to observe that what
Paulus praises as 'audacity' Francesco di Giorgio criticises as a 'mistake': '... tutti li
vacui debbano essare sopra li vacui ... colonna sopra colonna'. For the full text
see p.264, n.1 of the work cited above, p.335, n.2. Charles Perrault, to quote only one
more author, criticises in Versailles exactly the same 'negligence': '... les pilastres de
l'attique ... posent la plupart sur le vuide' etc.; see his *Parallèles des anciens et des modernes
en ce qui regarde les arts et les sciences* (Paris, 1688), p.165.
[1] Uffizi A 887 v.
[2] That is part of Antonio's criticism of Raphael's plan for St Peter's. See H. de Geymüller,
Les projets primitifs pour la basilique de Saint-Pierre de Rome (Paris, Vienna, 1880), p.300.
[3] See below, p.346.

Volpaia drew the remarkable conviction that they would be able to improve even the most celebrated ancient buildings from a perhaps unconscious continuation of a medieval *Bauhütten* tradition, Antonio da Sangallo based his far more severe criticism on his understanding of Vitruvius. He measured literally every single building and fragment of ancient Rome with the help of his *fratelli, cugini, cognati,* and *garzoni.* He produced and collected almost a thousand such studies, preserved in the Uffizi, trying to prove that the actual buildings in Rome, the rules of Vitruvius and his own architecture followed identical principles. If a deviation from these *regole* was discerned, the blame went either to imperfect knowledge of the object or to the ancient architect as in the case of the Pantheon. I have discussed his criticism of that most famous of ancient buildings in the eyes of the Renaissance in my paper at the 1969 conference together with Michelangelo's own view about the defects of the Pantheon and his devastating criticism of Antonio's plans for St Peter's.[1]

V

Michelangelo's opinion, related by Vasari and Cipriani, that the lack of coherence in the interior design of the Pantheon was due to the uneven talents of three masters working at different times, is an early testimony of our fifth type of criticism, based on historical arguments; but Michelangelo was perhaps preceded in this by Baldassare Peruzzi's analysis of the Pantheon.[2]

The Roman baroque architect, Carlo Fontana, also looked at the Pantheon and was unsatisfied with its present state. He attempted to reconstruct what he thought was a more austere temple, reflecting Roman piety in republican times: the real or '*Ur*-Pantheon' which did not have the overornate appearance supposedly given to the building later by Agrippa (Pl. 9*a, b*). He eliminated the columns and carried the arches of the sidechapels right into the eliminated attic and up to the foot of the cupola.[3]

If we look, with Carlo Fontana's purified Pantheon in mind, at the

---

[1] See the paper quoted above, p.335, n.2.
[2] See H. Burns, 'A Peruzzi Drawing in Ferrara', in *Mitteilungen des Kunsthistorischen Instituts in Florenz* XII (1966), 249 f., n.16.
[3] C. Fontana, *Templum Vaticanum et ipsius origo* (Rome, 1694), pp.454 ff. See the plates on pp.457, 465, 467.

interior of Bernini's church at Ariccia dedicated like the Pantheon to the Virgin, we shall perhaps understand Bernini's church as an attempt to produce such a pious, 'republican' reduction of Agrippa's splendid imperial temple.

At the exterior, Fontana reduces Agrippa's rich porch with its giant columns to a simple entrance. That again is taken over in Ariccia. Thus Bernini criticises the existing Pantheon's external appearance and interior design by 'quoting' an alleged republican predecessor more suitable for the desired pious and humble appearance of the church.[1]

VI

This criticism of the splendour of Roman imperial architecture on the basis of republican simplicity might be held to reflect the taste of the Counter-Reformation and what I should like to call its *ars humilis* criticism of ancient pagan art and architecture.

In the Sala di Costantino of the Vatican, the Triumph of Christianity represented in enormous frescoes on all four walls is quietly accompanied by two small neglected monochrome paintings by Giulio Romano in the window-embrasures, which I may be allowed to discuss in this context.[2] One shows Pope Gregory the Great in his study, writing under the inspiration of the dove. Opposite (Pl. 10) we see the atelier of a sculptor with unfinished statues and blocks of stone and a man dressed as a sculptor destroying with a hammer his own statues of the pagan gods. It is a good illustration of the widespread opinion of humanist historians, including Ghiberti and Vasari, that with the rise of Christianity the *artes* came to an end; a universally deplored process, which this painting interprets in a veiled criticism levelled against the Christian Church and depicted as a savage act of self-destruction. In the Stanza della Segnatura, Leo X's concern for the preservation of the relics of Rome's ancient grandeur is manifest in the picture of Augustus

---

[1] R. Wittkower, *Art and Architecture in Italy 1600 to 1750* (Harmondsworth, 1958), pp.118,f., pls. 62, 64. The Dutch architect J. Boumann's French Church in Potsdam of 1752 (Pl. 9c) is another striking example of Carlo Fontana's 'republican' Pantheon as a church. See H. Kania, *Potsdamer Baukunst* (Potsdam, 1916), pp.22 f. The widespread discussion of the 'original' Pantheon led to a complete misconception of that building and Roman architecture far into the nineteenth century.

[2] T. Buddensieg, 'Gregory the Great, the destroyer of pagan idols', in *Journal of the Warburg and Courtauld Institutes* 28 (1965), 62 ff., pls. 6, 7.

preventing Virgil from burning the *Aeneid*. Gregory the Great did not prevent, but induced our sculptor, perhaps encouraged him, to destroy his works. But what two years before the *Sacco di Roma* was considered a deplorable event, became at the end of the sixteenth century a glorification of the victory of Christ over paganism. In the ceiling of the Sala di Costantino by Tommaso Laureti a golden crucifix has replaced the smashed marble of a Mercury.

The zeal of the Counter-Reformation, particularly of Pope Sixtus V, who criticised the generous display of ancient statuary in public and private places in Rome and removed, even destroyed statues, has one surprising parallel, so far as I know, in the architecture of the end of the sixteenth century. In 1582 Vincenzo Scamozzi designed a church for the rich nuns of S. Maria delle Celestia near the Arsenal in Venice. Ten years later the church lacked only the roof, when a controversy arose about the suitability of its form, *poco o nulla dissimile della Rotonda di Roma*. Finally, the church was pulled down, a different one was begun and consecrated in 1611, which also has disappeared. We have only a detailed description of Scamozzi's design, no visual record of its appearance.[1] Nevertheless, I should like to associate an unpublished drawing of a church, certainly to be attributed to Scamozzi and preserved at Chatsworth,[2] with some stage in the planning process of S. Maria delle Celestia (Pl. 11*a*) although it is different from the description given by Stringa of his design. Scamozzi's interpretation of the Pantheon was critical and austere, but for all that it did not escape the criticism of the Venetian nuns. The *opaion*, the general grandeur of his rotunda, were still too Pantheon-like not to clash with the rigid prescription of Carlo

[1] The church was situated east of S. Francesco della Vigna. We owe a careful description to G. Stringa, *La Venezia gia descritta da Messer Francesco Sansovino* (Venice, 1604), pp.426f. T. Temanza, *Vita di Vincenzo Scamozzi* (Venice, 1770), pp.xvi f. F. Barbieri, *Vincenzo Scamozzi* (Verona and Vicenza, 1952), pp.100 f., 129.

[2] Chatsworth, Duke of Devonshire, Bookcase 25, shelf A[a], Drawings vol.xxxv, fol.63: careful pen drawing with various shades of brown wash, outside the rotunda blue; 70.5 × 40.5 cm on Burlington mount, watermark Lamb with banner (?). The style of the drawing and of the design point decidedly to Scamozzi, an attribution confirmed by Howard Burns with whom, and with Caroline Elam who made the photograph, I had the pleasure of studying the architectural drawings at Chatsworth. The rotunda, inscribed in a square, is certainly more Pantheon-like than any other church by Scamozzi or generally in Renaissance Venice. The resemblance with the Rocca Pisano is obvious. Stringa, op. cit., 427, with remarkable precision gives the two reasons, one iconographical, one formal, for Scamozzi's design: '. . . in forma d'una bella ritonda; parendo che cosi propriamente si convenisse alla Vergine . . . et anco perche in questa città tanto copiosa di fabriche, non si vedeva (come in Roma et altrove) una simile maniera di edificio.'

Borromeo that contemporary architects should follow the style of the humble early Christian churches, round plans were used for the temples of pagan idols.[1] The decision of the zealous nuns to pull down Scamozzi's tribute to the Santa Maria Rotonda in Rome reminds us of that early Christian sculptor in the *Sala di Costantino*. After exactly one thousand years, it concludes the history of the criticism and appraisal of that building with the argument of the hammer.

VII

Our last form of reassessment of ancient art and architecture lacks any trace of the hand of criticism described above. We must speak now of Raphael. To reconstruct the far-reaching influence of his ideas about the art of the ancients, it would be necessary to study the considerable number of architectural drawings of ancient buildings which are or should be associated with his workshop or his initiative; and the result of such a study might well be that Raphael was assisted in his last years by as many architectural assistants as by painters.

One of these architects or architectural draughtsmen is an Anonymus whose drawings are preserved in Vienna (Pl. 8*d*). I should like now to return to his remarkable ground plan of Santa Costanza which we mentioned above.[2]

Only modern standards of archaeological scholarship (Pl. 8*a*) would find details in this drawing not in accordance with the actual building, and they would be few. The undeniable fact that such a correct drawing is unknown before Raphael, and the further fact that it appears for the first time in the workshop of Raphael leads to the inevitable conclusion, I think, that accuracy in the case of this drawing means an acceptance of ancient architecture as such and, furthermore, a deliberate refusal to alter or to 'improve' it by 'correcting' its alleged mistakes.

If all attempts to reconstruct ancient architecture before Raphael

---

[1] Carlo Borromeo, *Instructiones fabricae et supellectilis ecclesiasticae* in *Trattati d'arte del Cinquecento*, ed. P. Barocchi (Bari, 1962), III, 9 ff. See S. Sinding-Larsen, 'Some functional and iconographical aspects of the centralized Church in the Italian Renaissance', in *Acta ad archaeologiam et artium historiam pertinentia* II (Rome, 1965), 205 ff.

[2] H. Egger, *Kritisches Verzeichnis der stadtrömischen Architekturzeichnungen* I (Vienna, 1903), 13, 18, nr.9 v. For the correct date 1519 on one of the drawings see *Münchner Jahrbuch der bildenden Kunst* 13 (1962), 44, nr.11. For the Raphaelesque style and related drawings see the article quoted below, p.347, n.2, p.68.

led to what we called a romantic equation of the supposedly ancient with Quattrocento architecture, to mainly fantastic dreams of ancient architectural grandeur, and to a supposedly improved antiquity according to a post-antique building practice and aesthetic, then, I should think, the appearance of precise drawings of ancient buildings testifies not so much to the beginnings of archaeology and architectural history but rather, when taken together with Raphael's own architectural designs, to his vision and belief that he would be able to revive ancient architecture to an unprecedented extent. Certainly, this new approach towards ancient architecture must be associated with Leo X's tremendous commission to Raphael to undertake an archaeological reconstruction of ancient Rome, which was interrupted by his early death in April 1520. It seems to me that this synthesis of factual correctness in the reconstruction of the architecture of a distant past and the immediate influence it had on Raphael's own designs is what distinguishes these drawings from the archaeologically useful, but architecturally unproductive, studies of ancient buildings of which the work of the so-called Anonymus Destailleur of the second half of the sixteenth century serves as an example.

What needs to be laboriously reconstructed in the architectural drawings produced under Raphael's influence can be grasped immediately in Raphael's own extraordinary drawing (Pl. 11*b*) of the 'Praxiteles' horse on the Quirinal, preserved at Chatsworth,[1] transfiguring it to the greatness of a Parthenon horse. But in surpassing the late antique statue, Raphael does not just give us a study of a lively horse like Heemskerck and most of the artists who admired the Quirinal *Colossi*. His drawing calls to mind all its great classical precedents. Yet, at the same time, it remains a portrait of an ancient statue in Rome. Raphael wants us to note his measurements and his careful documentation of its state of preservation. Knowledge and imagination, historic distance and eternal presence, Antiquity and High Renaissance – it is a miraculous fusion. This was the kind of revival of ancient sculpture Raphael must have hoped and planned for his own tomb in the Pantheon where his sculptural assistant, Lorenzetti, tried with a remarkable degree of success to represent the Virgin Mary in the appearance of the Roman statue of a Hygieia.[2]

[1] J. B. Shaw, *Old Master Drawings from Chatsworth* (London, 1973), 10, nr.56. John Shearman kindly pointed out to me the importance of this drawing in our context.
[2] T. Buddensieg, 'Raffaels Grab', in *Munuscula discipulorum. Festschrift für Hans Kauffmann* (Berlin, 1968), pp.45 ff.

Michelangelo, whose approach to antiquity was radically different, followed Raphael in his refusal to criticise ancient architecture according to a handy list of rules that defined a simple method for distinguishing good from bad and in his refusal to correct according to these rules the alleged mistakes of the ancients into what in the case of Antonio da Sangallo's St Peter, Michelangelo considered an almost tragic fall back into the errors of Gothic architecture.

Nobody has so far been able to define the impact of ancient architecture in, say, Michelangelo's Campidoglio design. But we know that in spite of his refusal to quote, correct, reconstruct, circumscribe or copy the ancients, he ensured a continued greatness for the Capitol and *public* (and civic) life and function for the only ancient statue to have it still, the Marcus Aurelius.

27

BAROQUE ARCHITECTURE AND CLASSICAL ANTIQUITY

ANTHONY BLUNT

The seventeenth century witnessed a great advance in the scientific study of classical archaeology. Men like Fabri de Peiresc and Cassiano dal Pozzo at the beginning of the century and Bernard de Montfaucon at the end collected the available evidence in a much more scientific manner than their predecessors and brought together a body of material which is still of interest to students, even if much of the interpretation put upon it at the time has to be rejected.

In the sixteenth century artists and archaeologists had made drawings of ancient buildings and statues, but in both cases their choice had been limited to the most celebrated works, though some, notably Fulvio Orsini, the librarian of Cardinal Alessandro Farnese, had greater curiosity and covered a wider field. Seventeenth-century archaeologists approached the subject in a much more encyclopedic spirit. Pozzo, who lived in Rome, was well placed to satisfy his ambition which was, quite simply, to collect or have made drawings of every accessible ancient object whether it was a building, a statue, a lamp, a bronze pin, or a fragment of pottery, anything in short which could help him to build up a picture of ancient life as well as ancient art. Montfaucon went a step further and published his material in the fifteen folio volumes of the *Antiquité expliquée* which appeared between 1719 and 1724 and contained upwards of a thousand plates, many illustrating ten or a dozen objects;[1] but Pozzo's drawings, which are mainly now at Windsor,[2] were available to any artist in Rome and were avidly studied by painters

---

[1] An English edition appeared between 1721 and 1725.

[2] The drawings have been studied by C. Vermeule in a series of articles: 'The Dal Pozzo–Albani drawings of classical antiquities', *Art Bulletin* XXXVIII (1956), 31 ff.; 'Aspects of scientific archaeology in the seventeenth century', *Proceedings of the American Philosophical Society*, CII (1958), 193 ff.; 'The Dal Pozzo–Albani drawings ... in the British Museum', *Transactions of the American Philosophical Society*, NS I, pt.5, pp.1 ff. The last article deals with the two volumes which got separated from the main body when they were bought by George III in 1762 and were eventually given to the British Museum.

like Poussin and sculptors like François Duquesnoy. These artists were professed classicists, who would obviously have drawn sustenance from the study of this collection, but it is often assumed that their rivals who created the Baroque style – Rubens, Bernini, Lanfranco, Pietro da Cortona and Borromini – did not study ancient works of art at all, because they were accused of flouting all the principles of classical art. In fact however it would be quite wrong to suppose that the partisans of the Baroque were not interested in antiquity. Rubens drew ancient statues with as much passion as Poussin – and in a much more precise and detailed manner – and Bernini appealed to the authority of the ancients as often as his more consciously orthodox French contemporaries such as Fréart de Chambray, a friend of Poussin, who put forward the most rigid – and arid – doctrines of any seventeenth-century writer on architectural theory.

Borromini can be taken as a basis for studying this paradox because on the one hand he was vilified by his opponents as having degraded art by departing from the principles of classical architecture and on the other he repeatedly and vehemently affirmed that his works were based on a study of ancient buildings and the principles on which they were constructed.[1]

The explanation of this apparent contradiction is that Borromini and Fréart de Chambray looked at different ancient models and looked at them in different ways. The supporters of the classical party took their stand on the notoriously conservative Vitruvius, and confirmed his doctrines by reference to the most 'classical' works of Roman architecture – the Temple of Fortuna Virilis, the Maison Carrée at Nîmes or the Pantheon. They ignored the other freer, more 'Baroque' types of building which flourished most conspicuously in the eastern Mediterranean and which we associate with Baalbek, Petra, Leptis Magna and Sabratha.[2]

[1] See particularly his own statements in the *Opus architectonicum*, published in 1725 from a manuscript prepared by his friend Virgilio Spada, and those of his friend Fioravante Martinelli in *Roma Ornata* (published by Cesare d'Onofrio, *Roma nel Seicento*, Rome, 1969).

[2] In the same way the more classical French sculptors ignored the Laocoon and the Barberini Faun and took as their models the Vatican Antinous and the Apollo Belvedere, works regarded in the seventeenth century as 'classical'. Poussin and Duquesnoy were the only artists of the time to distinguish between Greek and Roman art and to proclaim the superiority of the former a century before Winckelmann – a remarkable intuitive judgement, since they only knew it, apart from the descriptions given by ancient writers, through a few Roman copies (see the present writer's *Nicolas Poussin* (London, 1967), pp.232 ff.).

It was precisely this kind of architecture that Borromini admired and certain of his buildings are so close to ancient models of this kind that a direct connection seems almost demonstrable; but the question immediately arises: How could he have known them? In certain cases the answer is quite easy. The dome of S. Andrea delle Fratte is like the Conocchia, a Roman tomb standing beside the Via Appia near Capua which Borromini probably saw on his way to Naples and of which earlier drawings were available in Rome.[1] Some of his more unusual types of fluting are also taken from models still traceable in Rome. The exceptionally rich fluting on the fireplace of the Sala di Ricreazione in the Oratorio di S. Filippo Neri goes back to a type to be found, for instance, in columns in the Forum of Nerva, and the alternating broad and narrow flutings which he used in many of his churches has a model in a column from the temple of Apollo Sosianus, near the Theatre of Marcellus which was visible in his day and had been drawn in an early sixteenth-century sketch book, the Codex Coner, which belonged to Pozzo and is now in Sir John Soane's Museum, from which he is known to have made copies.

In other cases it is fairly certain that, though the surviving buildings which appear to be models for Borromini's works were not excavated till long after his time, other similar models existed in his day. For instance the oval fountains in the Flavian Palace on the Palatine, which are strikingly Borrominesque in their form, were only excavated in the present century, but engravings and drawings of the Palatine in the sixteenth century show similar fountains which have since disappeared. There may also have been models for him among the tombs on the Via Appia. These are now almost shapeless masses of brickwork but old engravings show them as having more precise forms, often of a kind which could legitimately be called Baroque. Borromini certainly did not know the architecture of Petra (discovered in the 1840s) or Leptis Magna and Sabratha (excavated in the present century) and probably did not have good drawings of Baalbek which was visited by pilgrims and traders much earlier, but there is ample evidence to show that in the sixteenth and seventeenth centuries there were buildings of similar character available to architects working in Rome, either in the

[1] For instance in Giuliano da Sangallo's sketchbook then in the library of Cardinal Francesco Barberini to whom Pozzo was secretary.

originals or in drawings, and it can be demonstrated that Borromini drew on such sources.

The most important corpus of material of this kind is a series of drawings by the Milanese architect Giovanni Battista Montano, or Montanus (1534–1621), who spent almost the whole of his career in Rome, building little and devoting the greater part of his energies to the study of antiquity. The drawings, which are now in Sir John Soane's Museum, belonged in Borromini's day to Pozzo, whose seal some of them bear, and about eighty-five of them were published in engravings between 1624 and 1638 together with further plates of the orders and others after Montanus's own designs for altars and tabernacles.[1] These drawings and engravings contain some features of Borromini's architecture which have generally been regarded as among his most fanciful 'inventions'.[2] There is, for instance, a circular temple with concave bays separated by coupled columns which was certainly the model for the lantern of S. Ivo della Sapienza (Pl. 12a, b) and saves us from the necessity of supposing that Borromini knew the round temple at Baalbek (Pl. 13a) with which the lantern has obvious affinities. Even more surprising is the engraving illustrated in Pl. 14a, which shows a building with a colonnade forming a false perspective, like that in Borromini's colonnade in the Palazzo Spada (Pl. 14b) in which the columns decrease in height and the distance between the rows diminishes as the colonnade recedes from the spectator standing in the court in front of it, producing the effect that it is far longer than is actually the case. It is clear, however, that the idea of producing this deception was due to Borromini and was not in Montanus's mind, because in his design the visitor would enter at the narrow end of the colonnade and would therefore be looking, so to speak, through the wrong end of the telescope.

Borromini was not the only architect of his generation to borrow from Montanus's drawings and engravings. Bernini made use of the false perspective colonnade in the Scala Regia of the Vatican, though he may have derived the idea through Borromini whose work

[1] The engravings were published by his pupil G. B. Soria and were reissued in 1691 in a single volume under the title *Li cinque libri di Architettura di Gio. Battista Montani Milanese.*

[2] The importance of Montanus was pointed out in a paper read by the present writer to the twentieth congress of the History of Art held in New York in 1961 and published in *Studies of the History of Western Art* (Princeton, 1963), III, pp.1 ff.

on the Palazzo Spada dates from some years earlier. He also used another design by Montanus as the basis for his church at Ariccia, and Pietro da Cortona's façades owe something to other engravings after Montanus.[1]

Montanus, was not, however, the only source available. There is, for instance, a drawing among the Pozzo series at Windsor (Pl. 15*a*) which shows a reconstruction of an ancient theatre and includes many features used by Baroque architects. This drawing is presumably based on a study of the theatres at Orange and elsewhere which were known in the seventeenth century but it is closer in character to that of Sabratha (Pl. 15*b*) which the draughtsman certainly did not know, particularly in the use of rectangular blocks projecting from deep curved recesses, which remind one of buildings by Pietro da Cortona. Here again, some evidence, now lost, must have been available to the artist who made this drawing.

Montanus claimed that his drawings were reconstructions of ancient buildings, a claim which, for obvious reasons, has been laughed out of court by classical archaeologists. He may, as has already been said, have known buildings now lost on which he based his 'reconstructions' but his work can be seen more clearly in its true perspective if it is realised that he was the last of a long line of architect–archaeologists who had produced imaginative reconstructions of ancient buildings, based on a free interpretation of the available evidence in terms of contemporary taste. This tradition goes back to the fifteenth century when it is traceable in Giuliano da Sangallo's drawings in the Codex Barberini, in the treatise of Filarete and in the illustrations to Colonna's *Hypneroto-machia*. It continued through the sixteenth century in the third book of Sebastiano Serlio's treatise on architecture which appeared in 1540, the treatise of Antonio Labacco[2] as well as in many drawings by unidentified architects. An example particularly relevant to the present discussion is a drawing by Raphael's follower, Polidoro da Caravaggio (Pl. 13*b*) which represents a circular temple which at first sight seems to postulate a knowledge of Baalbek. Did Polidoro in fact know a drawing of the eastern temple, or did he base his drawing on some other building like it in Italy which was also

[1] The two relevant engravings are reproduced in Blunt, op. cit. figs. 10 and 11, and the seventeenth-century buildings in R. Wittkower, *Art and architecture in Italy 1600–1750* (Pelican History, Harmondsworth, 1958, pls. 64B, 80, 82, 83).
[2] *Libro appartenente all'Architettura* (Rome, 1558).

known to Montanus? The problem is a matter on which scholars are still not agreed.

The fact that the reconstructions of Montanus and his like have been rejected as fantastic by modern students of ancient architecture is irrelevant to the problem discussed in this paper. It is quite clear that in the seventeenth century they were accepted at their face value and that the architects who borrowed from them believed that they were imitating ancient models. In fact it could be maintained that these 'reconstructions' exercised as fruitful an influence on Borromini and his contemporaries as did Palladio's more orthodox reconstructions on English architects of the eighteenth century, or the measured drawings of the Parthenon and the Theseion on neo-classical architects of the early nineteenth century. Archaeologically this may appear to be nonsense, but art-historically it is true.

INDEX

Figures in heavy type indicate that the topic in question is discussed at some length. Figures in italics indicate that a reference is given with the full title of a work. Where the reference is to a modern work on the topic, the name of the author follows in brackets. With a few exceptions, such as Petrarch, the names of writers after the sixth century A.D. are given in the form used in the country of their origin, unless the Latin form is much better known. Where this might lead to difficulties of identification, cross-references have been provided. Dates are A.D. unless shown otherwise.

Aalders, G.J. D. *312 n.5.*

Abel, son of Adam, 276

Abel, Michael, Bohemian Neo-Latin poet, 47, *47 n.3* (J.Heynic–J.Martinek), 52

Abraham, Hebrew patriarch, 278, 330

Abrams, H.M., *160 n.2*

Acciaiuoli, Zanobio, Florentine humanist and patristic scholar (1461–1519), 200

Accursius, Franciscus, Italian jurist (1182–1260), 241 n.2

Achebe, C., 108 n.1

Achilles, Homeric hero, 101, 186

Aconcio, Girolamo, Italian philosopher and pioneer of religious toleration (1492–1566?), 75

Actium, naval battle (31 B.C.), 382

Adam, 143, 143 n.3, 271, 272, 272 nn.2–3, **273, 273 n.1, 275–8**; in art, 330, 332, 333; 'new Adam', 69; *see also* Pre-Adamism

Adams, H.M., 35, *35 n.2*

Addison, Joseph, English man of letters (1672–1719), 165 n.4

Admetus, mythical Thessalian king, husband of Alcestis, 327, Pl. 2*a*

Aelianus Tacticus, late-first-century Roman writer on military subjects, 319, *319 n.1* (W.Hallweg), *320 n.2* (G. Oestreich)

Aeneas Sylvius (Enea Silvio Piccolomini, 1405–64, Pope Pius II, 1458), *Cinthia*, 172, 173, *173 n.1* (J.Cugnoni)

Africa, 100, 101; oral literature, *108 n.1* (E.Obiechena, B.Lindfors)

Agricola, Georgius (Georg Bauer), German medical writer and mineralogist (1494–1555), **318**; his classical scholarship, *318 n.2* (H.Prescher); *De re metallica*, 318, *318 n.2* (H.Wilsdorf)

Agricola, Gnaeus-Julius, Tacitus's father-in-law (37–93), 299

Agricola, Rudolphus (Roelof Huysmann), Rhineland humanist (1444 85): influenced by Valla, 147, *147 n.4* (C.Vasoli); innovations in dialectic,

7, **12–13**, *13 n.1* (L.Jardine), 74, *74 n.1* (W.J.Ong, N.W.Gilbert, C. Vasoli), 141 n.2, **148–9**, 151, 152 n.1, 153–4; use of commonplaces, 92

De formando studio, 148 n.3; *De inventione dialectica*, 147, 147n.4, **148–50**, 15 on. 4

agriculture, 27, 316; use of classical authorities, 318, **320**, *320 nn.4–5* (O.Brunner), **321**

Agrippa, M.Vipsanius, right-hand man of the Emperor Augustus (63 B.C.–A.D. 12), 292; his Pantheon, 343–4

Agrippina the Younger, mother of Nero (16–59), 287

Alain de Lille (Alanus ab Insulis), medieval Latin poet (1128–1204), 73

Alberti, Leon Battista, Italian humanist and architect (1404–72); imitations of Lucian, 5; on architecture, 339, *339 n.2*

Della famiglia, *24 n.1*

Albertini, R. von, *290 n.2*

Albertus Magnus, scholastic philosopher (1193–1280), 133, *144 n.4*, 305

Alcala de Henares, Spanish university, 227

Alcestis, mythical heroine, wife of Admetus, 327, Pl. 2*a*

Alciati, Andrea, Italian jurist and humanist (1492–1550): on Livy and Tacitus, 291, *291 n.3* (A.Momigliano); use of allegories, 262

Emblemata, 130, 184 n.6

Alembert, Jean le Rond d', French mathematician (1717?–83) 117

Alexander of Aphrodisias, Greek commentator on Aristotle (*fl.* 198–211), 251, 251 n.2

Alexander the Great (356–323 B.C.), 114, 202

Alfonso V (king of Aragon 1416–58), 282

allegory: in art, Pl. 4*c*, 4*d*; in Calderón, **23**, **264–70**; in Cicero, **239**; in Lotichius, 189, *189 n.3*; in Vivès, 22, **241–2**; its effect on style, 191; use of animals in, *189 n.3* (H.C.Schnur)

All Souls' College, Oxford, 212
Allen, C.G., *207 n.1*
Allen, D.C., *96 n.1, 91 n.3*, 110 n.1
Allen, P.S., 208, 208 n.1, 209, 225
alphabetical arrangement, 11, 83, **104–5**, 107, **109–11**
Alpheus, river in the Peloponnese, also the river-god, 101
Alsted, Johann Heinrich, German encyclopedist and theologian (1588–1638), 125
Altamura, A., *172 n.5*
Alva (Alba), Duke of, Spanish general (1508–83), 45
Amalteo, Giovanni Baptista, Italian Neo-Latin poet (1525–73), 64
Ambrogini, *see* Politian
Ambrose of Milan, Saint (340?–97), 18, 214
Amelot de la Houssaye, A.N. French translator and historian (1634–1706): on Machiavelli, 287, 288, 288 n.1; on Tacitus, **296**, 296 nn. 4–6
Tibère, 301, 301 nn.3–4
Amelung, W., *326 n.1*
Amerbach, Boniface, Basel printer (1495–1562), 112
America, 186; effects of its discovery, 273–4; identified with Atlantis, 274
American Indians, 274, *274 n.1* (L.E. Huddleston)
Ammianus Marcellinus, Roman historian (*c.* 330–after 391), 286 n.6
amor, 9, 101; *see also* Cupid
Amsterdam edition of Erasmus, 3
Amyot, Jacques, French hellenist and translator (1513–93), 191
Anabaptists, populist protestant sect, 114
'Anatomy' as book title, 115, *115 n.3* (L.A.Beaurline, K.J.Höltgen)
Anaxagoras, Ionian philosopher (d. 428 B.C.), 249
Andrelino, P.Fausto, Italian Neo-Latin poet (1462–1518), cited by Textor, 84, 85
Andromeda, mythical Ethiopian princess, 259, 260, 262; play by Calderón, 264
Anglicus, Michaelis, Flemish law professor in Paris and Neo-L tin poet (*fl.* 1505–7), cited by Textor, 84
animal poems, 184, *184 n.6* (G.Herrlinger, J.Hutton); similes, *189 n.3* (H.C. Schnur)
Annan, Lord, v
Annona, Roman goddess of the yearly produce, 328
Anonymous Destailleur, late-sixteenth-century draughtsman, 347
Anonymous (Vienna), early-sixteenth-century architectural draughtsman, 346, 346 n.2 (H.Egger), Pl. 8*d*
Anthologia Planudea, Planudes's 1301 abridgement of the tenth-century anthology of Cephalas, 184 n.6

anthologies, 8, 9, **118–19**; medieval, 103; Neo-Latin verse: (ed. J.Sparrow), 4, **57–64**, (in Germany) 57 *n.2*, (in Italy) *57 nn.2–3*
anthropology, 273–74, 274 *n.2* (J.S. Slotkin, T.Bendysche)
Antinous, favourite of the Emperor Hadrian (d.122), statue in the Vatican, 350 n.2
antiqui et moderni, renaissance controversy, **67–71**
Antoninus Pius (Roman emperor 138–61), 288
antonomàsia, substitution of epithet etc. for proper name, 73
Antwerp, works printed in, 95
Anysius, Janus, Neapolitan Neo-Latin poet (1475–1540), *52*
Apellus, J., pseudonym, *see* Eberle
Apollo, pagan god, 9, 83, 110, 182 n.4; in art, 331, 333, Pl. 6*b*; Apollo Belvedere (Vatican), 350 n.2; Apollo Sosianus, temple of (Rome), 351
Appian, second-century A.D. Greek historian, 285 n.1, 286 n.6
Apuleius, Lucius, Roman novelist and philosophical populariser (*c.* 123–after 180), 46, 251
Aquino, Carlo d', Neapolitan Neo-Latin satirist (1654–1737), *53*
Arabia, 100, 101
Arabic, 134
Aratus, third-century B.C. Greek didactic poet, 88
Arcadia, 100
Arcerius Sixtus, Dutch classical scholar, 319
archaeology, classical, 344, **349–53**, 350 n.2 (A.Blunt)
Archimedes, Greek mathematician (287–212 B.C.), 114, 317 n.2, 318, *318 n.1* (L.Olschki)
architecture, 316, 318, **335–48**; attitudes to classical buildings: (medieval) 336–38, (fifteenth-century naive) 338, *338 n.5* (A.Bartoli, G.Scaglia, T. Buddensieg, G.Schweikhart), 339, 339 n.1, (analytical) 339–41, (Vitruvian dogmatic) 342, (historical) 343, (counter-reformation) 344–5; drawings, *339 n.3* (W.Lotz); Tuscan, 338–9
Arco, Niccolò d', Italian Neo-Latin poet (1479–1546), 63; *Numeri*, 61 n.1
Arezzo, Tuscan city, 71
Argo, Jason's boat in the Golden Fleece legend, 261
Argonauts, crew of the *Argo*, 261–2
Ariccia, Bernini's church in, 344, 353
Ariosto, Lodovico, Italian and Neo-Latin poet (1474–1533), 63; *Carmina*, 60 n.1
Aristotle (384–322 B.C.), 78, 148 n.3, 278; Bodin on, 26, **306–13**; commentaries

Aristotle (*cont.*)
on, 251, 257, 305; humanist attitude to, **305–6**, 316; Petrarch on, 71; possessed by students, 153; Valla on, 12, 13, 71, 73, **141–5**, *142 n.4* (A.J. Ashworth), 144 n.3 (W. and M. Kneale); Vivès on, 22, 242, 242 n.1, **245–58**
De interpretatione, 254; *Ethics*, 242 n.1; *Metaphysics*, 132–3; *Organon* (in its entirety), 74, 75, 157, 250, 253–4; *Physics*, 242, 257; *Poetics*, 75, 157, 159, *160* (L.J.Potts), 161, 190 n.4; *Politics*, 26, **305–13**; *Posterior Analytics*, 254; *Prior Analytics*, 254; *Rhetoric*, 157; *Topics*, 12, 13, 102, 114, 157, 254
see also scholasticism
Arnobius Afer the Elder, Christian apologist (*fl. c.* 300), 49
Ascham, Roger, English educationist (1515–68), 121, 121 n.3, 123
Ashworth A.J., *142 n.4*
Asia, 273, 310
Assyria, ancient kingdom on the Tigris, 190, 311
astrology, 182 n.4
Athenaeus, Greek miscellanist (*fl. c.* 200), 29
Athens: as a political model, 25, 322; its building code, 115; the four Athens, 115 n.2
Atlantis, 274
Atropos, one of the Fates, 241, 243
Audebert, Germain, French Neo-Latin poet (1518–98), 193
Augurello, Giovanni Aurelio, Italian humanist and Neo-Latin poet (*c.* 1440–1524), cited by Textor, 84, 85
Augustine of Hippo, Saint (354–430), 18, 203, 305; Colet on, 214; criticises pre-Adamism, 272, 272 n.2, 273; influence on Ignatius Loyola, 233; Vivès on, 245, *245 n.3*, 246, 251, 253
Augustus (Roman emperor 63 B.C.–A.D. 14), 166, 283 n.4, 297–8, 344; his testament, 296, 296 n.2
Aulus Gellius, Roman miscellanist (*c.* 123–65), 130–1; his definition of 'humanitas', 141 n.1; imitated by Angelo Decembrio, 152, 152 n.5
Aurelius Marcus (Roman emperor 161–80), 288; statue in Rome, 348
Ausonius, Decimus Magnus, Roman poet (*c.* 310–*c.* 395), cited by La Peyrère, 277
Averroës (Ibn Rushd), Arab philosopher (1126–98), 71; condemned by Vivès, 251, 252, 257, 257 n.3
Avienus, R.Festus, late-fourth-century (?) Roman poet, echoed by Buchanan, 88 n.3
Aztecs, 274, *274 n.1* (L.E.Huddleston)

Baalbek (Syria), the ancient Heliopolis, 350–3, Pl. 13*a*

Babylonia (= Chaldea), ancient Near-Eastern kingdom, 24, 272 n.2, 276–7, 311; its esoteric wisdom, 76, *76 n.1* (*extensive bibliography*)
Bacon, Francis, jurist, essayist and philosopher (1561–1626): his bilingualism, 5 n.2; his use of induction, 108, 109, 112; on 'poesy', 159; on rhetoric and logic, 156–7
Baeyens, H., *67 n.1*
Baglione G., Italian art historian (*c.* 1573–1644), 336
Baines, Richard, an informer, 274
Baker-Smith, Dominic, 21, 22, 25
Balde, Jacob, Jesuit and German Neo-Latin poet (1604–68), 48, 49 n.1, *53*
Baldus de Ubaldis, Italian jurist (1327–1406), 128, 241 n.2
Baldwin T.W., 20, *20 n.1*, 92, 95 n.2, 121, 151 n.1
Bale, John, English antiquary (1495–1563), 216, *216 n.5*, 217
Barberini Faun, Roman copy of a Greek statue probably of the third century B.C., 350 n.2
Barberini, Cardinal Francesco, 276 n.3
Barcelona, Spanish university, 227
Barclay, John, Scots Neo-Latin novelist and satirist (1582–1621), 49, *49 n.3*, 50, 54
Baron, Hans, 25, *68 n.1*, *283 n.4*
Baroque: classical models for its art, **350–3**; influence of Lucan on, 179, *179 n.1*
Barthélemy de Loches, Nicholas, Parisian Neo-Latin poet and professor (1478–1540), cited by Textor, 84
Barthius Caspar (von Barth), German medievalist and Neo-Latin poet (1587–1658), 52
Bartholinus, Ricardus, sixteenth-century Neo-Latin poet, 90
Bartoli, A., *338 n.5*, 340, *340 n.1*
Bartolo di Sassoferato, Italian jurist (1313/14–57), 241 n.2
Basil of Caesarea, Saint (331–79), 17, 158; *Ad adolescentes*, 18, *18 n.2* (L.Schuhan), 200, 201; *Adversus Eunomium*, 200
Basini, Basinio, Neo-Latin poet from Parma (1425–57), *Cyris*, 173
Basle, 115, 116, 194, 225; printers in, 37, 112; the Swiss Athens, 115 n.2; works printed at, 45, 82, 82 n.2, 83 n.2, 95, 305, 317
Bassus, Cassianus, Byzantine agronomist (*fl.* early tenth century), *Geoponica*, 320
Baudoin, François, French jurist and reformer (1520–73), 306
Baumgartner, J., *42 n.8*
Bayle, Pierre, French encyclopedist (1647–1706), 279
Bayonne (France), 338 n.5
Beaurline, L.A., *115 n.3*

INDEX

Bebel, Heinrich, German humanist and Neo-Latin poet (1472–1518), 52
Beccadelli, Antonio (Panormita), Italian humanist and Neo-Latin poet (1394–1471), 41 n.1, 282, *282 n.4*
Beck, A., 92, *92 n.1*
Beda, Natalis (Noël Bédier), Sorbonne theologian (d. 1536/7), 228, 229
Behrens, I., *174 n.1*
Beissner, F., *171 n.2*, 172, 172 nn.2 and 4
Bellarmine, Robert, Saint, Jesuit theologian (1542–1621), 220, *220 n.3* (D.P.Walker)
Bellum discars Sophiae et Philautiae, 130
Belaucus, Jean, principal of the Collège de Navarre, 95
Bembo, Pietro, Italian humanist (1470–1547), 5 n.2, 63
Bendysche, T., *274 n.2*
Benesić (Benessa), Damianus, Croatian Neo-Latin poet (*fl.* 1513), *52*
Beowulf, Old English epic, seventh or eighth century, 119
Bérault, Nicole, French humanist (1473–1550), 85
Bering, Lyons printer, 112
Bernard of Clairvaux, Saint (1091–1153), 202
Bernini, Giovanni Lorenzo, Italian sculptor and architect (1598–1680), 344, 350, 352, 353; *see also* Ariccia, Scala Regia
Beroaldo, Filippo the Elder, Italian humanist and Neo-Latin poet (1453–1505), cited by Textor, 84
Beroaldo, Filippo the Younger, Italian classical scholar (1472–1518), 295, 300
Berosus, *see* Pseudo-Berosus
Berryman, J., *171 n.1*
Bertelli, S., *289 n.2, 290 n.1*
Berthelet, Thomas, English printer (*fl. c.* 1530), 206, 206 n.2
Besançon (France), 82 n.1
Bibbiena (Bernardo Dorizi called), cardinal and patron of humanists (1470–1520), 331
Bible
    Old Testament: accuracy of text questioned, 275; *Genesis*, 272, 272 n.2, 275, 276, 278; inconsistencies in, 276; *Pentateuch*, 276; *Psalms*, 13 n.2; Sapiential books, 102
    New Testament: Erasmus, *Paraphrases*, 230, 237–8; Erasmus's translation, 208, 208 n.1 (P.S.Allen), 209; Meghen's MS, 209, 210, *210 n.1* (W.Schwartz, J.K.McConica); reinforced by classical studies, 231, 231 n.2; source of knowledge of primitive Christianity, 20; Valla's annotations, 208
    see also Paul, Saint
Biblical figures linked with figures from

pagan myth, **264–70**, *325 n.1* (N. Dacos), **330–3**
Bibliothèque Nationale (Paris), 33
Bilingualism, 5 n.2, 10, 11; in German poetry, 179, *179 n.1* (R.Haller); in Montaigne, 136–40; translation of French into Latin, 53
Billanovich, Giuseppe, 281, *281 n.2*
Bilscius, Joachim (Bielski, Marcin), bilingual Polish and Neo-Latin poet (1495–1575), *52*
biography, 94 n.1, 102
Biondo Flavio (Flavius Blondus), Italian antiquarian and humanist (1388–1463), 285
Blunt, Sir Anthony, 29, 353 n.1; publications, *350 n.2, 352 n.2*
Boas, G., *272 n.1*
Boas, M., *78 n.1, 316 n.1*
Boccaccio, Giovanni (1313–75): his anti-scholasticism, 71; his influence on taste for classical art, 337–8, *338 n.1*; on Livy, 283; on Tacitus, 283, 285, *285 n.3* (A.Hortis), 289; translation of Livy, 282
    Amorosa Visione, 283, 283 nn.2–3; *Decameron*, 282; *De genealogia deorum*, 263
Boccati, Giovanni, Italian painter (b. 1420), Pl. 7*b*
Bodecherus Benningius, Janus, Dutch Neo-Latin satirist (1606–42), 50, *55*
Bodenham, John, English miscellanist (*fl.* 1600), *119*
Bodin, Jean, French political theorist (1530–96); on Aristotle's *Politics*, 26, **306–13**; on mixed governments, **309–10**; on monarchy, **311–13**; on sovereignty, **308–9**
    De la république, 5 n.2, **305–13**; *Methodus ad historiarum cognitionem*, 306, *306 n.1*
Bodleian Library, Oxford, 36, 38, *38 n.1*, 39, *111 n.1*
Boethius, Anicius Manlius Severinus, Roman philosopher (*c.* 480–524): cited by Textor, 84; Valla on, 73, 142, 145, 145 n.2; Vivès on, 251
Bohemia, Neo-Latin verse in, *47 n.3* (J.Hejnic–J. Martinek), *51* (K.Hrdina)
Boiardo, Matteo Maria, Italian poet (1430–94), 173
Boileau, Nicolas, French satirist and literary critic (1636–1711), 46; his satires translated into Latin, *53*
Bojana (Jugoslavia), 336 *336 n.2* (K. Mijatev)
Bolgar, R.R., v, vi, 103, 120, 191, 335 nn.1–2; publications, *78 n.1, 103 n.4*
Bologna (Italy), 71, 178, 182
Bombelli, Raffaele, Italian engineer and mathematician (1530?–72), 318, *318 n.1* (L.Olschki)
Bonaspes, Nicolas, *see* Dupuy
Boniface IV (Pope 608–15), 336

358

Bordeaux, 229, 275
Borromeo, Carlo, Saint (1538–84), 29, 346, *346 n.1* (S.Sinding-Larsen)
Borromini, Francesco, Italian architect (1599–1667), 29, **350–4**, Pls. 12*a*, 14*b*; *Opus architectonicum*, *350 n.1* (C. d'Onofrio); *see also* S. Andrea delle Fratte, S.Ivo della Sapienza, Oratorio of S.Filippo Neri, Palazzo Spada
Bosque, A.de, *338 n.4*
Bouelles, Charles de (Carolus Bovillus), French humanist and mathematician (1470–1533), 129
Bouhours, Père Dominique, Jesuit man of letters (1628–1702), 292
Boumann, Johann, Dutch architect (1706–76), *344 n.1* (H.Kania), Pl. 9*c*
Bourbon, Nicolas, French Neo-Latin poet (1503–*c*. 1549), 64, 81, 193, 194
Bouricius, Johannes, Dutch jurist and Neo-Latin satirist (d. 1671), *55*
Bowen, B., 136, *196 n.1*
Boyde, P., v
Bradner, L., *42 n.7*
Bramante (Donato d'Angelī Lazzari called), Italian architect (1444–1514), 325, *325 n.2* (D.Redig de Campos)
Brant, Sebastian, German Neo-Latin satirist (*c*. 1455–1521), 64
Brantôme, Pierre de, French biographer (1535–1614), 136
Brébœuf, Guillaume de, French translator and poet (1618–61), 164 nn.3–4, 166, *166 n.5*, 169
Bregolini, Ubaldo, bilingual Italian and Neo-Latin satirist (1722–1807), *54*
British Library (formerly British Museum Library), 34, 36, 39, 82 n.1, 209, 215, 215 n.5; catalogues, *34 n.1*, *35*, *35 n.3* (V.F.Goldsmith), 282
British Museum, 328 nn.1–2, 349 n.2
Brodeau, Jean, French hellenist (1503–63), 184 n.6
Brunelleschi, Filippo, Florentine architect (1377–1446), 336–7
Bruni, Leonardo (Aretinus), Italian humanist (1369–1444), 152 n.4; his translations, 200, 305; his view of history, 283, *283 n.4* (H.Baron); on correct Latin, 6, **71**, **72**; on Tacitus, 283, 289, 292
Dialogi ad Petrum Histrum, 71, *72 n.1*; *Historia florentini populi*, 71, 72, *72 n.1*
Brunner, O., *320 n.5*
Bruno, Giordano, Italian philosopher (1548–1600), 79, 274, *274 n.2*, 275
Buchanan, George, Scots humanist (1506–82), 9, 58, 88, 138, 228; his use of Textor, **88–90**
Elegia, 88–9; *Franciscanus*, 41 n.5, 90; *Sphaera*, 88, 88 nn.2–3; *Vita*, *88 n.1* (J.M.Aitken)
Buchwald Pelcowa, P., *43 n.1*
Buck, A., *67 n.1*, *180 n.4*, *316 n.1*, 321 n.1

Buddensieg, T., 28, 29, 336 n.3, 345 n.2; publications, *335 n.1*, *338 n.5*, *341 n.1*, *344 n.2*, *347 n.2*
Budé, Guillaume, French humanist (1467–1540): cited by Textor, 83
Annotationes in Pandectas, 128–9; *De transitu Hellenismi*, 231
Bühler, C.F., *209 n.7*
Burckhardt, Jacob, Swiss historian (1818–97), 30
Burdach, K., *71 n.3*
Burmann, Pieter I, Dutch classical scholar (1668–1741), 167 n.3, 169 n.1, *319 n.3*
Burmann, Pieter II, Dutch scholar and Neo-Latin poet (1714–78), 180 n.1, 182 n.2, 189 n.3
Burmeister, K.H., *180 n.4*
Burns, Howard, 28–9, *343 n.2*, 345 n.2
Burton, Robert, English moralist (1577–1640), 98, 115
Bush, Douglas, *281*, **285**
Bywater, Ingram, *62 n.1*
Byzantine humanism, 6, *6 n.1*, 74
Byzantium: military science, 315, 319 n.1; technical literature, 316; *see also* Hagia Sophia

Cabbala, 76, *76 n.1* (*bibliography*), 77, 214
Caesar, Gaius Julius (101–44 B.C.), 315 n.1; judgements on, 165, 165 n.5, 166, 283 n.4, 284, 289; owned by Cosimo de' Medici, 282, *282 n.4*
Calderini, Domitio, papal secretary and classical scholar (*c*. 1447–78), 42, *42 n.2* (R. Malaboti)
Calderón de la Barca, Spanish dramatist (1600–81), 22–4; combines pagan and Christian myths, **264–70**; his *autos sacramentales*, 264–6; his use of allegory, 267–8; list of his plays, 264; mirror theme in, 267
Celos aun del aire matan, 264; *El verdadero Dios Pan*, *259 n.1*, **265–70**; *No hay mas fortuna que Dios*, 265, 267
Calentius, Johannes Elisius, Italian Neo-Latin poet (1430?–1503?), *51*
Caligula (Gaius) (Roman emperor 37–41), 283 n.4, 288, 292, 300
Callimachus, Alexandrian poet (*c*. 310–*c*. 235 B.C.), 190, *190 n.3*
Calveras, J., *224 n.1*
Calvin, Jean (1509–64), 202, 229; his French style, 191; *Institutio*, 5 n.2
Calvus, 174
Cambridge, University of: curriculum, *13 n.1* (L.Jardine), 147, 147 n.3 (J.B. Mullinger); inventories of students' books, 153, *153 n.2* (L.Jardine); libraries, various, *35 n.2* (H.M. Adams), 111 n.1, 215, 215 nn.2–3, 216, 216 n.3; university library, 82 n.1, 209, 215–16
Camerarius, Joachimus (Leibhard), Ger-

Camerarius (*cont.*)
man classical scholar and Neo-Latin poet (1500–74), 62, 178–80, 180 n.1, 182 n.2

Campana, Marquis of, Italian collector and antiquarian, 328, 328 n.3

Campano, Gianantonio, Italian humanist (*c.* 1427–77), 41 n.1, *61 n.1*

Camporeale, S.I., *73 n.2, 142 n.2,* 144 n.4

Canaan (biblical), 332, Pl. 4*a*

Cannae, Battle of (216 B.C.), 320, 320 n.3

Cantalycius (Joannes Baptista Valentini), Italian Neo-Latin poet (*c.* 1450–1515), 42, *42 n.3* (V.Zappacosta)

Cantimori, D., *67 n.1*

Capella, Martianus, Roman encyclopedist (*fl. c.* 410–27), 84, 251

Caprara, Antonia, 173

Carariensis, Johannes (Johannes Michael de Carraria), Italian physician and Neo-Latin poet (1438–90), *51*

Caravaggio, Polidoro da, Italian painter (1495–1543), 353, Pl. 13*b*

Cardoner, river in Catalonia, 223–4, *224 n.1* (J.Calveras, L.R.Silos), 225, 226 n.1, 227

Carlson, G., *119 n.1*

Carolus Aurelianensis, *see* Charles d'Orléans

Cartari, Vincenzo, Italian mythographer (*c.* 1520–*c.* 1570), 263

Casa Maffei (Rome), 327

Casaubon, Isaac, French humanist (1559–1614), 5, 29; *Misoponeri Satyricon, 54*

Cassirer, E., 316, *316 n.1*

Castellus, Gulielmus, French Neo-Latin poet, cited by Textor, 84

Castelvetro, Lodovico, Italian literary critic (1505–71), 15

Castiglione, Baldassare, Italian writer on courtesy and Neo-Latin poet (1478–1529), 63

Castruccius, Bonamicus, German Neo-Latin satirist, *54*

Catherine of Aragon, queen of England (1485–1536), 219

Catherine of Siena, Saint (1347–80), 336, *336 n.1* (G.Fiocco)

Cato, M.Porcius, the Elder, orator and agronomist (232–147 B.C.), 320, 320 n.4

Cato, M.Porcius, the Younger, republican idealist (95–46 B.C.), 164, 165 n.4, 166, 166 n.2

Cattaneo, P. (Prandino dei Cattanei), architect in the service of the Visconti (*fl.* 1461–76), 339 n.1

Catullus, C.Valerius, Roman poet (*c.* 84–*c.* 50 B.C.): cited by Textor, 84–5, by Montaigne, 137, 137 n.2, 138; echoes of, 45, 138, 173, *179 n.5* (B.Coppel), *184 n.1* (B.Coppel)

Celtes (Celtis or Keltis) Conrad (Conrad Tickel), German humanist and Neo-Latin poet (1459–1508), 62; cited by

Textor, 84–5; imitated by Lotichius, 182, 182 n.4, 183
Amores, 60 n.1, 182, 182 n.4; *Odae, 60 n.1*

Cesarini, Giuliano, cardinal and humanist patron (1389–1444), 200

Ceva, Thomas, S.J., Milanese Neo-Latin satirist and philosophical poet (1649–1736/7), 53

Chalcondyles, Demetrius, Byzantine humanist (1424–1511), 8

Chaldea, *see* Babylonia

Chambray, Fréart de, French art critic (1609–76), 350

Charles V (1500–58), Holy Roman emperor 1519, 291, 296

Charles V (1337–80), king of France 1364, 305

Charles d'Orléans (Carolus Aurelianensis), French poet (1391–1465), 96 n.1

Chartres, School of, 246

Chatsworth, 345, 345 n.2, Pl. 11 *a–b*

cherrie and the slae, The, 5 n.2

China, 277, 277 n.2, 278

Christ, 73, 200, 225, 237, 241; represented by Raphaël, 330, by Calderón, 266–9

Christian humanism: at Sainte-Barbe, 229; changing aims of, 18, 19; Erasmus's attitude to pagan culture, 195, 197, **230–3**; Jesuit attitude to pagan culture, **235–7**; patristic age as ideal, 19; the mixing of pagan and Christian myths: (by Calderón) 23–4, 265–6, (by Lope de Vega) 259–62, (by Raphaël) 330–4; views on the *Somnium Scipionis,* 244; *see also docta pietas*

Christianity: its opposition to worldliness, 226 n.2; its puritanism in art, 344–5; rejected by Montaigne, 136–7; *see also Index librorum prohibitorum*

Chrysoloras, Manuel, Byzantine humanist (*c.* 1350–1415), 6, *6 n.1*

Chrysostom, John, Saint (347–407), 18, 202, 214

Chytraeus, Nathan, Rostock Latin professor and late-16th-century traveller, 178 n.4

Cian, V., 42, *42 n.1*

Cicero, Marcus Tullius (106–43 B.C.), 93, 139 n.1, 148 n.3; attitudes to his thought, 7, 19, 78, 134, 147, 226, 226 n.1, 239, 240–1, 305; cited by Textor, 83; his moral ideal, 21, 241; imitation of his language and style, 5, 7, 27, 76, 134, 192, 194; influence, 147, 151, 154, 239, 240, 243 n.3, 244; popularity, 38; read: (by Cambridge students) 153 n.1, (by Colet) 214, (in Jesuit schools) 233, (by La Peyrère) 277; reconciled with Christianity, 231, 244; reputation, 284 n.3, 292
De inventione, 147; *De officiis,* 134; *Somnium Scipionis,* 21, 25, 239, **241–3**,

Cicero (cont.)
   243 n.3, 244, commentators on, **240–2**, 244, 246; *Tusculanae disputationes*, 226 n.1, 231
Ciceronianism, 2, 5, *5 n.1* (I.Scott, G.Williamson, H.W.Croll), 46, 47, 47 n.2 (D.Gagliardi), 104, 146, 192, 194–7
Cinna, Cornelius, Roman politician (d. 84 B.C.), 284
Cipriani, Cipriano, priest at the Pantheon (*fl.* 1623–44), 343
Clarius, Johannes, Tungrensis, Flemish Roman Catholic controversialist and Neo-Latin satirist (1547–1611), *52*
Classen, J., *185 n.6*
classification, *see* information retrieval
Claudian (Claudius Claudianus), Roman poet (*fl. c.* 395–404): cited by Textor, 84–5; echo in Buchanan, 90; used by La Peyrère, 277
   De raptu Proserpinae, 8
Claudius (Roman emperor 41 54), 283 n.4, 292
Clement VII, Pope (1523–34), 286
Clement of Alexandria, Greek theologian (*c.* 160–*c.* 215), 200
Cleopatra, queen of Egypt (d. 30 B.C.), 165, 165 n.5
Cleophilus, Franciscus Octavius, Italian Neo-Latin poet (1447–1490/7), 84, 89
Clichtove, Josse, Flemish theologian (1472–1513), 233
Clotho, one of the Fates, 241
Clusius, Carolus (Charles de l'Ecluse), French medical writer (1525–1609), 183 n.6
Cluvius Rufus, Marcus, consul A.D. 45, 301
Cockx-Indestege, E., *36 n.4*
Codex Barberini, drawings by Giuliano da Sangallo, 351, 351 n.1, 353
Codex Coner, early-sixteenth-century sketchbook, 339, 341, *341 n.1* (T. Ashby, T.Buddensieg), 351, Pls. *7a, 8c*
Codex Pighianus (*c.* 1550), 327, *327 n.4* (O.Jahn), Pl. *2b*
Codrus, *see* Urceus
Coleman, Dorothy, 10
Coler, Jacob, theologian and agronomist (*fl.* 1593–1603), 321
Coleridge, Samuel Taylor, English critic and poet (1772–1834), 101
Colet, Sir Henry, father of John (d. 1505), 210
Colet, John, humanist Dean of St Paul's (*c.* 1467–1519), 19, 20, **205–22**, Pl. 16*a d*; early education, *221 n.2* (W.R.Godfrey); editions of his works 3, 205, *205 n.2* (*full bibliography*); lectures at Oxford, 207, 207 n.3 (S.Jayne, P.Duhamel); MS works, 215–18, *218 n.2* (E.W.Hunt), 219
   Aeditio, 206–7; *Oratio in convocatione*, 206, *206 n.1*; *Right fruitful monition*, 207, *207 n.2*

see also St Paul's School
Coliseum (Rome), 327
Collardeau, Julien III, French jurist and Neo-Latin poet (1595–1669), *54*
Colleoni, Bartolomeo, soldier of fortune (1400–75), 115
Colombus, Christopher (1451–1506), 278
Colonna, Francesco (*c.* 1449–1527), *Hypnerotomachia*, 353
Colonna, Landolfo, fourteenth-century collector of MSS, 282
Columella, L.Junius Moderatus, Roman agronomist (*fl. c.* 65), 318, 320, *320 n.4*, 321, 321 n.1 (A.Buck); cited by Textor, 83, 90; echo in Buchanan, 90
Comes, Natalis (Natale Conti), Italian mythographer (*c.* 1520–82), *263*
Commines, Philippe de, French historian (1445–1509), 296
commonplace material: arrangement of: (alphabetical) 11, 83, **104–5**, 107, **109–11**, (Ramist) 115, 115 nn.2–3, 116–17; Ascham's attack on, 121, 121 n.3; collections: (by Erasmus) 85, 94, **94 n.1**, (by Maffei) 110–11, (by Textor) 11, **81–90**, **95–101**, (by Zwinger) 14, **102–20**, (owned by students) 153, *153 n.2* (L.Jardine); links with oral culture, 118; theoretical considerations, **91–5**, **102–7**, **127–9**, 134; use in literature: (du Bellay) **130–1**, (Montaigne) **131–3**, (Rabelais) **129–30**, (Shakespeare) **120–6**
Conan, François de, French jurist, pupil of Alciat (1506–52), 306
Concord, personification, 328
Condé, Louis II, Prince de, French general (1621–86), 276
Cono of Nuremberg (Johann Kuno), German translator of the Fathers (1463–1513), 200
Conocchia, Roman tomb on the Via Appia, 351
Conrady, K.O., *179, 179 n.4*
Constantine I, Roman emperor (306–37), 17
Cop, Michel, French reformer (*fl.* 1530–64), 229
Copernicus, Nicholas, Polish astronomer (1473–1543), 78, 279
Copia verborum et rerum, 8, 9, 12, 14, 91–4, 97, 191
Coppel, B., 44, *179 n.5*
Corbinelli, Jacopo, Italian publicist working in France (b. 1535), 302, *302 n.6* (G.Procacci)
Cordara, Giulio Cesare, Jesuit Neo-Latin satirist and literary historian (1704–85), *53*
Cordier, Mathurin, French pedagogue (1478–1564), 82
Cordus, Euricius (Heinrich Solde), German epigrammatist (1486–1535), 41 n.1

Corneille, Pierre, French dramatist (1606–84), *165 n.2*, 169, *270*

Coronea, district of Boeotia, Greece, 100

Corpus Christi College, Cambridge, 215, *215 n.3*, 217, Pl. 16*c*

Corpus Christi College, Oxford, 209, *209 n.3*

Corrarius, Gregorius, Venetian satirist (1411–64), *51*

Cortona, Pietro da, Tuscan painter and architect (1596–1669), 350, 353

Cosenza, M.E., *152 nn.1 and 4*

Counter-Reformation, 235–6; change in poetic style, 49, 58; hostility to paganism, 322, 344–5; study of the Fathers, 203

Cracow, Poland, 182 n.4

Cranevelt, Franciscus, Flemish lawyer and humanist (1485–1564), 241, *241 n.1* (H. de Vocht)

Cranz, Edward, 199

Crassus, L.Licinius, first-century B.C. Roman orator, 241

Crassus, Marcus, Roman politician (115–53 B.C.), 284

Cratylus, one of Plato's dialogues, 252

Crinitus, Petrus, Italian Neo-Latin poet (1465–1504), cited by Textor, 85

Croll, M.W., *5 n.1*

Crombie, A.C., *316 n.1*

Cronaca, *see* Pollaiuolo

Cszemiczei, János, *see* Janus Pannonius

Cugnoni, J., *173 n.1*

Cupid, 176 n.1, 331

Curii, Roman *gens*, noted for M' Curius Dentatus who conquered the Samnites, 282

Curtius, E.R., 91, *91 n.2*, *180 n.4*

Curtius (Q.Curtius Rufus), Roman historian, (*fl. c.* 50), owned by Cosimo de' Medici, 282

Cyprian, Saint, Latin theologian (*c.* 200–58), read by Colet, 214

Dacos, Nicole, 27, 29, *328 nn.2–3*, *329 n.2*, *330 n.1*, *331 nn.1–2*; publications, *325 n.1*, *327 n.1*

Dainville, F.de, *233 n.2*, *234 n.4*

Dalmatia (Croatia, Yugoslavia), its Neo-Latin literature, *43 n.2* (V.Gortan–V.Vratović), 59, 64

Damaso, Cortile di (Vatican), 27

Dampierre, Jean, French Neo-Latin poet (d. 1550), 193, *193 nn.2 and 4*, 194–7

Damste, Petrus, present-day Dutch Neo-Latin satirist 55

Danchin, F.C., 275 n.1

Dante Alighieri (1265–1321): his knowledge of Livy, Tacitus and Virgil, 282–3

Convito, 133; *Paradiso*, 283

Daphne, river god's daughter, chased by Apollo, 333, Pl. 6*b*

David, king of Israel (*c.* 1000 B.C.), 296, 330, 333

Decembrius, Angelus, Italian man of letters (*c.* 1415–66), 152, *152 n.1* (M.E.Cosenza), 153; debt to Guarino, *152 n.3* (R.Sabbadini)

Politia literaria 152, *152 n.3* (A.della Guardia)

Decii, noted Roman *gens*, 282

Dedekind, Friedrich, German satirist (1525–98), *41 n.5*

Degenhart, B., *339 n.3*

Deichmann, F.W., *340 n.3*

Delaruelle, L., 10, *10 n.1*, 14

Delbrück, R., *325 n.2*

Della Barba, Pompeo, Neapolitan physician and philosopher (d. 1582), 244

Della Casa, Giovanni (Johannes Casa), Italian writer on courtesy, and Neo-Latin poet (1503–56), *52*

Della Guardia, A., *152 n.3*

Della Porta, Giacomo, Italian architect (*c.* 1485–1555), 336

Della Volpaia, Bernardo, Italian architect, 339, 341–3, *341 n.1* (T.Ashby, T.Buddensieg), Pls. 7*c* and 8*c*

Deloney, Thomas, English writer of narrative (1543?–*c.* 1600), *96 n.1* (H.Rollins), 121

Delprat, G.H., *315 n.1*

Democritus, Greek atomist (*c.* 460–*c.* 370 B.C.), 252

Demosthenes, Athenian orator (384–22 B.C.), 78, 234, 241

Denmark, 36 n.4

De Sanctis, Francesco, Italian literary critic (1818–83), 300

Descartes, René (1596–1650), 70, 116

Desgraves, L., *36 n.4*

Despauterius, Johannes, Flemish grammarian (*c.* 1460–1520), 81

Des Périers, Bonaventure, French story writer and humanist (1498?–1544), 136

Devil (Satan), 23, 224, 225, 237, 268, 336–7

Devotio moderna, 2, **19**, 235

dialectic: educational role of, 13, *141 n.3*, **145**, **149–51**; Harvey's views on, 13, **145–7**, **150–3**; humanist reform of, 11, 12, 14, 14 n.2 (W.S.Howell, W.J.Ong, C.Vasoli), 73–5, *141 n.2*, **142–5**; **147–51**, (its implications for rhetoric) 15, 157; place of Aristotle in, 12, 13, 74–5, **248–58**, 316; Ramus's views on, 13, 74–5; Rudolphus Agricola's views on, 12, 13, 74, **147**, *147 n.4* (C.Vasoli), **148**, **150–1**; use of induction in, 145, 145 n.2; Valla's views on, 7, 11, 12, **73–4**, **141–5**, *144 n.3* (W. and M.Kneale, W.Risse), **150–1**; Vivès's views on, 75, 240, **248–58**; *see also* scholasticism

dialogues, 41, 41 n.3; by Textor *96 n.1* (*extensive bibliography*)

Diana, goddess, 184 n.3; in Calderón, 23, 264, 268
dictionaries, 8, 10, *10 n.1* (W.T.Starnes and E.W.Talbert)
Diderot, Denis, French philosopher (1713–84), 117, 295, 301–2
Diodorus Siculus, Greek historian (*fl.* 60–21 B.C.), 276
Diomedes, late-fourth-century Roman grammarian, 175, *175 n.1*
'Dionysius the Areopagite', name given to a fifth-century Neoplatonist philosopher: Grocyn's lectures on, 219; studied by Colet, 19, 214, 218–19; Valla and Erasmus on, 219
Dionysius, Saint (S. Denys), patron saint of France (d. 97), 337
Dionysius of Halicarnassus, Greek literary critic (*fl.* 30–8 B.C.), 102
Dionysus, god, 28, 327–8, *328 n.1* (C. Picard, C.Vermeule) *and n.2* (N. Dacos), 333, Pls. 3*a*, 3*d*, 4*b*
Diophantus of Alexandria, third-century A.D. Greek mathematician, 318, 318 n.1 (L.Olschki)
Dioscorides, Pedianos, Greek medical writer and botanist, first century A.D., 317, *317 n.2* (A.Koyré)
discourse, its importance for the Renaissance, **7–17**, **141–54**, **155–8**
docta pietas, 18–22, 24, 201, **229–36**
Dogaer, G., *208 n.3*
Dolet, Etienne, French reformer and Neo-Latin poet (1509–46), 53, 193
Dolet, Martin, Neo-Latin poet (*fl. c.* 1513), 82
Dominicans, 236
Domitian (Roman emperor 81–96), 299, 337
Domus aurea, Nero's palace in Rome, 326–7, *326 n.1* (W.Amelung, F. Weege), *327 n.1* (N.Dacos), 331, 331 n.1
Donatus, Aelius, fourth-century A.D. Roman grammarian, 131
Donne, John, English metaphysical poet (1572–1631), 156
Dorat, Jean (Auratus), French humanist and Neo-Latin poet (*c.* 1502–88), 85
Dörrie, Heinrich, 16
Douai (North France), works printed at, 82, 95
Dousa, Franciscus, Dutch humanist (1577–1606), 44
Dousa, Janus, Dutch academic and Neo-Latin poet (1545–1604), 45, 48, *52*, 178 n.4
Du Bellay, Joachim, bilingual French and Neo-Latin poet (1522–60), 10, 62–3; commonplaces in 130; on *copia*, 191; on imitation, 192
Regrets, 17, 130–1
Duhamel, P.A., *207 n.3*
Dupuy, Nicole (Bonaspes), early-sixteenth-century French grammarian, 82, 131

Duquesnoy, François, Flemish sculptor (1594–1642), 350, 350 n.2
Durandus, Gulielmus, anti-Thomist scholastic philosopher (1270/5–1332), 214
Durling, R.J.A., *317 n.1*
Durm, J., *340 n.1*

Eberle, Josef (Apellus), present-day German Neo-Latin satirist, 42, *42 n.6*, *54*
echoes, literary: from classical authors, *see* Avienus, Catullus, Horace, Lucan, Propertius, Terence, Tibullus, Valerius Flaccus, Virgil; from renaissance authors, *see* Celtes, Flaminio, Mantuanus, Pontano, Remacle d'Ardenne
Ecphantus, Greek astronomer, pupil of Hicetas (? fourth century B.C.), 78
Edinburgh, libraries 34, 35, 83 n.1
education: for civil life, 24, 149, 166–7, 242; in grammar schools, 20, 121 n.3; Jesuit aims for, 46, **233–4**, **236**; Ramist influence on, 13–14, 114–17; study of Greek, 20, 103, *103 n.4*, *151 n.1*, 230–3; teaching of *copia verborum*, 83–5, 100–2, 191, of *copia rerum*, 91–2, 97–100, 114–17; textbooks, 81–2, 153, *153 n.2* (L.Jardine); university curricula, 13, *13 n.1* (L.Jardine), *141 n.3* (J.Weisheipl, J.P.Mullally, T.Heath), 146–7, *147 n.3* (J.B.Mullinger), 151; *see also* Christian humanism, *copia* and dialectic (humanist reforms in)
Egger, H., *346 n.2*
Egypt, 24, 76, *76 n.1*, 134, 166 n.2, 272–8
Elam, Caroline, 345 n.2
elegy: classical, 171, *172 n.2* (G.Luck), **174–5**; history of, *171 n.2* (J.W.Tibble, F.Beissner), *172 n.2* (J.Wiegand, C.M.Scollen); imitation in, 16, **180–1**, 188; influence of Petrarch on, 173, *173 n.2* (J.Sparrow, L.Forster); J.C. Scaliger on, 16, 17, **175**, 175 n.4, 176 n.1, **177**; Lotichius as elegist, **177–90**; modern, 171, *171 n.1* (A.F. Potts, K.Weissenberger); *querimonia* in, 16, **174–7**, 183, 183 n.4, 185; theory of, 16, *171 n.1* (J.Berryman etc.), *174 n.1* (I.Behrens), 175, *175 n.4* (R.M.Ferraro), **176**, 176 n.1, 177, 190, *190 n.4*; used in love-cycles, **172–3**; use of animal themes in, 184 n.6 (G.Herrlinger, J.Hutton); use of autobiographical detail in, 17, 179, 182, 182 n.4, 183–4
Ellinger, G., *172 n.3*, 179, *179 n.3*
Emden, A.B., *205 n.2*
Emmanuel College, Cambridge, 215, *215 n.2*
encomia, 41, *41 n.4*
encyclopedias, 102, *102 n.1*, 117, 125, 134
England, 100, 277, 321; Latin verse in, *42 n.7* (L.Bradner), 64; Renaissance in, 58; Textor's popularity in, 82

English language: replaces Latin, 39; use of Latin commonplace material in, 9, 10, *10 n.1* (W.T.Starnes, E.W. Talbert), 96 n.2, 100, 118–25

Ennius, Quintus, Roman epic poet (239–169 B.C.), 240

Enzinger, M., *49 n.2*

epicedia, 177, 184 n.6, 185, 185 n.4

Epicharis, slave who heroically endured Nero's tortures, 285, 285 n.3

Epicurus, Greek philosopher (341–270 B.C.), 78

epigrams, 41, *41 n.1* (F.-R.Hausmann, H.C.Schnur, K.-H.Mehnert), 130

Epiphanius, Christian Greek biographer (310–403), 94 n.1

Erasmus, Desiderius (1466–1536), 82, 112, 242; cited by Textor, 97, 100; editions of his works, 3; his attitude to classical learning, 226 n.1, **229–32**; his collections of commonplace material, 8, 9, 92 n.2; his condemnation urged, 229; his educational ideas, 92, **229–32**; his influence: (at Sainte-Barbe) 229, (on Rabelais) 10, *10 n.1*, (on the Jesuits) 223, 225–7, 233–4, 236, (on Vivès) 240, 246; his integration of Christian and classical values, 19–22, 226, 226 n.1, **229–36**; his study of Greek, 223, 229, 232; his patristic studies, 18, 200, 203, 233; his rejection of scholasticism, 230; his relations with Colet, 207, 207 nn.4–5, 214, 229; his use of classical genres, 5, 232; his views on: (Cicero's salvation) 231, (*copia*) 8, 12, 191, (dialectic) 74, (fable) 159, (Seneca) 231–2, (Socrates's sanctity) 231, 246–7, (style) 17, 104, **192–6**, 193 n.1 (H.Friedrich), 230; impression made on him by: (the *devotio moderna*) 235, (More) 21, 230, (Neoplatonism) 229, 233, 235, (Origen) 230

Adagia, 8, *9 n.1*, 129–31, 196, 223, 230, 232; *Antibarbari*, 192; *Apophthegmata*, 8, 9 n.1, 151 n.1; *Ciceronianus*, 47, 191, 192, 196, 230–1; *Colloquia*, 94 n.1, *207 n.4*, ('Convivium religiosum') 231, 246–7; *De duplici copia verborum et rerum*, 8, *8 n.1*, 85, *85 n.2*, 94, 94 n.1, 191; *De libero arbitrio*, 231; *De pueris . . . instituendis*, 231; *De recta Latini et Graeci pronuntiatione*, 18; *Encheiridion militis christiani*, 192, 230, 233, 235; *Moriae Encomium* (*The Praise of Folly*), 5, 41 n.4, 230, 235; *Novum Testamentum* (translation), 208–9, 235; *Parabola* 94 n.1, 97 n.3, *151 n.1* (J.C.Margolin); *Paraphrases in Evangelia*, 225, 227, 230; *Poems*, 60 n.1, 63–4, 94 n.1; *Tusculanae disputationes* (edition), 226, 231

Erythraeus, Ianus (Gian Vittorio Rossi), bilingual Italian and Neo-Latin poet (1577–1647), 55

Eskimos, 277, *277 n.1*

esoteric wisdom, *see* Cabbala

Esseiva, Peter, Swiss Neo-Latin poet (1823–99), 42, *42 n.8* (J.Baumgarten), 54

Estienne, Charles, French encyclopedist (1504–64), 10, *10 n.1* (W.T.Starnes and E.W.Talbert), 321

Etter, E.-L., *322 n.1*

Euclid, third-century B.C. Greek mathematician, 76, 318, *318 n.1* (L.Olschki); editions, 317, *317 n.2* (A.Koyré)

Euripides, Athenian tragic poet (480–406 B.C.), 78

Europa, Phoenecian princess abducted by Jupiter, 261–2

Eusebius, Greek ecclesiastical historian (265–340), 282; *In Hieroclem*, 200; *Praeparatio evangelica* 18, *18 n.2* (L. Schuhan), 200–1, 266

Eve (Biblical), 332

Everaerts, J., *see* Joannes Secundus

exempla, 8, 103, 113

exploration, its effects on ideas, 277

Fabricius, Georg, German classical scholar (1516–71), 180 n.1

Fabritii, Roman *gens*, noted for C.Fabritius Luscinus, the conqueror of Pyrrhus, 282

Farnaby, Thomas, English schoolmaster (1575–1647), 167, 167 n.1

Farnese, Cardinal Alessandro, patron of humanist learning (1520–89), 349

Farnesina, villa in Rome, 331

Fasolo, F., *325 n.2*

Fathers of the Church, humanist interest in, 17–18, 20–1, 72, **199–203**, 214, 230, 241 n.3

Fénelon, François de la Mothe de, French theologian and educator (1651–1715), *292 n.3*

Ferdinand V, king of Aragon (1468–1516), 97

Ferguson, W.K., *67 n.1*, 70 n.3

Fernel, Jean, French medical writer and mathematician (1497–1558), 228

Ferrari, Gaudenzio, Italian painter and sculptor (1484–1546), 331 n.1

Ferraro, R.M., *175 n.4*

Ferrucius, Aloisius, late-nineteenth-century Italian Neo-Latin satirist, 55

Festugière, A.J., *76 n.1*

Ficino, Marsilio, Florentine Neoplatonist and translator (1433–99): studied by Colet, **212–14**, *213 n.1* (S.Jayne), 219; *Theologia Platonica*, 244

fiction (or fable), 15, **158–62**

Filarete, Antonio, writer on architecture (*c.* 1400–*c.* 1470), 353

Filelfo, Francesco, Italian humanist (1398–1481), 42, *42 n.4*, *51*, 64

Fiocco, G., *336 n.1*

Fischli, W., *169*

Flaminio, Marcantonio, Italian Neo-Latin poet (1498–1550), 63; echoes in Lotichius, 188, 188 n.3
Flavian Palace (on the Palatine), 351
Fleming, D.A., *49 n.3*, 50
Fleming, Paul, bilingual German and Neo-Latin poet (1609–40), 47, 47 nn.4–5, 53
Florence (Firenze), 25, *71 n.2* (D.Thompson, A.F.Nagel), 213; Bibliotheca Nazionale at, 340, 340 n.1; Guicciardini's view of, 290, *290 n.2* (R.von Albertini), 295, 297, 299; its architecture and painters in the fifteenth century, 338; its historians, *71 n.1* (D.J.Wilcox); its Neo-Latin poets, *51* (G.Bottigliani); Machiavelli's view of, 285–6
fiorilegia, see anthologies
Florus, Lucius(?), second-century epitomist of Livy, 286 n.6
Flynn, W.J., *207 n.1*
Folly, in Rabelais, 120–1; *see also* Erasmus, *Moriae encomium*
Fontana, Carlo, Italian architect (1638–1714), 343, *343 n.3*, 344, 344 n.1, Pl. 9 *a–b*
Fontenay, Guy de, early-sixteenth-century French grammarian, 82
Forrer, Mme Veyrin, 33 n.2
Forster, L.W., v, *173 n.2*
Fortuna: in Rabelais 128, in Textor 86; personified in art, 328
Fortuna Virilis, temple of, 350
Forum, see Nerva, Trajan
Fracastoro, Girolamo, Italian doctor and Neo-Latin poet (1483–1553), 48, *61 n.1*, 63
Fraenkel, E., 164, *169*
Fraiman, K.A. O'Rourke, *178 n.2*, 182 n.1, 183 nn.2–3
Frame, D.M., *135 n.1*
France: agriculture in, 321; British Library holdings of books printed in, 34, *34 n.1*, 35, *35 n.2*; development of elegy in, *172 n.2* (C.M.Scollen); Italian books held by libraries in, 35 n.4 (S. and P.M.Michel); La Peyrère's attitude to, 272, 279, 279 n.5; Lotichius's visits to, 182, 185; Neo-Latin verse in, 64; *see also* Gallia, Maison Carrée
Franchini, Francesco, Italian Neo-Latin poet (*fl.* 1541–9), 64
Francis I (king of France 1515–47), 86, 201, 296
Frank de Frankenau, G., eighteenth-century Dutch Neo-Latin satirist, *53*
Frankfurt/Main, 178
French language: stylistic influence of Latin on, 191–2, 195–7; use of commonplace material in, 10, 100, **127–34**; use of Latin to complete meaning of, 10–11, **135–40**

Friedländer, P., *341 n.2*
Friedrich, Hugo, 133, 192, 196
Frischlin, Nicodemus, bilingual German and Neo-Latin poet (1547–90), *52*
Froben, Johann, Basle printer (1460–1527), 225, 227
Frontinus, Sextus Julius, Roman writer on military science (*c.* 30–104), 295 n.3, 320 n.2
Fulgentius, Roman allegorist (468–533), 262
Furnival (Fournival), Richard de, medieval French fabulist (1200–*c.* 1255), 132–3

'Gaeomemphion du Cantal' (? François Guyet, 1575–1655), pen name of French Neo-Latin satirist, 54, 50, *50 n.1*
Gagliardi, D., *47 n.2*
Gaguin, Robert, French historian and Neo-Latin poet (1425–1502), 81, 84
Galba, C. Sulpicius, Roman Emperor (68 A.D.), 292
Gale, Thomas, English schoolmaster (1635–1702), 216
Galen (Claudius Galenus), Greek medical writer (129–*c.* 201), 76, 78, 256; renaissance editions of his works, 316–17, 317 n.1 (R.J.A.Durling), 318 n.1
Galilei, Galileo (1564–1642), 70
Gallenfels, Carolus, Austrian Neo-Latin satirist, *53*
Gallia, 83
Galvan, E.T., *322 n.1*
Garcia-Villoslada, R., *233 n.1*, 234 n.3
Garin, E., *67 n.1*, *68 n.1*, 70 nn.1 and 3, 76 n.1, *78 n.1*
Garnier, Robert, French tragic poet (1534–90), 165 n.3
Gaspar Veronensis, professor of Latin at Rome (1400–74), 42, *42 n.1* (V.Cian, P.O.Kristeller)
Gassendi, Pierre, French physicist and freethinker (1592–1655), 292
Geldenhauer, Gerardus, Dutch Neo-Latin satirist, *52*
Gelida, Johannes, Spanish academic and reformer (d. 1556), 228
Geneva, works printed at, 38
genre-theory, *172 n.1* (K.W.Hempfer)
Geoponica, see Bassus
Germanicus, Roman general, nephew of Tiberius (d. A.D. 19), 292, 301
Germany: agriculture in, 321; blamed for Gothic style, 337; catalogue of libraries in, *36 n.4* (W. Nijhoff and M.E.Kronenberg); Bodin's view of its government, 310; books in its libraries, *36 n.4*; British Library holdings of books printed in, 34, *34 n.1*, 35; epigrammatists in, *41 n.4* (H.C.Schnur); Lotichius in, 182–3, 183 n.4, 185; Neo-Latin literature in,

Germany (*cont.*)
52 (Ranutius Gherus), 64, *172 n.3*
(G.Ellinger), *179 nn.1–5* (M.Rupprich, A.Schroeter, B.Coppel, K.O. Conrady), *189 n.3* (H.C.Schnur); satirists in, *44 n.2* (G.Hess)
Gerson (Jean Charlier), French theologian (1362–1428), 191, 224
Gesner, Conrad, Swiss humanist and naturalist (1516–65), 318
Geymüller, H. von, *340 n.1*, 342 n.2
Gherus, Ranutius, pseudonym, *see* Gruter, Janus
Ghiberti, Lorenzo, Italian sculptor and art historian (1378?–1455), 344
Giannoti, Donato, Italian political thinker (1492–1573), 289
Gideon (biblical), 23, 269
Gilbert, N.W., *74 n.2*
Gilmore, M.P., *68 n.1*
Gilson, J.P., *208 n.5*
Giocondo, Fra (Giovanni di Verona), Italian architect and sculptor (1457–1525), *339 n.1*
Giorgio Martini, Francesco di, Italian architect (*fl.* 1486), 338 n.5, 339, *339 n.1*, 340
Giovanni da Udine, Italian painter and architect (1487–1564), 325 n.1, 327
Giovanni, Matteo di Giorgio, Italian painter, 338 n.5
Giraldi, Lilio Gregorio, Italian poet and mythographer (1492–1552), 263
Glorieux, G., *36 n.4*
Goddaeus, Conradus, Dutch writer of paradoxical encomia (d. 1658), *41 n.4*
Godfrey, W.R., *221 n.2*
Golden Age, 78, *78 n.1*; in Spain, 259, 262
Golden Fleece (legend), 269–70
Golzio, V., *325 n.3*
Gómez-Moreno, M., *338 n.4*
Gongora y Argote, L. Spanish mannerist poet (1561–1627), 259
Gottsched, J. C., German literary critic (1700–66), 169
Gouvea, Andrea de (Goveanus), Portuguese jurist and reformer (d. 1548), 228–9
Gouvea, Diego de (Goveanus), Portuguese theologian (1505–66), 228, *228 n.1* (M.Bataillon), 229
Gozzoli, Benozzo, Florentine goldsmith and painter (1420–98): *Babilonia*, 338; Rotterdam sketchbook, 339, *339 n.3* (B.Degenhart, A.Schmitt), Pl. *7a*
Gratianus, Franciscus, compiler of the first systematic work on canon law, (*c.* 115), 292
Gravina, Gianvicenzo, Italian tragedian and critic (1664–1718), 48
Greece, ancient, 7, 17, 20, 24, 63
Greek language: Byzantine teaching of, 6 n.1; extent to which it was studied, 103, 103 n.4, 233; grammars owned by students, 153, *153 n.2* (L.Jardine);

Harvey lectures in, 151 n.1; learnt by Erasmus, 223; quotations latinised by Textor, 97; value of, 20
Gregg Press, 3, 129, *245 n.1*
Gregorio di Rimini, Italian logician (d. 1358), 241 n.2
Gregory I, Saint (Pope 590–604), 344, *344 n.2* (T.Buddensieg), 345
Gregory of Nyssa, Greek theologian (*c.*330–*c.* 400), 200
Grenan, Benignus, Paris classical professor and translator (1681–1723), *53*
Griffiths, Carlotta, vii, 8
Grillparzer, Franz, Austrian dramatist (1791–1872), 270
Grocyn, William, English theologian and humanist (*c.* 1446–1519), 219
grotesques, 326–32
Grotius, Hugo, Dutch jurist and Neo-Latin poet (1583–1645), 164, 166
Gruter, Jan, Dutch scholar and anthologist (1560–1627), *52*, 193, *193 n.3*, 320 n.1
Gualengo, Giovanni, fifteenth-century Italian humanist, 152
Guarino da Verona, Italian humanist (1374–1460): relations with Chrysoloras, *6 n.1*, with Angelo Decembrio, 152, *152 n.3* (R.Sabbadini), with Poggio, 284, *284 n.2* (H.Baron)
Guglielmini, Bernardo, Italian Neo-Latin poet, *54*
Guicciardini, Francesco, Florentine historian (1482–1540): influence, 302, 322; political opinions, 295–8, 300–1; relations with the Medici, 25, 290, *290 n.2* (R.von Albertini); use of Tacitus, **295–9**, 299 n.1, 302
Le cose fiorentine, 295; *Ricordi*, 295–7, 299, 302
Guicciardini, Lodovico, Italian historian and geographer (1478–1551), 290 *290 n.3*
Guidi, V.G., *286 n.1*
Gullini, G., *325 n.2*
Gundolf, F., *169*
Guy, A., 252, *252 n.2*, 254
Guyenne, Collège de, Bordeaux, refounded as a humanist school in 1534, 229
Guyet, François, *see* 'Gaeomemphion'

Haddon, Walter, English pamphleteer and Neo-Latin poet, 64
Hadrian (Aelius Hadrianus) (Roman emperor 117–38), 288; his villa, 326, *326 n.1* (W.Amelung, F.Weege)
Hagia Sophia, Constantinople, *341 n.2* (P.Friedländer, H.Jantz, C.Mango)
Hagius, Johannes, 181, 181 n.1
Hajnal, I., *103 n.3*
Halevi, Judah ben Samuel, Jewish poet-philosopher (*c.* 1085–1190), 272, 272 n.3
Haller, R., *179 n.1*

Hallie, P.P., *135 n.1*
Hamlet, the gravedigger scene, 96 n.1
Hannibal, Carthaginian general (247–183 B.C.), 113
Harding, Thomas, Anglican divine and controversialist (1516–72), 205, 205 n.1, 207
Harig, G., *316 n.1*
Harington, Sir John, English man of letters (1560–1612), 159, *159 n.3*, 160
Hariot, Thomas, English mathematician (1560–1621), 274, *275 n.1* (J.Jacquot)
Harvey, Gabriel, English scholar and critic (c. 1545–c. 1630), 13, **145–53**; his education, *151 n.2* (V.F.Stern); his Greek lectures, *151 n.1* (T.W.Baldwin) *Marginalia*, 149, *149 n.4* (Moore Smith), *150 n.1* (J.C.Margolin)
Hassenstein a Lobkowic, Bohuslav, Bohemian Neo-Latin satirist (d. 1510), 51
Hausmann, R., *41 n.1*
Havelock, E., 94, *94 n.2*, 118
Havraeus, Joannes, Flemish Neo-Latin poet (1549–1625), 52
Hay, Denys, 2, 324; publications, *67 n.1*
Haydn, H., *70 n.2*
Heath, T., *141 n.3*
Hebrew, 134
Heckscher, W.S., *338 n.2*
Heerkens, Gerardus, Dutch physician and Neo-Latin satirist (1726–1801), 54
Heidelberg (Palatinate, Germany), 178, 186, 186 n.4
Heinsius, Daniel, Dutch classical scholar (1580/1–1655), *165 n.1*
Hempfer, K.W., *172 n.1*
Henry II (king of France 1547–59), 296
Heraclides of Pontus, Greek astronomer (c. 388–c. 315 B.C.), 78
Herbert, George, English religious poet (1593–1633), 121, *121 n.1* (V.R. Mollenkott)
Hercules, 202, 327; the Gallic, 83
Herde, P., *68 n.1*
Heresbach, Conrad, German agronomist and educationist (1491–1576), 321
Hermann of Fritzlar, German mystic (*fl. c.* 1350), 336
Hermes, god, 269; 'Trismegistus', 277
Hermogenes, second-century A.D. Greek rhetorician, 74, 102
Hermophilus, *see* Bodecherus
Herodian, Greek historian translated by Politian (170–240), 286 n.6, 287
Herodotus, Ionian historian (c. 484–c. 425 B.C.), 276
Herrick, M. T., *160 n.2*
Herrlinger, G., *184 n.6*
Hervet, Gentien, French ecclesiastic and translator (1499–1584), 245
Hesperides, daughters of Atlas, 261
Hess, G., *44 n.2*
Hessus, Eobanus, German humanist translator (1488–1540), 185 n.6, *189 n.2*

Higman, F.M., 191
Hippocrates, supposed author of a body of Greek medical literature (460–377 B.C.), 78
Hirsch, E.T., 128
historiography: humanist, *71 n.1* (N. Struever, D.J.Wilcox), 282–3, 283 n.4 (H.Baron); Ramist, **111–16**
Hobbes, Thomas, English political theorist (1588–1679), 311
hodoeporicon (an itinerary, an account of a journey), 185, *185 n.6*
Hog (G.Hogaeus), Latin translator of *Paradise Lost* (1690), 5 n.2
Holberg, Ludwig, Scandinavian satirist and dramatist (1684–1754), 50, *50 n.3*
Holdsworth, Richard, Cambridge academic (*fl.* 1613–43), 215
Höltgen, K.J., *115 n.3*
Homer, 119, *119 n.1* (G.Carlson), 249, 277; *Iliad*, 118, 186; *see also* Ulysses
Horace (Q.Horatius Flaccus), Roman lyric poet, critic and satirist (65–8 B.C.), 293; cited, 84, 276; echoes of his verses, 41, 42, 45, 46, 180 n.4, 190, 190 n.3; his popularity, 38, 137 n.2, 153, *153 n.2* (L.Jardine); his theories on elegy, **174–7**, 183 n.4
Ars Poetica, 160, *160 n.2* (M.H.Abrams, B.Vickers, M.T.Herrick), 161, 168, 174, 176, 176 n.1
Horman, William, English schoolmaster, 121 n.3
Hortensius, Lambertus, Dutch Neo-Latin poet, 52
Hortis, A., *285 n.3*
Hotman, François, French jurist and political thinker (1524–90), 310
Housman, A.E., English poet and classical scholar (1859–1936), 3
Houtisberus, scholastic philosopher, 241 n.2
Howell, W.S., 14, *14 n.2*, 74; publications, *156 n.1*
Hrdina, K., *51*
Huddleston, Sir John, 210 n.1
Huddleston, L.E., *274 n.1*
Huet, Pierre Daniel, French scholar and Neo-Latin poet (1630–1721), 47, *47 n.6*
Hugo de Flavigny, chronicler (c. 1065–after 1111), 337, *337 n.2*
Hulsen, C., *340 n.2*
humanism
   definition of, 141 n.1
   importance of *copia* for, 8, 9, **82–90**, **91–101**, 120, 191; *see also* commonplace material
   importance of discourse for, 6, 7, **67–76**, **141–54**
   its campaign for correct Latin, 4, 5, 5 n.1, 6, 6 n.2, 46–7, 71–2, 81–2, 104, 192, 240–2
   its changing aims, 4, 8, 20–1, 67–80

humanism (*cont.*)
  its cult of style, 71–5, 192, 195–7, 240–2, 246
  its contribution: in dialectic, 7, 11–14, 73, 141–54, **249–52**; in literary criticism, 14–16, 155–62, 163–5, 168–9, 171–7; in philosophy, 19, 22, 212, 218–21, 245–58; to educational reforms, 20, 210, 223, 232–4; to esoteric learning, 24, 76, 271–80; to information retrieval, 11, **102–19**, 125, 306; to biblical and patristic studies, 3, 17–19, **195–204**, 207, 210 n.1, 214–16, 218, 230, 237–8; to political thought and behaviour, 6, 18, 24–6, 165–7, 239–43, 281–93, 295–303, 304–16, 321–3; to scientific and technical progress, 6, 26, 78, **313–21**; to vernacular literature, 5, 5 nn.1 and 2, 9, 120–5, 127–34, 191–7
  its emphasis on the understanding of texts, 19, 20, 73, 225, 226, 226 n.1, 229–32, 235
  its excursions into bilingualism, 5 n.2, 10, 127–34, 135–40
  its high valuation of liberty, 72, 165–9, 283–9
  its literary achievements, 4, 41–51, 57–64, 81, 177–90
  its treatment of pagan mythology, 259–70, 327–34
  its valuation of pagan ideas, 226, 229–37, 239–44, 245–58, 281
  regarded as heretical, 230
  rôle of imitation in, 5, 5 n.1, 6, 6 n.1, 16, 19, 41, 41 nn.1–5, 45, 76, 134, 165, 171–81, 192, 194
  the need for editions and catalogues of its literature, 33–9, 43–4
Hume, David, Scottish historian and philosopher (1714–76), 279
Hungary, 59, 64
Hunt, E.W., *218 n.2*
Hussovianus, N., Polish Neo-Latin poet (*c.* 1480–*c.* 1533), 64
Hutten, Ulrich von, German polemist and satirist (1488–1523), 41 nn.1 and 3, *52, 60 n.1* (Boecking), 82, 189 n.3
  Aula. Dialogus, 96, 97, *97 n.1*; *Epistolae obscurorum virorum*, 41 n.2, 46
Hutton, J., *184 n.6*
Hygieia, goddess of health, 347, *347 n.2* (T.Buddensieg)

Iamblichus, Syrian Neoplatonist philosopher (*c.* 250–*c.* 326), 276
Ibn Wahshiyya, Arab philosopher (*fl. c.* 904), 272, 272 n.3
Iceland, 36 n.4
IJsewijn, J., 2, 3, 39; publications, *41 n.1*, *185 n.6*
Imitatio Christi (Thomas à Kempis), 19
imitation, 75–6, 192, 195–6; in architecture, 339–44, 349–54; in art, 326–34;

of language, 5 n.1, 6, 103–4, 192, *see also* copia; of literary genres, 5, 16, 41, *41 nn.1–5*, 46, 49, 152; of literary style, 173, 179, 179 n.5, 180, 180 n.2, 191, *see also* echoes, literary; techniques of, 6 n.1, 191; *for imitations of literary content, see* commonplace material *and* mythology; *in general see also* Lucan, Lucian, Lucilius
Index Aureliensis, 36, 36 n.3
Index librorum prohibitorum, 38, *38 n.1* (F.Reusch), n.2 (H.J.Martin and A. Rotondo)
indexes, *see* alphabetical arrangement
India, 24, 228
information retrieval, 11, **102–19**, 125, 306
Inquisition, Roman, 38, 227
inventio, 8, 12–13, 107, **142–9**
Isaac, biblical, 330
Israel, lost tribes, 274
Isidore of Seville, Roman encyclopedist (*c.* 570–636), 267
Italy: academies in, 48, 48 n.1 (I.Carini); activity of presses in, 37, 38; agriculture in, 321; catalogues of books printed in, 34, 34 n.1, 35, *35 n.5* (S. and P.Michel), 36, 36 n.2; Colet visits, 213; epigrammatists in, *41 n.1* (F.R.Hausmann); Lotichius visits, 182, 185; Neo-Latin verse in, 60–1, 63–4; satirists in, 42, *44 n.2* (U.Limentani)

Jackson, W.A., 37
Jacob, biblical, 332
Jacquot, J., *275 n.1*
Jahn, O., *327 n.4*
James, Thomas, librarian of Bodley, 38, 38 n.3
Jantzen, H., *341 n.2*
Janus Pannonius (Csezmiczei János), Hungarian humanist poet, 16, 62, 64
Jardine, Lisa, 7, 11, 15 *142 n.3*; publications, *13 n.1*, *141 n.3*, *153 n.2*
Jason, leader of the Argonauts in the quest for the Golden Fleece, 261, 265
Jauregui, Juan de, Spanish literary critic and translator, 164 n.4
Jayne, Sears, *205 n.2*, *206 n.1*, 213, *218 n.2*
Jean d'Udine, *see* Giovanni da Udine
Jericho, biblical city, 333
Jerome, Saint (331–420), 85, 94 n.1, 213; studied by Erasmus, 18, 200, 214, 229, 231, 232
Jesuits, 228; early prejudice against Greek, 230–1, *231 n.1* (G.Schurhammer); educational ideas, 21, 46, 168, *168 n.1* (J.Müller), 223, 233–6; interest in natural science, 233; satirists among, 46, 49
  Constitutiones, 224, 233, 235; *Regulae communes*, 228; *Regulae concionatorum*, 233

Jewel, John, Anglican divine, 205, 219, 219 n.7
Joannes de Garlandia, medieval grammarian and Latin poet (*fl.* 218–52), 175
Joannes Secundus (Jan Everaerts), Flemish Neo-Latin poet (1511–36), 62–4, 86, 176 n.1, 178, 178 n.5
John III (king of Portugal 1521–57), 228, 252
John of Salisbury, English political thinker and philosopher (1110–80), 73
Johnson, A.F., 35, *35 n.1*, 38, *38 n.5*
Johnson, Samuel (1709–84), 98
Johnson, Thomas, English botanist and collector of commonplaces (d. 1644), 96 n.1
Jonas, Justus, canonist (1493–1555), 207
Jonson, Ben (1572/3–1637), 10, *10 n.1* (W.T.Starnes and E.W.Talbert), *115 n.3* (T. A Beaurline); *Timber,* 159, *159 nn.5–6* (L.J.Potts)
Jordan, river in Palestine, 332
Joseph, biblical, 330, 332–3, Pl. 6*a*
Josephus Flavius, Greek historian of the Jews (37–95), 276
Joshua, biblical, 330
Joyce, James, Irish novelist, 125
Judaism, 23, 268–9, **271–80**
Judith, biblical heroine, 23, 268
Julius II, Pope (1503–13), 325
Jupiter, god, 261–2
Juvenal (Decimus Julius Juvenalis), Roman satirist (*c.* 50–after 127), 3, 44; cited by Textor, 85; commentary, *42 n.1*; imitations, 41–2, 46
Juvencus, Vettius Aquilinus, Christian Latin poet (*fl.* 332), cited by Textor, 84

Kania, H., *344 n.1*
Kassel, R., 341 n.2
Kelcz, Emericus, S.J., Hungarian theologian and Neo-Latin satirist (1707–92), *53*
Keltis, *see* Celtes
Kempo of Texel, Dutch Neo-Latin poet (*fl. c.* 1515), *51*
Kenney, E.J., v
Ker, N.R., 212
King, William, English Neo-Latin satirist (1663–1712), 42, *42 n.7* (L.Bradner), 53
King's College, Cambridge, 335 n.1; 1969 conference, v, vii, 28–9, 335; 1974 conference, v, 1, 3–6, 14, 16–18, 41
Kirk, G.S., 22, *22 n.1*
Klopstock, Friedrich, German lyric poet (1724–1803), 179
Kneale, W. and M., *144 n.3*
Kochanowski, Jan, bilingual Polish and Neo-Latin poet (1532–84), 5 n.2, 64
Kocher, P.H., *272 n.1*, *275 n.1*
Koschaker, P., *317 n.3*

Koyré, A., *78 n.2*, *317 n.2*
Kratzer, Nicolas, German astronomer working in England (1486/7–1530), *208 n.3* (O.Pächt), *217 n.7*
Kraus, T., *340 n.3*
Kris, E., *329 n.1*
Kristeller, P.O., *67 n.1*, *76 n.1*, 91, *91 n.1*, 118, *141 n.2*, *199*
Kronenberg, M.E., *36 n.4*

Labacco (Antonio dell'Abacco), Italian architect (b. 1495), 353, *353 n.2*
La Boétie, Etienne de, French political thinker (1530–63), 308
Lachesis, one of the Fates, 241
Lactantius, Caecilius Firmianus, Roman patristic writer (*c.* 250–317?) cited by Textor, 84
Lambin (Lambinus), Denys, French classical scholar (1520–72), 85, 305
Lampridius, Aelius, Roman historian (d. 300), 286 n.6
Lanciani, R., *338 n.2*
Landi, Ortensio, Italian humanist (1500–after 1543), 47, *47 n.2* (D.Gagliardi)
Landino, Cristoforo, Florentine Neoplatonist (1424–1504), 173
Lanfranco, Giovanni, Italian painter (1580–1647), 350
La Penna, A., 25, 30
La Peyrère, Isaac (1596–1676), **271–80**, *271 n.1* (R.H.Popkin), *273 n.1* (O.Zöckler), *275 n.4* (R.H.Popkin) *Prae-Adamitae,* 271, 276
Laocoon, first-century B.C. Rhodian statuary group by Agesander, Polydorus and Athenodorus, *350 n.2*
La Ramée, *see* Ramus
Latin: archaism in verse, 46–7; cult of correct Latin, 4–7, 6 n.1, 71–3, 103–4, 192, 239; Montaigne's Latin quotations, 137; required for understanding Christian literature, 21; *see also* bilingualism, Ciceronianism, imitation
latinisation of names, 62, *62 n.1* (I.Bywater)
Lauremberg, Joannes, German Neo-Latin dramatist (1590–1658), 46, *52*
Laureti, Tommaso, Italian painter and architect (1530–1602), 345
law, 27, 128–9, 134, 317, *317 nn.3–4* (P.Koschaker, F.Wieacker)
Leach, A.F., *210 nn.2* and 4
Lechner, J.M., 92, *92 n.3*
Leeds, Duke of, 218, 218 n.2
Lefèvre d'Etaples, Jacques, French theologian and educator (*c.* 1455–1536), 82; his commentary on Aristotle's *Politics,* 305–6; his recension of the pseudo-Dionysius, 219
Lefranc, P., *275 n.1*
Legenda aurea, hagiographical work by Jacobus da Voragine (1230–98), 336–7

Leibhard, J., *see* Camerarius, J.
Lemaire de Belges, Jean, French *rhéto-riqueur*, poet and historian (d. after 1515), 191
Leo VI (Byzantine emperor 886–912), 319, 319 n.1
Leo X (Giovanni de' Medici) (Pope 1513–21), 286, 334; his interest in ancient monuments, 344–5; his part in Raphaël's loggias, 325, 325, n.3 (V.Golzio), 328–9, 329 n.1
Leonello d'Este, ruler of Ferrara (1407–50), 152
Le Palmier, Jacques (Le Paumier de Grentemesnil, Palmerius), French scholar and traveller (1587–1676), 167 n.4
Lepidus, M.Antonius, consul A.D. 6 (d. before 36), 299–301
Leptis Magna, ancient North African city, 350–1
Le Roy, Louis (Regius), French philosopher and translator (1510–77), 305–6, 310
Levi, A.H.T., 20–2; publications, 67 n.1
Levin, H., 78 n.1
Leyden, 38
l'Hôpital, Michel de, French statesman and Neo-Latin poet (1505–73), 61 n.1, 63
Liberale da Verona, Italian painter (c. 1445–1528/9), 338 n.5
Liberty, personified, 328
libraries, 33–9; *see also* Bibliothèque Nationale, British Library, Cambridge University, Corpus Christi College, Edinburgh University, Emmanuel College, Florence, Trinity College
Ligota, C.R., 240 n.1
Lily, William, headmaster of St Paul's School (1468–1522), 206, 207, 207 n.1 (V.J.Flynn, C.G.Allen)
Limentani, U., 44 n.2
Linacre, Thomas, English physician and humanist (c. 1460–1524), 82
Lindfors, B., 108 n.1
Lippius, Laurentius, Florentine Neo-Latin satirist (c. 1440–85), 51
Lipsius, Justus, Flemish scholar (1547–1606): on military organisation, 315 n.1, 319 nn.2 and 4; on Tacitus, 291–2, 291 n.4
Politica, 26–7, 319, 322, 322 n.2 and 323 n.1 (both G.Oestreich)
Somnium, 49
literary criticism, 15, 155–62
Livy (Titus Livius), Roman historian (59 B.C.–A.D. 17), 34, 281 n.6, 285, 292; Alciat on, 291, 291 n.3; cited by Textor, 85; early humanists on, 25, 281–2, 281 n.5 (G.Billanovich), 283; editions and translations, 282, 285; Machiavelli on, 286, 289, 290, 289 n.2 and 290 n.1 (both S.Bertelli); Sicco Polentone on, 284, 284 n.3

LOC project, 36–7, 39
Loggia of Psyche (Villa Farnesina), 331
logic, *see* dialectic
London, works printed in, 82, 95
Lorenzetti (Lorenzotto, Lorenzo Lotti), Italian sculptor, assistant to Raphaël (1490–1541), 347
Lotichius, Christianus, brother of Petrus, 178
Lotichius, J.P., 180 n.1
Lotichius, Petrus, German Neo-Latin poet (1528–60), 16–17, **177–90**; biography, 178, 178 n.2 (H.Rupprich, K.A. Fraiman), 179 n.2, 181, 181 n.1, 182–6; editions, 178, 178 n.3 (A. Heimpel, K.Fraiman, P. Burmann); indebtedness to classical poets, **179–80**, **182–4**; reputation, 179, 179 n.3 (G.Ellinger, A.Schroeter), 180 n.1
Elegies III.1, 185–90
Lotz, W., 339 n.3
Louis XIV, king of France (1643–1715), 16, 167 n.3, 169
Louvain, University of, 240, 241, 246
Louvre (Paris), 333
Lovejoy, A.O., 272 n.1
Loyola, Saint Ignatius, founder of the Society of Jesus (1491–1556), attitude to Erasmus, 223, **233**, 233 n.1 (R.Gracia-Villoslada), **235–6**; Cardoner experience (*eximia illustratio*), **223–5**, 224 n.1 (L.Calveras, L.R. Silos), 227; life in Paris, 227–9; on classical studies, 20, **233–6**
Constitutiones, 224, 233, 235; *Exercitia spiritualia*, 224–7, 224 n.4, 226 nn.1–2, 233
Łoz Poninski, Antoni, Polish Neo-Latin poet (late seventeenth century–1744), 43, 43 n.1 (P.Buchwald-Pelcowa), 53
Lucan (M.Annaeus Lucanus), Roman epic poet (39–65), 16, 163–9, 276; cited by Textor, 84, 84 n.1, 85; echoes: (in Buchanan) 89, (in Petrarch) 164, (in renaissance tragedy) 164–5, 165 nn. 1–6; opinions on: (favourable) 164–7, (unfavourable) 167–8, 168 n.1
Lucchesini, Joannes, Italian Neo-Latin poet, 53
Lucian, Greek satirist (c. 125–c. 192), imitations of, 5, 94 n.1, 232
Lucilius, Caius, Roman satirist (180–102 B.C.), imitations of, 44, 46, 47
Lucretius (Titus Lucretius Carus), Roman philosophical poet (94–55? B.C.), cited (by Montaigne) 136, 137 n.2, (by Textor) 84–5
Ludwig, W., 5, 16, 30
Luna, personified as goddess, 23, 266–9
Lupset, Thomas, English humanist (d. 1530), 214 n.1
Lupton, J.H., 205–7, 205 nn.2–4, 216, 218–19

Luschis (Luscus), Nicolaus de, Italian humanist (d. 1437/9), *51*
Luther, Martin (1483–1546), 202–3
Lutheranism, 228–9
Lycosthenes, Conrad (Wolffhardt), Alsatian collector of commonplace material (1518–61), 112; his edition of Textor, 98, 109–10, 110 n.1
Lyly, John, English euphuist (1554?–1606), 121
Lyons, works printed in, 82, 83 n.2, 95, 178, 316
Lysias, Athenian orator (*c.* 440–*c.* 380 B.C.), 248

(*Mc has been indexed as Mac*)
McConica, J.K., *210 n.1*
McDonnel, M.F.J., *210 n.2*
Macek, J., *71 n.3*
McFarlane, I.D., 9
Machiavelli, Niccolò, Florentine political theorist (1469–1527), 165, 309; his influence, 302, 309, 322; his political views, **285–9, 297–8**; on Livy, 290, see also *Discorsi* below; on Tacitus, 285, *285 nn. 3–5* (A.Hortis, D.Bush, G.Toffanin), 286–9, 299 n.1, 300, 312 *Arte della guerra*, 289; *Discorsi su Tito Livio*, **286, 288–9**, 297, 300; *Discursus florentinarum rerum*, 286, *286 n.1* (V.G. Guidi); *Il Principe*, **286–8**, 291, 297
Macrin, Salmon, French Neo-Latin poet (1490–1557), 64; cited by Textor, 84, 87, 87 n.2; echoes Pontano, 87
Macrobius, fourth- or fifth-century A.D. Neoplatonist, not certainly identical with the Ambrosius Theodosius Macrobius who wrote the *Saturnalia c.* 400, 242; his influence, 239, *239 n.1* (P.M.Schedler), 240, *240 n.1* (C.R.Ligota)
Maffei, Giovanni Pietro, biographer of Ignatius Loyola (Venice, 1585), (1535–1603), 223
Maffei, Raffaele (Vollaterranus), Italian humanist (1455–1522), 9 n.1, 110, 110 n.4
Magdeburg, 185 n.2, 189 n.3
Maimonides, Moses, Jewish philosopher (1135–1204), 272, *272 n.1*
Maison Carrée (Nîmes), pagan temple of the Augustan period, 350
Malaboti, R., *42 n.2*
Malmesbury, the Monk of, medieval English chronicler (*fl.* 1367), 337, *337 n.3*, 338
Mango, C., *341 n.2*
Manilius, Marcus, first-century A.D. Roman didactic poet, cited by Textor, 84, 85
Mantuanus, Baptista Spagnuoli, Italian ecclesiastic and Neo-Latin poet (1448–1516), 151 n.1; cited by Textor, 82,

84, 85; echoed by Buchanan, 88 n.4, 89
MSS, Colet's, 208–9, 215–17; copied from printed books, *209 n.7* (C.F.Bühler)
Marcellus, Theatre of (Rome), 351
Marck, Erard de la, patron of Vivès (*fl.* 1520), 240
Margolin, J.C., 21, 22, 251 n.3; publications, *151 n.1*
Marguerite d'Angoulême, queen of Navarre (1492–1549), 229
Marius, Gaius, Roman general and populist politician (156–86 B.C.), 284
Marius Cyrillus, *see* Heerkens
Marivorda, Adeodatus, Neo-Latin epigrammatist (d. 1576), 46 n.4
Marlowe, Christopher, English dramatist (1564–93), 161; his alleged pre-Adamite theories, 274, *275 n.1* (D.C. Danchin, P.H.Kocher)
Marmontel, J.F., French man of letters (1723–99), 169 n.1
Marrano, name given in Spain to Jewish converts to Christianity, 271, *271 n.1* (R.H.Popkin), 276, 279
Marrasio, Giovanni, Sicilian Neo-Latin poet, 172, *172 n.5* (A.Altamura)
Martial (M.Valerius Martialis), Roman epigrammatist (*c.* 40–104), 10, *41 n.1* (K.H.Mehnert), 44; cited: (by Montaigne) **137–40**, *137 n.4* (P.Villey), (by Textor) 83
Martin, H.J., 38, *38 nn.2 and 4*
Martinelli, Fioravante, Italian archaeologist (*fl.* 1647–68), *350 n.1*
Martines, L., *68 n.1*
Marullus, Michaelis Tarchaniota, Greek Neo-Latin poet (*c.* 1450–1500), *60 n.1*, 63, 87
Mary I (Tudor), queen of England (1516–58), 244
Mason, S.F., *316 n.1*
Massebieau, L., *96 n.1*
'Master C' of 1519, Pl. 8*d*
mathematics, Greek, 78, 318, *318 n.1* (L.Olschki)
Mattingly, H., *329 n.1*
Matz, F., *328 n.2*
Maurice of Nassau, Prince of Orange, Dutch general (1567–1665), 319 nn.1 and 3
May, Thomas, English translator and poet (1595–1650), 164 n.4, 167, 167 n.2
Medea, heroine of the Golden Fleece legend, 328
Medici, Florentine ruling family, 25, 285, 290–1, 297, 299; *see also* Leo X
Medici, Alessandro de', duke of Florence (1510–37), 290
Medici, Cosimo de', the Elder, Florentine patron of humanism (1389–1464), 282, 282 n.4
Medici, Cosimo de', the Younger, duke of Florence (1519–74), 290

Meghen, Peter (Magius), Dutch copyist (d. 1529), 208–9, *208 nn.3–4* (G. Dogear, O.Pächt), 212, 214 n.8, 215–18, 220, Pl. 16*c*

Mehnert, K.H., *41 n.1*

Mela, Pomponius, first-century A.D. Roman geographer, 276

Melanchthon, Phillipus (Schwarzerd), German reformer, educationist and Neo-Latin poet (1497–1560), 63, 74

Memmius Regulus, P., Roman senator (d. A.D. 62), 301

Menasseh ben Israel, seventeenth-century Jewish scholar, 275 n.2

Menendez Pelayo, M., 273 n.1

'Menippus Redivivus' pseudonym of seventeenth-century Neo-Latin satirist, 50–1, *55*

Menot, Michel, French preacher (*fl.* 1519–25), 224

Meres, Francis, English critic (1565–1647), *96 n.1* (D.C.Allen), 97 n.3, 101 n.1

Merleau-Ponty, M., 106, 106 n.1

Mersenne, Père Marin, French mathematician (1588–1648), 276

Meursius, Johannes, French hellenist (1579–1639), 319

Mexico, 274, 276, 278

Michelangelo Buonarotti (1475–1564), 343, 348

Michiel, Marcantonio, Venetian diarist (1484–1552), 325 n.3 (V.Golzio)

Micyllus (Molsheym), Jacobus, Alsatian humanist (1503–58), *185 n.6* (J. Classen)

Mignon, M., *96 n.1*

Mijatev, K., *336 n.2*

Milan, 25; *see also* S. Maria delle Grazie

military science, 27, 315, *315 nn.1–2* (W. Hahlweg), 319, *319 nn.1–5* (G.J. Aalders, G.Oestreich), 320 nn.1–3

Milton, John, bilingual English and Neo-Latin poet (1608–74), 5 n.2, 119

mining, 318, 318 n.2 (H.Wilsdorf)

Miroir de l'âme pécheresse, see Marguerite d'Angoulême

Modestus, Roman writer on strategy (*fl.* 275–6), 320 n.2

Molière (J.-B.Poquelin) (1622–73), 48

Mollenkott, V.R., *121 n.1*

Moltedo, Franciscus, late-nineteenth-century Italian Neo-Latin satirist, *54*

Molza, Francesco Maria, bilingual Italian and Neo-Latin poet (1489–1544), *61 n.4*, 64, 188, 188 n.3

Momigliano, A., vi, *291 n.3, 322 n.1*

Monsegu, B., 253, *253 n.4*

Montaigne, Michel de (1533–92): ideas on style, 17, **191–7**; influenced by Erasmus, *192* (H.Friedrich), **193**, **195–6**; on Lucan, 166; use of commonplaces, 92, 128, **131–4**; use of Latin quotations, 10, **136–40**; view

of sex, 135, *135 n.1* (D.M.Frame, P.P.Hallie, R.Sayce)

Essais: (De l'Amitié) 138, (De l'expérience) 132, (Des menteurs) 131–2, (Sur des vers de Virgile), 10, 136–7

Montaigu, Collège de (Paris), 227–8, 233

Montano, Giovanni Battista, Milanese architect (1534–61), 29, 352, *352 nn.1–2* (A.Blunt), 353, 353 n.1, 354, Pls. 12*b*, 14*a*

Montanus, Petrus, Dutch humanist and Neo-Latin satirist (1468–1507), 46, *46 n.3* (J.Prinsen), 48, *51*

Montesquieu, Charles de Secondat de, French political theorist (1689–1755), 309

Montfaucon, Bernard de, classical archaeologist (1655–1741), 349

Montpellier, 184, 185 n.1

More, Thomas, Sir (1478–1535), 21, 58, 62, 207; cited by Textor, 84; his influence on Erasmus, 230, *230 n.1* (M.Mann Phillips), 235; his Neo-Latin verse, 62, 64; his opinion on Vivès, 240

Apologye, 206 n.3; *Utopia*, 205, 235

Morisot, Claude, seventeenth-century French Neo-Latin satirist, 54

Morrison, Paul, 37

Moscherosch, Hans Michael, German satirist (1601–69), 165 n.6

Moses, biblical, 276–7, 330

Morgues, Odette de, v

Mullally, J.P., *141 n.3*

Mullinger, J.B., *147 n.3*

Müntz, E., *338 n.2*

Muret, Marc-Antoine, French humanist and Neo-Latin poet (1525–85), 64, 85, 300–1, 300 n.2

Murmellius, Johannes, Flemish humanist and Neo-Latin poet (d.1517), 82

Mussato, Albertino, Italian humanist and Neo-Latin poet (1261–1329), *51*

Mutii, Roman *gens* noted for C.Mutius Scaevola who burnt off his right hand, 282

mythology, classical, 259 *259 n.1* (L. Schrader); allegorical interpretation, 262–3; in Calderón, 23–4, 264–70; in Lope de Vega, 23, 259–62; in Vivès, 22, 241–2; its exploitation by Raphaël, 327–33; manuals in the Renaissance, 263; relation to astrology, 263

Nadal, Jerome, Jesuit educator (1507–80): on education, 233, *233 n.2* (F.de Dainville); on Ignatius's spiritual experience, 224, *224 n.1* (J.Calveras)

Naogeorgus, Thomas (Kirchmayer), German Neo-Latin satirist (1511–63), 45, *45 n.1* (H.Roloff), *52*

Naples, 351

Narcissus, 259, *259 n.1*, 264

Nardi, Jacopo, Florentine historian (1476–1563), 289, 290, *290 n.1* (S.Bertelli)

Nashe, Thomas, English critic and novelist (1567–1601), 121, 160

Nassau, Wilhelm Ludwig von, seventeenth-century writer on strategy (d. 1665), 320, *320 n.3*

Natalis, Antonius, seventeenth-century Italian Jesuit and Neo-Latin satirist (d. 1701), *53*

Naudé, Gabriel, French man of letters (1600–53), 276 n.3

Navagero, Andrea, Italian Neo-Latin poet (1483–1529), 61 n.1

Navarre, Collège de (Paris), 95

Nazaréens (Nazarenes), early-nineteenth-century school of painters in Germany, 333

Nelli, Francesco (Francescus Nicolai), Florentine humanist (d. 1363), 338 n.1

Nemesius of Emesa, Greek Christian philosopher (*fl.* 390), 200–1

Nemrod, (Nimrod), mythical Chaldean monarch, 311

Neo-Latin: its decline in the seventeenth century, 5, 30, **39**; need for catalogues and editions of its literature, 2, 3, **33–9, 42–3**, 50; present ignorance of, 4, 127, 134; verse: (anthologies) 4, 57–64, (in Bohemia) *51* (H.Hrdina), (in Croatia) *43 n.2* (V.Gortan–Vl. Vratović), (in England) *42 n.7* (L. Bradner), (in Germany) *52* (Ranutius Gherus), *57 n.2* (H.C.Schnur), (in Italy) *57 nn.2–3* (F.Arnaldi etc., F.A.Gragg), *173 n.2* (J.Sparrow); *see also* bilingualism, Ciceronianism, elegy, epigram, Latin (cut of correctness), satire

Neoplatonism, 2; in Colet, 214–20, *220 n.3* (D.P.Walker); in Erasmus, 229, 233, 235; in Loyola, 233; in Thomas More, 235; in Vivès, 242, 246, 258

Nepos, Cornelius, Roman biographer (99–24 B.C.), *see* Probus, Aemilius

Nero (L.Domitius Ahenobarbus) (Roman emperor 54–68), 16, 283 n.4, 287–8, 292, 300; *see also* Domus aurea

Nerva, M.Cocceius (Roman emperor 96–8), 288; his forum, 351

Nespoulos, P., 87 n.1

Netherlands, 45; British Library holdings of books printed in, 34, *34 n.1*; catalogue of libraries in, 36 n.4 (E.Cockx-Indestege and G.Glorieux); classical contribution to military reforms in, 315, 315 n.2, 318–20; Neo-Latin verse in, 64, *see also* satire

Niccolò Fiorentino, Italian painter (*fl.* 1445), 338, *338 n.4* (M.Gomez-Moreno, A. de Bosque)

Nicetas, a corruption for Hicetas (fourth-century B.C. Greek astronomer) in early editions of Cicero's *Academica*, 78

Nicholas de Troyes, French writer of tales (*fl.* 1535), 136

Nicolas, Saint, Lycian abbot, patron of Russia (late fourth or early fifth century), 336, 336 n.2 (K.Mijatev)

Nicolaus, Franciscus, eighteenth-century Italian Neo-Latin satirist, *55*

Niger, Dominicus Marius, late-fifteenth-century Venetian humanist, 183 n.6

Nijhoff, W., *36 n.4*

Nile, river, 100

Nîmes (France), 350

Nizolio, Mario, Ciceronian scholar (1498–1566), 75

Noah (biblical), 28, 330, 332–3, Pl. *3c*

Nodot, Francesco (Nodotius), French romance writer and Neo-Latin satirist (*fl.* 1698–1700), *55*

Nomi, Franciscus, Flemish Neo-Latin satirist, *53*

Nonius Marcellus, late-third-century Roman grammarian, 46

Nordholt, H.S., *67 n.1*

Noreña, C.G., *246 n.3*, 247, *273 n.2*

Norway, 36 n.4

Obiechena, E., *108 n.1*

Ockham, William of, English Nominalist philosopher (*c.* 1300–49), 75, 241 n.2

Odyssey, see Ulysses

Oestreich, G., 3, *26–7, 320 n.2*; publications, *319 n.5, 322 n.2, 323 n.1*

O'Kelly, P.B., 221, *221 n.1*

Olivier de Serres, French agronomist (1539–1619), *321*

Olschki, L., *316 n.1, 318 n.1*

Olympiodorus Diaconus, sixth-century A.D. biblical commentator, 200

Ong, Walter, J., v, 9, 11, 14, 74, *74 n.1, 93 n.1, 105 n.1, 107 n.1, 114 n.1, 115 n.1*; publications, *14 n.2, 94 n.4, 95 n.1, 105 n.2*

Onofrio, C.d', *350 n.1*

Onosander, first-century A.D. Greek writer on military science, 320 n.2

Ophir, unidentified region where Solomon obtained gold, 274

Opitz, Martin, German poet (1597–1639), 178, *178 n.5*, 179

Oporinus, Johannes, Basle printer (1507–65), 112

oral culture, 94–5, 102–3, *103 nn.2–3* (W.J.Ong, F.Hajnal), 108, *108 n.1* (E.Obiechena, B.Lindfors), 117–19

Orange (Vaucluse, France), 353

Oratorio di S. Filippo Neri (Rome), 351

Oresme, Nicolas, French physician, mathematician and translator (1323?–82), 305

Orestes, figure of Greek legend, 328

Origeb, Greek exegete and theologian (185–254), 200–1, 214, 230

Orosius, Paulus, Christian Latin historian (*fl.* 415), 283

Orpheus, mythical musician, 259, 264–5

Orphism, *see* Cabbala

Orsini, Fulvio, Italian humanist and antiquarian (1529–1600), 49, 349

Orti Oricellari, Florentine Academy to which Machiavelli belonged, held in the gardens of the Rucellai, 286

Othello, 101

Otho, M.Salvius, (Roman emperor A.D. 69), 292

Ovid (P.Ovidius Naso), Roman poet (43–17 B.C.): cited (by Montaigne) 137 n.2, (by Textor) 83, 84 n.1, 85, 97; his handling of elegy, 174–6; later indebtedness to, 173, 183–4, 184 n.3, *see also individual works below*; reputation, 38, 153, 153 n.2, 168, 178 *Amores*, 16, 189, echoes (Joannes Secundus) 176 n.1, (Lotichius) 183 nn.5-6, 184 n.6; *Fasti*, echoes, 186 n.3; *Ibis*, echoes, 187 n.5; *Metamorphoses*, 153, 262–4, illustrations, 333, 333 n.1 (Y.F.Giraud), Pl. 6*b*; *Tristia*, 16–17 echoes, (Lotichius) 183, 183 n.4, 184 n.3

Owen, John, English Neo-Latin epigrammatist (*c.* 1560–1622), 41 n.1

Oxford, 36, 72, 229, 338 n.5

Oxford Book of Medieval Latin Verse, 57, 64

Pächt, O., *208 n.3, 209 n.6, 217 n.6*

Pacuvius, Marcus, Roman tragedian (220–*c.* 180 B.C.), 47

Padua: Averroists at, 71, 251, 251 n.3; Italian Athens, 115 n.2; Lotichius at, 182, 185, 190

paganism: attitude recommended by Erasmus, 232; its account of early man, 272, 272 n.1 (P.Kocher, A.O. Lovejoy, G.Boas); reconciliation with Christianity: (allegorical) 264–8, (decorative) 259–62

Pagliari del Bosco, Italian commentator on Tacitus (1550–1613), 301

Palatine Hill (Rome), 351

Palladio, Andrea, Italian architect (1518–80), 335, 354

Palladius, Rutilius Taurus, fourth-century A.D. agronomist, 320 n.4

Palmerius, *see* Le Palmier

Palmieri, Matteo, humanist and political theorist (1406–75), *24 n.1*, 243, 243 n.3

Pamphilus Saxus (Sassi, Panfilo), bilingual Italian and Neo-Latin poet (1455–1527), cited by Textor, 84

Pan, god, 259 n.1, 265–9

Panchatantra, Indian collection of beast fables from the fourth century A.D. or earlier, 103

Panormita, *see* Beccadelli

Pantheon (Santa Maria Rotonda), 28, 331, 335–7, *341 n.2* (M.Gosebruch), 343–4, *344 n.1* (R.Wittkower), 345–7, 350

Paracelsus (Theophrastus Bombastes von Hohenheim), German physician and alchemist (1493–1541), 274, *274 n.1* (J.S.Slotkin, T.Bendysche)

Paris, 33, 100, 310; books printed in, 38, 82, 95, 178, 316; French Athens, 115 n.2; university of, 72, 95, 241

Paris, Trojan prince, 328

Parker, Henry, Lord Morley, English translator (1476–1556), 244

Parmenides, Greek philosopher (b. *c.* 540 B.C.), 250

Parnassians, nineteenth-century school of French poets, 260

Parnassus, mountain in Greece sacred to the Muses, 265

Parrhasius, Aulus Janus, Italian humanist (1470–1534), 8, 24

Parthenon, temple of Athene (Athens), 347, 354

Pascalis, Ludovicus, Croatian Neo-Latin poet (*c.* 1500–51), 64

Passerat, Jean, French classical scholar (1534–1602), 85

Paul, Saint, apostle, 224, 241 n.3, 278; Colet's devotion for, 210

Epistles, 19, 209

Paulus Silentiarius, sixth-century Byzantine poet, *341 n.2* (P.Friedländer, H.Jantzen, C.Mango)

Paulus Venetus (Paolo Nicoletti), scholastic philosopher (d. 1429), 241 n.2

Peace, personified, 328–9, *329 n.1* (H. Mattingly, E.Kris)

Pecka, Michael (Pieczkonides), seventeenth-century Bohemian Neo-Latin poet, 53

Pedioneus, Johannes, Swiss schoolmaster (*fl.* 1520–50), 180, *180 n.4* (K.H. Burmeister)

Peiresc, Nicolas Fabre de, French classical archaeologist (1580–1637), 349

Perez de Moya, Juan, Spanish mathematician and mythographer (1513?–97), 263

Pericles, Athenian statesman (499–29 B.C.), 311

Peripatetics, philosophers, followers of Aristotle, 248, 256

Perna, Peter, Basle printer, 112

Perosa, A., 57 n.4

Perotti, Niccolò, Italian humanist (1430–80), 82

Perrault, Charles, French man of letters (1628–1703), 341 n.2

Perseus, mythical hero, 259, 264

Persius (A.Persius Flaccus), Roman satirist (34–62), 41, 45–6

personification: of abstractions (in art) 328, 329 n.1, Pl. 4*c*, 4*d*; of cities, 189 n.3; of elegy, 183 n.6; of religions, 268–9; various, 241

Perugia (Italy), 339, Pl. 7*b*

Peruzzi, Baldassare, sculptor and architect (1481–1536), 343, *343 n.2* (H.Burns)

Peruzzi, Sallustio, Italian painter, 339 n.1

Peter Lombard, Italian logician and theologian (d.1160), 202, 236

Peter of Spain (Petrus Hispanus), scholastic logician, Pope (as John XXI, 1276–8), 241 n.2; *Summulae logicales, 141 n.3* (J.P.Mullally), 142, *142 n.3* (L.Jardine), 144, 147 n.4

Peterson, D.L., *122 n.1*

Petra (Jordan), ancient city, 350–1

Petrarch (Francesco Petrarca), humanist and bilingual Italian and Neo-Latin poet (1304–74), 62, 72, 283; cited by Textor, 84; echoes Lucan, 164; his *docta pietas,* 18–19, 201; his influence on artists and architects, 337; his interest in practical affairs, 18, 24, 71, 71 n.3; his interest in style, 6, 12, 20; his Neo-Latin verse, 58, 64; his study of Livy, 281, *281 n.2* (G. Billanovich), 282; multiple character of his humanist ideal, 7, 29, 240; on imitation, *180 n.2* (A.Buck)
Africa, 164, 240, 243, 282; *Canzoniere,* 173, *173 n.2* (J.Sparrow, L.Forster); *De viris illustribus,* 282

Petronius Arbiter, Roman novelist and poet (d. 66, if identical with Nero's favourite), 55

Petrucci, Palazzo, 330

Peutinger, Conrad, German patron of learning (1465–1547), 200–1

Phaethon, son of Apollo, 259, 264

Philargyrius, fifth-century Virgilian commentator, 266

Philip II (king of Spain 1558–98), 296

Philips, D., *67 n.1*

Phillips, M.Mann, 5, 16–17; publications, *230 n.1*

Philolaos, fifth-century B.C. Greek mathematician, 78

Philoponus, Johannes, Christian Greek commentator on Aristotle (475/80– c. 565), 251

Phrissemius, Ioannis Matthaeus, sixteenth-century German humanist, 147 n.4, 148, 148 n.1

Picard, C., *328 n.1*

Piccolomini, Alessandro, Italian astronomer and educationist (1508–78), 321

Piccolomini Library (Siena), founded in the late fifteenth century, 330, Pl. 5a

Pickel, *see* Celtes

Pico della Mirandola, Giovanni, Florentine Platonist and Cabbalist (1463–94), 212, 214, *214 n.5* (S.Jayne)

Pindar, Greek lyric poet (521–441 B.C.), 190

Pinturicchio (Bernardo Betti), Italian painter (1454–1513), 330, Pl. 5a

Piso, L.Calpurnius, senator who died of old age under Tiberius (d. 32), 301

Pits, John, English antiquary and Roman Catholic divine (1560–1616), 216

Plato (429–347 B.C.), 305; attitudes to, 78, 306; his criticism of democracy, 311; read by Colet, 214; relation to esoteric learning, *76 n.1* (*bibliography*); used by La Peyrère, 277; Vivès on, 22, 242 n.1, 245–7, 248–53, 257–8
Euthydemus, 250; *Timaeus,* 277

Plautus, T.Maccius, Roman writer of comedy (*c.* 254–184 B.C.), 46

Pléiade, mid-sixteenth-century school of humanist French poets, 86

Pliny the Elder (C.Plinius Secundus), Roman writer on science (23/4–79), 102; cited by Vivès, 249 n.2; renaissance editions of, 317, *317 n.2* (A. Koyré); used in sixteenth century, 320–1

Pliny the Younger (C.Plinius Caecilius Secundus), Roman letter-writer (61/2– before 114), cited by Textor, 84

Plotinus, Greek Neoplatonist philosopher (204–70), 78, 214

Plutarch, Greek moralist and biographer (*c.* 50–*c.* 115), 94 n.1, 102, 158, 282, 286 n.6, 315 n.1; *De defectu oraculorum,* 266

poetics, 15, 155–62; *artes versificatoriae,* 81–2, 174–5; *see also* elegy (theory of)

Poggio Bracciolini, Gianfrancesco, Italian humanist (1380–1459), 152 n.4; echoes Tacitus, 284, 289; his political views, 25, 284, *284 n.2* (H.Baron)

Polanco, A.de, biographer of Ignatius Loyola (1516–76), 223, 226 n.1; educational ideas, 233

Poland, 59, 64

Polentone, Sicco, Italian humanist (1375/6–1447), 284, 284 n.3

Politian (Angelo Ambrogini Poliziano), humanist and bilingual Italian and Neo-Latin poet, 62; cited by Textor, 84

politics, 7; education for, 24; organisational aspects of, 321–2; theoretical considerations, 305–13

Pollaiuolo, Simone de, called il Cronaca (1457–1508), 340, *340 n.1* (C.von Stegmann, H.von Geymüller, J. Durm), Pl.7d; drawings showing reconstructions of ancient architecture incorrectly attributed to him (Ps.-Cronaca series), 338, *338 n.5* (A. Bartoli, G.Scaglia, T.Buddensieg), 339 n.1, Pl. 7e

Pollak, R., *43 n.1*

Pollard, A.W., 35, 37, *206 n.1*

Pollius, Johannes, sixteenth-century German Neo-Latin satirist, *52*

Polybius, Greek historian of his times (210/5–*c.* 125 B.C.), 285 n.1, 298, 310; Lipsius on, 319–20

Pompeius Magnus, Gnaeus, Roman general and politician (107–48 B.C.), 284; plays about, 46–7, 165, 165 n.2

Pontano, Giovanni Gioviano, Italian humanist and Neo-Latin poet (1426–1503), 41 n.3, 60 n.1, 63, 87, *87 n.1* (P.Nespoulos), 173; cited by Textor, 84–5; echoed by Macrin, 86, 86 n.1

Pope, Alexander (1688–1744), 42, 43 n.1

Popkin, R.H., 24; publications, *271 n.1, 275 n.4, 276 nn.4–5*

Porphyry, Syrian Neoplatonist (*c.* 232–301/6), 276

Portugal, 64, 100, 228

Postel, Guillaume, French orientalist and mathematician (1510–91), 228

Potiphar's wife, 332, Pl. 6*a*

Potts, A F., *171 n.1*

Potts, L.J., 159–60, *159 n.6*

Poussin, Nicolas, French painter (1594–1665), 350, *350 n.2* (A.Blunt)

Pozzo, Cassiano dal, classical archeologist (d. 1657), 330, 349, *349 n.2* (C. Vermeule), 351–3, 351 n.1

Praxiteles, fourth-century B.C. Athenian sculptor, 347, *347 n.1* (J.B.Shaw), Pl. 11*b*

Pray Bober, Phyllis, 27, 326

Pre-Adamism, 24, **271–80**; outline of La Peyrère's theory, **276–8**; relation to modern anthropology, *273 n.1* (O. Züchler); Vivès on, 273

Premlechner, Johannes Baptista, S.J., Austrian historian and Neo-Latin poet (1731–89), *54*

Probus, Aemilius, fourth-century A.D. Roman historian to whom the works of Nepos were wrongly attributed: MS (of Nepos) in Cosimo de' Medici's library, 282

Procacci, G., *302 n.6*

Proclus, Neoplatonist philosopher (410–85), 252

Procopius, Greek historian (*fl.* 527–62), 286 n.6

Proctor, John, English anthologist and historian (1521–84), 119

Prometheus, mythical Titan who brought fire from heaven, 259, *259 n.1*

Propertius, Sextus, Roman elegiac poet (54/8–after 16 B.C.): echoes in Lotichius, 184 nn.1, 4–5, 187 n.5, 189 n.1; renaissance indebtedness to, 16, 173; reputation, 178, *178 n.5*, 190, 190 n.2

Proserpine, queen of the underworld, identified with Luna, 268

Protagoras, Greek sophist (*c.* 480–411 B.C.), 252

Protestants, 20, 38, 51, 203; on teaching of Greek, 233

Psellus, Michael, Byzantine philosopher and humanist (1018–78), 251

Pseudo-Berosus, Chaldean history forged by G.Nanni, 1498, 76, 83

Pseudo-Cronaca, *see* Pollaiuolo

Pseudo-Dionysius, *see* Dionysius the Areopagite

Psyche, bride of Cupid, *333 n.1*

Ptolemaeus, Claudius, second-century B.C. geographer, 252

Publilius Syrus, Roman first-century B.C. mime writer, 130

Puteanus, Erycius, Netherlands humanist (1574–1646), 46, 46 n.1

Pynson, Richard, English printer (*fl.* 1494–1526), 206

Pythagoras, sixth-century B.C. Greek philosopher, 78, 129, 252

Quellenforschung, 10

Quintilianus, M.Fabius, Roman educationist and rhetorician (*c.* 35–after 95): cited by Textor, 85, *85 n.1*; in Vivès, 241 n.3; Montaigne's echoes of, 132, 193; source for the reform of dialectic, 73–4, 78, 93, 108, 142, *142 n.2* (S. Camporeale), 145–7, 149, 150 n.1, 151, 151 n.3, 152 nn.1–2, 153, 153 n.1, 154

Quintinaus Stoa, Joannes Franciscus, Neo-Latin poet and tragedian (1484–1557), 84

Quirinal, 347

Quondam, A., *48 n.3*

Rabelais, François, French author and humanist (*c.* 1490–1553), 98, 136; borrowings from Erasmus, 10, *10 n.1* (L.Delaruelle), 14, *14 n.1* (W.F. Smith), 129; commonplaces in, 128–30; on *discretio spirituum*, 224–5; pseudo-Rabelaisian Almanach of 1544 132

Almanach of 1535, 133; *Gargantua*, 50, 120, 129; *Pantagruel*, 120; *Tiers Livre*, 128–30, 224–5

Raby, F.J.E., *57*

Racine, Jean (1639–99), 28

Radinus, Thomas, O.P., Italian theologian and Neo-Latin poet (1490–1527), 84–5

Raleigh, Sir Walter, English historian and political theorist (1552/4–1618), 274, 275, *275 n.1* (P.Lefranc)

Ramus, Petrus (Pierre La Ramée), French philosopher and educationist (1515–72): his Method, 14, *74 n.1* (N.W. Gilbert, C.Vasoli), 75, 115, *115 n.1* (W.J.Ong), *n.3* (K.J.Höltgen), 120 n.1, 306; his reform of dialectic, 13, 141 n.2; influence (on Harvey) 146 n.4, (on Zwinger) 115–17; lectures on the *Somnium Scipionis*, 244, 244 n.1

Basilea, 115, 115 n.4; *Dialectica*, 105, 105 n.2, 106

Raphaël Sanzio (1483–1520): his handling of ancient architecture, 346–8, *346 n.2* (H.Egger); his mingling of biblical and antique subjects, 330–3; his tomb, 347, *347 n.2* (T.Buddensieg);

Raphaël (*cont.*)
his use of antique models, **326–31**, *326 n.1* (W.Amelung, F.Weege), 328 nn.2–3, 331 n.1 (N.Dacos); his use of biblical themes, 330–2; on gothic style, 337; St Peter's, *342 n.2* (H.v.Geymüller); the Bibbiena apartments, 331; the loggia of Psyche, 331; the Praxiteles horse, 347, *347 n.1*, Pl. 11*b*; the Vatican loggias, 27–9, **325–34**, *325 n.1* (N.Dacos), *n.2* (P.Redig de Campos, V.Wanscher), *n.3* (V.Golzio), Pls. 1*a*, 2*a*, 3*a–c*, 4*a*, 4*c*, 5*b*, 6*a*
Raphelengius (Franz van Ravelinghen), printer and orientalist (1534–97), 319 n.3
Redgrave, G.R., 35, 37, *206 n.1*
Redig de Campos, D., *325 n.2*
Reguli, Roman surname, distinguished by the heroism of M.Atilius Regulus in the first Punic War, 282
Remacle d'Ardenne, Flemish Neo-Latin poet (1480–1524): cited by Textor, 84, 90; echo in Buchanan, 90
Renaissance, concept of the, 1–2, 57 8, 67, *67 n.1* (*bibliography*); *for particular developments see* allegory, alphabetical arrangement, architecture, Bible, bilingualism, Christian humanism, commonplace material, dialectic, education, historiography, humanism, imitation, Jesuits, Latin, literary criticism, Neo-Latin, mythology, politics, pre-Adamism; *also* Aristotle, Erasmus, Machiavelli, Petrarch, Ramus, Raphaël, Valla, Vivès
republicanism, 300
research opportunities:
(a) bibliographical and editorial:
collation of the MSS of Colet's commentaries, 218
collection of bibliographical data: on Neo-Latin works in general (a continental S.T.C.) 33–9; on renaissance translations and commentaries of patristic works (particularly on those by Erasmus), 200; on the renaissance editions, translations and commentaries of ancient technical works, 323–4
(b) themes in literary and cultural history:
a study of Latin/vernacular bilingualism in the renaissance, 5
an investigation of publishing and book-buying after 1500, 38
a literary interpretation of Lotichius, 181 (or indeed of any of the poets listed on p.63)
the nature of the commonplace collections and their influence, 134
a study of Erasmus's patristic works, 200
individual studies of patristic translators and editors, 200

the view of the primitive church in the works of the German humanists, 200
patristic scholarship 1560–1640, 203
the influence of the pseudo-Dionysius on Colet's thought, 220
a reassessment of the relations between evangelical humanism, reform and counter-reform, 236
the fortuna of certain seminal conceptions (e.g. *otium, negotium, tranquillitas animi, dignitas hominis*), 241
the character of renaissance commentaries on classical authors, 244
the *fortuna* of certain seminal works (e.g. the *Somnium Scipionis*), 244
the gradual decline after Raphaël of the precision with which pagan motifs were used, 334
the sources of G. B. Montano's architectural drawings, 352–4
Resti, Junius, Croatian Neo-Latin poet (d. 1814), 43, *43 n.2* (V.Gortan–V. Vratović)
Rettenpacher, Simon, Austrian Neo-Latin poet (1634–1706), *44 n.1*, 49, 49 n.2 (M.Enzinger), *53*
Reuchlin, Johann, German humanist and orientalist (1455–1522), 96 n.1, 200
Reusch, F., *38 n.1*
Rhenanus, Beatus, Alsatian Latinist (1485–1547), 200
rhetoric, 12–15, 69, 70, 73, **155–8**, **195–7**, 243; in education, 145, 145 n.1; Harvey on, 146, *146 nn.1, 3–4*; true and false varieties of, 250; Valla on, 144–5; *see also* copia, commonplace material
Rhetorica ad Herennium, 12, 12 n.1
Rhodes, 100
Rhône, river, 114
Ribadaneira, Pedro de, biographer (1572) of Ignatius Loyola (1527–1611), 223
Rice, E.F., 3, 18, 219; publications, *219 n.1*
Richelieu, Cardinal (Armand Duplessis) (1585–1642), 276 n.2
Rienzo, Cola di, Italian patriot and populist (*c.* 1313–54), 71, *71 n.3* (K. Burdach, J.Macek)
Risse, W., *144 n.3*
Robathan, D., *42 n.1*
Robinson, Clement, English song-writer and editor (*fl.* 1566–84), 119
Robortelli, Francesco, Italian humanist and literary critic (1516–67), 190, 190 n.4
Rogge, H., *41 n.2*
Rollins, H., *96 n.1*
Roloff, H.G., 45, *45 n.1*
Romano, Giulio, Italian painter (1482–1546), 344, *344 n.2* (T.Buddensieg), Pl. 10
Rome, ancient, 2, 17, 20, 24; decline with loss of liberty, 6, 72, 283–4, 288; its

Rome, ancient (*cont.*)
archaeological remains, 27-8, **326-9,
339-42, 350-2,** 350 n.1; its administrative organisation as a model, 26,
322-4; its military organisation as a
model, 318-19; personified, 189 n.3;
328; selective character of its literary
tradition, 63; variety of its artistic
tradition, 29, 350-4
Rome, modern, 325, 352; archaeology in,
349; its rebirth, 71; printing at, 37;
sack of, 189, 291, 395; *see also*
Pantheon, S. Andrea delle Fratte,
S. Costanza, S. Ivo della Sapienza,
S. Maria Maggiore, Oratorio i
S. Filippo Neri, St Peter's
Romulus, first king of Rome, 289
Rondelet, Guillaume, French naturalist
(1507-66), 184 n.6
Ronsard, Pierre de, classicising French
poet (1524-85), 29, 178; on *copia*, 191
Rotondò, A., *38 n.2*
Rouen (France), 227, 229; printing at, 82,
95
Roussel, Gérard, almoner to Marguerite de
Navarre (1480-1550), 229
Royzius, Petrus Maureus (Piotr Roizjusz),
Spanish Neo-Latin poet writing in
Poland (*c.* 1505-71), *52*
Rubens, Peter Paul (1577-1640), 350
Rupprich, H., *178 n.2,* 179 n.2
Russia, 36 n.4
Russo, F., *316 n.2*
Ruthall, Thomas, bishop of Durham
(d. 1523), 231

Sabbadini, R., *152 n.3*
Sabellicus, Marcus Antonius (M.Coccio),
Venetian historian (1436-1506), 112
n.1
Sabinus, Georgius, German literary critic
and Neo-Latin poet (1508-60), 82, 84,
180 n.3 (M.Töppen), 182 n.4, 189 n.3
Sabratha (Tripoli), ancient city of imperial
times, 350-1, 353, Pl. 15*b*
Sacro-Bosco, Johannes de (John of Holy-
wood), English mathematician (d.
1256), *151 n.3*
Saint, *for individual saints see under respective
names*
S. Andrea delle Fratte, Rome, by Borro-
mini, 351
S. Anna in Caprena, convent at Pienza
near Siena, 33
S. Costanza, church, Rome, 340-2, 346,
346 n.2 (H.Egger)
S. Ivo della Sapienza, church, Rome, by
Borromini, 352, Pl.12 *a* and *b*
S. Margherita, chapel, *331 n.1*
S. Maria delle Celestia (projected church,
Venice), 345, 345 nn.1-2 (G.Stringa,
T.Temanza), Pl. 11*a*
S. Maria delle Grazie, church, Varallo
(Milan), 331 n.1

S. Maria Maggiore, church, Rome,
382
S. Maria Rotonda, *see* Pantheon
St Paul's school, London, 210, 210 n.2
(M.F.McDonnell, A.F.Leach); its
Colet MS, 216, Pl. 16 *b* and *d*;
statutes, 210-11, 217
St Peter's, basilica, Rome, 342 n.2 (H.von
Geymüller)
S. Spirito, Hospital of, Rome, 213
S. Vitale, church, Ravenna, 342
Sainte-Barbe, Collège de (Paris), 227-9,
228 n.2 (J.Quicherat)
Salamanca (Spain), 227
Sallust (C.Sallustius Crispus), Roman
historian (86-*c.* 34 B.C.), 282, 286 n.6
Salutati, Colluccio, Florentine chancellor
and humanist (1330-1406), 71-2,
284, 289, 292
Sandys, J.E., 18, 18 n.1, 19
Sangallo, Antonio da, the Elder, Italian
architect (1455.?-1534), 339
Sangallo, Antonio da, the Younger,
Italian architect (1485-1546), 342-3;
his criticism of Raphaël, 342 n.2;
his plans for St Peter's, 343, 348
Sangallo, Giuliano da, the Elder, Italian
architect (1445-1516), 28, 29, 29
n.1 (H.Burns), 339, 340, 340 n.2
(C.Hülsen), 341-2, 351 n.2, 353
Sangenesius, Joannes, seventeenth-century
French Neo-Latin poet, *53*
Sannazaro, Jacopo, bilingual writer of
Italian and Neo-Latin pastoral (1458-
1530), 178, *178 n.5*
Sarton, G., *316 n.1*
Sansovino, Jacopo, Italian painter (1486-
1570), 339 n.1
satire, Neo-Latin: general, 3, **41-55,**
42 n.1 (V.Cian), *44 n.2* (G.Hess,
U.Limentani, H.Schaller, D.J.Shaw);
in America, 42, 42 n.5, 50, 50 n.2;
in Dalmatia, 43, *43 n.2* (V.Gortan-
V.Vratović); in England 42, 42 n.7
(L.Bradner), 49, *49 n.3*; in France,
50, *50 n.1*; in Germany, 45, *45 n.1,* 46,
47, 47 nn.1 and 4, 48-9, 49 nn.1-2;
52 (Ranutius Gherus); in Italy, 42,
42 n.1 (V.Cian), 48, 48 nn.1 and 3;
in the Netherlands, 44, 44 n.3, 45,
45 n.2, 46, *46 nn.2-4,* 48-50; in
Scandinavia, 50, *50 n.3*; in Switzerland, 42, *42 n.5*
literary, 46-8; medical, 48-9; Menippean, 43, 49-51
Satire Ménippée, satirical pamphlet composed by the moderates during the
French religious wars (1594), 50
Saumaise, Claude de (Salmasius), French
classical scholar and polymath (1588-
1653), 277
Savonarola, Girolamo, Italian preacher
(1452-98), 214, *214 n.8* (J.K.Mc-
Conica)

Sayce, R.A., 35 n.3, 135, 137, *137 n.1*
Scaglia, G., 338 n.5, 339 n.1
Scala Regia (Vatican) by Bernini, 352
Scaliger, Joseph Justus, French and Netherlands humanist (1540–1609), 5; cited as expert on China, 277; on Lucan, 167 n.4
Scaliger, Julius Caesar, Italian humanist domiciled in France (1489–1558), 15, 16, 85; on Dampierre, 193–4; on elegy, 175, 175 n.4 (R.M.Ferraro), 176, 176 n.1; on Lucan, 167–8, *167 n.5*
Scamozzi, Vincenzo, Italian architect (1552–1616), 345, *345 nn.1–2* (G. Stringa, T.Temanza) 346, Pl. 11a
Schalk, F., vi, 22–3
Schaller, H., *42 n.2*
Schedler, P.M., *239 n.1*
Scheffer, S., German Neo-Latin poet (b. c. 1530), 64
Schellhase, R.C., *287 n.1*
Schlayer, C., *169*
Schmidt, L., 264
Schmitt, A., *339 n.3*
Schmitt, C.B., *76 n.1*, *244 n.2*
Schnur, H.C., modern classical scholar and Neo-Latin satirist, *41 n.1*, 42, 42 n.5, *54*, *55*, 189 n.3
Schoek, R.J., 217 n.6
Scholae Piae, Fathers of the (Piarists – teaching order founded in the seventeenth century), 49
scholasticism: characterised, 73, *141 n.3* (J.P.Mullally), 142, *142 n.3* (L. Jardine) and n.4 (J.Ashworth), 251; humanist rejection of the '*moderni*', 2, 6, 19, 71–5, 148, 201, 230, 240–58, 316; Jesuit acceptance of, 234, 236
Scholderer, V., 38
Scholirius, Peter (Pierre Scholiers), Flemish Neo-Latin poet (1582–1631), 45, *45 n.2*, *53*
Schoppe, Kaspar (Scioppius), German classical scholar, historian and Roman Catholic pamphleteer (1576–1649), *52*, 292
Schrader, L., *259 n.1*
Schroeter, A., *179 n.3*
Schüling, H., *141 n.3*
Schurhammer, G., *231 n.1*
Schwarz, W., *210 n.1*
Schweikhart, G., *338 n.5*
Science: editions of scientific works, *316 n.2* (F.Russo); humanist support for, *78 n.2* (A.Koyré, M.Boas, E.Garin); in Jesuit education, 233; use of classical sources for, 316, *316 n.1* (*bibliography*)
Scioppius, *see* Schoppe
Scipio Africanus, conqueror of Hannibal (234–183 B.C.), 240, 242–3
Scoti, 85–6
Scoto, Fr. Tomás, fourteenth-century pre-Adamite, *273 n.1* (M.Menendez-Pelayo)

Scott, Isora, 5 n.1
Scotus, Joannes Duns, scholastic philosopher (c. 1270–1308), 214, 241, 241 n.2
Screech, M.A., 10
Seckendorff, Veit Ludwig von, German Scholar and statesman (1626–92), 164 n.4
Secret, F., *76 n.1*
Seneca, L.Annaeus, the Younger, Roman philosopher (5/4 B.C.–A.D. 65), 148 n.3, 153 n.1, 180 n.4, 241 n.3, 301; Erasmus finds spiritual stimulus in, 231–2; renaissance indebtedness to, 41, 43, 49, 165, 285
Apocolocyntosis, 41, 49
Sens, Council of, 233
Sepinus, Gervase, French Neo-Latin poet (*fl.* 1553?), 63
Sepúlveda, Juan Ginés de, Spanish humanist (*fl.* 1525–55), 305
Serbaldi della Pescia, Pier Maria, Italian engraver (*fl.* 1454/5), 328
Sergardi, Lodovico (Quinto Settano), bilingual Italian and Neo-Latin satirist (1660–1726), 48, *48 nn.1–3* (I.Carini, A.Quondam), *53*
Serlio, Sebastiano, Italian architect (1475–1552), 353, *353 n.2*
Servius (M.Servius Honoratus), Virgilian commentator (b. c. 355), 266
Seznec, Jean, *263*
Shakespeare, William (1564–1616), 161; his possible use of Textor, 95, *95 n.2* (T.W.Baldwin), 121–2, *122 n.1* (D.L. Peterson), 123–6
Shaw, D.J., *44 n.2*
Shaw, George Bernard (1856–1950), 165 n.5
Shearman, J., *329 n.1*
Shire, Helena, 5 n.2
Sidney, Sir Philip, English critic, novelist and poet (1554–86), 159–60, *159 n.2*
Sidonius Apollinaris, Roman poet and letter-writer (c. 430–after 479), cited by Textor, 84, 84 n.1
Siena, Pl. 5a, *see* Piccolomini Library, Pollaiuolo (for ps.-Cronaca)
Signorelli, Luca, Italian painter (1441–1523), 339 n.1
silenus, a satyr, 332
Silius Italicus, Roman epic poet (25/6–101), 84, 84 n.1, 85
Silla, *see* Sulla
Silos, L.R., *224 n.1*, *226 n.1*
Silver Latin, in Textor 84
Simon, Richard, French biblical scholar (1638–1712), 276
Simon Stylites, name of three saints, all from the Near East in the fifth and sixth centuries, 224
Simone, F., *67 n.1*
Simplicius of Cilicia, sixth-century A.D. pagan commentator on Aristotle, 251 n.2

Sinding-Larsen, S., *346 n.1*
Sisgoreus, G., Dalmatian Neo-Latin poet (*c.* 1440–1509), 64
Sixtus IV (Pope 1471–84), 338, *338 n.2* (E. Müntz, R.Lanciani, W.S.Heckscher)
Sixtus V (Pope 1585–90), 345
Slotkin, J.S., 274 n.2
Smith, G. Moore, *149 n.4*, 150 nn.1–5
Smith, W.F., 14, *14 n.1*
Soane (Sir John) Museum, London, 341, 351–2, Pls. 7*c*, 8*c*, 12*b*
Socrates (468–400 B.C.), 250; the saintly simpleton, 200–1, 231, 246–7
Sodoma (Giovanni Bazzi), Italian painter (1477–1549), 331 n.1
Solomon, king of Israel, tenth century B.C. 274, 296, 330, 332
Solon, Athenian lawgiver (640–558 B.C.), 115
Sophocles, Athenian tragic poet (*c.* 495–405 B.C.), 83
Sophronius, fourth-century Greek Christian biographer, 94 n.1
Sorbonne, 228
Soria, Giovanni Battista, sculptor working in Rome (1581–1651), 352 n.1
Spada, Palazzo, by Borromini, 352–3, Pl. 14*b*
Spada, Virgilio, Italian draughtsman (1596–1662), 350 n.1
Spain, 227; agriculture in, 321; British Library holdings of books printed in, 34, 34 n.1; La Peyrère in, 277
Spanish literature, 164 n.1, 259–70
Sparrow, John, 4, 5; publications, *173 n.2*
Sparrow Simpson, W., 212, *212 nn.5–6*
Spartianus, Aelius, Roman biographer (*fl.* 285), 286 n.6
Spenser, Edmund, English poet (1552–99), 119
Spinoza, Baruch, Jewish philosopher (1632–77), 279
Stackelberg, J.von, *295 n.6*, 297 n.2, 298 n.2, 300 n.2, 302 n.6, *322 n.1*
Stagyrite, name given to Aristotle after his birthplace Stageira, 249, 253
Standonck, Jean, Paris academic (d. 1504), 228, 233
Starnes, W.T., *10 n.1*
Statius, T.Papinius, Roman epic poet (*c.* 45–96): cited by Textor, 84, 84 n.1, 87; *Silvae*, 183 n.6
Stephanus, *see* Estienne
Stern, H., *340 n.3*
Stern, V.F., *151 n.2*
Sterne, Lawrence, English novelist (1713–68), 98
Steyn, location of Augustinian priory to which Erasmus belonged, 229
Stibar, Daniel, German nobleman with humanist interests (1503–55), 185 n.4
Stiblinus, Caspar, late-sixteenth-century Swiss satirist, 44, 44 n.3, *52*

Stigel Johannes (1515–62), 185 n.5
Stoicism, 246, 267, 323, *323 n.1* (G. Oestreich)
Stone, Lawrence, 33
Stringa, G., 345, *345 n.1*
Strozzi, Palazzo, Florence, 340, *340 n.1* (C.von Stegmüller, H.von Geymüller, J. Durm)
Strozzi, Tito Vespasiano, *51*; cited by Textor, 84, 85
Struever, N.S., *71 n.1*
Suetonius Tranquillus, C., Roman biographer (*c.* 69–140), 282, 286 n.6
Suiseth (Swineshead), Richard, English scholastic philosopher (*fl.* 1348), 241 n.2
Sulla, L.Cornelius, Roman general (136–78 B.C.), 284
Sun King, *see* Louis XIV
Sussanée, Hubert, French grammarian (1512–after 1550), 81
Sweden, 36 n.4
Swift, Jonathan, English satirist and moralist (1667–1745), 50
Syrinx, nymph hunted by Pan, 267

Tabularium (Vatican), 325, *325 n.2* (F.Fasolo, G.Gullini, R.Delbrück)
Tacitus, Cornelius, Roman historian (*c.* 55–after 115); editions and translation, 285; influence, *322 n.1* (*bibliography*); renaissance knowledge of, **285–93, 295–303**, 322
  Agricola, 300; *Annales*, 285–7, 295–8, 300; *Germania*, 298; *Historiae*, 283, 285
Talbert, E.W., *10 n.1*
Tarentum, 100
Tartaglia, Niccolò, Italian mathematician (1499–1557), 317, 318, *318 n.1* (L.Olschki)
technology: classical contribution to, 3, 7, 27, **315–24**; editions of technological works, 316 n.2 (F.Russo)
Telesio, Bernardino, Italian philosopher and Neo-Latin poet (1508–88), 63, 78
Temanza, T., *345 n.1*
Terence (P.Terentius Afer), Roman writer of comedies (*c.* 195–159 B.C.): popularity, 38, 153, *153 n.2* (L.Jardine); *Eunuch*, echoed, 130–1
Textor, Johannes Ravisius (Jean Tixier de Ravisi), French compiler of *copia* manuals (*c.* 1475–1524), 9, 10, **81–90, 95–102**, 108, 113, 117, 119–21, 121 n.3, 122–4, 126; arrangement of his material, 11, 83, **107–11**; authors cited, **83–5**, 97; his debt to Maffei, 110; his edition of Hutten, 96–7, 97 n.1; his plays, *96 n.1* (*bibliography*); used by Buchanan, 88–90; usefulness for vernacular writers, 96 n.1, 100, **121–6**
textual criticism, 5, 49

'Theatrum', used as title, 114
Themistius, Greek rhetorician and Aristotelian commentator (310/20–c. 395), 251
Theocritus, Greek bucolic poet (fl. 272 B.C.), 83
Theodoret, Bishop of Cyrus, Syria (386–c. 458), 200–1
Theophilus of Antioch, Greek Christian theologian (fl. 170), 272, 272 n.1 P.H.Kocher)
Theseion, fifth-century B.C. temple, Athens, 354
Thomas Aquinas, Saint (1226–74), 133, 236, 305; Vivès on, 257
Thompson, C.R., 207 n.4
Thrasea Paetus, P.Clodius, leader of senatorial opposition under Nero (d. 66), 302
Tibble, J.W., 171 n.2
Tiberius (Roman emperor 14–37), 283, 283 nn.2 and 4, 286, 292, 292 n.3, 296–300
Tibullus, Albius, Roman elegiac poet (48–19 B.C.), 16, 173–5; echoed by Lotichius, 181, 181 n.1, 183, 184 nn.2 and 4, 186, 188, 188 n.3; reputation, 178, 178 n.5, 180, 180 n.2, 190, 190 n.2
Tieghem, P.van, 172 n.3
Times, The, newspaper, 37 n.1
Titus (Roman emperor 79–81), 288; arch of, 333
TLF, Textes littéraires français, scholarly editions of French authors, 130
Toffanin, G., 25, 285–6, 288, 322 n.1
Tomiczki, Peter, Polish humanist and statesman (1465–1535), 231
Tootill, Miss, 132
topos, see commonplace material
Töppen, M., 180 n.3
Toronto edition of Erasmus, 3
Torquatus a Frangipani, A.J., see 'Menippus Redivivus'
tragedy, influence of Lucan on, 165
Trajan (M. Ulpius Traianus) (Roman emperor 98–117), 288; column of, 333; Forum of, 340, 340 n.1 (A. Bartoli)
Trapp, J.B., v, 3, 19, 39; publications, 208 n.3, 213 n.10
Traversari, Ambrogio, Carmelite monk and humanist (1386–1435), 200, 218
Trebizond, George of (Georgius Trapezuntius), Cretan immigrant and translator (1395–1484), 200
Trent, Council of (1545–63), 234
Tribrachus, Gaspare (Tribraco de'Tirimbocchi), Italian Neo-Latin satirist (1439–c. 1495), 51
Trinity College, Cambridge, library, 216, 216 n.3 (M.R.James)
Trinkaus, C., 79 n.2
Truchon, sixteenth-century French poet, 193

Tunstal, Cuthbert, Bishop of London, mathematician and humanist (1474–1559), 217
Turnèbe, Adrien, French classical scholar (1512–65), 85
Tuscany, architecture, 338–9, 339 n.1 (C.Scaglia, T.Buddensieg and G. Schweikhart)
tyranny, 165–9, 290–3, 295–301
Tyrollf, J., 45 n.1

Ulysses (Odysseus), 114, 182, 182 n.3, 187, 187 n.2, 259, 259 n.1 (L. Schrader)
Ulysses, Joyce's novel, 125
Umbritius Cantianus, pseudonym, English Neo-Latin satirist (fl. 1729), 53
Urceo, Antonio, called Codrus, Italian humanist (d. c. 1500), 51
Urswick, Christopher, Dean of York (1448–1522), 208 n.4, 210 n.1, 216, 217 n.6
Ussher, James, Archbishop, English scholar and preacher (1581–1656), 275
Utrecht, Holland (Ultraiectum), 45

Vadianus, Joachim, Swiss literary critic and geographer, 180 n.2, 190 nn.2 and 4
Valeriano, Giovanni Pierio, Italian Neo-Latin poet (1476/7–1558/60), 52, 64
Valerius Flaccus, Roman epic poet (d. c. 90): cited by Textor, 84; echo in Buchanan, 90
Valerius Maximus, Roman historical anecdotist (fl. 14–37), 282
Valla, Lorenzo, Italian humanist and philosopher (1407–57), 73 n.1 (S. Camporeale, C.Trinkaus), 147, 151, 152, 152 nn.1–2, 153, 289; advocacy of correct Latin, 6, 71, 73–4; on Albertus Magnus, 144 n.4; on historiography, 282, 282 n.2; on induction, 145 n.2; on Livy, 282, 282 n.1, 289; on Peter of Spain, 142, 142 n.3 (A.J. Ashworth), 144; on the pseudo-Dionysius, 219; reform of logic, 7, 11, 13, 73–4, 141–4, 144 n.3 (W. and M.Kneale), 145, 151, 154
Annotationes in Novum Testamentum, 208, 208 n.1 (P.S.Allen); Dialecticae disputationes, 7, 74, 141, 141 n.2 (P.O. Kristeller, C.Vasoli) 142, 144 n.4, 145, 149–50, 150 n.1
Valladolid (Castile), 229
Vanini, Lucilio, physician and free-thinker (1585–1619), 275
Varanne, Valéran de, French early-sixteenth-century Neo-Latin poet, 84
Varro, M.Terentius, Roman scholar (116–27 B.C.), 85, 276, 320, 320 n.4
Vasari, Giorgio, Italian art historian (1511–74), 326, 336, 343–4; on gothic style, 337

Vasoli, C., 6, 7, 11, 15, 141 n.2, 147 n.2; publications, *14 n.2, 71 n.2, 74 n.1*

Vatican, 200, 325; Bibbiena's apartment, 331; Raphaël's loggias, **325–34**; Sala di Costantino, 344–6, Pl. 10; Stanza della Segnatura, 344–5; Scala Regia, 352; Tabularium, 325, *325 n.2* (F.Fasolo–G.Gullini, R.Delbrück); *see also* Antinous, Apollo, Laocoon

Vega, Garcilaso de la Spanish and Neo-Latin poet (1503–36), 64

Vega Carpio, Lope de, Spanish poet and dramatist (1562–1635): his dramas, 262, 266–7; his style, 259; his use of mythology, 22–3, 260–2, 270
Maja, 266–7

Vegetius (F.Vegetius Renatus), late-fourth-century A.D. writer on military science, 315 n.1, 320, 320 nn.1–2

Vegius, Mapheus, Italian Neo-Latin poet (1406–58), 152 n.4

Venice, 188; its constitution, 310; works of art in, 115, 333, 345; works printed in, 37, 95, 317

Venus, goddess, 176 n.1, 183, 183 n.6; in art 331, *331 n.2* (N.Dacos)

Vergara, Joannes, Spanish humanist (1492–1557), 195

Vergerio, Pier Paolo, humanist writer on education (c. 1370–c. 1445), *24 n.1*

Vergil, Polydore, humanist historian (1470?–1555), 33, 201

Verinus, Ugolinus, Florentine Neo-Latin satirist (1438–1516), *51*

Vermeule, C.C., *328 n.1, 349 n.2*

vernaculars: development of, 5, 5 n.2, 9–10, 17, 39; usefulness of commonplace material in, 96 n.1, 100, **121–34**; usefulness of Latin style for, 191–7

Verocchio, Andrea, Italian painter and architect (1435–88), 115

verse: depicting actualities, 17, 64, 183–9; nineteenth-century teaching of, 117; textbooks, 81–2; *see also* Neo-Latin verse

Verwey, De la Fontaine, 33 n.2

Vesalius, Andreas, anatomist (1514–64), 49

Vettori, Francesco, diplomatist and traveller (1474–1539), 286 n.6, 288, 290–1, *290 n.4, 291 n.1*

Vettori, Piero (Victorius), Florentine classical scholar (1499–1585), 320

Via Appia, from Rome to Capua, 351

Via Salaria, from the Porta Collina at Rome to the country of the Sabines, 327

Viart, sixteenth-century French poet, 193

Vickers, B., *160 n.2*

Vico, Giambattista, Italian philosopher (1688–1744), 298 *298 nn.1–4*

Vida, Marcus Hieronymus, Italian Neo-Latin poet (c. 1490–1566), 63

Villani, Nicola (N.de Villanis), bilingual Italian and Neo-Latin poet (1590–1639), 53

Villey, P., *137 n.4*

Villon, François, French poet (1431–89), 96 n.1

Vincent de Beauvais, mediaeval encyclopaedist (c. 1190–1264), 102, 282

Virgil (P.Vergilius Maro), (70–19 B.C.), 166, 241, 284 n.3, 344–5; cited (La Peyrère) 276, (Machiavelli) 287, (Montaigne) 136, 137 n.2, (Textor) 83, 85, 97; compared with: (Homer) *119 n.1* (G.Carlson), (Lucan) 163–4; echoes in: (Buchanan) 88 n.3, (Calderón) 266, (J.Dousa) 45, (Lotichius) 185 n.4, 187 nn.2–3 and 5; imitation of, 19, 27; popularity, 38, 87, 153, 153 n.2, 292
Aeneid, 45, 119, 187 nn.2, 3 and 5; *Georgics*, 185 n.4, 266

Virgin Mary, 336–7, 344, 347, *347 n.2* (T.Buddensieg), Pl. 7*b*

Vitellius, Aulus, Roman emperor (A.D. 69), 283 n.4, 288, 292

Vitoria, Fray Baltasar de, seventeenth-century Spanish mythographer, 263

Vitrier, Jehan, 230

Vitruvius Pollio, Roman writer on architecture (*fl.* 10 B.C.), 29, 318, 342–3, 350

Vivès, Juan Luis, Spanish humanist working in the Netherlands (1492–1540), **239–58**; criticism of scholastics, 144 n.1, 241, 241 n.2, **251–3**, 257; his ideal statesman, **240**, **242–3**; on Aristotle, 22, 242 n.1, 245, **247–58**, *253 n.4* (B.Monsegu); on Neo-Platonism, 242, 246, 258; on Plato, 22, 242 n.1, **245–8**, **249–53**, **257–8**; on Pre-Adamism, 273, *273 n.2* (C.G. Noreña); rejection of authorities, **252**, **255–6**
Aedes Legum, 240; *Censura de Aristotelis operibus*, **247–9**, **253–5**; Commentary on Augustine's *De civitate Dei*, 245 n.3; Commentary on Cicero's *Somnium Scipionis*, 21, 25, **240–2**, 241 n.2, 246, *246 n.3* (C.G.Noreña), 249; *De causis corruptarum artium*, 249, 253, 255; *De initiis, sectis et laudibus philosophiae*, **247, 249**; *De tradendis disciplinis*, 247, 249, 250, 252, 255, 257; *In pseudo-dialecticos*, 142 n.4, 240

Vocht, H. de, *241 n.1*

Vodoz, J., *96 n.1*

Volpi, Giovanni Antonio, Italian Neo-Latin poet (1686–1766), *52*

Voltaire, François Marie Arouet de (1694–1778), 73 n.1, 279

Volusenus, *see* Wilson, Florens

Volz, Paul, German reformer (1480–1544), 230

Vossius Borchlonius, Gerardus, Dutch scholar, *not* the great Vossius (1550–1609), 240

Vratović, V., 43 n.2

Walker, D.P., *76 n.1, 220 n.3*
Wanscher, V., *325 n.2*
Warburg Institute, 36, 36 n.2, 326, 328 n.5
Warner, G.F., 208, *208 nn.5–6*
Watson, G., v
Webbe, William, English literary critic (*fl.* 1568–91), 160
Weber, H., 26, 30
Weisheipl, J.A., *141 n.3*
Weisinger, H., *67 n.1*
Weissenberger, K., *171 n.1*
Whitfield, J.H., 25, 29
Whittinton, Robert, early-sixteenth-century English schoolmaster, 121 n.3
Wieacker, F., *317 n.4*
Wilamowitz-Moellendorf, Ulrich von, German classical scholar (1848–1931), 3
Wilcox, D.J., *71 n.1*
William of Moerbeke, Flemish translator of Aristotle (1215–86), 305
Williams, B.A.O., v, vi
Williamson, G., *5 n.1*
Wilsdorf, H., *318 n.2*
Wilson, Florens (Florentius Volusenus), Scottish humanist (*c.* 1504–47), 244, 244 n.1
Wilson, Thomas, English writer on rhetoric (1525?–81), 156, 158
Wimpfeling, Jacob, German humanist (1450–1528), *42 n.4*
Winckelmann, Johann Joachim, German art historian (1717–68), 350 n.2
Windsor Castle, 349, 353, Pl. 15*a*
Wing, D.J., 34
Wittkower, R., *344 n.1, 353 n.1*

Wolsey, Thomas, Cardinal (1471–1530), 208 n.4, 217 n.7
Woodward, W.H., *24 n.1*

Xenophon, Athenian historian, memorialist and writer on domestic economy (*c.* 427–after 355 B.C.), 320–1, *321 n.1* (A.Buck)

Yates, F., *76 n.1*
Yuen, T., 328 n.3

Zanchius, Basilius, Italian Neo-Latin poet (1501–58/61), *61 n.1*
Zaninus de Solcia, Spanish heretic, condemned 1459, *273 n.1* (M. Menendez-Pelayo, O.Zöckler)
Zanobi da Strata, grammar teacher at Florence (1315–61), *51*, 283
Zappacosta, V., *42 n.3*
Zeno of Citium, Stoic philosopher (335–263 B.C.), 156, 158
Zeno of Elea, Greek philosopher (b. 490/85 B.C.), 250
Zobel, Melchior, bishop, 44
Zöckler, O., *273 n.1*
Zwinger, Jakob, son of Theodore, 112
Zwinger, Theodore, the Elder, Swiss polymath (1533–88), 14, 109–12, 111 n.1, 112 n.1 (J.Karcher), 119; his Ramism, 115–18
  Methodus apodemica, 115, *115 n.2;*
  Theatrum humanae vitae, 110 n.3, 111 n.1, 112 n.1, 113, *113 nn.1–4, 114 nn.1–6*
Zwingli, Huldrich, Swiss reformer (1484–1531), 202